A Financial Bestiary

A Financial Bestiary

Introducing Equity, Fixed Income, Credit, FX, Forwards, Futures, Options and Derivatives

Ramin Nakisa

Chesham Bois Publishing

Chesham Bois Publishing
21 Chestnut Close, Amersham, HP6 6EQ

First published in 2011 by Chesham Bois Publishing

Printed and bound in Great Britain by Lightning Source UK Ltd.

Typeset using L$_Y$X

Calculations in R

British Library Cataloguing in Publication Data. A catalogue record for this book is available from the British Library.

Rev : 1509

ISBN 978-0-9566635-0-4

To my family

Acknowledgements

I would like to thank Walter Braegger for generously sharing his encyclopedic knowledge and intuitive understanding of finance whenever he was asked, which was very often, Joe Troccolo for teaching Walter and the rest of the team in the first place, Kai-Hing Lum for showing how to convey technical topics like interest rate derivatives and still have a class like you afterwards, Bojana Pejic for keeping my knowledge up to date and laughing at my jokes, and Lindsey Matthews for sharing the broken-arm-third-principal-component joke.

This book benefited from all the people who read it and found ways to improve it. I would like to thank my wife Melanie who finally learnt what it is I do and spent so much time reading drafts and tactfully pointing out problems while simultaneously keeping the family alive and managing her own career. I would also like to thank Philip French who read the book cover-to-cover in a miraculously short space of time and yet managed to suggest several improvements, Stefano Nappo for Nappo's Razor, Sumit Gupta for help with inflation, James Martin and Andreas Razen whose enthusiasm reassured me that the book may be useful after all, Yuriy Bystrov for suggesting that there should be exercises and Alan Langworthy for helpful comments on an early draft. Finally I would like to thank all the people who agreed to have their profile in the Bestiary. Banking attracts many bright and, contrary to received wisdom, amiable people and can be a stimulating and exciting choice of career. I hope that this book will help others understand and appreciate the beauty of finance, and to find a suitable role within the industry.

Contents

Part I

The Bestiary

> **Bestiary** Books that had great vogue between the 11th and 14th centuries, describing the supposed habits and peculiarities of animals both real and fabled, with much legendary lore and moral symbolism. They ultimately derived from the Greek *Physiologus*, compiled by an unknown author before the middle of the 2nd century AD, while those in English were mostly translations of continental originals. Among the most popular were those of Philippe de Thaun, Guillaume le Clerc and Richard de Fournival, the latter's 14th-century *Bestiaire d'Amour* applying the allegory to love.
>
> *(Brewer's Dictionary of Phrase and Fable)*

Financial instruments, like living things, have evolved and adapted to particular financial environments. New instruments are continually created. Some survive and thrive, others are doomed to extinction. The instruments in this book are the survivors, the assets that have been fine-tuned through financial scandals and economic down-turns and shown their ability to weather all that the markets can throw at them. Well, so far at least. Structured products and derivatives took a battering during the Credit Crisis but as their ecological niche in trading risk now is now firmly established, and because they are useful, they inevitably recovered.

In this section we begin by briefly summarising each key instrument in a "bestiary", which is a medieval name for a book of exotic and mythical beasts. In this context the bestiary is simply a picture-book with descriptive text. The bestiary is intended as a quick reference, so that if you have forgotten the relationship between modified duration and DV01, or the approximate value of an at-the-money-forward call option, you can refer to the appropriate page in the bestiary without having to wade through a lot of text. The bestiary does not contain all the instruments mentioned in the book, instead focussing on the ones that are fundamental building blocks. For example the bestiary does not in include straddles but it does include calls and puts which can be used to construct a straddle. At the bottom of each page there is a list of pages in Bloomberg that are relevant to the security being described. Bloomberg is a widely-used application providing market data, news and various price calculators. Bloomberg is to finance what the Amazon jungle is to biodiversity. Using Bloomberg it is possible to rapidly look up definitions of standard financial terms, find up to the minute prices in a wide range of markets and to quickly generate trades. Like the Amazon jungle Bloomberg is continually changing and adapting as markets change, and it is easy to get lost. Hopefully the pointers in the bestiary will help users navigate through the jungle.

Finance is not just about mathematics, or complicated theories, it is ultimately about people who work in finance and their shared culture. Finance has a language and vocabulary all of its own. It is impossible to gain an understanding of finance without understanding the people and institutions who make finance happen. For this reason the second part of the bestiary describes some of the important financial roles with a brief description of each role, an example of someone who works in that role, and their description of what they do in their own words.

Bestiary of Financial Instruments

Asset Type	Detail	Risk
Cash Equity	*Section 1.6 (page 67)*	*Bankruptcy, price risk, dividend risk*

EQUITY

Description

A share in a company issued by a company to raise capital. This gives the owner voting rights in corporate decisions voted upon at company general meetings and participation in the company's profit through the payment of dividends. Equity capital is never repaid to investors, but shares can be bought and sold in an active secondary market.

Cash flows

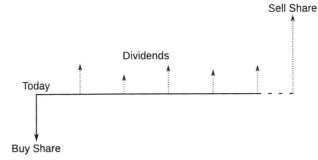

Identifier

Ticker and exchange code, ISIN, CUSIP

Quote

Price.

Example Trade

Buy 100 Apple Inc. shares at $315 a share.

Reason to buy

Believe that the company share price will rise, so the investor can sell their stock at a profit. Being a shareholder entitles an investor to receive some of the company profit as dividend payments but dividend payments are optional and are paid at the discretion of the company. As part-owners of the company shareholders also get to vote on important corporate decisions.

Bloomberg Pages

<Ticker> <Exchange> to select one equity then DES to describe the equity, GP to show its price history, EE to give earnings estimates, FA to see financial reports, ANR for analyst recommendations, DVD for dividend information, BDVD for dividend forecasts, EA for recent earnings announcements, EQS equity search, WPE for world price/earnings ratios, WEI for world equity indices, IMOV equity/index movers, MOST most actively traded stocks, MARB M&A arbitrage spread data, TOP STK top stock news, RSE research search, WECO world economic calendar, WE world economic data, ECFC economic forecasts/indicators.

Asset Type	Detail	Risk
Foreign Exchange	*Section 9.1.2 (page 330)*	*FX risk price risk*

FX SPOT

Description

On the spot market for currency conversion. Involves physical exchange of one currency for another e.g. buy EUR and sell USD.

Cash flows

Today

15,000,000 USD

10,000,000 EUR

Identifier

Each currency has a three letter symbol:

Major Currencies	USD (US dollar), EUR (European euro), CHF (Swiss franc), JPY (Japanese yen), GBP (British pound), CAD (Canadian dollar), AUD (Australian dollar), NZD (New Zealand dollar), SEK (Swedish krona), NOK (Norwegian krone), DKK (Danish krone)
Emerging Europe	ZAR (South African rand), PLN (Polish zloty), CZK (Czech crown), HUF (Hungarian forint), SKK (Slovak crown), ILS (Israeli shekel), RUB (Russian rouble), SAR (Saudi Arabian riyal), TRY (Turkish lira)
Asia	CNY (Chinese renminbi/yuan), HKD (Hong Kong dollar), IDR (Indonesian rupiah), INR (Indian rupee), KRW (South Korean won), MYR (Malaysian ringgit), PHP (Phillipine peso), SGD (Singaporean dollar), THB (Thai baht), TWD (Taiwanese dollar)
Americas	ARS (Argentinian peso), BRL (Brazilian real), CLP (Chilean peso), COP (Columbian peso), MXN (Mexican peso nuevo), PEN (Peruvian new sol), VEB (Venezuelan bolivar)
Metals	XAU (gold), XAG (silver), XPT (platinum), XPD (palladium)

Quote

Quoted as a currency pair e.g. EUR|USD is the number of US dollars required to buy one Euro.

Example Trade

Buy $15,000,000 and sell €10,000,000 today for settlement in two days time.

Reason to trade

To convert one currency into another enabling someone to trade goods and conduct business in the new currency.

Bloomberg Pages

FXC (real-time table of cross-rates), EURUSD Crncy GP (price history).

Asset Type	Detail	Risk
Fixed Income, Money Market	*Section 4.3.1 (page 137)*	*Interest rate (rates rise, price goes down)*

TREASURY BILL

Description

A bond that pays no interest but is sold at a discount and redeems at par. The return on the bond is due solely to the increase in value from the original discounted price to the redeption value at maturity. These are issued by the United States Treasury which calls them Treasury bills, or T-bills. T-bills are a way for the US government to raise funds. They are a low-risk investment that offers a fixed return. They are issued with three maturities: 28 days, 91 days, 182 days and 364 days.

Cash flows

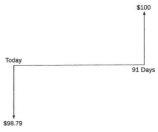

Identifier

CUSIP

Quote

Price or discount rate or yield

Example Trade

Term	91 Days
Issue Date	May 24 2007
Maturity Date	August 23 2007
Discount Rate %	4.775
Investment Rate %	4.914
Price Per $100	98.792986
CUSIP	912795ZW4

Reason to trade

To receive an extremely safe and small income, preserving investor capital. T-bills give a small interest rate risk exposure due their short duration.

Bloomberg Pages

CB3 <GOVT> for the three month T-bill, CT10 for the 10 year T-note.

Asset Type	Detail	Risk
Fixed Income, Money Market	*Section 4.3.1 (page 137)*	*Lose value when interest rates risk or credit risk increases*

COMMERCIAL PAPER

Description

A bond issued by high credit quality corporates, including banks, to raise capital. Commercial paper (CP) is quoted as a discount to face like T-bills and is issued with maturities of 2 to 270 days. Issuers can use CP to borrow money at rates that are slightly lower than a bank loan. Investors buy CP because it is seen as a safe investment and carries a higher rate of return than government debt. CP usually comes with a credit rating giving investors a measure of credit risk. CP has a short maturity so has little interest rate risk. The size of the CP market in the US in 2007 was over 1 trillion USD.

Cash flows

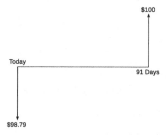

Identifier

CUSIP

Quote

Price or discount rate or yield

Reason to trade

Generating a small, safe return from exposure to a small amount of interest rate risk (short duration) and also some credit risk as they are issued by corporates. Return on CP is greater than equivalent duration T-bills because the investor is compensated for their exposure to credit risk.

Bloomberg Pages

FDCP lists outstanding CP, CPPR lists commercial paper issuers, MMCV gives money market curves including CP curves, DOCP lists direct issuer commercial paper, ECPX Euro CP offerings, SPBDCP <Index> is the S&P commercial paper index.

Asset Type	Detail	Risk
Fixed Income	*Section 4.5.3 (page 150)*	*Interest rate risk and some credit risk as OTC*

FORWARD RATE AGREEMENT

Description

An agreement between a bank and a borrower to borrow at some date in the future at a fixed rate, term and nominal principal. FRAs are OTC instruments which entail counterparty risk but have the flexibility to be tailored to start and end at any date in the future. They are cash settled on the forward expiry date using the difference between the agreed rate and a reference rate, and do not actually involve borrowing of the notional amount.

Cash flows

Identifier

Not applicable as these are OTC instruments. Notation used for showing start and end dates is $s \times e$ where s is the start time forward in months and e is the end time in months. The most frequently traded contracts are 1×4, 1×7, 3×6, 3×9, 6×9 and 6×12.

Quote

Forward rate as an annualized percentage of notional

Example Trade

Term	3×6
Trade Date	May 24 2007
Spot Date (T+2)	May 28 2007
Fixing Date (Settlement-2)	August 24 2007
Settlement Date	August 28 2007
Reference Rate	3M LIBOR
FRA Rate %	4.914
Amount paid on Settlement	$N \frac{\left(r_{ref} - r_{fra}\right)t}{1 + r_{ref}t}$

The amount paid depends on notional N, the value of the reference rate (usually LIBOR) at expiry r_{fra}, and time to expiry t.

Reason to trade

Certainty of locking in a fixed borrowing or lending rate in future. Being OTC allows flexibility in start and end dates and notional.

Bloomberg Pages

FWCV for forward curve analysis

Asset Type	Detail	Risk
Fixed Income	*Chapter 6 (page 241)*	*Counterparty default risk (OTC), interest rate risk*

INTEREST RATE SWAP

Description

An OTC agreement to swap a set of fixed cash flows for floating cash flows. Entering into a swap incurs no up-front payment as these are unfunded instruments.

Cash flows

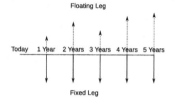

Identifier

OTC so has no identifier.

Quote

Par swap rate which is the interest rate on the fixed leg

Example Trade

Term	5 years
Issue Date	May 24 2007
Payer/Receiver	Payer
Maturity Date	May 24 2012
Fixed Rate %	4.775

Reason to trade

Converting a set of fixed cash flows into floating cash flows and *vice versa*. Used to convert bonds from fixed to floating cash flows by issuers (liability swap) and investors (asset swap). Used to hedge interest rate risk (pension funds LDI) or to get leveraged exposure to interest rate risk (hedge fund curve trades and interest rate speculation). A payer swap makes money if rates rise and a receiver swap makes money if rates fall.

Bloomberg Pages

SWPM for pricing, IYC to get swap curves

Asset Type	Detail	Risk
Fixed Income	*Section 4.5.4 (page 152)*	*Interest rate*

INTEREST RATE FUTURE

Description

An exchange-traded contract that fixes the cost of borrowing or lending over a set period of time in the future. Buyers of IR futures lose money as interest rates increase. Contracts are marked to market which requires regular margin payments.

Cash flows

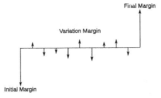

Identifier

ED<Month><Year> (Chicago Mercantile Exchange) e.g. EDH8 is a Eurodollar future expiring in March 2018.

Quote

100 - index rate

Example Trade

Underlying Instrument	Eurodollar Time Deposit having a principal value of USD $1,000,000 with a three-month maturity.
Price Quote	Quoted in IMM Three-Month LIBOR index points or 100 minus the rate on an annual basis over a 360 day year (e.g., a rate of 2.5% is quoted as 97.50). 1 basis point = 0.01% = $25.
Tick Size (minimum fluctuation)	One-quarter of one basis point (0.0025% = $6.25 per contract) in the nearest expiring contract month; one-half of one basis point (0.005% = $12.50 per contract) in all other contract months. The "new" front-month contract begins trading in 0.0025% increments at 7:20 a.m., Central Time (CT), after the "old" expiring front-month contract ceases trading at 11:00 a.m. London time on the expiring contract month's last trading day.
Contract Months	March, June, September, and December, extending out 10 years (total of 40 contracts) plus the four nearest serial expirations (months that are not in the March quarterly cycle). The new contract month terminating 10 years in the future is listed on the Tuesday following expiration of the front quarterly contract month.
Last Trading Day	The second London bank business day prior to the third Wednesday of the contract expiry month. Trading in the expiring contract closes at 11:00 a.m. London Time on the last trading day.
Final Settlement	Expiring contracts are cash settled to 100 minus the British Bankers' Association survey of 3-month U.S. Dollar LIBOR on the last trading day. Final settlement price will be rounded to four decimal places, equal to 1/10,000 of a percent, or $0.25 per contract.

Reason to trade

Gain exposure to interest rates with a particular maturity. Used to hedge interest rate risk (pension funds LDI) or to get leveraged exposure to interest rate risk (hedge fund curve trades and interest rate speculation). Being long a future will profit if rates fall because price is 100 - LIBOR rate.

Bloomberg Pages

EDS for Eurodollar strip curve

Asset Type	Detail	Risk
Fixed Income	*Chapter 5 (page 163)*	*Issuer's credit, interest rate*

FIXED COUPON BOND

Description

Bonds are issued by governments and companies to raise cash. The buyer provides a loan to the issuer. In return for the loan of the face amount the buyer receives a regular coupon payment of fixed size. Bonds issued by G7 governments have little credit risk; corporate bonds vary in risk from low to high risk which is reflected in the size of their coupon and their credit rating. In the event of bankruptcy and liquidation, bond holders are repaid before share holders.

Cash flows

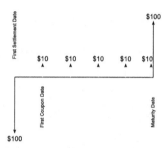

Identifier

ISIN or CUSIP code.

Quote

Price or yield to maturity

Example Trade

Term	5 Years
Issuer	General Electric Capital Corporation
Issue Date	September 30, 2004
Maturity Date	September 15, 2009
Coupon	3.45% fixed, paid quarterly
Price Per $100 face	$100.40
CUSIP	36966RSR8
ISIN	US36966RSR83
Credit Ratings	Aa2 (Moody's), AA+ (S&P)
Amount Issued	$3.314 million

FIXED COUPON BOND continued...

Risk

Credit risk of issuer defaulting, interest rate risk. Greatest loss limited to principal paid. Interest rate risk is measured by duration, so if the yield curve shifts by Δy the change in present value of a bond is the yield shift scaled by modified duration D_{modified},

$$\Delta \text{PV} = -D_{\text{modified}} \times \Delta y \times \text{PV}.$$

The present value of a bond with coupon c paid with compounding frequency f, face value P and yield to maturity y, discount factor $\delta_i = \frac{1}{\left(1+\frac{y}{f}\right)^{f t_i}}$ is

$$\text{PV} \quad = \quad \sum_{i=1}^{N} c\delta_i + P\delta_i = \frac{c}{y}\left[1 - \delta_T\right] + P\delta_T$$

The yield sensitivity is

$$\frac{\partial}{\partial y}\text{PV} = -\frac{c}{y^2}\left[1 - \delta_T\right] - \left(P - \frac{c}{y}\right)\frac{T\delta_T}{1 + \frac{y}{f}},$$

which gives modified duration when divided by $-PV$ and the dollar value of one basis point DV01 when divided by $-\frac{1}{10000}$. Modified and Macaulay duration are related by $D_{\text{modified}} = \frac{D_{\text{macaulay}}}{1+\frac{y}{f}}$.

All these risk measures are related to one another by $\text{DV01} = \frac{\text{PV} \times D_{\text{modified}}}{10000} = \frac{\text{PV} \times D_{\text{macaulay}}}{10000\left(1+\frac{y}{f}\right)}$.

Bloomberg Pages

<Ticker> <Coupon> <Maturity> CORP will pull up a single bond, or ID followed by the ISIN or CUSIP code, WBI for World Bond Indices, BTMM for general bond and money market prices, YA for yield analyis, YAS for yield and spread analysis, CSHF to see cash flows, ASW for asset swap margin calculation, HG for interest rate and credit hedging calculations

MORTGAGE BACKED SECURITY

Description

Bonds issued in the United States that are in some way dependent on cash flows generated by property mortgages. Agency-backed MBS have their principal and coupon payments guaranteed by one of the US mortgage agencies such Fannie Mae, Freddie Mac and Ginnie Mae. The simplest mortgage-backed securities are called pass-throughs because they pass through coupon and interest payments on pools of mortgages.

Cash flows

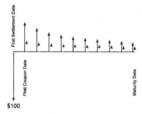

Identifier

ISIN or CUSIP code or a combination of ticker, coupon and maturity e.g. FNMA $4\frac{3}{8}$ Sep 2010.

Quote

Price or yield to maturity.

Example Trade

Term	3 Years
Issuer	Federal National Mortgage Association
Issue Date	September 13, 2007
Maturity Date	September 13, 2010
Coupon	$4\frac{3}{8}$% fixed, paid semi-annually
CUSIP	31398AGU0
ISIN	US31398AGU07
Credit Ratings	Aaa (Moody's), AAA (S&P), AAA (Fitch)
Amount Issued	$3 billion

Reason to trade

Gives investor exposure and compensation for interest rate risk like any fixed coupon bond but this is complicated by prepayment giving MBS the unpleasant characteristic of having negative convexity. Almost no credit risk of issuer defaulting or loss of principal due to defaults if backed by the US Government via an agency.

Bloomberg Pages

POOL for main MBS analysis menu, APX for TBA pricing and analysis, BBTM for TBA composite prices, MYS for yield spread history, HSST for housing economic statistics and delinquency rates, CPH for historical prepayment trends, CLASS for ABS/MBS class definitions, CLC collateral composition, YT price MBS varying prepayment assumptions, CMOR for CMO/ABS/CMBS market reports, MBSS to search for agency pass-throughs, MCFR for mortgage forward rates, MOAS to track mortgage collateral option adjusted spreads, BBMD for mortgage delinquency monitor, DELQ for credit card delinquency rates, CLPS deliquency rate by shelf, DQRP to rank deals by collateral performance.

Asset Type	Detail	Risk
Fixed Income	*Section 5.8 (page 195)*	*Issuer's credit, almost no interest rate*

FLOATING RATE NOTE

Description

Floating rate notes (FRN) or "floaters" are issued by companies to raise funds. The buyer provides a loan to the issuer. In return for loan of the face amount the buyer receives a set of variable but regular coupon payments. Coupons are set by regularly observing some index rate, such as LIBOR and adding a fixed margin e.g. LIBOR plus 20 basis points. Floaters carry very little interest rate risk due to their floating coupon, but still carry the issuer's credit risk and are often seen as pure credit instruments. Credit risk is reflected in the size of the fixed margin.

Cash flows

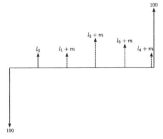

Identifier

ISIN or CUSIP code.

Quote

Price or discount margin

Reason to trade

Gives investor exposure to credit risk of issuer defaulting, and almost no interest rate risk as coupons are reset periodically from an interest rate index. Floaters are therefore based on investor beliefs about the credit quality of issuers.

Bloomberg Pages

YA will give the discount margin of the floater

BOND FUTURE

Description

Bond futures are an exchange-traded contract for buying and selling government bonds at some date in the future. If a contract is held until expiry the seller chooses which bond to deliver to the buyer. Bond futures give investors a way of getting exposure to the government bond market without investing a lot of capital.

Cash flows

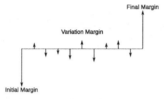

Identifier

Ticker in the form <underlying bond><delivery month><year> e.g. TYU7 would be the ten year US Treasury contract expiring in September 2017.

Quote

Price tracks cheapest to deliver government bond so usually about 100. For US Treasury futures quoted in thirty-secondths by appending "-" followed by two digits and sixty-fourths (+) so 117-09+ means $117 + \frac{9}{32} + \frac{1}{64}$.

Example Trade

Name	US 10 year Treasury note future expiring September 2009
Ticker	TYU9
Exchange	Chicago Board of Trade (CBOT)
Underlying (Notional)	US Treasury 10 year 6% coupon bond
Contract Size	$100,000
Tick Size	$0\text{-}00+ = \frac{1}{64}$
Tick Value	$\$15.625 = \frac{100,000}{100 \times 64}$
Price	117-30
Contract Value	$\$117,937.5 = 100,000 \times \frac{117+\frac{30}{32}}{100}$

		Speculator	Hedger
Margin Limits	Initial	$2,430	$1,800
	Secondary	$1,800	$1,800

	Trade Date	*First*	Jun 20, 2008
		Last	Sep 21, 2009
Related Dates	**First Notice**		Aug 31, 2009
	Delivery Date	*First*	Sep 1, 2009
		Last	Sep 30, 2009
Cycle	March (H), June (M), September (U), December (Z)		

Asset Type	Detail	Risk
Fixed Income	*Section 5.12 (page 204)*	*Interest rate*

BOND FUTURE continued...

Reason to trade Exposure to interest rate risk either to hedge an existing position, such as a bond portfolio, or to speculate on the movement of interest rates. Buying a bond future is equivalent to a leveraged position in a government bond where leverage is the reciprocal of the conversion factor.

Bloomberg Pages WBF (world bond futures), CT (contract table), CTD (cheapest to deliver bonds), DLV (cheapest to deliver bonds), FAC (conversion factors), HCD (historical cheapest to deliver), HCA & HCG (CTD analysis and graph)

CREDIT DEFAULT SWAP

Description

Credit default swaps provide protection against a debt issuer defaulting on its payments. A buyer of credit protection has sold away their credit risk so is short credit and will profit if credit spreads widen. Buyers of credit protection pay a quarterly premium to the seller of protection.

Cash flows

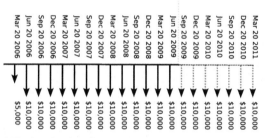

Identifier

RED identifier for reference entity

Quote

Price or discount rate or yield

Example Trade

Reference Entity RED	912795ZW4
Term	5 years
Issue Date	May 24 2007
Maturity Date	August 23 2007
Issue Premium	47 bp
Seniority	Senior
Restructuring	Modified
Currency	USD

Reason to trade

Buyer of protection will profit if spreads increase, seller of protection will profit if spreads tighten. Can be used to hedge existing issuer credit risk of owning issuer's bond by buying protection or taking a naked credit position to speculate on credit movements.

Bloomberg Pages

CDSW to price a CDS, QCDS quick CDS valuation and horizon analysis, CRVD to compare CDS spread and ASM, HGBD for bond credit hedging, VCDS to value bond using CDS spread, CDS to look up a reference entity, GCDS to see spread histories for the global CDS market, CDSV for CDS curve search, FWCS forward CDS curve, HGCS for CDS curve trade valuation, CAST capital structure of company, DDIS for company debt repayment profile, RATC issuer credit rating changes, CRPR for current and historical issuer ratings, ECCG credit spread alongside equity price and implied option volatility, GV for equity and credit trading volume, CMOV for CDS biggest spread changes, CXEV for credit/equity monitor, WCDS for world CDS pricing, SNAC for ISDA standardization portal, REDL for list of reference entity database identifiers.

Asset Type	Detail	Risk
Credit	*Section 7.5 (page 304)*	*Credit risk of index reference entities*

CREDIT DEFAULT SWAP INDEX

Description Credit default swap indices provide broad protection against any debt issuer in a published list of names in an index defaulting on its payments.

Cash flows

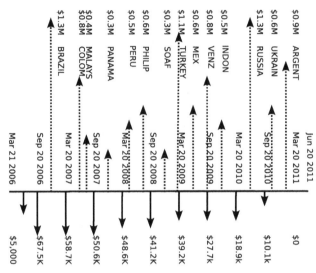

Identifier RED identifier

Quote Price or discount rate or yield

Example Trade

Reference Entity RED	2I666VAK1
Term	5 years
Issue Date	March 17 2009
Maturity Date	June 20 2014
Issue Premium	185 bp
Currency	EUR

Risk Buyer of protection will profit if index spread increases, seller of protection will profit if spreads tightens. Can be used to hedge "general" credit risk by buying protection or taking a naked credit position to speculate on credit movements.

Bloomberg Pages CDSW to price an index, CDSI to see and search a list of on-the-run and off-the-run CDS indices, CDX for credit index monitors, CDIA for credit index analysis, MEMB for credit index members, CINS for credit index member search.

Asset Type	Detail	Risk
Credit	Chapter 8 (page 315)	Credit risk of reference entities and their risk correlation

SYNTHETIC CDO TRANCHE

Description

Synthetic collateralised debt obligation.

Cash flows

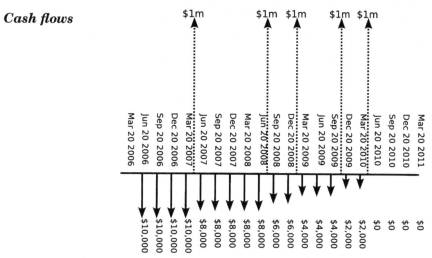

Identifier

OTC so no standardized identifiers.

Quote

Price or implied correlation.

Reason to trade

Seller of protection earns premium which is lost if the tranche is wiped out by defaults. Buyer of protection pays premium but receives payment if a default occurs. Equity tranche will gain in value as correlation increases, super-senior tranche will lose as correlation increases.

Bloomberg Pages

CDST for synthetic CDO tranche valuation, CDOT for credit index tranche data, CORR for customized correlation matrix, XCOR for correlation spreadsheet, CIX for customized index construction

Asset Type	Detail	Risk
Option	*Chapter 10 (page 347)*	*Loss of premium if underlying premium expires below break-even*

CALL OPTION

Description   The right, but not the obligation, to buy the underlying at a fixed price at a fixed time in the future.

Cash flows

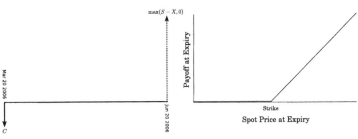

Pricing   According to the Black-Scholes model the price of a call option with underlying stock price S, cash lending rate r_l, carry rate r_c, strike price X, volatility σ and expiry t is

$$C = SN(d_1)e^{-(r_l - r_c)t} - Xe^{-r_l t}N(d_2).$$

And d_1 and d_2 are defined as

$$d_1 = \frac{\ln \frac{S}{X} + \left(r_c + \frac{\sigma^2}{2}\right)t}{\sigma\sqrt{t}}$$

$$d_2 = \frac{\ln \frac{S}{X} + \left(r_c - \frac{\sigma^2}{2}\right)t}{\sigma\sqrt{t}} = d_1 - \sigma\sqrt{t}.$$

For at-the-money-forward calls where the strike is equal to the forward $X = F = Se^{r_c t}$ the approximate value of the option is

$$C \approx \frac{2}{5}X\sigma\sqrt{t}.$$

Identifier   OTC so no standardized identifiers.

Quote   Premium quoted as a monetary amount.

Example Trade   Buy a \$500 strike call on Sprocket Corporation expiring in three months.

Reason to trade   If buying a call option the investor will profit from the underlying increasing past its break-even point. If selling a call option investor will take in a premium payment initially then lose if the underlying increases and they are assigned. The most a buyer can lose is their option premium and their upside is unlimited. A seller gains the premium initially then has potentially unlimited losses.

Bloomberg Pages   OMON option monitor, OV option valuation, OSA option scenario analysis, OHT option horizon analysis, OVX exotic options, OVDV vol surface, OVML FX options

Asset Type	Detail	Risk
Option	Chapter 10 (page 347)	Loss of premium if underlying premium expires below break-even

PUT OPTION

Description

The right, but not the obligation, to sell the underlying at a fixed price at a fixed time in the future.

Cash flows

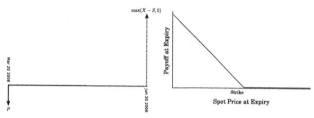

Pricing

According to the Black-Scholes model the price of a call option with underlying stock price S, cash lending rate r_l, carry rate r_c, strike price X, volatility σ and expiry t is

$$P = -SN(-d_1)e^{-(r_l - r_c)t} + Xe^{-r_l t}N(-d_2)$$

And d_1 and d_2 are defined as

$$d_1 = \frac{\ln\frac{S}{X} + \left(r_c + \frac{\sigma^2}{2}\right)t}{\sigma\sqrt{t}}$$

$$d_2 = \frac{\ln\frac{S}{X} + \left(r_c - \frac{\sigma^2}{2}\right)t}{\sigma\sqrt{t}} = d_1 - \sigma\sqrt{t}.$$

For at-the-money-forward puts where the strike is equal to the forward $X = F = Se^{r_c t}$ the approximate value of the option is

$$P \approx \frac{2}{5}X\sigma\sqrt{t}.$$

Identifier

OTC so no standardized identifiers.

Quote

Premium quoted as a dollar value.

Example Trade

Buy a $500 strike put on Sprocket Corporation expiring in three months.

Risk

If buying a put option the investor will profit from the underlying decreasing past its break-even point. If selling a put option investor will take in a premium payment initially then lose if the underlying decreases and they are assigned. The most a buyer can lose is their option premium and their upside is limited to the strike. A seller gains the premium initially then has a loss up to the strike.

Bloomberg Pages

OMON option monitor, OV option valuation, OSA option scenario analysis, OHT option horizon analysis, OVX exotic options, OVDV vol surface, OVML FX options

Bestiary of Financial Roles

Role Type	Detail
Front Office	*Section 2.3 (page 85)*

TRADER

Role   Making a market in an asset class, hedging to avoid any directional risk and profiting from bid-offer spread.

Skills   Extremely detailed knowledge of a particular market or asset type. A broad range of backgrounds. Good numerical skills and the ability to think fast under extreme time pressure.

Hours   Typical for a trading desk, very long but most intense around market trading hours.

Working Day   Making a market means that the trader is willing to buy and sell their asset class to clients at any time, creating liquidity. However the trader sets and continually adjusts their buying price (bid) and selling price (offer). They make profit from the bid-offer spread (their edge), buying low and selling high. As their profit is not driven by making directional bets market makers will try and sell their inventory as quickly as possible or hedge their directional risk using other instruments.

Profile - Joaquin Perez

Education   B Eng. Civil Engineering, Universite Libre de Bruxelles

Role   Senior Trader in Scandinavian Rates

Experience   14 years in finance in Mitsubishi UF (7 years), WestLB (2 years) and Nordea (3 years). Has run trading books in all G7 currencies and Scandies across the whole yield curve (0 to 30 years) in different instruments (bonds, derivatives, inflation linked instruments and FX).

The job consists of facilitating the buying and selling of debt and fixed income instruments (derivatives or bonds) for our clients. The specific action of market making improves the liquidity of markets and as a result allows companies and governments to issue debt to investors.

The decisions taken by traders on a daily basis are based on a combination of relative value analysis (finding discrepancies between correlated markets that allow for a profit to be made), macro-economic views (generated by the study of economic statistics and figures), trend-following and understanding the existing positions of the players in a specific market at a specific time, particularly those positions and trends related to dealing with the flow generated by the client base of the bank.

Apart from managing the risk taken on behalf of a bank, traders spend their days on their telephones talking to brokers (middle-men in most transactions), sales people and economists as well as reading reports on their specific markets. These days most traders in fixed income instruments have a strong mathematical background e.g. engineers or people with a PhD in a mathematical subject.

Role Type	Detail
Front Office	*Section 2.3 (page 85)*

SALES

Role

Interacting directly with the investment bank's clients. Sales people, also known as marketers, are the people on the end of the phone if a client wants to speak to a bank. Sales people liase between clients and traders.

Skills

An overview of the market place and a knowledge of all sectors of your coverage (e.g. European large caps). The gift of the gab, and good numerical skills. An ability to get on with anyone is a useful asset in making the job as enjoyable as possible. An ability to get the gist of a point and summarize it in a memorable way is vital to avoid blending into the crowd of coverage available to clients.

Hours

Hours are long, days are varied.

Working Day

Reading news, phoning clients, researching and suggesting trading ideas relevant to individual client needs, getting prices from traders, entertaining clients.

Profile - Ben Morton

Education   M. Chem. Oxford University

Role   Equity Derivative Sales

Experience   Joined as graduate.

There are two main aspects to work in sales:

Client relationship Trades & Ideas

The client relationship means that you are the face that the client associates with the bank for a particular type of coverage, in this case derivatives. As a salesman you spend time trying to understand the goals and demands of the client, as well as their quirks in order to personalise the most mutually advantageous relationship possible.

Trades & Ideas

This is both trade facilitation and superimposing your own collated views on the marketplace to suggest potentially profitable positions. This coverage can consist of clients to products that the bank has produced such as new research or creating new trade ideas that fit their remit. The salesman is there to facilitate the coverage that helps the client get the most from the bank. Equally, when this coverage means the client wishes to trade the salesman acts as the doorway to the bank, understanding what the client is asking for and liaising with the appropriate specialists.

Role Type	Detail
Corporate Governance	Section 2.3 (page 85)

AUDIT

Role

Internal audit reviews business activities and forms an opinion on whether the resulting range of risks are being managed adequately by the bank's management and control functions. In many organizations, recommendations for improvements are also made.

Skills

Most internal auditors trained with large accountancy firms, though some bring analytical skills from other areas. Knowledge of financial products, transaction processes and risk management techniques is important, but the most important quality for an auditor is an ability to unravel a complex situation and identify any risks to the bank, whether reputational or financial. A good auditor is able to talk to anyone in the bank about their role, listen well and draw out the issues. An ability to deliver difficult messages clearly and impartially is essential, as is dealing constructively with the occasional hosility this can generate.

Hours

Varied, with quieter and more intense periods. Each audit is a discrete project.

Working Day

On a typical day a lot of time is spent getting to understand the part of the business being audited. "Q&A" meetings are common, but so is time spent with sales and trading on the desk and with risk management and finance talking through the models and valuations. Data is sometimes analyzed directly by auditors to confirm understanding or to look for the unexpected. Detailed documentation of the audit is needed and, finally, an audit report is written and agreed.

Profile - Mark Roddick

Education	BSc Natural Sciences, Cambridge, MSc Risk Management, LSE
Role	Investment Bank Auditor
Experience	Trained with international accountancy firm, worked in internal audit for several investment banks with spells in product control and risk management

Occasionally you come across some process in the bank which is clearly not right. You would think this is a simple case of banging the table. But the challenge is recognizing it as wrong in the first place, when everyone else thinks it's normal, and then getting someone to recognize the danger which they are creating for the bank. More likely you come across situations which are in varying degrees of "rightness". Here it is more of a balancing act - trying to move things forward where needed but not getting it out of perspective. Once or twice in a career you might catch a rogue red-handed. This can be very rewarding, but it's not the main aim. A judge once described auditors as `watchdogs, not bloodhounds'.

Role Type	Detail
Asset Management	*Section 2.4 (page 89)*

FUND MANAGER

Role   Investing client funds on their behalf. Fund managers are the people who invest money which goes into pensions, savings and insurance plans.

Skills   Ability to assess and willingness to take calculated risks. Ability and desire to keep up to date on financial markets and the sectors that comprise your portfolio. Excellent analytical skills and ability to think strategically. Good numerical skills, ability to use computer systems and learn quickly, independence of thought.

Hours   Actual office hours can be reasonable but you will often find yourself thinking about and researching your portfolio during your off hours by watching and reading financial news. Days are varied.

Working Day Reading financial news research and messages from brokers, attending company presentations, researching and implementing investment ideas.

Profile - David Rollier, CFA

Education BA History, Yale University; MBA from the Kellogg School of Management at Northwestern University

Role   Credit fund manager

Experience Corporate commercial banking, debt capital market origination, credit sales at investment banks. Switched from "sell-side" (commercial and investment banking) to "buy-side" (asset management).

There are three main aspects to working in fund management: portfolio management, research and dealing. Some firms also add marketing their funds to clients to this list.

Research: Research entails studying the underlying issuers of the bonds (typically a company or a country), in order to assist the fund manager in properly assessing their proper valuation and/or creditworthiness. A research analyst typically analyzes to a greater depth than a portfolio manager. Often they write reports for the fund manager and for the fund's files to demonstrate that the work was properly done. It helps to be curious about how companies operate so that one finds company presentations more interesting. To be good you must enjoy always learning new things, really understanding how companies work, analyzing financial statements, following the financial markets and writing well.

Portfolio Management: The portfolio manager is generally the main decision maker. You must constantly monitor the progress of the fund's investments and generate new ideas to improve the portfolio, research those ideas to see if the stack up holistically within the context of the overall portfolio and meet the fund's investment criteria. Essentially you buy investments that you think will do better than the ones you have and vice versa. To be good you must be confident enough to be able to say no to some of the things that salesmen are trying to persuade you to do and to go against what other market participants are doing sometimes and yet also, at the same time, realize your own limitations and try not to be too clever. Markets have a tendency to humble those who think they are more clever than they really are. You will likely be inundated with information and must be able to quickly locate the most relevant and important information and prioritize your day despite many people making great efforts to compete for your time and attention. It is a job in which you are constantly learning and the day can be varied. It can be very exciting to put one's ideas into practice and watch how they turn out. While it is thrilling to watch ideas work out well, one must also have the mental strength to endure the fact that not all ideas will work out well and must be able to limit the damage as much as possible on the ones that don't. The goal is to get as high a percentage right as possible for as long as possible because things are in a state of flux and good ideas have a certain shelf life before they don't work any more.

Dealing: Dealing is the implementation of the researchers' and portfolio managers' ideas. Typically an investment manager is given guidelines as to how and what bond to purchase or sell. Often these guidelines can be quite strict and so dealing can be quite process oriented (almost mechanical) at times. The best dealers are sometimes given more leeway. The dealer determines the best and most efficient way to execute a portfolio manager's order, and to some degree the timing as well. It is the dealer's job to analyse and make judgements with regards to market liquidity (e.g. assessing how much of a market demand exists for either the purchase or sale of a bond). Dealers will be the ones who actually perform the trades although some portfolio managers do their own dealing. There is really no margin for error and a dealer must be organized, be able to work under pressure, be extremely detail oriented and prioritize quickly and well. It helps to have a good memory for prices of things. A well executed trade can give one a bit of an adrenaline buzz as well as praise from the portfolio manager, particularly if large amounts of money are involved.

Role Type	Detail
Capital Investment	*Section 2.7 (page 92)*

PRIVATE EQUITY

Role
Managing a fund of committed capital to generate financial returns by investing in controlling stakes in businesses across a number of different sectors. Post-acquisition, managing those businesses to generate value over what is typically a 3-5 year time frame. Selling those businesses on to yield a profit for the underlying investors in the fund.

Skills
Ability to assess businesses, identify growth and value potential and then work with management to deliver that value.

Hours
In the midst of an acquisition hours can become very long - it is a very intense process to assess every aspect of an entire company in a short space of time. The final negotiation almost invariably involves an all-night session - partly by tradition and partly because that kind of fatigue is really the only way to get buyers, sellers and all the lawyers to reach sensible compromises.

Working Day
Meeting people and working on relationships to identify businesses for sale. Board meetings of investee companies. Analysis of potential acquisitions.

Profile - Simon Oakland

Education   BA Mathematics, Oxford University; MBA from Cranfield University

Role   Private equity

Experience   Four years in management consulting, 2 years in operational management, 2 years in investment banking, 12 years in private equity and venture capital.

The role is hugely varied both in terms of skills and industries. The start of the process is networking and relationship building in order to get the chance to look at acquiring businesses - some are sold by wide auction, but the better opportunities generally come through bilateral discussions ("off-market"). Each company is a unique business and they span many different sectors (finance, retail, IT etc.) and so there is tremendous variety almost on a daily basis. Each business needs to be assessed and a strategic plan researched and developed for the company. This then needs turning into a financial valuation and requires a deep understanding of the risks involved to assess potential returns.

If the business still looks interesting, then this moves into a phase of negotiation of a complex set of legal documents covering the terms of the purchase, warranties, incentivisation arrangements and very probably banking/debt financing arrangements. In parallel there will be a complex set of "due diligence" to manage, researching at a minimum every aspect of the historical financial performance, legal position and tax; depending on the particular type of business there may also be an investigation of environmental issues, future commercial prospects, pensions provision, management assessment and other areas.

After acquisition the investment case needs to be delivered - this will typically involve joining the board as Chairman and working with executive management on a monthly basis to deliver the plans. At any one time I will probably be on the boards of 3-4 companies and assessing another 1-2 companies at any advanced stage and a further 10-20 at an early stage... and the investments still need to be sold at the end of the period to generate the profit!

MARKET RISK

Role
Understanding the exposure to various risk factors in the positions held by traders, evaluating whether the risk/return trade-off of a given strategy fits the bank risk appetite, and setting limits on specific exposures and monitoring their daily utilisation.

Skills
Being able to learn fast about new markets and develop your own views, good numerical skills to analyze exposures, being bold enough to challenge traders and your own managers about specific risks. Most risk analysts have a PhD in Mathematics, Physics or Computer Science.

Hours
Long, but not as bad as the front office.

Working Day
The first half of the day is consumed by catching up with the markets, figuring how our portfolios changed the day before, analyzing new risk exposures and discussing them with the traders, and then reporting any findings to management. The rest of the day is about ad-hoc analysis of specific risks, fire-drills or more long-term projects such as analysis of hedging strategies or design of Greek-based P&L explanatory tools.

Profile - Gilles Daniel

Education   PhD Computer Science.

Role   Market Risk Analyst

Experience   Joined investment bank after PhD.

Main aspects of the job: Market risk is often referred to as "a second pair of eyes", and that's what we are. We need to create a distance between ourselves and the trading desk, as traders usually perceive market risk as yet another form of Red Tape. However market risk is very important because senior managers need to know what kind of exposures traders are taking. This is about building trust while challenging assumptions again and again. What most of us enjoy most about this job is that it is at the intersection between (i) following the markets live, (ii) following the bank positions, and possibly impacting them, and (iii) working along with the quants on enhancing the risk representation itself.

Role Type	Detail
Risk	*Section 2.3 (page 85)*

CREDIT RISK

Role

To control credit risk on a portfolio of a bank's clients. Credit Officers are analysts and decision makers, giving opinions on transactions from large debt underwritings to volume FX transactions, and providing input to capital market instruments such as bond and equity issues. Credit also remains aware of market-related risks and overall issuer risk positions. Credit liaises with all parts of the business.

Skills

You should have a good knowledge of credit principles with a focus on analytical skills and problem-solving ability. Good written and verbal communication skills are vital. Accuracy, attention to detail and knowledge of the bank's policies are also important in this role. Managing a portfolio of credit risk counterparties also requires close following of the companies and their sectors and an awareness of how events can impact credit quality. A rigorous and questioning approach is necessary.

Hours

Hours vary according to transaction volume levels. During times of focus on large or structured transactions days can be very long.

Working Day

Writing internal analytical reports, appraising financial statements, news items and data, answering communications from marketers on lending, FX trades and interest rate swaps, attendance at committees, monitoring the portfolio including any excess positions.

Profile - Ian Cook

Education   BSc (Statistics) University of St Andrews.

Role   Credit Officer, Credit Risk Control

Experience   18 years in credit-related roles in three financial institutions.

The main aspect of the credit officer's role in credit risk control are analysis and decision making.

Analysis: Analysis involves assimilation of a large amount of information to develop an understanding of the counterparty's business, the main influences on the counterparty's revenues, earnings, cash flow, balance sheet and reputation and accordingly what risks it faces. Most businesses face numerous risks, and while it is important to consider as many as possible, the focus should be on the most important ones. The credit officer also needs to determine what mitigating factors exist within the client's business, such that the risks are eliminated or are not as significant as initially envisaged. The same skills are employed in analysing the risk in transactions.

Decision making: A credit officer takes decisions that create counterparty risk for the banks i.e. one is agreeing that the bank will face additional credit risk as a consequence of approving the transaction. This means having all of the available information to hand, assimilating this information, analysing what is important and making a confident decision that can withstand scrutiny, considering the bank's existing exposure to the counterparty and how this could change over time. If the decision is outside one's personal authority, the credit officer should make the appropriate recommendation, as if the decision were his/her own. The credit officer needs to balance the control of the credit risk with an understanding of the aims of the institution. Therefore the credit officer may be involved in helping to structure a transaction using credit risk mitigation techniques. Good written and verbal communication skills are essential. Credit officers are often part of deal teams where teamwork and interpersonal skills should be evident, whilst remaining firm on risk control.

OPERATIONAL RISK

Role

Operational risk is the risk of control failure arising from people, processes, technology or external factors. This requires understanding the risks in each business and how effectively these are controlled. Risks have to be identified, properly assessed and recorded and plans have to be made to reduce risk to an acceptable level. For example this could include finding ways to keep the business running during a flu pandemic or managing the reputational risk of employee criminal activity.

Skills

Good process analysis skills, influence and persuasiveness, a thick skin, persistence and tenacity and relationship and partnering skills. Wide experience is helpful as it's about identifying things that can go wrong and putting controls in place to avoid the same problems in future.

Hours

Depend on workload and risks. Many operational risks are of great interest to regulators, with whom interactions can be quite time-intensive, but a typical day would be 8 to 6.

Working Day

Varied. Operational risk will spend time reporting their findings to senior management on a quarterly and possibly monthly basis. If doing a deep review then this will involve spending time around the business seeing processes in action or looking at policies and procedures and developing metrics to measure the effectiveness of controls. A considerable amount of time is spent talking to staff and understanding the issues on the ground.

Profile - Philip White

Education	MSc Strategic Management Consultancy (LMU); ACMA
Role	Operational Risk Controller
Experience	Bank of England, Lloyds Banking Group, i2 Consulting. Roles encompassed programme management, finance, industry research, product development, operations management, client credit control, SOX.

Operational Risk Control is a bit of a cross between a soothsayer and a naysayer but hopefully based on facts rather than psychedelic visions. It's about predicting what might go wrong based on how things currently operate. You're looking for weaknesses in the control environment from process, people and technology perspectives or things outside the firm that could affect our ability to operate. You don't need to have specific or detailed experience of a particular industry or operation to be a controller but you do need to have a keen interest in how things work and it ideally suits someone who has "been around a bit". It suits people with a process re-engineering or management background and I know a lot of auditors in Ops Risk as they have seen a raft of issues in different companies and in different industries and know where things start to go wrong. A lot of former army officers end up in this kind of role as well. They have the ability to quickly understand the point of a process and to analyse the weaknesses - too many hand-offs, poor communication, excessive manual intervention, etc. - a friend of mine ran a consultancy firm that only employed exiting army officers for that very reason.

Role Type	Detail
Front Office Research	*Section 2.3 (page 85)*

ECONOMIST

Role

An economist researcher is a jack of all trades. Their main role is to write economic research and forecast the performance of specific regions with a focus on implications for asset markets. They then have to market that research directly to external clients (e.g. hedge funds) and internal clients (e.g. traders / salespeople) and hopefully in the process help make some returns for both.

Skills

You need to have good ideas about how the economic situation in a country / region will develop and how that will translate in to market moves. You have to be able to write those ideas in client-friendly language – i.e. not too technical. An advanced degree in Economics is not necessary but it helps. An ability to analyse and be creative with data is a must. That's half the job – the research. The other half is the talking. A good manner with clients is therefore an absolute must – you need to have the gift of the gab just like a salesperson.

Hours

Long.

Working Day

Varies. Comment on daily economic data to the press, traders and clients. Work on research ideas or phone / visit clients – always selling them ideas.

Profile - Sunil Kapadia

Education	MA (Economics) Edinburgh University and MSc (Economics) LSE
Role	Economist
Experience	Four years at the Bank of England

Economic research is a very varied role. The two main aspects are:

Writing Research and Producing Trade Ideas

Economists usually cover a certain region, in my case Europe. Our role is to forecast the economy – e.g. to project economic growth, inflation, unemployment and interest rates – using economic theory and analysis but also hunches!. We then use this analysis to come up with a view on interest rates, FX and even top down equity calls, so our research is highly market relevant.

Talking to Clients

Different clients want different services from us. Some just want data provision and analysis, while others want to talk to us about bigger picture themes like central bank policy or government indebtedness. Others may want access to our forecasting models, but they all have one thing in common: they want to achieve returns.

Role Type	Detail
Investment Banking Department / Equity Capital Markets	*Section 2.3 (page 85)*

ORIGINATOR

Role

Helping companies raise capital by issuing either bonds or shares in return for a fee which is a percentage of the capital raised.

Skills

Ability to match up a corporate client's strategic financing objectives with financial products which investors will be willing to buy. Judgement calls on market conditions in order to advise clients on likely success of their funding. Numeracy, familiarity with legal or accounting considerations and/or language and cultural influences depending on area of specialisation e.g. product complexity or particular country bias. Good client skills, whether marketing the bank (the majority of the work) or advising and guiding during deal execution.

Hours

Very long, 8 until late.

Working Day

Whatever it takes - from developing ideas and pitch materials with colleagues to address corporate client needs via calling and travelling to meet clients to capture the elusive deal through to deal execution. Execution involves coordination of a large team of internal and external parties in preparing a deal for market then announcing and marketing it to institutional investors. Usually there are several of these projects at different stages on a given day.

Profile - Derek Lowe

Education	BA in Mathematics with Statistics, Oxford University
Role	Convertible bond originator in Capital Markets, Investment Banking Department
Experience	Joined bank after completing university.

Understanding corporate clients: each corporate client will have their own motivations which determine their objectives, such as strategic direction of capital expenditure or acquisition of other companies, uninterrupted development of their products, lowest interest cost financing, maximum protection of shareholder interests etc. Developing an understanding of these drivers with the relationship bankers (who are typically country- or sector-focused).

Understanding markets: achieving a client's financing objectives is a very practical exercise in what the markets will accept (in size, pricing and features of a financing such as boosting their balance sheet by issuing shares, borrowing via bonds or managing risk). Developing a transaction that will be saleable to investors as well as meeting corporate clients' demands is the key, often in the face of competition with other banks and changing market conditions. A crystal ball is a typical part of the toolkit.

Marketing: the capital markets specialist will be the client's main contact at the bank on the particular deal, so demonstrating how our capabilities can best serve the client, and building rapport, will be important aspects of the deal-winning process. Whether during any introductory meetings or subsequent joint development of ideas, competition between banks will be very high and so it is key that the corporate client sees our bank as the leading source of experience and capability in meeting their financial needs.

Deal execution: after a company has decided to go ahead with a transaction, the capital markets specialists co-ordinate a team of internal colleagues (relationship bankers, sales/trading, operations etc.) and external parties (many lawyers, some accountants, a stock exchange and not forgetting the client) in preparing the deal for announcement which can take from 2 days to 2 months (longer if delays come from corporate events or market condition changes). Then the deal is announced and marketed to institutional investors by the sales team, alongside their daily calls on trade ideas, market trends etc. Within as little as 1 day from announcement there will be enough demand from investors and the corporate client will have secured their funding with another week or month of paperwork before cash changes hands.

Role Type	Detail
Quantitative / Analysis	*Section 2.3 (page 85)*

QUANT

Role

Pricing financial instruments through the creation of mathematical models. Quant is an abbreviation for "Quantitative Analyst".

Skills

Usually quants are mathematicians or physicists, often with a PhD in one of the numerate disciplines. Most models are implemented in Excel so wizard-like knowledge of Excel is a must.

Hours

Long if working alongside traders as a desk quant.

Working Day

Answering trade and sales questions, pricing new products.

Profile - Richard Martin

Education   BA (Hons) Mathematics, Cambridge, PhD Mathematics/Engineering University College, London

Role   Head of Credit Trading and Strategy

Experience   Joined BNP Paribas in 1998 working mainly on credit portfolio modelling, moved to Credit Suisse in 2003 to the Credit Portfolio Strategy Group, then head of Quantitative Credit Strategy. Moved to AHL (part of Man Group PLC) in 2008 as head of credit trading and strategy.

Quantitative analysts are found in a variety of disciplines. Traditionally on the sell side they price derivative securities and work out how to replicate them with simpler instruments, which involves also the risk management of the products by delta-, gamma- and vega-hedging. However, quants are found in other disciplines too. Strategists attempt to mathematically model the market and try to understand how prices should relate to each other, either within an asset class (such as trading credits against each other, or different CDO tranches against each other) or across asset class (for example credit vs. equity trading). In general these quants are less concerned with fitting the market instruments exactly, or hedging; their role is to find mis-pricings (or "alpha value"), and view themselves as price-takers, as do proprietary traders on the sell-side and also the buy-side professionals. There are also modellers who use macroeconomic data to make predictions about the general direction of the market or markets. Finally in the last ten years risk management has attracted a large amount of quantitative attention. These are a different type of problem again: desks, funds and banks often hold positions that they cannot or do not wish to hedge - for example a bank's proprietary books and its loan portfolios. As well as modelling individual risks, a difficult problem when many events are "unforeseen", the risk quants have the problem of understanding how risks accumulate in a portfolio and how to attribute risk to the positions and to the risk-factors that drive it.

Role Type	Detail
Middle Office Support	*Section 2.3 (page 85)*

SALES SUPPORT

Role

Sales support assist the sales team by doing all the administrative tasks generated through the course of business. This frees time for sales people to have more contact with clients.

Skills

Sales support people need to be diligent, have high attention to detail, good interpersonal skills for dealing with clients, high stress resilience and the strength of character to challenge the status quo so processes and controls can be improved. A sense of humour and a thick skin are essential.

Hours

Hours are consistently long.

Working Day

The day starts with reviewing the previous day's trades, checking for unbooked trades and margin requirements, comparing positions with brokers, other banks and between desks, a process called reconciliation. Sales support act as liaison between confirmation, settlement and front office teams. They deal with front office trade queries providing information or amending bookings, and they book trades entered in the sales blotter. Trades are booked into internal risk systems and external systems such as MarkitWire, Bloomberg and TradeWeb.

Profile - Laura-Louise White

Education	BA French, German and Business Studies
Role	EMEA head of OTC Interest Rate Derivative Sales Support
Experience	Joined investment bank as a graduate, worked in a variety of roles within OTC derivative sales support

Sales support is a very varied role which at its centre focuses on controlling the bank's risk. This entails everything from change management and process re-engineering to client and vendor management. Each member of the team is expected to gain a thorough understanding of the risk implications related to the queries and the systems used to book the trades, whilst simultaneously assessing front office and downstream operational impact. It is essential each person has a conscientious and thorough approach to work and the confidence to review established processes if they can be enhanced.

Our client base is varied but can be divided into internal and external groups. Externally our relationships are with our hedge fund, real money and interbank clients who we liaise with for pre- and post-execution related queries as well as our counterparts within the G14 who we work with on industry regulation and straight-through processing projects. Internally our clients are both in the front office who we support in our run the bank roles as well as our clients within operations, legal, finance and credit risk.

TRADE SUPPORT

Role

Trade support ensure all trades are correctly reflected in the system so that risk can be monitored accurately and downstream departments have sufficient information to settle. It is often referred to as middle office because it forms a key link between back and front office functions, gaining exposure to all areas of the bank.

Skills

A typical trade support team will be composed of a variety of skill bases. To satisfy the constant strive for efficiency and control, one skill set is attention to detail, problem-solving and process improvement. For the trade capture element you would need strong knowledge of financial products teamed with numerical and IT skills. Finally, to manage the trade lifecycle it is beneficial to have a good understanding of the front-to-back process from trade execution right down to settlement with the client.

Hours

Hours are consistently long.

Working Day

Morning checks and reports; trade capture; helping with issues for sales, trading, confirmations, settlements, business control (accounting), market risk, collateral management etc; processing coupon and expiry calculations; market close P&L and risk checks.

Profile - Andy Hartwell

Education	Exotic equities trade support
Role	BA(hons) Finance, Accounting and Management Nottingham
Experience	Joined as a graduate

Trade support is at the heart of Operations. As the main contact point for practically any query about a trade it gives you the broadest exposure to the key business areas and a strong appreciation of the front-to-back workflow. Responsibility for trade capture gives good visibility over a trading book, providing you with the opportunity to develop an understanding of the fundamentals of finance, the mechanics of financial products, how they are traded and the steps of risk management.

I would recommend this role for those individuals who like to work in a fast-paced environment and can maintain a high level of accuracy whilst working under pressure. The hours can get demanding at times of high activity, however the opportunity to develop a broad financial skill set and network is unparalleled within Operations.

Role Type	Detail
Quantitative / Trading	*Section 2.3 (page 85)*

STRUCTURER

Role Producing new products to address particular financial requirements.

Skills Extremely detailed knowledge of a particular market or asset type. Possibly an academic background. Good numerical skills.

Hours Typical for a trading desk, very long.

Working Day Creating, pricing, hedging complex, new financial structures.

Profile - Lev Babiev

Education	BS Georgetown University, MBA NYU Stern
Role	Hybrid Exotics Structurer
Experience	Derivatives Strategy, US asset management firm

Lev has a keen intellect and a deep knowledge of finance. Known on his MBA course as "Arb" in recognition of his relentless pursuit of arbitrage opportunities, he is the kind of person who spends a weekend trying to solve a mathematical problem for fun. His role as a structurer is to create new products. Once he dreams up a new structure he has to sell it to clients and work out how to hedge its risk. Lev spends a lot of time figuring out how to price his structures by building mathematical models. To implement his models he uses spreadsheets, although he could implement them in a number of computer languages if so inclined. Despite his cerebral nature, Lev is partial to heavy metal which, remarkably, has not yet destroyed his mind.

Part II

Foundations

1 The Big Picture

1.1 Who invests and why?

An investor is someone who tries to increase their wealth by buying things at a low price and selling them at a high price. The things that investors buy and sell are financial products called INSTRUMENTS. An instrument bought in order to generate profit either by increasing in value before sale or by generating a stream of income payments is an ASSET. Companies obtain CAPITAL to invest in assets by borrowing money through issuing a loan called a BOND or selling part ownership of their company in the form of SHARES (a share is also known as EQUITY or STOCK) and these sources of capital are called LIABILITIES. A financial instrument can be a share, a bond, gold, property, or even cash itself. A SECURITY is an instrument that comes with a certificate of ownership and this certificate can be easily sold to other investors transferring ownership as the certificate changes hands. Bonds and shares are securities but gold and cash are not. Investors range from individuals who buy a few thousand dollars worth of shares to hedge funds that invest billions in a single trade. Individuals who trade their personal wealth are called RETAIL INVESTORS and large companies that trade their capital are INSTITUTIONAL INVESTORS. Although few people understand finance and investment almost everyone is investing in financial markets in some way.

Figure 1.1 shows a simplified view of financial players and markets where those players buy and sell financial instruments. In this simplified world the BUY SIDE is made up of institutions that buy and sell financial instruments in financial markets. The institutions that provide access to financial markets are the SELL SIDE. The sell side is dominated by investment banks and broker-dealers. Investment banks also play a role in helping companies create new financial instruments by issuing new bonds and shares and this is called the PRIMARY MARKET. Once created, bonds and shares can be bought and sold between investors in the SECONDARY MARKET. Although people are generally unaware of the primary market because the secondary market of share and bond prices dominates the news, without primary issuance there would be no secondary market. Retail investors fit into this world via their dealings with pension companies, insurance companies, retail banks and mutual funds. When paying money into their bank account depositors are in fact making a loan to that bank. These deposits then become part of that bank's assets. These banks can lend this money out and receive a higher rate of interest than they pay to their depositors. Such banks are DEPOSITARY BANKS (or RETAIL BANKS in the United Kingdom). Depositary banks will be active in the financial markets because they invest their depositors' capital in assets to generate a profit for their shareholders and to pay interest to depositors.

Many people pay money into insurance policies to insure their house, their car or even their life. Insurance companies accumulate these premia into excess cash that is then re-invested in instruments that they hope will match their future insurance claim payments. If the income from their assets exceeds their claims they can give this to their shareholders as a cash DIVIDEND. Not only is an insurance company trying to get a good return on their investments, they also have to time the cash flows of their assets to coincide with the payments on their liabilities. Bonds are ideal for pension companies because they provide constant, predictable streams of income. Life insurance companies have to generate income far into the future so they are natural buyers of long-dated bonds.

If a retail investor doubts their own ability to invest they may put their money into a fund that is managed by a professional ASSET MANAGER or INVESTMENT MAN-AGER. In the United States these asset management companies are called MUTUAL FUNDS, in the UK they are known as OPEN ENDED INVESTMENT COMPANIES (OEIC, pronounced "oik"), and more generally they are called INVESTMENT FUNDS. Investment funds make their money by charging clients an annual fee which is a percentage of their investment. In return they use their expertise and access to financial information to try and increase their fund capital by buying instruments that increase in value or that generate an income. Investment funds are on the buy side because they buy and sell instruments from brokers and investment banks on the sell side. Pension funds are asset managers, and when you pay money into a pension during the course of your career your capital is being invested by a fund manager. If your pension fund manager loses all your money you will have no pension, so there are strict regulations for pension funds restricting the securities they may buy and the risk that they can take. In particular pension funds have limits on how much money they can borrow to boost their return and the derivatives they can buy.

A HIGH NET WORTH INDIVIDUAL (HNWI means a very rich person) can afford to buy the services of better asset managers and so invest via HEDGE FUNDS which have the top tier investment managers. Hedge funds opt out of regulation so that they have complete freedom in their investment strategy. For example hedge funds can buy any sort of derivative or borrow money to boost their fund returns. Pension funds and mutual funds are sometimes called REAL MONEY funds to distinguish them from hedge funds whose invested capital may be mostly borrowed. Boosting return in this way increases risk that the better fund managers can keep under control. Another reason why investment in hedge funds is limited to HNWI is to protect people that have a small amount of capital that they cannot afford to lose. High net worth individuals frequently have a FAMILY OFFICE which deals with their global financial affairs and the office may employ its own asset managers. The family office will deal with investment banks and broker-dealers directly and the size of their trades may be comparable with those of institutional investors.

Governments collect money in the form of taxes and through issuing bonds. They must manage their expenditure and their income and this is their FISCAL POLICY. When the government issues bonds to raise money it is usually with the help of investment banks from the sell side. The government may also have excess cash from its natural resources such as oil reserves. This can be put into a fund called a SOVEREIGN WEALTH FUND which is then invested in financial instruments to increase its value. The size of some sovereign wealth funds is staggering with the largest, such as the

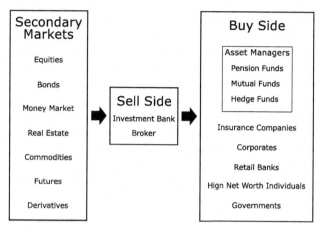

Figure 1.1:
Relationship between investors, investment banks and secondary markets.

fund for the United Arab Emirates, approaching $1,000,000,000,000 (a trillion dollars). Governments sometimes intervene in the foreign exchange market to either devalue or increase the value of their own currency, a process called FOREIGN EXCHANGE INTERVENTION, and they will do this by executing foreign exchange transactions with the sell side. A country that exports its goods abroad will want to have a currency that is weak relative to the currency of the countries that receive its goods. By weakening its currency the exporting country's goods will be cheaper to buy. In order to devalue its own currency it will sell its domestic currency and buy the currency of the country to which it exports. Importing countries want to strengthen their currency so that their currency will buy more imported produce for the same price.

PRIVATE EQUITY companies are on the buy side and they specialize in buying entire companies. They do this because they are expert in restructuring businesses to be more profitable and therefore more valuable. The companies they buy will probably be flagging financially so they will have a low valuation. If a company has shares that trade on the stock market it is PUBLICLY OWNED, but if a private equity company buys up all the available shares the company becomes PRIVATELY OWNED, hence the name "private equity". Then if the private equity company succeeds in turning around a company's fortunes they will sell the company at a profit. They can either sell the company to another company in a private sale, or they can issue shares in the company which are sold in the stock market, placing the company back in public ownership. A stock market share sale is called a FLOTATION. The private equity company may enlist the help of one or more investment banks in the purchase of the company. Investment banks will lend money to the private equity company and also advise in any subsequent stock market flotation as part of its EXIT STRATEGY.

1.2 What is investment?

Investment is a battle between fear and greed. Everyone would like to make a large return, but it is impossible to make large returns without taking a large risk. If your life is governed by a desire for safety, and you live in one of the industrialized nations such as the United States of America, the safest investment is to lend money to your government. People lend to the government by buying government bonds, known as GOVVIES, in the knowledge that as a last resort the government can pay its debts by printing more money[1]. Buying government bonds keeps your fear to a minimum but does not satisfy your greed as govvies pay small rates of interest. At the other extreme, if your greed is unchecked by fear and you are willing to risk losing all your capital in return for the highest potential profit you could buy shares in start-up companies. You may be lucky enough to invest in the next Google and make a significant profit. But for every successful start-up like Google there are a thousand failures. This high risk strategy is like betting on "00" in roulette in that most of the time you will lose all your money but infrequently you will hit the jackpot.

Investment is a trade-off between fear, which is quantified as a number called RISK, and greed, which is quantified as RETURN. Professional investors spend a great deal of time and money estimating these two numbers and then adjusting their investments to keep an acceptably low level of risk and high level of return. One of the many measures of risk might be "How much money could I lose by buying X?". And a measure of return might be "If I buy X how much money do I expect to make?" Return is quantified as the percentage increase in an investment over a year. If we invest $100 today and have $110 after a year that is a return of 10%. If we invest $100 today and have $110 after one month we annualize the return by scaling it up. This would be a return of 10% over one month or twelve times as much over one year, or an ANNUALIZED RETURN of 120%. Risk is usually measured by working out the average day-to-day variability or VOLATILITY of the value of an investment. The volatility of the S&P 500 index is published as a volatility index called VIX. Officially VIX is the Chicago Board Options Exchange Volatility Index, and unofficially it is called the FEAR INDEX. When markets are tumbling VIX increases in value, and when they are in a period of steady growth VIX decreases. The value of the S&P 500 alongside the VIX is shown in Figure 1.2. The words "volatility", "uncertainty" and "fear" are almost synonymous.

1.2.1 Return

When you buy assets what you are really buying is a distribution of returns. For this discussion we will think about daily return, which is how much our investment increases or decreases in value over a single day, expressed as a percentage. What we are after is a set of positive daily returns, and the larger the better. Unfortunately it is impossible to buy an asset that will always give positive returns without any negative returns. When we calculate things such as expected return, volatility and other risk measures what we are doing is summarizing our distribution of returns. If

---

[1]Printing more money can lead to inflation, as demonstrated by Zimbabwe which issued a 100 trillion ($100,000,000,000,000) Zimbabwean dollar banknote in 2009 shortly before the currency ceased to exist.

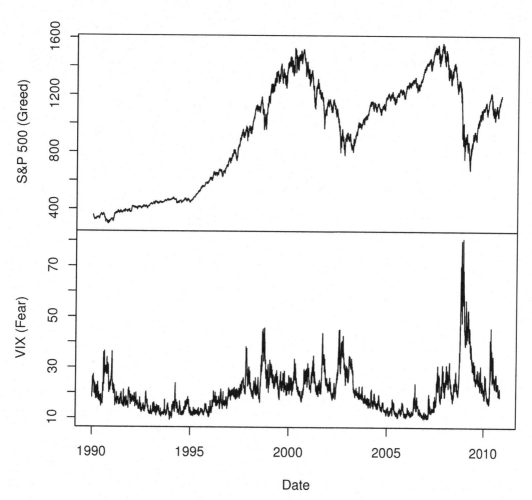

Figure 1.2: S&P 500 stock index vs. CBOE VIX volatility index.

we use return distributions to compare investments implicitly we are assuming that the returns in future will resemble those in the past. Of course this need not be true, but it is a good start.

To show how we calculate return here is the set of closing prices in UK Sterling pence (one hundred pennies make one pound Sterling) from October 26th to November 6th for the pharmaceutical company Astrazeneca as traded on the London Stock Exchange. This is a period of two weeks.

Mon	Tue	Wed	Thu	Fri	Mon	Tue	Wed	Thu	Fri
2775.5	2830	2789	2752	2742	2721	2690.5	2702	2701.5	2696.5

The two common methods for working out returns are SIMPLE RETURN and CONTINUOUS RETURN (continuous return is also called LOG RETURN). Simple returns take the difference in price over a given period and look at the change over the period divided by the price at the beginning. So if price at the beginning of the period is p_{begin} and price at the end of the period is p_{end} and the time period in years is t then the annualized simple return is defined as

$$r_{simple} = \frac{1}{t} \frac{p_{end} - p_{begin}}{p_{begin}}$$

Continuous return assumes that the price is growing exponentially and is defined as

$$r_{continuous} = \frac{1}{t} \ln \frac{p_{end}}{p_{begin}}$$

For our time series the simple return from Monday to Tuesday of the first week would be $\frac{2830-2775.5}{2775.5}$ or 2.0%. We could annualize this by scaling up by the number of trading days in a year, but here we will look at the unannualized returns. The continuous return (or log-return) over the same one day period would be $\ln \frac{2830}{2775.5}$ or 2.0%. If we take more decimal places then the two returns are different, the simple return 1.9636% and the continuous return is 1.9626%. The returns for each day over this two week period are as follows:

Day	Mon	Tue	Wed	Thu	Fri	Mon	Tue	Wed	Thu	Fri
AZN Share price	2775.5	2830	2789	2752	2742	2721	2690.5	2702	2701.5	2696.5
Simple return %		1.96	-1.45	-1.33	-0.36	-0.77	-1.12	0.43	-0.02	-0.19
Continuous return %		1.94	-1.46	-1.34	-0.36	-0.77	-1.13	0.43	-0.02	-0.19

There is one other important consideration when calculating returns which is the period of returns. It may sometimes make sense to use weekly returns rather than daily returns. If there is a consistent weekly pattern to prices, such as slow trading mid-week and lots of trading on Friday, then weekly returns will iron out such patterns. So the first simple weekly return in our period will be from the first Monday to the second Monday $\frac{2721-2775.5}{2775.5}$ which is -1.96%. The second simple weekly return would be from the first to the second Tuesday $\frac{2690.5 - 2830}{2830}$ or -4.93%. On average the weekly returns will be larger than the daily returns if they are not annualized because stocks move further in a week than they do in a day.

1.2.2 Risk

Risk comes in a variety of forms. Fluctuation in prices due to market forces gives rise to MARKET RISK. If you buy shares in or lend money to a company it may become bankrupt and you may lose your entire investment. The risk of losing money due to bankruptcy or refusal to repay debt is called CREDIT RISK. If the value of your assets depends on interest rates then you will have INTEREST RATE RISK. Market, credit and interest rate risk can be reduced by buying instruments that react in the opposite direction to your assets or selling instruments that react in the same direction as your assets and this deliberate cancellation of risk is called HEDGING. Other types of risk are difficult to model and nigh impossible to hedge, such as LIQUIDITY RISK. Liquidity is the ability to easily and quickly sell an asset for cash. Liquidity tends to become a problem when markets are in turmoil as the market is flooded with people trying to sell their assets and buyers are scarce.

Going back to the Astrazeneca example there are many methods for quantifying the risk of owning that stock. VOLATILITY or VOL is a simple and commonly used measure of risk, so we will look in detail to see how this is calculated. Our continuous returns over the two week period were +1.94%, -1.46%, -1.34%, -0.36%, -0.77%, -1.13%, 0.43%, -0.02%, and -0.19%. There was a five day period where the stock price dropped every day, then a one day respite, then two more falls. Volatility can be thought of as the typical size of move of the stock over a given time period. Volatility, like interest rates, is always annualized. To work out volatility we first find the mean return which is -0.32% then find the squared differences between each return and the mean. We square to get rid of the sign, so a value of +0.68% contributes the same amount toward volatility as -1.32 because the differences to the mean are -1% and +1% which when squared both give +0.0001. Then we sum these squared deviations and take their average. Finally we work out the square root because we want our answer in currency, not currency squared[2].

$$\text{Volatility} = \sqrt{\frac{1.94^2 + 1.46^2 + 1.34^2 + 0.36^2 + 0.77^2 + 1.13^2 + 0.43^2 + 0.02^2 + 0.19^2}{9}}$$

And so we arrive at a volatility of 1.1%. Because we used daily returns our answer is a typical daily return so we would expect Astrazeneca's returns to be around plus or minus 1% on a typical day. If we see a return of +5% or -10% we would be surprised. Volatility is annualized so we scale up by the square root of time. A good rule of thumb is called the RULE OF 16 which converts daily vol into annual vol by multiplying by 16. The number 16 comes from the square root of the number of trading days in a year which is a little bit more than 256, and the square root of 256 is 16. So if volatility is 1% in a day we would expect volatility of about 16% in one year. For an annual

---

[2]There is a twist which is that we divide by one less than nine because this gives an unbiased estimate of the standard deviation of the population of returns that we are trying to measure.

volatility of 50% daily volatility would be about 3%. On the news you may sometimes hear the presenter give the value of a STOCK INDEX. An index is like a barometer for the whole market because it is an average price of many stocks. Each currency and each market has its "standard" index, so US stocks have the S&P 500 index and the Dow Jones Industrial Average, the UK stock market has the FTSE 100, the Japanese stock market has the Nikkei 225. If all the stocks in the index go up one day there will be a large increase in the index. If some go up and some go down then the index will not change much. If all the stocks go down, the whole index would go down sharply. Volatility lets you interpret the percentage moves in an index. If the annual volatility of the S&P 500 stock index is, say, 30% then you know that the daily volatility is about 2%. So if you hear the S&P 500 index has gone down 2% in one day you can go on about your business as this is a typical daily move. If the S&P 500 has gone down 6% in a single day you know that a drama is unfolding.

From our two week history of Astrazeneca's closing price we obtain nine daily returns. Earlier we said that when we buy an asset we are buying a distribution of returns. What do we mean by a return distribution? To explain a return distribution we introduce the idea of return "buckets". The buckets chop up the range of returns into regions and we count how often returns fall into each region or bucket. For example we could have the following buckets:

Return bucket	< -3%	-3% to -2%	-2% to -1%	-1% to 0%	0% to 1%	1% to 2%	2% to 3%	>3%
Returns	-	-	-1.46, -1.34, -1.13	-0.36, -0.77, -0.02, -0.19	0.43	1.94	-	-
Count	0	0	3	4	1	1	0	0
Frequency %	0	0	33.3	44.4	11.1	11.1	0	0

We can see that the buckets with small returns have the most counts and that large positive and negative returns happen less frequently. As we add more buckets and more returns a clearer picture emerges. Here are the 1,721 continuous daily returns between January 1, 2003 and November 20, 2009 as counted in our return buckets.

Return bucket	< -3%	-3% to -2%	-2% to -1%	-1% to 0%	0% to 1%	1% to 2%	2% to 3%	>3%
Count	60	85	244	486	437	258	84	67
Frequency %	3.5	4.9	14.2	28.2	25.4	15.0	4.9	3.9

It is striking that these returns are positive just 49.16% of the time but the positive returns were slightly larger on average (1.26%) than the negative returns (-1.18%). This slight imbalance is sufficient to increase the share price from 1,889p on January 1, 2003 to 2,695p on November 20, 2009. This is because the sum of all the continuous daily returns is +35.54% so the final share price is $1889 \times e^{0.3554}$ which is 2,695. It takes very little to shift the balance of returns into negative territory and tip our investment from profit to loss. We like positive returns and we dislike negative returns. But what we utterly abhor are very large negative returns, or DRAWDOWNS, because it can take a long time to recover from a price crash. A fund manager may never recover from a drawdown on their fund as they are likely to lose their job. The worst return over this time period for Astrazeneca was -11.5% when the price dropped from 2,805 to 2,501 from close to close between November 18 and November 19, 2008. It is possible to protect against such crashes by buying a PUT OPTION, as we shall see later (Section 12.1.4 on page 427).

Now that we can think in terms of return distributions we can reinterpret the rather vague statement that greater risk means greater return. Over the long term our Astrazeneca return was based on the slight excess of positive returns over negative returns. We paid for this return by having to erode our capital with all the negative returns that came with an investment in this stock. If we wanted to buy a stock with greater return than Astrazeneca it would have a greater volatility. The distribution would again be centred around zero but would have a greater width with propotionately more very large positive and very large negative returns. This distribution would have a greater volatility because vol is just another measure of the "width" of a distribution. The price we pay for the larger positive returns for this more volatile stock is the larger negative returns which could easily wipe out our profit.

Volatility is obviously not a perfect measure of risk. We worry on days when our return is negative and rejoice on days when our return is positive. But when we square deviations from the mean we are saying that these two outcomes contribute equally to risk. Volatility is a symmetric risk measure because it weighs positive and negative returns equally. To address this problem we can use asymmetric measures of risk. One approach is to say that the returns follow a normal distribution with volatility set by historical observations over some time period. For Astrazeneca the mean of the distribution of continuous daily returns was 0.02% and the volatility was 1.70%. Then we can ask what return value corresponds to a once in 100 day loss, or a once in 1000 day loss. This approach is called VALUE AT RISK.

If we assume that the returns follow a normal $N(0.02, 1.7)$ distribution then the 1 in 100 day loss is -3.9% and the 1 in 1000 day loss is -5.2% (see Section 3.1 on page 97 and following sections for background on probability distributions and statistics). The probability of getting our minimum return of -11.47% is 0.00000000000707. In other words the normal distribution says that such a return should occur once every 390 million years. Experience tells us that such returns occur much more frequently, so our normal model is too short-tailed and should credit outliers with more likelihood. For this reason some dispense with the normal distribution in favour of heavier tailed distributions, such as a Student's t or the Levy distribution that have much heavier tails. Alternatively we can dispense with parametric distributions altogether and take the first percentile of the returns to get the once in 100 day loss. We do this by sorting the returns into ascending order and as there are 1,721 returns we take the $(0.01 \times 1,721)$-th which is the 17th return which is -4.50. Or if we wanted the 0.001 percentile we would take the $(0.001 \times 1,721)$-th or second lowest return which is -9.84. The more extreme the percentile the more samples are required to get a meaningful estimate.

1.2.3 Alpha and Beta

Stock price variations are driven partly by the fate of the company, but the company is itself swept along with the market. There is a commonly accepted language that is used to split up the return of an asset into an asset-specific component and a market-driven component. In order to guage the health of the general market we might use a stock index. Our example stock Astrazeneca is a member of the FTSE 100 stock index and its share price is somehow entangled with the index. Some stocks are more index-entangled than others, and our measure of entanglement is usually called BETA. Beta is a statistical measure called the linear correlation coefficient which measures whether the returns of an asset move in tandem or independently of an index. If $\beta = +1$ then the asset and the index are perfectly correlated; that is, if the index increases by 1% then the asset also increases in value by 1%; if $\beta = 0$ then the return of the asset and the index are not at all correlated with one another, they are INDEPENDENT; if $\beta = -1$ then the return of the asset and the index move in exactly opposite directions. If the index increases by 1% then the asset will decrease by 1%. Beta can be greater than 1 and less than -1, which means that the movements are greater or smaller than those of the index. The stock-specific return is called ALPHA and measures how much return one would expect from the asset if the return on the index were zero. The way we estimate alpha and beta is to do a linear regression of the asset returns on the index returns as shown in Figure 1.3 (see Section 3.6 on page 114 for an explanation of linear regression). As an equation we are saying that

$$
\begin{array}{ccccccccc}
r_a & = & \alpha & + & \beta & \times & r_m & + & \varepsilon \\
\text{Asset} & = & \text{Asset-Specific} & + & \text{Market Correlation} & \times & \text{Market} & + & \text{Error}
\end{array}
$$

If we imagine that we have an investment fund where $\beta = 1$ and $\alpha = 0$ then we are simply tracking the market, and this would be called a TRACKER FUND or INDEX TRACKER. If we swap the coefficients around and so $\beta = 0$ and $\alpha = 1$ we would have an ABSOLUTE RETURN or PURE ALPHA fund. Such a fund should be completely unaffected by market crises or market booms. It should steadily increase in value at a fixed rate α. Inflation-linked UK government bonds are weakly negatively correlated with the FTSE 100. If stocks are increasing in value then government bonds, which are a safe-haven, lose their lustre and fall in value. If stocks are going down inflation-linked government bonds seem more attractive and go up in value. However beta is just -0.09 so the anti-correlation is weak. Similarly the return on gold is largely independent of the FTSE 100 return with a beta of just 0.13. This is why gold is a useful asset class to diversify a stock portfolio. HSBC Holdings, the financial services company is almost perfectly correlated with the FTSE 100 with beta equal to 0.99, so buying HSBC stock is like buying the index. Finally Kazakhmys PLC the mining company has beta 2.3 and is therefore like a boosted, or LEVERAGED position in the FTSE 100. Leverage means that if the FTSE 100 goes up 1% then Kazakhmys will go up about 2.3% and if the FTSE goes down 1% Kazakhmys will go down 2.3%. Alpha is practically zero for all of these assets.

Alpha and beta are not just statistical coefficients, they are a language used widely in the fund industry to describe the aim of a fund. If you want exposure to the market as a whole, as measured by an index, you want "beta". If you want to have steady returns that can be relied upon independent of the movement of markets as a whole

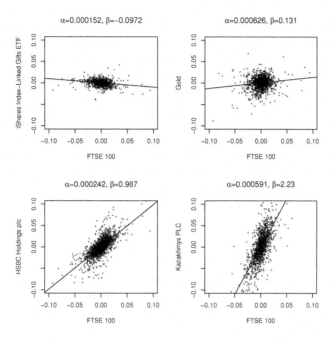

Figure 1.3: Regression of returns against the FTSE 100 index.

you want "alpha". Beta is easy to create but alpha is elusive. To create beta a fund manager simply has to buy the assets in the index with the money they are given. A fund that tracks the S&P 500 index simply has to buy the stocks in the index in the correct proportions then the fund will have a beta value of 1. This can be done quite cheaply and easily so investors would be willing to pay very little for this index-tracking service, in the range of 20 to 50 BASIS POINTS per year. A basis point is one hundredth of a percent, so 20 to 50 basis points is 0.2% to 0.5% of assets under management. What has proved much more difficult is to create alpha, particularly in times of crisis. It is almost impossible to create a portfolio that always maintains growth in good times and during market crashes. The few fund managers who do manage to generate alpha are paid well to do so. Generally investors who seek alpha will go to hedge fund managers, and the fees that they pay for their services are high. Typically hedge funds charge 2% on assets under management and take 20% of any return that they make, and this fee structure is called TWO-AND-TWENTY.

When we invest our capital by buying an asset we are deliberately exposing our capital to risk. Each asset that we can buy is a bundle of risks. Different assets expose investors to different risks and in return investors receive payment for their RISK EXPOSURE. In return for exposing their capital to risk investors earn a RISK PREMIUM. For example bonds expose bondholders to PRICE RISK as the price of bonds fluctuate in the bond market. Bonds are also sensitive to interest rates, so if rates go up bonds lose value, so bonds come with significant INTEREST RATE RISK. And as a bond is effectively a loan it comes with the risk that the bondholder will not be repaid, and this is CREDIT RISK. Investors can either buy this bundle of risk called a "bond" and reap the reward in the form of a high yielding stream of interest payments, or they can do away with the bond and take the pure interest rate risk or credit risk by buying and selling DERIVATIVES. The greater the risk the greater the risk premium an investor would expect, otherwise the investment is not worthwhile.

Derivatives are a way of taking an asset and skimming off different types of risk that can then be traded in pure form. The value of a derivative depends on the value of other instruments. Its value is derived from these UNDERLYING instruments. If an investor likes the credit risk of a company but is not interested in interest rate risk she can buy their bond and hedge away the interest rate risk with an interest rate derivative called an INTEREST RATE SWAP. Or if it is the interest rate risk she is after she would hedge away the credit risk of the bond with a credit derivative called a CREDIT DEFAULT SWAP. If the investor is allowed to buy pure derivatives then it is possible to do away with the bond altogether and trade pure interest rate or credit risk via interest rate swaps or credit default swaps. Trading the derivative without owning the underlying is called a NAKED POSITION. For example, instead of buying shares in a company an investor could buy equity derivatives on that company's shares such as calls and puts. An equity derivative exposes an investor to the price risk of the underlying equity but the investor does not have to commit as much capital to get that risk exposure. Getting risk exposure with minimal outlay of capital is called either LEVERAGED EXPOSURE , UNFUNDED EXPOSURE or SYNTHETIC EXPOSURE.

1.3 What can you buy?

Just as an artist has a palette on which they can combine paint to create works of art, so investors have a palette of financial instruments that can be combined in a portfolio in order to achieve a particular balance of risk and return. The broadest categorisation of financial instruments is between mass-produced standardized instruments traded in bulk in the equivalent of a financial supermarket and more bespoke instruments that are traded directly between buyer and seller. Mass-produced instruments are traded through an intermediate company called an EXCHANGE. These are called EXCHANGE-TRADED instruments. When trading on an exchange buyers and sellers never face one another directly, they buy from the exchange and sell to the exchange. The other class of instruments are hand-crafted for each deal and the deal is transacted directly between a buyer and seller. These hand-crafted instruments are known as OVER-THE-COUNTER (OTC).

Every market can suffer a downturn. When this happens you want to sell your position as quickly as possible. If nobody is willing to trade with you then you can be wiped out. The speed with which you can turn an asset into cash by selling it is called LIQUIDITY or the DEPTH of the market. Exchange traded markets are usually very deep and liquid which makes them extremely attractive to investors. Over-the-counter markets are usually illiquid because there is no "marketplace" in which they trade and this makes OTC instruments more risky. Even exchange traded securities such as shares may be illiquid when trading shares of small companies. If you hold 100,000 shares of a small company for which the average daily trading volume is 10,000 shares it may take several days to sell your shares, which could be disastrous if the share price is plummeting. Liquidity is extremely important.

Another variation in the way an investor gets exposure to an asset class is the timing of their purchase. If they pay money to buy an asset today then this is a SPOT TRADE. Spot is short for on-the-spot. If they defer the hand-over of cash in return for the asset to some fixed time in the future this is called a FORWARD if traded over-the-counter or a FUTURE if traded on an exchange.

Equities Equities (also called shares or stock) are traded on exchanges through a broker. When you buy shares you are buying ownership of part of a company. You may receive some share of the profits as a dividend and will get a vote at shareholder meetings. The upside, or maximum potential return, on shares is unlimited, but you may lose your entire investment if the company becomes bankrupt.

The Money Market By lending money to governments, banks or companies short term you receive a small return but take very little interest rate risk. Short-term generally means instruments that mature in a year or less. Money market investments are safe havens for parking capital while earning a modest return. Money market instruments include short-term bonds and loans such as COMMERCIAL PAPER (CP), CERTIFICATES OF DEPOSIT, short-dated government bonds, longer dated bonds that have only one year or less remaining until maturity, and the REPO market which is a form of collateralized lending.

Government Bonds Lending money to the government. This is a very safe investment with low return if the government is one of the G7 countries[3] and has a small debt burden as a proportion of GROSS DOMESTIC PRODUCT (GDP). If the government becomes bankrupt then this leads to widespread turmoil in financial markets. Some countries have been known to default in the past, such as Argentina and Ecuador. These governments' bonds are considered to be risky and must pay a high rate of interest. Other countries have not defaulted for the last century or longer, such as the US Treasury and the UK Treasury and these entities can fund themselves cheaply because of their credit-worthiness. Short-term government bonds are a significant part of the money market, and longer dated government bonds which carry greater interest rate risk are not.

Corporate Bonds Lending money to a company. Corporate bonds are riskier than government bonds because the company may become bankrupt and you may lose your capital, so you are taking a credit risk. Buying corporate bonds is less risky than buying equity from the same company as you will recover more of your investment in the event of bankuptcy. Bond markets tend to be illiquid which carries a risk if there is a crisis.

Commodities Buying things such as precious metals (gold, silver, platinum), non-precious metals (copper, aluminium, tin, lead, zinc, nickel), agricultural products (corn, soybeans, wheat, live cattle, cocoa, coffee, sugar, cotton, crude palm oil, robusta coffee) or various types of oil (crude, heating oil, natural gas, Brent crude, gas oil). Usually these are bought and sold as derivatives such as futures rather

---

[3]G7 countries include France, Germany, Italy, Japan, United Kingdom and United States of America.

than actual stockpiles of physical commodities. Commodities such as gold, which can be stored over long periods of time, are safe in that commodities have intrinsic value, hence the rush to buy gold in financial crises. Commodity futures are exchange-traded.

FX If a company has to buy foreign goods or trades in many countries then it will at some point have to convert cash from one currency into another. This business is called foreign exchange or FX and is a large and liquid market both in cash FX where phyisical currency is traded and derivatives based on foreign exchange rates. FX is dominated by the OTC market but can also be exchange-traded.

Real Estate & Commercial Property Land is an asset that can be bought and sold, and although the focus is usually commercial property in the centre of large cities some institutional investors such as hedge funds deal in agricultural land in recognition of its economic importance in the face of global population growth. The drawback with real estate is that it is a very illiquid market which means that when a crash occurs it may take a very long time to sell these assets. An indirect way to get exposure to property prices is via a Real Estate Investment Trust (REIT) which uses pooled capital from its investors to buy real estate then pays the capital appreciation on sale or rental income back to its investors.

Funds Rather than buy assets directly you can buy into the expertise of a professional asset management company to invest your money on your behalf. If you want to track a published index like the FTSE 100, the S&P 500, or the DAX then you can buy an INDEX TRACKER FUND. If you want exposure to corporate bonds then you might buy a CORPORATE BOND FUND. Some funds trade directly on stock exchanges and these are called Exchange Traded Funds (ETF), and even though they trade like shares they offer exposure to many different asset classes usually for a very small fee. ETFs are usually very liquid and allow investors to trade intra-day. HEDGE FUNDS charge high fees but usually employ the best fund managers, and usually only deal with high net worth individuals.

Derivatives Contracts whose value depend in some way on the values of equities, commodities, bonds, currency exchange rates or even the weather. Most derivatives are now very well understood but some are so complex that few people understand how to calculate their value. Derivatives can be exchange-traded or OTC.

1.4 Where can you buy it?

Assets are usually bought from MARKET MAKERS and BROKERS. When you see film clips on the news of people on trading floors surrounded by computer displays covered in brightly coloured numbers, phone in hand, shouting excitedly at one other, these people will almost certainly be market makers. Most trading jobs at investment banks are market making jobs. A market maker must be willing to buy and sell in their market whenever a client wants to buy or sell, so they add value to the market by creating LIQUIDITY. By the nature of their role a market maker is usually left holding an INVENTORY of their assets which they must carefully risk-manage as they do not want to be exposed to price risk.

Invariably the price at which market makers sell something will be more than the price at which they buy. The difference in price at which the market maker buys (their BID PRICE), and sells (their OFFER PRICE or ASK PRICE) is known as BID-OFFER SPREAD[4] or more informally as the trader's EDGE. A market maker will try and make the bid-offer spread as large as possible because this is how they make money. Competitors in a market will force a market maker to tighten their bid-offer spread. When a new asset comes along it usually trades at a large spread. As the market in the new asset becomes more liquid spreads tighten. Eventually volumes may become immense, as they have for the spot foreign exchange market, and computers are used to make the market as the only way to make money is to have large trade volume and to make split-second adjustments in price. At this point the market has become a FLOW TRADING business.

Market makers make their money through their bid-offer spread. Brokers act on behalf of their clients buying and selling assets on an exchange as instructed by the client. Brokers make their money through charging a fee called a COMMISSION. Since brokers do not need to hold any instruments directly they have no inventory. Brokers add value by giving investors exposure to instruments traded on exchanges by having a seat on those exchanges. For example the Chicago Board Options Exchange does not allow people to walk in off the street and start trading. To trade on the CBOE you must be a member of the exchange or you have to deal with a broker who has a seat on the exchange. Some brokers also deal using their own capital and these are called BROKER-DEALERS. However brokers cannot be both a broker and a dealer in the same transaction in order to avoid a conflict of interest, so they have to be clear for each transaction whether it is a trade on behalf of their client or on their own book.

To understand the difference between brokers and dealers it may help to draw on analogies in our daily lives. When you buy a house you buy from an estate agent in the United Kingdom or a realtor in the United States. Estate agents/realtors are brokers because they charge you a fee for selling you a house that is some percentage of the value of the house. As brokers they do not possess an inventory of property, their job is simply to match buyer and seller. In contrast a supermarket is like a market maker in that they buy at a low price from producers and sell at a higher price to shoppers in their stores. Supermarkets, like market makers, have to maintain an inventory of products that they sell and make their money through buying low and selling high. And just like supermarkets, market makers are always there to provide a market where clients can buy, so they provide liquidity. Market makers, unlike supermarkets, provide a two way market and allow clients to buy or sell. It is as if you could walk into your supermarket and sell a can of beer to the supermarket at $0.99 or buy a can of beer from the supermarket at $1.01.

The most liquid markets are those traded on an exchange and the largest exchanges by volume are futures exchanges. Historically futures exchanges grew up around agriculture allowing farmers to lock in a profitable price for their future crop well before harvest time. The futures markets now trade a bewildering variety of contracts

---

[4]A useful way of remembering the meaning of bid and offer from the investor's point of view is: "bid to get rid".

which still include things such as grain and pork bellies, but have expanded to include futures on interest rates or even the weather. By centralizing all trading the exchange is an informational hub, collecting such information as who traded, what they traded, when they traded and how much they traded. The exchange will disseminate this information in aggregate form, so that all market participants know volume and price data and this data is updated by the second while markets are open. Whereas buying an OTC asset directly from a counterparty incorporates credit risk, inserting an exchange between buyer and seller removes this risk, as exchanges have impeccable credit quality. In the aftermath of the Credit Crisis governments and regulators wanted to move trading of all OTC instruments onto exchanges and as a result credit derivatives such as credit default swaps became exchange traded. In the futures market most institutions trade via a broker, but investment banks will probably be members and can trade directly on the exchange and they are usually broker-dealers. Futures exchanges include:

CBOT Chicago Board of Trade. Offers a wide range of futures: agricultural (corn, soybeans, wheat, ethanol, rice), interest rates (government bonds, interest rate swaps), indices (DJIA futures) and metals (gold, silver).

CME Chicago Mercantile Exchange. Trades a wide range of futures including commodities (butter, milk, cheese, cattle, lean hogs, pork bellies), equities (futures on the S&P 500, NASDAQ Composite, Russell 2000, Nikkei 225), foreign exchange, interest rates, housing indices, and weather.

ICE Intercontinental Exchange. Operates ICE Futures U.S., ICE Futures Europe and Winnipeg Commodity Exchange. Specialises in agricultural and soft commodities (cocoa, sugar, coffee, orange juice, cotton and grains).

MDEX Bursa Malaysia Derivatives Berhad. Although it offers other types of future, its specialty is crude palm oil futures (FCPO) and crude palm kernel oil futures. Palm oil is widely used in food products, cosmetics, soap, and washing powder.

LIFFE London International Financial Futures and Options Exchange. Pronounced to rhyme with "strife". Specialises in interest rate futures, but also some equity index, single equity futures and options.

LME London Metal Exchange. Offers futures and options contracts for aluminium, copper, nickel, tin, zinc and lead and aluminium alloy.

NYMEX New York Mercantile Exchange. Trades fossil fuel products (crude oil, gasoline, heating oil, natural gas, propane, coal), metals (uranium, gold, silver, copper, aluminum, platinum, palladium) and electricity. Merged with COMEX on August 3, 1994.

COMEX New York Commodities Exchange. Merged with NYMEX in 1994, although a division of labour still exists: COMEX deals mostly in metals and NYMEX in oil and gas.

Just like commodity futures, equities are traded through exchanges and so incur no counterparty risk. Many countries have their own stock exchanges. Retail investors in stocks usually trade through a broker so they do not interact with the exchange directly. In addition to shares which provide part ownership of a company there are now many ETFs that trade just like equities on an exchange even though they may provide exposure to any portfolio of assets such as gold or bonds. There are rules for each exchange which govern codes of conduct for the companies that trade on the exchange. For example companies that trade on an exchange must provide publicly available, standardized financial reports on a regular basis so that investors have a clear view of their financial performance and can make informed investment decisions. The exchange will also keep records of who owns what stock called a share register. This is important if a company pays a dividend to its shareholders because the register determines who gets paid and their share of the dividend. To see the latest volume data on the number of shares traded globally on each exchange see the web site for the World Federation of Exchanges[5]. The top five exchanges by total year to date value of share trading in April 2009 are:

Europe		Americas		Asia-Pacific	
Deutsche Börse	EUR	Nasdaq	USD	Tokyo S.E.	JPY
London S.E.	GBP	NYSE Euronext (US)	USD	Shanghai S.E.	CNY
NYSE Euronext (Europe)	EUR	TSX Group	CAD	Korea Exchange	KRW
BME Spanish Exchanges	EUR	BM&FBOVESPA	BRN	Hong Kong Exchanges	HKD
SIX Swiss Exchange	CHF	Santiago S.E.	CLP	Shenzhen S.E.	CNY

Buying and selling bonds is usually done through a broker. The minimum investment for bonds, the MINIMUM PIECE , is typically greater than buying single shares and this may put off retail investors. The risk-reward profile of bonds makes them attractive to institutional investors like pension funds and insurance companies who know that they must invest for the long term. Institutional investors will either speak directly to bond sales desks at investment banks or to bond brokers. Another way that retail investors can get exposure to the bond market is by buying into bond funds managed by asset managers. The remit for these bond funds is to use their pool of investor money to purchase bonds and to actively manage the risk of the fund by buying and selling bonds that give a good reward but do not incur too much risk. Buying such a fund is less risky for a retail investor because the fund is diversified. If you have only $1,000 to invest this will be the minimum piece of a single bond. If your bond issuer defaults you will lose almost all of your capital. If you invest your $1,000 in a bond fund which pools your money with that of other investors to buy a diversified and well-managed bond fund then the default of a single bond in that fund will hardly matter at all. The drawback with a fund is that it is only as good as its asset manager and you pay a fee for the asset manager whether they are good or bad.

The foreign exchange market, or FX market, is divided into SPOT FX and FX DERIVATIVES. By spot FX we mean that someone wants to sell one currency in return for another. When you buy foreign currency when going on holiday you are doing a deal in the spot FX market. Spot FX is for people who simply need to do transactions in a non-domestic currency. For large companies that operate globally FX can pose a

---

[5]World Federation of Exchanges http://www.world-exchanges.org

significant risk to their profit. For this reason corporates use the FX market to hedge their FX risk, and to do this they typically use FX derivatives such as FX forwards or FX options. The FX market is still largely OTC and even during the Credit Crisis it operated efficiently as an OTC market. However FX derivatives can be traded on exchanges in the form of exchange-traded options or FX futures. Institutional investors will usually deal with the FX sales desk at investment banks and as this is a flow business the entire transaction will probably be electronic for a simple trade. If the client wants an exotic FX derivative then the sales desk would be involved.

1.5 How do you balance risk and return?

We have seen that greater risk is the way to greater return. The unattainable ideal is to buy securities which have a large return while incurring a small risk. This led to the creation of a number called the SHARPE RATIO. Firstly the return R of a portfolio is measured relative to that of a risk-free investment R_{rf} or RISK-FREE RATE. The risk-free rate is usually taken to be the return on government bonds. If we are taking a risk above that of buying govvies then we are entitled to a better return than the risk-free rate, and the amount by which the return on our investment exceeds the risk-free rate is its EXCESS RETURN. The Sharpe Ratio takes this excess return $R - R_{rf}$ and divides it by risk. Dividing by risk produces an adjusted return that penalises risky investment strategies. When comparing two investments with a 3% excess return the Sharpe ratio will reward the one that took the smallest risk. Risk is quantified by measuring the volatility of the excess return σ_P.

$$\text{Sharpe Ratio} = \frac{\text{excess return}}{\text{risk premium}} = \frac{R_P - R_{rf}}{\sigma_P}$$

But the Sharpe ratio does not give us a method for deciding how to choose assets in our portfolio. If we decide to use volatility of returns as a measure of risk then we can use a simple result from statistical theory to reduce our risk. If we have many assets and their returns are not correlated and each has the same volatility σ then a portfolio of n such assets has volatility[6]

$$\sigma_P = \frac{\sigma}{\sqrt{n}}.$$

If the volatility of each asset is 30% and we own 100 of these assets then the volatility of our portfolio will be $\frac{30}{\sqrt{100}}$ or just 3%. And if we had 10,000 assets the volatility of our portfolio would be 0.3%. This is the DIVERSIFICATION effect and is a result of the fact that individual asset return fluctuations tend to cancel one another out if assets are not moving in the same direction at the same time. So diversification cannot eliminate the concerted movement of prices for an entire market. Individual asset price fluctuations that are specific to the circumstances and news flow for a particular asset

---

[6]As the assets are not correlated the portfolio return is the weighted average of each asset return, and as the assets are equally weighted this is the average return. The portfolio variance σ_P^2 is the variance of the average return, $\text{Var}\left(\frac{1}{n}\Sigma_{i=1}^n r_i\right) = \frac{1}{n^2}\Sigma_{j=1}^n \sigma^2 = \frac{1}{n^2} n\sigma^2$, hence $\sigma_P = \frac{\sigma}{\sqrt{n}}$.

are known as IDIOSYNCRATIC RISK and large-scale concerted movements in markets are called SYSTEMATIC RISK. Idiosyncratic risk can be reduced by diversification but systematic risk cannot.

There is an elegant theory describing the relationship between risk and return. The theory must be elegant otherwise it would not have survived so long given that its assumptions are universally agreed to be flawed. Say we have two assets with expected returns r_1 and r_2. To measure risk we will use the return volatilities σ_1 and σ_2. We have one dollar to invest, so we assign a fraction x of our dollar into asset 1 and $1 - x$ into asset 2. The return we would now expect in our portfolio will be a combination of returns from the two assets weighted by the amount of money we have allocated to each,

$$r_P = xr_1 + (1-x)r_2$$

The portfolio variance σ_P^2 is also a weighted average of the variance of the first asset σ_1^2 and second asset σ_2^2 with a third term that includes the CORRELATION ρ between the returns of the assets. The variance of our portfolio σ_P^2 will be

$$\sigma_P^2 = x^2\sigma_1^2 + (1-x)^2\sigma_2^2 + \rho\sigma_1\sigma_2 x(1-x).$$

If the correlation ρ is zero then the portfolio variance is the weighted sum of variances for the assets. In order to get a relationship between return and variance we can rearrange the returns formula to get the asset 1 investment in terms of the portfolio and asset returns

$$x = \frac{r_P - r_2}{r_1 - r_2},$$

then the risk return relationship becomes

$$\sigma_P^2 = \left(\frac{r_P - r_2}{r_1 - r_2}\right)^2 \sigma_1^2 + \left(\frac{r_1 - r_P}{r_1 - r_2}\right)^2 \sigma_2^2 + \rho\sigma_1\sigma_2 \frac{(r_P - r_2)(r_1 - r_P)}{(r_1 - r_2)^2}.$$

Straight away we can see that the volatility of the portfolio contains quadratic terms in portfolio return, so we would expect a parabola of some kind. Say the two asset returns are $r_1 = 3\%$ and $r_2 = 12\%$ but that these returns come with volatilities of $\sigma_1 = 30\%$ and $\sigma_2 = 40\%$. We can vary the value of correlation from $\rho = -1$ where the two asset returns are perfectly negatively correlated, through $\rho = 0$ where the asset returns are independent of one another, to $\rho = +1$ where the asset returns are perfectly correlated. The results are shown in Figure 1.4. For each curve there is one portfolio with minimum risk but the composition of this portfolio and the minimum risk depends on correlation. The minimum risk portfolios corresponding to the left-most point on each curve, are shown in the following table.

Correlation (ρ)	Asset 1 Allocation	Volatility	Return
-1	57%	0%	6.9%
-0.5	60%	17.1%	6.6%
0	64%	24.0%	6.2%
0.5	77%	28.8%	5.1%
1	100%	30%	3%

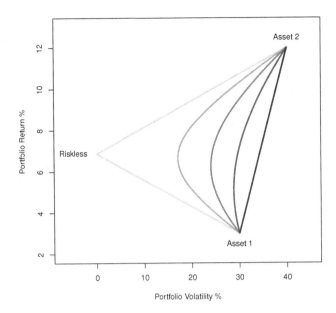

Figure 1.4:
  Portfolio risk and return for two assets varying correlation. Correlations are -1,
  -0.5, 0, 0.5 and 1 (light grey to black).

  Increasing correlation decreases the diversification effect and so reduces the effectiveness of any hedge. So we can achieve a volatility of zero when $\rho = -1$ if we invest
$0.57 in asset 1 and $0.43 in asset 2. This is a perfect hedge and means we can earn
6.9% while taking no risk at all. The volatility minimum increases to 30% when $\rho = 1$
because the best we can do is put all our money into the single asset with the lowest
volatility, which is asset 1.
  Slicing the graph vertically we can see that for a given level of risk there are two
portfolios one with a higher return and one with a lower return. Clearly if we have
two portfolios with the same risk we would always choose the one with higher return
so we will only be interested in the upper half of each curve. Slicing the graph horizon-
tally we are aiming to achieve a portfolio return of, say, 6%. Looking at the diagram
the lowest risk given a return of 6% and a correlation of 0.5 is 29.1%. This is the case
where we allocate $0.67 to asset 1 and $0.33 to asset 2. For any return we can find a
single portfolio with minimum risk and the portfolios on this line as we vary return
form the EFFICIENT FRONTIER. Increasing correlation increases the risk of the efficient frontier for a given return. To take the extreme case where the two assets have
a correlation of -1, this means that returns for asset 2 are opposite to those of asset 1
making it the perfect hedging instrument. When correlation is +1 then the two assets
are perfectly correlated so buying asset 2 is exactly like buying more of asset 1 (if we
could short asset 2 then we could still hedge perfectly but in this example we do not
consider short positions).
  The two asset case is odd because all portfolios must sit somewhere on the efficient
frontier. If we extend our analysis to three assets then portfolios can exist that do not

sit on the efficient frontier. The asset allocation of our dollar is now represented by x_1 in asset 1, x_2 in asset 2 and $x_3 = 1 - x_1 - x_2$ in asset 3. The return of the portfolio is

$$r_P = x_1 r_1 + x_2 r_2 + (1 - x_1 - x_2) r_3$$

and the variance of the portfolio is

$$\sigma_p^2 = x_1^2 \sigma_1^2 + x_2^2 \sigma_2^2 + x_3^2 \sigma_3^2 + 2 \left(x_1 x_2 \rho_{12} \sigma_1 \sigma_2 + x_1 x_3 \rho_{13} \sigma_1 \sigma_3 + x_2 x_3 \rho_{23} \sigma_2 \sigma_3 \right)$$

As we increase the number of assets the notation gets rather messy so we will use matrices to represent return, allocation and COVARIANCE. Covariance will now be a 3 by 3 matrix Σ. The diagonal elements of Σ are the variances of each asset. The off-diagonal elements incorporate the linear correlation ρ_{ij} between every pair of assets multiplied by the product of the asset volatilities $\sigma_i \sigma_j$. Asset allocation is now a vector $\mathbf{x} = (x_1, x_2, x_3)$ which, when multiplied by the returns of each asset, which is also a vector $\mathbf{r} = (r_1, r_2, r_3)$, gives us the portfolio return r_P. So portfolio return is now simply

$$r_P = \mathbf{x}^T \mathbf{r},$$

and the portfolio variance σ_P^2 is given by

$$\sigma_P^2 = \mathbf{x} \Sigma \mathbf{x}^T.$$

The efficient frontier can be defined as the line that minimizes risk and maximizes return. Expressing this optimization problem in the form of an equation,

$$\min \left[\text{risk} - \text{risk appetite} \times \text{return} \right] = \min \left[\sigma_P^2 - u r_P \right]$$
$$= \min \left[\mathbf{x} \Sigma \mathbf{x}^T - u \mathbf{x}^T \mathbf{r} \right],$$

where u is a multiplier that weights the importance of return over risk. A bold investor that is willing to take a lot of risk to get a potentially high return would have a large value for u. When u is large there will be a tendency to favour high return portfolios at the cost of incurring some additional risk. A nervous and risk-averse investor would have u close to zero so return would only matter a little and the minimization procedure would favour portfolios that took the smallest risk at the cost of having low returns.

We can use a simple example to illustrate the efficient frontier. We will look at four possible investments: the S&P 500 total return index (which includes the effect of reinvested dividends), a US corporate bond index (the JP Morgan U.S. Aggregate Bond Index), gold (London afternoon closing price) and light, sweet crude oil as traded on the New York Mercantile Exchange (the near crude light futures contract price) using twenty year time histories. The price histories are shown in Figure 1.5 along with their daily continuous returns and the efficient frontier is shown in Figure 1.6. The average returns and volatilities over this period of 20 years are:

	S&P 500	Bond Index	Gold	Oil
Return %	5.7	6.9	5.4	6.2
Volatility %	22.7	4.9	19.2	49.3

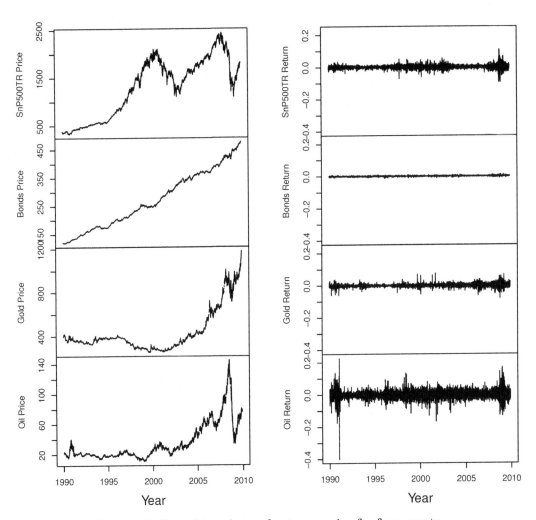

Figure 1.5: Price histories and return series for four assets.

Immediately we can see that although the returns are broadly similar there is a marked difference in the risk of these four assets. Oil has very high volatility of about 50%. The stock index and gold have comparable volatilities of about 20% and the least volatile asset is the bond index with a volatility of just 5%. We might expect that the returns follow the same pattern as volatility with oil giving the greatest return. This is not the case. In fact over this time period the bond index provided the greatest average return and the least risk. But can we do better than invest all of our money in bonds? The answer is yes, because we can reduce our risk through diversification. The left-most point on the efficient frontier, which has the lowest risk of 4.6% has a return of 6.7%. So we have sacrificed a little return by buying lower yielding assets but this diversification gave a lower risk. The allocation in this case was:

Asset	S&P 500	Bond Index	Gold	Oil
Allocation %	5.1	88.5	5.1	1.3

In this portfolio we are still putting the majority of our money, almost 90%, into bonds with the remaining 11.5% split evenly between stocks and gold with just a smidgeon in oil. Bonds had a high return and a low volatility so took the greatest allocation while oil had a very high volatility hence its low allocation. The last thing we will consider is the riskless asset which would be something like US Treasury bonds. These offer a small return for taking interest rate risk and almost no credit risk, but we can boost this return by combining the riskless asset with a combination of the four risky assets. By incorporating this "riskless" asset the efficient frontier is a straight line that passes through a riskless return point on the y axis where the risk is zero. The risk-free return is chosen to be a rather unrealistic 6.5% in order to fit the scale of the diagram nicely. Our covariance matrix shows that the risk-free asset has zero covariance with other assets because its volatility is zero:

$$\Sigma = \begin{bmatrix} & \text{S\&P 500} & \text{Bonds} & \text{Gold} & \text{Oil} & \text{Risk Free} \\ \text{S\&P 500} & 0.051438 & -0.000591 & -0.002949 & 0.003730 & 0 \\ \text{Bonds} & -0.000591 & 0.002437 & 0.000060 & -0.002142 & 0 \\ \text{Gold} & -0.002949 & 0.000060 & 0.036722 & 0.013531 & 0 \\ \text{Oil} & 0.003730 & -0.002142 & 0.013531 & 0.243117 & 0 \\ \text{Risk Free} & 0 & 0 & 0 & 0 & 0 \end{bmatrix}$$

We can see that in Figure 1.6 we have drawn a line called the CAPITAL ALLOCATION LINE (CAL) from the return of the riskless asset (6.5%) on the y-axis to touch the upper half of the efficient frontier. The point at which this line touches the efficient frontier is very special because it defines the TANGENCY PORTFOLIO. The tangency portfolio has the highest Sharpe ratio on the efficient frontier. This means it has the highest return adjusted for the risk that is being taken. We can create a portfolio for any point on the thick black capital allocation line by combining an investment in the riskless asset and the tangency portfolio. By combining the riskless asset and the tangency portfolio we can always "beat" the efficient frontier in terms of return for a given level of risk because the CAL is to the left of the efficient frontier. To extend the CAL beyond the tangency portfolio and get even higher returns we would use leverage

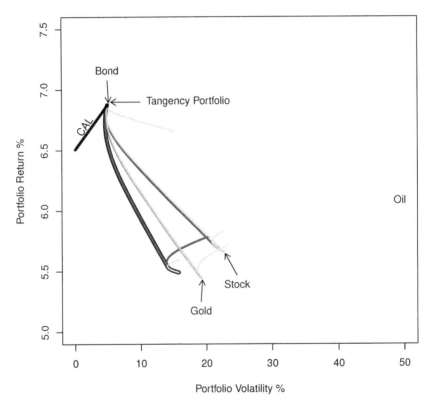

Figure 1.6:
Efficient frontiers for stocks, bonds, gold and oil. The black Capital Allocation Line (CAL) connects the risk-free asset and the tangency portfolio on the efficient frontier which is also black. The darker grey curves are the efficient frontiers incorporating three assets, and the lighter grey lines are frontiers with two assets.

by shorting the riskless asset and use the proceeds to buy increasing amounts of the tangency portfolio.

1.6 What is a company and how does it raise funds?

Before the industrial revolution there was little need for companies or investment banks. Large-scale engineering projects like railways, mines and factories created a need for marshalling resources on a large scale. The way this was done in some countries was to have a legal entity called a COMPANY and a system of raising money, or CAPITAL, for the company. Companies are owned by shareholders who give their capital to the company. This capital is used to buy assets which generate an income. Then if the income of the company after tax is greater than its costs the company grows organically and is fulfilling its primary purpose of generating a return on its invested capital. The excess cash can either be re-invested in the company so that it can expand by buying more assets that generate more income or the profit can be paid out to the owners, who are the shareholders, as a dividend. A company can either grow ORGANICALLY by re-investing its profits or it can grow by using its capital as a WAR CHEST to purchase other companies through takeovers. Investment banks are there to assist with every stage from capital raising through a share issue or advising on takeovers. In return for their services they earn an ADVISORY FEE.

Sometimes existing companies need to raise fresh capital to fund expansion or to cover losses. There are three ways that companies can raise capital to run their business: issuing shares, issuing bonds or taking out bank loans. When a company issues shares they are selling part ownership of their company. With ownership comes the right to vote on how the company is run, so by buying shares a third party also gains partial control of the company. If someone owns more than 50% of a company's shares then they effectively have control of the company. Another benefit of owning shares is participation in the profits by receiving a dividend. The amount of dividend paid to a shareholder is proportional to the amount of stock they own. The board of directors makes a decision on how much net profit should be kept as a CASH RESERVE, how much should be paid to shareholders as a dividend, how much debt they repay, and how much should be ploughed back into expanding the business and growing the balance sheet. There is no obligation to pay dividends but refusal to pay dividend may disgruntle equity holders and have an adverse affect on the stock price. Issuing new shares DILUTES the existing shares, which means that each shareholder's dividend share will be reduced and their voting power will be reduced. Dilution upsets existing shareholders which is why companies are reluctant to raise capital through new share issues.

Bonds are another avenue for raising capital. In return for lending cash to a company bond holders receive interest payments called coupons. Unlike shares, where investors give capital to the company and never receive that money back, bond holders get their money back at the maturity date of the bond. Bond holders do not own a part of the company like shareholders, which means that they have no voting rights. However companies do have an absolute obligation to pay their bond coupons. If they fail to make a single coupon payment on a bond this is called a DEFAULT and they are declared bankrupt. If a company encounters difficult trading conditions and has reduced profits they must still pay interest on their bonds. So bonds carry a risk because they have to be paid whereas dividends to shareholders can be cut. Having the choice to stop paying dividend is one benefit of issuing shares over issuing bonds. A company that has issued large amounts of bond debt must be confident that its assets will generate enough income to service this debt burden otherwise it faces bankruptcy. Bond issuers usually build in a feature to protect themselves if the general rate of interest rates drops. If rates are lower then it makes sense to pay back the debt that is financed at a high rate of interest and borrow again at the new, lower rate. This option to repay debt early is called a CALL FEATURE, and a bond with a call feature is a CALLABLE BOND.

Companies issue standardized reports called company accounts, which are usually published on their website in a section called "Investor Relations". This report, called the BALANCE SHEET, contains a snapshot of what the company owns and owes as illustrated in Figure 1.7. A company's balance sheet is a way of showing its ASSETS and LIABILITIES. Assets are things that are owned by a company that generate an income. Liabilities show how the company financed the purchase of those assets. The fundamental principle of accounting is that any action or transaction performed by a company must have an equal effect on the assets and liabilities so the two will always be exactly equal.

$$
\begin{aligned}
\text{Assets} \quad &= \quad \text{Claims} \\
&= \quad \text{Liabilities} + \text{Shareholder Equity}
\end{aligned}
$$

Another way of understanding the balance sheet is that the company itself owns nothing. The assets are owned by the people and insitutions who have a claim to those assets. These are the shareholders, the bond holders and anyone else to whom the company owes money. These claimants are the company's CREDITORS. The company is just a framework for organizing the raising of capital and the generation of revenue through use of the assets. This becomes clear when a company becomes bankrupt and is liquidated because the assets are sold and the creditors are paid off. The order in which they are paid off is clearly defined. Firstly bond holders are repaid their capital then if there is any money left the shareholders are paid off. This order of priority is called CAPITAL STRUCTURE and is illustrated in Figure 1.9 for a bank.

Banks usually have a more complicated capital structure than other companies. The repercussions of bank bankruptcy can be severe, so regulators insist on certain rules to ensure banks are well capitalized. These rules try to enforce a minimum amount of equity capital relative to debt capital because equity absorbs loss. As assets lose value the asset side of the balance sheet shrinks. Because assets and liabilities must balance the liabilities must also shrink and it is equity value that is reduced. When the value of a company's assets have been written down by more than the value of the company's equity the company is bankrupt. Equity provides a cushion against bankruptcy. By issuing more bonds a company is able to buy more assets and potentially amplify its revenue, but this also comes with an increased risk that it has more debt that it may not be able to repay. The ratio of bond debt to equity is called LEVERAGE because the return on a fixed amount of equity can be boosted or levered by purchasing more assets with borrowed money. The other risk with leverage is that levered asset values are

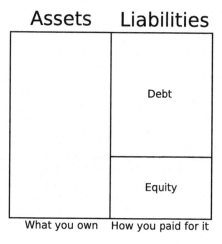

Assets   Liabilities

Debt

Equity

What you own   How you paid for it

Figure 1.7: A balance sheet. Debt can be a combination of bonds and loans.

proportionately larger and so a given percentage drop in asset value when amplified by leverage may wipe out all equity value and cause bankruptcy.

Figure 1.8 shows the 2009 year-end liabilities of three US companies: Google Incorporated, McDonalds Corporation and Goldman Sachs Group Incorporated. The size of the balance sheets are wildly different with Goldman weighing in at $849 billion, dwarfing both Google at $40 billion and McDonald's at $30 billion but in the illustration they are scaled to the same size to show the differences in capital structure more clearly. What is striking is that we have a progression of increasing balance sheet leverage. For Google 89% of their capital is shareholder equity, for McDonald's 46% and for Goldman just 8.4%. Technology stocks in the United States typically have the majority of capital in the form of shares. For companies with very volatile income, such as technology startups, the risk of bankruptcy would be high if each year they were forced to pay fixed interest on their bonds. Dividend payments on equity are at the discretion of the company so in years of meagre income they can choose not to pay a dividend. As Google matures it may choose to raise more of its capital in debt form. McDonald's is a very well-established company with relatively predictable and steady income so it can safely raise some of its capital in the form of debt. Banks are lending businesses and as such they can only generate enough return on their equity capital by levering up their balance sheet.

To take an extreme and simplified example say we have a bank that has raised $1 billion through issuing shares. It lends out this money in the form of mortgages. The bank can borrow money at 3% and it charges its mortgage customers a rate of 4%. Its profit is driven by this difference between a low cost of borrowing and a higher rate of lending known as NET INTEREST MARGIN. In this case net interest margin is 4%-3% which is 1%. The annual revenue for our bank is 1% of the money we lend as mortgages and 1% of $1 billion is $10 million. The value of the mortgages will vary due to interest rates and credit concerns and if the value of the mortgage assets has to be written down by 1% then we will also have to write down the value of shareholder equity by 1%, or from $10 million to $9.9 million. Our equity has absorbed our loss

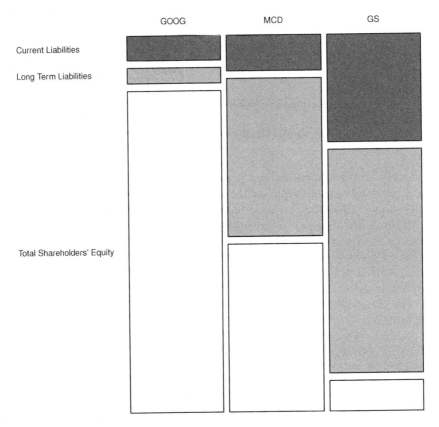

Figure 1.8:
Balance sheet capital structure and leverage. Liabilities for the year 2009 for Google (GOOG), McDonalds (MCD) and Goldman Sachs (GS) broken into shareholder equity (white), long-term liabilities (grey) and current liabilities (black). Source: Bloomberg.

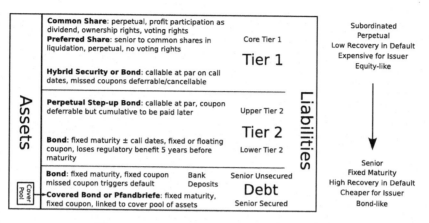

Figure 1.9: Capital structure of a bank.

but we are not bankrupt. If we want to increase our profit then we simply lend more money. We could do this by issuing more shares but we choose to lever up by issuing $99 billion in bonds bringing the size of our balance sheet up to $100 billion. We now lend out $99 billion in new mortgages and our annual revenue goes up to 1% of $100 billion which is $1 billion. This sounds great. But if the value of our assets, our mortgages, drops by 1% as before then our equity will have to absorb a loss of 1% of $100 billion which is $1 billion. Our equity of $1 billion is entirely wiped out and we are bankrupt. We have learned our lesson in leverage, unless the government bails us out, and if the government bails us out it learns its lesson in moral hazard.

Bank regulators, such as the Bank for International Settlements (BIS), impose constraints on the leverage of bank balance sheets through lower limits on the BIS TIER 1 CAPITAL RATIO. Tier 1 capital ratio is the amount of BIS Tier 1 capital, which includes only loss-absorbing liabilities such as equity and preferred shares, divided by the risk-weighted assets. A set of weighting rules, defined by BIS, are applied to assets according to their probability of generating a loss so that things such as US Treasury bonds have a zero weighting but riskier corporate bonds carry a higher weighting. The larger the amount of loss-absorbing equity relative to risky assets the greater the Tier 1 capital ratio and the lower the risk of bankrupcy. The smaller the number of risky assets the greater the Tier 1 capital ratio and the lower the risk of bankruptcy. So setting a lower limit on this ratio sets a cap on the riskiness of a bank's capital structure.

$$\text{BIS Tier 1 Capital Ratio} = \frac{\text{BIS Tier 1 Capital}}{\text{BIS Risk-Weighted Assets}}$$

Figure 1.9 shows the capital structure of a typical bank. The instruments listed in this diagram are all issued in order to raise capital for a bank. The continuum ranges from the most subordinated instrument at the top which is equity down to the most senior instrument on the bottom which is a secured bond. In the event of liquidation the assets of the bank are sold and the banks creditors are paid off in order of their seniority in the diagram starting at the bottom and working upward until the proceeds of the asset sale are exhausted. There is seldom any money left over for equity holders who typically lose everything in the event of liquidation. The percentage of capital that is recovered in liquidation, the RECOVERY RATE, is greatest at the bottom and least at the top of the diagram. This means that equity and other subordinated instruments bear the greatest risk and senior instruments the least. From the bank's point of view the riskiest, most subordinated instruments are the most expensive to issue so the banking industry has created these hybrid instruments that trade off cost of funding with capital requirements imposed by regulators. If it was up to regulators there would just be equity and senior debt and that would be the end of it.

Starting with the most senior type of liability, senior bonds are paid out first. There is a distinction between SECURED and UNSECURED senior debt. Secured debt has a COVER POOL of high quality assets set aside specifically for the purpose of repaying that debt in the event of liquidation. Secured bonds are also called COVERED BONDS or PFANDBRIEFE and have very high recovery of capital in the event of liquidation as ensured by the existence of the cover pool, hence they have a low coupon and are a source of cheap capital for the issuer. Once the sale proceeds of the cover pool are paid to the secured bond holders, if there is still any principal outstanding the secured debt ranks equally, or PARI PASSU (literally "on the same step") with senior unsecured bonds. In this way secured debt has two claims on the assets of the issuer: the first is exclusive and applies to assets in the cover pool and the second claim is on the remaining assets. Senior unsecured debt has no such relationship with particular assets, but is still uppermost in the capital structure. Senior debt coupons must be paid in full on a pre-arranged schedule either annually, semi-anually or quarterly, and failure to pay will result in bankruptcy. In the case of depository banks senior bonds are on a par with bank depositors. Below senior bonds are subordinated bonds which are subdivided into finer grades: SENIOR SUBORDINATED and JUNIOR SUBORDINATED.

One layer up the capital structure on our journey from bonds to equity brings us to Tier 2 debt. This is sub-divided into Lower Tier 2 (LT2) which is closer to bonds and Upper Tier 2 (UT2) which is closer to equity. Usually Lower Tier 2 bonds have a defined maturity date when the bondholders' principal must be returned and they cannot defer any coupon payments. Upper Tier 2 bonds are equity-like in that they are usually perpetual, which means that the issuer need never return principal to the investor and the bond does not have a maturity date. This is similar to equity capital which never has to be returned to the investor. Upper Tier 2 bonds do however have a call date after which the coupon steps up to a punitively high level of interest and issuers almost always choose to call the debt and repay the bondholders on this date. Above Tier 2 debt is Tier 1 debt which is also usually perpetual, meaning that the principal need never be repaid. These instruments are also called hybrids because they have are combination of bond and equity. Tier 1 bond coupons can be deferred without incurring bankruptcy, but if a dividend payment is made to common shareholders then coupon must be paid on Tier 1 bonds. And if Tier 1 coupons are deferred they accumulate and must be paid at a later date.

The final layer above debt is equity. This has the lowest level of subordination so is last to be paid out in the event of liquidation. At this level in the capital structure recovery rates are very low so in the event of liquidation the investor will likely lose all of their capital. Equity is the riskiest part of a company's capital structure from the point of view of the investor. Equity is sub-divided into COMMON EQUITY or COMMON SHARES and PREFERRED SHARES that are senior to common shares but junior to any form of debt. Preferred shares sometimes have the bond-like property of guaranteed dividends which are rather like a bond coupon. And if a dividend is paid on common shares then a dividend must be paid on preferred shares. Preferred shares often do not have voting rights which is attractive to issuers as they are not ceding control by issuing preferred shares. From the point of view of a bank preferred shares are beneficial because they count toward regulatory Tier 1 capital.

As a result of the Credit Crisis it became extremely expensive for banks to fund themselves by issuing bonds because banks were suddenly seen as a credit risk, particularly after the collapse of Lehman Brothers in September 2008. In December 2008 Deutsche Bank shocked the market by not redeeming its LT2 debt on its first call date. These bonds had a face value of €1 billion and were set to mature in January 2014, with their first call date in January 2009. As a result the coupon changed to Euribor plus 88 basis points. At the time that this bond was issued funding at Euribor+88 bp was unthinkably expensive. After the collapse of Lehman, however, 88 basis points seemed like a very small payment to take the credit risk of a bank. So although this non-call decision upset subordinated bondholders it was quite rational on the part of Deutsche Bank who kept their debt capital funded at pre-Credit-Crisis levels. In June 2009 another $650 million of Tier 1 Deutsche Bank bonds reached a call date and again they chose not to redeem.

1.7 How do you transform an opinion into money?

Investors express their opinion about future evolution of markets in the financial instruments that they buy and sell. The list of things you own at a particular time is a POSITION or a PORTFOLIO. For institutional traders the list of assets is known as the TRADING BOOK. If you expect Google shares to increase in value you can do a number of things depending on your certainty and risk appetite. Say you have a million dollars to spend. The simplest is to buy Google shares. The most that you can lose is your entire capital investment of a million dollars, because the Google share price could become zero if the company becomes bankrupt. Your DOWNSIDE, or maximum loss, is limited to a million dollars and your UPSIDE, or maximum gain, is unlimited.

If you are even more certain that the share price will increase you can use LEVERAGE. Just as a mechanical lever seems to magnify strength, financial leverage increases potential profit and loss. In addition to using your own money you can borrow $9 million to buy a $10 million stake. If Google does increase in value by 10% you will make $1 million. As a fraction of your initial investment this is a return of 100% (ignoring interest on your borrowing). Without leverage your return would have been a mere 10%. Leverage means you can satisfy your greed at the cost of increasing your fear. If Google had slumped to zero the downside would be that you would have lost your capital of $1 million and would also owe your creditor $9 million. A loss of $10 million would be ten times your initial investment, so leverage could boost your loss to -1000%.

If you own Google shares you are LONG Google. You want the price of Google to increase, and the act of buying their shares was expression of your belief that the Google share price would increase. What if you want to be SHORT Google? If you were short then you would make a profit if the Google share price were to decrease. This would involve selling something you do not own. What you can do is borrow Google shares from someone else, and sell them at today's market price. If Google does drop, say 10%, you can buy the shares back at the lower price and hand them back. You pocket the 10% difference. That's the upside. Unfortunately the downside is unlimited. If Google's share price quadrupled you would make a massive loss. And since share prices are unlimited your loss is potentially unlimited, so short positions are not for the faint-hearted. If you believe a security will increase in value you are said to be BULLISH, and the opposite opinion is described as BEARISH. People also bandy about phrases such as BULL MARKET and BEAR MARKET which mean that prices overall are increasing or decreasing.

Sometimes you may want to take a position which does not expose you to the full risk of the underlying asset. You want some of the upside, but are willing to sacrifice some of that upside in order to limit your downside. You can HEDGE your position. Hedging is the purchase of financial instruments in order to mitigate risk. To take our Google example you could go long half a million dollars of Google and short half a million dollars of Yahoo. Now if technology stocks, or the whole stock market, drops your loss in Google will be compensated by your short position in Yahoo. You are now taking a position called a PAIR TRADE that assumes Google will outperform Yahoo, but is neutral as to whether the market will rise as a whole.

Table 1.1 shows various instruments and the factors that affect their price. All these instruments are described in detail later in this book. When you buy a corporate bond you are exposing your capital to risk and you should be rewarded appropriately for taking that risk. The extra amount you are paid relative to the risk-free interest rate, which is roughly what you would receive by putting your money in the bank, is your RISK PREMIUM. For a corporate bond you are taking the risk that the company that issued your bond will go bust, which is credit risk. Interest rates may rise, which will drive down the value of your bond. Inflation may rise which will erode the value of your bond. You will receive compensation for all these risks which means that the instruments that are most risky give the highest returns. If you take too much risk the chance of losing your capital increases which means that investors have to strike a balance between risk and return. Your choice of investment will depend on your view on the direction of the risk factors. The corporate bond would be a good investment if you believe the credit risk of the issuer will fall, interest rates will fall and inflation will remain low.

1.8 Arbitrage

ARBITRAGE is the ability to make risk-free profit. If you can buy a television on eBay from Hong Kong for $1,000 and sell it in France for $1,200 then you would have found an arbitrage opportunity. As a shrewd arbitrageur you would buy as many of the cheap televisions as the supplier could provide, sell them on at the higher price and pocket $200 for each television. This would not work for ever. As other people spot the

	Risk Factor Exposure				
	Real interest rate	Inflation	Credit	Earnings	Foreign Exchange
Inflation-linked government bond	-				
Government bond	-	-	*		
Corporate bond	-	-	-		
Equity			-	+	
Interest rate swap (payer)	+	+			
Interest rate future (long)	-				
Credit default swap (buy protection)			+		
Foreign currency strengthens vs. domestic currency					+

Table 1.1:

> Where to harvest risk premium. The symbol "+" denotes positive exposure, "-" denotes negative exposure and * shows that government bonds have sovereign credit risk.

opportunity the prices for the television in France and Hong Kong would converge.

The value of assets are built on the assumption that markets are free of arbitrage. Of course this does not mean that arbitrage opportunities do not arise. It simply means that they do not last long, so securities spend almost all of their time in an arbitrage-free state. An arbitrage-free market gives rise to an important principle. Physicists have Conservation of Momentum, biologists have Natural Selection, chemists have the Periodic Table, and finance has the Law of One Price.

The Law of One Price There can only be one price for any instrument, otherwise there would be an arbitrage opportunity.

This statement sounds obvious, but the subtlety lies in the definition of "instrument". A corollary of the Law of One Price is that if you can copy the future cash flows of instrument I by buying and selling a portfolio P of other securities, then the value of instrument I and portfolio P must be the same.

Replicating Cash Flows If a portfolio of securities P replicates the future cash flows of an instrument I then, by the Law of One Price, the price of P must equal the price of I.

To give an example, and introduce another important concept, imagine you are approached by someone who offers to sell you a contract whereby you will receive a dollar one year in the future. How much would you be willing to pay for that dollar-in-the-future contract today? The transaction, for the sake of argument, is guaranteed. Furthermore you also have the option to borrow or invest money with a bank, risk free, at an annual rate of 5% interest. If you buy the dollar-in-the-future contract you have a cash flow of $-f$ today and $+1$ in one year's time. If you sell the dollar-in-the-future contract you receive $+f$ today and pay -1 in one year. We can use an arbitrage argument to price this deal. Here is our "arb". First we replicate the future cash flows using other securities that we can price, in this case a single cash flow of $+1$ in one year. In order to receive 1 in one year we could invest an amount a with our bank. At the end of one year this will become $1.05a$. If we want the final amount to replicate the deal cash flow of $+1$ in one year then $1.05a = 1$, so $a = \frac{1}{1.05} = 0.9524$. By investing \$0.9524 today we will receive \$1 in a year from our bank.

	Today	One Year
Contract Cash Flow	$-f$	$+1$
Replicating Cash Flow	-0.9524	$+1$

We can now price the contract fairly. If the contract price f were greater than 95 cents, say \$1, then it would be expensive. Today we would sell the dollar-in-the-future contract for \$1 and put the money in the bank. In one year we would hand over a dollar as promised in our dollar-in-the-future contract and receive a dollar and five cents interest from our bank. That would be five risk-free cents in our pocket for each contract we sold.

	Today	One Year
Contract Cash Flow	$+1$	-1
Bank Account	-1	$+1.05$
Money in Pocket	0	$+.05$

If the contract price f was less than 95.24 cents, say 90 cents, we would do the reverse trade. Today we would buy the cheap dollar-in-the-future contract at 90 cents by borrowing 90 cents from the bank. In one year we would receive a dollar but would repay just 1.05×90 or 94.5 cents to the bank. We would earn 5.5 cents risk free for each contract we bought.

	Today	One Year
Contract Cash Flow	-0.90	$+1$
Bank Account	$+.90$	-0.945
Money in Pocket	0	$+.055$

Any deviation of the dollar-in-the-future contract from 95.4 cents will result in somebody getting fleeced. What we have demonstrated is that if there is an agreed-upon rate of risk-free borrowing and lending then using a simple arbitrage argument the future value of money is less than the value today. This is called the TIME VALUE OF MONEY.

Arbitrage is not just a theoretical concept. There are many examples in financial markets where prices are kept in a strict relationship by arbitrage trades. Because there is a cost to trade arbitrage ensures that these sets of arb-entangled instruments trade within certain bounds. Automated systems can spot when prices move outside the bounds and quickly scoop up the risk-free profit. During crises some arbitrageurs may not be able or willing to trade and in these situations there may be profits to be made.

Exercise 1 *An exchange sells a contract that promises to sell the owner a Troy ounce[7] of gold in one year at $g. The value of a Troy ounce of gold today is $820. You have a bank that offers to borrow or lend at an annual rate of 5%. Use arbitrage to price the value of this contract.*

Exercise 2 *Someone offers to buy or sell the contract for delivery at $900 a Troy ounce in one year. You smell an arb. What's the trade? How much money will you make on each contract?*

Exercise 3 *Someone offers to buy or sell a contract for delivery at $800 a Troy ounce in one year. Now what's the trade and how much will you make?*

Exercise 4 *While arbing the precious metals market your neighbour has the misfortune of having his garden gold hoard plundered. You realize that the garden might not be the safest place to store gold. A precious metal storage company offers to house and guarantee your gold for $2 per Troy ounce per year. How does this effect your two previous trades?*

---

[7]In case you were wondering, a Troy ounce is the weight of a cubic inch of distilled water at 62 degrees Fahrenheit and 30 inches barometric pressure. In SI units a Troy ounce is 31.1034768 g. The name Troy stems from a town in northeastern France called Troyes (pronounced like the number three in French "troi") which evidently hosted a vibrant commodities market in the Middle Ages. Troy ounces are used to measure the mass of precious metals, jewels and gunpowder.

Answers to Exercises

1 *An exchange sells a contract that promises to sell the owner a Troy ounce of gold in one year at $g. The value of a Troy ounce of gold today is $820. You have a bank that offers to borrow or lend at an annual rate of 5%. Use arbitrage to price the value of this contract.*

Today we buy a Troy ounce of gold for $820 with money we have borrowed from the bank and bury it at the bottom of the garden. After a year we dig up, wash and deliver the gold to the buyer of our contract who in turn gives us $g. In order to be arbitrage-free the payment we receive must equal the amount we repay to the bank, so $g = 1.05 \times 820 = 836$ dollars.

2 *Someone offers to buy or sell the contract for delivery at $900 a Troy ounce in one year. You smell an arb. What's the trade? How much money will you make on each contract?*

We sell the expensive contract, we borrow $820 and buy and bury our gold. After a year we deliver the gold to the buyer of the contract in return for $900. We pay the bank $836 and pocket $64.

3 *Someone offers to buy or sell a contract for delivery at $800 a Troy ounce in one year. Now what's the trade and how much will you make?*

We buy the cheap contract, we sell a Troy ounce of gold short at $820 and invest the proceeds in our bank account. After a year we receive the gold and return it to the person we borrowed it from. The bank pays us $836 and we pay $820 for the gold. We pocket $16.

4 *While arbing the precious metals market your neighbour has the misfortune of having his garden gold hoard plundered. You realize that the garden might not be the safest place to store gold. A precious metal storage company offers to house and guarantee your gold for $2 per Troy ounce per year. How does this effect your two previous trades?*

The profit on the first trade would be reduced by the storage cost of $2 to $62. The second trade is unaffected as we did not hold the gold over the year of the trade. But shorting the gold would incur a borrow cost.

2 Institutions

2.1 Governments

Governments can raise money by taxation, but this tends to make them unpopular. Alternatively they can borrow money in the form of loans from investors in search of a safe haven. These loans are called GOVERNMENT BONDS and the market as a whole is called SOVEREIGN DEBT. In democracies, where popularity with taxpayers is at a premium, governments have an insatiable appetite for debt. For domestic investments government debt is usually the safest. If Treasury funds are running low the Treasury can print more money. Countries which have no control over their currency, such as those that use the Euro, cannot control the supply of money in this way. Because governments are keen to borrow and investors are keen to lend to such a safe borrower, there is a huge market for government debt. The U.S. Treasury issues about $5 trillion worth of debt each year through the auction of various types of bond. When stock markets are in crisis investors usually turn to government bonds.

Bonds sold to national investors are classified as INTERNAL DEBT and those held by foreign investors are EXTERNAL DEBT. Government bonds vary in their duration, coming in short (one year or less), medium (one year to ten years) and long term (more than ten year) form. The United States Treasury calls these T-bills, T-notes and T-bonds respectively. Regional governments get in on the act in the United States by offering Municipal Bonds. If an investor who lives in California buys a Californian "muni" they are entitled to tax breaks. The state gets an inexpensive source of capital and local investors get a reasonably safe, tax-free investment and get a warm feeling from helping their local community. Munis are used to fund about 60,000 entities in the US ranging from small issues for local schools and libraries to issues by entire states.

The US Treasury debt market is the largest ($5.8 trillion in 2008) but almost all governments issue sovereign bonds. For example in the United Kingdom the UK Treasury issues bonds called GILTS because British bond certificates used to have a distinctive silver edging. Japan issues JAPANESE GOVERNMENT BONDS (usually abbreviated as JGBs), Germany issues BUNDS, France issues OATs, Spain issues Bonos, and Italy issues BTPs. Table 5.6 on page 208 contains a list of names for government bonds of short, medium and long term maturity issued by various sovereigns and Figure 2.1 shows the size of the sovereign debt market for the largest issuers. Of all government bonds US Treasuries are considered safest because of the strength and maturity of the US economy. Neither the US Treasury nor the UK Government has defaulted on a single payment of their bonds in recent history, although see Reinhart and Rogoff (2009) for a complete and fascinating history of sovereign defaults going back to the Middle Ages. Some governments carry significant credit risk because they have defaulted in the past or look as if they may default in future. For

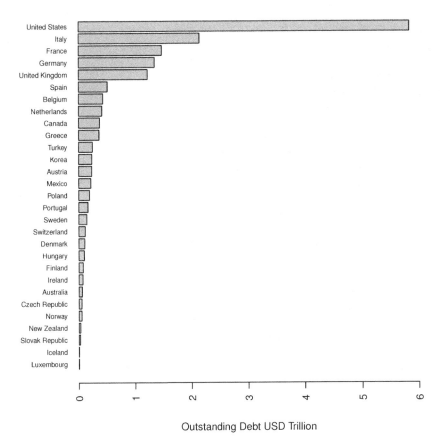

Figure 2.1:
Size of the sovereign debt market in 2008 as total amount outstanding in trillions of dollars. Source: OECD.

example Argentina failed to make some of its bond payments in 2002 and as a result of this sovereign default Argentinian bonds carry a much higher coupon than US Treasury bonds or other South American countries. Similarly in 2010 it looked likely that Greece would default on their debt so their cost of funding increased significantly as a result of this increased credit risk.

Governments control their economy through their FISCAL POLICY and indirectly through the central bank their MONETARY POLICY. Fiscal policy adjusts the amount that the government spends and earns. If the government is not earning enough to pay for its debt repayments, infrastructure projects, health system, state pensions, military spending etc., this means that it is running a FISCAL DEFICIT (or BUDGET DEFICIT), then it can either raise taxes or boost its capital by issuing more bonds. If the government has a FISCAL SURPLUS then it can reduce taxes, reduce its debt or set up a SOVEREIGN WEALTH FUND to invest the excess. However issuing too many bonds comes with the danger that the national debt can spiral out of control with no way to repay the debt. The three ways out of this situation are to grow the economy and increase tax revenue which can be used to pay off debt, default on the debt or print money to repay the debt and risk a high level of inflation. Monetary policy draws on another power of the government which is its control of interest rates and its own currency. It is commonly believed that interest rates can be used to control inflation. Increasing short-term interest rates is supposed to slow down an overheating economy and reduce inflation. Reducing interest rates is supposed to kick-start an economy that is not growing quickly enough, as measured by the growth in GROSS DOMESTIC PRODUCT.

2.2 Central Banks

Central banks are responsible for setting MONETARY POLICY. Governments grant them a monopoly on the issuance of domestic currency so they quite literally control the SUPPLY OF MONEY in the economy. The central bank is responsible for maintaining the PRICE STABILITY of its currency for buying goods, in the form of INFLATION or DEFLATION, and against other currencies in the foreign exchange market. And after the Credit Crisis we now know that the central bank is also a LENDER OF LAST RESORT to domestic banks. A central bank has few levers by which it can control the economy. The most important lever is the interest rate at which the government borrows and lends because this sets the risk-free rate. We have already seen the importance of risk-free lending to the pricing of all financial instruments in Section 1.8.

Governments use the rate of borrowing to tread the knife-edge between economic growth and recession. Investment banks and other corporations like an environment in which it is cheap to borrow money, or an EASY MONETARY POLICY (alternatively described as a LOOSE MONETARY POLICY or ACCOMODATIVE MONETARY POLICY) because they can use borrowed money to expand their enterprise. For the populace low interest rates mean cheap mortgages but low interest on savings. If your savings in the bank are earning next to no interest it encourages investment in risky assets like the stock market and new startup businesses in search of higher returns on your capital. So a RATE CUT means the government is putting more money in borrowers' pockets and fuelling growth in the economy. A RATE HIKE has the opposite effect, damping growth and reducing disposable income and is therefore called a TIGHT MONETARY POLICY. The drawback with low rates is that this leads to salary growth and price rises for basic goods, which is inflation. The central bank runs the risk that it will keep rates low for too long which may lead to an ASSET BUBBLE. For example Japan suffered a mild recession in 1986 and lowered interest rates to stimulate its economy back into growth. However the rate was kept low for 30 months leading to a surge in the Japanese stock and housing markets up to the end of 1989 when the bubble popped. The ensuing economic disaster that ravaged the Japanese economy in the 1990s has become known as the LOST DECADE.

The means by which rates are set differ from country to country. In the United States monetary policy is set by the Federal Open Market Committee (FOMC), which is part of the Federal Reserve System or Fed. There are twelve Federal Reserve Banks each covering large regions of the country. The committee has twelve voting members consisting of seven members of the Federal Reserve Board and five of the twelve Federal Reserve Bank presidents. The Chairman of the Board of Governors of the Federal Reserve is the most influential figure, Alan Greenspan being the longest serving Chairman. The committee meets every six weeks and the outcome of their meetings are changes in the target for the FEDERAL FUNDS RATE. The Federal Funds Rate is the target rate at which depository institutions lend balances at the Federal Reserve to other depository institutions overnight. Although the Fed cannot force banks to borrow at this target rate the effective rate is usually very close to the target. Because the decisions of the committee are so important each of the members' public, and sometimes private, utterances are scrutinized closely by the markets. Statistical models are built to predict their decisions. The Fed has been criticized for holding meetings in secret, however the Federal Reserve web site publishes minutes of past FOMC meetings three weeks after they have taken place[1]. The Fed is also criticized for the incomprehensibility of its press statements, phrased in its own version of English called FEDSPEAK.

In the United Kingdom monetary policy is set by the Monetary Policy Committee (MPC) which meets monthly. The committee consists of the governor of the Bank of England, its chief economist, two deputy governors, its executive director for market operations, and four external people appointed by the Chancellor of the Exchequer. The MPC sets the official interest rate in order to meet an inflation rate target set by the Chancellor of the Exchequer in his or her annual budget. Perhaps in response to complaints about the opacity of the FOMC, minutes of MPC meetings are published on the Bank of England website after a delay of just two weeks. Members of the FOMC and MPC that are keen to keep interest rates low are called DOVES and those that are in favour of interest rate increases are HAWKS. The financial press often refer to monetary policy views as being dovish or hawkish.

Central banks seldom deal directly with businesses as this is the role of commercial banks. If the economy is growing too quickly and inflation is on the rise then the central bank wants to drain liquidity out of the financial system and reduce the amount that companies are allowed to borrow. Commercial banks are required to hold a fraction of their deposits with the central bank in order to ensure that they can pay this money back to their customers. This is enforced as a minimum RESERVE REQUIREMENT RATIO (RRR) of central bank cash as a percentage of customer deposits. In some countries a minimum RRR is not enforced by the central bank and reserves are voluntary, as in the United Kingdom. In other countries the central bank imposes a reserve requirement and uses it as part of their monetary policy. For example China and Brazil both raised their reserve requirements in 2010 to drain money out of the financial system to avoid inflation and asset price bubbles. Some central banks, such as the US Federal Reserve, the European Central Bank and the Bank of England, prefer to use OPEN MARKET OPERATIONS to control the supply of money. When a central bank buys assets such as bonds or gold it can electronically print more money for the purchase. This money then sits on the balance sheet of the seller and the supply of money has been increased and the effect is to decrease short-term interest rates. When the central bank sells these assets it decreases the money supply and increases short-term interest rates.

In an attempt to formalize the process by which a central bank tries to balance

---

[1] http://www.federalreserve.gov/monetarypolicy

inflation and growth the economist John B. Taylor produced a simple rule to set the short-term interest rate (John B. Taylor, 1993). His rule includes two terms that represent the main concerns of monetary policy. The first term is the deviation of inflation i_t from its target i_{TARGET}. If inflation at time t, which is i_t, is above its target then the central bank should raise rates, so this term is proportional to $i_t - i_{TARGET}$. The second term concerns gross domestic product (GDP). Assuming that there is some theoretical potential value for GDP, which is $g_{POTENTIAL}$, then if GDP at time t, which is g_t, exceeds this potential level of GDP the bank should raise rates in order to cool off the economy by an amount proportional to the excess $g_t - g_{POTENTIAL}$. Economists call $g_t - g_{POTENTIAL}$ the OUTPUT GAP. If the short term interest rate at time t is r_t, and the equilibrium real interest rate is r_{EQ}, then Taylor's rule is

$$ r_t = r_{EQ} + i_t + \frac{1}{2}(i_t - i_{TARGET}) + \frac{1}{2}(g_t - g_{POTENTIAL}). $$

Taylor set the equilibrium interest rate r_{EQ} equal to 2% and the target inflation rate i_{TARGET} equal to 2%. This means that the short term rate should be set to one plus one-and-a-half times the inflation rate plus half the output gap,

$$ r_t = 2 + i_t + \frac{1}{2}(i_t - 2) + \frac{1}{2}(g_t - g_{POTENTIAL}) $$
$$ = 1 + \frac{3}{2}i_t + \frac{1}{2}(g_t - g_{POTENTIAL}). $$

If the economy is "on target" according to this rule, when $i_t = i_{TARGET}$ and $g_t = g_{POTENTIAL}$ then the real interest rate (nominal rate minus the expected inflation rate) equals the equilibrium real interest rate $r_t - i_t = r_{EQ}$. Taylor found that even though the Federal Reserve was not following an explicit rule, historical observations of the short term rate showed that Fed rate decisions seemed to fit his model. Unfortunately there may be disagreement about the potential value for GDP and so the Taylor Rule is subjective.

The other weapon in the central bank arsenal is more extreme, and only drawn upon in emergency. This is known as QUANTITATIVE EASING. One of the properties of bonds is that their prices and yields move in opposite directions. When a bond's price goes up its yield goes down. In quantitative easing central banks purchase long-term government bonds which pushes up their prices and drives down their yields. Driving down government bond yields means that the cost of borrowing decreases for all bonds because goverment debt is a benchmark for many bonds and loans. The central bank can also purchase corporate bonds injecting cash directly into corporate balance sheets. The drawback is that the central bank's balance sheet has to increase. Whereas setting interest rates affects short-term borrowing, quantitative easing affects long-term borrowing. The size of the US Federal Reserve balance sheet is shown in Figure 2.2. Quantitative easing is clearly visible as a sharp increase in the size of the balance sheet after the default of Lehman Brothers in September 2008. The increase in assets was initially due to loans to financial institutions and liquidity provision to key markets. This was followed by the Fed buying long-term Treasuries and taking a very large stake in Mortgage Backed Securities following the conservatorship of the US mortgage agencies.

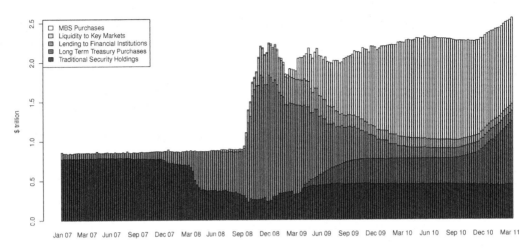

Figure 2.2:
Size and asset composition of the Federal Reserve balance sheet. Source: Cleveland Fed.

In addition to setting interest rates a central bank may intervene to protect its own currency, a process known in the FX market as FX INTERVENTION. For exporting countries the aim is usually to keep the price of their currency weak relative to the currencies of countries to which they export because this keeps the price of their exports competitively low. If their currency becomes too strong they may intervene by selling their own currency in return for the foreign currency of countries to which they export. For example the central bank in Switzerland, the Swiss National Bank, interceded in the FX market to keep the Euro-Swiss Franc exchange rate above 1.5 in March 2009 by selling Swiss Francs and buying Euros. Japan is also known for its willingness to intervene in FX markets to keep the value of the Yen low relative to the countries to which it exports, in particular the US dollar. When the Yen grows too strong the central bank will often sell Yen and buy US Dollars which acts to lower the USDJPY exchange rate

A central bank will also act as a LENDER OF LAST RESORT to investment and depositary banks under its jurisdiction. Although people believe that their money is safe in their private bank account and may be withdrawn in the form of cash immediately this is not strictly true. A look at the balance sheet of any bank will show that the amount of cash that the bank holds is sometimes much smaller than the size of its deposits. This means that if all of the customers decide to withdraw their money at the same time the bank will not be able to return their money, a phenomenon dreaded by bankers and known as a RUN ON THE BANK. This happens in times of panic when customers believe that their bank may itself become bankrupt, such as during the Great Depression in the USA in the 1930s, and the panics of 1893, 1896 and 1907. In September 2007 the UK bank Northern Rock suffered a banking run which resulted in the nationalisation of the bank in February 2008. In order to avert banking runs the government can guarantee deposits up to some maximum amount. In the United States this guarantee is provided by the Federal Deposit Insurance Corporation[2] (FDIC) which guarantees $250,000 per depositor per member bank. The FDIC requires that its member banks display a sign that says "Deposits are backed by the full faith and credit of the United States Government".

2.3 Investment Banks

Investment banks exist to provide financial services for companies. They help raise money for companies by issuing their shares in the equity capital market or bonds in the debt capital market, they manage and advise in mergers and takeovers, and they make secondary markets by buying and selling financial instruments. They help companies throughout their life cycle, from managing their initial flotation on the stock market, through helping the company expand by raising capital or acquiring other companies, and in some cases through to "death" via bankruptcy and liquidation. There are many distinct financial businesses which are called a bank. The kind of bank where you deposit your monthly salary and do your personal banking is a retail bank. Although some investment banks do have retail subdivisions the retail and investment banking arms are very different businesses, as summarized here:

Investment Bank Helps companies raise cash through issuing shares and bonds.

Commercial Bank Takes deposits and makes loans, usually to companies.

Retail Bank Banking for people. Bank takes deposits in checking and savings accounts and and makes loans as mortgages or personal loans or in the form of credit cards.

Private Bank Banking for high net worth people. Provides all the services of a retail bank with a focus on investment advice and asset management.

The dividing line between different types of bank is blurred because financial companies often operate two or more of the businesses in this list. Some believe that it is best to offer all services, a business model called the UNIVERSAL BANK. To illustrate some of the large investment banking players and how they make their money see Figure 2.3. The width of the bars represents the total income in USD for the financial year 2009, so Citi generated the greatest income in this group. The height of the bars show the amount of income that was generated by the bank broken down according to categories on the 2009 annual income statement. The categories include both interest income and net interest income giving some idea of the interest expense which is the cost to each bank over 2009 of the interest that they had to repay on their own borrowing. For a lending company it is critical that the net interest income is positive and this can only be true if the lender can borrow money more cheaply than the rate at which it lends. To check the health of the lending business we would take a look at the following numbers in the income statement:

$$\text{Net Interest Income} = \text{Interest Income} - \text{Interest Expense}$$

---

[2] http://www.fdic.gov

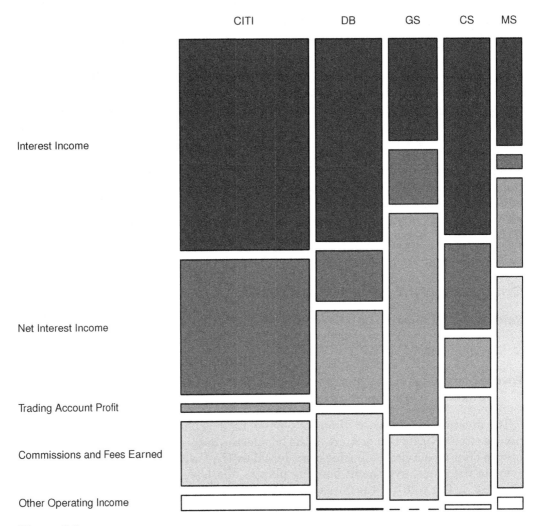

Figure 2.3:
   Investment bank income broken down by income type for year-end 2009 for Citibank
   (CITI), Deutsche Bank (DB), Goldman Sachs (GS), Credit Suisse (CS) and Morgan
   Stanley (MS). Bar width represents total 2009 income. Categories are shaded: Interest Income (black), Net Interest Income (dark grey), Trading Account Profits
   (medium grey), Commisions and Fees Earned (light grey) and Other Operating Income (white). Source: Bloomberg.

For Citibank the numbers in 2009 for interest income, in billions of dollars, were:

$$\text{Net Interest Income} \quad = \quad \text{Interest Income} \quad - \quad \text{Interest Expense}$$
$$48.9 \quad = \quad 76.6 \quad - \quad 27.7$$

Lending includes corporate loans and mortgages but also lending to hedge funds in the prime brokerage business. While Citibank, Deutsche Bank and Credit Suisse generated roughly half their income from lending money, Goldman Sachs generated most of their income from trading with their own capital. This is called PROPRIETARY TRADING or more casually PROP TRADING. History shows that proprietary trading is a very volatile source of income generating very large profits in some years and very large losses in others. Morgan Stanley made about half their income from commissions and fees. This would include things such as brokerage fees and advisory fees in mergers and acquisitions and issuance of new bonds and shares on behalf of companies to help them raise money. The income-generating activities can be broken down more finely as follows:

Mergers and Acquisitions For a fee the M&A team advise companies on how to fund and execute takeovers. Companies seldom merge with other companies and so corporate management cannot reasonably be expected to have much experience of the complex process of melding two companies. It is therefore common practice to work with a team from an investment bank that specializes in M&A and which can help with legal issues, valuation of the companies involved, assessing market impact, and financing the deal. The fee is usually about 2% of the deal value, and the deal value can be in the range of billions of dollars.

Wealth Management High net worth individuals often leave the day to day management of their wealth to others. In return for a fee some investment banks provide this wealth management service. This service can range from managing an investment portfolio to providing loans to building an art collection.

Asset Management Investors may not have the ability or the time to manage a portfolio of investments on a daily basis. So they can buy into a fund that is managed by experts with particular investment goals. For example an investor in the United States could gain exposure to the Chinese market by buying into a fund that invests in Chinese companies. Usually funds are benchmarked against an index whose return they have to track or exceed by a certain amount. Asset management earns a fee on the total assets under management and its success is measured by the size of assets under management and the fee charged.

Prime Brokerage Servicing hedge funds by providing them with all the facilities that would be available to a trader within the bank, such as funding, stock borrowing and lending, trade clearing and balance sheet accounting. This frees the fund manager to do what they do best which is to come up with and execute trade ideas.

Market Making and Brokerage

Rates Trading of interest rates. This is usually done through the sale and purchase of instruments such as interest rate futures, interest rate swaps, Treasury bonds, bond futures and more esoteric fixed income derivatives.

FX Foreign exchange trading. Investors can take a punt on the direction of rates by buying the currency directly or by the use of derivatives such as currency forwards and currency swaps.

Commodities Derivatives based on the price of commodities such as oil, gold, soya bean. Seldom trading in the underlying asset itself.

Fixed Income Buying and selling bonds, either government or corporate.

Credit Corporate bonds, credit derivatives such as credit default swaps or structured credit products such as collateralised debt obligations.

Equities Buying and selling shares on behalf of clients (acting as a broker), also known as CASH EQUITIES and making a market in EQUITY DERIVATIVES such as call and put options on equities.

An investment bank usually has several trading and sales desks for different asset types with specialized staff for each. There are usually desks for equities, fixed income, credit, FX and commodities, usually broken down into smaller desks with their own specialized asset. For example "Equities" would be sub-divided into "Cash Equities", a desk that buys and sells common stock, and "Equity Derivatives" which buys and sells options on those underlying stocks. The structure of each desk is fairly consistent. When a client wants to buy or sell something the person they talk to will work in SALES. Sales people at a bank will do their best to win business with a client, preferably repeat business, so they are keen to please. When a sales person receives a request from a client to buy they will talk to, or alternatively shout at, a TRADER (traders are also called MARKET MAKERS). The job of the trader is to very quickly come up with a price at which they are willing to buy and sell. Their buying price is their BID, their selling price is their OFFER and the difference between the two is how they make their money. The bid-offer spread (difference) is the trader's EDGE. Traders tend to care less about the client and more about their edge, and usually have a deeper, more technical knowledge of the asset that they trade. Sales people often travel out to visit their clients whereas traders spend most of their time on the desk managing their positions which are recorded in their TRADING BOOK. Each desk will usually have a handful of people working in RESEARCH. Researchers are specialized analysts that spend their time looking for trade ideas which they publish and distribute as a service to clients.

This combination of sales, trading and research is replicated for each desk. Collectively sales, trading and research come under the title FRONT OFFICE because these roles are client-facing and directly generate revenue for the bank and consequently these roles are usually highest paid. For each person in front office sales and trading roles there are scores of support staff. These include risk analysts, operations, sales and trade support, information technology, finance, and product control. These are BACK OFFICE roles and because they are a cost to the bank rather than revenue generators these jobs are usually not as well paid as front office roles. People who act as go-betweens between the front and back office are the MIDDLE OFFICE.

2.4 Pension Funds

If you work for a company you probably pay into a corporate pension scheme. The amount that comes out of your salary is paid, along with the contributions of thousands of others, into a pension fund. The idea is that this money will be invested wisely until you retire at which time it will have grown in value sufficiently to give you a cash payment some of which will purchase an annuity that will pay for your retirement. But who decides where to invest your fund's money? This is the job of a PORTFOLIO MANAGER (PM) or FUND MANAGER at a pension fund.

Pension funds are awash with cash, and are powerful forces in global markets. Pension funds are REAL MONEY investors because, unlike hedge funds, they cannot borrow money to make money. The investment strategies and instruments that they can use are strictly regulated. In theory this regulation reduces the risk of a pension fund losing all its capital, but in recent years it seems that this regulation has not always been effective. In the short term bonds have historically been safer than shares, although they have a limited upside. In good years equities sometimes give spectacular performance, but in bad years equities can lose a large proportion of their value. If a stock loses 50% of its value in one year it must gain in value by 100% to recover its previous value, so volatility can result in bad years from which recovery can take a very long time. Fund managers try to avoid the DRAWDOWN effect of these bad returns by reducing the volatility of their assets through diversification or strict stop-losses. Funds that invest the money of younger people tend to invest in riskier assets such as shares. Funds for people close to retirement sacrifice potential increased return for safer bond investments, concentrating on government bonds and highly rated corporate bonds.

Decisions about which assets to buy for a large pension fund are often made in a hierarchical fashion. Firstly the asset manager decides which asset classes will offer the best return over the coming period, a process called ASSET ALLOCATION. This will be a mixture of bonds, equities, commodities and perhaps the geographical distribution of investments. For example in a volatile market the fund may favour government bonds and AAA rated corporate bonds. If equity markets in the Far East are growing strongly the fund may allocate more of their portfolio in selected sectors in those markets. Once the percentage allocations have been decided portfolio managers choose individual assets to buy and sell within an asset class, region and sector. As a guideline PMs are often given a BENCHMARK INDEX, such as the S&P 500, with which they have match or exceed returns.

If you are a PM whose fund must match returns on the S&P 500 which has risen by 5% over the past year then your bonus will depend on your fund matching or exceeding 5%. In advertising brochures and performance reports for pension companies you will often see which benchmark is being used for each fund and how well the fund outperforms the benchmark. Advertising seldom shows the cases where the fund has performed worse than the benchmark even though this occurs frequently. As the fund manager charges you a fee for their expertise in investment they should always outperform their benchmark, particularly as for many indices it is now possible to buy a fund, called an exchange traded fund (ETF), that exists solely to track that index and does so as cheaply as possible. A fund manager that charges more than an ETF would be expected to earn their extra management fee by generating alpha (market outperformance) rather than just beta (market tracking). The best asset managers tend to move to where their personal return will be highest, either hedge funds or their own investment fund. This may explain why some pension funds perform poorly.

Pension funds perform a complex financial balancing act. Using statistical models they can calculate how long their existing pensioners will survive and receive payments. These are their liabilities. They can also model income from people paying into their pension before retirement and income generated from investing their excess cash and assets purchased with this cash. This balancing act is called ASSET LIABILITY MANAGEMENT.

2.5 Hedge Funds

Hedge funds manage the wealth of high net worth individuals and institutional investors. They differ from pension funds in that they are subject to almost no regulations. This means they can use all the tools in the financial engineer's toolbox to generate return. Firstly they can borrow money to make money. This is called LEVERAGE because just like a mechanical lever it can amplify profits and losses. Hedge funds can also buy financial derivatives. In return for hiring the best fund managers they receive a management fee of about 2% annually and keep about 20% of any gross profits as a performance fee. Although risky as a whole the best hedge funds often outperform any other investment so investors are willing to pay hefty management and performance fees.

Hedge funds come with a significant risk of losing your investment so in the United States the government restricts investors to people who should be well-informed about that risk. These are called ACCREDITED INVESTORS. An accredited investor is, according to the US Securities and Exchange Commission "a natural person who has individual net worth, or joint net worth with the spouse, that exceeds $1 million at the time of the purchase; a natural person with income exceeding $200,000 in each of the two most recent years or joint income with a spouse exceeding $300,000 for those years and a reasonable expectation of the same income level in the current year" [3].

Unlike mutual funds which are totally transparent and open about the assets that they own hedge funds are typically very secretive about their investment strategy and their investment portfolio. If their competitors know about their strategy they could copy it and reduce the profit in the trade. Some hedge funds will invest in illiquid assets making it difficult to assess the market value of a fund. For example bonds to fund the building of a dam in South America may never trade in the secondary market and will be hard to price whereas millions of shares in IBM change hands daily. This is why IBM shares are easier to price and, more importantly, sell for cash. If investors try to pull their money out of an illiquid fund it is forced to sell assets, which by definition takes a long time if the assets are illiquid. Funds usually have GATES which are barriers to redemption that come into being after a certain percentage of capital is pulled out of a fund. Investors may only find out the net asset value of their fund a few times a year. For example an investment in a hydro-electric

---

[3]http://www.sec.gov/answers/accred.htm

dam in Indonesia may take months to sell, whereas IBM stock can be sold for cash almost immediately. This combination of secrecy and reduced frequency and detail of reporting make an environment where it is easier to perpetuate a fraud, as was spectacularly demonstrated by BERNARD MADOFF.

Global Macro An opportunist strategy involving the fund manager's belief in global economic trends. This can be as simple as buying shares in glaziers in countries recently hit by an earthquake or it could be a complex trade-off of interest rates in two countries.

Micro Trading small pricing differences against one another for a particular asset type.

Convertible Arbitrage A play on the value of convertible bonds, which are bonds that can be converted into shares if the share price reaches an agreed level. These may not be priced correctly, and by judicious purchase of both the convertible bond and selling the related equity, hedge funds can profit from the mis-pricing.

Merger Arbitrage Takeovers are complex and often protracted affairs. This strategy hinges on the oscillations in share price as the bidders perform a complex dance of "will they/won't they". As the merger becomes more likely the share price of the target will shoot up to the bidder's offered price. As the merger becomes less likely the share price reverts to its value before the merger was announced which is usually substantially lower.

Distressed Securities When companies run into trouble "vulture" funds swoop and lend money, or offer to write off debt in return for a share of the company and its profits if it returns to good health. These funds perform well during economic downturns such as those in 1991 and 2001. For example Appaloosa Management LP returned 170% to investors in 2003 by trading the debt of bankrupt companies. Historically around 5% of companies default each year.

Event Driven Any strategy that is driven by corporate events. The price of a company's equity or debt will be affected by news of mergers, litigation against the company, approval of a drug for a pharmaceutical company or financial distress.

Equity Market Neutral The goal here is to choose a portfolio of equities that always increase in value and are not correlated to the market as a whole. If the Dow Jones Industrial Average drops dramatically in a market crash the theory is that these funds will not be affected.

Equity Long/Short The oldest and therefore most tried and tested type of hedge fund. The fund manager simply buys equities that they believe will rise in value and shorts equities that they believe will decrease in value. This strategy is not as dependent on leverage as proceeds from selling short can be used to fund the long positions.

Fund of Funds A fund that buys investments in other funds, dynamically allocating its capital according to the perceived performance and risk of each strategy as market conditions change.

2.6 Insurance Companies

Insurance companies generate income from premium payments and their costs include payments made when policies pay out. What surprises some people is that their income is hugely boosted by investing the excess premium payments. This extra cash is called FLOAT. Just like pension funds, who are also in possession of cash, insurance companies are major players in financial markets buying equities and bonds in order to boost income. There are different types of insurance company each of which has a unique pattern of investment. But all insurance companies have to balance their income and their payments and like pension funds are concerned with ALM, continually balancing their future profile of liabilities and income.

Life "Lifers" offer insurance against dying too soon. If this happens the insured's nominated beneficiaries receive a lump sum or a stream of payments over a period of time. Life insurance company investments are usually long term because human lifespans are long relative to most financial investments.

Non-Life Insurance for automobiles, boats, houses, theft of assets and so on. This tends to be shorter term than life insurance and this is reflected in the investment profile of non-life insurers which is shorter term.

Reinsurance Insurance for insurers. If insurance companies want to pass on some of their risk they strike reinsurance deals. In order to make a profit insurance companies must charge their customers a greater premium than they pay the reinsurer. There are a few huge reinsurance companies, such as Swiss Re and Munich Re in Europe and General Re in the United States. Reinsurance allows small insurance companies to increase the number of policies that they can write by reducing the risk of each individual policy.

Insurance companies are concerned about MORAL HAZARD which is the tendency of people to act recklessly once they are insured. Moral hazard has the effect of increasing claims and decreasing their profit. For example someone with fire insurance may consider the insured value of their property exceeds its true value and deliberately commit an act of arson. A less extreme example is car insurance. Drivers may be less careful about damaging their car if they know that their insurance company has to pay for repairs which is why insurance companies have their insureds pay a certain amount before the insurance company steps in to cover further payments. This is related to the problem of ASYMMETRIC INFORMATION, namely the fact that insurance companies do not know what their insureds are up to. This is a problem because insurance company income and ALM strategy depends on their ability to calculate the risk of a payout. The more they know about their insureds' behaviour the more elaborate and accurate their risk models.

2.7 Private Equity

Private equity refers to companies that profit from buying and selling other companies. Private equity companies use their capital, business knowledge and management skill to make the companies they buy more valuable, and then sell them for a profit. Some private equity companies specialize in VENTURE CAPITAL where they buy a stake in fledgling companies in return for money, advice and contacts. The private equity company makes its profit when the company is floated on the stock market in an INITIAL PUBLIC OFFERING (IPO). Venture capital is very risky as few small companies are successful, but success stories abound, such as Microsoft and Google. Slightly less risky is mezzanine capital which courts more established pre-IPO companies.

Another private equity strategy is to buy ailing companies and turn them around. For example Tommy Hilfiger Corp was a famous sportswear brand from the United States which traded on the New York Stock Exchange. It had a preppy image that became fashionable in the 1990s, then transformed into a more urban style which lost popularity. A private equity company called Apax Partners raised $1.6 billion in May 2006 for a management-led buyout. Noticing that the brand was still popular in Europe Apax Partners moved the headquarters to Amsterdam and marketed the brand for the European market. The strategy worked and the company explored an IPO on the Amsterdam Euronext exchange for between $2.9 and $4.4 billion at the end of 2007 which fell through due to the Credit Crisis. Eventually Apax Partners sold Tommy Hilfiger to Phillips-Van Heusen Corporation for $3 billion in May 2010, roughly doubling its investment in four years.

Private equity companies are exclusive as they require a large initial investment, usually around $1 million. Once invested money cannot be withdrawn, possibly for many years. Consequently these investments are only suitable to people or institutions that have large sums of money that they do not need immediately. Investors in private equity firms are usually pension funds, endowments, sovereign wealth funds or high net worth individuals. In the United States only accredited investors are able to invest in private equity. Unlike a mutual fund where there are several thousand investors in a fund a private equity company typically has 50 or so investors which are partners in the company. Some of the largest private equity firms include Kohlberg Kravis Roberts, CVC Capital Partners, Apax Partners and Blackstone Group. Private equity firms rely on capital being available through debt markets because this is often how they fund acquisitions. Typically about 60% of the purchase price of acquired companies in LEVERAGED BUYOUTS is funded with debt issued by the acquired company. Consequently the performance of private equity is cyclical as money becomes harder or easier to borrow. During crises in the debt markets, such as the Credit Crisis, or during cyclical downturns it becomes more difficult to fund leveraged buyout deals, so these strategies became less profitable and less frequent.

2.8 Sovereign Wealth Funds

Some governments find themselves in the fortunate position of having surplus cash to invest. The cash usually comes from having mineral resources such as oil fields or the ability to produce goods that the rest of the world is keen to buy. These excess funds are pooled into funds that are controlled by a government agency and invested in international markets by SOVEREIGN WEALTH FUNDS (SWF). Table 2.1 lists some sovereign wealth funds along with the size of their assets, when the fund was created and the source of the money. The source of data is the Sovereign Wealth Fund Institute in California, USA. Notice that the origin of sovereign wealth funds is dominated by oil with Abu Dhabi Investment Authority having the largest assets at $627 billion followed by Norway's Government Pension Fund at $445 billion and Saudi Arabia's SAMA Foreign Holdings fund with $431 billion. China and Singapore obtain their capital from savings of their citizens.

The sheer amount of capital owned by sovereign wealth funds means that they wield considerable power. Some have seen this as a threat to their national security. For example when an Arabian fund called Dubai Ports World bought the British company P&O they obtained control of six major US ports. Possibly due to pressure from the US Government in March 2006 Dubai Ports World handed control of the US ports to domestic authorities. Dubai also attempted without success to buy Auckland International Airport in New Zealand. The Credit Crisis meant that the United States banking system was willing to accept cash from a wider range of investors and as a consequence Abu Dhabi Investment Authority injected cash into Citigroup in the form of shares and came to own about 5% of the company.

2.9 Further Reading

"Barbarians at the Gate" (Burrough and Helyar, 2004) is a detailed and readable account of a leveraged buyout deal for RJR Nabisco in the late 1980's, and describes the perils of buyouts financed by the company's own debt. "Lords of Finance" (Ahamed, 2010) is about the role of central banks around the two World Wars and the Great Depression, and describes how a few larger-than-life characters muddled through a series of catastrophes and arrived at the central banking system that we have today. "Inside the House of Money" (Drobny and Ferguson, 2009) is a series of interviews with hedge fund managers and gives an account of what they do in their own words.

Country	Fund Name	Assets $ bn	Inception	Origin
UAE - Abu Dhabi	Abu Dhabi Investment Authority	$627	1976	Oil
Norway	Government Pension Fund – Global	$445	1990	Oil
Saudi Arabia	SAMA Foreign Holdings	$431	n/a	Oil
China	SAFE Investment Company	$347.1**		NC
China	China Investment Corporation	$288.8	2007	NC
Singapore	Government of Singapore Investment Corporation	$247.5	1981	NC
Kuwait	Kuwait Investment Authority	$202.8	1953	Oil
Russia	National Welfare Fund	$168.0*	2008	Oil
China	National Social Security Fund	$146.5	2000	NC
China - Hong Kong	Hong Kong Monetary Authority Investment Portfolio	$139.7	1993	NC
Singapore	Temasek Holdings	$122	1974	NC
Libya	Libyan Investment Authority	$70	2006	Oil
Qatar	Qatar Investment Authority	$65	2005	Oil
Australia	Australian Future Fund	$49.3	2004	NC
Algeria	Revenue Regulation Fund	$47	2000	Oil
Kazakhstan	Kazakhstan National Fund	$38	2000	Oil
Ireland	National Pensions Reserve Fund	$30.6	2001	NC
Brunei	Brunei Investment Agency	$30	1983	Oil
France	Strategic Investment Fund	$28	2008	NC
South Korea	Korea Investment Corporation	$27	2005	NC
US - Alaska	Alaska Permanent Fund	$26.7	1976	Oil
Malaysia	Khazanah Nasional	$25	1993	NC
Iran	Oil Stabilisation Fund	$23.0	1999	Oil
Chile	Social and Economic Stabilization Fund	$21.8	1985	Copper
UAE - Dubai	Investment Corporation of Dubai	$19.6	2006	Oil
UAE - Abu Dhabi	Mubadala Development Company	$14.7	2002	Oil
UAE - Abu Dhabi	International Petroleum Investment Company	$14	1984	Oil
Bahrain	Mumtalakat Holding Company	$14	2006	Oil
Canada	Alberta's Heritage Fund	$13.8	1976	Oil
Azerbaijan	State Oil Fund	$13.4	1999	Oil
US - New Mexico	New Mexico State Investment Office Trust	$12.9	1958	NC
New Zealand	New Zealand Superannuation Fund	$11.0	2003	NC
Nigeria	Excess Crude Account	$9.4	2004	Oil
Brazil	Sovereign Fund of Brazil	$8.6	2009	NC
Oman	State General Reserve Fund	$8.2	1980	Oil & Gas
Botswana	Pula Fund	$6.9	1996	Diamonds & Minerals
Saudi Arabia	Public Investment Fund	$5.3	2008	Oil

Table 2.1:
Sovereign wealth funds. Origin NC is non-commodity. *This includes the oil stabilization fund of Russia. **This number is a best guess estimation. ***All figures quoted are from official sources, or, where the institutions concerned do not issue statistics of their assets, from other publicly available sources. Some of these figures are best estimates as market values change day to day. Source: Sovereign Wealth Fund Institute (December 2009).

3 Mathematics Refresher

3.1 Descriptive Statistics

When faced with lots of data it is often useful to boil it down to a few numbers that summarize its essence. For example we may be interested in buying a stock. We would definitely be interested in the following information about daily returns on the stock.

Information	Description	Summary Statistics
Location	What is the typical value?	Mean, median, mode
Dispersion	How spread out is the data?	Standard deviation (vol), inter-quartile range, median absolute deviation
Shape	Which values are favoured?	Skew, kurtosis
Extremes	Are there any extremely large or small values?	Outliers

The mean, or average, or expected value indicates the location or typical value of the data, and is usually labelled μ. The expected value of a random variable X is a function $\mathrm{E}(X)$ and is defined as

$$\mu = \mathrm{E}(X) = \frac{1}{n} \sum_{i=1}^{n} x_i.$$

Alternatively the location of the distribution is roughly at its peak value, which is called the MODE. For some distributions the mean and the mode are the same, such as the normal distribution. It is also useful to know how far the data lies from the mean, on average. This is the mean deviation from the mean, called STANDARD DEVIATION, or VOLATILITY (often shortened to VOL) in finance, and usually labelled σ,

$$\sigma = \sqrt{\frac{1}{n} \sum_{i}^{n} (x_i - \mu)^2}.$$

If we don't bother to take the square root we can use σ^2 which is called the VARIANCE. Notice that squaring the difference between each value and the mean throws away the sign. In measuring variance we concentrate on the distance between the value and the mean not whether it is below or above the mean. Another way of thinking about mean and variance is to use expectation. The mean of a random variable X is the expectation $\mu = \mathrm{E}(X)$, and the variance is the expected squared difference from the mean

$$\sigma^2 = \mathrm{E}(X - \mathrm{E}(X))^2 = \mathrm{E}(X^2) - (\mathrm{E}(X))^2.$$

Exercise 5 *Show that* $E(X - E(X))^2 = E(X^2) - (E(X))^2$.

Mean and variance are sometimes called the first and second moments of a distribution. The third moment is known as SKEW and measures whether the distribution is squashed to the left with a long tail of high values (positive skew) or the right with a long tail of low values (negative skew) of the maximum value as illustrated in Figure 3.1. Skew is defined as

$$\text{Skew} = \text{E}\left[\left(\frac{x - \mu}{\sigma}\right)^3\right].$$

The fourth moment is known as KURTOSIS and measures whether the distribution is more peaked in the centre and heavy-tailed than a normal distribution (LEPTOKURTIC) or less peaked and less heavy-tailed than a normal distribution (PLATYKURTIC) or whether the kurtosis matches that of a normal distribution (MESOKURTIC). The fourth moment about the mean is

$$\mu_4 = \text{E}\left[\left(\frac{x - \mu}{\sigma}\right)^4\right],$$

however most statistical functions in software such as excel calculate EXCESS KURTOSIS, which is defined as

$$\text{Kurtosis} = \frac{\mu_4}{\sigma^4} - 3,$$

where the subtraction of 3 ensures that the kurtosis of a normal distribution is zero. The lowest possible value of excess kurtosis is -2. Most market prices are leptokurtic which means that they move by a small amount and by a very large amount more often than would be predicted by a normal distribution. Figure 3.2 shows a way of remembering the meaning of platykurtic and leptokurtic devised by William Sealy Gosset (Student, 1927). Gosset had to operate under the pseudonym "Student" because he was working for the brewer Guinness which at the time operated under a strict policy of secrecy.

There are non-parametric equivalents to these descriptive statistics. For finding the location of the distribution we sort the samples and take the middle value. This is called the MEDIAN. For finding the dispersion we use the median absolute deviation (MAD[1]). MAD is the median absolute difference from the median,

$$MAD = \text{median}\,|x_i - \text{median}(X)|$$

Median and MAD are less sensitive to outliers than mean and standard deviation. So if we have five numbers, 4, 2, 4, 5, 1000, then their mean is $\frac{4+2+4+5+1000}{5} = 203$ and their median is found by sorting the values (2, 4, 4, 5, 1000) and finding the middle value which is 4. The mean was knocked out of kilter by the outlier of 1000, whereas

---

[1]Which supports the hypothesis that statisticians have a sense of humour.

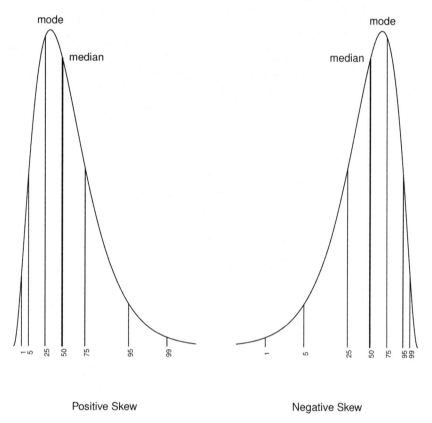

Figure 3.1:
Examples of distributions with positive and negative skew. The 1%, 5%, 25%, 50% (median), 75%, 95% percentiles are shown with vertical lines.

* In case any of my readers may be unfamiliar with the term "kurtosis" we may define mesokurtic as "having β_2 equal to 3," while platykurtic curves have $\beta_2 < 3$ and leptokurtic > 3. The
important property which follows from this is that platykurtic curves have shorter "tails" than the

normal curve of error and leptokurtic longer "tails." I myself bear in mind the meaning of the words
by the above *memoria technica*, where the first figure represents platypus, and the second kangaroos,
noted for "lepping," though, perhaps, with equal reason they should be hares!

Figure 3.2:
William Sealy Gosset's *aide-mémoire* for distinguishing between platykurtic and
leptokurtic distributions. Source Student (1927).

the median ignored the outlier completely. The standard deviation would be

$$\sigma = \sqrt{\frac{1}{5}[(4-203)^2 + (2-203)^2 + (4-203)^2 + (5-203)^2 + (1000-203)^2]}$$

$$= \sqrt{\frac{1}{5}[39601 + 40401 + 39601 + 39204 + 635209]}$$

$$= 398.50,$$

and the MAD would be

$$MAD = \text{median}(|4-4|, |2-4|, |4-4|, |5-4|, |1000-4|)$$

$$= \text{median}(0, 2, 0, 1, 996)$$

$$= 1.$$

In order to make MAD and standard deviation comparable we can multiply MAD by
1.4826. For large numbers of samples, MAD scaled by 1.4826 and standard deviation
converge if the samples are normally distributed.

Extending the idea of the median we can derive information about the shape of a
distribution using PERCENTILES. If we take 100 samples from some distribution and
sort them into ascending order then the first sample with be the first percentile, the
second sample the second percentile and so on up to the last sample which will be the
100th percentile. If there were 100,000 samples then the 100th sorted value would
be the first percentile and the 200th would be the second percentile. For example we
could take the following set of 21 numbers

552	542	524	498	482	471	543
559	431	555	367	563	514	499
465	451	556	476	598	410	483

To find the percentiles we sort the numbers.

0%	5%	10%	15%	20%	25%	30%
367	410	431	451	465	471	476
35%	**40%**	**45%**	**50%**	**55%**	**60%**	**65%**
482	483	498	499	514	524	542
70%	**75%**	**80%**	**85%**	**90%**	**95%**	**100%**
543	552	555	556	559	563	598

The median is the 50% percentile, which is 499 in this case. Alternatively we could use fractions other than percentages, such as quarters, to describe the distribution. The first quartile would be the same as the 25% percentile, which is 471. The third quartile would be the same as the 75th percentile, which is 552. If we were to use quintiles then the first quintile would be the same as the 20% percentile, which is 465. A commonly used measure of dispersion is the inter-quartile range (or IQR), which is the 75% percentile minus the 25% percentile, and in our case the IQR would be $552 - 471$ which is 81. The general name that covers percentiles, quartiles and quintiles is QUANTILES.

3.1.1 Correlation and Covariance

When we are looking at more than one variable we have to consider each of the variables on its own but also how the variables relate together. Take the case of two stocks such as Ford Motor Company and General Motors. When Ford and GM stock prices change do they go up and down together? A very simple measure of this lock-step behaviour is CORRELATION. If Ford and GM move in perfect synchrony then correlation would be +1. If one moves up when the other moves down so that the two stock prices mirror one another, then the correlation would be -1. If the two stock prices move completely independently of one another then correlation is zero. It is important to realize that people usually talk about LINEAR CORRELATION. This means that we are assuming that on average the change in Ford is some constant factor times the move in GM, so a plot of daily change in Ford and GM stock price would fall on a straight line. Many relationships are non-linear which means that they may not be picked up by linear correlation.

In order to measure linear correlation between Ford (F) and GM (G) stock prices we would start by calculating their means $E(F)$ and $E(G)$. Then we would work out, for each day, how far Ford was trading above or below its average $F - E(F)$ and do the same for GM $G - E(G)$. Finally we would scale this deviation because the share prices may be hugely different. We scale by dividing each deviation by the standard deviation. This process of subtracting the mean and dividing by standard deviation is called STANDARDIZATION and the number it produces is called the Z-SCORE. The z-score for Ford would be

$$z_F = \frac{F - \mathrm{E}\,[F]}{\sigma_F}.$$

If Ford's z-score z_F is zero then Ford is sitting at its mean value. If the z-score is +1 the Ford's stock price is high relative to its average, and if the z-score is -1 then

Ford is trading low relative to its average. In terms of correlation the question we are asking is: are the two stocks consistently surprising us in the same way? When Ford is above average is GM also above average? When Ford is below average is GM also below average? If the two are correlated then the expected product of the z-scores will be large. We could draw up a table as follows and score the stock prices each day.

	Ford Surprisingly Low	Ford Surprisingly High
GM Surprisingly Low	$z_F \times z_G > 0$	$z_F \times z_G < 0$
GM Surprisingly High	$z_F \times z_G < 0$	$z_F \times z_G > 0$

If Ford and GM are strongly positively correlated we would expect a lot of days to fall into the top-left and bottom-right parts of the table where the product of z_F and z_G are positive. If the correlation is negative we would see lots of entries in the top-right and bottom-left parts of the table where the product of z_F and z_G is negative. The larger the surprise the greater the effect on our correlation measure, so $z_F = +3$ and $z_G = +2$ would suggest a strong positive correlation, as would $z_F = -3$ and $z_G = -2$. If there is little correlation between Ford and GM then there should be roughly equal counts in each element of the table. By taking the average product of the z-scores we have a good estimate of linear correlation. The linear correlation between F and G is

$$\rho_{F,G} = \mathrm{E}\left[\frac{F - \mathrm{E}\,(F)}{\sigma_F} \times \frac{G - \mathrm{E}\,(G)}{\sigma_G}\right] = \frac{\mathrm{E}(FG) - \mathrm{E}(F)\mathrm{E}(G)}{\sigma_F \sigma_G}.$$

Numerically the value of ρ lies between -1 and +1 and has no dimension, which means that if F and G are measured in dollars then ρ is not measured in dollars. If we want to know about the combination of correlation and volatility then we need covariance. The covariance between F and G combines the volatility of F and G with their linear correlation $\rho_{F,G}$,

$$\mathrm{cov}\,(F, G) = \rho_{F,G}\sigma_F\sigma_G = \mathrm{E}(FG) - \mathrm{E}(F)\mathrm{E}(G).$$

Exercise 6 *Show that* $E\left[\frac{F - E(F)}{\sigma_F} \times \frac{G - E(G)}{\sigma_G}\right] = \frac{E(FG) - E(F)E(G)}{\sigma_F \sigma_G}$.

If we have n variables $X_1, X_2 \ldots, X_n$ rather than two we create a covariance matrix by calculating the covariance between all pairs of variables. The correlation between variable i and variable j given the linear correlation ρ_{ij} and the volatility σ_i and σ_j is

$$C_{ij} = \sigma_i \sigma_j \rho_{ij}.$$

If we have a small sample size to work with then covariance is modified slightly. Instead of dividing the sum of the product of z-scores by the number of data points n we divide by $n - 1$. This is called an UNBIASED ESTIMATE of the covariance of the population from which our n samples originated. The difference between biased and unbiased estimators gets smaller as n increases, but you may notice that your mathematical software gives you

$$C_{ij} = \frac{\sum_{i=1}^{n} x_i y_i}{n - 1} - \frac{\sum_{i=1}^{n} x_i}{n - 1} \times \frac{\sum_{i=1}^{n} y_i}{n - 1},$$

and for volatility you may find that you are getting the unbiased estimator

$$\sigma = \sqrt{\frac{1}{n-1} \sum_{i}^{n} (x_i - \mu)^2}.$$

Exercise 7 *Find the correlation and covariance of these two series: (1,2,3,4,5) and (10,19,32,39,51).*

A common mistake is to assume that if there is a correlation between two variables then there is a causal relationship between those variables. However correlation is not the same as causation. Finance is rife with SPURIOUS CORRELATIONS which are pairs of variables that are statistically correlated but have no causal relationship. Another difficulty is that linear correlation is often inappropriate because almost all relationships are non-linear. More generally it is conditional dependence that is interesting, and although it is harder to define conditional dependence can be non-linear. Conditional dependence can be summarized as follows: if I know the value of F does that tell me anything about the distribution of G? If so then G is conditionally dependent on F. For simple examples of distributions that have the same mean, variance, and linear correlation and yet strikingly different conditional dependence refer to Anscombe's Quartet. Anscombe constructed these four sets of data, containing just 11 data points each, in order to show the importance of visually exploring distributions before performing standard numerical analyses.

3.2 Probability Distributions

When we toss a coin there are three outcomes: heads, tails and landing on an edge. Throwing a dice has six outcomes. If we were to make a list of all the things that could happen this would be our OUTCOME SPACE. Note that this could be an infinitely large list in the case of real numbers. All that we know about the world now, in the past, or in the future can be stated as weightings for each outcome. Probability is just this weighting, with the nice property that the outcome weightings add up to one because if we have truly listed all possible outcomes and they are mutually exclusive then the world will choose one of those outcomes. The distributions in this section are called PARAMETRIC because their shape is described by a set of numeric parameters.

Using just a few parameters and an equation, a PROBABILITY DISTRIBUTION describes the pattern in which probability is smeared out over the outcome space. If the outcomes are discrete such as the result of tossing a coin or rolling a die we have a discrete probability distribution like the Poisson distribution or the Binomial distribution. If the outcomes are continuous then we have a continuous probability distribution such as the normal distribution or Student's t-distribution. If the distribution describes the outcome of a single variable it is UNIVARIATE. Models with two outcomes are called BIVARIATE and with three outcomes TRIVARIATE and more generally any model with two or more variables is MULTIVARIATE.

Once you have a probability distribution there are lots of interesting things you can do with it. Given an outcome you can calculate its likelihood, which is the amount of probability that is assigned to it by the density function with a given set of parameters. Multivariate distributions are more interesting than their univariate siblings because they allow the calculation of MARGINAL and CONDITIONAL distributions. These are methods for throwing variables out of a distribution. A marginal distribution is one in which we integrate out parameters that do not interest us. If we have a bivariate model of a company's share price and credit spread and suddenly decide that credit spread is not interesting we can integrate out all possible values of credit spread to give a univariate share price model. A conditional distribution is one in which we fix the value of a subset of the variables giving a distribution of the remaining variables. So we could fix the value of the credit spread at a certain value and see what distribution that gives us for share price.

So if we have a probability model M and a set of data D the likelihood is $p(D|M)$ which is read as "the probability of the data *given* the model" or "the probability of the data *conditioned* on the model". If the two variables we are modelling are credit spread C and share price S then we would have a bivariate model $p(S, C)$. The marginal distribution of share price S would be

$$p(S) = \int p(S|C)dC$$

and the marginal of the share price for a given value of C, say 73 basis points, would be $p(S|C = 73)$. The marginal distribution removes some variables completely whereas a conditional distribution is a slice through the probability density. The normal distribution is interesting because both its marginals and conditionals are also normal distributions.

The Russian RTS index is an index of 50 stocks which is said to be strongly correlated to the value of oil. Figure 3.3a shows the monthly returns of the stock index against the monthly returns of the price of oil over a period from mid-2004 to the end of 2009. Each point on the graph is the return over one month of Russian stocks and oil. Superimposed on the plot is a set of contour lines showing the joint probability density $p(\text{RTS}, \text{Oil})$. If Russian stock prices and oil were perfectly correlated the returns would fall on the straight line. The linear correlation coefficient is 0.7 and this positive correlation is reflected in the diagram as an elongation of the probability density. At the sides of the figure are two histograms that show the marginal distributions of the two time series with oil returns on the right hand side and RTS index returns along the top. Figure 3.3b shows the conditional distribution of RTS returns given that the return of oil is +0.2 or -0.2, corresponding to a slice through the density visible as a horizontal dashed or dotted line in Figure 3.3a. Notice that the conditional density $p(\text{RTS}|\text{Oil} = 0.2)$ is mostly positive and the conditional density $p(\text{RTS}|\text{Oil} = -0.2)$ is mostly negative as we would expect given positive correlation.

3.2.1 Normal Distribution

This distribution crops up everywhere, so you've probably come across it before. It is defined by two parameters, a location and a breadth. If the location is μ and the

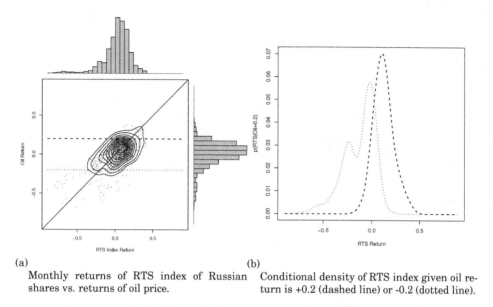

(a)   (b)

Monthly returns of RTS index of Russian   Conditional density of RTS index given oil re-
shares vs. returns of oil price.   turn is +0.2 (dashed line) or -0.2 (dotted line).

Figure 3.3: Joint, marginal and conditional densities for RTS index and oil.

breadth is σ then the distribution is

$$p(x|\mu, \sigma^2) = \frac{1}{\sigma\sqrt{\pi}}e^{-\frac{(x-\mu)^2}{\sigma^2}}$$

The normal distribution has some special properties. It is symmetric about its peak value, also known as the mode, and the tails of the distribution fall off very quickly, dropping to very small densities beyond three or four standard deviations from the mean. Because the distribution is symmetric about its mode the mode is equal to the mean. It is also very frugal in terms of parameters. All that is required to fully describe a normal distribution are two numbers: the mean μ and the standard deviation σ. Other distributions require some additional shape parameters. Another interesting property is that when many observations are taken from other distributions, such as the Binomial distribution or the Poisson distribution, they converge on the normal distribution. It is sometimes useful to ask the question "What is the chance that some value lower than x will be observed from a normal process?". This is called the cumulative normal distribution. Figure 3.4 illustrates the normal density and also the cumulative normal distribution.

The cumulative normal distribution appears in the Black-Scholes formula. The cumulative normal distribution is the area under the normal density curve up to some point x. In mathematical terms it is described as $N(x|\mu, \sigma) = \frac{1}{\sigma\sqrt{\pi}}\int_{-\infty}^{x}e^{-\frac{(y-\mu)^2}{\sigma^2}}dy$. Intuitively if $x = 0$ then the sum of the area to the left of the peak of the curve will be 0.5 because half of the density is to the left of the peak and half is to the right. This is because the normal distribution is symmetric about its mode. If x is a large

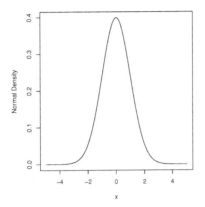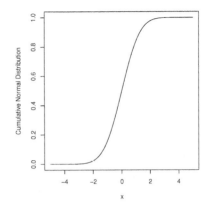

Figure 3.4:
Normal density (left) and distribution (right) functions with $\mu = 0$ and $\sigma = 1$.

negative number that is more than three standard deviations *below* the mean then $N(-x)$ will be close to zero. If x is a large positive number that is more than three standard deviations *above* the mean then $N(x)$ will be close to 1. The symmetry of the distribution leads to another property relating the density for negative and positive values of x, namely $N(-x) = 1 - N(x)$. In words this means that the probability of lying above some value $+x$ is equal to the probability of lying below $-x$.

In its multivariate form the likelihood of a set of observed data x for a $N(\mu, \Sigma)$ distribution is

$$p(x|\mu, \Sigma) = \frac{1}{(2\pi)^{\frac{k}{2}} |\Sigma|^{\frac{1}{2}}} \exp\left(-\frac{1}{2}(x - \mu)^T \Sigma^{-1}(x - \mu)\right).$$

The term $(2\pi)^{\frac{k}{2}} |\Sigma|^{\frac{1}{2}}$ is a normalisation constant that ensures the probability adds to unity. The exponent term $(x - \mu)^T \Sigma^{-1}(x - \mu)$ is just a scalar, a single number, called the Mahalanobis distance. It is called a distance because it measures how far the data x lie from the centre of the distribution μ where distances are scaled by the shape of the distribution Σ. In two dimensions we can draw a line through points of constant probability density and this would be an ellipse. The shape of the ellipse is determined by Σ and the location of the ellipse, its centre, is given by μ.

3.2.2 Log-Normal Distribution

A log-normal probability distribution is the logarithmic twin of the normal distribution. If a random variable is log-normal then taking the logarithm of the variable will yield a normal distribution. The probability density is

$$p(x|\mu, \sigma^2) = \frac{1}{\sqrt{2\pi}\sigma x} e^{-\frac{(\ln x - \mu)^2}{2\sigma^2}},$$

and the mean and variance are $E(X) = e^{(\mu + \frac{\sigma^2}{2})}$ and $Var(X) = e^{(2\mu + \sigma^2)}\left(e^{\sigma^2} - 1\right)$. Note that this distribution is only meaningful for positive values of x and that it has a long tail. A common assumption is that the returns on equities are log normal however this is questionable (see Section 10.7 on page 358 for an example).

3.2.3 Poisson Distribution

The probability of k events with the expected number of events per interval λ is

$$p(k, \lambda) = \frac{e^{-\lambda}\lambda^k}{k!}$$

The time to the first event has an exponential distribution $e^{-\lambda t}$.

3.2.4 Binomial Distribution

For a binary outcome with "success" probability p, the probability of getting exactly k successes in n independent trials is

$$p(k, n, p) = \left(\begin{array}{c} n \\ k \end{array} \right) p^k (1 - p)^{n-k}$$

The value $\left(\begin{array}{c} n \\ k \end{array} \right)$ read "n choose k" is the BINOMIAL COEFFICIENT and is also written C_n^k, $_nC_k$ or $C(n, k)$. It enumerates the number of ways of choosing k things from n options. The name binomial coefficient stems from the fact that the numbers are the coefficients in th expansion $(x+y)^n$. The equation for calculating a binomial coefficient is

$$C(n, k) = \frac{n!}{k!(n - k)!}$$

The notation $n!$ is a factorial and is the product of all the integers from 1 to n, so $5! = 5 \times 4 \times 3 \times 2 \times 1 = 120$. Say we have a hamburger restaurant where customers can choose from a wide variety of toppings. Say there are 10 different toppings and each burger is allowed exactly 3 different toppings then the number of possible burger topping combinations is $C(10, 3) = \frac{10!}{3!7!} = \frac{10 \times 9 \times 8}{3 \times 2 \times 1} = 120$. An intuitive explanation of $C(n, k)$ is that there are 10 ways of choosing the first topping, 9 ways of choosing the second, and 8 ways of choosing the third. Because the order does not matter, a bacon, cheese and pickle burger being the same as a cheese, bacon and pickle burger, this over-estimates the number of combinations, so we divide by the possible orderings of 3 things, which is $3! = 3 \times 2 \times 1 = 6$.

We can build a picture out of binomial coefficients which is called PASCAL'S TRIANGLE. This is despite the fact that the triangle pre-dates Pascal by two milennia having first been described in a Sanskrit text on phonology by Pingala at some time in the first millenium BC. It was re-discovered in the Middle Ages and is still known in China as YANG HUI'S TRIANGLE and in Iran as KHAYYAM'S TRIANGLE. Whatever its name, the triangle of coefficients is shown in Table 3.1. The coefficient we have already calculated $C(10, 3)$ is on the tenth row down, three steps into the pyramid.

n											
						1					
1						1	1				
2					1	2	1				
3				1	3	3	1				
4			1	4	6	4	1				
5		1	5	10	10	5	1				
6	1	6	15	20	15	6	1				
7	1	7	21	35	35	21	7	1			
8	1	8	28	56	70	56	28	8	1		
9	1	9	36	84	126	126	84	36	9	1	
10	1	10	45	120	210	252	210	120	45	10	1

Table 3.1: Binomial coefficients.

3.3 Sampling from Distributions

3.3.1 Univariate Normal

The old-fashioned way of drawing a sample from the univariate normal distribution is the Box-Muller method. The idea is to use two draws from a uniform distribution $u(-1,1)$, call them x and y, then find whether this would fall inside the unit circle by calculating $s^2 = x^2 + y^2$. If not the samples are thrown away, which means that this is a REJECTION SAMPLING method. The process is repeated until we have a pair of variables that lie inside the unit circle, then two normal samples are generated using the transforms

$$z_1 = x\sqrt{\frac{-2\ln s}{s}}$$

and

$$z_2 = y\sqrt{\frac{-2\ln s}{s}}$$

The problem with a rejection sampling method such as Box-Muller is that the rejection rate may be very high which slows down the generation of valid samples. Most mathematical packages have their own highly efficient random number generators. Matlab, for example, uses something called the Ziggurat algorithm. This uses a very efficient rejection sampling method where the envelope function is constructed by a set of n rectangles of equal area. Increasing n results in more memory usage, but a lower rejection rate. In practice it is worthwhile using an efficient method for numerically intensive calculations.

3.3.2 Multivariate Normal

The first step is to calculate the Cholesky decomposition of the covariance matrix Σ. The Cholesky matrix L is often likened to the square root of a matrix since $LL^T = \Sigma$. Then a vector n of independent $N(0,1)$ samples are drawn and premultiplied by L.

The samples are calculated using

$$S = \mu + Ln,$$

where μ defines the centre of the samples.

3.3.3 Normal Copula

The normal copula is a method for sampling from a multivariate distribution. The normal copula separates the correlation and marginal distributions of a set of random variables. When using the copula to generate samples a multivariate normal distribution is used to generate correlated variables, then by a quantile mapping procedure the samples are kneaded into the correct marginal distributions. The sampling procedure can be broken down into the following steps:

1. Draw n $p \times 1$ samples from a $N(0, \Sigma)$ distribution where Σ is a $p \times p$ dimensional covariance matrix.

2. Transform the n normally distributed samples to probabilities using the inverse normal distribution ϕ^{-1}.

3. Inverse-transform the probabilities using the cumulative distributions for the marginals.

3.4 Comparing Distributions

A common question in finance is whether two distributions are the same. For example when we look for conditional dependence between X and Y we are really asking whether the probability distribution of Y tells us anything about the distribution of X. In other words we are comparing the probability distribution of X alone, $p(X)$, and the probability of X conditioned on the value of Y, $p(X|Y)$. If $p(X) = p(X|Y)$ then there is no conditional dependence and this is very important in finance, in particular for constructing a diversified portfolio that has low volatility.

If the distributions are derived from return time series then a good place to start is a scatterplot because the human visual system is very good at spotting subtle patterns. The next step would be to look at individual histograms for the series. We would then compare the summary statistics to see if the means and volatilities differ or whether there is a difference in skew or kurtosis. A very powerful comparison tool to compare the shape of probability distributions is called a QUANTILE PLOT. Say we have two series that have the same distribution but very different means and volatilities. The shape of the distribution is the same but one is shifted and stretched relative to the other. If it is the shape that interests us then we can sort the two sets of returns, find the percentiles, and plot these percentiles against one another. If their distributions have the same shape then the matched percentiles will fall on a straight line. To test whether a distribution is normal we can plot its percentiles with those of a normal distribution and see whether these fall on a straight line.

As an example we will take samples from two distributions: a normal distribution and a log normal distribution. We generate 100,000 samples from both distributions and the percentiles are:

Percentile	10%	20%	30%	40%	50%	60%	70%	80%	90%
X	423.1	449.4	468.3	484.4	499.7	515.0	531.0	550.2	577.1
Y	78.4	97.8	114.3	130.8	148.5	168.2	192.7	225.9	281.8

If these two distributions had the same shape then a plot of the percentiles of X and Y should fall on a straight line. We can also compare the percentiles with those of known distributions. With astonishing foresight we could use those of the normal and log normal distributions. Starting with X:

Percentile	10%	20%	30%	40%	50%	60%	70%	80%	90%
X	423.1	449.4	468.3	484.4	499.7	515.0	531.0	550.2	577.1
Normal	423.3	449.6	468.6	484.8	500.0	515.2	531.4	550.4	576.7
Log Normal	424.5	447.9	465.6	481.2	496.3	511.9	529.1	550.0	580.3

Clearly the quantiles for X match those of a normal distribution very closely, but not those of a log normal distribution. We can do the same for Y:

Percentile	10%	20%	30%	40%	50%	60%	70%	80%	90%
Y	78.4	97.8	114.3	130.8	148.5	168.2	192.7	225.9	281.8
Normal	53.7	93.0	121.3	145.6	168.2	190.8	215.0	243.4	282.7
Log Normal	78.3	97.6	114.3	130.9	148.5	168.5	192.9	226.0	281.6

In this case the percentiles match those of a log normal distribution very closely, but not those of a normal distribution. In practice a plot of the two sets of quantiles is the best way to compare the shape of distributions, and the quantile plots for X and Y are shown in 3.5. The quantile plots clearly show that the distribution of X is normal and the distribution of Y is log normal. We can see this because the quantile plot of X against the normal distribution (top left graph) is a straight line, and the quantile plot of Y against a log normal distribution (bottom right) is a straight line. We know that a log normal distribution has a truncated lower tail and an extended upper tail relative to a normal distribution. This is shown in the top right graph because the upper tail of distribution Y veers off well above and is longer than the upper tail of a normal distribution. The lower tail also lies above and is shorter than that of a normal distribution. The opposite is true when we compare X with a log normal distribution (bottom left graph); the upper tail of X is shorter and the lower tail of X is longer than those of the log normal distribution.

To see a comparison between returns of an equity with a normal distribution refer to Section 10.7 on page 358. The distribution of daily share price movements is leptokurtic which means that the centre and tails have more density than the normal distribution. In the normal quantile plot of Google daily returns we can see that the upper tail lies well above the normal tail and the lower tail lies well below the normal tail. This means that in the stock market we see more extreme daily stock price movements and more small stock price movements than predicted by a normal distribution.

3.5 Monte Carlo Sampling

There are many Monte Carlo sampling techniques. They fall into different classes depending on the aim of the simulation. In finance one is usually trying to calculate the expectation of some distribution. In one dimension it is quite easy to draw samples from any probability distribution $f(x)$ using draws from a uniform distribution $U(0,1)$. This is simply a matter of calculating the cumulative probability distribution

$$F(x) = \int_{-\infty}^{x} f(y)dy,$$

then looking up values using the inverse cumulative distribution $F^{-1}(x)$. For example the following probability density function, which is a mixture of four normal distributions,

$$f(x) = \frac{1}{7\sqrt{\pi}} \left[e^{-(x+5)^2} + \sqrt{3}e^{-\frac{(x+1)^2}{3}} + \sqrt{10}e^{-10(x-2)^2} + 2e^{-(x-7)^2} \right],$$

is shown in the top left hand panel of Figure 3.6 along with its cumulative distribution in the top right hand panel. The probability density consists of four peaks. Notice that where the probability density is zero the cumulative distribution is flat. To draw samples from $f(x)$ we generate many samples distributed evenly in the range 0 to 1 and look up the x value that corresponds with that value. In other words we are using the inverse of the cumulative distribution $F^{-1}(u)$ to "shape" the flat samples. For example our uniform random number generator might produce the following five numbers in the range 0 to 1, which are transformed by looking up x from the inverse cumulative distribution function in Figure 3.6

Uniform $U(0,1)$ Sample	$F^{-1}(u)$
0.2655087	-1.8841211
0.3721239	-1.3510916
0.5728534	-0.4475368
0.9082078	6.7938957
0.2016819	-2.2994819

The bottom left panel in Figure 3.6 shows the simulated distribution for ten million samples. It fits the original probability distribution well. But the bottom right hand panel shows how well the mean of the distribution is estimated as we increase the number of samples. For this distribution the mean can be calculated exactly and it is -0.05. It takes about a million samples to get close to the true mean. In other words the

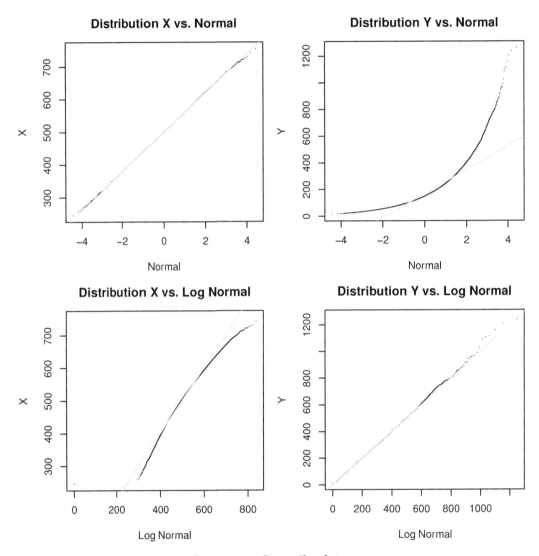

Figure 3.5: Quantile plots.

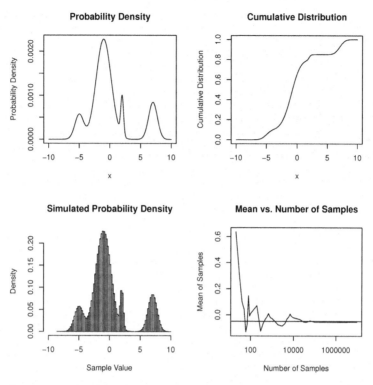

Figure 3.6: Probability density and cumulative distribution.

mean of the generated samples converge slowly on the distribution mean. If we are
solely interested in the expectation of the distribution then we can use some tricks to
make the samples converge toward the true expectation with less samples. But note
that in other applications the subject of interest is the full probability distribution
where these tricks to speed convergence of the expectation may not help.

The slow convergence of the mean lies in the fact that we are using pseudo-random
numbers. Because computers are deterministic it is actually quite difficult to make
them generate what seem like random numbers. Computer scientists exert themselves trying to come up with random number algorithms that pass rigorous tests of
randomness. But in finance we are focussed on finding the fair price of assets. The
fair price equates to the present value of an asset which is the expectation of some
function of a set of random variables. We simply require rapid convergence of the
expectation, randomness be damned. To this end there are quasi-random sequence
generators that aim to fill the space evenly in as few samples as possible, ensuring
rapid convergence of the expectation.

There are two popular quasi-random generator algorithms named after their cre-
ators: Sobol and Halton. Figure 3.7 compares a pseudo-random sequence with a
quasi-pseudorandom sequence. The left hand panels show a pseudo-random sequence
and a Sobol sequence. Notice that the quasi-random sequence does not seem random.
There seem to be regular patterns in the samples, but they fill the range 0 to 1 more

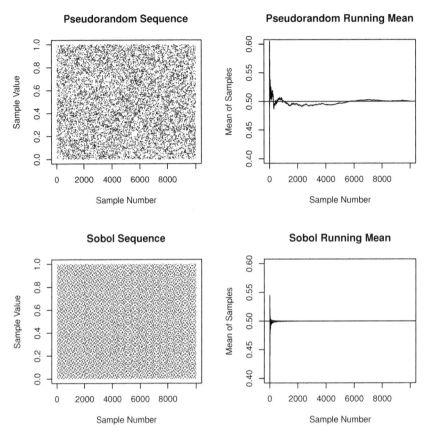

Figure 3.7: Comparison of Sobol and pseudorandom sequences.

evenly than the pseudo-random numbers. Most importantly the running average of the mean for the Sobol generator converges after just a few hundred samples, whereas the pseudo-random generator is still wandering around after several thousand samples. A good resource for Monte Carlo sampling for financial applications is the book by Jaeckel (2002). More advanced methods can be found on Radford Neal's web site `http://www.cs.utoronto.ca/~radford` which hosts some of his publications and software implementing some of his Monte Carlo algorithms.

3.6 Linear Regression

Linear regression takes sets of variables and looks for straight-line relationships between these variables. In finance this usually means looking at relationships between the prices of assets. As an example we will look at the relationship between the log returns on the FTSE 100 stock index and one of its component stocks, a mining company called Kazakhmys. We will start with returns for just 20 days so that we can see what is going on, then scale up to more data. The returns over this time period were as follows:

Date	FTSE 100	Kazakhmys
2009-09-08	0.00285	0.06219
2009-09-09	0.01146	0.00370
2009-09-10	-0.00332	-0.00278
2009-09-11	0.00476	0.01563
2009-09-14	0.00148	-0.00825
2009-09-15	0.00461	0.00916
2009-09-16	0.01613	0.03229
2009-09-17	0.00776	0.00704
2009-09-18	0.00172	-0.01501
2009-09-21	-0.00747	-0.03347
2009-09-22	0.00160	0.01098
2009-09-23	-0.00062	0.00273
2009-09-24	-0.01176	-0.03509
2009-09-25	0.00057	-0.00849
2009-09-28	0.01630	0.01785
2009-09-29	-0.00116	0.00000
2009-09-30	-0.00501	0.00000
2009-10-01	-0.01691	-0.03506
2009-10-02	-0.01178	-0.04992
2009-10-05	0.00711	0.01559

Just looking at the data makes it hard to see any pattern, so we could ask a very simple question. If the FTSE goes up does Kazakhmys go up too? And if the FTSE goes down does Kazakhmys go down too? Here is a table showing how often both go up and down with the cases where both went up together and down together in bold:

	Kazakhmys Down	Kazakhmys Up
FTSE Down	**7**	1
FTSE Up	3	**9**

It does seem that returns for the FTSE and Kazakhmys are related. We see many cases where both the FTSE and Kazakhmys go up and down together and relatively few cases where they go in different directions. Now that we have summary data we can use longer time-series, so expanding the period of time from January 4th 2000 to December 21, 2009 we find the following pattern:

	Kazakhmys Down	Kazakhmys Up
FTSE Down	**850**	339
FTSE Up	322	**907**

To summarize this table, if the FTSE falls then it is three times as likely for Kazakhmys to fall as it is for Kazakhmys to rise. If the FTSE rises it is about three times more likely that Kazakhmys will rise rather than fall. We seem to have a strong correlation. But this table does not tell us how much Kazakhmys will rise or fall given that we know how much the FTSE rises or falls. We are going to assume that the relationship between the FTSE return and stock return is linear. This means the Kazakhmys return is equal to some constant, α, plus the correlation β times the FTSE return, plus some residual noise ϵ,

$$r_{KZK} = \alpha + \beta r_{FTSE} + \epsilon.$$

The RESIDUAL for each data point is the difference between the value that the model predicts $\widehat{r_{KZK}}$ and the actual value that we observe r_{KZK}. If the model were perfect, and all of our data sat on a straight line the residuals would all be zero $\widehat{r_{KZK}} - r_{KZK} = 0$. We do not care whether residuals are positive or negative so we can square the difference to get rid of the sign. We can then tell how "good" the model is by summing these squared errors,

$$SSE = \Sigma_i \left(\widehat{r_{KZK},i} - r_{KZK,i} \right)^2.$$

Finally we need to find the value of α and β that best fit the data. In terms of our sum of squared errors we need to find values for α and β that minimize the sum of squared errors. We could just use a solver to do this but for linear regression it is fairly easy to do this analytically and the result is a value for β of

$$\beta = \frac{\mathrm{E}(r_{FTSE}r_{KZK}) - \mathrm{E}(r_{FTSE})\mathrm{E}(r_{KZK})}{\mathrm{E}(r_{FTSE}^2) - \mathrm{E}^2(r_{FTSE})} = \frac{\mathrm{cov}(r_{FTSE}, r_{KZK})}{\mathrm{var}(r_{FTSE})} = \frac{\sigma_{KZK}}{\sigma_{FTSE}}\rho_{FTSE,KZK}$$

where $\rho_{FTSE,KZK}$ is the linear correlation coefficient between the FTSE returns and the Kazakhmys returns and

$$\alpha = \mathrm{E}(r_{KZK}) - \beta\mathrm{E}(r_{FTSE}).$$

For our 20 returns the expected values that we need to estimate α and β are:

$\mathrm{E}(r_{FTSE}r_{KZK})$	0.0001569855
$\mathrm{E}(r_{FTSE})$	0.0009149138
$\mathrm{E}(r_{KZK})$	-0.0005459111
$\mathrm{E}(r_{FTSE}^2)$	0.00007423523

So

$$
\begin{aligned}
\beta &= \frac{0.0001569 - 0.0009149 \times (-0.0005459)}{0.00007424 - 0.0009149^2} \\
&= \frac{0.0001575}{0.00007340} \\
&= 2.1456,
\end{aligned}
$$

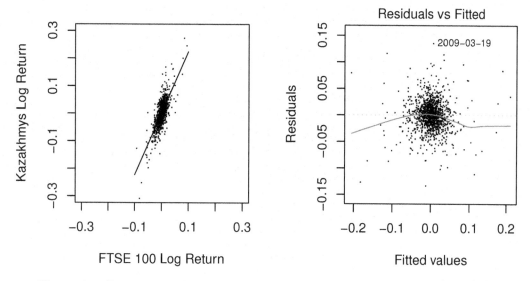

Figure 3.8: Regression of Kazakhmys log returns against FTSE 100 returns.

and

$$\begin{aligned} \alpha &= -0.0005459 - 2.1456 \times 0.0009149 \\ &= -0.002509 \end{aligned}$$

This means that the relationship between the FTSE returns and the Kazakhmys returns, if linear, would be best fit in the least-sum-of-squared-error sense by

$$r_{KAZ} = -0.0025 + 2.15 \times r_{FTSE} + \epsilon.$$

The value of α is tiny and β is about 2, so on average the Kazakhmys returns are twice the FTSE returns. It always pays to plot the data to see how well the model, a straight line in this case, fits the data. The returns and the least squares straight line fit are shown in Figure 3.8. It looks like the data are very noisy so that although on average the Kazakhmys returns are twice as large as the FTSE returns there is a huge amount of day-to-day variation from this pattern due to trading activity that is company-specific to Kazakhmys rather than generated by market sentiment as a whole. It is also apparent that for very high upward and downward shifts in the FTSE Kazakmys reacts even more strongly than a straight line would suggest. This is more evident if we plot the RESIDUALS, which is the error ϵ in our prediction. If our predicted value for Kazakhmys is $\widehat{r_{KAZ}}$ and the observed value is r_{KAZ} then the residual is the difference between the two $\widehat{r_{KAZ}} - r_{KAZ}$. The residuals are shown in the right hand panel of Figure 3.8.

In more general terms, if we are looking to predict a variable y based on our knowledge of variable x assuming a straight-line relationship then we define a gradient β and the value of y where the line crosses (when $x = 0$) and we will call this offset term α. Because we know that the model will never be *exactly* correct we also add the noise term ϵ.

$$\hat{y} = \alpha + \beta x + \epsilon,$$

If we mimimize the sum of squared residuals, which are the differences between predicted and actual values of y it can be proven that

$$\beta = \frac{\mathrm{E}(xy) - \mathrm{E}(x)\mathrm{E}(y)}{\mathrm{E}(x^2) - \mathrm{E}^2(x)} = \frac{\mathrm{cov}(x, y)}{\mathrm{var}(x)} = \frac{\sigma_y}{\sigma_x}\rho_{x,y}$$

and once we know β we calculate α using the means of x and y.

$$\alpha = \mathrm{E}(y) - \beta\mathrm{E}(x).$$

3.7 Sum of a Geometric Series

If we have the sum of say $3^5 + 3^6 + 3^7 + \ldots + 3^{20}$ we can save some legwork by finding an expression that does not require lots of addition. Our sum

$$S = \sum_{t=a}^{b} z^t,$$

or

$$
\begin{aligned}
S &= z^a &+ z^{a+1} &+ z^{a+2} &\ldots &+ z^b \\
zS &= &z^{a+1} &+ z^{a+2} &\ldots &+ z^b &+ z^{b+1}
\end{aligned}
$$

Subtracting the bottom line from the top line removes all the terms on the right hand side except for z^a and z^{b+1} so

$$S = \frac{z^a - z^{b+1}}{1 - z}.$$

In the special case where $a = 1$, then $S = z + z^2 + \ldots + z^n$ this simplifies to

$$S = \frac{1 - z^n}{z^{-1} - 1}. \tag{3.1}$$

In our previous example where we were calculating the sum of the series $3^5 + 3^6 + 3^7 + \ldots + 3^{20}$ we set $z = 3$, $a = 5$, $b = 20$ and the sum should be $\frac{3^5 - 3^{21}}{1 - 3} = 5,230,176,480$. Equation 3.1 is useful for valuing an annuity where we have a stream of cash flows each with value c with present value

$$\mathrm{PV_{ann}} = \frac{c}{\left(1 + \frac{r}{f}\right)^f} + \frac{c}{\left(1 + \frac{r}{f}\right)^{2f}} + \ldots + \frac{c}{\left(1 + \frac{r}{f}\right)^{nf}},$$

so $z = \frac{1}{\left(1 + \frac{r}{f}\right)^f}$, $a = 1$ and $b = n$ giving

$$\mathrm{PV_{ann}} = c\frac{1 - \frac{1}{\left(1 + \frac{r}{f}\right)^{nf}}}{\left(1 + \frac{r}{f}\right)^f - 1}.$$

When the payments are annual $f = 1$,

$$\text{PV}_{\text{ann}} = c \frac{1 - \frac{1}{(1+r)^n}}{r}.$$

3.8 Maclaurin Series Approximations

Any Function $f(x)$ Around $x = a$

$$f(x - a) \simeq f(a) + \left.\frac{df}{dx}\right|_{x=a} (x - a) + \frac{1}{2}\left.\frac{d^2 f}{dx^2}\right|_{x=a} (x - a)^2 + \frac{1}{6}\left.\frac{d^3 f}{dx^3}\right|_{x=a} (x - a)^3 + O(x - a)^4$$

Natural Logarithm

$$\ln(1 + x) = x - \frac{x^2}{2} + \frac{x^3}{3} - \frac{x^4}{4} \cdots = \sum_{i=0}^{\infty} \frac{(-1)^i}{i + 1} x^{i+1}$$

if $|x| < 1$.

Exponential

$$e^x = 1 + x + \frac{x^2}{2!} + \frac{x^3}{3!} \cdots = \sum_{i=0}^{\infty} \frac{x^i}{i!}$$

Binomial

$$(1 + x)^n = 1 + nx + \frac{n(n - 1)}{2!} x^2 + \frac{n(n - 1)(n - 2)}{3!} x^3 \cdots = \sum_{i=0}^{\infty} \binom{n}{i} x^n$$

3.9 Principal Component Analysis

Often we have to deal with data which has more than three dimensions. This causes a difficulty because it becomes impossible to visualise the data directly. This is sometimes called the "curse of dimensionality". Extra dimensions do not provide much new information. For example if we were to measure the price to earnings ratio of various companies and also their share price the two numbers are directly proportional to one another. The share price is what you would pay for a share in the market and the price to earnings ratio is the price per share divided by the earnings per share. The two time series are driven by the same underlying process, which is the value of the equity on the open market. Earnings will be updated occasionally, but we will assume that they are constant whereas the share price varies throughout each trading day. How could we throw away the useless dimension and focus on the PRINCIPAL COMPONENTS of the data? This is the purpose of PRINCIPAL COMPONENT ANALYSIS (PCA).

PCA is a statistical method for rotating a data set such that the new axes capture the maximum amount of variation. To take our simple two-dimensional case of share price and price to earnings ratio all of our measurements of these two numbers, when plotted against one another, would fall on a straight line. PCA would rotate the data such that the data would fall on the first axis. When describing each data point we would only need one number, not two because the first principal component captures all of the variation of the data. It is often interesting to see what axes are chosen by PCA. In this case the axis would correspond directly with share price.

If we have a set of observations in a data matrix M such that each row is one observation, then the steps in calculating the principal components are as follows:

1. Centre the data by subtracting the mean of all the observations $m_j = \frac{\sum_i^n M_{ij}}{n}$, resulting in a "centred" data matrix $X_{ij} = M_{ij} - m_j$.

2. Calculate the covariance matrix $\Sigma = \mathbf{X}^T \mathbf{X}$.

3. Find the matrix V such that the product $\mathbf{V}^{-1} \Sigma \mathbf{V} = \mathbf{D}$, where $\mathbf{D}$ is a diagonal matrix (all the off-diagonal elements are zero).

V is a rotation matrix that diagonalizes the covariance matrix Σ. The columns of V are called EIGENVECTORS of the covariance matrix and are the new, rotated axes. The diagonal of the diagonal matrix D contains the EIGENVALUES. Eigenvalues show how much variance is captured by projecting the data onto each of the eigenvectors. Sometimes the third step can break down if the covariance matrix is SINGULAR, or almost singular. This occurs when two of the columns in $\mathbf{X}$ are very strongly or perfectly correlated. In this case there is a numerical method for finding the eigenvectors and eigenvalues called SINGULAR VALUE DECOMPOSITION (SVD). For an entertaining introduction to SVD see Press et al. (2007).

In order to explain why PCA is useful we can use an example from the world of fixed income. The price of bonds is driven largely by movements in the yield curve, and by other factors that we discuss elsewhere such as the issuer's credit curve. The yield curve is a snapshot at one point in time of the yield of fixed income instruments with different maturities. The curve we will examine is the US dollar interest rate swap curve using historical data obtained from Bloomberg covering a period from January 2006 to March 2010. There are quotes for interest rate swaps of maturity ranging from one year out to thirty years. Longer maturities are available but these are not liquid. The time-series for the USD swap data are shown for each of thirteen maturities in Figure 3.9. Typically the short end of the curve is more variable than the long end, and this is certainly true for the USD swap rates over this period of time. However if we take the daily changes in rate measured in basis points, and find the daily standard deviation it is fairly flat across the term structure and in fact drops off at the short end:

1Y	2Y	3Y	4Y	5Y	6Y	7Y	8Y	9Y	10Y	15Y	20Y	30Y
5.39	6.95	7.44	7.63	7.80	7.70	7.69	7.66	7.63	7.58	7.38	7.29	7.46

The covariance matrix of daily changes in the swap curve in basis points looks as follows:

USD Swap Rate History

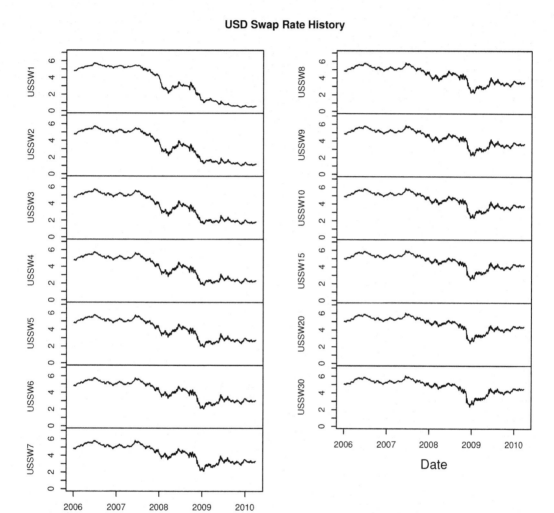

Figure 3.9:
    USD interest rate swap rate history for 1 to 10, 15, 20 and 30 year maturities.

$$\Sigma = \begin{pmatrix}
29.00 & 34.30 & 34.79 & 33.99 & 32.97 & 31.72 & 30.56 & 29.56 & 28.62 & 27.74 & 24.86 & 23.34 & 22.30 \\
34.30 & 48.29 & 50.72 & 50.61 & 49.92 & 48.37 & 46.88 & 45.54 & 44.29 & 42.98 & 39.15 & 36.98 & 35.57 \\
34.79 & 50.72 & 55.42 & 55.88 & 55.74 & 54.44 & 53.25 & 51.91 & 50.72 & 49.46 & 45.65 & 43.28 & 41.83 \\
33.99 & 50.61 & 55.88 & 58.17 & 58.74 & 57.59 & 56.76 & 55.65 & 54.55 & 53.30 & 49.61 & 47.38 & 46.09 \\
32.97 & 49.92 & 55.74 & 58.74 & 60.85 & 59.53 & 59.13 & 58.04 & 57.10 & 56.07 & 52.50 & 50.31 & 49.11 \\
31.72 & 48.37 & 54.44 & 57.59 & 59.53 & 59.34 & 58.62 & 58.16 & 57.39 & 56.43 & 53.17 & 51.25 & 50.09 \\
30.56 & 46.88 & 53.25 & 56.76 & 59.13 & 58.62 & 59.07 & 58.38 & 57.92 & 57.17 & 54.33 & 52.41 & 51.66 \\
29.56 & 45.54 & 51.91 & 55.65 & 58.04 & 58.16 & 58.38 & 58.65 & 58.13 & 57.26 & 54.51 & 52.84 & 52.12 \\
28.62 & 44.29 & 50.72 & 54.55 & 57.10 & 57.39 & 57.92 & 58.13 & 58.15 & 57.39 & 54.92 & 53.36 & 52.90 \\
27.74 & 42.98 & 49.46 & 53.30 & 56.07 & 56.43 & 57.17 & 57.26 & 57.39 & 57.40 & 55.17 & 53.70 & 53.32 \\
24.86 & 39.15 & 45.65 & 49.61 & 52.50 & 53.17 & 54.33 & 54.51 & 54.92 & 55.17 & 54.52 & 53.48 & 53.68 \\
23.34 & 36.98 & 43.28 & 47.38 & 50.31 & 51.25 & 52.41 & 52.84 & 53.36 & 53.70 & 53.48 & 53.14 & 53.59 \\
22.30 & 35.57 & 41.83 & 46.09 & 49.11 & 50.09 & 51.66 & 52.12 & 52.90 & 53.32 & 53.68 & 53.59 & 55.64
\end{pmatrix}$$

Recall that the covariance matrix Σ is the product of the volatility vector and the correlation matrix

$$\Sigma = \sigma^T \rho \sigma,$$

the volatility vector σ is

$$\sigma = (\ 5.3851 \quad 6.9491 \quad 7.4441 \quad 7.6268 \quad 7.8006 \quad 7.7033 \quad 7.6854 \quad 7.6585 \quad 7.6255 \quad 7.5761 \quad 7.3836 \quad 7.2897 \quad 7.459\ ).$$

and the correlation matrix ρ is

$$\rho = \begin{pmatrix}
1.00 & 0.92 & 0.87 & 0.83 & 0.79 & 0.77 & 0.74 & 0.72 & 0.70 & 0.68 & 0.63 & 0.59 & 0.56 \\
0.92 & 1.00 & 0.98 & 0.96 & 0.92 & 0.90 & 0.88 & 0.86 & 0.84 & 0.82 & 0.76 & 0.73 & 0.69 \\
0.87 & 0.98 & 1.00 & 0.98 & 0.96 & 0.95 & 0.93 & 0.91 & 0.89 & 0.88 & 0.83 & 0.80 & 0.75 \\
0.83 & 0.96 & 0.98 & 1.00 & 0.99 & 0.98 & 0.97 & 0.95 & 0.94 & 0.92 & 0.88 & 0.85 & 0.81 \\
0.79 & 0.92 & 0.96 & 0.99 & 1.00 & 0.99 & 0.99 & 0.97 & 0.96 & 0.95 & 0.91 & 0.89 & 0.84 \\
0.77 & 0.90 & 0.95 & 0.98 & 0.99 & 1.00 & 0.99 & 0.99 & 0.98 & 0.97 & 0.94 & 0.91 & 0.87 \\
0.74 & 0.88 & 0.93 & 0.97 & 0.99 & 0.99 & 1.00 & 0.99 & 0.99 & 0.98 & 0.96 & 0.94 & 0.90 \\
0.72 & 0.86 & 0.91 & 0.95 & 0.97 & 0.99 & 0.99 & 1.00 & 1.00 & 0.99 & 0.96 & 0.95 & 0.91 \\
0.70 & 0.84 & 0.89 & 0.94 & 0.96 & 0.98 & 0.99 & 1.00 & 1.00 & 0.99 & 0.98 & 0.96 & 0.93 \\
0.68 & 0.82 & 0.88 & 0.92 & 0.95 & 0.97 & 0.98 & 0.99 & 0.99 & 1.00 & 0.99 & 0.97 & 0.94 \\
0.63 & 0.76 & 0.83 & 0.88 & 0.91 & 0.94 & 0.96 & 0.96 & 0.98 & 0.99 & 1.00 & 0.99 & 0.98 \\
0.59 & 0.73 & 0.80 & 0.85 & 0.89 & 0.91 & 0.94 & 0.95 & 0.96 & 0.97 & 0.99 & 1.00 & 0.99 \\
0.56 & 0.69 & 0.75 & 0.81 & 0.84 & 0.87 & 0.90 & 0.91 & 0.93 & 0.94 & 0.98 & 0.99 & 1.00
\end{pmatrix}$$

Notice that rates that have similar maturity are more strongly correlated than rates that have very different maturities. For example the one and two year rates have a correlation of 0.9165 whereas the one and thirty year swap rates have a correlation of just 0.552. To find the covariance of the one and three year swap rates we simply multiply the correlation with the one year swap and three year swap standard deviations

$$
\begin{aligned}
\sigma^2_{1Y,3Y} &= \sigma_{1Y} \sigma_{3Y} \rho_{1Y,3Y} \\
&= 5.3851 \times 7.4441 \times 0.8679 \\
&= 34.79
\end{aligned}
$$

PCA is a rotation of the data X such that the covariance matrix Σ becomes a diagonal matrix D with no cross-terms. The rotation ensures that the linear correlation between each variable is zero. All the volatility is contained on the diagonal of the new covariance matrix D. If we add up each variance term on the diagonal of D the total is 707.62. This is exactly equal to the total variance of all the swap tenors $\sigma^2_{1Y} + \sigma^2_{2Y} + \sigma^2_{3Y} + \ldots + \sigma^2_{30Y}$ because our rotation preserved all of the variance in the original data X. In fact the variance is now concentrated onto just the first three of the new dimensions. As a fraction of the total variance of 707.62 the first three components make up $650.31 + 42.92 + 7.48$ or 700.7 of the total variance 707.62, which is

99.02% of the total variance. In other words, by projecting our data onto just the first three principal components and throwing the other ten principal components away we are still capturing most of the variation of our data. To see what this means graphically see Figure 3.10. This is a plot of the thirteen principal components over the four year time period. The first principal component is varying a great deal, the second less so, and the third less still. Beyond the first three components there is little variation over time. The diagonalized covariance matrix D containing the eigenvectors is:

$$D = \begin{pmatrix}
650.31 & 0.00 & 0.00 & 0.00 & 0.00 & 0.00 & 0.00 & 0.00 & 0.00 & 0.00 & 0.00 & 0.00 & 0.00 \\
0.00 & 42.92 & 0.00 & 0.00 & 0.00 & 0.00 & 0.00 & 0.00 & 0.00 & 0.00 & 0.00 & 0.00 & 0.00 \\
0.00 & 0.00 & 7.48 & 0.00 & 0.00 & 0.00 & 0.00 & 0.00 & 0.00 & 0.00 & 0.00 & 0.00 & 0.00 \\
0.00 & 0.00 & 0.00 & 2.80 & 0.00 & 0.00 & 0.00 & 0.00 & 0.00 & 0.00 & 0.00 & 0.00 & 0.00 \\
0.00 & 0.00 & 0.00 & 0.00 & 1.21 & 0.00 & 0.00 & 0.00 & 0.00 & 0.00 & 0.00 & 0.00 & 0.00 \\
0.00 & 0.00 & 0.00 & 0.00 & 0.00 & 0.79 & 0.00 & 0.00 & 0.00 & 0.00 & 0.00 & 0.00 & 0.00 \\
0.00 & 0.00 & 0.00 & 0.00 & 0.00 & 0.00 & 0.54 & 0.00 & 0.00 & 0.00 & 0.00 & 0.00 & 0.00 \\
0.00 & 0.00 & 0.00 & 0.00 & 0.00 & 0.00 & 0.00 & 0.53 & 0.00 & 0.00 & 0.00 & 0.00 & 0.00 \\
0.00 & 0.00 & 0.00 & 0.00 & 0.00 & 0.00 & 0.00 & 0.00 & 0.33 & 0.00 & 0.00 & 0.00 & 0.00 \\
0.00 & 0.00 & 0.00 & 0.00 & 0.00 & 0.00 & 0.00 & 0.00 & 0.00 & 0.27 & 0.00 & 0.00 & 0.00 \\
0.00 & 0.00 & 0.00 & 0.00 & 0.00 & 0.00 & 0.00 & 0.00 & 0.00 & 0.00 & 0.18 & 0.00 & 0.00 \\
0.00 & 0.00 & 0.00 & 0.00 & 0.00 & 0.00 & 0.00 & 0.00 & 0.00 & 0.00 & 0.00 & 0.14 & 0.00 \\
0.00 & 0.00 & 0.00 & 0.00 & 0.00 & 0.00 & 0.00 & 0.00 & 0.00 & 0.00 & 0.00 & 0.00 & 0.13
\end{pmatrix}$$

Each column of the rotation matrix V is an eigenvector or principal component and each row corresponds to increasing swap maturities from one year to thirty years. The first principal component (column of matrix V) is a flat upward shift of about 0.3 basis points for every maturity (except for the first two elements which fall below 0.3). The second principal component is a fairly straight line running from +0.4 basis points at the short end to -0.4 basis points at the long end. The third principal component is a twist in the curve with an inflection point at about five years. The first three principal components in V are in bold typeface.

$$V = \begin{pmatrix}
0.16 & 0.42 & -0.65 & -0.53 & 0.22 & -0.06 & 0.02 & -0.17 & 0.02 & 0.00 & 0.01 & -0.01 & 0.02 \\
0.24 & 0.44 & -0.20 & 0.31 & -0.31 & 0.17 & 0.03 & 0.67 & -0.14 & -0.02 & -0.15 & 0.03 & -0.06 \\
0.28 & 0.35 & 0.02 & 0.40 & -0.32 & -0.13 & -0.13 & -0.51 & 0.35 & -0.29 & 0.20 & -0.03 & 0.01 \\
0.29 & 0.24 & 0.17 & 0.22 & 0.18 & 0.03 & 0.02 & -0.34 & -0.51 & 0.61 & -0.04 & 0.01 & 0.03 \\
0.30 & 0.13 & 0.29 & 0.01 & 0.56 & -0.21 & -0.15 & 0.34 & 0.09 & -0.16 & 0.42 & 0.00 & 0.32 \\
0.30 & 0.06 & 0.25 & -0.07 & 0.15 & 0.03 & 0.68 & 0.00 & 0.45 & 0.08 & -0.38 & -0.03 & -0.04 \\
0.30 & -0.02 & 0.20 & -0.12 & 0.19 & -0.10 & -0.43 & -0.02 & -0.12 & -0.29 & -0.44 & -0.16 & -0.55 \\
0.30 & -0.07 & 0.19 & -0.29 & -0.16 & 0.43 & 0.14 & -0.10 & -0.25 & -0.30 & 0.25 & 0.57 & -0.09 \\
0.30 & -0.13 & 0.12 & -0.29 & -0.30 & 0.36 & -0.12 & -0.02 & -0.04 & 0.00 & -0.02 & -0.63 & 0.41 \\
0.29 & -0.18 & 0.03 & -0.25 & -0.32 & -0.24 & -0.26 & 0.17 & 0.36 & 0.54 & 0.21 & 0.18 & -0.24 \\
0.28 & -0.29 & -0.15 & 0.02 & -0.17 & -0.48 & -0.02 & -0.02 & -0.19 & -0.14 & -0.40 & 0.31 & 0.50 \\
0.27 & -0.34 & -0.25 & 0.13 & -0.04 & -0.29 & 0.42 & 0.04 & -0.28 & -0.13 & 0.38 & -0.34 & -0.33 \\
0.27 & -0.41 & -0.43 & 0.38 & 0.33 & 0.46 & -0.18 & -0.04 & 0.25 & 0.08 & -0.06 & 0.10 & 0.02
\end{pmatrix}$$

Figure 3.11 shows the one and two year swap rates shown plotted against each other. The one and two year rates are clearly strongly correlated because they fall close to a straight line. The first principal component lies along the ellipse of data points. This is precisely where we would draw a line by eye that captures the greatest variation in the data. The second principal component lies at right angles (is OR-THOGONAL) to the first, although it is orthogonal in thirteen dimensions, not in the two that we can see. The graph to the right shows the data projected onto the first two principal components. In the rotated coordinate system we can see that the first two principal components are now at right angles and the data has been transformed to lie naturally along the axes of greatest variation.

Because we have chosen axes that capture the variation of our data it is likely that our axes are meaningful. For our swap example the three first three principal components describe how the curve moves. The first eigenvector is a simple up and down shift of the curve across the entire term structure. This captures a huge amount of the daily variation of the swap curve (using the variance from D it captures $\frac{650.31}{707.62}$ or 92% of the total variance). We could describe the yield curve dynamics very well with

USD Swap Rate Principal Component History

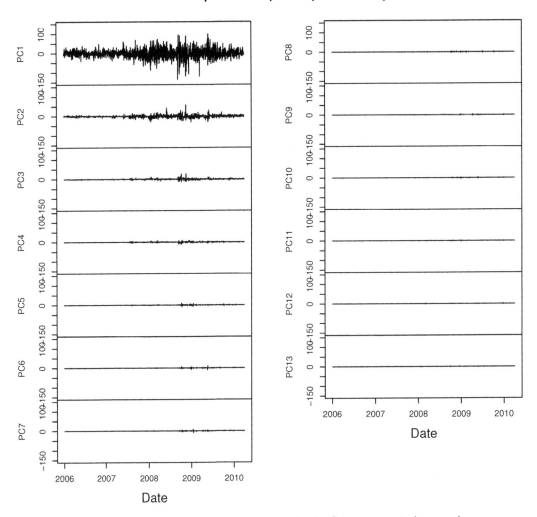

Figure 3.10: USD interest rate swap principal component time series.

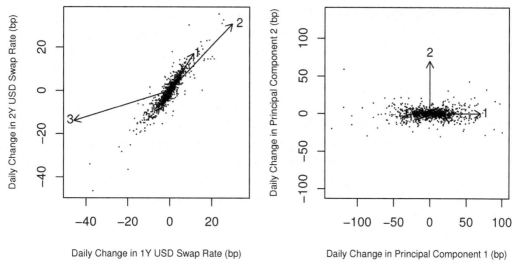

Figure 3.11:
USD one year and two year rate scatterplots showing the first three principal components (left) and data projected onto the first and second principal components (right).

just this single number. If we refine our curve description with the second principal component, the second eigenvector is a steepening or flattening of the yield curve. This refinement captures a further 6% of our variance. The third principal component is harder to describe, except as a kink, or twisting of the curve, but now we are just explaining 1% of the total variance. We could use more principal components but there is only 1% of the total variance left, so this greater complexity would gain very little in terms of explanatory power. We can now describe the term structure in terms of just three numbers rather than 13. If we were to build a risk model that uses the covariance of the swap rates this would be a huge cost saving in terms of storage and computation. The number of elements in the covariance matrix would reduce from $13 \times 13 = 169$ to just $3 \times 3 = 9$.

PCA works well in reducing the number of dimensions to describe swap curves because swap rates are strongly correlated. PCA is not so useful for dimension reduction if all of the factors are independent. This is because the eigenvalues for a set of independent factors would all be roughly equal, so we can not throw away factors without losing a significant amount of variance. It may still be interesting to use PCA in this case because it may produce an interesting new set of factors for describing a set of data, but PCA cannot be used to reduce the size of the data when factors are uncorrelated. There are other, faster methods for teasing apart underlying factors in a large set of data such as INDEPENDENT COMPONENT ANALYSIS (ICA) and these have proved successful in engineering applications such as separating the mixed up voices of individual speakers.

Answers to Exercises

5 *Show that* $E(X - E(X))^2 = E(X^2) - (E(X))^2$.

$$
\begin{aligned}
E(X - E(X))^2 &= E\left[(X - E(X))(X - E(X))\right] \\
&= E\left[X^2 - 2X E(X) + (E(X))^2\right] \\
&= E\left(X^2\right) - 2E\left[X E(X)\right] + E\left[(E(X))^2\right]
\end{aligned}
$$

We can now make use of the fact that $E\left[X E(X)\right] = E\left[X\right] E\left[E(X)\right]$ and that $E\left[E(X)\right] = E(X)$ which, when combined, mean that $E\left[X E(X)\right] = E(X)E(X)$ and so,

$$
E(X - E(X))^2 = E\left(X^2\right) - 2E(X)E(X) + E\left[(E(X))^2\right].
$$

Because $E\left[(E(X))^2\right] = E\left[E(X)E(X)\right] = E\left[E(X)\right]E\left[E(X)\right] = E(X)E(X)$ we can see that

$$
\begin{aligned}
E(X - E(X))^2 &= E\left(X^2\right) - 2E(X)E(X) + E(X)E(X) \\
&= E\left(X^2\right) - E(X)E(X) \\
&= E\left(X^2\right) - E^2(X)
\end{aligned}
$$

6 *Show that* $E\left[\frac{F - E(F)}{\sigma_F} \times \frac{G - E(G)}{\sigma_G}\right] = \frac{E(FG) - E(F)E(G)}{\sigma_F \sigma_G}$.

We start by multiplying the terms then apply the expectation operator to each of the terms,

$$
\begin{aligned}
E\left[\frac{F - E(F)}{\sigma_F} \times \frac{G - E(G)}{\sigma_G}\right] &= \frac{1}{\sigma_F \sigma_G} E\left[(F - E(F)) \times (G - E(G))\right] \\
&= \frac{1}{\sigma_F \sigma_G} E\left[FG - F E(G) - G E(F) + E(F) E(G)\right] \\
&\quad \frac{1}{\sigma_F \sigma_G}\left[E(FG) - E(F E(G)) - E(G E(F)) + E(E(F) E(G))\right]
\end{aligned}
$$

Because we can split up the expectation of the product $E(E(F) \times E(G))$ into the product of expectations $E(E(F)) \times E(E(G))$ and then using $E(E(F)) = E(F)$ (and of course $E(E(G)) = E(G)$) the expression above simplifies into

$$
\begin{aligned}
E\left[\frac{F - E(F)}{\sigma_F} \times \frac{G - E(G)}{\sigma_G}\right] &= \frac{1}{\sigma_F \sigma_G}\left[E(FG) - E(F) E(G) - E(F) E(G) + E(F) E(G)\right] \\
&= \frac{E(FG) - E(F) E(G)}{\sigma_F \sigma_G}
\end{aligned}
$$

7 *Find the correlation and covariance of these two series: (1,2,3,4,5) and (10,19,32,39,51).*
The numbers we need are:

Statistic	Calculation	Value
$E[X]$	$\frac{1+2+3+4+5}{5}$	3
$E[Y]$	$\frac{10+19+32+39+51}{5}$	30.2
$E[X^2]$	$\frac{1^2+2^2+3^2+4^2+5^2}{5}$	11
$E[Y^2]$	$\frac{10^2+19^2+32^2+39^2+51^2}{5}$	1121.4
$E[XY]$	$\frac{1\times10+2\times19+3\times32+4\times39+5\times51}{5}$	111

Now it is a simple matter to calculate the volatilities,

$$
\begin{aligned}
\sigma_X^2 &= E\left(X^2\right) - E(X)E(X) \\
&= 11 - 3^2 \\
&= 2
\end{aligned}
$$

and

$$
\begin{aligned}
\sigma_Y^2 &= E\left(Y^2\right) - E(Y)E(Y) \\
&= 1121.4 - 30.2^2 \\
&= 209.36
\end{aligned}
$$

which means that the volatilities are $\sigma_x = \sqrt{2}$ and $\sigma_Y = \sqrt{209.36}$ which is 14.47. Now the correlation is

$$
\begin{aligned}
\rho_{X,Y} &= \frac{E(XY) - E(X)E(Y)}{\sigma_X \sigma_Y} \\
&= \frac{111 - 3 \times 30.2}{\sqrt{2 \times 209.36}} \\
&= 0.9969,
\end{aligned}
$$

which is almost +1 implying that a plot of X versus Y will fall almost on a straight line. We can find the covariance of X and Y by multiplying the correlation by the volatility of X and the volatility of Y, or we could use $E(XY) - E(X)E(Y)$,

$$
\begin{aligned}
C_{XY} &= E(XY) - E(X)E(Y) \\
&= 111 - 3 \times 30.2 \\
&= 20.4,
\end{aligned}
$$

or using the unbiased estimator we would increase the covariance estimate by a factor $\frac{n}{n-1}$, or 1.2, giving 25.5.

Part III

Fixed Income

4 Interest Rates

4.1 Cash Flows

Finance is all about the flow of cash. The most complex financial instruments can be broken down into CASH FLOWS. Cash flow diagrams are a useful way of understanding who gets paid, when they get paid and what they are paid. Time is represented along the horizontal axis increasing from left to right. The convention is that an upward pointing arrow is money that is received from a counterparty and a downward pointing arrow is money that is paid to a counterparty. Figure 4.1 shows some example cash flows. The solid arrows represent fixed cash flows. Sometimes the value of

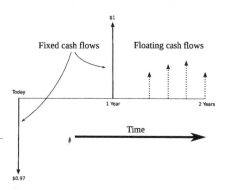

Figure 4.1: A cash flow diagram.

the cash flow is dependent on some interest rate that is not yet known, and this is known as a floating cash flow. Usually these are represented as wiggly arrows instead of solid arrows, but in this book floating cash flows will be represented as an arrow with a dotted stem.

Some cash flows are guaranteed. Others depend on some unknown event occurring or not occurring. Derivatives usually have cash flows that are conditional on the value of some rate or the occurrence of some event making them harder to price. If the cash flow depends on the value of a share it is an equity option which we deal with in Chapter 10. If the cash flow depends on the default or bankruptcy of a company it is a credit derivative which we deal with in Part IV. If the cash flows are known ahead of time then we have a fixed income product such as a bond and it is these instruments that we deal with in detail in this chapter.

4.2 Interest Rate Calculations

Jesus told a parable about a man who went on a trip to a distant land and invested some of his money with three different fund managers, or "servants" as they were known at the time. One was given five talents, another two talents and another one talent. The allocation was based on their fund-managing ability. After the master returned the best fund manager had doubled his investment from five talents to ten talents. The second-best manager had also doubled his investment to four talents. But the third-rate fund manager had opted for the low-risk strategy of burying his money in the ground. The master was not pleased: "And cast ye the unprofitable servant into utter darkness: there shall be weeping and gnashing of teeth". When comparing investments today we are still concerned about the growth of our principal, although usually less harsh in condemning poor performance.

Interest rates tell us how much interest we will receive if we invest over a given period of time. Increasing the term or the rate will increase our interest. Interest rates are always quoted as annual rates. Other than that there are many variations in the way interest rates are used and quoted. If someone quotes an interest rate you should ask the following questions:

- Is the interest rate simple or compound?

- If it is a simple interest rate, is it a discount rate or an add-on rate?

- If compound, what is the compounding period?

- What is the day count convention used in calculating interest?

After reading this section you should be able to understand these concepts and to calculate interest using the combination of all these factors. As the amounts involved are usually very large rates are usually quoted as percentages. People also talk about POINTS and BASIS POINTS abbreviated as "bp" and pronounced as "bip" or "beep". A point is 1%, and a basis point is 0.01%. To introduce the terminology up-front this is a list of the symbols we will use:

Symbol	Description
r	Interest rate, always annualized
t	Time until cash flow is received in years
FV	Future value, the value at a time in future of cash invested today
PV	Present value, the value today of cash received at a time in future
δ	Discount factor, a multiplier used to convert future value to present value
$r_{m \times n}$	Forward rate starting at time m and ending at time n
f	Compound frequency for compound rates
r_{bey}	Bond equivalent yield

4.2.1 Simple Interest

The process of putting a dollar in the bank now and collecting a dollar plus interest a year from now is like stepping through a time portal. Interest rates are always positive, so going into the future increases the amount of money we have. Stepping back through the portal the other way, from the future to the present, reduces the amount of money we have. If we call the amount of money that we have today the PRESENT VALUE (PV) and the amount of money in the future the FUTURE VALUE (FV) then we can describe travelling into the future with this equation

$$FV \quad = \quad PV(1 + rt). \tag{4.1}$$

Another way of thinking about this is that in the future our invested capital, or PRINCIPAL, is returned to us along with some extra cash that is called INTEREST. After a time t we will receive two cash flows: our principal and an interest payment equal to the interest rate r times the time we travel into the future t in years.

$$\text{Future Value} = \text{Present Value} + \text{Interest}$$
$$\text{FV} = \text{PV} + \text{PV} \times r \times t$$

We can rearrange Equation 4.1 to get the equation for travelling back from the future to the present,

$$\text{PV} = \frac{\text{FV}}{1 + rt}. \tag{4.2}$$

Equation 4.1 is probably familiar if you have a bank account, but in finance one normally tries to price the cash flows today that people have promised in the future, so one deals with Equation 4.2. Notice that there is a simple factor relating future and present value. The factor $\frac{1}{1+rt}$ is known as a DISCOUNT FACTOR because the present value is less than the future value. These equations define SIMPLE INTEREST which is the convention for short-term investments of up to one year. The rate r is also called SPOT RATE, or the ADD-ON RATE. Spot rate reflects the fact that this is a rate for today, it is the on-the-spot rate. Add-on rate is used because the interest is added on to the amount we have today. As there is an add-on rate you have probably guessed that there is a take-away rate. This is called a DISCOUNT RATE and is used for Treasury bills (T-bills), which are short-term government bonds issued by the US Treasury. When an investment is quoted as a discount rate, the rate tells you how much you reduce the future value to get the present value

$$\text{PV} = \text{FV}(1 - rt).$$
$$\text{Present Value} = \text{Future Value} - \text{Discount} \tag{4.3}$$

Exercise 8 *We buy a contract that promises to pay \$1 million in one year, \$1 million in two years and \$5 million in three years. If the risk-free interest rate is 6% how much should you pay for the contract today i.e. what is the present value of the three cash flows? Bear in mind that T-bills assume 360 days in a year.*

Exercise 9 *We buy \$100,000 face of a 13 week T-bill and the discount rate is 1%. What is the discount and what is the present value of the T-bill?*

4.2.2 Compound Interest

For longer-term investments, where long term is an investment of over one year, we use COMPOUND INTEREST. Compound simply means that we break down time into periods, and at the end of each period interest is added to the original amount, and that becomes the new invested amount. With compound interest the future and present value relationships become

$$\text{FV} = \text{PV} \left(1 + \frac{r}{f} \right)^{ft}, \tag{4.4}$$

Compounding Frequency	Future Value	Discount Factor
2	1.1941	0.8375
4	1.1956	0.8364
8	1.1964	0.8358
16	1.1968	0.8356
32	1.1970	0.8354
64	1.1971	0.8353
128	1.1972	0.8353
256	1.1972	0.8353

Table 4.1:
Effect of increasing compounding frequency on future value and discount factor $\left(1 + \frac{0.06}{f}\right)^{\pm f \times 3}$.

and

$$PV = \frac{FV}{\left(1 + \frac{r}{f}\right)^{ft}}. \tag{4.5}$$

Notice we have a new term f which is the COMPOUNDING FREQUENCY (number of compounding periods per year) and t is time in years. Another thing to notice is that just like simple interest there is still a simple factor relating future and present value. The discount factor for compound interest is $\frac{1}{(1+\frac{r}{f})^{ft}}$. For example a cash flow of \$3 million in three years at a rate of 6% compounded twice per year would have $f = 2$ compounding periods per year, and $t = 3$ years. The present value would be $\frac{3}{\left(1+\frac{0.06}{2}\right)^{2\times 3}}$ which is \$2.51 million. Increasing the compounding frequency increases $\left(1 + \frac{r}{f}\right)^{ft}$ but only up to a limit. In our example $\left(1 + \frac{0.06}{2}\right)^{2\times 3} = 1.194$, but as we increase f it reaches a limiting value as shown in Table 4.1. The limit as f becomes infinite is called CONTINUOUS COMPOUNDING. In continuous compounding the discount factor becomes much simpler,

$$PV = FVe^{-rt}$$

for the present value and

$$FV = PVe^{rt}$$

for the future value.

It may seem strange to use continuous compounding given that interest is never received at more than a daily rate. The reasons are threefold. Firstly by setting the compounding frequency f to infinity it is effectively being ignored and drops out of all calculations. Secondly the discount factor becomes much neater. The expression e^{-rt} is much more compact than $\frac{1}{(1+\frac{r}{f})^{ft}}$, missing out fractions and clumsy addition of 1 to all rates. Finally, quantitative analysts are usually physicists and mathematicians to whom e^x is an old friend which is easy to integrate and differentiate. Ultimately the choice of compounding is irrelevant as it is easy to convert from one rate convention to another. For example, to convert between the continuous rate and the compound rate simply equate the future value of one dollar compounded for time t using the two types of rate,

$$e^{r_{cont}t} = \left(1 + \frac{r_{comp}}{f}\right)^{ft}.$$

Taking logs of both sides gives

$$r_{cont} = f \ln\left(1 + \frac{r_{comp}}{f}\right)$$

and reversing the equation

$$r_{comp} = f\left(e^{\frac{r_{cont}}{f}} - 1\right).$$

In our example above the continuous discount factor for a rate of 6% and a period of three years would be $e^{0.06 \times 3}$ which is 1.19722. And just to show that rates are easily interchangeable, the compound rate r_{comp} of 6% with two payments per year $f = 2$ is equivalent to a continuously compounded rate of $2\ln\left(1 + \frac{0.06}{2}\right)$ or 5.912%. Check this by finding the future value of a dollar compounded both ways for a year, and you will find that 1.03^2 is equal to $e^{0.05912}$. Converting between rates that have different day count conventions is done in the same way. Equate the value of a dollar invested using the two rates and re-arrange.

$$1 + r_{simple}t_{360} = \left(1 + \frac{r_{comp}}{f}\right)^{ft_{365}}$$

This gives

$$r_{comp} = f\left[(1 + r_{simple}t_{360})^{\frac{1}{ft_{365}}} - 1\right]$$

Exercise 10 *If we have a single cash flow with future value $3 million in six months, find the present value, given that the simple interest rate is 7%.*

Exercise 11 *Re-arrange equation 4.1 to give rate r in terms of PV, FV and time t.*

Exercise 12 *Re-arrange equation 4.1 to express t in terms of PV, FV and rate r.*

Exercise 13 *Assume annual compounding ($n = 1$) and re-arrange Equation 4.4 to find the number of years to double your investment.*

Exercise 14 *Using the answer to the previous question find an approximate linear equation to express t in terms of r.*

4.2.3 Pricing a Stream of Cash Flows

We are now in a position to value any asset that can be broken down into a stream of fixed cash flows. We calculate discount factors for each cash flow date then add up the present value of all the cash flows. For example, say we buy a contract that promises to pay us $1.23 million in six months. If the six month semi-annually compounded interest rate is 4.6% then the present value from equation 4.5 would be $\frac{1.23}{(1+\frac{0.0046}{2})^{2\times0.5}}$ which is \$1.202 million.

A useful equation that crops up frequently is the present value of a stream of equally spaced equally valued future payments. This is called an ANNUITY. If we have n equal payments with future value c and the constant interest rate is r then the present value of all the cash flows is given by

$$\mathrm{PV}_{\mathrm{ann}} = c\frac{1 - \frac{1}{(1+r)^n}}{r},\tag{4.6}$$

and taking the limit as n becomes infinite gives the value of a PERPETUITY which is the present value of an infinite number of payments

$$\mathrm{PV}_{\mathrm{perp}} = \frac{c}{r}.\tag{4.7}$$

If the cash flows are not equally spaced in time with equal values, then we calculate the present value of each cash flow and add them.

Exercise 15 *A retiree turns out to be immortal. They will receive \$50,000 each year for the rest of their life. What is the value of this annuity given the interest rate is 5%?*

Exercise 16 *Another retiree will live for exactly thirty years after retirement. They will receive \$50,000 each year for the rest of their life. What is the value of this annuity given the interest rate is 5%?*

Exercise 17 *Derive the present value of an annuity from the present value of a single cash flow. Hint: write out each term in the series, then take out the common factor of the series and use the standard result for the sum of a geometric series $\sum_{k=0}^{n} af^k = \frac{a(1-f^{n+1})}{1-f}$ where $a = 1$ and $f = \frac{1}{1+r}$.*

4.2.4 Day Count Convention

There are two types of time: absolute time and relative time. A date, such as January 1st 2000, is an absolute time and relative time is the difference between two dates. A trade agreement will usually use specific dates from the Gregorian calendar, such as a start date of May 10th, 2007 and an end date of May 10th, 2008. Absolute time is uncontroversial and the Gregorian calendar is the *de facto* standard for trade agreements. However difficulties arrive when calculating the difference between two dates as a fraction of a year. The reason why we need relative time is for interest calculations such as t in Equations 4.1 and 4.2. To calculate the value of t we divide the number of interest-bearing days between two calendar dates by the number of days in a year. Both these numbers depend on the market in which an asset is traded. If this seems strange to you remember that this is simply a matter of historical convention, and stems from a time before calculations could be performed rapidly on a computer. The convention used for USD transactions is called ACTUAL 360, abbreviated ACT/360 or A/360. This means that t is the actual number of calendar days divided by an imaginary 360 day year. If the security issuer is domiciled in one of the Commonwealth countries, such as the United Kingdom, Canada, Australia or New Zealand then it will usually abide by an ACTUAL 365 (A/365) convention, which is the number of calendar days divided by a slightly less imaginary year of 365 days. The third convention that is widely used is 30/360 which assumes there are 30 interest-bearing days in a month and 360 days in a year. See Appendix A.1 for more detail on day count convention.

4.3 A Trinity of Yield Curves: Zero, Forward and Par

Each type of short-term instrument in the money market has its own rate. For example, there are many securities that look like Figure 4.2. If the term of the loan or deposit is one year or less the instrument is part of the MONEY MARKET. We will focus here on three types of rate that form the bedrock on which one can build yield curves. These are the zero rate for borrowing today at a fixed rate, the forward rate for borrowing in the future at a fixed rate and par rate which is quoted for swaps and par bonds. Each money market instrument seems to be different in the way that it is quoted and priced, but as we will see the rates for each security are related in a rather elegant way.

4.3.1 Zero Rate

The two cash flows in Figure 4.2 represent a very simple deal. You lend someone $98.79, wait for 91 days, then receive $100 on the MATURITY DATE. The amount you receive, the FACE VALUE, is more than the amount you gave, the difference being the interest of $1.21. This is a simple instrument with a complicated name, it is a ZERO COUPON BOND. These are issued by companies and by governments to raise cash. The US Treasury calls the instrument in Figure 4.2 a TREASURY BILL or T-BILL. The US Treasury makes the largest market in zero coupon bonds, but

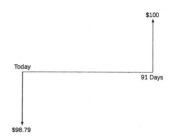

Figure 4.2: T-Bill cash flows.

other countries, such as the UK, also issue T-bills. If a company issues a short-term zero coupon bond it is called COMMERCIAL PAPER often abbreviated CP. Commercial paper has a maturity between 2 and 270 days, comes with a credit rating and is only issued by companies with the highest credit worthiness.

One of the beautiful aspects of zero coupon bonds is that one can simply read off discount factors from their price. In the example above the 91-day discount factor is 0.9879. To get the discount factor we simply divide the present value of $98.79 by the face value of $100. One oddity of zero coupon bonds is that they are usually quoted as a discount rate, so you invest an amount worth less than the face value at issue, then receive your principal plus interest at maturity which gives you the face value of the bond.

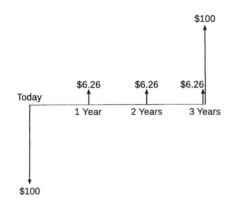

Figure 4.4: Three year par bond.

Zero coupon bonds define a zero coupon rate, or ZERO RATE. This is the rate that would be quoted for a zero coupon bond of some maturity. Zero rates do not have to be based on zero coupon bonds which is just as well because T-bills come with a very limited set of maturities up to one year. Forward and par rates can be converted to a zero rate, but zero rates are often used as a standard for building yield curves because they are easily converted into discount factors, as we will see in Section 4.4.

4.3.2 Forward Rate

Figure 4.3:
Forward rate agreement.

The rates we have come across so far assume we are borrowing money today. Sometimes it is useful to arrange borrowing in the future by fixing the rate today. Fixing the rate ahead of time avoids any uncertainty about the rate that will be paid. Say that Sprocket Corporation knows that it will need to deposit $10 million three months in the future for a period of six months. The treasurer of Sprocket dislikes uncertainty. Who knows what interest rates will be like in three months? He wants to fix the rate now for a loan in the future. He approaches an investment bank which agrees a rate of 5.5% today for a six month deposit of $10 million starting in three months time as illustrated in Figure 4.3. The two cash flows look exactly like a six month zero coupon bond except that both have been shifted three months into the future. The bank has set a FORWARD RATE which has been bought by Sprocket Corporation. See Section 4.5.3 on page 150 for details about forward rate agreements.

4.3.3 Par Bond Coupon and Par Swap Rate

The PAR RATE or PAR COUPON has two manifestations: the BOND par rate and the INTEREST RATE SWAP par rate. We will discuss bonds and swaps in more detail later on. For now we will look at a simplified bond and use it to illustrate the concept of a par coupon. Say we buy a zero coupon bond that will pay $100 in three years. Because zero coupon bonds trade at a discount the value today, given a three year zero rate of 6.3%, will be $\frac{100}{(1+0.063)^3}$ which is $83.25. We like round numbers, so we ask the issuer to pay us a fixed payment of c at the end of each year. At the end of year one, two and three the issuer will give us c. Assuming that zero rates for one and two years are 5.5% and 5.7% what value of c will top up the present value to $100? The present value of the zero coupon bond and the annuity must add up to 100, so

ZRY1: 5.5%

ZRY2: 5.7%

ZRY3: 6.3%

$$\underbrace{\frac{c}{(1+0.055)} + \frac{c}{(1+0.057)^2} + \frac{c}{(1+0.063)^3}}_{\text{annuity}} + \underbrace{\frac{100}{(1+0.063)^3}}_{\text{zero coupon bond}} = \underbrace{100}_{\text{par today}} \qquad (4.8)$$

The fourth term $\frac{100}{(1+0.063)^3}$ is the present value of the principal of $100 paid in three years, and the first three terms are the annuity. Solving for c (see example) gives an annual payment of $6.26. If we receive an annuity with a rate of 6.26% then given today's zero rates the present value of all our cash flows is $100. The special annuity rate that tops up the zero coupon bond present value to 100 is known more succinctly PAR RATE
as the PAR RATE. The word par, which means "equal", reflects the fact that this rate equates the FV of $100 (for the principal payment in three years) and PV of $100 (for the $100 in three years and the annuity).

The cash flows for this combined instrument are shown in Figure 4.4. We have constructed a three year par bond. The bond has a par coupon of 6.26%, which is the coupon required to make its present value exactly $100. This also shows that a bond can be decomposed into an annuity and a zero coupon bond. As we shall see in chapter 5 the par rate for bonds is equal to the par swap rate.

Exercise 18 *You own a fixed coupon bond. Interest rates increase. What effect will this have on the value of your bond?*

Exercise 19 *Solve Equation 4.8 for the par coupon c.*

4.4 Interest Rate Arbitrage

Although money market instruments seem to be very different, they are entangled by arbitrage. This is because it is possible to reconstruct one money market instrument from others. The universal building block security which can be used to synthesize any asset with fixed cash flows is a zero coupon bond. Assuming we have a zero coupon bond that exactly matches the maturity of each cash flow we can simply read the discount factor straight from the present value of the matching bond.

Figure 4.5 shows how three forwards reconstruct the cash flows of a three year par bond. This immediately sets up a possible arbitrage. If you notice that it is cheaper to buy the bond than the three forwards you can make an instant, risk-free profit by buying the bond and selling three forwards. If the forwards were cheaper than the bond you would reverse the trade. Because there are an army of eagle-eyed traders

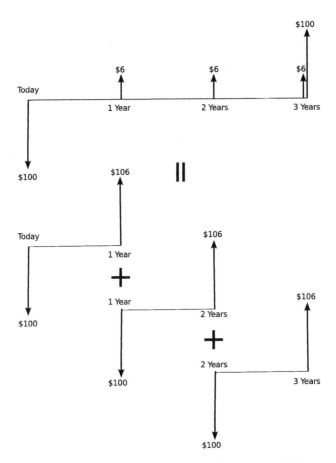

Figure 4.5: Synthesizing a bond from three FRAs.

exploiting each arb the price of the three forwards will be very similar to the price of the three year bond.

Arbitrage arguments allow us to relate the three rates: zero rate, forward rate and par rate. Given any one of the three we can infer the other two. The relationships generate several equations, perhaps too many equations. The simple thing to remember is the arbitrage trades that generate the equations, as these will allow you to derive the relationships for yourself and generally understand what is going on. Take the following zero rates:

Term	1 Year	2 Years	3 Years	4 Years	5 Years
Zero Rate	4.1%	4.5%	4.8%	5.0%	5.1%

These zero rates determine the forward rates. Why? Because there is an arbitrage trade that relates them. For example the three year zero rate is 4.8%. This means you can invest a dollar today and receive $(1 + 0.048)^3$ or $1.15 in three years. Alternatively you could invest a dollar today and buy a daisy-chain of three end-to-end forwards, the 0×1 the 1×2 and the 2×3 (see Section 4.5.3 on page 150 for an explanation of the forward rate $m \times n$ naming convention). The first forward is actually not a forward at all because a 0×1 forward is actually a one year zero coupon bond (try drawing the cash flow diagram if this is not obvious). So at the end of year one your dollar becomes $1 + r_1$. The second instrument increases your investment by a guaranteed rate of $r_{1 \times 2}$ to give you $(1 + r_{0 \times 1})(1 + r_{1 \times 2})$. The 2×3 forward increases your investment at the end of year three to $(1 + r_{0 \times 1})(1 + r_{1 \times 2})(1 + r_{2 \times 3})$. The cash flows for the daisy-chained forwards trade would be exactly the same as those of the three year zero coupon bond, so the interest earned must also be the same. If this were not the case arbitrageurs would leap on the opportunity and batter the rates into alignment.

We can now calculate the forward rates. The 0×1 forward rate is the same as the one year zero rate, which is 4.1%. The 1×2 rate is how much we would make if we deposited an amount in one year for a period of a year. This must give the same interest as the two forwards: 0×1 and 1×2. After the first forward expires we re-invest the amount into the second forward. So

$$(1 + r_{0 \times 1})(1 + r_{1 \times 2}) = (1 + r_2)^2.$$

We know $r_{0 \times 1} = 4.1\%$ and we are given the zero rate $r_2 = 4.5\%$ so we know that $r_{1 \times 2} = \frac{(1+r_2)^2}{1+r_{0 \times 1}} - 1$ which is 4.9015%. To find the 2×3 forward rate we construct the arbitrage again. This time we equate the value of a dollar invested successively in three forwards, the 0×1, 1×2 and 2×3 with the value of a dollar invested today at the three year zero rate.

$$(1 + r_{0 \times 1})(1 + r_{1 \times 2})(1 + r_{2 \times 3}) = (1 + r_3)^3,$$

which gives us

$$r_{2 \times 3} = \frac{(1 + r_3)^3}{(1 + r_{0 \times 1})(1 + r_{1 \times 2})}.$$

Putting in the values gives 5.4026%. Calculating the rest of the forwards in this way produces

Term	1 Year	2 Years	3 Years	4 Years	5 Years
Zero Rate	4.1%	4.5%	4.8%	5.0%	5.1%
Forward Rate	4.1%	4.9015%	5.4026%	5.6023%	5.5010%

Finally we can calculate the par rate from either the zero rates or the forward rates. Again we have to consider the arbitrage relationship that would reproduce the cash flows of a par bond using zero coupon bonds. The first par rate is the one year rate. As interest is paid annually we would receive one coupon c_1 at the end of the year and would also receive our principal of $1,

$$\begin{aligned} \text{Present Value} &= \text{PV(coupon)} + \text{PV(Principal)} \\ 1 &= \frac{c_1}{1+r_1} + \frac{1}{1+r_1} \end{aligned}.$$

Re-arranging shows that $c_1 = r_1$, the one year par rate is the same as the one year zero rate, which is 4.1%. We can simplify the equations by introducing the following notation for discount factors. The one year discount factor $\delta_1 = \frac{1}{1+r_1}$, the two year discount factor $\delta_2 = \frac{1}{(1+r_2)^2}$, the three year discount factor $\delta_3 = \frac{1}{(1+r_3)^3}$ and the ith year is $\delta_i = \frac{1}{(1+r_i)^i}$. The discount factors calculated from the zero rates are as follows:

Term	1 Year	2 Years	3 Years	4 Years	5 Years
Zero Rate	4.1%	4.5%	4.8%	5.0%	5.1%
Discount Factor	0.9606	0.9157	0.8688	0.8227	0.7798

The definition of the two year par rate is that we pay 1 today to receive a coupon payment of c_2 in one year and the combination of our principal of 1 and coupon c_2 in two years. As an equation we have

$$1 = c_2\delta_1 + c_2\delta_2 + \delta_2,$$

so

$$c_2 = \frac{1-\delta_2}{\delta_1 + \delta_2}.$$

For the third par rate we equate 1 and the present value of three coupon payments and the principal repayment

$$\begin{aligned} 1 &= c_3\delta_1 + c_3\delta_2 + c_3\delta_3 + \delta_3 \\ c_3 &= \frac{1-\delta_3}{\delta_1 + \delta_2 + \delta_3}. \end{aligned}$$

Generally we have

$$c_i = \frac{1-\delta_i}{\Sigma_{t=1}^i \delta_t}.$$

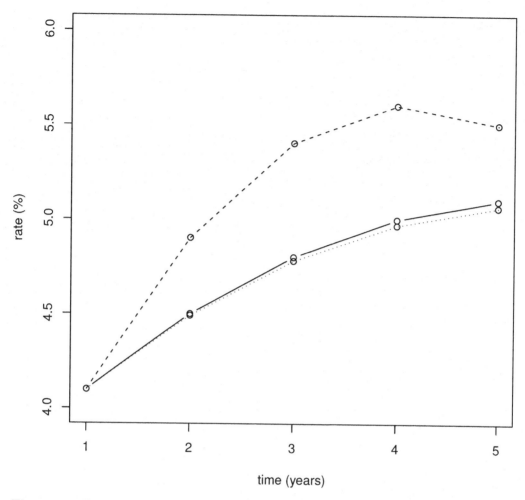

Figure 4.6: Zero rate is the solid line, forward rate is dashed and par rate is dotted.

So the par coupon c_i is the ratio of $1 - \delta_i$ and the cumulative discount factor $\sum_{t=1}^{i} \delta_t$. Filling in our table using these formulae gives

Term	1 Year	2 Years	3 Years	4 Years	5 Years
Zero Rate	4.1%	4.5%	4.8%	5.0%	5.1%
Discount Factor	0.9606	0.9157	0.8688	0.8227	0.7798
Cumulative Discount Factor	0.9606	1.8763	2.7451	3.5678	4.3476
Forward Rate	4.1%	4.9015%	5.4026%	5.6023%	5.5010%
Par Rate	4.1%	4.4912%	4.7796%	4.9693%	5.0647%

All three rates are shown in Figure 4.6. The zero curve is upward sloping, and this is considered to be a typical yield environment. In this environment the par rate is

From	To	Relationship
Discount Factor	Cumulative D.F.	$\Delta_i = \delta_1 + \delta_2 + \delta_3 \ldots + \delta_i = \sum_{t=1}^{i} \delta_t$
Zero Rate	Forward Rate	$r_{i\times 1} = \frac{(1+r_{i+1})^{i+1}}{(1+r_i)^i}$
Zero Rate	Discount Factor	$\delta_i = \frac{1}{(1+r_i)^i}$
Forward Rate	Discount Factor	$\delta_i = \frac{1}{1+r_1}\frac{1}{1+r_{1\times 1}}\frac{1}{1+r_{2\times 1}}\cdots\frac{1}{1+r_{i-1\times 1}} = \frac{\delta_{i-1}}{1+r_{i-1\times 1}}$
Par Rate	Discount Factor	$\delta_i = \frac{1-\Delta_{i-1}c_i}{1+c_i}$
Discount Factor	Zero Rate	$r_i = \sqrt[i]{\frac{1}{\delta_i}} - 1$
Discount Factor	Forward Rate	$r_{i\times 1} = \frac{\delta_{i-1}}{\delta_i} - 1 = \frac{\delta_{i-1}}{1+r_{i-1\times 1}}$
Discount Factor	Par Rate	$c_i = \frac{1-\delta_i}{\Delta_i}$
Forward Rate	Zero	$r_i = \sqrt[i]{(1+r_1)(1+r_{1\times 1})(1+r_{2\times 1})\ldots(1+r_{i-1\times 1})} - 1$

Table 4.2: Rate conversion table for annual compounding.

slightly lower than the zero rate. The forward rate is much higher than the other two rates. The zero rate is the geometric average of the forward rates. A geometric average of n numbers is the nth root of their product. The three year zero rate is

$$[(1+r_1)(1+r_2)(1+r_3)]^{\frac{1}{3}} - 1.$$

And the four year zero rate is

$$[(1+r_1)(1+r_2)(1+r_3)(1+r_4)]^{\frac{1}{4}} - 1$$

which is

$$[(1+0.041)(1+0.049015)(1+0.054026)(1+0.056023)]^{\frac{1}{4}} - 1.$$

This is equal to the zero rate of 0.05. The geometric average has the property that it lies between the smallest value and the highest value averaged, so we know that the zero rate has to lie between the smallest and largest forward rate. Consequently when the zero curve is downward sloping the forward curve lies below it.

Exercise 20 *Given the following zero rates, find the forward rates and the par rates: 1 year 5.5%, 2 years 5.4%, 3 years 5.2%, 4 years 4.9%, 5 years 4.5%.*

4.4.1 Rate Conversion

To convert from one rate to another we can apply our arbitrage principle. We equate the future value of one unit of currency using any pair of conventions. This is because we must end up with the same amount of money whatever compounding convention we use. Then we simply re-arrange to get one rate in terms of the other. Conversion formulae are easily derived from the following three relationships:

	Simple	Compound	Continuous
Simple		$r_s = \dfrac{\left(1+\frac{r_p}{f}\right)^{ft_p}-1}{t_s}$	$r_s = \dfrac{e^{r_ct_c}-1}{t_s}$
Compound	$r_p = \left[\sqrt[ft]{1+r_st_s}-1\right]f$		$r_p = \dfrac{e^{\frac{r_ct_c}{ft_p}}-1}{f}$
Continuous	$r_c = \dfrac{\ln(1+r_st_s)}{t_c}$	$r_c = f\dfrac{t_p}{t_c}\ln\left(1+\dfrac{r_p}{f}\right)$	

Table 4.3: Rate compounding conversion table.

Simple and continuous	$1 + r_st_s = e^{r_ct_c}$
Compound and continuous	$\left(1+\frac{r_p}{f}\right)^{ft_p} = e^{r_ct_c}$
Simple and compound	$1 + r_st_s = \left(1+\frac{r_p}{f}\right)^{ft_p}$

Rearranging these equations, as shown in the exercises, leads to the set of conversion equations in Table 4.3. Notice that time in the equations has a subscript. This is because the day count convention may differ as well as the type of rate. For example a simple rate may be 30/360 whereas a compound rate may be A/365, so even though the rate is quoted for the same two dates the time in years may be different.

Exercise 21 *Rearrange the relationship between simple and continuous future value to get an equation for simple rate in terms of continuous rate and vice versa.*

Exercise 22 *Rearrange the relationship between compound and continuous future value to get an equation for compound rate in terms of continuous rate and vice versa.*

Exercise 23 *Rearrange the relationship between simple and compound future value to get an equation for simple rate in terms of compound rate and vice versa.*

4.5 Money Market Instruments

In the world of fixed income the instruments that carry the least interest rate risk are the ones that have the shortest duration. If you have bought a bond and are receiving a fixed coupon of 5% then if rates go up to, say, 7% then your 5% looks less attractive as you will be losing out by 2% every year for five years. If you have a ten year bond then you suffer that 2% loss for a longer period of time than you would with a five year bond. If rates drop below 5% then you have locked in a high rate relative to the market. The ten year bond locks in that advantage for longer than the five year bond. So the ten year bond gains more when rates drop and loses more when rates increase compared to the five year bond. The ten year bond is more sensitive to interest rates than the five year bond because it has greater duration. Money market instruments have maturities of up to one year and so are characterized by having a small duration.

The money market is an appropriate investment for capital that has to be stored somewhere that carries almost no risk and gives little return. The alternatives are

Enter all fields and hit \<GO\>.

TRADE: 5/16/07   **LIBOR RATES**   SETTLEMENT: 5/23/07

DOLLAR   (A/R5.36)   STERLING (A/R5.7481)   D-MARK   (A/R4.0684)

	LIBID	LIBOR	LIMEAN	LIBID	LIBOR	LIMEAN	LIBID	LIBOR	LIMEAN
1 MONTH	5.195	5.32	5.2575	5.5256	5.6506	5.5881	3.7699	3.8949	3.8324
2 MONTH	5.215	5.34	5.2775	5.5556	5.6806	5.6181	3.8883	4.0133	3.9508
3 MONTH	5.235	5.36	5.2975	5.6231	5.7481	5.6856	3.9434	4.0684	4.0059
4 MONTH	5.235	5.36	5.2975	5.66	5.785	5.7225	3.9805	4.1055	4.043
5 MONTH	5.235	5.36	5.2975	5.69	5.815	5.7525	4.025	4.15	4.0875
6 MONTH	5.235	5.36	5.2975	5.73	5.855	5.7925	4.065	4.19	4.1275
9 MONTH	5.215	5.34	5.2775	5.815	5.94	5.8775	4.1703	4.2953	4.2328
12 MONTH	5.185	5.31	5.2475	5.8738	5.9988	5.9363	4.2423	4.3673	4.3048

YEN   (A/R0.6663   SWISS FR. (A/R2.41)   EURO   (A/R4.0684)

	LIBID	LIBOR	LIMEAN	LIBID	LIBOR	LIMEAN	LIBID	LIBOR	LIMEAN
1 MONTH	0.5025	0.6275	0.565	2.1358	2.2608	2.1983	3.7699	3.8949	3.8324
2 MONTH	0.5225	0.6475	0.585	2.235	2.36	2.2975	3.8883	4.0133	3.9508
3 MONTH	0.5413	0.6663	0.6038	2.285	2.41	2.3475	3.9434	4.0684	4.0059
4 MONTH	0.5694	0.6944	0.6319	2.3217	2.4467	2.3842	3.9805	4.1055	4.043
5 MONTH	0.5975	0.7225	0.66	2.365	2.49	2.4275	4.025	4.15	4.0875
6 MONTH	0.6231	0.7481	0.6856	2.415	2.54	2.4775	4.065	4.19	4.1275
9 MONTH	0.6838	0.8088	0.7463	2.525	2.65	2.5875	4.1703	4.2953	4.2328
12 MONTH	0.7338	0.8588	0.7963	2.615	2.74	2.6775	4.2423	4.3673	4.3048

For complete information on current LIBOR fixings see BBAM \<GO\>

Australia 61 2 9777 8600   Brazil 5511 3048 4500   Europe 44 20 7330 7500   Germany 49 69 920410
Hong Kong 852 2977 6000 Japan 81 3 3201 8900 Singapore 65 6212 1000 U.S. 1 212 318 2000 Copyright 2007 Bloomberg L.P.
G405-1070-0 16-May-2007 17:35:11

Figure 4.7: Source: Bloomberg.

to buy one of the following money market instruments directly or to gain exposure indirectly by buying into a money market fund. The money market fund manager has few assets from which to choose and generally money market funds charge very small fees, usually less than 50 basis points. One of the other advantages of being invested in short-term highly liquid instruments is that investors can withdraw their money quickly rather like a savings account at a bank because the fund can quickly sell their assets to redeem the investor's cash. The return you receive in a money market fund is usually a little more than a deposit account at a bank.

4.5.1 LIBOR Rate

Floating rates are usually quoted as offsets from the LIBOR curve. LIBOR stands for LONDON INTERBANK OFFERED RATE. Investment banks actively lend one another money in what is called the interbank market. In the 1980s banks wanted to ensure that the loans they made to corporate clients, known as syndicated debt, never exceeded the rate at which the banks were themselves funded. What was required was a publicly available and frequently updated average rate for the interbank market. Then the loans could be quoted at a "spread" to the average funding rate for banks. So a very well funded and large corporation might be able to get loans at LIBOR plus a spread of half a percent. And a very risky loan might trade at LIBOR plus 5%. LI-BOR is a rate for unsecured short-term lending meaning that it is not collateralized and therefore carries the risk that the other bank will not be able or willing to re-pay their debt. LIBOR therefore reflects the perceived credit risk amongst banks and trades above, sometimes well above, risk-free government rates. Another measure of this perceived credit risk is LIBOR-OIS spread which is described in detail in Section 6.4 on page 259.

Each morning by 11 a.m. London time, the British Bankers Association (BBA) polls a set of 16 investment banks to find the rate at which they are willing to lend in size in USD to other prime banks in the London interbank market (see Figure 4.8). The top and bottom 4 rates are discarded and an averate rate calculated from the remaining 8 rates. The number produced is called the LIBOR FIXING and "the fix" is published on the BBA web site and through other sources such as Bloomberg. Two other less frequently used numbers provided by the BBA are LIBID, the London Interbank Bid Rate, and LIMEAN which is the average of LIBOR and LIBID. LIBOR fixings are published for ten currencies.

Currency Name	Currency code	Currency Name	Currency code
Pound Sterling	GBP	Australian Dollar	AUD
US Dollar	USD	Euro	EUR
Japanese Yen	JPY	Danish Kroner	DKK
Swiss Franc	CHF	Swedish Krona	SEK
Canadian Dollar	CAD	New Zealand Dollar	NZD

The LIBOR rates page on Bloomberg (code LR) showing rates sourced from the British Bankers Association is shown in Figure 4.7, but for those without Bloomberg access all LIBOR rates and their full histories are available for download from the BBA web site free of charge[1]. The size of panels for different currencies varies. For example GBP, EUR, and JPY LIBOR rates all have panels of sixteen banks, whereas other currencies have smaller panels. The LIBOR panels for Australian dollar (AUD), New Zealand Dollar (NZD), Danish Krone (DKK) and Swedish Krona (SEK) LIBOR have just eight banks each. Contributor Panel Banks are chosen by the BBA's FX and Money Markets Advisory Panel on the basis of "reputation, scale of activity in the London market and perceived expertise in the currency concerned, and giving due consideration to credit standing". Contributors change over time, so when HBOS was taken over by Lloyds Banking Group it was replaced by other banks in all of the panels in which it took part e.g. Société Générale replaced HBOS on the USD contributor panel on February 9th, 2009.

If a bank wants to borrow at the LIBOR rate it would structure the deal as a short term loan. For example, if a bank wants to borrow $10 million for one month it would phone round the trading desks of other banks who would quote a one month offered

---

[1]British Bankers Association http://www.bba.org.uk

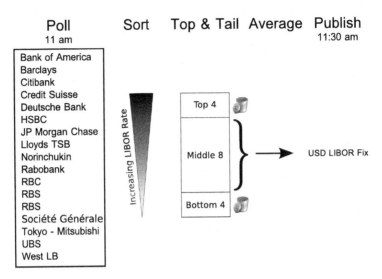

Figure 4.8: LIBOR panel for USD as of February 2009.

rate that would be scattered around the value of LIBOR on that day. From Figure 4.7 the offered rates would be around 5.32% for May 16th 2007. The trade would be agreed on May 16th, and settled on May 23rd when the $10 million would be transferred from one bank to another. After three months it would pay back the original $10 million with interest $10 \times 0.0532 \times \frac{30}{360}$ or $44,333.33.

LIBOR is not the only offered rate for unsecured lending. There are equivalents on other exchanges throughout the world. For example EURIBOR is the equivalent for lending in euro. Sometimes people refer to IBOR without any prefix, meaning a generic unsecured interbank offered rate. Table 4.4 provides a non-exhaustive list of some of the other flavours of IBOR.

4.5.2 T-Bills

The United States Government borrows cash to fund its activities. It does so by selling bonds, and its short term bonds are called Treasury bills, abbreviated to T-bills. To see how easy it is to buy a T-bill have a look at the United States Treasury Direct site[2]. T-bills are the safest possible investment because they are backed by the largest and strongest economy in the world. As you would expect for a low risk security T-bills have a very low return. US Treasury bills are issued with terms of 28 days, 91 days and 182 days. One of the T-bills listed on the Treasury Direct site is a 91-day bill that was issued on May 10th 2007 with a maturity date of August 9th 2007. The Treasury web site says that the discount rate is 4.760%, the investment rate is 4.898% and the price on May 11th was 98.796778. The discount rate is the percentage reduction that is paid now, as a present value, for a future value of $100 in 91 days time. In other

---

[2]United States Treasury Direct http://www.treasurydirect.gov

Interbank Offered Rate	City	Country	Currency	Interbank Offered Rate	City	Country	Currency
AIDIBOR	United Arab Emirates	Abu Dhabi	AED	MEXIBOR	Mexico	Mexibor	MXN
RIGIBOR / RIGIBID	Latvia	Riga	LVL	MIBOR / MIBID	Mumbai	India	INR
BAIBOR	Buenos Aires	Argentina	ARS	MOSIBOR	Moscow	kk Russia	RUB
BKIBOR	Bangkok	Thailand	THB	OIBOR / NIBOR	Oslo	Norway	NOK
BRAZIBOR	Sao Paulo	Brazil	BRL	PRIBOR	Prague	Czech Republic	CZK
BRIBOR / BRIBID	Bratislava	Slovakia	SKK	REIBOR / REIBID	Reykjavik	Iceland	ISK
BUBOR	Budapest	Hungary	HUF	PHIBOR	Manila	Philippines	PHP
CHILIBOR	Santiago	Chile	CLP	SABOR	Johannesburg	South Africa	ZAR
CHIBOR	Beijing	China	CNY	SHIBOR	Shanghai	China	CNY
CIBOR	Copenhagen	Denmark	DKK	SIBOR	Singapore		SGD
COLIBOR	Bogota	Columbia	COP	SOFIBOR	Sofia	Bulgaria	BGN
EURIBOR	Europe		EUR	STIBOR	Stockholm	Sweden	SEK
HIBOR	Hong Kong		HKD	TAIBOR	Taipei	Taiwan	TWD
JIBAR	Johannesburg	South Africa	ZAR	TELBOR	Tel Aviv	Israel	ILS
JIBOR	Jakarta	Indonesia	IDR	TIBOR	Tokyo	Japan	JPY
KAIBOR	Astana	Kazakhstan	KZT	TRLIBOR	Tr	Turkey	TRL
KIBOR	Karachi	Pakistan	PKR	TURKIBOR	Istanbul	Turkey	TRL
KLIBOR	Kuala Lumpur	Malaysia	MYR	VNIBOR	Hanoi	VietNam	VND
KORIBOR	Seoul	South Korea	KRW	WIBOR	Warsaw	Poland	PLN

Table 4.4: Global interbank offered rates.

words the discount, using an A/360 discounting convention, is $100 \times 0.0476 \times \frac{91}{360} = 1.203$, and the original amount of \$100 minus the discount of \$1.20 gives the present value of $100 - 100 \times 0.0476 \times \frac{91}{360} = 98.7968$. As investors we are probably interested in how much return we will make if we lend money in this way. Our return over the 91 day period would be $\frac{1.2032}{98.796778}$ or 1.22%, and annualising using A/365 would give $\frac{365}{91} \frac{1.2032}{98.796778}$ or 4.88%.

There are two implicit conventions in the calculations above. Firstly, if you are looking at the US Treasury Direct web site it will use A/360. Secondly, when comparing returns on bonds you use the A/365 convention. Discounting convention is not mentioned on the web page listing recent US Treasury issues. That is probably because US government bonds are the biggest debt market in the world usually valued at about one trillion dollars (\$1,000,000,000,000) in outstanding issues.

Some government borrowing rates are considered to be "risk-free" because these governments can print their own money to meet their domestic obligations. Government borrowing in these countries defines the RISK-FREE RATE. Note that this only applies to domestic lending. If Argentina were to issue a dollar-denominated bond they could not print US dollars to meet their payments. When the US Treasury issues a T-bill they are not just borrowing money for the government they are also defining another rate called the ZERO RATE. Zero rates are easily converted to discount factors that in turn are used to calculate the present value of cash flows for any asset.

4.5.3 Forward Rate Agreements

A forward rate agreement is a way of arranging a fixed rate of borrowing for a fixed amount of principal and a fixed term in the future. Forward rate agreements or FRAs (FRA is pronounced to rhyme with "spa") are OTC instruments tailor-made by the seller for the buyer. For example, Sprocket Corporation knows that it will receive \$10 million two months in the future which it will deposit for a period of three months. The rate of interest for this forward deposit is unknown today and the treasurer of Sprocket Corporation is concerned that rates will decrease. So she decides to lock in a forward rate today for her two month forward three month deposit. This would be called a 2×5 FORWARD RATE AGREEMENT. The "2×5" is read "two by five" and means that the deposit starts in two months, ends in five months and is therefore for a three month deposit. A 3×9 would be a three month forward six month deposit. The first number is the number of months in the future on which the trade settles, which when added to today's date gives the SETTLEMENT DATE or FORWARD EXPIRY DATE, and the second number is the number of months in the future when the future LIBOR loan or deposit ends:

$$\text{Settlement} \quad \times \quad \text{LIBOR Maturity}$$
$$2 \qquad \times \qquad 5$$

When Sprocket's 2×5 FRA is settled no money changes hands. In two months time no deposit is actually made, instead the deal is cash settled using the value of the observed 3 month LIBOR rate observed in two months time. The counterparties exchange the difference on the contract, so that if the agreed fixed rate was 6% and the 3 month LIBOR rate turned out to actually be 5.5% in two months time

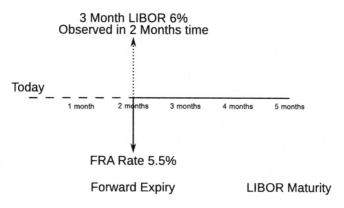

3 Month LIBOR 6%
Observed in 2 Months time

Today

1 month   2 months   3 months   4 months   5 months

FRA Rate 5.5%

Forward Expiry   LIBOR Maturity

Figure 4.9: 2×5 FRA cash flows.

then the payment would be $\$10,000,000 \times (0.055 - 0.06) \times \frac{1}{4}$ which is $12,500 paid to Sprocket Corporation. And because the payment would have been made at maturity it is discounted back from the maturity date to the expiry date $\frac{10,000,000 \times (0.055 - 0.06) \times \frac{1}{4}}{1 + 0.055 \times \frac{1}{4}}$ or $12,330.46. In this case the treasurer made a shrewd decision because the three month rate did decrease to 5.5% and she effectively locked in a rate of 6%. The cash flows are illustrated in Figure 4.9.

Because FRAs are over-the-counter they can carry significant COUNTERPARTY RISK. Say that rates had dropped massively in the next three months. Sprocket corporation stood to lose a very large sum of money which they did not have to settle until expiry of the FRA. Until the payment was made their counterparty was taking a significant risk that their money would not be repaid. Contrast this with interest rate futures where everyone trades with an exchange and all accounts are marked to market at the end of each day. Futures are designed to carry almost no counterparty risk. But there are circumstances in which only an FRA would do. This would be the case if the date on which a deposit was to be made did not fall on an IR future expiry date, or the period of lending did not match an IR future.

The forward rate can be determined from the yield curve. To make our previous example a little bit more realistic say the trade date is October 21st, 2009. Our yield curve tells us that the discount 2 month and 5 month discount factors on the trade date are 0.999571 and 0.997970 respectively. The settlement date (and the effective date) of the FRA would be in two months time on December 21, 2009. The value of three month LIBOR would be observed on the reset date of December 17th 2009 because USD LIBOR deposits settle T+2. The forward rate would be $\left(\frac{0.999571}{0.997970} - 1\right) \frac{360}{91}$ or 0.635%. Say the value of 3 month LIBOR observed on the reset date on December 17th is 0.3%. At maturity this would have resulted in a cash flow of $10,000,000 \times (0.00635 - 0.003) \times \frac{91}{360}$ or $8,468.06. To find the value on the settlement date we discount for three months at the observed LIBOR rate of 0.3% $\frac{8468.06}{1 + 0.003 \times \frac{91}{360}}$, a value of $8,461.64. The cash flows would look as follows:

151

Trade Date	October 21, 2009	↑		0
		61 days		
Settlement Date	December 21, 2009	↓	↑	$8,461.64
			91 days	
LIBOR Maturity	March 21, 2010		↓	0

Exercise 24 *If you buy a forward rate agreement are you agreeing to borrow or lend forward? Will you make or lose money if LIBOR increases?*

Exercise 25 *What would have happened to Sprocket's 2×5 FRA fixed at 6% if the 3 month LIBOR rate had instead increased to 6.5%?*

4.5.4 Interest Rate Futures

We saw in Section 4.3.2 that some rates are forward rates, which means that they are an agreement to lend at a fixed rate at some time in the future. A forward rate agreement, or FRA, is one way of achieving this. But each FRA is a tailor-made agreement between two counterparties, and therefore carries counterparty risk. If you change your mind and want to close out a position by buying the opposing contract the FRAs do not cancel out, and you may end up facing counterparty risk with two counterparties. There is a huge demand for a cheap way of getting future rate exposure, either to reduce interest rate risk or for speculation on the direction of short term interest rates. To satisfy this demand there is an exchange-traded version of an FRA called an INTEREST RATE FUTURE, or SHORT TERM INTEREST RATE FUTURE (STIR).

Futures have almost no counterparty risk, as all trades are carried out with a clearing house that guarantees contracts will be settled. As futures contracts have to be shrink-wrapped and sold in volume they have standardised maturity dates and contract sizes. Contracts are offered which mature in March (H), June (M), September (U) and December (Z) with maturities ranging up to ten years (see Table 9.6 on page 342 for a complete list of month codes). Each futures contract has a code, such as EDZ3. "ED" means that it is a Eurodollar contract, Z is the month code for December and 3 means that it matures in the next year ending in 3 (2013 at the time of writing). Prices are defined as 100 minus the future rate. So a price of 95.23 would correspond with a rate of $100 - 95.23$ or 4.77%. It is important to note that the price of a Eurodollar contract, unlike the price of a bond, is nothing to do with the present value of cash flows. It is just a convention for quoting the contract rate. Futures contracts are not for the faint-hearted as the size of each contract is $1,000,000.

Say we were to buy a single EDZ3 contract at a price of 95.23. This corresponds to a three month rate of 4.77%. Eurodollar contracts are unfunded so we do not need to put up much capital. Clearing houses protect themselves by asking for INITIAL MARGIN. This is usually a small amount equal to the size of a typical gain or loss for a single day move in the underlying rate. Say we buy 20 contracts each worth $1 million notional. The next day the three month LIBOR rate decreases by 12 basis points (a basis point is 0.01%). We are then required to hand over the difference in value of our contract, to provide VARIATION MARGIN. We would pay $20 \times 1,000,000 \times 0.0012$ or

	3M Eurodollar	3M Sterling	3M Euro	3M Swiss Franc
Currency	USD	GBP	EUR	CHF
Period	3 months	3 months	3 months	3 months
Unit of trading	$1 million	£500,000	€1 million	SFr 1 million
Value of 1 bp	$25 per lot	£12.50 per lot	€25 per lot	SFr 25 per lot
Quotation	100 - rate	100 - rate	100 - rate	100 - rate
Min. Price Move	0.5 bp ($12.50)	1 bp (£12.50)	0.5 bp (€12.50)	1 bp (SFr 25.00)
Last Trading Day	Two business days prior to the third Wednesday of the delivery month.	Third Wednesday of the delivery month, following if not a business day.	Two business days prior to the third Wednesday of the delivery month.	Two business days prior to the third Wednesday of the delivery month.
Interest Rate Basis	A/360	A/365	A/360	A/360

Table 4.5: Interest rate future contracts traded on the NYSE Euronext exchange.

$24,000 margin. As you can see, we pay or receive $2,000 for each basis point move in three month LIBOR. The next day the three month LIBOR rate drops by 8 basis points. We can either take $16,000 out of our margin account or leave it there to cover future losses. Clearing houses greatly reduce their risk by forcing traders to mark their position relative to the current market value daily, a process known as MARK TO MARKET. Marking to market ensures that each day is started with a clean slate. Nobody can run up huge losses without settling them promptly and all traders in a futures market start the day afresh.

Eurodollar futures are not the only interest rate future that can be traded. There is also a market in Sterling futures, Euribor futures and Swiss Franc futures with minor differences from Eurodollar futures as summarized in Table 4.5.

The rate against which each contract settles is the official British Bankers Association LIBOR rate except for the euro contract which settles against EURIBOR. More detail on these and other short-term interest rate futures and options can be found on the NYSE Euronext web site[3].

4.5.5 Treasury STRIPS

T-bills come with limited maturities. For example the US Treasury issues T-bills with maturities of 28 days, 91 days and 182 days. This is fairly limited if we want to tailor-make sets of cash flows. It is therefore possible to chop up a Treasury bond into its individual cash flows and sell them separately. Each of the cash flows is a zero coupon bond issued by the government. These securities are known as SEPARATELY TRADED REGISTERED INTEREST AND PRINCIPAL SECURITIES or STRIPS. Interest cash flows, which are coupons, are C-STRIPS and principal cash flows occurring at maturity are

[3]NYSE Euronext http://www.euronext.com

P-STRIPS. STRIPS expand the zero coupon bond palette allowing greater creativity in constructing cash flows to order.

You may be wondering why it is useful to construct cash flow profiles. A typical use is in asset liability management for pension funds. Statistical models are used to predict when customers will retire and when they will die. This can be used to project the future cash flows required to service customers pensions, known as liabilities. Then the fund has to match these costs with cash flows generated by its assets. STRIPS can be used to ensure that the right cash flows occur at the right time to meet future requirements.

Exercise 26 *An unscrupulous trader wants to shift the LIBOR curve to suit her own position. The range of 6 month rates from her colleagues at the other 15 banks polled lie in the range 5.3% to 5.6%. Her rate is 5.7%. How much will her rate affect the published LIBOR fixing?*

4.6 Bootstrapping the Yield Curve

Bootstrapping is the process of taking a wide range of interest rate instruments and combining them into a single, unified yield curve. The process is sometimes called bootstrapping because it is a chicken-and-egg problem; it is impossible to price assets without the yield curve and it is impossible to build the yield curve without priced fixed income assets. We break this deadlock by calculating discount factors for short term securities, such as the overnight LIBOR rate. Then we use our short term discount factors to extend the curve to longer-term securities with a single cash flow poking into the unknown. Interest rate futures and LIBOR rates supply information for the shorter end of the curve and interest rate swaps and longer dated government bonds constitute the longer end of the curve.

Construction of yield curves is as much black art as science. Yield curves are also controversial because they affect trader profit and loss in the fixed income business. Often different desks will have their own preferred methods for curve building, so even within the same bank there may be different opinions about the current shape and levels of the yield curve. To see how curve building is done in practice there is an excellent paper by Hagan and West (2006) that explains the detail of choosing good interpolation methods. They show that some bootstrapping methods that are used in commercial software or in-house at investment banks violate the assumption that the curve should be arbitrage-free and suggest two bootstrap algorithms that overcome the problems they describe. The purpose in this section is merely to convey the idea of building a curve using no-arbitrage principles and readers should refer to papers such as Hagan and West if they need to build production-quality curves.

4.6.1 Cash Curve

When stipping a real yield curve one has to consider day count and compounding conventions for each currency. Here we will strip the USD yield curve, but the same principles apply to any other currency. At the short end of the curve we can use the interbank offered rates for the currency of interest. This is the rate at which banks lend to one another. Here are the U.S. dollar LIBOR rates (Eurodollar interest rates) published by the British Bankers Association on August 24, 2007:

o/n	5.19750	**3m**	5.50563	**8m**	5.31500
1w	5.42625	**4m**	5.46125	**9m**	5.27000
2w	5.44688	**5m**	5.43125	**10m**	5.24625
1m	5.50250	**6m**	5.41125	**11m**	5.22313
2m	5.50563	**7m**	5.36188	**12m**	5.20000

There are 15 maturities, the shortest being the overnight rate (o/n) which is quoted for deposits today maturing tomorrow, and the longest is one year. The Eurodollar interest rate is quoted A/360 simple. It is not a compounded rate. So if we invest principal p at the LIBOR rate $r_l(t_{360})$ for term t_{360} our interest i is

$$i = pr_l(t_{360})t_{360},$$

and we interpolate for terms that do not fall on the quoted maturities. If we were to invest $1 million for one month from August 24th, 2007 to September 24th, 2007 (31 actual calendar days) our interest would be $1,000,000 \times 0.055025 \times \frac{31}{360}$ which is $4,738.26. These are all zero rates, so we can calculate the discount factors directly from the rates. Since the rates are quoted as simple rates the discount factor is

$$\delta = \frac{1}{1+rt}.$$

We can now fill in the table of discount factors. What we are aiming to produce is a set of dates in the future and a single number associated with each date. The discount factor is the value today of receiving a dollar on that date. The precise number of days in the interval depends on whether the final date falls on a weekend, in which case the final date is shifted to the next business day. For example, the overnight rate is for three days rather than one.

Date	Discount Factor	Date	Discount Factor
Aug 24 07	1	**Jan 24 08**	$\frac{1}{1+0.0543125 \times \frac{153}{360}} = 0.977438$
Aug 27 07	$\frac{1}{1+0.0519750 \times \frac{3}{360}} = 0.999567$	**Feb 25 08**	$\frac{1}{1+0.0541125 \times \frac{185}{360}} = 0.972945$
Aug 31 07	$\frac{1}{1+0.0542625 \times \frac{7}{360}} = 0.998946$	**Mar 24 08**	$\frac{1}{1+0.0536188 \times \frac{213}{360}} = 0.969251$
Sep 7 07	$\frac{1}{1+0.0544688 \times \frac{14}{360}} = 0.997886$	**Apr 24 08**	$\frac{1}{1+0.0531500 \times \frac{244}{360}} = 0.965229$
Sep 24 07	$\frac{1}{1+0.0550250 \times \frac{31}{360}} = 0.995284$	**May 26 08**	$\frac{1}{1+0.0527000 \times \frac{276}{360}} = 0.961166$
Oct 24 07	$\frac{1}{1+0.0550563 \times \frac{61}{360}} = 0.990757$	**Jun 24 08**	$\frac{1}{1+0.0524625 \times \frac{305}{360}} = 0.957444$
Nov 26 07	$\frac{1}{1+0.0550563 \times \frac{94}{360}} = 0.985828$	**Jul 24 08**	$\frac{1}{1+0.0522313 \times \frac{335}{360}} = 0.953649$
Dec 24 07	$\frac{1}{1+0.0546125 \times \frac{122}{360}} = 0.981829$	**Aug 25 08**	$\frac{1}{1+0.0520000 \times \frac{367}{360}} = 0.949658$

4.6.2 Futures Curve

Another set of instruments that we can use to construct short term rates are interest rate futures, also known as Eurodollar futures. Eurodollar futures are standardised, exchange-traded contracts for future three month borrowing, and they mature on a fixed schedule each March, June, September and December. These are the closing quotes for Eurodollar futures on August 24th 2007:

Contract	Date	Days	Price	Rate	Contract	Date	Days	Price	Rate
Dec07	12/19	117	95.030	4.970	Mar09	3/18	572	95.180	4.820
Mar08	3/19	208	95.260	4.740	Jun09	6/17	663	95.130	4.870
Jun08	6/18	299	95.310	4.690	Sep09	9/16	754	95.085	4.915
Sep08	9/17	390	95.2765	4.725	Dec09	12/16	845	95.035	4.965
Dec08	12/17	481	95.225	4.775	Mar10	3/17	936	95.005	4.995

Eurodollar futures are quoted as a price by subtracting their interest rate index from 100. For example, the Jun08 contract had a closing price of 95.310 on August 24th, 2007 implying a rate of $100 - 95.310$ or 4.690%. By stringing together a series of Eurodollar futures we can re-invest a dollar today into each forward rate to give a future value for each contract. A sequence of futures with successive expiry dates is called a STRIP of futures. Then using the appropriate day count convention we can convert the future values into discount factors.

The first value of the Eurodollar discount curve does not come from the futures market at all. It comes from the LIBOR curve. This is because we need a spot rate, which is a rate quoted for lending on the spot today, to get us up to our first futures contract in December. The December contract starts on December 19th 2007 which is 117 days in the future. This lies between the three month and four month LIBOR rate, so we can use linear interpolation to find the rate at 117 days. The LIBOR rate for 90 day borrowing is 5.50563% and 120 day borrowing is 5.46125%. The interpolated rate for 117 day borrowing is $5.50563 + \frac{117-90}{120-90}(5.46125 - 5.50563)$ which is 5.46569%. If we invest a dollar at this rate for 117 days it will be worth

$$1 + 0.0546569 \times \frac{117}{360} = 1.017763.$$

Now we start to use futures contracts to build the curve. We invest our $1.017763 for 91 days at the Dec07 rate of 4.970%. Our investment now becomes

$$1.017763 \left(1 + 0.0497 \times \frac{91}{360}\right) = 1.030550.$$

The Mar08 contract is also for 91 days at a rate of 4.740% and will increase our investment to

$$1.030550 \left(1 + 0.0474 \times \frac{91}{360}\right) = 1.042897.$$

We carry on investing our proceeds in each successive future to find the accrued value of our investment:

Dec07	Mar08	Jun08	Sep08	Dec08	Mar09	Jun09	Sep09	Dec09	Mar10
117	208	299	390	481	572	663	754	845	936
1.017763	1.030550	1.042897	1.055261	1.067865	1.080754	1.093922	1.107389	1.121147	1.135218

These values for accrued interest are converted into zero coupon rates by setting them equal to the interest on a zero coupon bond. For example the Jun08 accrued is 1.042897

$$1 + r_{zero} \times \frac{299}{360} = 1.042897$$

Rearranging gives

$$r_{zero} = (1.042897 - 1) \times \frac{360}{299},$$

which is 5.164905%. If the accrued interest on a 299 day zero coupon bond was higher than our daisy-chain of forwards we could sell the zero coupon bond (which is expensive) and buy the daisy-chain of forwards (which is cheap). We would then make a risk-free profit. Arbitrageurs ensure that this cannot happen by doing this trade until prices come into alignment. One of the quirks of curve-building on Bloomberg and elsewhere is that a rate is quoted as a BOND EQUIVALENT YIELD if it has a term greater than one year. Because all bonds have differing compounding conventions and day count conventions, bond equivalent yield forces a standard convention, usually semi-annual compounding ($f = 2$) and an Actual/365 day count convention. Bond equivalent yield is useful because it creates a common measure for comparing yields across fixed income markets with different quoting conventions. Converting the Jun09 accrued to bond equivalent yield r_{bey} gives

$$\left(1 + \frac{r_{bey}}{2}\right)^{2\frac{663}{365.25}} = 1.093922$$

$$r_{bey} = 2\left(1.093922^{\frac{1}{2}\frac{365.25}{663}} - 1\right).$$

This works out as 5.007092%. We can easily fill in the rest of the bond equivalent rates.

	Dec07	Mar08	Jun08	Sep08	Dec08	Mar09	Jun09	Sep09	Dec09	Mar10
Days	117	208	299	390	481	572	663	754	845	936
Accrued	1.017763	1.030550	1.042897	1.055261	1.067865	1.080754	1.093922	1.107389	1.121147	1.135218
Rate	5.4657	5.2874	5.1649	5.1015	5.0487	5.0209	5.0071	5.0028	5.0044	5.0107
	←—	Simple A/360	—→	←—			Compound A/365			—→

4.6.3 Interest Rate Swap Curve

Interest rate swaps are very actively traded, and are used in conjunction with LIBOR rates to build the cash yield curve. Swap rates are quoted for much longer maturities than LIBOR, usually out to 30 years. For the one year swap rate in U.S. dollars rates are quoted on an annualised Actual 360 basis. In contrast to LIBOR where one rate is quoted and universally agreed upon, interest rate swaps are OTC. You will get slightly different quotes from each investment bank, and the quote will vary during the day. Here are some swap rates for August 24, 2007.

2y	3y	4y	5y	6y	7y	8y	9y	10y
4.994	5.002	5.017	5.069	5.122	5.163	5.206	5.242	5.275

The par swap rate is equal to the coupon of a par bond that sets the present value of the bond to 100. For a one year par bond that pays coupons twice per year the one year rate is given by setting the present value of the future cash flows to 100, then re-arranging. If the coupon is c, the discount factors in six months is $\delta(0.5)$ and in one year is $\delta(1)$ then

$$
\begin{aligned}
100 &= \frac{100c}{2}\delta(0.5) + \frac{100c}{2}\delta(1) + 100 \cdot \delta(1) \\
\delta(1) &= \frac{1 - \frac{c}{2}\left[\delta(0.5) + \delta(1)\right]}{1 + \frac{c}{2}}.
\end{aligned}
$$

By knowing the one year par swap coupon c and the discount factor δ at $t = 0.5$ and $t = 1$ we can creep forward in time to find the two year discount factor $\delta(2)$.

$$
\begin{aligned}
1 &= \frac{c}{2}\delta(0.5) + \frac{c}{2}\delta(1) + \frac{c}{2}\delta(1.5) + \frac{c}{2}\delta(2) + 1 \cdot \delta(2) \\
\delta(2)\left(1 + \frac{c}{2}\right) &= 1 - \frac{c}{2}\left[\delta(0.5) + \delta(1) + \delta(1.5)\right] \\
\delta(2) &= \frac{1 - \frac{c}{2}\left[\delta(0.5) + \delta(1) + \delta(1.5)\right]}{1 + \frac{c}{2}}
\end{aligned}
$$

If we don't have $\delta(1.5)$ we can interpolate $\delta(1.5) = \frac{\delta(1)+\delta(2)}{2}$,

$$
\begin{aligned}
1 &= \frac{c}{2}\delta(0.5) + \frac{c}{2}\delta(1) + \frac{c}{2}\frac{\delta(1) + \delta(2)}{2} + \frac{c}{2}\delta(2) + 1 \cdot \delta(2) \\
\delta(2)\left(1 + \frac{c}{2} + \frac{c}{4}\right) &= 1 - \frac{c}{2}\left[\delta(0.5) + \delta(1) + \frac{\delta(1)}{2}\right] \\
\delta(2) &= \frac{1 - \frac{c}{2}\left[\delta(0.5) + \frac{3\delta(1)}{2}\right]}{1 + \frac{3c}{4}}
\end{aligned}
$$

Putting in the values we already have from the LIBOR curve

$$
\delta(2) = \frac{1 - \frac{0.04994}{2}\left[0.9736565 + \frac{3}{2} \times 0.9505703\right]}{1 + \frac{3}{4} \times 0.04994}
$$

This is a two year discount factor of 0.9061445 and a one and a half year discount factor of $\frac{0.9505703 + 0.9061445}{2} = 0.9283574$. Now we can use our discount factors up to two years and the next par swap rate for three years to find the discount factor at two and a half years and three years and so on for the rest of the curve.

Answers to Exercises

8 *We buy a contract that promises to pay $1 million in one year, $1 million in two years and $5 million in three years. If the risk-free interest rate is 6% how much should you pay for the contract today i.e. what is the present value of the three cash flows? Bear in mind that T-bills assume 360 days in a year.*

The present value of the cash flows is $\frac{1}{1+0.05\times1} = 0.9524$ for the first year, $\frac{1}{1+0.05\times2} = 0.9091$ for the second and $\frac{5}{1+0.05\times3} = 4.3478$ giving a total present value of $6.21 million.

9 *We buy $100,000 face of a 13 week T-bill. What is the discount and what is the present value of the T-bill?*

The discount is the product of the discount rate and time in years. Thirteen weeks is 13×7 or 91 days and T-bills assume a 360 day year so the discount is $100000 \times \frac{91}{360} \times 0.01$ or $252.78. The present value is $100,000 minus the discount, which is $99,747.22.

10 *If we have a single cash flow with future value $3 million in six months, find the present value, given that the simple interest rate is 7%.*

$$\text{PV} = \frac{\text{FV}}{1+rt} = \frac{3}{1+0.07\times0.5} = 2.8986.$$

11 *Re-arrange equation 4.1 to give rate r in terms of PV, FV and time t.*

$$r = \frac{1}{t}\left(\frac{\text{FV}}{\text{PV}} - 1\right).$$

12 *Re-arrange equation 4.1 to express t in terms of PV, FV and rate r.*

$$t = \frac{1}{r}\left(\frac{\text{FV}}{\text{PV}} - 1\right).$$

13 *Assume annual compounding ($n = 1$) and re-arrange Equation 4.4 to find the number of years to double your investment.*

We know that $\text{FV} = 2\text{PV}$. So equation 4.4 becomes $(1+r)^t = 2$ and taking logarithms gives $t = \frac{\log 2}{\log(1+r)}$.

14 *Using the answer to the previous question find an approximate linear equation to express t in terms of r.*

For small r, $\ln(1+r) \approx r$ (see Section 3.8 on page 119), and $\ln 2 \approx 0.6931$ so $t \approx \frac{0.6931}{r}$. You can probably guess why this is called the "Rule of 72". If the interest rate is 6% the time taken to double your money is, by the Rule of 72, about $\frac{72}{6}$, 12 years. The exact value is 11.9 years. The approximation deteriorates for high interest rates.

15 *A retiree turns out to be immortal. They will receive $50,000 each year for the rest of their life. What is the value of this annuity given the interest rate is 5%?*

The present value of this perp is $\text{PV}_{\text{perp}} = \frac{c}{r} = \frac{50000}{0.05}$, or $1 million.

16 *Another retiree will live for exactly thirty years after retirement. They will receive $50,000 each year for the rest of their life. What is the value of this annuity given the interest rate is 5%?*

The present value of this annuity is $\text{PV}_{\text{ann}} = c\frac{1-\frac{1}{(1+r)^n}}{r} = 50000\frac{1-\frac{1}{1.05^{30}}}{0.05}$ or $768,622.60. Note that the difference in present value between a perpetuity and a longish maturity annuity is quite small because the present value rapidly approaches its limiting value as n increases. In other words a perpetuity is not as good as it sounds.

17 *Derive the present value of an annuity from the present value of a single cash flow. Hint: write out each term in the series, then take out the common factor of the series and use the standard result for the sum of a geometric series $\sum_{k=0}^{n} af^k = \frac{a(1-f^{n+1})}{1-f}$ where $a = 1$ and $f = \frac{1}{1+r}$.*

See text (Section 4.2.3 on page 135) for the value of an annuity.

18 *You own a fixed coupon bond. Interest rates increase. What effect will this have on the value of your bond?*

This will decrease the value of the bond. Mathematically this is because the discount factors have a larger denominator and so become smaller. Intuitively you are receiving a fixed level of interest that becomes less attractive as the general level of interest rates increase.

19 *Solve Equation 4.8 for the par coupon c.*

We are solving this equation for c,

$$\frac{c}{(1+0.055)} + \frac{c}{(1+0.057)^2} + \frac{c}{(1+0.063)^3} + \frac{100}{(1+0.063)^3} = 100$$

$$c\left(\frac{1}{1.055} + \frac{1}{1.057^2} + \frac{1}{1.063^3}\right) = 100\left(1 - \frac{1}{1.063^3}\right)$$

$$c = \frac{100\left(1 - \frac{1}{1.063^3}\right)}{\left(\frac{1}{1.055} + \frac{1}{1.057^2} + \frac{1}{1.063^3}\right)}$$

$$c = 6.26$$

Each annual coupon payment is $6.26 which when expressed as an annualized percentage of the face value of $100 is a par coupon rate of 6.26%.

20 *Given the following zero rates, find the forward rates and the par rates: 1 year 5.5%, 2 years 5.4%, 3 years 5.2%, 4 years 4.9%, 5 years 4.5%.*

Forward rates are 0.055000, 0.053001, 0.048011, 0.040051, 0.029152. Par rates are 0.055000, 0.054026, 0.052118, 0.049297, 0.045568. Discount factors are 0.947867, 0.900158, 0.858920, 0.825844, 0.802451.

21 *Rearrange the relationship between simple and continuous future value to get an equation for simple rate in terms of continuous rate and vice versa.*

Rearrange to get the simple rate in terms of the continuous rate

$$1 + r_s t_s = e^{r_c t_c}$$

$$r_s = \frac{e^{r_c t_c} - 1}{t_s}$$

To get the continuous rate from the simple rate take the logarithm of both sides,

$$r_c = \frac{\ln(1 + r_s t_s)}{t_c}.$$

22 *Rearrange the relationship between compound and continuous future value to get an equation for compound rate in terms of continuous rate and vice versa.*

To get the compounded rate in terms of the continuous rate take the ft_p-th root of both sides,

$$\left(1 + \frac{r_p}{f}\right)^{ft_p} = e^{r_c t_c}$$

$$1 + \frac{r_p}{f} = e^{\frac{r_c t_c}{ft_p}}$$

$$r_p = \frac{e^{\frac{r_c t_c}{ft_p}} - 1}{f}.$$

In the special case where the continuous rate and compound rate use the same day count convention the fraction $\frac{t_c}{t_p} = 1$ so the relationship simplifies to

$$r_p = \frac{e^{\frac{r_c}{f}} - 1}{f}$$

To get the continuous rate in terms of the compound rate take the logarithm of both sides,

$$\left(1 + \frac{r_p}{f}\right)^{ft_p} = e^{r_c t_c}$$

$$ft_p \ln\left(1 + \frac{r_p}{f}\right) = r_c t_c$$

$$r_c = f\frac{t_p}{t_c} \ln\left(1 + \frac{r_p}{f}\right).$$

Again, this simplifies if the day count convention for the continuous and compound rates is the same.

$$r_c = f \ln\left(1 + \frac{r_p}{f}\right).$$

23 *Rearrange the relationship between simple and compound future value to get an equation for simple rate in terms of compound rate and vice versa.*

To get the compound rate in terms of the simple rate take the ft_p-th root of both sides,

$$\left(1 + \frac{r_p}{f}\right)^{ft_p} = 1 + r_s t_s$$

$$1 + \frac{r_p}{f} = \sqrt[ft_p]{1 + r_s t_s}$$

$$r_p = f\left(\sqrt[ft_p]{1 + r_s t_s} - 1\right)$$

To get the simple rate in terms of the compound rate just rearrange,

$$1 + r_s t_s = \left(1 + \frac{r_p}{f}\right)^{f t_p}$$

$$r_s = \frac{\left(1 + \frac{r_p}{f}\right)^{f t_p} - 1}{t_s}$$

24 *If you buy a forward rate agreement are you agreeing to borrow or lend forward? Will you make or lose money if LIBOR increases?*

Buying an FRA is an agreement to borrow forward at a fixed rate. This is a position that will make money if rates increase because you have locked in a fixed rate which is lower than prevailing market rates.

25 *What would have happened to Sprocket's 2×5 FRA fixed at 6% if the 3 month LIBOR rate had instead increased to 6.5%?*

Sprocket Corp would have paid the bank $\frac{10{,}000{,}000 \times (0.06 - 0.065) \times \frac{1}{4}}{1 + 0.065 \times \frac{1}{4}}$ or \$12,300.12, in two months time, and the treasurer would be making excuses including the word "unforeseeable" because they would have locked in an unfavourably low rate for their deposit.

26 *An unscrupulous trader wants to shift the LIBOR curve to suit her own position. The range of 6 month rates from her colleagues at the other 15 banks polled lie in the range 5.3% to 5.6%. Her rate is 5.7%. How much will her rate affect the published LIBOR fixing?*

The trader's LIBOR rate will not affect the published LIBOR fixing at all. The top 4 and bottom 4 rates are discarded for this very reason. This procedure makes it difficult for a single bank to move the fixing significantly to suit its own interests.

5 Bonds

5.1 Introduction

Bonds provide a structured way for governments or companies to borrow cash. Bonds are classified as FIXED INCOME products because all their cash flows are known in advance so unlike an equity they do not have an unlimited upside. A bond is a loan where an investor hands over a sum of cash to a bond issuer for a fixed period of time with the understanding that if all goes well the investor will receive it back in full with interim interest payments called COUPONS. Once in possession of a bond an investor can simply hold it until it matures, receiving fixed coupons and remaining indifferent to fluctuations of its price in the market. Bonds are often seen as a safe haven in times when the equity markets become turbulent.

Of course, all may not go well even for safe investments such as bonds. If the issuer becomes bankrupt, or simply cash-strapped before the debt is repaid, the investor may not see their money again. Investors receive a risk premium to compensate for this possibility. The greater the risk of DEFAULT the greater the risk premium. Bonds issued by governments, usually referred to as GOVVIES, are seen as a safe bet. Bonds issued by companies, known as CORPORATE BONDS or CREDIT BONDS are more likely to default and carry a larger premium. A whole industry has grown up around estimating the risk of default. Bond issuers pay rating agencies such as Moody's, Standard and Poor's, and Fitch to rate their own debt.

5.2 An Idealised Bond

Seen from a distance a bond is a glorified bag of cash flows. This is illustrated in Figure 5.1 which shows a five year bond. Firstly there are the dates when the cash flows start and stop known as the bond's ISSUE DATE or FIRST SETTLEMENT DATE and MATURITY DATE. You will have noticed that some of the cash flows are grey and some black. The cash flows are dominated by two large black cash flows at the beginning and end of its life. These are the PRINCIPAL PAYMENTS of the bond where a nervous investor hands over a large amount of cash to a bond issuer who after five years reluctantly gives it back. Figure 5.1 shows cash flows from the investor's point of view because the initial principal payment is negative and the return of principal after five years is positive. The smaller cash flows shown in grey are a sweetener offered by the bond issuer to entice investors to lend them some money. These are known as COUPONS, or interest payments. In this case the coupon is 10% which means that at the end of each year 10% of the principal is paid to the investor. Some bonds have no coupon at all and are called ZERO COUPON BONDS. A five year zero coupon bond would look exactly like the one in Figure 5.1 with all the grey cash flows removed except for the last one on the maturity date. For a zero coupon bond the sweetener comes at the end of its life when accrued interest and principal is paid altogether.

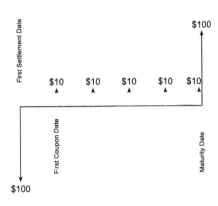

Figure 5.1: Bond cash flows.

One of the quirks of the bond market is that principal usually comes in chunks of $100. Principal goes under a variety of synonyms: face value, par value, redemption value or maturity value. There is no reason why principal should not be quoted using units of 1 rather than 100, but it does have the benefit that coupon calculations are easy, so in this case a 10% coupon on a principal of $100 would result in annual coupon payments of $10.

Coupons are sometimes paid more than once a year. This usually depends on the market in which the bond is issued. For example, the United States and Japanese bond markets usually pay coupon semi-annually, whereas annual payments are more common in the European bond market. A coupon of 10% paid semi-annually would be split into two payments of 5% one of which occurs half-way through the year and the other at the end of the year.

5.3 Dissection of a Real Bond

A bond is a complex beast. To summarise its attributes we will take a look at the way a bond is displayed in Bloomberg. Figure 5.2 shows the security description page (DES) for a bond issued by Ford Motor Credit Company, the "eight and five eighths of 2010". The DES page is like a Facebook page for a bond. DES tells you about the bond and its life history so far. We will dissect this description so that when we put the parts back together we have a fuller understanding of the whole. The page is split into areas describing the issuer, the bond, how the bond is identified using various naming systems, the current credit ratings of the bond from one or more credit rating companies, the size of the issue and links to other information about the bond and the issuer. If you want to know even more then the best place to look is the bond prospectus which may run to hundreds of pages, but it lays out in legal language exactly what you will get when you invest your money.

5.3.1 Issuer

A bond is an attempt by some entity, a bond issuer, to borrow money. In this case the issuer is Ford Motor Credit Company, the car loan financing offshoot of Ford Motor Company in the United States. Because the issuer is a company this is a CORPORATE BOND. If the issuer had been a government this would be a GOVERNMENT BOND or SOVEREIGN BOND. A bond investor will be weighing up two things: the risks they are taking by buying the bond and the coupon that they are paid to take those risks. The price behaviour of this bond will be driven in part by investor belief in the ability

DES Corp **DES**

SECURITY DESCRIPTION Page 1/ 1

FORD MOTOR CRED F $8\frac{5}{8}$ 11/01/10 100.000/100.000 (8.28/8.28) TRAC

ISSUER INFORMATION	IDENTIFIERS	1) Additional Sec Info
Name FORD MOTOR CREDIT CO LLC	Common 023447886	2) ALLQ
Type Finance-Auto Loans	ISIN US345397UJ05	3) TRACE Trade Recap
Market of Issue US Domestic	CUSIP 345397UJ0	4) TRACE Trade History
SECURITY INFORMATION	RATINGS	5) Corporate Actions
Country US Currency USD	Moody's Ba2	6) Cds Spreads/RED Info
Collateral Type Sr Unsecured	S&P B+	7) Ratings
Calc Typ(1)STREET CONVENTION	Fitch BB-	8) Custom Notes
Maturity 11/ 1/2010 Series	DBRS BB	9) Covenant/Default
NORMAL	ISSUE SIZE	10) Identifiers
Coupon $8\frac{5}{8}$ Fixed	Amt Issued/Outstanding	11) Fees/Restrictions
S/A 30/360	USD 500,000.00 (M)/	12) Prospectus
Announcement Dt 10/26/05	USD 500,000.00 (M)	13) Sec. Specific News
Int. Accrual Dt 11/ 2/05	Min Piece/Increment	14) Involved Parties
1st Settle Date 11/ 2/05	1,000.00/ 1,000.00	15) Issuer Information
1st Coupon Date 5/ 1/06	Par Amount 1,000.00	16) Pricing Sources
Iss Pr 99.13500	BOOK RUNNER/EXCHANGE	17) Related Securities
SPR @ ISS 437.50 vs T $4\frac{1}{2}$ 11/10	BCLY,DB,LASCM	18) Issuer Web Page
HAVE PROSPECTUS DTC	Multiple	66) Send as Attachment

SHORT 1ST CPN.

Australia 61 2 9777 8600 Brazil 5511 3048 4500 Europe 44 20 7330 7500 Germany 49 69 9204 1210 Hong Kong 852 2977 6000
Japan 81 3 3201 8900 Singapore 65 6212 1000 U.S. 1 212 318 2000
SN 826864 G378-607-2 20-Oct-2010 17:28:15

Figure 5.2: Bloomberg description of a bond (DES). Source: Bloomberg.

of this issuer to pay its debts and avoid bankruptcy, which is called the credit risk of the issuer. The simplest way for a bond investor to control their credit risk is to choose their issuers carefully. If the company issues many bonds then it is possible to plot the yield of those bonds against their remaining maturity and this is the ISSUER YIELD CURVE. The issuer will belong to a sector, such as the automobile sector or the finance sector, and this means that the price of the bond will also be driven by market sentiment towards that sector. This bond is classified as "Finance - Auto Loans". You may own very high quality financial sector debt, but if the entire industry is out of favour your bond will suffer. For more detail on yield curves see Section 5.13 on page 208.

```
ISSUER INFORMATION
Name FORD MOTOR CREDIT CO LLC
Type Finance-Auto Loans
Market of Issue US Domestic
```

Figure 5.3:
  Bond   issuer   information.
  Source: Bloomberg.

Our issuer is domiciled in the United States and has chosen to issue this bond in the domestic US market. If Ford Motor Credit had chosen to issue this bond in another country it would be described as a EUROBOND. This term is slightly misleading, as a Eurobond is a bond that is issued and traded in any country different from the one in which the issuer is domiciled. So if Toyota Motor Corporation were to issue bonds in dollars in the United States these would be Eurobonds and would trade in the US bond market. This affects not just the currency of payments but also the legal framework of the bond. Eurobonds are usually in the form of BEARER BONDS which means that their ownership is not registered centrally and may avoid witholding tax. If you own the bond certificate you are legally entitled to receive coupon and principal payment. Eurobonds come with a nickname which is based on the country where they are issued. For example Bulldog bonds are bonds issued in the United Kingdom, which often adopts the bulldog as its national mascot. Other Eurobonds include Matador bonds (Spain), Kangaroo bonds or Matilda bonds (Australia), Samurai bonds (Japan), Yankee bonds (USA), Sushi bonds (issued outside Japan by a Japanese domiciled company), Shogun bonds (issued in Japan but in the currency of company domicile), Dragon bonds (issued in Asia but denominated in USD) and Dim Sum bonds (issued in Hong Kong and denominated in Chinese renminbi).

5.3.2 Identifiers

```
IDENTIFIERS
Common    023447886
ISIN      US345397UJ05
CUSIP      345397UJ0
```

Figure 5.4:
  Bond   identifiers.
  Source: Bloomberg.

Humans do not like codes, so there has to be some unambiguous and easily intelligible way of describing bonds. At the coffee machine you might have heard traders talking about the bond in Figure 5.2 as the "Ford Motor Credit eight and five eighths of 2010", which specified the bond using its issuer name, coupon and maturity date. Tickers, harking back to the days when share prices would appear on a ribbon of paper called ticker-tape, are uppercase abbreviations of a company's name, usually about four letters or less in length. Ford Motor Credit's ticker is "F".

Corporate tickers are usually used in financial software because they are easy to type and well-known.

When it comes to making a trade we have to be exact, so various international organisations produce unique codes that identify each bond and for the case of US Treasury bonds, each coupon. Figure 5.4 shows three of these identifiers. The first is a common code, which is an identifier used for bonds which is produced jointly by two organisations: Clearstream (the clearing division of Deutsche Börse) and Euroclear (a Brussels-based company that offers a clearing and settlement system). ISIN stands for International Securities Identifying Number. This is broken down into three parts. The first two letters are the country code, although Clearstream and Euroclear have their own code "XS" for European bonds. Some UK bond ISINs start with "GB" rather than "XS". This ISIN starts with US because it is a bond issued in the United States. Each country has its own national numbering agency (NNA) that generates the National Securities Identification Number (NSIN) that forms the next nine digits. In the United Kingdom the NNA is the London Stock Exchange, and the NSIN they produce is the SEDOL code. SEDOL codes are seven digits, six of which identify the security followed by a seventh check digit. In the United States the NNA is the Committee on Uniform Security Identification Procedures (CUSIP) and the NSIN is the CUSIP code.

5.3.3 Security Information

Our issuer is domiciled in the United States and our bond is denominated in US dollars. This means that the bond is paid for in USD and pays investors coupon and principal in USD. Collateral type is an indicator of the position of the bond in the company's CAPITAL STRUCTURE (described in detail in Section 1.6 on page 67). In this case the bond is senior unsecured, which is the most common type of collateral. The bond's seniority is very important in the event that Ford Motor Credit were to become bankrupt. When a company is liquidated its assets are sold and proceeds are distributed in a strict order. Bond holders are usually paid before equity holders. And bond holders are themselves ordered into tiers of debt ranging from senior to junior. The lower a bond in the seniority hierarchy the greater the

```
SECURITY INFORMATION
Country US        Currency USD
Collateral Type Sr Unsecured
Calc Typ(  1)STREET CONVENTION
Maturity  11/ 1/2010 Series
NORMAL
Coupon        8 5/8      Fixed
S/A           30/360
Announcement Dt 10/26/05
Int. Accrual Dt 11/ 2/05
1st Settle Date 11/ 2/05
1st Coupon Date  5/ 1/06
Iss Pr  99.13500
SPR @ ISS 437.50 vs T 4 1/2  11/10
HAVE PROSPECTUS     DTC
```

Figure 5.5:
Security information. Source: Bloomberg.

risk that an investor holding that bond will not be able to recover their capital in the event of default, so decreasing seniority means increasing risk and all else being equal a greater coupon to compensate for that risk. At the bottom of the security information box is "Iss Pr 99.135" and "SPR @ ISS 437.50 vs T 4 ½ 11/10". This means that the issue price of the bond was $99.135 and it was issued at a spread of 437.5 basis points relative to a US Treasury of similar maturity (the 4½'s of 2010). This spread of 437.5 basis points reflected the market perception of the credit risk of the issuer at the time of issue.

In Europe a corporate bond is usually priced relative to interest rate swap rates because the government bond market is not as large and liquid as it is in the United States. Very high quality credits might be able to issue a bond at SWAPS FLAT. Most corporate issuers will trade at swaps plus a spread that reflects their credit risk. A further complication is that interest rate swaps have a bid and offer price. Bonds are priced relative to the mid-price, so a new ten year corporate bond issue might be priced at "mid-swaps plus 150", which means the fixed coupon would be the ten year mid-swap rate at the time of issue plus 150 basis points.

The rest of the information about our security fixes its precise cash flows. The company announced that it was issuing the bond on October 26, 2005. The interest accrual date and maturity date give us the start and end dates of the bond. Interest started accruing on this bond on the day that the company successfully raised $500 million in the PRIMARY MARKET on November 2, 2005. The bond was traded in the SECONDARY MARKET for five years. The issuer then repaid the principal of $500 million to its bond investors in full on November 1, 2010. This bond had an initial maturity of five years. Between the first settlement and maturity dates the company made interest payments starting with the first coupon on May 1, 2006. This bond had a fixed coupon of 8.625% paid semi-annually using the 30/360 day count convention. For a principal of $100 the investor received $4.31 twice a year until maturity. Figure 5.6 is the CSHF page that shows the cash flows for a principal of $1 million. The cash flows are broken into semi-annual interest payments of $43,125 on each May 1st and November 1st. At maturity on November 1st 2010 the investor received the last coupon of $43,125 and also the face value of $1 million.

5.3.4 Credit Ratings

RATINGS	
Moody's	Ba2
S&P	B+
Fitch	BB-
DBRS	BB

Figure 5.7:
Bond credit ratings.
Source: Bloomberg.

Bond investors need to assess the risk of losing their principal if an issuer defaults on their payments. This is known as CREDIT RISK, the word credit coming from the Latin *credere,* to believe. It is very difficult to assess the probability of default, so there are companies called RATING AGENCIES that specialize in assessing default probability and the size of loss given a default has occurred. When an issuer is about to issue a bond they usually pay one or more rating agencies to have their issue rated. Rating agencies are given privileged access to the issuer's accounts to try and determine whether their projected future income cash flows will cover their future liability cash flows. An agency will also have to collect historic information on the issuer's past history of defaults.

The largest rating agencies are Moody's, Standard and Poor's, and Fitch which are all based in the United States. Dagong Global Credit Rating, a Chinese rating agency, caused controversy in July 2010 when it produced ratings for global sovereigns and rated the United States, the United Kingdom, and Japan lower than China on the basis that Western rating agencies were biased. Further controversy followed when the

```
CUSIP:345397UJ0   BOND  PAYMENT  SCHEDULE      Page 1/   1
FORD MOTOR CRED  F 8 ⅝ 11/01/10    100.000/100.000   (8.28/8.28) TRAC
  PRICE   100.000000 SETTLEMENT DATE 11/ 2/05 ISSUE 11/ 2/05  MATURITY  11/ 1/10
  YIELD    8.625122 to M Maturity on 11/ 1/10 @ 100.000000
                                              FACE AMOUNT     1000.00 M

  Display C C=Cashflow or P=Present Value @         % compounded   2/YR
```

DATE	INTEREST	PRINCIPAL	DATE	INTEREST	PRINCIPAL
5/ 1/06	42885.42	0.00			
11/ 1/06	43125.00	0.00			
5/ 1/07	43125.00	0.00			
11/ 1/07	43125.00	0.00			
5/ 1/08	43125.00	0.00			
11/ 1/08	43125.00	0.00			
5/ 1/09	43125.00	0.00			
11/ 1/09	43125.00	0.00			
5/ 1/10	43125.00	0.00			
11/ 1/10	43125.00	1000000.00			

```
Australia 61 2 9777 8600 Brazil 5511 3048 4500 Europe 44 20 7330 7500 Germany 49 69 9204 1210 Hong Kong 852 2977 6000
Japan 81 3 3201 8900     Singapore 65 6212 1000    U.S. 1 212 318 2000    Copyright 2010 Bloomberg Finance L.P.
                                                              SN 826864 G378-607-2 20-Oct-2010 17:29:37
```

Figure 5.6: Bond cash flows. Source: Bloomberg.

US was downgraded by Dagong after the announcement of a second round of quantitative easing in November 2010 citing "its deteriorating debt repayment capability and drastic decline of the government's intention of debt repayment". Ratings downgrades are often controversial because they adversely affect bond prices. Some pension funds are not allowed to buy bonds below a certain rating which means that a downgrade may cause forced selling of bonds and large price drops.

Ratings take the form of letters ranging from A for the highest credit worthiness to C for junk bonds, with anything above BB (Moody's) and Ba (S&P) being considered as INVESTMENT GRADE. Each rating is sub-divided, so that Aaa is higher than Aa and AAA is higher than AA. These categories are further subdivided by appending + (Moody's) or a number (S&P). Fitch uses the same codes as S&P with the addition of a code "D" for defaulted entities. For details of rating definitions see Table 5.1. The third column shows the probability of defaulting within five years for each credit rating code. This shows how rapidly credit quality decreases as one crosses into non-investment grade ratings. It would take a very keen appetite for risk to buy something below B- where the probability of default in five years tops 50%.

Credit ratings can change over time as the financial health of issuers change. An improvement is called a credit UPGRADE and a deterioration is called a credit DOWN-GRADE and although most changes are by a single NOTCH multiple notch changes do occur. Possibly in response to complaints that rating agencies gave little warning of impending credit events, rating agencies produce CREDIT WATCHES that give expec-

Standard & Poor	Fitch	Moody	DBRS	R&I	p(Default in 5Y)	Quality
Investment Grade						
AAA	AAA	Aaa	AAA	AAA	0.06%	Highest quality
AA+	AA+	Aa1	AAH	AA+	0.10%	High quality
AA	AA	Aa2	AA	AA	0.22%	
AA-	AA-	Aa3	AAL	AA-	0.28%	
A+	A+	A1	AH	A+	0.37%	Upper Medium Grade
A	A	A2	A	A	0.46%	
A-	A-	A3	AL	AA-	0.69%	
BBB+	BBB+	Baa1	BBBH	BBB+	1.39%	Medium Grade
BBB	BBB	Baa2	BBB	BBB	2.32%	
BBB-	BBB-	Baa3	BBBL	BBB-	5.18%	
Sub Investment Grade						
BB+	BB+	Ba1	BBH	BB+	7.02%	Lower Medium Grade
BB	BB	Ba2	BB	BB	10.42%	
BB-	BB-	Ba3	BBL	BB-	14.60%	
B+	B+	B1	BH	B+	18.57%	Low Grade
B	B	B2	B	B	24.46%	
B-	B-	B3	BL	B-	34.33%	
CCC+	CCC+	Caa1	CCCH	CCC+	55.81%	Poor Quality
CCC	CCC	Caa2	CCC	CCC	70.04%	
CCC-	CCC-	Caa3	CCCL	CCC-	85.51%	
CC	CC	Ca	CC	CC+	100%	Very poor quality
C	C	C	C	CC	100%	Bankruptcy filed
D	D		D	CC-		In default

Table 5.1:
Long-term credit rating codes and probability of default within five years. Source: Bloomberg, S&P.

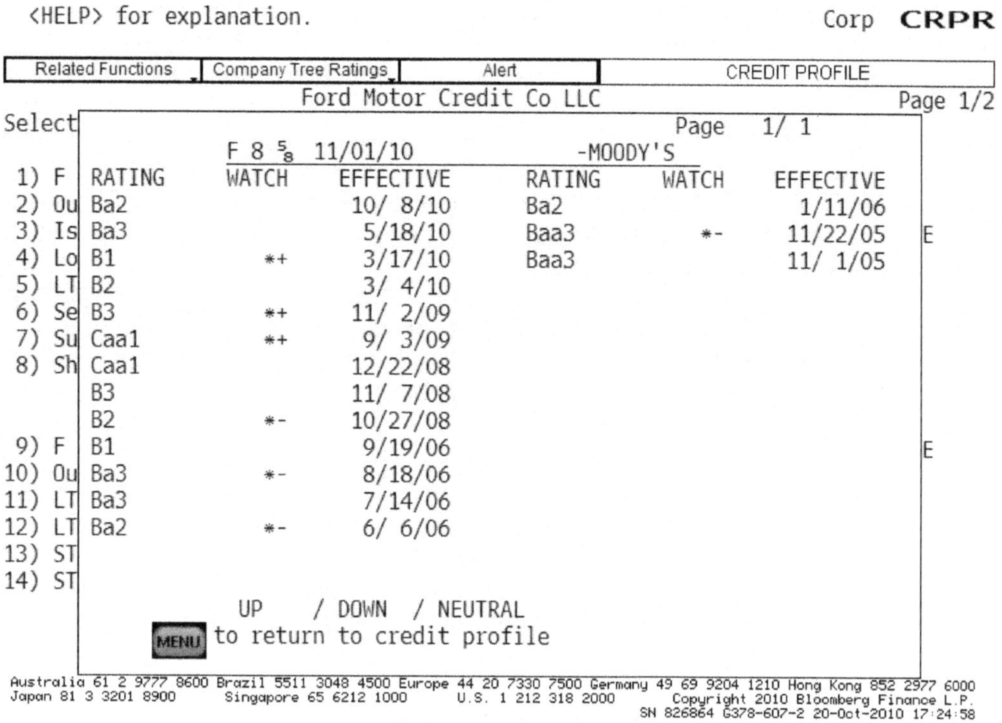

Related Functions	Company Tree Ratings	Alert	CREDIT PROFILE

Ford Motor Credit Co LLC   Page 1/2

Select   Page   1/ 1

F 8 ⅝ 11/01/10   -MOODY'S

1) F	RATING	WATCH	EFFECTIVE	RATING	WATCH	EFFECTIVE	
2) Ou	Ba2		10/ 8/10	Ba2		1/11/06	
3) Is	Ba3		5/18/10	Baa3	*-	11/22/05	E
4) Lo	B1	*+	3/17/10	Baa3		11/ 1/05	
5) LT	B2		3/ 4/10				
6) Se	B3	*+	11/ 2/09				
7) Su	Caa1	*+	9/ 3/09				
8) Sh	Caa1		12/22/08				
	B3		11/ 7/08				
	B2	*-	10/27/08				
9) F	B1		9/19/06				E
10) Ou	Ba3	*-	8/18/06				
11) LT	Ba3		7/14/06				
12) LT	Ba2	*-	6/ 6/06				
13) ST							
14) ST							

UP   / DOWN / NEUTRAL

MENU to return to credit profile

Australia 61 2 9777 8600 Brazil 5511 3048 4500 Europe 44 20 7330 7500 Germany 49 69 9204 1210 Hong Kong 852 2977 6000
Japan 81 3 3201 8900   Singapore 65 6212 1000   U.S. 1 212 318 2000   Copyright 2010 Bloomberg Finance L.P.
SN 826864 G378-607-2 20-Oct-2010 17:24:58

Figure 5.8: Changes in credit rating over time. Source: Bloomberg.

tations of upgrade or downgrade in the near term. Watches require less evidence than full-blown ratings, and as a result can be produced more quickly by the agencies. The Moody's rating history for our bond is shown in Figure 5.8. The bond started out with the lowest investment grade rating of Baa3 on its issue date of November 1, 2005. Three weeks later things started to go downhill with a negative downgrade watch on November 22, 2005 followed two months later by an actual two-notch downgrade to Ba2 which is sub investment grade. Several more downgrades followed taking the rating down to Caa1 at the end of 2008. Then the issuer's credit rating turned around in September 2009. By the time the bond was about to mature in November 2010 it almost made it back to investment grade with a rating of Ba2. If we were to look at the credit history from other agencies we would see that they tend to track each other quite closely.

5.3.5 Issue Size

Issue size is the amount borrowed by the issuer for this particular issue. This sum of money raised by the bond will sit on the liability side of the corporate balance sheet. An issuer may issue many bonds of various issue sizes depending on its borrowing requirements and on the amount of its debt that it believes the market is willing to buy. If the issuer tries to force a massive bond placement into the market then it may not be able to place the entire issue. The underwriters will then be left holding a large number of bonds that are probably trading at a discount. For this reason the debt capital market advisers in the investment banking department will advise clients on the size of issuance and ensure that the coupon is high enough to make it attractive to investors. Choosing the size of issue and coupon is based on experience and judgement. The advisers have to balance the interests of the issuer, which wants a low coupon, with what they believe the market is willing to accept as compensation for taking the credit risk of the issuer.

```
ISSUE SIZE
Amt Issued/Outstanding
USD    500,000.00 (M)/
USD    500,000.00 (M)
Min Piece/Increment
  1,000.00/  1,000.00
Par Amount   1,000.00
```

Figure 5.9:
Issue   size.
Source:
Bloomberg.

Our issue is $500 million and at this time there is still $500 million outstanding. If some of the debt has been redeemed early, which may happen if the bond is callable or puttable, then the amount issued may not equal the amount outstanding. This may happen if some of the bonds have been called by the issuer or put back to the issuer by investors. The smallest investment size if you were to buy this bond is $1,000. The coupon on this bond is $8\frac{5}{8}\%$. If funding costs for the issuer had dropped because the government yield curve had fallen or the issuer credit spread had dropped since issue then the issuer may choose to repay, say, $200 million of this bond. They would then issue new bonds at the lower rate and reduce their cost of funding. The amount outstanding would then be $300 million.

The par value is the principal amount that you will receive at maturity for each bond that you own and this is $1,000. The amount you pay for this par value today would of course not be $1,000 unless the bond happens to be trading at par. For some bonds the par value will change over time. This is true of inflation-linked bonds where the principal scales up in line with an inflation index. For some bonds the principal repays before maturity. For example European Asset Backed Securities that are based on pools of residential mortgages have principal values that pay down at a rate that depends on how quickly the mortgages pay down their principal. In this case the par value would fall over time.

5.3.6 Book Runner

```
BOOK RUNNER/EXCHANGE
BCLY,DB,LASCM
Multiple
```

Figure 5.10:
Book runners. Source:
Bloomberg.

Companies cannot issue bonds directly, they need an investment bank to issue the debt for them. The process usually involves several investment banks joining together to form a temporary legal entity called a SYNDICATE. In return for a fee the syndicate takes on the risk of buying all the debt from the issuer, then selling on the bonds into the market. The process of placing the bonds with investors is called BOOK BUILDING. The syndicate and the issuer work closely together to find the best coupon and size of issuance given the credit worthiness of the issuer and prevailing market conditions. For example they may specify a range of possible values for the coupon. In the language of debt capital markets this advice is called GUIDANCE and usually costs a few percent of the issue size. After the issuance takes place the investment banking department is pleased if the coupon was issued "within guidance" and if the issue was slightly over-subscribed because this shows that they chose the correct issue size and coupon. In this case the BOOK RUNNERS are Barclays Capital (BCLY), Deutsche Bank Securities (DB) and LaSalle Capital Markets (LASCM).

5.4 Price and Yield

Bonds are quoted in two equivalent ways: as a price or a YIELD TO MATURITY. At the top of Figure 5.11 on page 174 you will see the quote for our bond at the time the page was recorded. The quote is "F8$\frac{5}{8}$ 11/01/10 \$ C 100.000". This is the issuer ticker for Ford Motor Credit, "F", the coupon for this bond of 8$\frac{5}{8}$%, its maturity date of November 2010 and its price of \$100. Usually instead of one price you would see the bid and offer price followed by the bid and offer yield in parentheses. In this case the bond is being displayed on its maturity date so the price is equal to the face value of \$100 and the bid and offer are equal at \$100, something known as a CHOICE MARKET. Given a bond's cash flows one can determine yield to maturity from price, or price from yield to maturity. Price and yield have an inverse relationship, so that if the price of a bond goes up the yield goes down. This inverse relationship makes sense intuitively. If you are being paid a fixed rate of interest of 8$\frac{5}{8}$% and rates increase so that a newly issued bond would pay 10% then you are losing out on 1$\frac{3}{8}$% per year so your bond would be worth less. If rates decrease to 7% then you have locked in an extra 1$\frac{5}{8}$% per year so your bond price would increase.

Bond prices in the United States are unusual in that their price is quoted in fractions. Perhaps this is because of the American fondness for the arcane Imperial system of measurement. For example a bond price might be quoted as 97-17+. This means that the price as a decimal would be \$97 plus 17 thirty-secondths of a dollar. The plus sign means that we add another sixty-fourth of a dollar. The price as a decimal amount, which is what you actually pay, would be $97 + \frac{17}{32} + \frac{1}{64}$ which is \$97.55.

The daily price of a bond is driven entirely by market forces and the fortunes of its issuer. Figure 5.11 shows the price of our bond over its five year lifetime. Notice that it is always somewhere around the par value of \$100 except for the period of time just after the collapse of Lehman Brothers when all corporate bond credit spreads increased dramatically. The key drivers of bond price are shown in Table 5.2. If we were to see a sharp increase in the price of the bond it may be a rise in the entire bond market in response to the government lowering interest rates, or it could be a reduction in Ford Motor Credit's credit risk, or it could simply be that Ford Motor Credit has been in the headlines recently and its credit has become more desirable.

The present value of a bond is the sum of the present values of all its individual cash flows. Its YIELD TO MATURITY is the single rate which discounts the bond's cash flows to its current market price. If coupon payments are annual the price or present value (PV) of a bond, as a function of its coupon c, principal P, and yield to maturity y must satisfy the equation

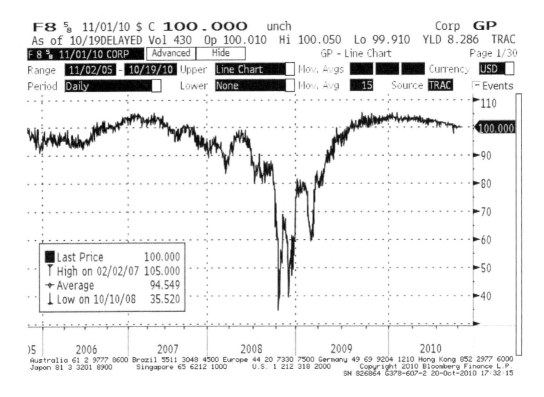

Figure 5.11: Bond price history graph. Source: Bloomberg.

Factor	Price Effect	Reason
Interest rates↑	↓	Stronger discounting of cash flows, coupon looks less attractive relative to risk-free rate
Credit risk↑	↓	Less likely to receive future coupon and principal as company may go bankrupt
Inflation↑	↓	Government may raise interest rates to stop economy overheating, eroding cash flow values and reducing price

Table 5.2: Factors affecting bond prices.

$$PV = \sum_{t=1}^{n} \frac{c}{(1+y)^t} + \frac{P}{(1+y)^n}. \tag{5.1}$$

The present value is dominated by the term $\frac{P}{(1+y)^n}$ on the right hand side. This large cash flow at the end of a bond's life is the return of principal from the issuer to the investor. The first term is the sum of interest, or coupon, payments. Coupon payments are smaller than the principal repayment, so for a principal of $P = 100$ the annual coupon payment c is seldom more than 10 for issuers with a good credit rating. This equation shows how PV can be derived from yield, but it is impossible to rearrange and calculate yield in terms of PV without a root-finding algorithm. If you have a bond calculator you may notice that calculating bond price is almost instantaneous, but calculating yield to maturity from price takes longer.

Equation 5.1 is for an annual bond with principal P, and as a matter of convention P is usually 100. Also some bonds pay coupons more than once a year. For example gilts, which are issued by the UK Treasury, and US T-bills have semi-annual compounding, paying two coupons per year. If we take compounding into consideration we can come up with a more general equation relating present value and yield,

$$PV = \sum_{i=1}^{N} \frac{\frac{c}{f}}{\left(1+\frac{y}{f}\right)^{ft_i}} + \frac{P}{\left(1+\frac{y}{f}\right)^{fT}}. \tag{5.2}$$

The time that each coupon is paid $t_i = \frac{i}{f}$ and the number of coupons to maturity time T is $N = fT$. For example a five year T-bill will pay coupons twice a year, so coupon frequency $f = 2$, and in total there are $N = 5 \times 2 = 10$ coupon payments.

Exercise 27 *Use the expression for the sum of a geometric series in Section 3.7 on page 118 to re-write Equation 5.2 in a form without summation.*

For a bond with lots of coupon payments it becomes tedious to add up the discounted future values of all the cash flows. Fortunately it is possible to re-write the price of a bond, using a result in the previous exercise, as

$$PV = \frac{c}{y}\left[1 - \frac{1}{\left(1+\frac{y}{f}\right)^{fT}}\right] + \frac{P}{\left(1+\frac{y}{f}\right)^{fT}}. \tag{5.3}$$

Equation 5.3 is elegant. It contains no summation, just coupon c and coupon frequency f, maturity T, yield y, and principal P. The only discount factor that appears is the one at maturity. Rewriting the discount factor at time T as $\delta(T)$ we can see how simple the price-yield relationship has become,

PV	=	$\frac{c}{y}$	$\times$	$[1 - \delta(T)]$	$-$	$P\delta(T)$
Bond Dirty Price	=	Annuity Price	$\times$	$[1 - \delta(T)]$	$-$	Zero Coupon Bond Price

This gives us a deeper insight into the behaviour of a fixed coupon bond. If the discount factor at maturity $\delta(T)$ is close to 1, which is the case if the bond is short-dated or if interest rates are very low, then $\mathrm{PV} \simeq P\delta(T)$ which is the value of a zero coupon bond maturing at time T. This means the bond is behaving like a zero coupon bond. If $\delta(T)$ is close to zero, which is the case for long-dated bonds or very high interest rates, then the bond behaves like an annuity where $\mathrm{PV} \simeq \frac{c}{y}$. The price behaviour of a bond can be seen as a combination of a zero coupon bond and an annuity with the sway of power determined by the discount factor at maturity.

5.4.1 Approximate Price and Return of a Bond

Equation 5.3 is all very well if you have a spreadsheet or a financial calculator to hand. But what if you want to work out the price of a bond in your head? This is actually quite simple for a fixed coupon bond. As an example, say we have a bond with three years to maturity with a coupon of 5% and a yield to maturity of 6%. We are receiving a fixed income of 5% when the rest of the market is enjoying an income of 6%. This means we are missing out on 1% each year for three years. So our bond will be trading at a discount of about 3%, which on a face value of 100 is a price of 97.

$$\mathrm{PV} \simeq 100 + (\text{coupon} - \text{yield}) \times \text{time to maturity}$$

We have ignored discounting so the amount we add or subtract is too large using this approximation. To be a little more accurate we would use the bond duration multiplied by the difference between the coupon and yield to maturity

$$\mathrm{PV} \simeq 100 + (\text{coupon} - \text{yield}) \times D.$$

For bonds we can also explain daily changes in value fairly well using a few approximations and assumptions. The price of a bond is driven by changes in the risk free rate r_{rf}, the credit spread of the issuer s and the passage of time t,

$$\mathrm{PV} = \mathrm{PV}(r_{rf}, s, t).$$

The change in price due to changes in the risk free rate and credit spread are simply approximated by multiplying the changes in the three factors (risk free rate r_{rf}, credit spread s and time t) by the bond's sensitivity to those three factors and adding these three contributions to the price change.

$$\Delta \mathrm{PV} \simeq \frac{\partial \mathrm{PV}}{\partial r_{rf}} \Delta r_{rf} + \frac{\partial \mathrm{PV}}{\partial s} \Delta s + \frac{\partial \mathrm{PV}}{\partial t} \Delta t.$$

For a fixed coupon bond the sensitivity to risk free rate and credit spread is the present value of a 1 basis point shift, the PV01. Sensitivity of price to the passage of time is well approximated by the yield to maturity (derive this by approximating the annually compounded discount factor $\frac{1}{(1+y)^t}$ by its first order Maclaurin series in Section 3.8 on page 3.8 then differentiate the expression for the present value of a bond with respect to time). If the risk free rate and spread change are in basis points then the change in price of the bond over a short period of time, such as a day, is then

$$\Delta \mathrm{PV} \simeq (\Delta r_{rf} + \Delta s) \times \mathrm{PV01} + y \times \Delta t.$$

For a corporate floater the sensitivity to rates is much smaller than the sensitivity to credit spread so we would probably have to split PV01 into two parts: sensitivity to a 1 basis point shift in interest rates, IR01, and sensitivity to a 1 basis point shift in credit spread CS01. An inflation-linked bond would have to include another factor for inflation i which would look like $\frac{\partial PV}{\partial i} \Delta i$. In this way we could explain where our profit and loss is coming from by attributing it to the various factors that drive the value of a bond.

Exercise 28 *A bond with three years to maturity and an annual coupon of 2% has a yield to maturity of 1%. What is its approximate price (without using a calculator)?*

Exercise 29 *A bond with two years to maturity and an annual coupon of 4% trades at a price of $96. What is its approximate yield to maturity (without using a calculator)?*

5.4.2 Special Cases

The price-yield relationship as shown in Equation 5.3 is extremely useful for exploring special types of bond. We will look at some special cases that will help us to better understand the price-yield relationship.

Par Bond

Setting $c = Py$ and the principal $P = 100$ we find that

$$PV^{par} = 100,$$

so we have a bond that has a price equal to its face value, and a coupon equal to its yield. This is called a PAR BOND.

Zero Coupon Bond

If we set $c = 0$ then Equation 5.3 simplifies to

$$PV^{zero} = P\delta(T),$$

which is simply the principal payment discounted at the maturity date.

Annuity

If there is no principal repayment, $P = 0$, then we have a set of constant payments lasting until time T, and this is called an annuity. The present value of an annuity is

$$PV^{ann} = \frac{c}{y}\left[1 - \delta(T)\right].$$

Perpetuity

A perpetuity is a bond with no maturity date. This means the principal is never repaid but the fixed coupons last indefinitely. Taking the limit as the maturity of the bond becomes infinite the terms with an exponent of T drop out and we are left with

$$\text{PV}^{perp} = \frac{c}{y}.$$

PERPETUITIES, or PERPS are rare beasts, but this relationship is useful nonetheless. This is because bonds with very long maturities (greater than about 20 years) have a price-yield relationship which is close to that of a perpetuity. For example a bond with an annual coupon of 5% and a yield of 6% would have a price of about $\frac{5}{0.06} = 83.33$. And if the yield were 5% the bond would be trading at par and its price would be 100.

Bond about to Mature

The opposite of a perpetuity is a bond that is about to mature. As $T \to 0$ the first term in 5.3 becomes very small, and the discount factor for the principal payment approaches 1, so

$$\text{PV}^{short} \approx P,$$

which makes intuitive sense, because in order to receive a principal of \$100 tomorrow you would only be willing to pay a little bit more or less than \$100 today. This tendency of bond prices to converge to their face value shortly before maturity is known as PULL TO PAR. Another consequence of pull to par is that a bond's price volatility reduces as it approaches maturity. You can see the effect of pull to par in Figure 5.11 where we see the entire life history of a bond. It starts life at a price of \$100 then enters a volatile youth. The price drops during the Credit Crisis to a distressed value below \$40 in a mid-life crisis. Because there is no default the promise of \$100 at maturity pulls the price up to and beyond \$100 and for a while the bond trades at a premium. It is important to notice that the bond becomes less volatile as it is about to mature and the price is drawn inexorably back to its par value of \$100.

5.4.3 Price from Yield for a Real Bond

We will calculate the bid price of a Boots bond on July 14, 2006 given a yield to maturity of 5.44%. Bloomberg quotes the bond price at £100.14. There are three remaining coupon payments on May 26 2007, May 26, 2008 and May 26, 2009 and on the final coupon date our principal is returned. The number of days until the coupon payments are 312, 672 and 1032 using a day count convention of 30/360. Our year fractions are $312/360 = 0.8667$, $672/360 = 1.8667$ and $1032/360 = 2.8667$

$$
\begin{aligned}
\text{Price} &= \frac{5.5}{(1.0544)^{\frac{312}{360}}} + \frac{5.5}{(1.0544)^{\frac{672}{360}}} + \frac{5.5}{(1.0544)^{\frac{1032}{360}}} + \frac{100}{(1.0544)^{\frac{1032}{360}}} \\
&= 5.2532 + 4.9822 + 4.7521 + 85.9115 \\
&= 100.8720
\end{aligned}
$$

What's wrong? We know the answer should have been 100.14. The difference between the two is the accrued interest since the last coupon date. If we were to buy this bond on July 14 it would have been accruing interest since May 26, which is 48 days in 30/360 day count convention. So we would have accrued $5.5 \times \frac{48}{360} = 0.7333$. Rather than hand back this accrued interest to the previous bond owner, we subtract it from the calculated price to give $100.8720 - 0.7333 = 100.14$ which is the bid price we saw in the quote. The price that includes accrued interest is called DIRTY PRICE or FULL PRICE or INVOICE PRICE and the price that excludes it is called CLEAN PRICE, and it is clean price that is used for bond quotes.

$$\text{Clean Price} = \text{Dirty Price} - \text{Accrued Interest}$$

If we were to plot dirty price over time then we would see little ramps superimposed on fluctuations in the clean price. The accrued interest resets to zero each coupon payment date, then ramps up to its maximum value of $\frac{c}{f}$ just before the next coupon payment date. For a semi-annual bond paying a coupon of 5% the value of accrued interest would ramp from zero to 2.5 during a coupon payment interval. The purpose of clean price is to iron out the ramps, producing a price that truly reflects the market value of the bond rather than the ugly mechanics of coupon payment. The value that you actually pay to buy the bond is the dirty price.

5.4.4 Yield from Price Calculation

Calculating price from yield is simple if we know all the cash flows. Calculating yield from price is possible but more difficult because we cannot rearrange equation 5.1 to give a closed form expression for y. Finding this root is simple as we have a closed form expression for the gradient, and we can initialise the root finding algorithm with the coupon.

Figure 5.13 shows that although the relationship between price and yield is non-linear, for small shifts in yield it is locally linear. This means that we can make approximate calculations of price changes given yield changes if we know the gradient of the price with respect to the yield. The gradient has great importance in the world of fixed income because it is a direct measure of interest rate risk as we will see in the following section.

5.5 Yield Sensitivity

There are two ubiquitous measures of interest rate sensitivity in fixed income: DURATION and DV01. Before launching into a detailed description of different measures of rate sensitivity, we will begin by saying why they are important. Duration tells you the fractional change in bond price for a change in yield. DV01 tells you the dollar change in bond price for a basis point[1] change in yield. These two numbers allow bond investors to quickly calculate the effect of interest rates on the value of their bonds. It turns out that the duration depends on the time that cash flows occur in the future.

---

[1]A basis point is a fraction of $\frac{1}{10000}$ or 0.01%.

The further out they occur the greater the duration and the greater the sensitivity of the price of the bond to changes in yield.

It is important to stress that this section deals with parallel shifts in the yield curve. In reality yield curves undergo all sorts of strange twists and contortions in response to market pressure. The price of a bond depends on the shape of the whole yield curve, not just shifts up and down. But it is hard to quote entire curves, so the market usually deals with the yield of particular maturities. For example the Wall Street Journal usually quotes the ten year Treasury bond yield when talking about fluctuations in the bond market. Those with statistical tendencies may find it stimulating to use principal component analysis (see Section 3.9) to decompose historical fluctuations of yield curves into a set of eigenvectors. This lonely numerical odyssey usually leads to the conclusion that the first principal component is a parallel shift, suggesting that the system is actually driven, to first order, by parallel shifts.

Here are some examples of the kind of simple mental calculations that bond traders do all the time. A bond that matures in 10 years has a duration of about 7 and a DV01 of $0.07. If we have a 10 year par bond, with price $100, a 1 bp drop in yield will result in a 7 bp increase in price, increasing value by 7 cents to $100.07. A five year bond has a duration of about 4, so the same 1 bp drop in yield will increase the price of a five year par bond by only 4 basis points, or 4 cents, to $100.04. Knowing this simple fact, a bond fund manager will buy bonds with a longer duration if she expects rates to decrease. This will maximize the increase in value of her portfolio. She will shorten duration if she expects rates to increase to cut her exposure. To get the interest rate risk of a bond we need the volatility of its present value. This is the bond duration multiplied by the volatility of interest rates, so duration is a direct measure of the interest rate risk of a bond.

Bond investors like another aspect of interest rate sensitivity which is convexity. This may seem rather abstract but in fact is very beneficial. Convexity acts as both a safety net in bad times and a boost to returns in good times. When interest rates decrease and the price of your fixed coupon bond decreases it decreases less than predicted by straight duration. When rates decrease and your bond increases in value the amount exceeds the value you would expect from straight duration. Convexity has real montetary value and the greater the maturity of the bond the greater the amount of convexity.

5.5.1 Macaulay Duration

Duration is important in fixed income. It is so important that many definitions of duration are used. Macaulay duration is a good place to start even though it is not often used in practice. However, it is useful for understanding the concept of duration. Macaulay duration is constructed by taking the derivative of the present value of each cash flow c_i with respect to the yield y. Using continuous compounding to simplify the derivatives, the present value is just the sum of the cash flows discounted by the yield

$$\text{PV} = \sum_i c_i e^{-y t_i},$$

which we differentiate with respect to yield y,

$$\frac{\partial}{\partial y}\text{PV} = \sum_i -t_i c_i e^{-yt_i}.$$

These sensitivities are given in dollar amounts, so by dividing by the total present value we have fractional sensitivities, and if we flip the sign we get Macaulay duration,

$$\begin{aligned} D_{macaulay} &\equiv -\frac{1}{\text{PV}}\frac{\partial}{\partial y}\text{PV} \\ &= \frac{\sum t_i c_i e^{-yt_i}}{\sum c_i e^{-yt_i}} \end{aligned}$$

Some people find it useful to visualise this as weights on a see-saw. The see-saw represents the life of the bond, and a weight equal to the present value of each cash flow is placed on the see-saw. The position of each weight is determined according to the time that the cash flow will occur. The Macaulay duration is the place where you would put a fulcrum to balance the see-saw. Because the final principal payment is very large this shifts the fulcrum to the right, toward the end of the life of the bond, as illustrated in Figure 5.12. The analogy is useful in understanding the effect of increasing the relative value of principal and interest payments. If we increase the value of principal, making the big dollar sign even bigger, this will tip the balance down on the right. We would have to move the fulcrum to the right, in other words increasing the duration. Increasing interest rates will decrease the value of all the payments by discounting them more heavily, but it will discount those further in the future most heavily. This would tip the balance to the left, so decreasing duration.

Macaulay duration for a zero coupon bond is very simple. Zero coupon bonds have just one future cash flow when we retrieve our principal payment P at maturity T.

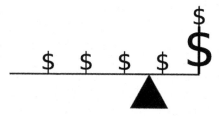

$$D^{zero}_{macaulay} = \frac{TPe^{-yT}}{Pe^{-yT}} = T$$

Figure 5.12:
Duration as the position of a fulcrum on a cash flow see-saw.

Macaulay duration for a zero coupon bond is its time to maturity. The present value of a bond can be replicated by the present value of a zero coupon bond portfolio $\text{PV}_{bond} = \sum_i \text{PV}^{zero}_i$. The present value of each zero $\text{PV}^{zero}_i = c_i e^{-yt_i}$. So we can rewrite the Macaulay duration in terms of the duration of the replicating portfolio of zero coupon bonds

$$D_{macaulay} = -\frac{1}{PV}\frac{\partial}{\partial y}PV$$

$$= \frac{\sum_i t_i c_i e^{-yt_i}}{\sum_i c_i e^{-yt_i}}$$

$$= \frac{\sum_i t_i PV_i^{zero}}{\sum_i PV_i^{zero}}$$

$$= \text{PV-weighted average of } t.$$

Instead of thinking about duration in terms of derivatives we can describe it as the average term of the cash flows weighted by their present value. The further out in the future cash flows occur the greater the duration of the bond. Reducing y increases the present value of the cash flows, and since present value weights the cash flows this increases duration. For a five year par bond with annual coupons of 10% we can calculate the duration of its replicating portfolio of zero coupon bonds. We can replicate the cash flows with five zero coupons that pay $10 in years 1, 2, 3, 4, and 5, and the principal is a payment of $100 at maturity in year 5.

Year	1	2	3	4	5	Total
Payment	10	10	10	10	110	
Present Value	$\frac{10}{1+0.1}$	$\frac{10}{(1+0.1)^2}$	$\frac{10}{(1+0.1)^3}$	$\frac{10}{(1+0.1)^4}$	$\frac{110}{(1+0.1)^5}$	100
	$= 9.0909$	$= 8.2645$	$= 7.5131$	$= 6.8301$	$= 68.3013$	
Macaulay Duration	1	2	3	4	5	
Duration$\times$PV	9.0909	16.5289	22.5394	27.3205	341.5067	416.9865

The Macaulay duration of the bond is the present-value weighted Macaulay duration of its cash flows. The present value of all the cash flows is $100 (9.090909 + 8.264463 + 7.513148 + 6.830135 + 68.301346), which is what we would expect as this is a par bond. The PV-weighted duration of the cash flows is

$$\frac{1 \times 9.090909 + 2 \times 8.264463 + 3 \times 7.513148 + 4 \times 6.830135 + 5 \times 68.301346}{9.090909 + 8.264463 + 7.513148 + 6.830135 + 68.301346} = 4.169865.$$

Another way of thinking of Macaulay duration is that we could replace a bond B with a zero coupon bond Z. If Z has maturity equal to the Macaulay duration of B, then B and Z would have roughly the same interest rate sensitivity. In fact this could be used as a very crude form of hedge, where one simply shorts a zero coupon bond with duration equal to that of a portfolio of bonds. The reason why this would be a poor hedge is that it would only guard against parallel shifts of the yield curve, not against changes in the steepness or curvature.

Exercise 30 *Calculate the Macaulay duration of a ten year annual par bond with a coupon of 10%.*

Exercise 31 *If we were to hedge interest rate sensitivity of the 10 year 10% par bond above with a single zero coupon bond, what would be the maturity of that zero coupon bond?*

5.5.2 Modified Duration

In the real world bond yields are rarely quoted using continuous compounding. Using continuous compounding in the previous section simply made the derivatives easier to calculate. If we take another look at the derivative of the present value of a single cash flow c_i at time t_i this time using periodic compounding, the present value PV_i is

$$PV_i = \frac{c_i}{\left(1 + \frac{y}{f}\right)^{ft_i}},$$

which when differentiated with respect to yield y gives

$$\frac{\partial}{\partial y} PV_i = -\frac{t_i}{\left(1 + \frac{y}{f}\right)} \frac{c_i}{\left(1 + \frac{y}{f}\right)^{ft_i}},$$

and you may have noticed that this is just the present value of cash flow c_i multiplied by the factor $-\frac{t_i}{1+\frac{y}{f}}$.

Exercise 32 *Try this for yourself by differentiating* $\frac{c_i}{\left(1+\frac{y}{f}\right)^{ft_i}}$ *with respect to* y.

If we were to calculate the derivative of the present value based on periodic compounding with frequency f for a series of cash flows, such as a fixed coupon bond,

$$\frac{\partial}{\partial y} PV = \sum_i -\frac{t_i}{1 + \frac{y}{f}} PV_i. \tag{5.4}$$

For periodically compounded yield we can find the fractional change in price if we divide Equation 5.4 by the total present value and flip the sign, just as we did for Macaulay duration. The result is called MODIFIED DURATION. Modified duration is more commonly used than Macaulay duration because yields are quoted as periodically compounded rates. Differentiating e^{-yt} with respect to y pulls down a term $-t$ whereas differentiating $\frac{1}{\left(1+\frac{y}{f}\right)^{ft}}$ with respect to y pulls down $-\frac{t}{1+\frac{y}{f}}$. The derivative of the discount factors differ by the factor $\frac{1}{1+\frac{y}{f}}$. For this reason modified duration with compounding frequency f is related to Macaulay duration by

$$D_{modified} = \frac{D_{macaulay}}{1 + \frac{y}{f}}.$$

We can use modified duration to calculate the corresponding fractional change in the value of a bond for a shift Δy in the yield,

$$\frac{\Delta PV}{PV} \simeq \frac{\frac{\partial}{\partial y} PV}{PV} \times \Delta y$$
$$= -D_{modified} \times \Delta y,$$

or alternatively

$$\Delta PV = -D_{modified} \times \Delta y \times PV.$$

Exercise 33 *If the modified duration of a bond portfolio is five years and the yield curve moves up by one basis point, will you make or lose money and how much will you gain or lose?*

5.5.3 DV01

Fractional changes in price, as measured by modified and Macaulay duration, are all very well. But what really matters is how much changes in rate hit the money in your pocket. The standard way of measuring the impact of yield on price is to take a tiny change in yield of one basis point and see how it affects present value. This is what is meant by "dollar value of an 01", abbreviated to DV01 and also called the present value of a basis point "PVBP" or "PV01". And if you want to tie it all together this is the relationship of DV01 to price and modified and Macaulay duration,

$$\text{DV01} = \frac{\text{PV} \times D_{modified}}{10000} = \frac{\text{PV} \times D_{macaulay}}{10000 \left(1 + \frac{y}{f}\right)}. \tag{5.5}$$

As we would expect, a greater price will mean a greater absolute hit in dollars when yield changes. And the greater the bond duration the greater the change in price when yields change.

Exercise 34 *If the modified duration of a bond portfolio with a present value of $10 million is five years and the yield curve moves up by one basis point, how much money will you gain or lose?*

5.5.4 First Derivative of Price by Yield

Equation 5.3, repeated here for convenience,

$$\text{PV} = \frac{c}{y}\left[1 - \frac{1}{\left(1 + \frac{y}{f}\right)^{fT}}\right] + \frac{P}{\left(1 + \frac{y}{f}\right)^{fT}},$$

can be differentiated to give an expression for the change in present value for a unit increase (100% or 10,000 basis points) in yield,

$$\frac{\partial}{\partial y}\text{PV} = -\frac{c}{y^2}\left[1 - \frac{1}{\left(1 + \frac{y}{f}\right)^{fT}}\right] - \left(P - \frac{c}{y}\right)\frac{T}{\left(1 + \frac{y}{f}\right)^{fT+1}}. \tag{5.6}$$

Using this equation it is simple to calculate modified duration and DV01. To get modified duration we multiply by $-\frac{1}{\text{PV}}$ and for DV01 we divide by $-\frac{1}{10000}$. The result in both cases is an equation that at first glance looks rather unwieldy. So we will start by looking at particular cases, just as we did with Equation 5.3, and hopefully we will gain some insight into the sensitivity of bond price to changes in yield.

Par Bond

When $P = 100$ and $c = Py$ (if principal $P = 100$ then yield is equal to coupon as yield is quoted as a percentage and coupon is a fraction of principal)

$$\frac{\partial}{\partial y}\text{PV}^{par} = -\frac{P}{y}\left[1 - \frac{1}{\left(1 + \frac{y}{f}\right)^{fT}}\right].$$

For long maturities we can effectively ignore the term in parentheses, so $\frac{\partial}{\partial y}\text{PV}^{par} \simeq -\frac{100}{y}$, interest rate sensitivity is approximately inversely related to yield. For the bond in the worked example above with a maturity of ten years ($T = 10$), a coupon of 10% ($c = 10$) and annual compounding ($f = 1$) the sensitivity is $-\frac{100}{.1}\left[1 - \frac{1}{(1+0.1)^{10}}\right] = -614.4567$, a number that is both huge and negative. It is huge because it is the change in price for a unit change in yield (100% or 10,000 basis points) and it is negative because price and yield have an inverse relationship. The DV01 of this bond would be $\frac{1}{10000}$ of the sensitivity, or 0.06144567. Its modified duration is $-\frac{1}{\text{PV}}$ times the sensitivity, which is 6.144567 years.

Zero Coupon Bond

Setting $c = 0$, Equation 5.6 becomes

$$\frac{\partial}{\partial y}\text{PV}^{zero} = -\frac{T}{1 + \frac{y}{f}}\frac{P}{\left(1 + \frac{y}{f}\right)^{fT}},$$

which is the present value of the principal payment multiplied by a factor $-\frac{T}{1+\frac{y}{f}}$. In other words the yield sensitivity of a zero coupon bond is just a constant multiplied by its maturity. If the maturity of the principal repayment is doubled the sensitivity is doubled.

Annuity

If $P = 0$ yield sensitivity becomes

$$\frac{\partial}{\partial y}\text{PV}^{ann} = -\frac{c}{y^2}\left[1 - \frac{1}{\left(1 + \frac{y}{f}\right)^{fT}}\right] + \frac{c}{y}\frac{T}{\left(1 + \frac{y}{f}\right)^{fT+1}}.$$

Perpetuity

For a perpetuity

$$\frac{\partial}{\partial y}\text{PV}^{perp} = -\frac{c}{y^2}$$

	Coupon Bond	**Zero Coupon**	**Par**	**Perp**	$T \to 0$
PV	$\frac{c}{y}[1-\delta(T)]+P\delta(T)$	$P\delta(T)$	P	$\frac{c}{y}$	P
$\frac{\partial}{\partial y}$PV	$-\frac{c}{y^2}[1-\delta(T)]-\left(P-\frac{c}{y}\right)\frac{T\delta(T)}{1+\frac{y}{f}}$	$-\frac{T}{1+\frac{y}{f}}P\delta(T)$	$-\frac{P}{y}[1-\delta(T)]$	$-\frac{c}{y^2}$	0
D_{mod}	$\dfrac{\frac{c}{y^2}[1-\delta(T)]+\left(P-\frac{c}{y}\right)\frac{T\delta(T)}{1+\frac{y}{f}}}{\frac{c}{y}[1-\delta(T)]+P\delta(T)}$	$\frac{T}{1+\frac{y}{f}}$	$\frac{1}{y}[1-\delta(T)]$	$\frac{1}{y}$	0
DV01	$\dfrac{-\frac{c}{y^2}[1-\delta(T)]-\left(P-\frac{c}{y}\right)\frac{T\delta(T)}{1+\frac{y}{f}}}{10000}$	$\dfrac{T}{\left(1+\frac{y}{f}\right)}\dfrac{P\delta(T)}{10000}$	$\frac{P}{10000y}[1-\delta(T)]$	$\frac{c}{10000y^2}$	0

Table 5.3: Special cases of price and yield sensitivity.

Short Maturity

When $T \to 0$ Equation 5.6 shows that interest sensitivity decreases to zero. This makes intuitive sense as a cash flow in the near future is all but independent of interest rates.

Exercise 35 *Using Table 5.3 on page 186 fill in the table for a five year and a ten year semi-annual bond. Assume the principal is $100 and the coupon is 5% for both bonds and that the yield curve is a flat 6% for all maturities. Which is the most sensitive to interest rates? Is this what you expected?*

5.5.5 Second Derivative of Price by Yield or Convexity

If we differentiate Equation 5.2 with respect to yield once again we get

$$\frac{\partial^2}{\partial y^2}\text{PV} = \frac{1}{\left(1+\frac{y}{f}\right)^2}\sum_{i=1}^{N}t_i\left(t_i+\frac{1}{f}\right)\frac{\frac{c_i}{2}}{\left(1+\frac{y}{f}\right)^{ft_i}}+\frac{T\left(T+\frac{1}{f}\right)}{\left(1+\frac{y}{f}\right)^2}\frac{P}{\left(1+\frac{y}{f}\right)^{fT}}$$

This leads to the definition of CONVEXITY which is always positive for fixed coupon bonds. This allows us to have a more accurate approximation to the change in value for a change in yield. For large changes in yield the non-linear relationship of price and yield becomes significant. Notice that the definition of convexity is a function of t^2 so bonds with cash flows occurring far in the future have the greatest convexity. For the owner of a bond convexity is beneficial. If rates go up then, as we know, the price of the bond goes down, but convexity means that the price will go down less than expected if the price-yield relationship were linear. If rates go down the price of the bond goes up, but it increases more than would be expected if the price-yield relationship were linear. So although bonds with a high duration carry a great deal of interest rate risk their saving grace is that they also have a large convexity.

The concept of DV01 and convexity is familiar to mathematicians because any price-yield relationship can be approximated by a power series. As we add more terms to the power series the approximation becomes more accurate. We could approximate the price-yield curve around the current price by a first-order, or linear approximation

$$\Delta\text{PV} \simeq \frac{d\text{PV}}{dy}\Delta y + \dots$$

This is only a good approximation if the size of the yield shift Δy is very small. We can make the approximation better by introducing a second-order term $(\Delta y)^2$ which makes our approximation a parabola,

$$\Delta PV \simeq \frac{dPV}{dy}\Delta y + \frac{1}{2}\frac{d^2 PV}{dy^2}\Delta y^2 + \ldots$$

In fixed income we never consider any higher-order terms. We can translate the parabola into fixed income terms such as $DV01$ and convexity,

$$\Delta PV \simeq 10000 \times DV01 \times \Delta y + \frac{1}{2} \times \text{Convexity} \times (\Delta y)^2 + \ldots$$

Another way of seeing convexity is in terms of the rate sensitivity of duration. Ideally what we would like as a bond investor is to minimize the loss in value of our bond if rates go up and to maximize the increase in value if rates go down. Like a ship unfurling her sail in a favourable breeze our bond would increase its duration when rates go down and furl the sail in stormy weather and reduce duration when rates go up. For a simple fixed coupon bond this is exactly what happens thanks to convexity. Duration decreases when rates increase reducing our loss, and duration increases when rates decrease maximizing our gain. Convexity for a fixed coupon bond is positive. However the convexity of bonds may be negative. For example callable bonds can have negative convexity (see Section 5.7 on page 192). Mortgage Backed Securities can have negative convexity as a result of prepayment (see Section 5.17 on page 222). Bond investors think twice about buying bonds with negative convexity as they are exposed to loss of yield when rates change in either direction. As a consequence bonds with negative convexity have additional yield compared to comparable bonds with positive convexity and for Mortgage Backed Securities this is called the MBS SPREAD.

Exercise 36 *We buy a five year fixed coupon bond for \$100. Tomorrow rates increase by 1%. Will the price of the bond go up or down? How would this be affected by convexity? What if rates had decreased by 1%?*

Exercise 37 *Earlier we found that the yield sensitivity of a fixed cash flow c_i at time t_i by differentiating its present value using compound interest $\frac{c_i}{\left(1+\frac{y}{f}\right)^{ft_i}}$,*

$$\frac{\partial}{\partial y}PV_i \;=\; \frac{\partial}{\partial y}\frac{c_i}{\left(1+\frac{y}{f}\right)^{ft_i}} \;=\; -t_i\frac{c_i}{\left(1+\frac{y}{f}\right)^{ft_i+1}}$$

Find the second derivative by differentiating again. Is convexity linear in t?

Exercise 38 *Show that*

$$\frac{\partial^2}{\partial y^2}PV \;=\; PV\left[D^2_{modified} - \frac{\partial}{\partial y}D_{modified}\right]$$

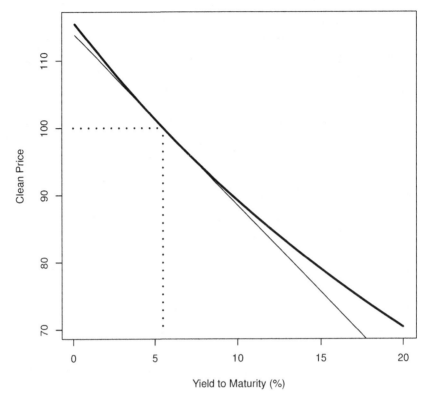

Figure 5.13:
Price-yield relationship of a three year bond paying an annual coupon of 5.5%. The dotted line shows that the yield to maturity of a par bond is equal to the bond coupon of 5.5%. Comparison with the straight line shows that the price-yield relationship is non-linear.

5.6 Graphical Price, Yield and Risk Relationships

5.6.1 Price and Yield

Figure 5.13 shows the relationship between yield and price for a three year bond paying an annual coupon of 5.5%. The gradient is always negative, so price and yield have an inverse relationship. Increasing yield reduces the price of a bond and decreasing yield increases the price of a bond. Furthermore the relationship is non-linear, so that increasing yield by a small fixed amount will have a greater effect on price for smaller yields than it would for larger yields. When the yield is equal to the bond coupon, which is 5.5% in this case, the price of the bond is $100. Because $100 is the par value, a bond that has yield equal to coupon is said to be TRADING AT PAR. When yield is greater than the coupon the price is less than 100 and the bond is TRADING AT A DISCOUNT. When yield is less than the coupon the price is greater than 100 and the bond is TRADING AT A PREMIUM.

trading at a premium	price > 100	yield < coupon
trading at par	price = 100	yield = coupon
trading at a discount	price < 100	yield > coupon

In Figure 5.14 we can see what happens to price when we fix the yield at 5% and vary coupon and maturity. A constant price of $100 runs down the middle of the graph when coupon is 5% for all maturities. For a par bond maturity does not matter, a bond trading at par is always worth $100. We can split the graph into two regions: the premium region and the discount region. In the premium region coupon is greater than the yield of 5% and price is always greater than $100. In the discount region on the left hand side of the centre-line coupon is less than 5% and price is always less than $100. Maturity has the opposite effect in the two regions. In the premium region maturity increases price and in the discount region maturity decreases price. At the bottom of the graph we see that the contours flare out. This shows that coupon becomes irrelevant as the maturity of the bond decreases. For very short maturities the price converges on $100 whatever the coupon. This is because the value of a short term bond or loan is dominated by the value of the principal and only marginally by the value of interest.

5.6.2 Duration

Figure 5.15 shows how maturity and coupon affect the Macaulay duration of bonds with a yield of 5%. A plot of modified duration would have the same shape but would be scaled by a factor $\frac{1}{1+\frac{0.05}{2}}$, reducing duration values by about 3%. The far left of the graph where coupon is zero shows that the Macaulay duration of zero coupon bonds is simply equal to their maturity. As we increase coupon, duration decreases. Recall that duration is the PV-weighted average arrival time of cash flows, and increasing coupon increases the PV-weighting of interest payments. Because interest payments occur before the principal, increasing their weighting reduces duration. The effect of coupon is more marked for bonds with longer maturity because these have more interest payments.

A seemingly obvious fact is that increasing the maturity of a bond increases its duration. It turns out that this is not true for bonds with small but non-zero coupon. For these bonds duration increases to a maximum then decays down to the duration of a perpetuity which is $\frac{1}{y}$ or 20 in Figure 5.15. For bonds trading at a premium on the right hand half of the graph increasing maturity steadily increases duration up to a limit of the duration of a perpetuity. A 30 year par bond with yield 5% has a Macaulay duration of 15.5 years. Increasing maturity to 100 years only increases duration to 19.9 years. A maturity of 1000 years would give duration just less than 20 years.

For short maturity bonds, at the bottom of the graph, contours of equal duration run almost parallel to the coupon axis. These bonds have few coupon payments and their duration is dominated, in PV terms, by the principal payment which occurs at the maturity date. They behave like zero coupon bonds whose Macaulay duration is equal to their maturity.

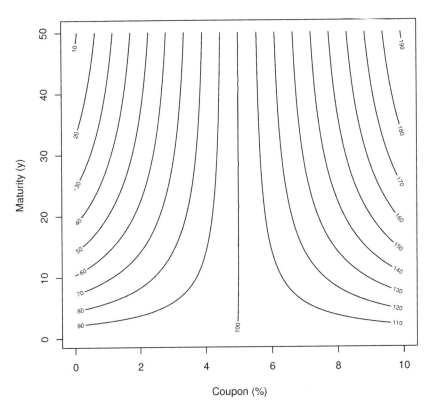

Figure 5.14:
Price of bonds with yield 5% varying coupon and maturity. Contours are labelled with the price of the bond in dollars.

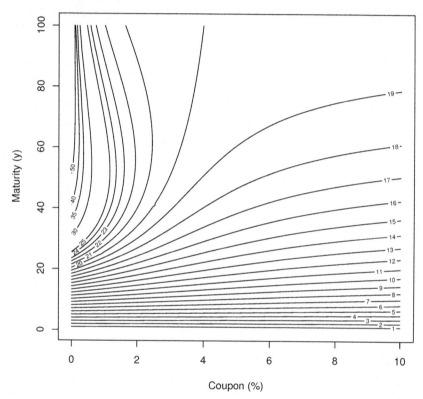

Figure 5.15:
Macaulay duration vs. maturity and coupon for 5% yield. Contours are labelled with the Macaulay duration of the bond in years.

5.6.3 DV01

DV01 is illustrated in Figure 5.16 and measures how much the price of a bond changes if the yield curve shifts up by one basis point. The dollar value of a single basis point is just the gradient in Equation 5.6 scaled by $-\frac{1}{10000}$. For bonds trading at a premium increasing maturity increases DV01. For bonds trading at a discount DV01 increases with maturity, reaches a maximum, then decreases with maturity. The "hump" in DV01 is most marked for zero coupon bonds for which $c = 0$ which runs up the far left hand side. For a zero coupon bond DV01 peaks at a maturity of about $\frac{1}{y}$, or a little over 20 years in this case (see exercise). The right hand side of the graph, which has tightly packed contours, shows that bonds with very high coupon exhibit the greatest affect of maturity on DV01.

The bottom of the graph shows that for short maturities DV01 decreases to zero, as price is dominated by the imminent principal payment and largely unaffected by interest over a short period of time. The top of the graph shows bonds with very long maturities. For these bonds which are *almost* perpetuities DV01 approaches a constant times the coupon, hence the regular spacing of contours at the top of the graph. DV01 for perps is $\frac{c}{10000y^2}$, and as the graph is for bonds with yield 0.05 DV01 is about 4% of the coupon.

Exercise 39 *Find an expression for the maximum DV01 of a zero coupon bond in terms of yield.*

5.6.4 Convexity

Figure 5.17 shows the price-yield relationship for a five year bond and a 30 year bond, both with 5% coupon. The duration of each bond is visible as the gradient of the price-yield line. The 30 year bond loses value more quickly than the five year as yield increases because it has a greater duration. Both lines pass through the point at yield 5%, present value 100 which is the point where both bonds are trading at par. Convexity is the curvature of the price-yield lines. The greater the maturity and duration of a bond the greater its convexity so the 30 year bond is much more convex than the five year bond.

Another way of understanding convexity is in terms of how duration changes as yield changes. As yield to maturity increases the curves flatten so duration decreases. As yield to maturity increases the curves flatten so duration decreases. This is good for a bond investor because as yield goes up the bond loses value but it loses less than it would if there was no convexity. Similarly if the yield goes down the price of the bond goes up, but it goes up more than it would if there was no convexity. The greater the convexity the better for the investor.

5.7 Callable and Puttable Bonds

When issuing a fixed coupon bond an issuer faces the risk that interest rates will drop and they are locked into an unfavourably high cost of funding. For this reason issuers

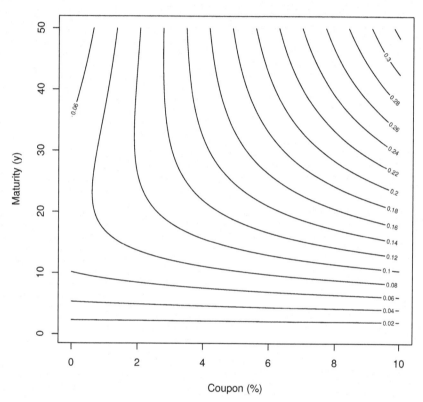

Figure 5.16:
DV01 vs. coupon and Maturity for 5% yield. Contours are labelled with the DV01 of the bond in dollars.

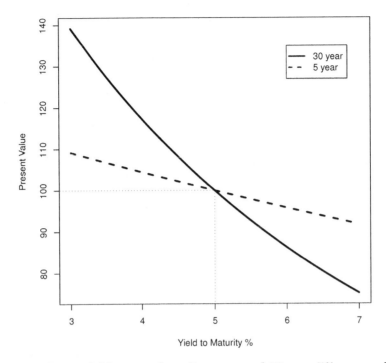

Figure 5.17: Price-yield curves for a five year and 30 year 5% coupon bond.

sometimes build in a CALL FEATURE into their bonds. CALLABLE BONDS grant the issuer the right to buy back their bonds at some fixed price before maturity. When rates drop this gives the issuer the right to stop paying a high coupon by repaying their outstanding callable bonds. Then they can raise fresh capital by issuing new bonds paying a lower coupon. The fixed CALL PRICE can be par but to appease bondholders callables can redeem to an amount that is greater than par. As the bond contains an embedded call option there are the usual variations on the option exercise type. EUROPEAN calls allow the issuer to call the bond only on one call date. BERMUDAN calls allow the issuer to call the bond on some schedule, often the coupon payment schedule, after the first call date. American call options allow the issuer to call the bond on any day after the call date. The most common exercise style for callable bonds is a schedule of call dates when the bond may be called at par, and this is the Bermudan exercise style.

Call features favour issuers rather than bond investors. A call feature caps the maximum price increase of the bond because the bond will be called when rates are low, and this is precisely when the bond has greatest value. In order to make callable bonds palatable to investors they pay a higher coupon than comparable non-callable bonds. This is because the bond investor is effectively selling a CALL OPTION to the issuer when they buy the bond (see Section 10.3 on page 352 for an explanation of call options). The more valuable the option the higher the coupon which means that an American exercise style will have the greatest option value and highest coupon, a Bermudan style will have intermediate value and coupon and a European style will have the least value and the lowest coupon. The value of the call option will increase roughly as the square root of time to expiry which means that quadrupling time to expiry will double the value of the call option. The value of the option will also increase with the volatility of the issuer yield curve. In addition to high coupons callable bonds have a HARD NON-CALL protection period during which the bond cannot be called. A ten year bond that has call protection for the first three years after issue would be summarized as 10NC3 or "ten non-call three".

When pricing a callable bond it is useful to compare it with non-callable comparable issues. For the 10NC3 example we would compare the price of the callable with 3 and 10 year bonds from the same issuer because the bond will either be called after three years or mature after ten years. If we make the unrealistic assumption that all three bonds have the same coupon of 5% then the value of the callable bond will always be lower than either of the non-callable bonds because the investor is paid by a discounted price rather than higher coupon. The callable bond price converges with either the three year or ten year non-callable according to the level of interest rates. If rates are low then the call has a lot of value and is likely to be exercised after three years. So the value of the callable bond will approach that of the three year non-callable bond. If rates are high then the call is almost worthless and is unlikely to be exercised so the bond will mature after ten years. In this case the callable price will approach that of the ten year non-callable bond.

PUTTABLE BONDS give the bondholder the right to force the issuer to redeem their bond. Sometimes investors will talk about redeeming their bond as "putting the bond back to the issuer". This PUT FEATURE gives bondholders protection because effectively they have bought a put option along with their bond. When buying a non-puttable bond the investor will lose money if interest rates increase or the credit quality of the issuer deteriorates. If the price of a bond drops massively and it is puttable then the investor could wait until the next put date then exercise their put to redeem at par. In turn this means that the coupon of puttable bonds is lower than comparable non-puttable issues because reduced coupon is the way the investor pays the put option premium. The price of a puttable bond is lower than a non-puttable bond by the value of the put option. Of course it is possible to have a bond that is both callable and puttable. To summarize the relationship of callable and puttable bonds with their comparable non-callable and non-puttable issue:

$$\text{Price}_{\text{callable}} = \text{Price}_{\text{non-callable}} - C$$
$$\text{Price}_{\text{puttable}} = \text{Price}_{\text{non-puttable}} + P$$

Here C is the value of a call option on the non-callable non-puttable comparable bond and P is the value of a put option on the non-callable non-puttable comparable bond.

5.8 Floaters

All the bonds we have looked at so far have had a fixed coupon. If we know the coupon, the first coupon date, coupon payment frequency and maturity date then we know immediately what cash flows a fixed coupon bond will pay in future. This foreknowledge comes at a price. By locking in a fixed coupon on the issue date we have to live with interest rate risk. From the point of view of a bond investor the risk is committing to a low rate of return when interest rates may increase. From the point of view of the issuer the risk is committing to a high cost of funding when in future there may be an opportunity to refund at a lower rate. At the time of issue the coupon is a snapshot of the state of interest rates and the credit quality of the issuer. The coupon may become inappropriate as interest rates and the credit quality of the issuer change.

If investors want a bond with almost no interest rate risk it is possible to buy FLOAT-ING RATE NOTES, also known as FLOATERS. The cash flows for a floater are shown in Figure 5.18. Floaters, like fixed coupon bonds, pay interest in the form of coupons. Floaters, like fixed coupon bonds, have principal payments on their issue and maturity dates. Unlike fixed coupon bonds the coupon rates are reset on a fixed set of dates from some universally agreed published rate, so the floater has a FLOATING COUPON. The floating coupon is usually set using the IBOR rate for the currency in which the floater is denominated, typically the three month LIBOR rate. So if you were to buy a floater you would not lose sleep at night worrying about the value of interest rates. If rates go up, then so will your coupon. If rates go down so will your coupon. By adapt-ing the coupon to the level of interest rates the issuer removes almost all interest rate risk. Buying a floater is almost like putting money into an interest bearing bank ac-count. You part with your money and in return receive a floating rate of interest. At any time you can take out your money and expect to receive exactly the amount you put into the account.

The value of a floater is almost insensitive to interest rates. It is almost insensitive because one of the coupons is already set. In Figure 5.18 the first coupon payment is 10, the rest are $l_1 + m$, $l_2 + m$, $l_3 + m$, and $l_4 + m$. The numbers l_1 to l_4 are the as yet unknown LIBOR rates in one, two, three and four years and m is a fixed margin that is added to the LIBOR fixing. Because we set the rate at the beginning of a coupon period the first coupon is already set at 10. Now the present value of any floating payment is insensitive to interest rates, but as we have already seen fixed payments are sensitive. So the first coupon carries an interest rate risk. On a coupon payment day all the future coupon payments are both fixed and discounted at LIBOR so the bond is worth par. It is a fair approximation to say that the value of a floater is always 100 (and a better approximation on or shortly after a coupon payment date). The duration of a floater the day after an interest rate reset is the time until that coupon is paid. If the floating leg resets quarterly then duration will be at most 0.25 years.

A floater carries little interest rate risk. However, it still has an associated credit risk. In other words you may not get your principal back if the bond issuer becomes bankrupt. By buying a corporate floater, which is a floating rate bond issued by a company, you are long the credit of the issuer. In this sense a floater is a "pure" credit instrument. By being long a fixed coupon bond and short a floater from the same issuer one can hedge out credit risk and create a "pure" interest rate risk instrument. Being long a fixed coupon bond and short a floater reproduces the cash flows of an interest rate swap, as described in Chapter 6. For an even "purer" credit instrument than a floater see Chapter 7. Floaters are quoted using a price just like fixed coupon bonds. However instead of also being quoted as a yield to maturity floaters are quoted in terms of DISCOUNT MARGIN measured in basis points. Discount margin is zero

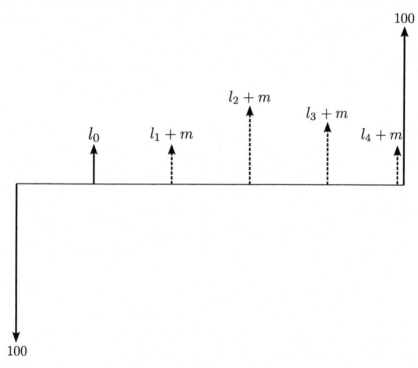

Figure 5.18:
Floater cash flows. Dashed cash flows are floating payments which will be set in the future depending on the value of LIBOR.

if the floater is trading at par, is positive if the floater is trading at a discount and negative if the floater is trading at a premium. Discount margin is calculated as the fixed amount that is added to the zero rates in order to discount the future cash flows to the observed market price of the floater. This is rather like the z-spread calculation for a fixed coupon bond.

In Figure 5.19 we compare two bonds issued by the same company at roughly the same time with the same maturity, but one pays a floating coupon and the other pays fixed. The issuer is General Electric Capital Corporation. Notice that the price of the fixed coupon bond fluctuates wildly in response to interest rates, ranging from 98 to 102 over its lifetime. In contrast, the floater gently coasts at around 100. By being less volatile floaters bear less risk than fixed coupon bonds and therefore offer lower returns. This makes floaters attractive to low risk investors, such as banks, who are seeking a slow but steady rate of return. Whereas fixed coupon bonds have their price driven by both interest rates and the issuer's credit quality, the price of floaters depends only on credit quality.

5.9 Asset Swaps & Liability Swaps

As an investor you may like the credit quality of an issuer but not want to take an interest rate risk. So buying a fixed coupon bond, which exposes you the investor to both risks, is not appropriate. But by buying a bond and entering a payer's swap you are paying away the fixed coupon and receiving floating so you have created a SYNTHETIC FLOATER (see Section 5.8, on page 195 for more detail on floaters). A floater is a pure credit instrument in that its price is sensitive to changes in the credit quality of the issuer but not to the general level of interest rates. This trade, buying a bond and paying away the fixed coupon with an interest rate swap, is called an ASSET SWAP. The floating coupon has an additional fixed spread which reflects the credit quality of the bond issuer. This fixed payment is called the ASSET SWAP MARGIN and is roughly equal to the credit default swap spread. See Section 7.2 on page 296 which shows how asset swap margin is calculated in detail.

One can also see the trade from the point of view of the issuer. Issuers often issue fixed debt because fixed coupon bonds are more popular with investors than floaters. From the point of view of the issuer a fixed coupon is unattractive because their income is uncertain whereas their debt payments are fixed. This means that they run the risk of not being able to meet their future obligations and becoming bankrupt. Also rates may drop which would mean the issuer would be lumbered with expensive funding when it would like to refinance at the lower rate. For these reasons issuers may want to convert their fixed liabilities into floating liabilities. This is done through a LIABILITY SWAP which is the reverse of the asset swap. In a liability swap you issue a fixed bond, so are paying fixed coupon payments. At the same time you enter into a swap receiving fixed and paying floating payments indexed to some IBOR rate, say the three month LIBOR rate. Synthetically you have issued a floating rate note.

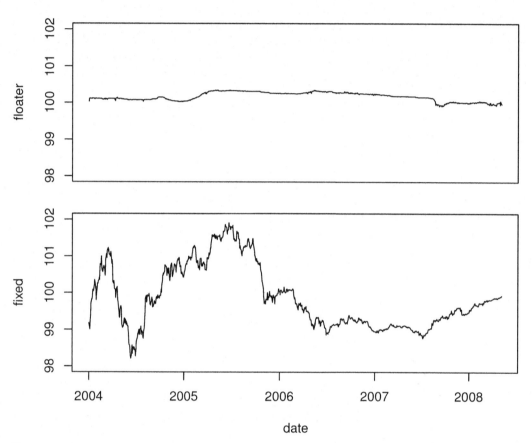

Figure 5.19:
Price histories for a fixed and floating rate bond from the same issuer, General Electric Capital Corporation. The floater was issued in October 2003, and matured in October 2008. The fixed rate bond was issued in June 2003, paid a coupon of $1\frac{3}{4}\%$ and matured in June 2008.

5.10 Repo

Holding bonds offers an opportunity called REPO which is a mangled abbreviation for "sale and repurchase agreement". Repo trades are usually very short-term, either overnight or in the case of TERM REPO for a few weeks. But why would anyone do a repo trade? Take the example of Penelope, who works as a pension fund portfolio manager. Penelope holds a large number of government bonds in her portfolio and one day decides that she needs $10 million in cash. This is to take advantage of a one week trade that she believes will have a higher return than holding bonds. She does not want to sell her govvies outright, so she temporarily sells one of her bonds in return for $10 million cash with an agreement to buy the bond back in a few days. Penelope calls Bob who works on the bond repo desk at an investment bank and arranges a one week repo. The trade agreement specifies the amount of interest charged for borrowing $10 million collateralised with her bond and this is the REPO RATE.

Bob is doing the opposite trade to Penelope, taking the bond as collateral for a very safe loan, and this is known as REVERSE REPO. If Penelope cannot repay the $10 million Bob can keep and sell the collateral so the repo rate incorporates a very small risk premium. For this reason the repo rate is usually just a handful of basis points above or below the risk-free rate. If Bob thinks that Penelope's pension fund carries a high risk of default, or that volatile interest rates may devalue the collateral, he may ask for more than $10 million worth of collateral. This excess capital is called a HAIRCUT. The term repo trade can be summarized as follows:

	Repo Trade	Reverse Repo Trade
Today	Pension fund lends bond to Bank, receives $10 million	Bank receives bond as collateral, pays pension fund $10 million
One week later	Pension fund retrieves bond from Bank, repays $10 million plus one week's interest at the repo rate	Returns bond to pension fund, receives $10 million plus one week's interest at the repo rate

So one reason to do a repo trade is to free up capital, which can be used for other investments. Repo may therefore offer a way to squeeze a little more return out of a bond portfolio. Rather than have the bonds sit in the portfolio they can be put on loan in the repo market. Another common use of repo is a way of funding purchase of a bond. Say Bob, who works at an investment bank, wants to buy $100 million face of a five year government bond. He could just borrow the money to fund the purchase in the money market. But if he buys the bond and immediately does a repo trade, then he receives the $100 million from the repo counterparty, which he can use to pay for the bond. As soon as he receives the bond he hands it over as collateral for the repo. This reduces his cost of funding because the repo rate, which is a secured rate, is lower than his bank's unsecured borrowing rate. The repo rate is less than the LIBOR rate because it tracks the risk-free rate, whereas the LIBOR rate reflects bank credit risk for unsecured borrowing and lending.

From the other side of the trade, reverse repo is a way to generate an extremely small and almost risk-free return. This is because reverse repo is a collateralized loan. Even if the counterparty is unable to pay back the loan the lender is left holding their collateral which is worth as much as or more than the loan principal. The lender can sell the collateral so they would lose nothing. Reverse repo is akin to a money market investment in that it is short-term, low-risk and low-return. When shorting a bond reverse repo provides a convenient way of laying hold of a bond. The repo rate reduces the cost of funding the bond purchase.

The repo rate depends on the bond. There are three types of published rate. The GENERAL COLLATERAL rate or GC rate is for government bonds. If you are doing a repo trade on government bonds then you would pay the general collateral rate, because you do not care about the particular bond you get as collateral as long as it is government quality. Then there are particular rates for corporate bonds depending on the credit quality of the issuer and the liquidity of the bond. And finally if a bond is in very high demand for repo it is said to be "on SPECIAL". The greater the demand for a bond the lower the repo rate. This is because the person borrowing the bond as loan collateral is willing to forgo some interest to get hold of the bond. In extreme cases the repo rate can even become negative. For the USD repo market the GC rate historically tracks the Federal Funds Target Rate, usually trading about ten basis points lower.

5.11 Combining and Decomposing Bond Risk

Bonds are rather crude instruments in that they carry several types of risk, such as interest rate risk, credit risk and liquidity risk. Investors demanded more targeted instruments that distilled different parts of a bond's risk and return. In this section we give a few examples where we combine and separate the cash flows of different instruments in a sort of "asset algebra". If we can reconstruct the cash flows of a complex instrument with simple instruments that can be priced we can use the law of one price to assign a value to the complex instrument. If we want to hedge the risk of the complex instrument we can use a portfolio of the simple instruments to put on or lift our hedge. So we can see that asset algebra is useful for pricing and risk control.

As an example we will look at what happens when we are long a fixed coupon bond and short a floater from the same issuer. The two bonds have the same principal and the same maturity. Firstly the principals cancel, so on the issue date the principal we pay for the fixed coupon bond we receive for selling the floater. At the maturity date the principals cancel again when we receive our principal for the fixed coupon and pay back the principal for the floater. What remains in between issue and maturity date are positive, fixed coupon payments and negative, floating coupon payments indexed off LIBOR. The risks are roughly as shown in Table 5.4.

In a word-equation this would be as follows,

$$\text{Fixed Coupon Bond} - \text{Floater} = \text{Interest Rate Swap (Receiver)}$$

	Credit Risk	Interest Rate Risk	Cash Flows
Long Fixed Coupon	$+C$	$+I$	
Short Floater	$-C$	0	
Total	0	$+I$	

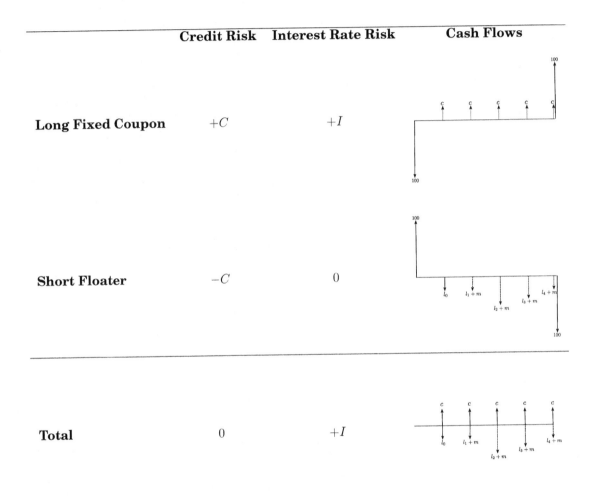

Table 5.4: Risk composition of a fixed coupon bond, floater and interest rate swap.

The fixed and floating bonds must be from the same issuer and have the same maturities. When we do an asset swap we convert a fixed coupon bond into a synthetic floater by rearranging this equation

$$\text{Floater} = \text{Fixed Coupon Bond} + \text{IRS (Payer)}$$

We can also decompose a bond into its two major risk components, a credit default swap and an interest rate swap.

$$\text{Fixed Coupon Bond} = \text{CDS (sell protection)} + \text{IRS (Receiver)}$$

This leads to the basis trade where we can harvest a mis-pricing in the spread of a synthetic CDS and the asset swap margin of a bond. In this trade we buy a fixed coupon bond and pay away the fixed coupon by entering a payer's interest rate swap and pay away the credit risk by buying a CDS on the issuer by doing the following re-arrangement of the formula

$$\text{Fixed Coupon Bond} + \text{CDS (buy protection)} + \text{IRS (Payer)} = 0$$

Here we have bought a bond, so we are receiving its fixed coupon and exposed to its credit risk. So we pay away the fixed coupon with the payer's swap and pay away the credit risk with the credit default swap. In theory we should have a flat trade with exposure to neither interest rate risk nor credit risk. In practice there are relative differences in the credit spread of a bond, as measured by its asset swap margin, and the credit default swap spread. The difference between an issuer's credit default swap spread and one of its issued bond's asset swap margin and is known as the credit BASIS.

$$\text{Credit Basis} = \text{CDS spread} - \text{ASM}$$

This combination of buying a bond, hedging credit risk with a credit default swap and hedging interest rate risk with an interest rate swap, which is an arb trade that harvests a situation in which credit basis is negative, is known as a NEGATIVE BASIS TRADE. If the credit basis were positive, which occurs when CDS spread is greater than asset swap margin then we reverse the trade and it is called a POSITIVE BASIS TRADE. The conditions for doing the negative and positive basis trade are as follows:

Basis	Bond	IR Swap	CDS
CDS spread < ASM, negative basis	Buy	Payer	Buy credit protection
CDS spread > ASM, positive basis	Short	Receiver	Sell credit protection

A useful way to think about these basis trades is in terms of what you would like to receive. If payments on CDS credit protection are high then you would like to receive those payments so you will sell CDS credit protection and hedge by shorting the bond (positive basis trade). If the credit risk premium, or ASM, paid in bond coupon is high then you would like to receive that bond premium so you will buy the bond and hedge by buying CDS credit protection (negative basis trade).

5.12 Bond Futures

A bond offers the investor a package of risks and reward. In return for interest and credit risk the investor receives an income in the form of coupon payments. Buying a bond requires tying up a lot of capital, and the market for some bonds can be quite illiquid. It can also be difficult to short a bond because this involves borrowing the bond in the repo market and not all market participants are equipped with the infrastructure to play in the repo market. Bond futures are used to get positive or negative exposure to government bond price risk, and indirectly interest rate risk, without having to invest a large amount of capital or taking on any credit risk. All that has to be paid upfront is the initial margin, then a continual set of payments into and out of the margin account as the future is marked to market daily due to fluctuations in price. Whereas shorting a bond is complicated by having to borrow bonds through reverse repo transactions it is as easy to be long a bond future as short. The US Treasury bond futures market has several underlying maturities giving exposure to bonds across the term structure. This is useful for hedging a fixed income portfolio with a wide range of maturities or for taking positions based on views about changes in the shape of the yield curve.

Bond futures have government bonds as their underlying securities and they are available for sovereign debt of any country with an active money market, such as the United States and the eurozone. Like any futures contract bond futures are traded on an exchange, which means that they have no counterparty risk. They have identifiers that depend on the underlying Treasury bond and the expiry date (see Table 5.5 for a list of tickers). Expiry dates occur on a quarterly cycle:

Expiry Month	March	June	September	December
Month Code	H	M	U	Z

The maturities that are available for US Treasury futures are:

Maturity	Two Year	Three Year	Five Year	Ten Year	Long Bond (30 year)
Ticker	TU	3Y	FV	TY	US

As an example we will use the TYU9 contract which is the US Treasury ten year note contract (hence "TY" in the ticker) traded on the Chicago Mercantile Exchange and expiring in September (code "U") 2009 (code "9"). The important dates in the life of a bond future are illustrated in Figure 5.20. The TYU9 contract has a trading period of just over a year starting June 20, 2008 and ending on September 21, 2009 but most trading takes place in the last four months after the previous contract TYM9 expires in June 2009. Almost all contracts are closed by trading the offsetting contract before the last trade date. If a contract is not closed before the last trade date the open position must be physically settled in the delivery month. In phyical settlement those short the contract deliver an appropriate face value of Treasury bonds to the those long the contract. For US and UK bond futures the contract is settled on any business day in the DELIVERY MONTH, because traditionally futures contracts were for delivery of agricultural products and spreading out delivery times avoided congestion. For

Bund futures delivery occurs on one day in the delivery month. The short has to give notice of delivery before delivery occurs and this notification must occur between the first and last delivery notice dates. For the TYU9 contract the important dates are:

Trade Date		First Notice	Delivery Date	
First	Last		First	Last
Jun 20, 2008	Sep 21, 2009	Aug 31, 2009	Sep 1, 2009	Sep 30, 2009

A bond future differs from other futures because of the complexity of bonds. It is easy to define an interest rate future because the underlying forward deposit has relatively few attributes, such as notional amount, index rate, term, and day count convention. Having a simple underlying means that it is easy to standardize interest rate futures. The same is true of commodity futures which are standardized by setting out the purity, quality and quantity of the commodity that must be delivered. For bonds however there are a lot of moving parts. Bond futures have government bonds as their underlying so the issuer is standardized. But bonds can have a variety of coupons and maturity dates, so how are these standardized? The solution is to define a fictional NOMINAL BOND with a standard coupon and maturity date. For example the CME 10 year bond future specifies the nominal bond as being a US Treasury 10 year 6% coupon bond. On the delivery date it is extremely unlikely that there will be a bond with a maturity of exactly 10 years and a coupon of exactly 6%. The exchange therefore allows some leeway in terms of maturity (between $6\frac{1}{2}$ and 10 years from the first day of the delivery month). This in turn means that there are a handful of treasuries that can be delivered by the person who is short the contract, and where there is choice there is optionality. The short (a name for the person who is short the contract) will choose to deliver the bond that is cheapest, or the CHEAPEST TO DELIVER (CTD) bond.

If a bond future is physically settled the invoice price paid by the long to the short is not simply the last traded price of the contract. The price paid for the bond depends on the futures settlement price but also depends on the bond chosen by the short from the basket of deliverable bonds. A delivered bond with a very high coupon should have a higher invoice price than a bond with a low coupon and a bond with a longer maturity date should have a higher invoice price than a bond with a short maturity. So the exchange defines a price adjustment factor that compensates for coupon and maturity called the CONVERSION FACTOR. Because the nominal bond has a coupon of 6% this is the yardstick by which the coupon of the delivered bond is measured. The conversion factor is defined by calculating the price of the delivered note with par value of $1 and a yield to maturity of 6%. And as with any bond we have to add accrued interest. If the coupon is c, maturity time is T and the underlying bond is semi-annually compounded the conversion factor (from Equation 5.2 on page 175) is

$$\text{Conversion Factor} = \sum_{i=1}^{N} \frac{\frac{c}{2}}{\left(1 + \frac{0.06}{2}\right)^{2t_i}} + \frac{1}{\left(1 + \frac{0.06}{2}\right)^{2T}},$$

and the invoice price is

$$P_{\text{invoice}} = F_{\text{settle}} \times \text{Conversion Factor} + \text{Accrued Interest}.$$

The definition of conversion factor satisfies our expectations about what is fair. The value of a bond with a coupon of exactly 6% and yield to maturity of 6% would be, by definition, $1 so the conversion factor would be 1 as the delivered bond would match the nominal bond. If the coupon is greater than 6% and the yield to maturity is 6% then the value of the delivered bond will be greater than 1, so the conversion factor will boost the invoice price above the futures settlement price. Conversely if the coupon is less than 6% the conversion factor will be less than 1. Maturity increases the value of the conversion factor as we would expect because if two bonds have the same coupon the one with greater maturity will have greater value.

With any forward or future the difference between the spot price and the forward price is called the basis. The basis is simply the cost of buying the underlying and carrying the position through time until delivery. In the case of a bond future the cost is the interest paid to fund the invoice price paid to buy the govvie bond for delivery and the benefit is the coupon received while holding the bond. The cost of funding for a government bond will depend on the repo rate because the bond can be lent in the repo market. This leads to the definition of carry basis as the cost minus the benefit of holding the deliverable bond.

$$
\begin{aligned}
\text{Carry Basis} \ &= \ \text{Funding Cost} - \text{Coupon Benefit} \\
&= \ \text{Dirty Price} \times r\text{repo} \times \frac{d}{365} - \text{Face} \times \frac{d}{365}
\end{aligned}
$$

GROSS BASIS is the difference today between the clean price of the bond and the price paid if the bond were delivered to settle the futures contract.

$$
\text{Gross Basis} = \text{Clean Price} - F_{\text{settle}} \times \text{Conversion Factor}
$$

NET BASIS is the gross basis adjusted for cost of carry until some delivery date in the future. In other words the net basis incorporates the costs and benefits of buying the delivery bond today and holding it until delivery in the future.

$$
\begin{aligned}
\text{Net Basis} \ &= \ \text{Gross Basis} - \text{Carry Basis} \\
&= \ \text{Bond Price} - F_{\text{settle}} \times \text{Conversion Factor} - \text{Funding Cost} + \text{Coupon Benefit}
\end{aligned}
$$

Consider the cash flows if we are short the futures contract and we buy a bond today to deliver into the futures contract on the delivery date. Firstly we have to pay for the bond today, and we pay the invoice or dirty price. On the delivery date we receive payment for our bond of the future settlement price adjusted by the conversion factor. The cash flows are like a zero coupon bond. If we pay B for the bond today and receive S when we settle the futures contract at delivery time t then we can define the rate of return as $\frac{S-B}{B}\frac{1}{t}$. The factor $\frac{1}{t}$ simply annualizes the rate. This rate is called the implied repo rate because this transaction is rather like a reverse repo where we lend money and take a bond as collateral. We also have to incorporate any coupon that we pick up between today and the delivery date by rolling it up into F. Expressed more

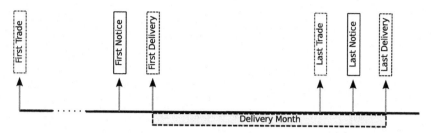

Figure 5.20: Bond future time-line of important dates.

Contract	Ticker	Issuer	Original Term	Remaining Term FDDM	Remaining Term LDDM	Tick Size	Price Change Per Tick	Coupon	Exchange
US 2y Note	TUU9	UST	< 5y3m	T>1y9m	T<2y	$\frac{1}{64}$	$15.625	6	CME
US 3y Note	3YU9	UST	<5y3m	T>2y9m	T<3y	$\frac{1}{64}$	$15.625	6	CME
US 5y Note	FVU9	UST	<5y3m	T>4y2m		$\frac{1}{128}$	$7.8125	6	CME
US 10y Note	TYU9	UST		6.5y<T<10y		$\frac{1}{64}$	$15.625	6	CME
US Long Bond	USU9	UST		call >15y, T>15y		$\frac{1}{64}$	$15.625	6	CME
Canadian 10y	CNU9	CT		8y<T<10.5y		0.01%	CAD 10	6	CDE
Long Gilt	G U9	UKT		8.75y<T<13y		0.01%	£10	6	Euronext
Euro-Schatz	DUU9	FDR/SC		1.75y<T<2.25y		0.005%	€5	6	Eurex
Euro-Bobl	OEU9	FDR/SC		4.5y<T<5.5y		0.01%	€10	6	Eurex
Euro-Bund	RXU9	FDR/SC		8.5y<T<10.5y		0.01%	€10	6	Eurex
Euro-Buxl 30y	UBU9	FDR/SC		24y<T<35y		0.02%	€20	4	Eurex
Swiss Federation	FBU9	SC		8y<T<13y		0.01%	CHF 10	6	Eurex
Spanish 10y	NTU9	TP		7.5y<T<10.5y		0.01%	€10	4	MEFF

Table 5.5:
Abbreviations: UST is US Treasury, FDR is Federal Republic of Germany, SC is Swiss Confederation, TP is Tesoro Público, FDDM/LDDM is first/last day of delivery month.

accurately the implied repo rate is

$$\text{Implied Repo} = \frac{F \times CF + AI_{\text{deliv}} + \text{coupon received} - DP_{\text{today}}}{DP_{\text{today}}} \times \frac{360}{\text{days}_{\text{deliv}}}$$

Exercise 40 *It is October 9th, 2009 and the FVZ9 contract (US Treasury five year note expiring in December 2009) is trading at 116-00+. The cheapest to deliver bond is the $1\frac{7}{8}\%$ Treasury maturing on February 28th 2014 which is trading at 99-00+. The conversion factor for this bond is 0.8499. Find the gross basis, carry basis and net basis of this bond assuming that delivery will occur in 89 days time on January 6th, 2010.*

Sovereign	Name	Bill	Note	Bond	Issuer
United States	US Treasuries	T-bill	T-note	T-bond	Bureau of the Public Debt
Japan	JGBs	T-bill	JGB	JGB	Ministry of Finance (MoF)
Germany	Bunds	Bubill, Schätze	Bobl	Bund	Finanzagentur GmbH
United Kingdom	Gilts	Short gilt	Medium gilt	Long gilt	UK Debt Management Office
France	OATs	BTF	BTAN	OAT	Agence France Trésor
Spain	Bonos	Letras del Tesoro	Bonos	Obligaciones del Estado	Spanish Public Treasury
Italy	BTPs	BOT	CTZ	BTP	Dipartimento del Tesoro

Table 5.6: Government bond names and issuers.

5.13 Yield Curves and Credit Risk

Governments need money to run their country and this is partly funded through taxes and partly through issuing debt in the form of government bonds. People usually call these bonds GOVVIES or more formally SOVEREIGN DEBT. The largest sovereign bond issuers are shown in Table 5.6. Companies also need money that they can obtain by issuing shares, taking out loans, or issuing CORPORATE BONDS. Traders usually just say that they trade "govvies" or trade "credit". The cheapest cost of borrowing in any currency is usually that of the government. Banks are usually next in terms of cost of funding because their lending business is predicated on their ability to borrow more cheaply than the rate at which they lend. To get an idea of the cost of borrowing for a particular length of time and for a particular issuer, it is useful to use yield curves. Figure 5.21 shows an imaginary set of yield curves. In order to build each curve we would plot the remaining maturity of every bond against its yield to maturity. Then we could draw a line that best fits a particular issuer or group of issuers. In Figure 5.21 we have shown the govvie curve, which carries the credit risk of the government, the swap curve which carries bank credit risk, and then a set of corporate bond curves broken down by credit rating. The lower the credit rating the greater the risk of default, the greater the cost of funding, and the greater the yield for that curve. Hence single B rated corporate bonds have the greatest cost of funding and triple A rated corporate bonds have the lowest cost of funding of the corporates. Banks are riskier than governments so the swap curve sits above the govvie curve.

Time to maturity also affects the yield of a bond. Lending for a longer time carries greater risk than lending for a short time so longer dated bonds have a greater yield than shorter dated bonds. For example US Treasury two year notes historically yield about 25 basis points more than short-term T-bills to compensate investors for the extra risk in the form of price volatility. The extra 25 basis points are called TERM PREMIUM and term premium is one of the reasons why, most of the time, yield curves are upward sloping. There are other explanations for the upward slope, such as greater investor demand for shorter-term bonds and greater liquidity for shorter-term bonds. The shape of the yield curve, whether it is upward or downward sloping, is called the TERM STRUCTURE OF INTEREST RATES. If markets expect a sharp drop in rates in future then the term structure would be downward sloping. For long-dated bonds at the LONG END of the yield curve inflation becomes a concern. Inflation would erode the value of an income that is fixed for a very long period of time so yields at the long end price in expectations about inflation.

The curves for corporate issuers broken down by credit rating in Figure 5.21 are called CREDIT CURVES. If you run a company that has been given a BB rating by the credit rating agencies, and you want to raise capital by issuing a 10 year bond, then you can look up the coupon you will have to pay on the bond using your credit curve. If today's credit curves look like Figure 5.21 then you know you will have to pay a coupon of about 5%. If you were to be upgraded to AAA then your cost of funding for your 10 year bond would drop to less than 1%. This is why credit ratings are important: they determine the cost of borrowing for an issuer. The reason why BB companies pay a higher coupon is that they are more likely to miss their coupon payments and become bankrupt, so investors demand a higher return for this higher risk. The credit-risky curves that sit on top of the government curve are an embodiment of the trade-off between risk and return. It is possible to create finer-grained credit curves by breaking down the universe of issued bonds by currency or by country of issue or by sector. For some issuers that issue a lot of bonds it is even possible to build a single ISSUER YIELD CURVE.

Models often require a risk-free rate, and this has to come from somewhere. Despite the fact that the government curve carries some credit risk the risk-free rate is often taken from the government bond curve. As models are often built by investment banks to price their instruments another choice is to use a combination of the interest rate swap curve, the LIBOR curve (up to 12 months) and interest rate futures. A bank may ask its counterparties for collateral in order to reduce its credit risk and for these safer deals the bank may discount cash flows with the overnight indexed swap curve. Setting aside doctrinal issues about the meaning of risk-free, it is important to have a BENCHMARK CURVE. Once we have a benchmark we can start to measure credit risk as a SPREAD TO BENCHMARK.

The job of an originator in the investment banking department is to raise capital for companies through issuing bonds. The expertise of an originator, apart from organizing an entourage of lawyers, traders and salespeople in a bond issue, is to advise the client on the coupon that their bond will pay. This will be done by looking at the appropriate issuer curve based on the company's rating, industry, currency and market sector. A debt capital originator also provides advice on the maturity of the bonds issued (equity has no maturity as it is perpetual capital that is never repaid, hence maturities are not relevant to equity capital markets). The coupon the originators produce as part of their issuance advice is usually expressed in terms of a benchmark. So they may say that a 10 year bond has been issued relative to a benchmark Treasury bond plus 200 basis points. The benchmark bond will be a recently issued government bond with a maturity that matches the corporate bond being issued as closely as possible. In this case we would be looking for a Treasury bond with a roughly 10 year maturity. The 200 basis points, or 2%, is a measure of the compensation required by investors to take the credit risk of that company relative to the benchmark government bond. This compensation is called GOVERNMENT SPREAD more informally SPREAD TO GOVVIE or GOVVIE SPREAD.

Another benchmark that we can use is the bank credit curve. This is a combina-

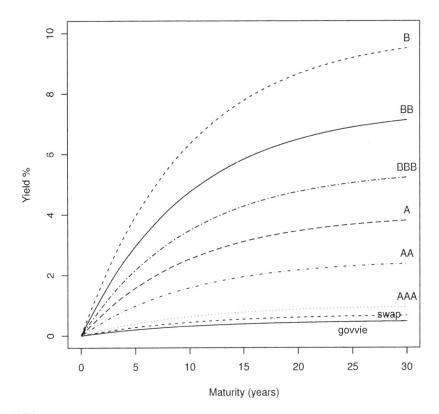

Figure 5.21:
Issuer yield curves showing cost of funding based on credit rating and bond maturity.

tion of the LIBOR curve and the interest rate swap curve as these carry bank credit risk. So another measure of credit risk is variously called SPREAD TO LIBOR, SWAP SPREAD or ASSET SWAP MARGIN (ASM). The least woolly of these definitions is ASM. Asset swap margin is a measure of how much additional credit risk a bond carries above bank credit risk. Asset swap margin is usually smaller than government spread because banks are riskier than the government. If a bond trades SUB-LIBOR then it carries less credit risk than banks. The only bonds that used to be sub-LIBOR before the Credit Crisis were government bonds, but after the Credit Crisis banks were downgraded and were perceived as being risky. This meant that the few remaining companies that were still rated AAA in 2009/2010 typically traded sub-LIBOR. They were, quite literally, perceived by the market as being safer than banks. For details of how to calculate various forms of credit spread with examples see Section 7.2 on page 296. The spread between the government bond curve and the swap curve is called the TED spread. This used to stand for Treasury-Eurodollar but as the swap market became liquid the meaning of the name shifted to refer to swaps rather than futures. The TED spread reflects credit quality difference between banks and the government but is also driven to some degree by the issuance of new debt by the Treasury.

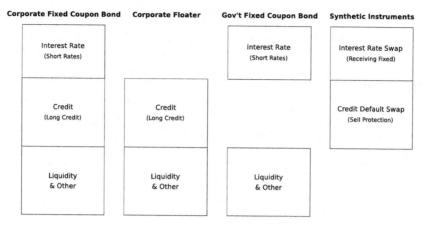

Figure 5.22:
Risk decomposition for a corporate bond, a corporate floater, and a govvie.

Figure 5.22 is a diagrammatic comparison of risk for three types of bond and their synthetic counterparts. Synthetic means that the instrument is unfunded, so we pay nothing up front and receive no lump sum back at expiry as we would for a bond. First we have a corporate fixed coupon bond that has a combination of interest rate, credit and liquidity risk. Second we have a floater issued by the same corporate that has (almost) no interest rate risk but carries exactly the same credit risk and liquidity risk as the fixed coupon bond. Third we have a government issued fixed coupon bond with the same duration as the corporate fixed coupon bond. The govvie has no credit risk but carries exactly the same interest rate risk and liquidity risk as the corporate fixed coupon bond. Finally we have "pure" risk instruments: an interest rate swap that carries the interest rate risk of the corporate and government fixed coupon bonds and a credit default swap that carries the credit risk of the corporate fixed coupon bond and corporate floater. This shows why it is possible to hedge away interest rate risk by entering a payer's swap and hedge away credit risk by buying CDS credit protection.

5.14 Convertible Bonds

Occasionally life on Earth, for one reason or another, is almost wiped out. Some species flourish after such an event, and in the plant world this is the ferns. The fossil record shows surges in the number of fern spores after mass extinction events and paleontologists call this a FERN SPIKE. We can see why fern spikes occur in the present day. When a volcano erupts and wipes its flanks clean of vegetation the first new colonizing plants are, as you have probably guessed, ferns. By providing food and shelter for insects and other animals ferns pave the way for other forms of life and help the ecosystem bootstrap itself to recovery.

Convertible bonds are the ferns of the fixed income world. While economies flourish and money is cheap and stock prices rise convertible bonds bide their time. But when disaster strikes, stock prices plunge and the cost of borrowing money through bond issues soars, converts come into their own. Convertibles are bonds that give the investor the right to convert their bond into a certain number of equities. In other words there is a call option embedded within the bond. If the equity price starts to rise then the investor will convert their bond into equity and benefit from all the upside. If the equity price falls the investor has the bond as a safety net which guarantees they will receive their investment in full at maturity. And while the investor waits for the equity price to increase they receive a coupon that is a little bit greater than the dividend paid by the stock. So when the investor buys the convert they are also buying an embedded call option on the stock. The issuer is selling a bond to raise capital but they are also selling an option on their own stock. This means that the issuer can pay a smaller coupon than they would with a non-convertible bond and reduce their cost of funding. And as the embedded option value increases with the volatility of their stock the issuer actually profits from their own volatility. Issuing a convertible bond is a way for a company to monetize their own volatility.

Convertible bonds exhibit equity-like and bond-like behaviour. If the stock price is low the equity call option has a very small value and the bond-like behaviour of the convert comes to the fore. This bond-like behaviour is sensitivity to interest rates and credit risk. If interest rates go up the price of the convert drops and if interest rates go down the price of the convert increases. As with any bond there is the risk of default in which case the investor may lose all of the capital they invested. So the credit spread of the issuer affects the price of a convert. A large credit spread means a default is more likely and this decreases the value of the convert. And when stock prices are low the price of the convert is insensitive to the stock price. If the stock price increases then the convert shifts into equity-like behaviour. This means that it is no longer as sensitive to interest rates and credit spreads and much more sensitive to the stock price. For very high stock prices then the convert is extremely likely to be converted to equity so its price tracks the price of the stock. In the middle ground between high and low stock prices the convert exhibits more mixed behaviour, being sensitive to stock price, interest rates and credit spread. In order to make sense of such complicated behaviour there are some standard numbers that are useful. But there are also measures that are specific to converts, as summarized in Table 5.7.

Figure 5.23 shows how the value of a convertible varies with stock price. When the stock price is low the convertible falls back onto its bond floor and starts to behave like a bond. This means it has almost no sensitivity to stock price movements and delta is roughly zero. The price of a convertible in the bond-like state is sensitive to interest rates and the issuer's credit spread just like a regular bond. Then as stock prices increase the convertible enters a region where it behaves both like a bond and like an equity. Delta in this "hybrid" state is about 50% and the bond is still sensitive to interest rates and the issuer's credit spread. As the stock price increases further the convertible exhibits equity-like behaviour. In the equity-like state the convertible becomes insensitive to interest rates but starts to track the equity price. If the issuer is close to bankruptcy then the convertible will be in the "busted" state where share

Conversion price	Specified in the bond prospectus and used to calculate the conversion ratio.	P_{conv}
Bond price	Price at which the convertible trades in the bond market	B
Bond coupon	Fixed coupon payment rate	c
Share dividend	Last dividend payment on share	d
Share price	Price at which the share trades in the equity market	S
Face value	Par value of convertible bond that is received at maturity if not converted	P_{face}
Conversion ratio	Number of shares into which each bond converts	$r_{conv} = \frac{P_{face}}{P_{conv}}$
Parity	Value of converted shares given today's share price	$S_{parity} = r_{conv} \times S$
Conversion premium	Bond market price expressed as a percentage of parity	$100 \times \frac{B - S_{parity}}{S_{parity}}$
Bond floor	Value of bond component of convertible with yield taken from issuer's comparable maturity non-convertible issues	$\sum_i \frac{c}{\left(1 + \frac{y}{f}\right)^{ft_i}} + \frac{100}{\left(1 + \frac{y}{f}\right)^{fT}}$
Bond running yield	Coupon return on bond investment	$y_{running} = \frac{c}{B}$
Share dividend yield	Dividend return on equity investment	$y_{share} = \frac{d}{S}$
Yield advantage	Difference between the running yield of the convertible and the dividend yield of the issuer's stock.	convert yield − stock dividend yield

Table 5.7: Attributes of a convertible bond.

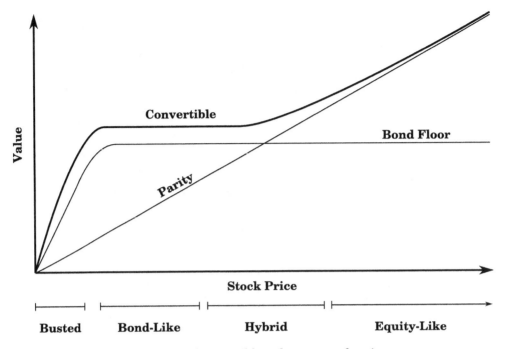

Figure 5.23: Convertible value vs. stock price.

prices are very low and the convertible price crashes through the bond floor. In other words the protection of the bond floor disappears when the issuer becomes distressed. This is precisely when you would like to have some protection of your capital and is one of the less attractive aspects of owning a convertible. However it is reassuring that historically few convertibles have entered the busted state.

As an example we will take a 15 year convertible bond issued by Adidas AG summarized in Table 5.8. The convertible was issued on October 8, 2003 with a coupon of 2.5% and a maturity date of October 8, 2018. The par value of this bond is €50,000 and its conversion price specified in the bond prospectus is €25.50. When the bond is trading at par this means that each bond converts into $\frac{50,000}{25.5}$ or 1960.7843 shares and this is the CONVERSION RATIO. The conversion ratio is not an even number, as is usually the case, and the conversion ratio for this convert remains at 1960.7843 until maturity. On August 24, 2009 Adidas stock was trading at €32.58. This gave a parity value for the convert of 1960.784359×32.58 which is €63,882.35. But this number is per €50,000 face of the bond and bond prices are usually quoted per €100 face. So we scale by a factor of $\frac{100}{50,000}$ to give a parity value of €127.76 per €100 face.

Once we have the parity value we would like to know how far above parity the bond is trading today, and this is called the CONVERSION PREMIUM, and we express the premium as a percentage. The convertible bond is trading today for €132.4728, so this is a little bit above parity, which is €127.76. The conversion premium is there-

Denomination	EUR 50,000
Issue size	EUR 400 million
Currency	Euro
Issue date	October 8, 2003
Maturity	October 8, 2018
Duration	15 years
Bond identification number (ISIN)	DE0009038968
Issue price	100%
Redemption price	100%
Coupon	2.5% payable annually in arrears
Conversion premium	40%
Conversion price	EUR 25.50

Table 5.8: Adidas convertible properties.

fore quite small: $100 \times \frac{132.4728 - 127.76}{127.76}$ or 3.68%. As the equity price increases and parity increases the convertible will start to behave like the underlying equity and the difference between parity and the convertible price decreases. So as the convertible becomes more equity-like the conversion premium decreases. The smaller the conversion premium the more likely it is that the convertible will be converted into equity. So for this bond we are on the cusp of equity prices for which conversion is likely. But there are good reasons not to convert immediately, such as the coupon and the option value. Typically the coupon of the convertible is greater than the dividend of the stock, and coupon must be paid otherwise the company faces bankruptcy. In contrast, dividend payments on equity can be cut completely without facing any legal penalty. This means that if we are confident that the stock price will remain high it is worth waiting until maturity to convert because by converting we would reduce our income. The yield of this bond is 1.89% on August 24, 2009 but the dividend yield of Adidas AG stock was just 1.53%. So the YIELD ADVANTAGE of the convertible is the difference of 0.352%. And the second we convert from bond to equity all of our call option value disappears, so it may pay to hold onto the convertible as long as possible. If the convertible is deeply in-the-money then the yield of the bond becomes meaningless, so to compare yield on the bond with dividend yield we would use RUNNING YIELD (also called CURRENT YIELD or INTEREST YIELD), which is the bond's coupon divided by its current market price.

Issuers often embed a CALL PROVISION into the convertible. This gives the issuer the right to force its convertible bond holders to choose whether they want their principal back or whether they would like shares before the bond matures. From the standpoint of the issuer this call provision makes a lot of sense. The reason why companies issue convertibles is that they provide a cheap form of funding. If the cost of funding has dropped then it is cheaper to refinance by recalling any convertible debt and issuing new bonds with lower coupons. The cost of funding will drop if the fortunes of the issuer are improving, its equity price is increasing and its credit rating is improving. And if its equity price is high then conversion will mean most investors choose to convert to stock. So instead of repaying investor principal the company issues new stock which costs almost nothing. This reduces the issuer's level of debt and increases the amount of equity on its balance sheet so reduces its leverage. The most important downside is that this may disgruntle existing investors whose shares will be diluted.

For a convertible investor call features are not advantageous. This is because the option embedded within the convertible has a value that scales up with time to maturity as this gives the equity more time to increase in value. If the convertible is callable by the issuer this decreases the maturity of the bond and its option value. Also by redeeming the bond early the investor loses out on coupon payments. So investors like to have a period during which a call cannot occur under any circumstance. This is HARD CALL PROTECTION or ABSOLUTE CALL PROTECTION. Often the documentation of a convertible bond includes the abbreviation "NC3" which means that the convertible has three year hard call protection and is "Not Callable" for three years. Once hard call protection disappears convertibles often have an extended period of call protection but protection is now conditional on certain events. These events are designed to be beneficial to the investor and to sweeten the pill of early redemption. This is called SOFT CALL PROTECTION or PROVISIONAL CALL PROTECTION. A common form of soft protection is to allow the issuer to call the bond only if the convertible has traded at a minimum conversion premium for a certain number of consecutive trading days. Another sweetener that may be attached to a convertible is a put feature. If a convertible bond is puttable this means that if the price of the bond drops significantly the investor can choose, on certain set dates, to get their par value back. The call and put features of the Adidas example are as shown in Table 5.9.

For the Adidas convertible the first date that a call can occur is October 2009. This is hard call protection that lasts from issue for the first six years of the life of the bond. But this convertible also has soft call protection because the call feature is then conditional on a trigger of the conversion premium reaching 130% and this protection lasts until October 2012. This soft protection is beneficial to investors because it guarantees a certain level of capital gain before the bond can be called. Because of the put feature the investor can also choose to put the bond back to the issuer at par on October 8, 2009, October 8, 2012 or October 8, 2015.

There are many variations on the standard convertible bond designed to make the structure fit the requirement of issuers and investors. A MANDATORY CONVERTIBLE is a convertible that forces conversion to equity at a fixed time in future. This takes all optionality out of the hands of the investor, and therefore carries a high coupon. But if an issuer has exhausted the equity market as a source of funding then it may issue a mandatory convertible. Until conversion the mandatory convertible will cost the issuer a sizeable rate of interest, but it defers dilution of equity until conversion occurs. Another variation is to take some of the coupon and defer its payment until maturity, so that instead of receiving a principal of 100 the investor receives a premium of 100 plus the deferred coupon. This is a PREMIUM REDEMPTION convertible bond. Taken to the extreme all of the coupon can be deferred until redemption in which case we have a ZERO COUPON CONVERTIBLE. Deferring payment of coupon until maturity is a benefit to the issuer and an increased risk to the investor.

Call protection	Contingent Protection	Put at Par
Hard non-call for 6 years; callable by the issuer, in whole but not in part from:	Convertible into shares:	Bondholders may redeem bonds at par value on Oct 8, 2009, Oct 8, 2012 or Oct 8, 2015 upon proper notification to the issuer. The bondholders may also redeem bonds at par upon a change of control event.
• October 8, 2009, to October 7, 2012, at Principal Amount plus accrued interest if Xetra quotation of the shares exceeds 130% of conversion price, for any 20 out of 35 trading days;	If at any time the stock trades above 110% of the conversion price for at least 20 trading days out of the last 30 trading days of any calendar quarter; The adidas AG share first traded above 110% (€ 28.05) of the conversion price of € 25.50 on more than 20 trading days within the last 30 trading days in the fourth quarter of 2004.	
• October 8, 2012, to October 7, 2015, at Principal Amount plus accrued interest if Xetra quotation of the shares exceeds 115% of conversion price, for any 20 out of 35 trading days; callable thereafter at Principal Amount plus accrued interest without conditions.	Consequently, bondholders have the right to convert their convertible bonds into equity since January 1, 2005.	
• Callable if less than 10% in aggregate amount of the bonds remain outstanding.		

Table 5.9: Adidas convertible optionality and call protection.

A CONTINGENT CONVERTIBLE (CoCo) is a convertible bond where conversion is triggered by an event. If the event is the tier 1 capital ratio falling below some threshold the CoCo is called an Enhanced Capital Note. A tier 1 capital threshold trigger offers a way for bank balance sheets to delever automatically during crises as some of their debt disappears from the balance sheet and reappears as loss-absorbing equity. Because these bonds may turn into equity and provide no optionality to the investor they would be expected to have a high coupon to compensate investors for the risk of conversion. Lloyds Banking Group in the United Kingdom used CoCo financing in 2009 to re-capitalize itself and to avoid the requirement for future bailouts by taxpayers. Some contingent convertibles do retain optionality for the investor and the trigger acts to reduce the probability of conversion by setting a price above the strike price that must be reached by the stock before conversion can occur. This feature was present in the Adidas 2003 bond above as "contingent protection". The Adidas share price had to trade above 110% (€28.05) of the conversion price of €25.50 on more than 20 trading days within the last 30 trading days before the shares could be converted. This occurred in the fourth quarter of 2004 and this triggered possible conversion after the beginning of 2005.

5.15 Covered Bonds

Bonds provide the reassurance that in the event of bankruptcy and liquidation of a firm's assets the bondholder is at the front of the queue for retrieving their capital. There is a form of bond that provides an even better guarantee called a COVERED BOND or SECURED BOND. In the event of liquidation covered bondholders have two claims: one on a pool of assets put aside exclusively for their bonds and secondly on the assets of the issuer. If selling off the pool of assets does not raise enough capital to repay the covered bondholders then they step into line with other senior bondholders. In the language of capital structure covered bonds rank *pari passu* (on the same level of seniority) with senior unsecured bonds.

The reason why issuers issue covered bonds is to lower their financing cost. If the issuer knows that they hold high quality assets and that they will continue to hold these assets for a long period of time then it may be worthwhile using those assets to secure a covered bond issue. This process may sound similar to the creation of mortgage backed securities and asset backed securities but it differs in some significant ways. For MBS and ABS the originator creates a special purpose vehicle (SPV), a separate legal entity, to which they sell their pool of assets. This means that if the originator goes bankrupt they have no claim on the pool of assets any more. The SPV and its assets are bankruptcy-remote from the originator. And this also means that for an ABS/MBS the assets no longer sit on the issuer's balance sheet. For a covered bond the pool of assets used to secure the bond still belong to the issuer and still sit on its balance sheet and the assets are called the COVER POOL. Furthermore it is the job of the issuer to maintain the quality of the pool of assets at all times, and it does so by continually changing assets in the cover pool to maintain its value in case of bankruptcy and liquidation.

Because covered bonds have an extra cushion protecting their capital they usually have a higher credit rating than other comparable bonds of the issuer. Typically covered bonds have AA or AAA ratings even though the issuer may have a credit rating several notches lower than AAA. During the Credit Crisis some banks used their higher quality assets to raise capital via covered bond issues. This was because they had suffered rating downgrades and needed some way to issue bonds with high credit ratings and low coupons. When a company announces that it is issuing covered bonds this may disgruntle existing bond holders because the high quality assets set aside for the cover pool are no longer available to repay the principal of other bond holders in the event of liquidation. The concept of covered bonds probably grew out of a type of bond issued in Prussia in the 18th century during the time of Frederick the Great. As a consequence of its long pedigree the covered bond market is very well established in Germany. German covered bonds secured by mortgages are called PFANDBRIEF (plural PFANDBRIEFE and pronounced with a silent "p") and are exceptional in that during their long history there has never been a default on a pfandbrief.

5.16 Inflation-Linked Bonds

Imagine that you have just retired and you have invested a lump sum of £1 million into government bonds that pay about 5%. Now you plan to live off your bond portfolio income of about £50,000 for the rest of your life. What could go wrong? If interest rates go up your bonds will drop in value but you probably don't care too much because you intend to hold those bonds until maturity anyway. Maybe as bonds mature you can reinvest the capital at a higher rate so this could even be good for you. But the real problem is that you may live for a long time (although some may not consider this to be a problem). If you live for a long time and the economy enters a period of severe inflation then that £50,000 may not cover your cost of living any longer. Pension funds are massive players in financial markets and have an appetite for inflation protection and consequently they are large players in the inflation-linked bond market. To satisfy this demand many governments around the World issue inflation-linked bonds. In the United States the Treasury issues TREASURY INFLATION PROTECTED SECURITIES (TIPS) and in the United Kingdom the Debt Management Office issues INFLATION-LINKED BONDS (ILB) or LINKERS. In Europe some bonds are linked to domestic inflation, denoted by the suffix "i" such as French OATi bonds, and others are linked to the Eurozone inflation denoted by the suffix "€i". Table 5.10 lists some of the larger issuers of inflation linked bonds with some of the attributes of those bonds.

Inflation is the steady increase in the value of goods, or seen another way it is a reduction in value of a currency. It is important to have some way of measuring inflation so governments pay statistical institutions to create an inflation index for their currency. In the United Kingdom there is the Retail Price Index (RPI) and Consumer Price Index (CPI), in the United States the main inflation index is also called the Consumer Price Index (CPI) and in Europe there is the Harmonised Index of Consumer Prices (HICP). Index linked bonds in the United States actually use a sub-index called CPI-U which is the CONSUMER PRICE INDEX FOR URBAN CONSUMERS. The way these indices are calculated is to define a basket of commonly bought goods that an "average" person buys. The basket of goods is supposed to track consumer spending

	Name	Floor	Index	Lag	Issued
USA	TIPS	Y	USA CPI-U	3m	1997
Canada	Canadian Real Return Bonds (CRRB)	Y	Canadian CPI	3m	1991
UK	Index-linked gilt (linker)	N	UK RPI	3m/8m	1981
France	OAT€i, BTAN€i	Y	HICP ex-tobacco	3m	2001
France	OATi	Y	French CPI	3m	1998
Italy	BTP€i	Y	HICP ex-tobacco	3m	1983
Germany	OBL€i	Y	HICP ex-tobacco	3m	2006
Sweden	SGBi	Y	Swedish CPI	3m	1994
Australia	Treasury Indexed Bond (TIB)	Y	Australian CPI	6m/12m ave.	1985
Japan	JGBi	N	Japanese Core CPI ex-fresh-food	3m	2004

Table 5.10: Inflation linked bonds.

habits and so includes costs for things such as food, transportation, clothes, entertainment, and housing. Once the basket is defined its cost is monitored and recorded to see how it varies over time. By comparing the cost of the basket on two dates, it is possible to work out an inflation value. In the UK the OFFICE FOR NATIONAL STATISTICS (ONS) calculates the RPI and CPI by collecting 120,000 prices per month on a basket of 650 goods. Of course the basket contents change over time as spending habits change so the ONS updates the basket each year to reflect these changes. In 2004 they started to include digital cameras and shortly afterward flat-screen TVs were added to the basket when these became a common part of many British households.

When we talk about inflation it is important to distinguish between two types of return. If we put money on deposit in a bank account and receive a fixed 5% rate of return, this is a NOMINAL RETURN. If the price of goods generally, as measured by something like the CPI, is increasing by 3% then this is eroding the true value of our money in terms of its buying power. To adjust our rate of return to reflect the effect of inflation we would subtract the rate of inflation. Our 5% less the 3% inflation gives a return of just 2%. This inflation-adjusted rate of return is the REAL RETURN. People seldom consider the effect of inflation on their wealth and instead hang onto a belief in the absolute value of money, a phenomenon called MONEY ILLUSION. If we have a nominal rate of return r_n and an inflation rate of r_i then when we invest $1 after one year we will have

$$\frac{1 + r_n}{1 + r_i} \simeq 1 + r_n - r_i,$$

where the approximation is derived using Taylor expansions of the numerator and denominator (see Section 3.8 on page 119). This leads to the definition of real return r_r as $r_r \simeq r_n - r_i$, and this is called the FISHER EQUATION after the economist Irving Fisher who was a pioneer in the formalization of our understanding of inflation. As a word-equation we could say that

real rate = nominal rate − inflation rate.

What we would like, going back to our hypothetical role as a retiree, is to link our bond payments to the inflation index. If the inflation index increases then so should our payments in direct proportion. If we own an inflation-linked bond then we would expect both our coupon payments and our principal that is returned at maturity to be scaled by inflation in some way. Each country varies in the precise way that they inflate their cash flows. For inflation-linked gilts the coupon and principal payments depend on the INDEX RATIO,

$$\text{Index Ratio} = \frac{\text{Reference RPI on cash flow date}}{\text{Reference RPI on issue date}}.$$

So if the reference RPI when a bond is issued is 110 and the reference RPI on the cash flow date is 120 then the index ratio is $\frac{120}{110}$ or 1.091 and the coupon is scaled up in value by 9.1%. A complication arises because the reference RPI used has an INDEXATION LAG. This means that the reference RPI for the first calendar day of a month is the RPI for the calendar month three months earlier. So the reference RPI for August is the RPI figure for May. For dates within a month the reference RPI is found by linear interpolation between the beginning of the month and the RPI at the start of the next month. So for example

$$\text{Ref RPI}_{\text{August 21}} = \text{Ref RPI}_{\text{August 1}} + \frac{21}{31}\left(\text{Ref RPI}_{\text{September 1}} - \text{Ref RPI}_{\text{August 1}}\right).$$

Both coupon and principal payments are scaled by the reference RPI on the date on which they are paid. Since the coupon on UK index linkers is semi-annual the payments for a nominal coupon of c are calculated as

$$\text{coupon payment} = \frac{c}{2} \times \text{index ratio}_{\text{coupon payment date}}.$$

Principal repayments are scaled in the same way. So if the face value of the linker is £100 then

$$\text{redemption payment} = 100 \times \text{index ratio}_{\text{maturity date}}.$$

From the point of view of the government issuing inflation-linked notes is a gamble on their own ability to keep inflation in check. When first issued inflation-linked bonds have a smaller coupon compared with comparable non inflation-linked notes and so provide cheaper capital. But if inflation rises rapidly the cost to the government of paying the coupon and principal of its linkers becomes punitive. Inflation-linked bond investors do not share the government's confidence in its ability to control inflation and take a bet that inflation will increase more than the rate priced into the linker. For each inflation-linked bond there is an INFLATION BREAKEVEN which is the amount by which inflation would have to increase to make the yield on the linker equal to the yield on a comparable non inflation-linked government bond. So index-linked bonds are doubly important instruments as they help retirees and pension funds protect their capital from inflation and they punish government when it fails to keep inflation in check.

An important difference between UK linkers and US TIPS is that the US Treasury guarantees the principal of each TIPS. This means that if there is deflation during the life of an inflation linked note a UK linker may pay an investor back less than the $100 principal that they paid originally. The US Treasury, however, guarantees the principal of $100 even if the inflation adjusted amount would be less than $100. During periods of deflation it may make sense for a TIPS investor to hold onto their bonds until maturity because their principal is protected. This very attractive feature of TIPS, and most other inflation-linked bonds is called a DEFLATION FLOOR. Both UK linkers and Japanese index-linked bonds are unusual in not having a deflation floor.

5.17 Mortgage Backed Securities

Mortgage backed securities (MBS) are any type of bond that is secured by mortgages. The MBS market is based purely in the United States but the MBS model for financing home purchases has spread across the world. The simplest type of MBS is called a mortgage pass-through. To gain familiarity with pass-throughs we can summarize their life cycle. An MBS begins with the demand to buy houses. People usually require loans to purchase a house, so they get a mortgage. A mortgage is a long-term, typically low-cost loan collateralized by the house being purchased. The loan has a lower rate of interest than borrowing money outright because any failure of the borrower to pay the mortgage will result in reposession and sale of the house. In this way the lender is reducing their credit risk by effectively owning the house until the mortgage is repaid. This kind of collateralized borrowing is similar to repo.

The story could and sometimes does end here: a bank lends money to its customers to buy houses and the home owners pay interest on their loans until they are all either repaid or in default. But the problem is that the bank itself has to borrow money to pay for the homes. The bank borrows at a lower rate than it is charging the customer and so makes a net interest rate margin. The bank is taking a considerable risk because if customers default on their mortgages it may not be able to recoup all of its losses. Also each time it issues new mortgages it is growing its balance sheet. The mortgage is a loan and appears on the balance sheet as an asset. The money borrowed to finance the mortgage appears as a liability and the more it borrows the more leveraged the bank becomes, as leverage is the ratio of equity capital to borrowed capital. A bank cannot grow their balance sheet indefinitely because this increases their leverage, increases their risk and will eventually breach their capital ratio.

One solution is to package up the mortgages and sell them off. This way the bank is no longer taking any risk of mortgage defaults and the mortgages no longer appear on its balance sheet. The drawback is the the bank no longer makes money from net interest margin. Instead they earn a fee for arranging the mortgages called an ORIGINATION FEE. Before approving a mortgage the originator should check the credit worthiness of the borrower and the value of the house they are buying which will be the collateral for the loan. Once the pool of loans is formed the originator can apply to one of the Federal Agencies for a guarantee. In order to get the guarantee the pool of mortgages has to pass certain criteria on the credit-worthiness of the borrower, as measured by something like a FICO score, loan to value (size of loan divided by value of house) and size of mortgage. For many mortgages this guarantee is provided by Fannie Mae (the Federal National Mortgage Association) or Freddie Mac (the Federal

Home Loan Mortgage Corporation). Ginnie Mae (Government National Mortgage Association) guarantees mortgages of MBS issuers but does not issue securities itself and is targeted at low income households and mortgages of the Veterans Administration and Federal Housing Agency. See Table 5.11 for a list of entities involved in the MBS market.

MBS that do not satisfy the criteria to be guaranteed by government agencies are called private label MBS. For example if the size of the mortgage exceeds the limit of $370,000 dollars then it is called a Jumbo loan. If the home owner does not provide documentary evidence for their income the mortgage is Alt-A. If the home owner has a low credit score then the mortgage is sub-prime.

MBS exhibit an ugly trait when rates fluctuate. With simple fixed coupon bonds we benefit from positive convexity. In keeping with most bonds when rates go up the price of MBS decrease and when rates go down the price of MBS increase. But unlike fixed coupon bonds whose positive convexity reduces our loss when rates increase MBS PREPAYMENT has the unleasant effect of increasing our losses more than we would expect if the price-yield relationship were linear. And when rates decrease and we would benefit from a greater than expected increase in value due to convexity for a normal fixed coupon bond we will see that prepayment reduces our gains. This is called NEGATIVE CONVEXITY. The reason why we see negative convexity is summarized as follows:

Rates	MBS Investor	Mortgage Payer	Prepayment Rate	Duration
Go up	Investor wants to get out of their fixed investment and buy bonds with higher yield.	Home owners do not refinance as rates are now high.	Decreases	Increases
Go down	Investor wants to keep receiving their high coupon as newly issued bonds have a lower coupon.	Home owners refinance to take advantage of low rates.	Increases	Decreases

In the US mortgage market there is no penalty for refinancing a mortgage. So when rates drop people REFINANCE to take advantage of the low rates. From the point of view of the MBS this refinancing is seen as a prepayment of principal. So when rates drop the prepayment rate of MBS increases. When rates are high home owners no longer refinance and hold onto their low-rate mortgages and consequently prepayment rates decrease. MBS duration increases when rates increase and decrease when rates decrease. This means that MBS are more sensitive to rates when they are losing value and less sensitive to rates when they are gaining in value. Negative convexity is bad for the MBS investor and decreases their appeal to fixed income investors so MBS have to compensate investors by having higher yields than equivalent non-mortgage-backed bonds with fixed coupons.

Name	Description	Role	History
Fannie Mae	Federal National Mortgage Association	Issues MBS and insures interest and principal payments of existing MBS with claims on conforming pools of mortgages for a fee of about 20 basis points on the principal insured.	Founded 1938, spun off from Government in 1968 as a public company, placed in government conservatorship 2008.
Freddie Mac	Federal Home Loan Mortgage Corporation	Same as Fannie Mae.	Founded 1970 as a government sponsored entity, became a publicly traded company in 1989.
Ginnie Mae	Government National Mortgage Association	Government agency that guarantees interest and principal payments of MBS with claims on pools of mortgages insured by the Federal Housing Authority and Veterans Association. Pools contain mortgages for lower income households.	Founded in 1968 within the Department of Housing and Urban Development.
Originator	Commercial banks, savings and loan associations (S&L) and mortgage banks	Create mortgages that are then put into pools and securitized as MBS. Commercial banks and S&L keep the mortgages on the balance sheet, mortgage banks do not.	
Investor	Global investors such as sovereign wealth funds, pension funds.	Provide capital for the US domestic housing market.	Not available to investors until the concept of securitisation took off

Table 5.11: Players in the US mortgage backed security market.

Pricing an MBS is more difficult than pricing a government or corporate bond because of prepayment. An MBS has interest rate and credit risk but also has prepayment risk. If you buy an MBS at a premium for, say, $105 and the whole bond prepays the next day repaying you the principal amount of $100, then you will have made a loss of 5%. If you buy an MBS at a discount at a price of $95 and the bond prepays the next day then you will have made a profit of 5%. Prepayment is good for investors that buy at a discount and bad for investors that buy at a premium. Pricing an MBS therefore requires a model that can predict whether people will repay their mortgages early, and predicting human behaviour is difficult. It turns out that for large numbers of people in a pool their behaviour is predictable and depends on demographic factors which can be derived from the published pool characteristics. For example the prepayment behaviour of a poor community in Louisiana will be different from the behaviour of a wealthy community in the suburbs of San Francisco, and models can be built to take these differences into account.

Because prepayment is so important in the MBS market an entire language has arisen to describe the rate of prepayment or PREPAYMENT SPEED. This is a chart of the months since the MBS was originated on the horizontal axis and the rate at which prepayment occurs on the vertical axis. The Bond Markets Association (BMA) defines a "standard" prepayment profile which starts at 0% prepayment rate on origination, rises steadily up to 30 months at a rate of 0.2% per month and is flat at 6% after 30 months. This standard prepayment profile is called PSA (because the BMA used to be called the Public Securities Association). When describing prepayment speed we would say that the MBS is, say, 70% PSA. This means that it is prepaying more slowly than the standard PSA profile. A percentage over 100% would mean the MBS is prepaying more quickly than PSA. Two other numbers are also used to describe prepayment speed. CONSTANT PREPAYMENT RATE (CPR) is the percentage of principal that is repaid over the course of a year. SINGLE MONTHLY MORTALITY (SMM) is the percentage of principal that is repaid per month. The two are related by

$$\text{SMM} = 1 - \sqrt[12]{1 - \text{CPR}}.$$

Pools are usually described in terms of "weighted average X" where the number is a weighted average and the weighting is done by amount of loan outstanding as listed in Table 5.12. For example to guage the remaining life of the mortgages in the pool one would consider WEIGHTED AVERAGE LIFE (WAL) or WEIGHTED AVERAGE (REMAINING) MATURITY (WARM/WAM). Seasoned pools will be safer because they contain mortgages that have been around for a while and so it is useful to look at WEIGHTED AVERAGE LOAN AGE (WALA). To guage the coupon that you will be paid you would look at WEIGHTED AVERAGE COUPON (WAC). For credit-worthiness of the mortgage holders you would be interested in a weighted average credit score as measured on the settlement date, or WEIGHTED AVERAGE ORIGINAL CREDIT SCORE (WAOCS) or a measure of how much debt the borrowers had taken on relative to their income or WEIGHTED AVERAGE ORIGINAL DEBT TO INCOME (WAODTI). An MBS prospectus may contain even more detailed information about the distribution of these numbers such as the percentiles, minimum, maximum, median and mean. Other interesting characteristics would include the percentage of loans with a particular loan purpose (re-finance or purchase), property type (single-family home, num-

Weighted Average	Acronym
Coupon	WAC
(Remaining) Maturity	WA(R)M
Life	WAL
Loan Age	WALA
Loan to Value	WALTV
Original Credit Score	WAOCS
Original Debt to Income	WAODTI

Table 5.12: Weighted average pool statistics for MBS.

ber of units for a condominium or housing co-op), occupancy type (principal residence, second home or investor), geographic distribution by state, origination year, and MBS servicer.

Institutional investors often buy and sell MBS before the pool characteristics are fully known. Agencies will publish rough characteristics including the mortgage agency involved, coupon, delivery date and principal amount. These are known as TBA's or TO BE ANNOUNCED. TBA's are bought as forwards which means that the trade will settle on a fixed delivery date in the future, with standardized settlement days in each month. The buyer and seller exchange details about the pool that will be delivered 48 hours before settlement. Some trades are STIPULATED TRADES where the buyer and seller agree on characteristics of the mortgage loans underlying the MBS that can be delivered, such as loan age, size or geographic location of the house. Others are SPECIFIED TRADES where the buyer and seller agree on the specific pool to be traded identified by its CUSIP number. TBA's are very useful for companies that originate home loans because they allow them to fix the interest rates for their clients without taking the risk that they cannot hedge this risk during the origination process.

5.18 Managing Bond Risk

Bonds have existed for over a century. The risks of owning a bond are very well understood. Bonds are loans, and as anyone knows the risk of a loan is that our debtor will not repay our capital. This is credit risk. As we have seen fixed coupon bond prices are affected by interest rates because they "freeze in" a rate when they are issued. If rates increase the bond looks less attractive to investors because they can get higher returns from new issues. So interest rates are a risk to fixed coupon bonds.

As often happens in finance the risks and returns of a bond can be chopped up into new financial instruments. The credit risk part of a bond has been isolated in an instrument called a credit default swap (see Chapter 7). And the interest rate risk part of a bond has been skimmed off into an interest rate swap (see Chapter 6). These pure interest rate and credit instruments can be used either to reduce risk (and return) for owners of bonds or used on their own to take a punt on rates or credit. A bond investor would hedge the interest rate risk of a bond by entering into a payer's swap, paying away the fixed coupons of the bond and receiving floating payments in return. This would create a SYNTHETIC FLOATER, which is a credit instrument with very little interest rate risk (see Section 5.8). In order to hedge credit risk one could buy a credit default swap, paying a premium in order to mitigate the risk of losing capital if the issuer cannot or will not return your principal.

Other risks cannot be hedged, such as LIQUIDITY RISK. This is the risk that an investor is not able to sell a bond when prices drop dramatically. In a crisis the usual response is to batten down the hatches until things blow over cutting trading volume dramatically and making it harder to sell. There are various ways to quantify liquidity risk. For corporate bonds one approach is to use the bond basis which is the difference between the swap spread and the CDS spread of the issuer (see Section 7.2.1 on page 296 for a description of this spread and how it is calculated). This is implicitly assuming that bond spread is composed of a credit risk premium and a liquidity premium. Another approach is to use covered bonds, as these have almost no loss given default and therefore carry almost zero credit risk, assuming the cover pool is of high quality (see Section 5.15 on page 218). Any spread difference between covered bonds and the risk-free rate may be due to liquidity premium. Bonds also have tax implications, and although tax risk is quite different from interest rate and credit risk in that it cannot be hedged, tax can have a significant impact on trading profit.

5.18.1 Managing Interest Rate Risk

The single most widely used measure of interest rate risk is duration. As we have seen the modified duration provides the sensitivity of present value to a small change in yield. So given modified duration $D_{modified}$ we can quickly calculate the change in value for a small shift in yield Δy,

$$\Delta \text{PV} = -D_{modified} \times \Delta y \times \text{PV}.$$

Clearly the change in value for a shift in yield is proportional to the duration. So doubling duration $D_{modified}$ doubles sensitivity to interest rate changes Δy. The single most important risk measure for a fixed income portfolio is its duration. If a portfolio manager runs a LONG-ONLY bond fund (this means that they can only buy bonds not sell bonds short) and they think that interest rates are about to increase they know they will lose money. This is because as yields go up bond prices come down. So the best they can do to mitigate their loss is to reduce the duration of their portfolio. They could do this by selling their long-maturity bonds and replacing them with short-maturity bonds. Or they can reduce duration by entering into interest rate swaps with carefully chosen maturities. If they believe that rates will decrease then they know that their bond portfolio will increase in value. They now want to be fully exposed to the yield change and will do the opposite, increasing their duration by buying longer-dated bonds and selling shorter-dated bonds.

If a fund is not restricted to be long-only then it is possible to short bonds. Being short a bond means that you are long interest rates, so you will make money on the short position if rates increase. This means that your bond has negative duration. If a bond fund manager believes interest rates will increase one way of expressing that view is to short bonds and to make the duration of their portfolio negative.

There are three instruments that are commonly used to hedge interest rate exposure. These are interest rate futures, interest rate swaps and bond futures. The interest rate futures market is attractive because it is extremely liquid, particularly for shorter maturities, and has very small bid-offer spreads. Interest rate futures have the added benefit of having no counterparty risk as they are traded on an exchange. But interest rate futures have some complexities in execution because of daily mark-to-market and maintenance of margin accounts. Interest rate swaps are an OTC alternative to interest rate futures, and also have an extremely liquid market. But they do carry credit risk because the swap counterparty may not be perfectly creditworthy. The benefit of being OTC is that the swap can be tailored to match the interest rate risk profile very accurately whereas the maturities and contract sizes of interest rate futures may not match up well with the cash flows of a portfolio. Bond futures are another liquid fixed income market that can be used to hedge interest rate risk. Bond futures are exchange traded so like interest rate futures they carry no credit risk but consequently they have the same drawbacks of fixed maturities and notionals.

Duration measures sensitivity to shifts of the entire yield curve by an equal amount across the term structure. If a bond portfolio is hedged in a duration sense then it is still sensitive, although usually to a lesser degree, to changes in the steepness and shape of the yield curve. It is possible to hedge the entire term structure using a combination of hedging instruments with successively increasing maturity. With interest rate futures a string of futures with successive expiries is called an interest rate future STRIP. By choosing the strip expiries and numbers of contracts appropriately it is possible to hedge the entire term structure. Of course this is also possible with interest rate swaps, in which case the set of hedging instruments is called a SWAP OVERLAY. Being OTC has the benefit that swaps can be chosen to match the portfolio maturities and notionals closely whereas a strip of futures may not meet requirements exactly. Bond futures are another alternative hedging instrument but come in a limited range of maturities. However bond futures may offer enough flexibility to hedge against flattening and steepening and a degree of flexing.

5.18.2 Managing Credit Risk

Any bond portfolio will carry credit risk. Credit risk is created whenever a future payment is promised by a counterparty. Before the advent of credit derivatives the only way for a bond investor to manage credit risk was to pick and choose their issuers carefully. If an issuer's credit started to deteriorate the only way to reduce risk was to sell their holding in that issuer's bonds. Pure credit instruments now exist, called CREDIT DEFAULT SWAPS (CDS), which can be used to insure against default (see Chapter 7). CDS protect against default by single issuers, so a large bond portfolio might need as many CDS as there are issuers to fully protect future principle repayments. The CDS contract specifies the notional amount that will be paid out in the event of default. This can be determined from the credit sensitivity of each bond. Either the bond can be hedged to be DV01-neutral, so that any shifts in credit spread cause no change in the value of the bond, or it can be hedged for its full replacement value. If the notional of the CDS is equal to the face amount of the bond then in the event of default the bond holder will be fully compensated for their loss.

It can be costly to insure each issuer in a portfolio. One alternative it to hedge credit risk by buying or selling credit indices (for a full description of CDS indices see Chapter 7.5). Indices exist for particular industries and sectors such as the automobile sector so that portfolios that are overweight one sector could be DV01 hedged fairly well. The danger is that the hedge will not be perfect as the composition of the index will not match that of the portfolio exactly creating some BASIS RISK. Unfortunately basis risk increases in precisely the environment in which protection is needed, namely when credit spreads are highest. A half-way house between buying CDS protection on each single name and a CDS index is to hedge with a credit linked note that contains a basket of names to which a portfolio has greatest exposure. These are OTC credit derivatives and would be cheaper than buying single name protection and which would match the credit exposure of the portfolio more accurately.

5.19 Securitization

To take an extreme and simplified example say we have a bank that has raised $100 million through issuing shares. We lend out this money in the form of mortgages. Each mortgage is $100,000 dollars, so we can afford to lend to 1,000 borrowers. Our bank can charge our mortgage customers a mortgage interest rate of 4%. The annual revenue for our bank is 4% of the money we lend as mortgages and 4% of $100 million is $4 million.

Assets ($ mn)		Liabilities ($ mn)	
1000 Mortgages	100	Equity	100

The value of our mortgages will vary due to interest rates and credit concerns and if the value of our mortgage assets has to be written down by 10% then we will also have to write down the value of shareholder equity by 10% of $100 million, from $100 million to $90 million. Our equity capital has absorbed our loss but we are far from bankrupt. Our equity cushions us from bankruptcy and we would have to write off all the mortgages before we became bankrupt.

Assets ($ mn)		Liabilities ($ mn)	
1000 Mortgages	90	Equity	90

But 4% is a very small return on our investment as shareholders. Equity investors expect a RETURN ON EQUITY for a bank to be about 20%. If we want to increase our revenue and our profit then we can simply lend more money. We could do this by issuing more shares but then the extra income would be divided among more shareholders so we would not increase our return on equity. Instead we choose to use LEVERAGE because bondholders do not participate in any profits, they simply receive a fixed coupon payment. We lever up by issuing $900 million in bonds paying a fixed coupon of 3% bringing the size of our balance sheet up to $1 billion. We have borrowed money at an interest rate of 3% and we lend it out at 4%. Our NET INTEREST MARGIN is 4%-3% which is 1%.

Assets ($ million)		Liabilities ($ million)	
10,000 Mortgages	1,000	Equity	100
		Debt	900

We now lend out $1 billion in 10,000 mortgages and our annual revenue goes up to 4% of $1 billion which is $40 million. Unfortunately we have to pay 3% of $900 million, which is $27 million, each year in bond coupon to our bondholders. But if the value of our assets, our mortgages, drops by 10% as before then our equity will have to absorb a loss of 10% of $1 billion which is $100 million. Our equity of $100 million is entirely wiped out and we are bankrupt.

Assets ($ million)		Liabilities ($ million)	
10,000 Mortgages	900	Equity	0
		Debt	900

It therefore seems that although it is possible to make a small income through mortgage lending there is no way to increase the return on equity for this business. Our gross return seems to be capped by our net interest margin and few investors would be willing to buy shares for such a paltry return. We have to use leverage to make this lending business work. Each mortgage that we produce increases the size of our balance sheet, and we need borrowed capital to boost our return. Regulators, quite rightly, cap our leverage and therefore cap our revenue in order to cap our risk of bankruptcy. This is not a scaleable lending process.

One solution is to take the assets off our balance sheet. We can create a new company, independent of our own, which is called a SPECIAL PURPOSE VEHICLE (SPV). We are the SPONSOR of this SPV. We can originate some mortgages which briefly live on our balance sheet. Then we can sell those mortgages to our new company. The company will need to issue bonds in order to fund its purchase of our mortgages. The final ingredient in this recipe for scaleable mortgage lending is to create a capital structure for the SPV's bonds. If the assets lose value either through write-downs or defaults on mortgage payments, the bonds lowest, or most SUBORDINATED in the capital structure will lose their principal first. Then the next tier in the capital structure will start to take losses, and so on up to the highest tier or TRANCHE. As the principal of a bond is wiped out by losses its coupon drops until it reaches zero when the tranche is said to be WIPED OUT. The most senior bonds, called the SENIOR TRANCHE, will have the highest credit rating, perhaps even AAA, because it would take a catastrophic sequence of losses to start to erode their principal. The senior tranche enjoys CREDIT ENHANCEMENT because of all the subordinated tranches beneath it in the capital structure. Consequently the senior tranche will pay a low coupon to reflect this low risk of losing invested capital. The most junior bonds will have an extremely high risk and must pay a very high coupon to recompense investors for the high risk of losing their capital. The most junior tranche is called the EQUITY TRANCHE or FIRST LOSS PIECE. Cynics usually call the equity tranche TOXIC WASTE but it can be a good investment because it pays such a high coupon that you may make your investment back with a significant profit before it is wiped out. In between the senior tranche and equity tranche we can insert a MEZZANINE TRANCHE or even several mezz tranches with intermediate levels of risk and intermediate coupons to reflect their risk. Above the senior tranche there may be a SUPER-SENIOR TRANCHE. The assets and capital structure of the SPV will look like this:

Assets ($ million)		Liabilities ($ million)	
10,000 Mortgages	1,000	Super-senior Bond (AAA)	200
		Senior Bond (AA)	200
		Mezzanine Bond (BB)	400
		Equity (not rated)	200

One way to think of tranches is like ranks of bathers marching down the beach into a stormy sea. The front line of bathers are taking the greatest risk and will be knocked over first, like the equity tranche. The second row of bathers, the mezzanine tranche, is shielded from the waves by the first row, until the first row is knocked over and then the second row starts to be pounded by the waves. The bathers who are safest are the ones at the back of the formation, and these bathers resemble the super-senior tranche. Senior tranches are protected by subordinated tranches.

After investors have bought the bonds and the SPV has bought its pool of assets the structure starts generating cash flows. The mortgage borrowers will pay mortgages that form the income of the SPV. Almost all of these cash flows are used to pay the interest and coupon and principal of the bondholders. Some of the asset income is kept back and not paid to the bondholders, and this is called EXCESS SPREAD. Excess spread is either siphoned into a cash reserve called the RESERVE ACCOUNT to cover losses on the assets or used to pay a servicing fee to the person who administrates the structure, the SERVICER. Usually the servicer is the sponsor so this servicing fee may generate a small income. If you are late on a mortgage payment you will receive a nasty letter from the servicer. Principal is often repaid in a particular order, usually starting with the most senior liabilities, but it can in theory occur in any order. The order that is used is called the CASH WATERFALL.

From the point of view of the investor, what are their considerations when investing in one of the bonds of our SPV? The most important consideration is credit risk. Very importantly the credit risk of one of the SPV's bonds depends entirely on the behaviour of the assets in the SPV. An SPV bond is secured by the assets of the SPV, hence the name of this off-balance-sheet lending model: SECURITIZATION. The SPV is BANKRUPTCY-REMOTE from us, its SPONSOR. If we, the sponsor, go into bankruptcy and are forced to liquidate our assets to pay off our creditors the assets in the SPV do not belong to us. Our creditors have no claim on the assets of the SPV. So the investor should focus on the quality of assets of the SPV. If the assets are of poor quality and very likely to default then the investor would expect a high coupon as compensation. So in the prospectus for the bond one would expect detailed information about the people taking out the mortgages and the properties that are being purchased, such as the credit history of the borrowers, the geographic location of the houses, and how many people have already defaulted. It is much safer to invest in one of these bonds once it is SEASONED, which means that it has existed for a few years. In this period of time it becomes clear what level of defaults to expect and typically defaults peak after a few years then decline. One could interpret seasoning as shaking the bad apples out of the tree.

A second important consideration for an investor buying one of the SPV's bonds is CORRELATION. To take an extreme example we can imagine that all the mortgage holders default together. Two things can happen: either everyone defaults simultaneously, or nobody at all defaults. The super-senior tranche is now looking much more risky. When defaults were happening in dribs and drabs and correlation was low, it was extremely unlikely that all the subordinated tranches would be wiped out. But now that everyone defaults together it is looking much more likely that the senior tranche will be wiped out entirely. For the equity tranche, which in low correlation environments will be nibbled away quite quickly, increased correlation means that it becomes more likely that there will be no defaults at all. So the senior tranches lose value when correlation increases, and the equity tranche gains value when correlation increases. To see why this is the case mathematically, see Section 8.3 on page 317 for a synthetic CDO.

From the point of view of the sponsor of this structure our business model is now completely different. Our job is to originate mortgages, for which we collect an origination fee. Then we briefly hold the mortgage on our balance sheet until we sell it off into an SPV. If we want to originate more mortgages we simply create a new SPV. Critically, the number of mortgages we originate is now not affecting our leverage. To maximize our profit we must now originate as many mortgages as possible. We have changed from a borrowing low, lending high business into a flow business. It is clear to see why it would be tempting to "overlook" poor credit scores and get as many mortgages through the door and into an SPV as quickly as possible. As the sponsor of the structure we will not pay the price for this credit time-bomb because the mortgage is no longer on our balance sheet. Property valuation and credit checks are the weak-points in mortgage origination and must be subject to strict regulation, otherwise securitization rewards those who lie about the credit quality of borrowers and the value of their property.

The assets that are securitized need not be mortgages, they can be anything that generates an income. If, as in our example above, the assets are residential mortgages then a bond issued by the structure is called a RESIDENTIAL MORTGAGE BACKED SECURITY (RMBS) or a COLLATERALIZED MORTGAGE OBLIGATION (CMO). If the assets are mortgages to build skyscrapers then these bonds are called COMMERCIAL MORTGAGE BACKED SECURITIES (CMBS). Other assets such as credit card liabilities, student loans, boat loans, or even the income from upmarket holiday parks like Center Parcs in Europe, are lumped into the catch-all category of ASSET BACKED SECURITY (ABS). If the assets are commercial loans a bond issued by the structure is called a COLLATERALIZED LOAN OBLIGATION (CLO), and if the assets are simply a pool of corporate bonds then we have a COLLATERALIZED BOND OBLIGATION (CBO). Each different type of securitization carries the risk of its assets and their correlation and in order to be an investor in one of these securitized bonds one should have expert knowledge. A prospectus for a securitized bond can run to hundreds of pages as these are complex products, but despite this complexity securitization is an elegant and scaleable way of generating large-scale funding.

5.20 Further Reading

For a comprehensive and clearly explained introduction to fixed income products and pricing see Tuckman (2002). This book is not too technical but Bruce Tuckman gives an excellent grounding in the theory of fixed income and how it is applied in practice. To understand the world of rates from the trader's perspective see Wiseman (2001). Wiseman's book is refreshingly short and non-technical but gives an intuitive understanding and introduces some language used by fixed income practitioners. Fabozzi has many books on fixed income, but I would recommend Fabozzi (2009) and Fabozzi (2005). For more detail on convertible bonds Calamos (2003) provides details on pricing and also convertible arbitrage. Deacon et al. (2004) is an excellent reference for inflation-linked securities.

Answers to Exercises

27 *Use the expression for the sum of a geometric series in Section 3.7 on page 118 to re-write Equation 5.2 in a form without summation.*

Equation 5.2 can be simplified by noticing that the first term is the sum of a geometric series, and can be rewritten using the result in Section 3.7 on page 118, namely $\sum_{t=a}^{b} z^t = \frac{z^a - z^{b+1}}{1-z}$. In this case $z = \frac{1}{\left(1+\frac{y}{f}\right)}$, $a = 1$, and $b = fT$ giving

$$\text{PV} = \frac{c}{f} \cdot \frac{\frac{1}{\left(1+\frac{y}{f}\right)} - \frac{1}{\left(1+\frac{y}{f}\right)^{fT+1}}}{1 - \frac{1}{\left(1+\frac{y}{f}\right)}} + \frac{P}{\left(1 + \frac{y}{f}\right)^{fT}}.$$

If we multiply the numerator and denominator by $\frac{1}{\left(1+\frac{y}{f}\right)}$ in the first term, then we arrive at a more elegant version of Equation 5.2 that contains no summation,

$$\text{PV} = \frac{c}{y}\left[1 - \frac{1}{\left(1 + \frac{y}{f}\right)^{fT}}\right] + \frac{P}{\left(1 + \frac{y}{f}\right)^{fT}}.$$

28 *A bond with three years to maturity and an annual coupon of 2% has a yield to maturity of 1%. What is its approximate price (without using a calculator)?*

The bond is paying a fixed coupon of 2% while the rest of the market is making just 1%. This is an advantage to the investor so we know that the bond will be trading at a premium (a price greater than its face value of $100). The benefit each year is $2\% - 1\%$ or 1% each year for 3 years, which gives a price of about $103.

29 *A bond with two years to maturity and an annual coupon of 4% trades at a price of $96. What is its approximate yield to maturity (without using a calculator)?*

The bond is trading at a discount to its face value of $100 so the market must be getting paid more than the bond coupon of 4% and yield to maturity must be more than 4%. Over two years the bond loses out on $100 - $96 or 4% of face, which is a loss of 2% per year. The yield to maturity will be about 2% more than the coupon of 4%, which is a yield to maturity of 6%.

30 *Calculate the Macaulay duration of a ten year annual par bond with a coupon of 10%.*

Present value is 9.090909 + 8.264463 + 7.513148 + 6.830135 + 6.209213 + 5.644739 + 5.131581 + 4.665074 + 4.240976 + 42.409762, which adds up to 100 because this is a par bond.

Year	1	2	3	4	5
Payment	10	10	10	10	10
Present Value	$\frac{10}{1+0.1}$	$\frac{10}{(1+0.1)^2}$	$\frac{10}{(1+0.1)^3}$	$\frac{10}{(1+0.1)^4}$	$\frac{10}{(1+0.1)^5}$
Macaulay Duration	1	2	3	4	5

Year	6	7	8	9	10
Payment	10	10	10	10	110
Present Value	$\frac{10}{(1+0.1)^6}$	$\frac{10}{(1+0.1)^7}$	$\frac{10}{(1+0.1)^8}$	$\frac{10}{(1+0.1)^9}$	$\frac{10}{(1+0.1)^{10}}$
Macaulay Duration	6	7	8	9	10

Adding the products of each present value by Macaulay duration ($1 \times \frac{10}{1.1} + 2 \times \frac{10}{1.1^2} + \ldots + 10 \times \frac{10}{1.1^{10}}$) and dividing by the total PV of 100 gives a duration of 6.759024.

31 *If we were to hedge interest rate sensitivity of the 10 year 10% bond above with a single zero coupon bond, what would be the maturity of that zero coupon bond?*

The Macaulay duration of a zero coupon bond is its time to maturity. So by shorting a zero coupon bond with 6.759024 years to maturity we could hedge against small parallel shifts upward and downward of the yield curve. This would not hedge against steepening, flattening or twisting of the yield curve or large shifts of the yield curve.

32 *Try this for yourself by differentiating* $\frac{c_i}{\left(1+\frac{y}{f}\right)^{ft_i}}$ *with respect to* y.

We can differentiate this with respect to yield y using the chain rule. Some people can do this in their head, but in case your differentiation is a bit rusty we will use the chain rule explicitly here. We can split up the partial derivative $\frac{\partial PV_i}{\partial y} = \frac{\partial PV}{\partial g} \frac{\partial g}{\partial h} \frac{\partial h}{\partial y}$, and we set $h = 1 + \frac{y}{f}$, $g = h^{-ft_i}$, and $PV_i = c_i g$, then $\frac{\partial h}{\partial y} = \frac{1}{f}$, $\frac{\partial g}{\partial h} = -ft_i h^{-ft_i-1}$, $\frac{\partial PV_i}{\partial g} = c_i$. Multiplying the derivatives together,

$$\frac{\partial}{\partial y}PV_i = -\frac{1}{f}\frac{ft_i}{\left(1+\frac{y}{f}\right)^{ft_i+1}}c_i$$

$$= -t_i\frac{c_i}{\left(1+\frac{y}{f}\right)^{ft_i+1}}$$

$$= -\frac{t_i}{\left(1+\frac{y}{f}\right)}\frac{c_i}{\left(1+\frac{y}{f}\right)^{ft_i}}$$

$$= -\frac{t_i}{\left(1+\frac{y}{f}\right)}PV_i$$

33 *If the modified duration of a bond portfolio is five years and the yield curve moves up by one basis point, will you make or lose money and how much will you gain or lose?*

The bond portfolio will lose money because we own bonds that have a fixed coupon that becomes less desirable as rates increase. If the yield curve has shifted up by one basis point (0.01%) then the bond portfolio's value will decrease by 5 basis points (0.05%),

$$\frac{\Delta PV}{PV} = -D_{modified} \times \Delta y$$

$$= -5 \times 0.0001$$

$$= -0.0005$$

Note that this is a fractional change in PV. To find the dollar change we would have to multiply by the present value of the bond portfolio.

34 *If the modified duration of a bond portfolio with a present value of $10 million is five years and the yield curve moves up by one basis point, how much money will you gain or lose?*

The bond portfolio will lose money because we own bonds that have a fixed coupon that becomes less desirable as rates increase. If the yield curve has shifted up by one basis point (0.01%) then the bond portfolio's value will decrease by 5 basis points (0.05%), and we scale by present value to give the change in value as a dollar amount

$$\Delta\text{PV} = -D_{modified} \times \Delta y \times \text{PV}$$
$$= -5 \times 0.0001 \times 10,000,000$$
$$= -5,000$$

We therefore lose $5,000.

35 *Using Table 5.3 on page 186 fill in the table for a five year and a ten year semi-annual bond. Assume the principal is $100 and the coupon is 5% for both bonds and that the yield curve is a flat 6% for all maturities. Which is the most sensitive to interest rates? Is this what you expected?*

For the five year 5% semi-annual bond $P = 100$, $T = 5$, $c = 5$. The discount factor at maturity $\delta(5)$ is $\frac{1}{\left(1+\frac{0.06}{2}\right)^{10}}$ which is 0.7441. We can fill in the table as follows:

	PV	$\frac{\partial}{\partial y}$PV	Modified Duration	DV01
Coupon	95.73	−415.63	4.34	0.0416
Zero Coupon	74.41	−361.21	4.85	0.0361
Par	100	−426.51	4.27	0.0427
Perp	83.33	−1388.89	16.67	0.1389
Short Maturity	100	0	0	0

For the ten year bond we can ignore the last two years because they ignore maturity ($T \to \infty$ for a perp, $T \to 0$ for a bond about to mature). The discount factor at maturity is now $\delta(10)$, $\frac{1}{\left(1+\frac{0.06}{2}\right)^{20}}$ which is 0.5537. The first three rows of the table are as follows:

	PV	$\frac{\partial}{\partial y}$PV	Modified Duration	DV01
Coupon	92.56	−709.49	7.67	0.0709
Zero Coupon	55.37	−537.55	9.71	0.0538
Par	100	−743.86	7.44	0.0744

The longer maturity bond has greater interest rate sensitivity as we suspected. This is true for both duration and DV01. The ten year has duration 7.7 years and the five year has duration 4.3 years. In dollar terms whereas the ten year loses 7 cents as yield increases by one basis point the five year loses only 4 cents for each basis point increase in yield.

36 *We buy a five year fixed coupon bond for $100. Tomorrow rates increase by 1%. Will the price of the bond go up or down? How would this be affected by convexity? What if rates had decreased by 1%?*

If rates go up the price of our bond will go down, but less than we would expect if the price-yield relationship were linear. If rates had decreased the price of the bond would increase but more than would be expected if the price-yield relationship were linear.

37 *Earlier we found that the yield sensitivity of a fixed cash flow c_i at time t_i by differentiating its present value using compound interest $\frac{c_i}{\left(1+\frac{y}{f}\right)^{ft_i}}$,*

$$\frac{\partial}{\partial y} PV_i \;=\; \frac{\partial}{\partial y}\frac{c_i}{\left(1+\frac{y}{f}\right)^{ft_i}} \;=\; -t_i\frac{c_i}{\left(1+\frac{y}{f}\right)^{ft_i+1}}$$

Find the second derivative by differentiating again. Is convexity linear in t?

We can differentiate with respect to yield y again using the chain rule. We can split up the partial derivative $\frac{\partial^2 PV_i}{\partial y^2} = \frac{\partial}{\partial y}\frac{\partial PV_i}{\partial y} = \frac{\partial}{\partial g}\frac{\partial PV_i}{\partial y}\frac{\partial g}{\partial y}\frac{\partial h}{\partial y}$, and we set $h = 1 + \frac{y}{f}$, $g = h^{-(ft_i+1)}$, and $\frac{\partial}{\partial y}PV_i = -t_i c_i g$, then $\frac{\partial h}{\partial y} = \frac{1}{f}$, $\frac{\partial g}{\partial h} = -(ft_i+1)h^{-(ft_i+2)}$, $\frac{\partial}{\partial g}\frac{\partial PV_i}{\partial y} = -t_i c_i$. Multiplying the derivatives together,

$$\frac{\partial^2}{\partial y^2}PV_i \;=\; t_i c_i\frac{ft_i+1}{\left(1+\frac{y}{f}\right)^{ft_i+2}}\frac{1}{f}$$

$$=\; t_i\left(t_i+\frac{1}{f}\right)\frac{c_i}{\left(1+\frac{y}{f}\right)^{ft_i+2}}$$

$$=\; \frac{t_i\left(t_i+\frac{1}{f}\right)}{\left(1+\frac{y}{f}\right)^2}PV_i$$

Convexity is quadratic in t so long-dated bonds will have very large convexity.

38 *Show that*

$$\frac{\partial^2}{\partial y^2}PV \;=\; PV\left[D_{modified}^2 - \frac{\partial}{\partial y}D_{modified}\right]$$

We can re-arrange the definition of Macaulay duration,

$$D_{macaulay} \;=\; -\frac{1}{PV}\frac{\partial}{\partial y}PV$$

$$\frac{\partial}{\partial y}PV \;=\; -PV D_{macaulay}$$

Then we differentiate with respect to yield again

$$\frac{\partial^2}{\partial y^2}\text{PV} = -D_{macaulay}\frac{\partial}{\partial y}\text{PV} - \text{PV}\frac{\partial}{\partial y}D_{macaulay}$$

$$= \text{PV}\left[D^2_{macaulay} - \frac{\partial}{\partial y}D_{macaulay}\right]$$

39 *Find an expression for the maximum DV01 of a zero coupon bond in terms of yield.*

The DV01 of a zero coupon bond in terms if its yield y, face value P, compounding frequency f and maturity T is $\frac{T}{1+\frac{y}{f}}\frac{P}{\left(1+\frac{y}{f}\right)^{fT}}$. First we differentiate this expression with respect to T. To differentiate the denominator set $z = \left(1+\frac{y}{f}\right)^{fT+1}$, take logarithms $\ln z = (fT+1)\ln\left(1+\frac{y}{f}\right)$, then differentiate $\frac{1}{z}\frac{dz}{dT} = f\ln\left(1+\frac{y}{f}\right)$ and so $\frac{dz}{dT} = f\ln\left(1+\frac{y}{f}\right)\left(1+\frac{y}{f}\right)^{fT+1}$.

$$\frac{\partial}{\partial T}\frac{PT}{10^4\left(1+\frac{y}{f}\right)^{fT+1}} = \frac{P}{10^4}\frac{\left(1+\frac{y}{f}\right)^{fT+1} - Tf\ln\left(1+\frac{y}{f}\right)\left(1+\frac{y}{f}\right)^{fT+1}}{\left(1+\frac{y}{f}\right)^{2fT+2}}.$$

To find the maturity T_{max} for which DV01 is at a maximum we set the derivative equal to zero

$$\left(1+\frac{y}{f}\right)^{fT_{max}+1} = T_{max}f\ln\left(1+\frac{y}{f}\right)\left(1+\frac{y}{f}\right)^{fT_{max}+1}$$

and re-arrange to give

$$T_{max} = \frac{1}{f\ln\left(1+\frac{y}{f}\right)}.$$

If $f = 2$, and $y = 0.05$ then $T_{max} = \frac{1}{2\ln(1+\frac{.05}{2})} = 20.24897$. If you take a look at the left hand side of Figure 5.16 where $c = 0$ the maximum DV01 for a zero coupon bond with yield 5% is indeed around 20 years. For small values of yield $\ln\left(1+\frac{y}{f}\right) \simeq \frac{y}{f}$ to first order, and so $T_{max} \simeq \frac{1}{y}$.

40 The clean price of the bond is $99 + \frac{1}{64} = 99.01562$. It has accrued interest for 39 days since the last coupon payment on August 31st (there are 39 calendar days between August 31st 2009 and October 9th 2009). The coupon period for a US Treasury is calculated using the Actual/Actual day count convention. The actual time between the last and next coupon payments is February 28th, 2010 which is a period of 181 days. So the accrued coupon is $\frac{39}{181}$ of the coupon payment, which is half of $1\frac{7}{8}$ as it is paid semi-annually,

$$\text{Accrued Interest} = \frac{39}{181} \times 1\frac{7}{8} \times \frac{1}{2} = 0.2020$$

The dirty price of the bond is

$$
\begin{aligned}
\text{Dirty Price} &= \text{Clean Price} + \text{Accrued Interest} \\
&= 99\frac{1}{64} + 0.2020 = 99.2176
\end{aligned}
$$

The gross basis is the clean price and the adjusted future settlement price

$$
\begin{aligned}
\text{Gross Basis} &= \text{Clean Price} - P_{\text{settle}} \times \text{Conversion Factor} \\
&= 99\frac{1}{64} - 116\frac{1}{64} \times 0.8499 = 0.4139
\end{aligned}
$$

For US Treasuries gross basis is expressed in fractions of $\frac{1}{32}$, so 0.4139 becomes 13.2 32nds. Carry basis, assuming that we will be delivering this bond in 85 days time on January 6th 2010, is the difference between funding cost to buy the bond and coupon benefit while holding the bond.

$$
\begin{aligned}
\text{Carry Basis} &= \text{Funding Cost} - \text{Coupon Benefit} \\
&= \text{Dirty Price} \times r_{\text{repo}} \times \frac{d}{365} - \text{Face} \times \frac{\text{Coupon}}{2} \times \frac{d}{\text{Coupon Period}} \\
&= 99.2176 \times 0.0005 \times \frac{85}{360} - 100 \times \frac{1\frac{7}{8}\%}{2} \times \frac{85}{181} \\
&= 0.0117 - 0.4403 = -0.4285
\end{aligned}
$$

Net basis is

$$
\begin{aligned}
\text{Net Basis} &= \text{Gross Basis} - \text{Carry Basis} \\
&= 0.4139 - 0.4285 \\
&= -0.0146
\end{aligned}
$$

And finally implied repo is

$$
\begin{aligned}
\text{Implied Repo} &= \frac{F \times CF + AI_{\text{deliv}} + \text{coupon received} - DP_{\text{today}}}{DP_{\text{today}}} \times \frac{360}{\text{days}_{\text{deliv}}} \\
&= \frac{116\frac{1}{64} \times 0.8499 + 100 \times \frac{128}{181} \times \frac{1\frac{7}{8}\%}{2} - 99.2176}{99.2176} \times \frac{360}{128} \\
&= 0.13\%
\end{aligned}
$$

6 Swaps

The asset in Figure 6.1 is called an INTEREST RATE SWAP. An interest rate swap is an agreement between two counterparties to swap cash flows on some notional amount. When an investor enters into an interest rate swap no money changes hands, so this is an UNFUNDED INSTRUMENT. As no money is paid up front it makes no sense to talk about buying or selling a swap so we say that we are "entering into" a swap. Swaps are widely used to hedge interest rate risk, so if someone has large interest rate exposure they can enter into swaps to reduce their exposure. If a corporation is issuing fixed coupon bonds to raise capital swaps can be used to convert a set of fixed liabilities into floating liabilities in a trade called a LIABILITY SWAP. If a bond investor such as a pension fund owns fixed coupon bonds as assets and wants to reduce its interest rate exposure it can convert some of the fixed cash flows into floating cash flows in an ASSET SWAP.

The fact that swaps are unfunded means that they are also a cheap way of taking a bet on rising or falling interest rates, which make them an attractive instrument for hedge funds. A notional amount is specified in the trade to scale the cash flows, but it is important to understand that the notional is never exchanged. Interest rate swaps are traded in staggering volumes because they have so many uses in fixed income markets. The Bank for International Settlements estimated that the size of outstanding swap notional worldwide was $349 trillion in December 2009. The most commonly traded interest rate swap is a fixed-for-floating swap and this is the kind of swap that we will deal with in detail in this section. Swaps are over-the-counter (OTC) which means that they carry counterparty credit risk. For this reason trading a swap often requires collateral to mitigate the risk that the counterparty will fail to pay. Pricing a swap typically also includes a modification based on the credit spread of the counterparty, and this correction is called a CREDIT VALUATION ADJUSTMENT (CVA).

A swap has two streams of of cash flows. One stream is paid, one is received. These streams are called LEGS, and in a fixed-for-floating swap one is the FIXED LEG the other the FLOATING LEG. A swap is created in such a way that on the day it is issued the present value of the fixed and floating legs are equal and opposite, so its present value is zero. The swap market maker sets the fixed rate, and the floating rate is reset to be equal to some published rate, usually LIBOR, at each RESET DATE. If the value of the fixed and floating legs cancel exactly and the swap is worth zero on the trade date then the fixed rate is known as a PAR RATE and is exactly equal to the par coupon of a fixed coupon bond. This is because the cash flows of an interest rate swap can be replicated by being long a fixed coupon bond and short a floater from the same issuer. The swap is also said to be ON MARKET. If a client wants to have a fixed leg that differs from the par coupon then the value of the two legs is not zero on the trade date. The amount paid for an OFF-MARKET SWAP can be spread out over the life of the swap or paid up front.

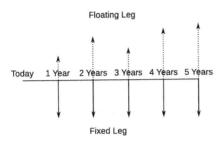

Floating Leg

Today 1 Year 2 Years 3 Years 4 Years 5 Years

Fixed Leg

Figure 6.1:
Interest rate swap cash flows for a payer's swap.

The cash flows for a five year swap are shown in Figure 6.1. The floating leg payments are dashed and variable in size reflecting the varying but as yet unknown value of the LIBOR rate at each reset date. Fixed rate cash flows are solid and all equal. Notice that there is no cash flow today because this is a par swap. The important dates in the life of an interest rate swap are its trade date on which a trade is agreed between buyer and seller, settlement date on which any exchange of money occurs, effective date (usually the same as the settlement date) when interest starts to accrue, and maturity date when the contract ends. In between the effective date and the maturity date are reset dates, when interest rate for the upcoming period is set from an index, and payment dates when fixed and floating payments are made. Sometimes fixed and floating payments coincide and rather than generate payments from buyer to seller and seller to buyer the exchange is netted off into a single payment.

Swaps are OTC instruments. This means that they are hand-crafted for each transaction rather than standardized and sold on an exchange. The benefit of an OTC instrument is that the buyer can adjust it to suit their needs exactly. The drawback is that there is no secondary market, so if interest rates turn against you getting out of the contract is not a simple matter of selling it on at a loss. Another consequence of being OTC is that interest rate swaps come with counterparty risk, which is the risk that the person from which you bought a swap or to whom you sold the swap reneges on the deal and stops making payments.

There are two useful ways of thinking of swaps. The first is that the swap is simply a portfolio of successively expiring forward rate agreements (FRAs). All the FRAs have the same notional as the swap and the same locked-in forward rate. Buying a FRA is like borrowing money forward at an agreed rate and as we are borrowing money we are paying a fixed rate. So entering a payer's swap is like buying a portfolio of FRAs.

To understand how swaps are priced we will take a simple example and calculate the par swap rate, then look at a realistic example once we have built up an intuitive sense of what "par swap rate" means. The current zero rates from the yield curve are as follows:

Year	1	2	3
Zero Rate	3%	4%	5%

Say we are working on the swaps desk at an investment bank and a client asks us to make a market in the three year interest rate swap. The quant is on holiday and all we have is a spreadsheet with the current one-, two- and three-year zero rates, and our own wits. We know that the fixed and floating legs pay annually at the end of years one, two and three. We must find the three year fixed leg rate that makes the floating and fixed legs equal in value because the client expects to pay nothing initially. This fixed leg rate will be the par swap rate given today's yield curve. We can quickly find the three discount factors using this formula: $\frac{1}{\left(1+\frac{r}{f}\right)^{ft}}$. For simplicity we will assume annual compounding $f = 1$.

Year	1	2	3
Zero Rate	3%	4%	5%
Discount Factor	0.9709	0.9246	0.8638

Now we know that if the par swap rate is r_{par} then the value of the fixed leg V_{fixed} will simply be the discounted value of this fixed annual payment. This will be

$$V_{fixed} = r_{par}\left(0.9709 + 0.9246 + 0.8638\right).$$

By the definition of par rate this must be equal to the value of the floating leg V_{float}. But how do we value the floating leg rates? We do not know the future value of LIBOR, so we use the forward rates for the appropriate periods. The forward rate for the first period from the trade date to the first coupon, f_1, will just be the one year zero rate. But the second period from year one to year two will be the one year rate one year forward. The third period floating rate from year two to year three is taken to be the one year rate two years forward. The first floating rate is the same as the zero rate, $f_1 = 3\%$. The second period rate must give a discount factor at the end of year two of 0.9246. So $\frac{1}{1+0.03}\frac{1}{(1+f_2)} = \frac{1}{(1+0.04)^2}$. Re-arranging $f_2 = \frac{(1+0.04)^2}{1+0.03} - 1$ so $f_2 = 0.0501$. Similarly the third period forward rate f_3 must give a discount factor equal to 0.8638 when multiplied by the year two discount factor, $\frac{1}{(1+0.04)^2}\frac{1}{1+f_3} = \frac{1}{(1+0.05)^3}$. The third period rate is the ratio of the two year discount factor and three year discount factor minus one, $f_3 = \frac{(1+0.05)^3}{(1+0.04)^2} - 1 = \frac{\delta_2}{\delta_3} - 1$ or 0.0703.

Year	1	2	3
Zero Rate	3%	4%	5%
Discount Factor	0.9709	0.9246	0.8638
Forward Rate	3%	5.01%	7.03%

Now we can find the par swap rate. This is the fixed leg rate that equates the value of the fixed and floating legs.

$$
\begin{aligned}
\text{fixed leg present value} &= \text{floating leg present value} \\
r_{par}\left(\delta_1 + \delta_2 + \delta_3\right) &= f_1\delta_1 + f_2\delta_2 + f_3\delta_3 \\
r_{par}\left(0.9709 + 0.9246 + 0.8638\right) &= 0.03 \times 0.9709 + 0.0501 \times 0.9246 + 0.0703 \times 0.8638 \\
r_{par} &= \frac{0.03 \times 0.9709 + 0.0501 \times 0.9246 + 0.0703 \times 0.8638}{0.9709 + 0.9246 + 0.8638}
\end{aligned}
$$

Our par rate is 4.93%. Notice that the par rate is just a weighted average of the forward rates where the weightings are the discount factors. So forward rates with shorter maturities will receive a greater weight than longer maturities. Just to check that 4.93% is truly a par rate we can check that the two legs have equal value. The fixed leg is worth $(0.9709 + 0.9246 + 0.8638) \times 0.0493$ and this is 0.1361. The value of the floating leg is $0.03 \times 0.9709 + 0.0501 \times 0.9246 + 0.0703 \times 0.8638$ which is also 0.1361 but opposite in sign so the two legs cancel out and the total value of the swap is zero. So 4.93% is indeed the par swap rate. Although this example is simplified it should show how the par rate is dependent on the yield curve. If we were to make a market in the three year swap we would add some bid offer spread around this value of 4.93%. Typically this spread would be tiny, perhaps a basis point, so our market would be 4.9250|4.9350. This means that we are willing to enter into a payer's swap with a client paying a fixed rate of 4.9250 or enter into a receiver's swap with a client receiving a fixed rate of 4.9350. Notice that we, as a market maker, always pay less than we receive, the difference being our profit or EDGE. Conversely our client, a market taker, will always pay more than they receive.

	Bid	Offer
	4.9250	4.9350
Us (market maker)	Payer	Receiver
Client (market taker)	Receiver	Payer

Exercise 41 *What is the cost of entering a par payer's swap on the trade date?*

Exercise 42 *Find the par swap rate if the one, two and three year zero rates are 1%, 2% and 3% respectively.*

6.1 Dissection of an Interest Rate Swap

We will look in detail at a $10 million five year receiver's swap struck at a par rate of 5.07032% on August 24, 2007. Receiver simply means we are receiving fixed cash flows and paying floating cash flows. The terms of the swap are as shown in Table 6.1 and cash flows are shown in Table 6.2 and Figure 6.2. The legs differ in their payment frequency. The fixed leg pays every six months, whereas the floating leg pays every three months. The fixed leg day count convention is 30I/360 and the floating leg is A/360. In Figure 6.2 it is clear that the fixed cash flows actually vary in size depending on whether the payment dates have been jostled by weekends. Although the rate is fixed the payments also depend on time intervals which are irregular. Floating payments look rather erratic because they depend on the shape of the forward curve.

By design the present value of the fixed and floating legs are equal and opposite ($10,001,486 and -$10,001,486) so they net off to zero. This means that the contract trades at par on the trade date. "Trades at par" is just a way of paraphrasing the fact that the present values of the two legs cancel one another.

Notional	10 million
Currency	USD
Effective date	2007-08-24
Maturity date	2012-08-24
Coupon	5.0703218%

Table 6.1: Terms of receiver's swap.

Date	Fixed	Floating	Net	Discount	Net PV
2007-11-26		-143578.47	-143578.47	0.985991	-141567.15
2008-02-25	254924.51	-132773.77	122150.75	0.973072	118861.43
2008-05-27		-124346.29	-124346.29	0.961120	-119511.76
2008-08-25	254924.51	-121320.76	133603.76	0.949600	126870.11
2008-11-24		-119452.83	-119452.83	0.938391	-112093.41
2009-02-24	250699.24	-119157.54	131541.7	0.927341	121983.96
2009-05-26		-114884.38	-114884.38	0.916808	-105326.9
2009-08-24	253516.09	-110792.58	142723.51	0.906762	129416.2
2009-11-24		-124629.17	-124629.17	0.895600	-111617.86
2010-02-24	253516.09	-125392.24	128123.85	0.884509	113326.67
2010-05-24		-121429.11	-121429.11	0.873897	-106116.55
2010-08-24	253516.09	-125679.80	127836.29	0.863050	110329.15
2010-11-24		-128246.25	-128246.25	0.852122	-109281.47
2011-02-24	253516.09	-128864.07	124652.02	0.841281	104867.38
2011-05-24		-125008.89	-125008.89	0.830894	-103869.16
2011-08-24	253516.09	-129598.89	123917.2	0.820264	101644.78
2011-11-25		-133019.92	-133019.92	0.809496	-107679.06
2012-02-24	253516.09	-130693.01	122823.08	0.799053	98142.11
2012-05-24		-129643.62	-129643.62	0.788826	-102266.27
2012-08-24	10253516.09	-10132911.96	120604.13	0.778479	93887.8
				Total	0

Table 6.2: Cash flows for a $10 million five year receiver's swap.

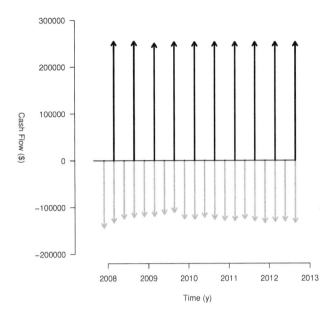

Figure 6.2:
   Cash flows for a receiver swap. Black arrows are fixed cash flows, grey arrows are
   floating cash flows.

Fixed Leg

The fixed leg pays semi-annually. The cash flows are calculated in the usual way as
the product of notional, rate and time. For the first fixed cash flow the year fraction is calculated using the difference in time between August 24, 2007 and February 25, 2008 using the 30I/360 day count convention. There are six months (August to February) and a day (24th to 25th) between the two dates, so that makes
$6 \times 30 + 1 = 181$ days (if we were using an "Actual" day count the difference would be
185 days). To convert to a year fraction we divide by 360, $181/360 = 0.5027778$. The
fixed leg has a coupon of 5.0703218% and the notional is \$10 million, so our cash flow
is $10,000,000 \times \frac{181}{360} \times 0.050703218$ which is \$254,924.51. Year fractions between the
next cash flows are calculated in the same way. There are 6 months between Febru-
ary 25, 2008 and August 25, 2008, a 30I/360 year fraction of $\frac{6 \times 30}{360} = 0.5$. The next year
fraction is one day short of three months $\frac{6 \times 30 - 1}{360} = 0.497222$, and so on. The final cash
flow has ten million added on for exchange of notional. Calculations for all fixed leg
cash flows are shown in Table 6.3.

Floating Leg

For the fixed leg it was a simple matter to calculate the cash flows because the coupon
was fixed. For the floating leg it is not so simple because future fixings are not known
in advance. The floating leg will be reset every three months from the USD three
month LIBOR rate. By convention these future fixings are inferred from the yield

Date	$t_{30I}/360$	Cash flow	Discount	PV
2008-02-25	0.502778	254924.51	0.973072	248059.82
2008-08-25	0.500000	254924.51	0.949600	242076.28
2009-02-24	0.497222	250699.24	0.927341	232483.58
2009-08-24	0.500000	253516.09	0.906762	229878.66
2010-02-24	0.500000	253516.09	0.884509	224237.21
2010-08-24	0.500000	253516.09	0.863050	218797.14
2011-02-24	0.500000	253516.09	0.841281	213278.29
2011-08-24	0.500000	253516.09	0.820264	207950.03
2012-02-24	0.500000	253516.09	0.799053	202572.71
2012-08-24	0.500000	10253516.09	0.778479	7982148.33

Table 6.3: Fixed cash flows for receiver's swap.

curve. The date on which the value of three month LIBOR for a floating payment is observed, or RESET is called a RESET DATE and the date on which it is paid is the PAY DATE.

The first rate is special because it is the only one that is actually known on the trade date. In fact the first floating payment is a *fixed* payment. On the trade date on August 24, 2007 the USD three month LIBOR rate, as issued by the British Bankers Association was 5.49875%. The day count convention is A/360 so the first payment is interest for the period from August 24, 2007 to November 26, 2007 which is 94 actual days and an A/360 year fraction of $\frac{94}{360}$. The payment is the product of notional, rate and time, which is $10^7 \times 0.0549875 \times \frac{94}{360}$ or -$143,578.47. Note that this is negative because we are paying the floating rate and it is roughly half the value of the first fixed payment $254,932.47 because the fixed payments are semi-annual and the floating payments are quarterly.

We will not deal with building the yield curve here. Our requirement for pricing a swap is simply to have discount factors on each payment date. This serves two purposes. Firstly it lets us discount our cash flows. Secondly it allows us to infer the forward rate for the floating payments. These payments follow money-market convention and so are calculated as A/360 simple rates. Recall that this means the discount factor is

$$\delta(t) = \frac{1}{1+rt}.$$

The forward rate between two times in the future t_1 and t_2 is given by

$$r_f(t_1, t_2) = \frac{1}{t_2 - t_1} \left(\frac{\delta(t_1)}{\delta(t_2)} - 1 \right). \tag{6.1}$$

So for the first *floating* payment, which is the second floating leg payment, the forward rate is $\frac{360}{91} \times \left(\frac{0.98599149}{0.97307165} - 1 \right)$ which is 5.252589%. The first floating payment is the product of notional, rate and time which is $10^7 \times 0.05252589 \times \frac{91}{360}$ which is -$132,773.77. Multiplying by the discount factor 0.973072 gives a present value of -$129,198.39. Full calculations for all the floating cash flows are given in Table 6.4.

Date	$t_{A/360}$	Discount	Rate	Cash flow	PV	Date	$t_{A/360}$	Discount	Rate	Cash flow	PV
26/11/07	0.261111	0.985991	5.498750%	-143578.47	-141567.15	24/05/10	2.788889	0.873897	4.911739%	-121429.11	-106116.55
25/02/08	0.513889	0.973072	5.252589%	-132773.77	-129198.39	24/08/10	3.044444	0.863050	4.917905%	-125679.80	-108467.99
27/05/08	0.769444	0.961120	4.865724%	-124346.29	-119511.76	24/11/10	3.300000	0.852122	5.018332%	-128246.25	-109281.47
25/08/08	1.022222	0.949600	4.799502%	-121320.76	-115206.17	24/02/11	3.555556	0.841281	5.042507%	-128864.07	-108410.91
24/11/08	1.272222	0.938391	4.778113%	-119452.83	-112093.41	24/05/11	3.802778	0.830894	5.056540%	-125008.89	-103869.16
24/02/09	1.527778	0.927341	4.662686%	-119157.54	-110499.62	24/08/11	4.058333	0.820264	5.071261%	-129598.89	-106305.26
26/05/09	1.780556	0.916808	4.544877%	-114884.38	-105326.90	25/11/11	4.316667	0.809496	5.149158%	-133019.92	-107679.06
24/08/09	2.030556	0.906762	4.431703%	-110792.58	-100462.46	24/02/12	4.569444	0.799053	5.170273%	-130693.01	-104430.60
24/11/09	2.286111	0.895600	4.876794%	-124629.17	-111617.86	24/05/12	4.819444	0.788826	5.185745%	-129643.62	-102206.27
24/02/10	2.541667	0.884509	4.906653%	-125392.24	-110910.53	24/08/12	5.075000	0.778479	5.200903%	-10132911.96	-7888260.53

Table 6.4: Floating leg for a payer's swap.

The par rate 5.07032% was set such that the present value of the fixed leg is exactly equal and opposite to the present value of the floating leg. The steps in calculating the par swap rate are

1. Build or borrow a yield curve in the currency of the swap. This gives a discount factor δ_i on each cash flow date.

2. Calculate the forward rates $r_{f,i}$ from the discount factors.

3. Calculate the present value of the floating leg by discounting the floating cash flows.

4. Calculate the single fixed rate that equates the present value of the fixed and floating legs.

The par swap rate r_{par} is calculated by equating the present value of the fixed and floating legs. If the floating cash flows are f_{float} and the fixed cash flows are f_{fixed}, then

$$\text{PV}_{fixed} = \text{PV}_{float}$$
$$\sum_i f_i^{fixed}\delta_i = \sum_j f_j^{float}\delta_j$$
$$\sum_{i=1}^{I} Nr_{par}\Delta t_i^{30/360}\delta_i = Nr_{fix}\delta_1 t_1^{A/360} + \sum_{j=2}^{J} Nr_{f,j}\Delta t_j^{A/360}\delta_j$$
$$r_{par} = \frac{r_{fix}\delta_1 t_1^{A/360} + \sum_{j=2}^{J} r_{f,j}\Delta t_j^{A/360}\delta_j}{\sum_{i=1}^{I}\Delta t_i^{30/360}\delta_i}$$

Note that the time between cash flows differs between the fixed and floating legs because they have different day count conventions. Forward rates are not really necessary, as we can infer cash flows directly from discount factors. Substituting the expression for forward rate from Equation 6.1 into our expression for the par rate

$$r_{par} = \frac{r_{fix}\delta_1 t_1^{A/360} + \sum_{j=2}^{J} \frac{\left(\frac{\delta_{j-1}}{\delta_j} - 1\right)}{t_j^{A/360} - t_{j-1}^{A/360}} \delta_j \Delta t_j^{A/360}}{\sum_{i=1}^{I} \delta_i \Delta t_i^{30/360}}$$

But $t_j^{A/360} - t_{j-1}^{A/360} = \Delta t_j^{A/360}$ so our expression for the par rate simplifies to a ratio of the total discount factor changes over the time-weighted discount factors,

$$r_{par} = \frac{r_{fix}\delta_1 t_1^{A/360} + \sum_{j=2}^{J} \delta_{j-1} - \delta_j}{\sum_{i=1}^{I} \delta_i \Delta t_i^{30/360}}$$

Looking at the numerator of our expression for par premium all the intermediate terms cancel and we are left with the difference between the first and last discount factors.

$$\sum_{j=2}^{J} \delta_{j-1} - \delta_j = \delta_1 - \delta_J$$

So our expression simplifies into its final form,

$$r_{par} = \frac{r_{fix}\delta_1 t_1^{A/360} + \delta_1 - \delta_J}{\sum_{i=1}^{I} \delta_i \Delta t_i^{30/360}}$$

Exercise 43 *Show that $\sum_{i=2}^{J} \delta_{i-1} - \delta_i = \delta_1 - \delta_J$. It may be helpful to write out the terms for, say, $J = 4$.*

6.1.1 Replicating Cash Flows

We have seen that floating rates are assumed to be forward rates, and we already know that forward rates can be inferred from any other kind of rate (zero or par) or from a pair of discount factors. If payment dates and fixing dates coincide then we can make a rather elegant simplification. We will start with a single floating payment, then see what happens as we add more floating payments.

Say we have a single floating payment that is fixed at time t_{fix} and pays at time t_{pay}. The size of the payment will be something like $Nr\,(t_{pay} - t_{fix})$, where the notional is N the floating rate is r and the time interval over which interest accrues is $t_{pay} - t_{fix}$. The rate over this interval is unknown, but we assume that it is equal to the forward rate over the time interval t_{fix} to t_{pay}, so $r = r_f(t_{fix}, t_{pay})$. If this is the case then we can replicate the floating payment with a small portfolio where we sell a zero coupon bond with maturity t_{fix} and buy a zero coupon bond with maturity t_{pay}. We set up the portfolio such that the present value of two trades is equal. The two trades are as follows:

Portfolio A Buy notional N of a zero coupon bond that matures at time t_{fix}, then re-invest the principal and interest at time t_{fix} at a pre-arranged forward rate $r_f(t_{fix}, t_{pay})$ from time t_{fix} to time t_{pay}.

Portfolio B Buy notional N of a zero coupon bond that matures at time t_{pay}.

If portfolios A and B have equal value then if the zero rate at time t_{fix} is $r_z(t_{fix})$ and at time t_{pay} is $r_z(t_{pay})$, remembering that we use a money market accrual convention for the forward rate, which is a simple rate of the form $1 + rt$,

$$e^{r_z(t_{fix})t_{fix}} \left[1 + r_f(t_{fix}, t_{pay})(t_{pay} - t_{fix}) \right] = e^{r_z(t_{pay})t_{pay}}.$$

Equivalently one can express this more succintly in terms of discount factors, so $e^{-r_z(t_{fix})t_{fix}} = \delta_{fix}$ and $e^{-r_z(t_{pay})t_{pay}} = \delta_{pay}$

$$\frac{1}{\delta_{fix}} \left[1 + r_f(t_{fix}, t_{pay})(t_{pay} - t_{fix}) \right] = \frac{1}{\delta_{pay}},$$

then we can re-arrange to get

$$r_f(t_{fix}, t_{pay}) = \frac{1}{t_{pay} - t_{fix}} \left(\frac{\delta_{fix}}{\delta_{pay}} - 1 \right). \tag{6.2}$$

The floating payment f made at time t_{pay} is the product of notional, forward rate and time, $Nr_f(t_{pay} - t_{fix})$,

$$f = Nr_f(t_{pay} - t_{fix}).$$

Substituting the expression for the forward rate from Equation 6.2,

$$f = N \left(\frac{\delta_{fix}}{\delta_{pay}} - 1 \right).$$

Then we discount the floating cash flow to get its present value

$$\begin{aligned} PV(f) &= N\delta_{pay} \left(\frac{\delta_{fix}}{\delta_{pay}} - 1 \right) \\ &= N \left(\delta_{fix} - \delta_{pay} \right). \end{aligned}$$

This is exactly the same present value as two fixed payments of $+N$ at time t_{fix} and $-N$ at time t_{pay}. Alternatively we can think of this as a way of re-stating the fact that we can generate a stream of floating payments by repeatedly investing some notional N at the beginning of each period. At the end of the period our notional is returned and we can skim off the LIBOR payment. Then we re-invest the notional and the process repeats until the stream of floating payments terminates. So a single floating payment can be replicated by two fixed payments. In the following diagram notice that the floating payment is much smaller than the replicating cash flows, as the forward rate generates an interest payment that is a few percent of the notional.

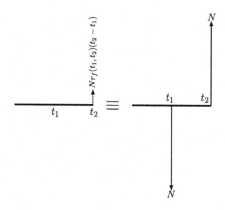

Now what happens when we add the next floating payment? The fixing time of the second coincides with the payment time of the first or equivalently $t^1_{pay} = t^2_{fix}$. We can re-label the cash flow times $t^1_{pay} = t^2_{fix} = t_1$, $t^2_{pay} = t^3_{fix} = t_2$, and so on.

Time	t_1	t_2	t_3
First Floating Payment	$-N$	$+N$	
Second Floating Payment		$-N$	$+N$
Net Payment	$-N$	0	$+N$

The intermediate cash flows cancel leaving fixed payments at times t_1 of $-N$ and t_3 of $+N$.

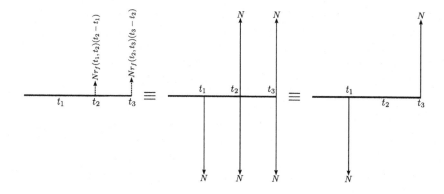

And if we were to add a third floating payment then the middle cash flows cancel again.

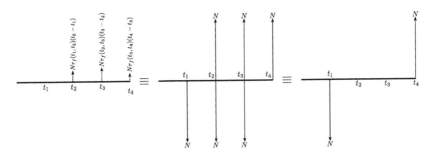

Alternatively here is the same information in tabular form.

Time	t_1	t_2	t_3	t_4
First Floating Payment	$-N$	$+N$		
Second Floating Payment		$-N$	$+N$	
Third Floating Payment			$-N$	$+N$
Net Payment	$-N$	0	0	$+N$

As we add more floating payments then given that the payment date of the previous and fixing date of the next coincide exactly we can cancel out all of the intermediate payments. So what remains is a fixed payment at time t_1 of $-N$ and another fixed payment at time t_n of $+N$.

6.1.2 Interest Rate Sensitivity

Owners of interest rate swaps want to know the sensitivity of their instrument to shifts in the yield curve. As with bonds, a useful measure of this sensitivity is DV01, the dollar value of an "01", which is the dollar amount by which the present value changes if there is a one basis point increase in the yield curve. Because swaps are unfunded it makes no sense to talk about the duration of a swap. By unfunded we mean that the value of a swap starts at zero on the trade date so any percentage change in value will involve division by zero, and as duration is a multiplier that gives the percentage change in value for a percentage rate change it will blow up for swaps. DV01 is a dollar amount not a percentage so it makes perfect sense to use DV01 as a measure of interest rate sensitivity for swaps. We have a choice of which curve we want to shift: zero, forward or par. We choose to shock the zero curve here but it is possible to shock any member of the rate trinity to find the zero, forward or par rate DV01, and each will give a slightly different answer.

Almost all of the interest rate sensitivity of an interest rate swap is at the maturity date. If we want to see where the greatest sensitivity lies in the term structure we can apply a 1 basis point shift at each term and see how it affects the value of the swap. If we are careful about how we "shock" the curve, such that we apply tent functions centred around each maturity of interest then the total sensitivities should add up to the total DV01. The places where we place our tent functions are the KEY RATES. As we will see, most of the interest rate sensitivity of an interest rate swap comes from the floating leg. As the floating leg can be replaced by two notional cash flows of $-N$

at the first float fixing date and $+N$ at the expiry date the final replicating cash flow will carry almost all the interest rate sensitivity.

Before embarking on an elaborate calculation it is always useful to build some intuition about the approximate answer. We know that a five year interest rate swap embodies the interest rate risk of a five year fixed coupon bond with a coupon equal to the par swap rate. A five year bond will have a duration of just over four years, and its DV01 on a present value of \$10 million will be about \$10 million times the duration divided by 10,000 (see Equation 5.5 in Section 5.5.3 on page 184). If we use the DV01 equation for a face value of \$10 million this is $\frac{10000000}{10000c}[1 - \delta(5)]$. The par coupon c is 5.0703218% and discount factor in 5 years $\delta(5)$ is 0.778479 giving a DV01 of \$4,369. To be still more precise we can replicate the swap cash flows by being long a fixed coupon par bond and short a floater from the same issuer with the same maturity. The floater will have a duration that is roughly the reset period, which is 0.25 years since our floating leg pays quarterly. If the floater duration D is 0.25 years, and the present value of a floater is almost exactly par just after a reset then DV01 is $PV \times D \times \frac{1}{10000}$, which is about \$250. Our total DV01 will be the fixed coupon DV01 minus the floater DV01 or $4369 - 250$ or about \$4,120.

Now that we know the approximate answer we can calculate DV01 more accurately. The total present value of a swap is the sum of the present value of the two legs, and we can differentiate this with respect to the underlying rate

$$\frac{\partial PV}{\partial r} = \frac{\partial PV_{fixed}}{\partial r} + \frac{\partial PV_{float}}{\partial r}.$$

First we will look at the interest rate sensitivity of the floating leg,

$$\frac{\partial PV_{float}}{\partial r} = N(1 + r_{fix}t_1^{A/360})\frac{\partial}{\partial r}\delta_1 - N\frac{\partial}{\partial r}\delta_J.$$

We have replaced the stream of 20 floating payments into two fixed payments because they have exactly the same interest rate sensitivity and are easier to calculate. The first cash flow is $-N$ and occurs at time t_1 and the second is $+N$ and occurs at t_J. These are discounted using compound rates so the derivative of the discount factor is $-\frac{\delta t}{1+\frac{r}{f}}$ where r is the zero rate and f is the compounding frequency. The interest rate sensitivity is

$$\frac{\partial PV_{float}}{\partial r} = Nt_J^{A/360}\frac{\delta_J}{1+\frac{r_J}{f}} - (1 + Nr_{fix}t_1^{A/360})t_1^{A/360}\frac{\delta_1}{1+\frac{r_1}{2}}.$$

To make the numbers more manageable we can look at DV01, which is $\frac{1}{10000}\frac{\partial PV_{float}}{\partial r}$. For our swap,

$$\frac{1}{10000}\frac{\partial PV_{float}}{\partial r} = 5075 \times \frac{0.77847913}{1 + \frac{0.049956}{2}} - (1 + 0.05498750 \times 0.261111) \times 2611.11 \times \frac{0.98599149}{1 + \frac{0.054767}{2}}$$

$$= 3854.504 - 254.1891 = 3600.315$$

This floating rate sensitivity can be broken down into three parts: the stub and two floating rate sensitivities,

	Stub	Floating	Floating
	$-r_{fix}\left(t_1^{A/360}\right)^2\delta_1^2$	$t_J^{A/360}\frac{\delta_J}{1+\frac{r_J}{f}}$	$t_1^{A/360}\frac{\delta_1}{1+\frac{r_1}{2}}$
	-3.606392	3854.504	-250.5912

The fixed leg is much simpler and includes the zero rate at the time of fixed cash flow i, which is r_i,

$$\frac{\partial \mathrm{PV}_{fixed}}{\partial r} = Nr_{par}\sum_{i=1}^{I}\Delta t_i^{30/360}\frac{\partial \delta_i}{\partial r}$$

$$= -Nr_{par}\sum_{i=1}^{I}\left(t_i^{30/360}-t_{i-1}^{30/360}\right)\delta_i\frac{t_i^{30/360}}{1+\frac{r_i}{2}}$$

For our swap the interest rate sensitivity of the fixed leg is \$571.53. The total sensitivity is

$$\frac{\partial \mathrm{PV}}{\partial r} = \frac{\partial \mathrm{PV}_{fixed}}{\partial r}+\frac{\partial \mathrm{PV}_{float}}{\partial r}$$

$$= 571.53 + 3600.32,$$

which is \$4,171.85. This is close to our rough estimate of \$4,120.

6.2 Flatteners, Steepeners and Butterflies

When we plot the current set of swap rates against their expiry time we have the swap curve. The volume of interest rate swaps traded is colossal and all this liquidity means that the swap curve for all major currencies is very smooth. If we were to plot the swap curve every day we would see that the shape of the curve is continually changing. An analysis of the way it moves shows that three changes dominate: 93% of day to day movement is a parallel up and down shift of the entire curve, 6% is a steepening or flattening and 1% is twisting (see Section 3.9 on page 119 for details). If you believe that swap rates of a particular maturity will increase then you would enter a payer's swap, and if you think rates will fall you would enter a receiver's swap. However some people have opinions about whether the curve will steepen or flatten. To make money from flattening and steepening an investor has to enter into two swaps: a payer where rates will rise and a receiver where rates will fall. The shorter and longer dated maturities are usually called the short end and long end and this class of trades is known as a CURVE PLAY. Assuming that the swap curve is upward sloping these are the trades that would harvest curve steepening or flattening:

	Short End	Long End
Curve Steepens	Falls, receive fixed	Rises, pay fixed
Curve Flattens	Rises, pay fixed	Falls, receive fixed

The maturities will depend on how an investor sees the curve shape changing, but a common choice is to use maturities of two years and ten years. This would be called a 2's 10's steepener or flattener. A very important consideration is how to choose the notional amounts of the two swaps. Ideally the investor would like to be paid while they wait for the curve to steepen or flatten. The amount paid to maintain a trade is called the CARRY RATE and investors naturally favour trades with POSITIVE CARRY over trades with NEGATIVE CARRY. Two standard ways of choosing the notionals are to have trades that are:

DV01 neutral where the notionals are chosen to have equal and opposite sensitivity to parallel up-shifts and down-shifts of the entire swap curve. This sensitivity is the change in value of the swap, as a dollar amount, for a 1 basis point shift in the curve. If the DV01 of the payer and receiver swap are exactly equal and opposite then the overall position will not make or lose money as the swap curve shifts up and down. However this position may result in negative carry.

Carry_neutral so that the amount received on the receiver swap is exactly equal to the amount paid on the payer swap. This suffers the drawback that the position may be sensitive to parallel upward and downward shifts in the swap curve rather than just steepening and flattening.

Swaps are by no means the only way to put on a curve play. Using bonds one would go short a bond at the maturity that is expected to rise and buy a bond at the maturity where rates are expected to fall and the face values can also be chosen to be DV01-neutral or carry-neutral. Using bond futures is similar, as they behave like leveraged positions in government bonds, and the sign is therefore the same as for bonds; sell a bond future at the maturity that will rise and buy a bond future at the maturity that will fall. Interest futures are another means to put on a curve play. Because the value of an interest rate future is 100 minus the LIBOR rate, as rates rise the price of the future drops. So you would buy bond futures at the maturities where you would expect rates to fall and sell bond futures at the maturities you would expect to rise. Buying a forward rate agreement is an agreement to borrow forward at a fixed rate, and this position will benefit if rates rise, so FRAs are bought at maturities where rates are expected to rise and sold at maturities where rates are expected to fall. The direction of these trades is summarized in Table 6.5.

Although the examples we deal with in this section deal exclusively with interest rate curve plays the same ideas apply to any kind of rate curve. For example investors with a view about the evolution of the term structure of interest rates can express this view using either index-linked bonds or in synthetic form with inflation-linked swaps. Similarly, credit investors can put on single-name credit curve steepeners and flatteners. Instead of using sensitivity to a one basis point shift in interest rates to decide on notional amounts, an inflation curve play would use sensitivity to a one basis point shift in inflation, and a credit curve play would use sensitivity to a one basis point shift in credit spread. Another more complex trade would be to trade steepness of the interest rate curve in one currency against the steepness of another while taking some foreign exchange risk. This could reflect an opinion about a divergence in monetary policy between two central banks such as the Fed and the European Central Bank.

	Rate Increase	**Rate Decrease**
Interest Rate Swap	Payer (pay fixed)	Receiver (receive fixed)
Fixed Coupon Bond	Sell short	Buy
Bond Future	Sell	Buy
Interest Rate Future	Sell	Buy
Forward Rate Agreement	Buy	Sell

Table 6.5: Trade direction to benefit from rate changes.

Options also have a term structure of volatility which can be traded via buying and selling options with different expiries.

The language used to explain bond yield curve changes is also used to explain swap yield curve changes. When many investors buy a bond with a particular maturity it drives up the price and drives down the yield, as yields and prices move inversely. If the curve is upward sloping and steepening this could be caused by heavy investor buying at the short end pushing down short-term yield, or it could be heavy selling of long term bonds pushing up long-term yield, or a combination of both. The buying explanation is bullish and the selling explanation is bearish. So the following language is used:

Bull Steepening Intense buying of bonds with short maturities is pushing down short-term rates.

Bull Flattening Intense buying of bonds with long maturities is pushing down long-term rates.

Bear Steepening Intense selling of bonds with long maturities is pushing up long-term rates.

Bear Flattening Intense selling of bonds with short maturities is pushing up short-term rates.

Bond prices are driven by expectations of interest rates, inflation and credit concerns. For the short end of the curve monetary policy is very important. This is because the central bank will set the short term rate in order to keep inflation under control while maintaining growth. If the central bank changes the short term rate the rate on all bonds, both government and corporate, will track that rate. In the United States bond investors have the adage "Don't Fight the Fed" suggesting it is wisest to buy what the Fed buys, particularly if the Fed is doing something exceptional such as quantitative easing. For the short end of the curve inflation is less important than the long end because during the brief life of the bond inflation will not greatly affect its value. At the long end however inflation plays a dominant role because over long periods of time what investors should look for is a real rate of return, which is the nominal yield minus the rate of inflation. A rise in inflation expectations will cause a sell-off of long dated bonds and a rise in yield. Finally credit risk drives prices for corporate

	N_2	N_{10}
DV01 & Pitch	$-\dfrac{N_5}{2}\dfrac{D_5}{D_2}$	$-\dfrac{N_5}{2}\dfrac{D_5}{D_{10}}$
Carry & Pitch	$-\dfrac{r_5}{r_2+\frac{D_2}{D_{10}}r_{10}}N_5$	$-\dfrac{D_2}{D_{10}}\dfrac{r_5}{r_2+\frac{D_2}{D_{10}}r_{10}}N_5$
DV01 & Carry	$-\dfrac{N_5r_5+N_{10}r_{10}}{r_2}$	$-\dfrac{1}{r_2}\left(r_5+r_{10}\dfrac{r_5D_2-r_2D_5}{r_2D_{10}-r_{10}D_2}\right)N_5$

Table 6.6: Constructing swap butterflies.

bonds, and after the sovereign debt crisis in Europe, this includes credit risk for some government bonds. Bond investors will punish poor credits by selling their bonds and reward good credits by buying their bonds. An increase in credit risk will spark selling of bonds and push up yields, particularly for longer dated bonds.

Sometimes a kink appears in a swap curve where the swap rate at a particular maturity is low or high relative to the rest of the curve. Historically the swap curve tends to be smooth so one would expect that this kink would iron itself out over time. To harvest this de-kinking we can trade the kink against the two swaps with neighbouring maturities. The trade is called a BUTTERFLY because we are trading the body, where the kink lies, against the wings either side. Again we have to choose the size of each trade but now we have three notionals to choose which gives us an added degree of freedom. Ideally we would like the trade to have positive carry, while being insensitive to general upward and downward changes in rates and insensitive to steepening and flattening of the curve, or PITCH-NEUTRAL. Because we have three degrees of freedom we can achieve any two of the three properties: DV01-neutral, carry-neutral and pitch-neutral. If the "belly" of the butterfly is at 5 years and the wings are at two years and 10 years (a 2s 5s 10s butterfly), we can fix the belly notional to be N_5 then choose the two year notional N_2 and ten year notional N_{10} using our choice of constraints. If the DV01s of the three swaps are D_2, D_5 and D_{10} per dollar notional then the overall duration of the butterfly position is just the weighted DV01 of the three swaps,

$$D = N_2 D_2 + N_5 D_5 + N_{10} D_{10},$$

the carry will be

$$C = N_2 r_2 + N_5 r_5 + N_{10} r_{10},$$

and the pitch sensitivity, or sensitivity to steepening and flattening, will be the sum of sensitivity on the right wing $N_{10}D_{10} - N_5D_5$ and on the left wing $N_5D_5 - N_2D_2$

$$
\begin{aligned}
P &= (N_{10}D_{10} - N_5D_5) + (N_5D_5 - N_2D_2) \\
&= N_{10}D_{10} - N_2D_2
\end{aligned}
$$

We can set the overall size of the trade with the belly notional and then use two of the constraints to find the left and right wing notionals. The three solutions to the notionals are shown in Table 6.6 and are derived in more detail in the solutions to the exercises.

If we were to use government bonds to put on our butterfly trade we would start worrying about cost. Whereas an interest rate swap is an unfunded instrument and has no upfront payment a bond requires a payment of roughly the principal amount upfront. The additional constraint we are worried about with a bond butterfly is cost so we can add a constraint that the price to put on the butterfly must be zero. The sum of the present value of the three bonds must be zero. We are either buying the belly and selling the wings or selling the wings and buying the belly. In either case the proceeds from shorting bonds must equal the cost of buying bonds.

$$N_2 PV_2 + N_5 PV_5 + N_{10} PV_{10} = 0$$

Bond futures require a small margin payment up-front so the cost-neutral constraint would be less important. Furthermore bond futures make it just as easy to have a short position in a government bond as having a long position in a government bond whereas shorting the actual cash bonds involves the complications of the repo market. Another approach to choosing the size of the notionals is to use a regression model. Using the historical distribution of returns of the belly against the wings may give a more realistic picture of expected return and risk.

Exercise 44 *Find the two year and ten year notionals N_2 and N_{10} for a 2s 5s 10s butterfly given that the five year notional N_5 is $10 million, and the DV01s for the two year, five year and ten year swaps per $10 million notional are $1,770.37, $4,801.25 and $8,729.53. For a DV01-neutral and pitch-neutral butterfly find the two year notional N_2 and ten year notional N_{10} in terms of the five year notional N_5, the two year duration D_2 and the ten year duration D_{10}. Given that the two year, five year and ten year par swap rates are 0.7864%, 2.144%, and 3.418% construct the carry-neutral, pitch-neutral and DV01-neutral and carry-neutral butterflies.*

Exercise 45 *For a DV01-neutral and pitch-neutral butterfly find the two year notional N_2 and ten year notional N_{10} in terms of the five year notional N_5, the two year duration D_2 and the ten year duration D_{10}.*

Exercise 46 *For a carry-neutral and pitch-neutral butterfly find the two year notional N_2 and ten year notional N_{10} in terms of the five year notional N_5, the two year duration D_2, ten year duration D_{10}, the two year swap rate r_2, five year swap rate r_5 and ten year swap rate r_{10}.*

Exercise 47 *For a DV01-neutral, carry-neutral butterfly find the two year notional N_2 and ten year notional N_{10} in terms of the five year notional N_5, the two year duration D_2, ten year duration D_{10}, the two year swap rate r_2, five year swap rate r_5 and ten year swap rate r_{10}.*

6.3 Forward Starting Swap

If an issuer wants to convert a fixed coupon bond to a floating coupon bond it can do a liability swap. But what if the corporate treasurer knows she will issue a five year fixed coupon bond in one year's time and she wants to set up a swap using today's swap rates? In this case she would enter into a one into five year forward starting receiver swap. The code used to describe forward starting interest rate swaps (and also swaptions which are options to enter into a forward-starting swap) is $s \times m$ where s is when the swap starts and m is its maturity. Our example would be a 1×5, read "one into five" swap because it starts in one year at which time we enter into a five year swap.

An attractive feature of a forward starting swap is that it gives interest rate exposure without any cash flows being paid until the start date. If you want to speculate on interest rates without having to pay or receive any cash flows then you could enter into a payer or receiver swap that starts forward. The direction of interest rate sensitivity is not affected by the fact that your swap starts forward. If you enter into a payer's swap then you will profit from rates increasing and lose if rates decrease. If you enter into a receiver's swap then you will profit if rates decrease and lose if rates increase. Exactly the same is true of a forward starting payer or receiver swap.

Exercise 48 *Find the par swap rate for the one year forward-starting two year swap (the 1×2 or "one into two" swap) if the one, two, three and four year zero rates are 1%, 2%, 3% and 4% respectively.*

6.4 Overnight Indexed Swap

Yield curves are generally upward sloping, so that long-term rates are greater than short-term rates. For this reason banks try to obtain short-term funding through overnight borrowing which is the shortest and cheapest term possible. Banks earn income with assets such as loans and mortgages which are longer term and which provide income at a higher rate because long-term rates are usually greater than short-term rates. If all goes well the bank can borrow at a low rate and lend at a high rate and profit from the NET INTEREST MARGIN which is the difference between the two. However the danger for banks is that they are exposed to increases in the overnight rate. Clearly there is the need for an instrument that allows banks to hedge this exposure. This instrument is known as an overnight indexed swap, abbreviated as OIS SWAP.

An OIS swap, just like a plain fixed to floating interest rate swap, has two legs. The fixed leg is an annuity and the floating leg depends on the geometric average of actual overnight lending rates over the term of the swap. The floating leg index rate depends on the currency of the OIS. For OIS denominated in US dollars the index is the effective federal funds rate, for OIS denominated in euros it is the Euro Overnight Index Average (EONIA) and for OIS denominated in pounds sterling it is the Sterling Overnight Index Average (SONIA). LIBOR can be quoted but need never be traded whereas the effective federal funds rate, EONIA and SONIA are averages of actual rates of overnight borrowing. Another difference between LIBOR and OIS index rates is that LIBOR is an unsecured wholesale money market rate and therefore carries bank credit risk. OIS index rates, such as the federal funds rate, do not incorporate bank credit risk. This means that banks are sometimes willing to pay a hefty premium to lock in a funding rate that gets rid of credit risk.

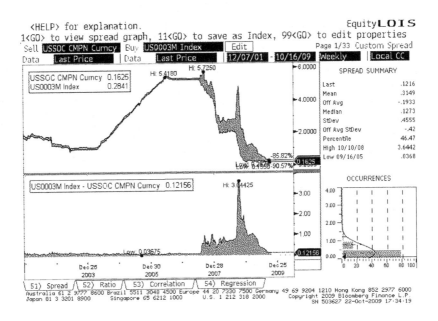

Figure 6.3: LIBOR-OIS spread.

Historically the spread between LIBOR and OIS was about 5 to 10 basis points, but during the Credit Crisis this spread blew out. To take a very extreme example, on October 10th 2008 three month LIBOR was 4.8187% and the OIS rate was 1.1745%. A bank funding itself at three month LIBOR and entering an OIS receiving the OIS rate would have been paying the federal funds rate plus 364 basis points which is a massive premium. Banks were willing to pay this premium in order to avoid the credit risk of other banks and the risk that the overnight lending rate would increase. In fact each time there was a new shock during the Credit Crisis the LIBOR-OIS spread would increase, as shown in Figure 6.3.

For example if the bank borrowed one euro on day 1, then the next day they would roll the borrowing including the interest from the previous day. The amount borrowed accrues interest until the next floating payment. In common with fixed to float interest rate swaps an OIS fixed rate payer profit when rates increase and a fixed rate receiver profits when rates decrease. Say we enter into a one week payer's OIS swap at 1.3031% on a notional of €100 million. Over the term of the OIS swap the observed EONIA rates are as shown in Table 6.7.

At the maturity date the accrued rate of the floating leg is obtained by re-paying and re-investing €1 repeatedly each night at each overnight rate. The rate on Friday is invested over the weekend for three nights. Then the rate is annualized by multiplying the total interest by $\frac{360}{7}$ to give the average rate. The total calculation is as

Date	EONIA	Value of Rolled €Debt
Wed Feb 8, 2012	1.303%	100,003,620
Thu Feb 9, 2012	1.304%	100,007,241
Fri Feb 10, 2012	1.312%	100,018,101
Mon Feb 13, 2012	1.321%	100,021,724
Tue Feb 14, 2012	1.320%	100,025,345

Table 6.7: Cash flows for a payer's OIS swap.

follows:

$$\frac{360}{7}\left[\left(1+\frac{0.01303}{360}\right)\left(1+\frac{0.01304}{360}\right)\left(1+\frac{0.01312\times3}{360}\right)\left(1+\frac{0.01321}{360}\right)\left(1+\frac{0.01320}{360}\right)-1\right]$$

The "average" rate is 1.312% and this would be the rate on the floating leg of the OIS. The amount that changed hands at maturity would be the difference between 1.312% and the fixed payment of 1.303% scaled up by the notional and the period of the swap. This would be $(0.01312-0.01303)\times100,000,000\times\frac{7}{360}$ or €175.

6.5 FX Swap

An FX swap is a way of swapping one currency for another for a period of time without taking FX risk. For example a European company may want to have US dollars for three months. They could do a three month EUR|USD FX swap. On the settlement date they would pay EUR and receive USD converted at the spot rate. They would have USD to play with for three months then at expiry they would pay USD and receive EUR at the three month forward FX rate (see Section 9.1.2 on page 330 for more detail on how FX forward rates are calculated). The FX risk they take with the spot transaction is offset by the FX risk of the forward transaction so overall this trade has no FX risk.

There are strong similarities between an FX swap and an FX forward and this is reflected in they way these products are named. An FX forward is sometimes called an FX OUTRIGHT FORWARD, or just outright forward, and an FX swap is sometimes called an FX SPOT-FORWARD SWAP. To give an example that illustrates the cash flows for an outright forward and an FX spot-forward swap we will buy 10 million EUR forward against USD. Say EUR|USD spot is 1.5, and the one year EUR rate is 3% and the one year USD rate is 5%. Then the outright forward will have no cash flows until maturity when we receive 10 million EUR and pay 15,291,262 USD (the three month forward rate is $1.5\times\frac{1+0.05\times0.25}{1+0.03\times0.25}$ which is 1.5291262). The FX swap will have the same cash flows as the outright forward at expiry but also a spot exchange where we pay 10 million EUR and receive 15 million USD. The cash flows for this FX outright forward and FX spot-forward swap are shown in Figure 6.4.

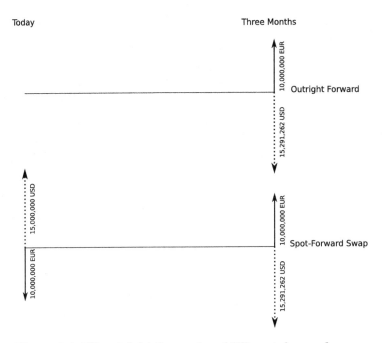

Figure 6.4: FX outright forward and FX spot-forward swap.

6.6 Cross-Currency Basis Swap

When a company wants to issue debt in another currency they can transform the cash flows back into their domestic currency using a cross currency basis swap. It may want to do this because it has exhausted the domestic debt market and feels it has sufficient brand recognition in another market to create demand for its debt and so find a new and cheaper source of capital. In this example we will use the case of a British company that wants to issue debt in the United States. For simplicity this example uses fixed rates even though it is more common to use floating rates. The cash flows would look as follows:

	GBP Issuer		Swap		USD Investors
Issue Date	Receives £50 M	←	Converts $100 M to £50 M	←	Pay $100 M
First Coupon	Pays 10% coupon £5 M	→	Converts £5 M to $10 M	→	Receive $10 M
Second Coupon	Pays 10% coupon £5 M	→	Converts £5 M to $10 M	→	Receive $10 M
...	...		...		...
Maturity Date	Pays 10% coupon £5 M	→	Converts £5 M to $10 M	→	Receive $10 M
Maturity Date	Repays £50 M	→	Converts £50 M to $100 M	→	Receive $100 M

These cash flows are also shown as a cash flow diagram in Figure 6.5. On the issue date the entire bond issue is placed successfully with investors in the United States generating an income of $100 million. The cross currency swap then swaps this $100

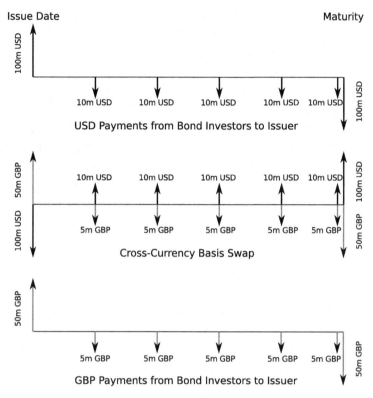

Figure 6.5: FX cross-currency basis swap.

million into £50 million which the UK company can then use to run its business. As each coupon payment comes due the issuer pays 10% of the face value in Sterling, or £5 million, then this is converted by the swap into $10 million that is divided amongst the bond investors. At maturity the last coupon of £5 million and the principal of £50 million is repaid in Sterling, converted to $110 million and the investors are repaid their principal and last coupon.

Basis swaps are quoted as a fixed spread added to one of the legs, and are usually quoted against USD. Figure 6.6 shows the euro basis swap rate over the period from 2000 until early 2011. For example, an investor wanting to swap euros for dollars would pay USD LIBOR flat (i.e. no spread) and receive euribor plus a fixed basis swap rate. When the EURUSD basis swap rate is negative it is subtracted from the Euribor payment and shows a willingness to receive less euro interest in order to satisfy the demand for dollars. For example European banks with loans in USD would use a basis swap to convert their capital from euros to US dollars to service their dollar-denominated debt.

Dollar Demand vs. Euro	Basis Swap Rate	Swap EUR→USD	Swap USD→EUR
High	Decrease (more negative)	More expensive	Less expensive
Low	Increase (more positive)	Less expensive	More expensive

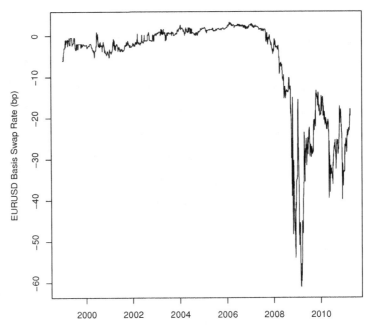

Figure 6.6: EURUSD basis swap rate history. Source: Bloomberg.

As demand to swap euros into dollars increases the increasing cost is reflected as the basis becoming more negative. Figure 6.6 clearly shows the effect of the Credit Crisis on the euro basis swap rate. From 2000 until 2007 the rate was close to zero. The euro basis swap rate turned sharply negative just after the Lehman default in September 2008 as European banks needed to convert euros to dollars to service their dollar loans and trading book transactions. The next two downward spikes are due to the European sovereign debt crisis as investors sought to swap their euros for the safe haven of US dollars. Both financial and non-financial European companies can take advantage of such strongly negative basis swap rates to issue debt in US dollars, swap it back into euros, and lock in a low cost of funding.

6.7 Total Return Swap

Instead of buying an asset and holding it on your own balance sheet it is possible to get an investment bank to buy the asset on your behalf and pay you the income or you pay the loss generated by that asset. In return you can pay the investment bank their funding cost to buy the asset. This is a TOTAL RETURN SWAP because you are swapping the return on the asset for funding payments. So the two sets of cash flows are that you receive any increase in value and pay any decrease in value on one leg and pay LIBOR plus some spread on the funding leg. There is a risk that the bank will go bankrupt while owing you money, so total return swaps come with the bank's credit risk. An investor can go long or short the underlying asset or assets by choosing to receive or pay the total returns. If the underlying asset is a stock then the return will include the share price performance as well as any dividends paid. If the underlying is a bond then the return will include bond price performance as well as any coupon paid.

Total return swaps are quoted as a bid and offer funding spread. For example a quote might be -10|20. This means that if you want to go long the underlying you will pay LIBOR + 20 basis points funding in return for receiving the total return on the asset. If you want to go short the underlying you will be paid LIBOR - 10 basis points in return for paying the total return on the asset. The margin that is required by the issuer of the swap depends on several factors. There will be a base margin, say 10%, that depends on the credit-worthiness of the buyer of the swap. Then there will be various add-ons that depend on the asset itself. This will include add-ons for

Volatility Greater volatility results in greater margin add-on because it means greater risk.

Illiquidity Assets that take a long time to sell are illiquid. The thinner the market and the greater the illiquidity the greater the margin add-on. If the owner of the swap closes their position it may take a long time to unwind the issuer's hedge leaving them exposed to price risk, so the issuer has to be compensated for this risk.

Concentration If one asset dominates the portfolio this makes the portfolio returns more volatile and will require greater margin than a diversified portfolio.

Duration Bonds with greater duration have greater interest rate sensitivity and greater interest rate risk.

Total return swaps are extremely flexible. For example the asset can be anything, such as a single equity, a single bond, or an entire portfolio combining equities and bonds. Why would an investor choose to have a total return swap rather than own the assets on its own balance sheet? The most compelling reason is leverage. If you buy a stock for $100 then you have to put that capital on the table as soon as the trade settles. If you get exposure to the stock price and dividends through a total return swap on the stock you will only have to pay a fraction of the $100 in margin, maybe $10, and you will still get the same price exposure and dividends as if you had bought the stock directly. Secondly total return swaps can give exposure to markets that are usually unavailable. For example a hedge fund based in the United States may want to buy LG Electronics stock in Korea. The hedge fund could ask a global investment bank, which has a seat on the Korean Stock Exchange, for a total return swap on LG Electronics. The investment bank will hedge itself by buying the stock in Korea then pay any returns to the hedge fund. In return the hedge fund will pay the funding cost for purchasing LG stock to the bank. Thirdly there may be tax incentives for using a total return swap. If Korea did not have a tax treaty with the United States the hedge fund may have to pay tax on their LG stock in both Korea and the United States. The total return swap ensures that the hedge fund will only have to pay one set of taxes (WITHOLDING TAX) because the investment bank can hold the stock in an account in Korea and pay local Korean axes. Investors in the UK have to pay a tax called STAMP

DUTY on every equity trade but market makers do not, so by having the bank buy the stock the benefit can be passed on to the hedge fund. Fourthly there may be funding benefits for using a total return swap. If the hedge fund does not have a good credit rating it may have to pay a high rate to borrow money to fund the purchase. A bank will probably have access to cheaper funding which it can pass on to the hedge fund through the total return swap.

There are many variations on the total return swap theme. If the swap pays only the price increase and decrease and not the dividend or coupon then it is a PRICE RETURN SWAP. We can also vary the payment frequency and resets on both legs of the swap. A RESET on the interest leg can incorporate two things. The funding leg is exactly like the floating leg of an interest rate swap in that it will reset the interest rate based on the observed value of some published interest rate index like LIBOR with a spread e.g. LIBOR + 50 basis points. The funding leg differs from the floating leg of a fixed for floating interest rate swap because the notional can reset based on the current market value of the underlying. So say that we have agreed to pay LIBOR + 50 basis points on the funding leg for a purchase of $1 million worth of a stock and these are annual payments. If the value of one year LIBOR is 3% then our first annual interest payment would be $1,000,000 \times (0.03 + 0.005)$ or $35,000. If we have no notional reset we will pay this amount each year for the life of the swap. If the notional of the funding leg resets then we would observe the market value of the underlying on the reset date then pay the next funding payment based on the new notional. If the stock has fallen in value by 20% then we would pay just $28,000 on the next year's funding payment.

If a hedge fund wants to trade large volumes through total return swaps then it will probably create a PORTFOLIO SWAP. Portfolio swaps are offered by investment banks to their hedge fund clients as part of their services as a PRIME BROKER. A prime broker is an investment bank with which a hedge fund does most of their business. Portfolio swaps require some additional legal documentation in the form of a Portfolio Swap Master Confirmation in addition to the normal ISDA documentation for OTC swaps. Once this is in place the hedge fund can very easily trade equity swaps. This is simply a matter of a single flag in their trade request saying "I want to buy/sell amount X of stock Y on swap" rather than another flag that says "I want to buy/sell amount X of stock Y on equity". Trading on swap means that the asset sits on the prime broker's balance sheet which means that the hedge fund does not have to worry about clearing or custody. The prime broker will partly fund the purchase giving the hedge fund leverage. For example if a hedge fund buys $10 million notional of a bond the prime broker will lend $7 million toward the purchase and the hedge fund will pay just $3 million. Trading on swap can come with tax advantages such as not having to pay stamp duty on equity trades in the UK. It may also mean reduced fees because the purchase is being done by the prime broker which sits directly on the exchange.

One of the benefits of having a prime broker is CROSS-MARGINING. If a hedge fund has a huge position in a single stock the value of that position will fluctuate a great deal day to day, it will therefore have a high volatility and a large margin add-on for volatility. If the fund has many diversified stocks the overall fluctuation will be smaller and less volatile, so the margin requirement imposed by the prime broker will be smaller. From the hedge fund's point of view cross-margining is a strong argument for keeping their positions with a single prime broker because less margin means more leverage. Against this the hedge fund has to balance the credit risk of being entangled with an investment bank that may go bankrupt while holding onto their margin. The compromise is usually to have several prime brokers.

6.8 Swaps with Varying Notional

With a plain vanilla fixed-for-floating swap the notional never changes. For corporates who have time-varying interest rate exposure it would be expensive to keep buying and selling swaps to match their exposure because they would have to cross the bid-offer spread continually. If their interest rate exposure is gradually decreasing with time the appropriate swap would be an AMORTIZING SWAP. An amortizing swap is useful for hedging the interest rate exposure of a pool of mortgages where the principal pays down over time. If the exposure is increasing with time the appropriate product would be an ACCRETING SWAP. Increasing interest rate exposure would be expected from a long-term infrastructure project where more money is scheduled to be borrowed in future. If the interest rate exposure of a company is seasonal then it is possible to enter into a swap where the notional varies with time in a predictable way and this is called a ROLLERCOASTER SWAP.

If we own a callable bond then the issuer can choose to call the bond on or after certain dates. If we have hedged the interest rate risk of this callable asset with a payer's swap then we are hedged until the issuer calls the bond. Once the bond is called we are left with the hedge which gives us an unwanted interest rate exposure. For this reason it is useful to have a CANCELLABLE SWAP that gives us the option to get rid of the swap if the issuer calls. It is possible to construct a cancellable swap from a vanilla swap and a SWAPTION, which is an option to enter into a swap. Using the example of hedging a callable bond, our hedge would be a vanilla payer's swap but we would also buy a receiver's swaption. If the bond is called then we would exercise our receiver's swaption and the cash flows of the receiver's swap would cancel those of the original payer's swap. By combining a vanilla swap with a swaption it is also possible to create an EXTENDIBLE SWAP that allows the life of the swap to be extended. If we wanted to extend a payer's swap then we would buy a payer's swaption with expiry falling on the termination date of the first swap.

6.9 Inflation Swaps

Inflation is a measure of the value of money and is a concern for long-term investors because positive inflation erodes the value of capital. This leads investors to seek some type of hedge against inflation. This comes in two forms, one funded and one unfunded. The funded form of protection is to buy government inflation-linked bonds as described in Section 5.16 on page 219. Unfortunately these are issued in finite amounts so the maturity and amount may not meet all requirements. The unfunded form of protection is an inflation swap where unfunded means that we pay nothing up-front to enter into the swap.

Being over-the-counter has all the usual benefits and drawbacks. Inflation-linked swaps can be traded in large size with any maturity but the investor will have to consider the creditworthiness of their inflation-linked swap counterparty. And just as with fixed-for-floating interest rate swaps investors can use inflation swaps either to hedge away their inflation risk or they can use inflation swaps to take on inflation risk seeking speculative return. If a pension fund has index-linked funds then the link with inflation can be created by having non-inflation-linked bonds combined with inflation swaps. Hedge funds can use inflation swaps to take speculative positions that express a view on inflation as they are able and willing to use the inherent leverage of this unfunded instrument.

An inflation swap has a fixed leg where the payments are a fixed rate times some notional amount and a floating leg where the cash flows depend on the value of an inflation index, such as the US Consumer Price Index (CPI). This seems very similar to a fixed for floating interest rate swap, but for an inflation swap the floating leg is indexed to CPI rather than LIBOR plus some fixed spread. However one critical difference is that if there is a period of deflation during which the value of CPI decreases the investor would have to pay on *both* legs. Furthermore there is no theoretical limit on the size of deflation and although this extreme downside is unlikely investors should beware. If the swap notional is N and the inflation index for cash flow n is $I(n)$ and the length of the nth period is Δt_n then the floating payment will be

$$ N \times \left[\frac{I(n)}{I(0)} - 1 \right] \times \Delta t_n. $$

The index at the effective date of the swap is $I(0)$ and if $I(n) > I(0)$ then the floating payment will be positive if we are receiving floating and paying fixed. If $I(n) < I(0)$ due to deflation over the life of the swap then the floating payment will be negative so the investor will pay on both legs. There is a twist, just as there is for inflation-linked bonds. The index I will depend on the lagged value of the inflation index, usually based on a three month lag. This lag is also used to calculate cash flows for inflation-linked bonds. The fixed leg would simply be the fixed swap rate r times the notional and the payment period $Nr\Delta t_n$.

Inflation swaps are usually long-dated with maturities ranging up to 30 years, sometimes to 50 years. The most popular form of inflation-linked swap is a ZERO COUPON INFLATION SWAP. Instead of paying periodic coupons on the fixed and floating legs all the cash flows are rolled up into one fixed and one floating payment at the termination date. The value of the fixed rate will be chosen such that the value of the two legs are equal and opposite and future inflation rates will be taken from the inflation forward curve. The mark to market value of the swap will be positive if realized rates of inflation exceed those priced into the swap on the trade date if the investor is paying fixed.

6.10 Variance Swaps

Extending the concept of a swap further we could pay a regular fixed amount and receive the realized volatility of some underlying. We can draw an analogy with a fixed for floating payer's interest rate swap where we would profit if the index interest rate increased. If the realized volatility at expiry has increased above the level priced into the swap on the trade date then the investor will profit. If realized volatility is less than the amount priced into the swap the investor will lose money. If the investor thinks volatility will increase they will receive realized volatility and pay a fixed amount and if they believe volatility will fall they will pay realized volatility and receive a fixed amount. Having a view on the direction of volatility is quite natural to option investors so this product is a pure way to take a view on the future behaviour of volatility. By taking positions at two or more expiries the investor can express views about the steepness or curvature of forward volatility curve.

The payoff of a variance swap is the difference between the realized variance and the strike variance. The strike variance is the square of the strike volatility so it is usually written σ_X^2. If the daily prices for the underlying are P_i then the daily log returns are $r_i = \ln \frac{P_i}{P_{i-1}}$ and scaling the payoff by the contract dollar notional N the payoff at expiry is

$$
\begin{aligned}
V &= \text{Notional} \times (\text{realized variance} - \text{strike}) \\
&= N \times (\sigma^2 - \sigma_X^2) \\
&= N \times (\tfrac{252}{n} \sum_{i=1}^{n} r_i^2 - \sigma_X^2)
\end{aligned}
$$

Another way of looking at this payoff is in terms of daily payments. Each day the investor receives the realized variance $\frac{252}{n} r^2$ for that day and they pay some fixed amount $\frac{X^2}{n}$. If the realized variance they receive is greater than the fixed amount they pay they will make a profit on that day. If the realized variance is less than the amount they pay they will make a loss on that day. The final payoff is just a sum of these daily profits and losses. Because this is a pure volatility instrument it makes sense to think of it in terms of vega. Vega is sensitivity of the value of the variance swap to volatility and it is measured in dollars per volatility point. Vega is used because investors want to know how much money they will make if volatility changes. Differentiating with respect to volatility σ it is easy to show that if we have dollar notional N vega is

$$
\nu = \frac{\partial V}{\partial \sigma} = 2\sigma N.
$$

If we want vega to be \$100,000 then this means we make \$100,000 if realized volatility increases by 1%. As a simple example of variance swap pricing we will use the returns on the S&P 500 Index between May 12th and May 27th, 2010. These are shown in Table 6.8. We will assume we have an 11 day variance swap and that the fair strike on May 12th was 26% (actually 25.888% in case you want to work through the example) which was set such that no money changed hands on the settlement date. Now that we know the strike σ_X^2 we can calculate the dollar notional

$$
N = 100 \times \frac{\nu}{2\sigma_X}
$$

where we scale by 100 because vega is quoted as a percentage. Our dollar notional will be $100 \times \frac{100000}{2 \times 0.25888}$ or \$19,313,968. This seems rather large, but like any swap notional this amount is simply used as a scaling factor and never actually changes hands.

Date	S&P 500	Log-Return	Log-Return^2	Daily Vol.	P&L
May 12	1171.67				
May 13	1157.44	-0.0122	0.00014931	19.40	-51,606.43
May 14	1135.68	-0.0190	0.00036021	30.13	41,705.74
May 17	1136.94	+0.0011	0.00000123	1.76	-117,128.69
May 18	1120.80	-0.0143	0.00020442	22.70	-27,221.73
May 19	1115.05	-0.0051	0.00002646	8.17	-105,967.18
May 20	1071.59	-0.0398	0.00158052	63.11	581,651.56
May 21	1087.69	+0.0149	0.00022239	23.67	-19,274.05
May 24	1073.65	-0.0130	0.00016880	20.62	-42,986.66
May 25	1074.03	+0.0004	0.00000013	0.56	-117,617.32
May 26	1067.95	-0.0057	0.00003223	9.01	-103,412.78
May 27	1103.06	+0.0323	0.00104634	51.35	345,297.53

Table 6.8: S&P 500 variance swap from May 12 to 27, 2010.

Every day the investor pays their swap counterparty a fixed amount of \$117,672.70 (which is $N \times \frac{X^2}{n} = 19313968 \times \frac{0.25888}{11}$). What they are hoping is that the S&P 500 will have a daily volatility that exceeds the strike of 25.888%. We can see that this occurs on May 14, 20 and 27. On May 14th the realized volatility of the S&P 500 was 30.13%. The investor receives a payment of $N \frac{252}{n} r^2 = 19313968 \times \frac{252}{11} \times 0.0190^2$ which is \$159,378.47 creating a net profit of \$41,705.74 for that day. Notice that the variance swap investor does not care about which direction the market moves. All they care about is that it moves a lot in either direction and keeps moving each day.

The total realized volatility over this 11 day period is found by taking the square root of the summed squared log returns and then annualizing the result. This is $\sqrt{\frac{252}{11} \Sigma_{i=1}^{11} r_i^2}$ which is 29.47403% and good news for our swap investor as it is greater than the strike volatility which was 25.888%. The total value of the swap after 11 days is

$$19313968 \times \left(0.2947403^2 - 0.25888^2\right),$$

which is \$383,440. Alternatively we could add up the daily profits and losses and come up with the same final value.

Sophisticated investors may want to hedge or take a position in correlation. This can be structured with variance swaps. If the investor wants to buy correlation exposure they can buy a variance swap on an index, such as the S&P 500 and sell variance swaps on the members of the index. Thinking in terms of a covariance matrix for equities in the S&P 500 buying the var swap on the index is creating exposure to the entire matrix. Selling individual member variance swaps sets the diagonal of the covariance matrix to zero. All that remains are the off-diagonal elements that depend on correlation. Hedging mechanics are complicated because index member weightings change over time requiring adjustment of notional exposure of the single-equity var swaps. Alternatively an investor can buy or sell the whole package which is called a CORRELATION SWAP and leave the details of construction to the structurer.

Answers to Exercises

41 *What is the cost of entering a par payer's swap on the trade date?*
Nothing, as this is the definition of a par swap.

42 *Find the par swap rate if the one, two and three year zero rates are 1%, 2% and 3% respectively.*

Year	1	2	3
Zero Rate	1%	2%	3%
Discount Factor	0.9901	0.9612	0.9151
Forward Rate	1%	3.01%	5.03%

A rough estimate is that the par swap rate would be the average forward rate $\frac{1+3+5}{3} = 3$. The actual par swap rate is $\frac{0.08486}{2.866}$ which is 2.96%.

43 For $J = 4$ the summation is

$$\sum_{i=2}^{4} \delta_{i-1} - \delta_i = \delta_1 - \delta_2 + \delta_2 - \delta_3 + \delta_3 - \delta_4$$
$$= \delta_1 - \delta_4.$$

If we increase J the intermediate terms still cancel so we are left with just the first and last terms of the summation δ_1 and δ_J,

$$\sum_{i=2}^{J} \delta_{i-1} - \delta_i = \delta_1 - \delta_2 + \delta_2 - \delta_3 + \ldots - \delta_{J-1} + \delta_{J-1} - \delta_J$$
$$= \delta_1 - \delta_J.$$

44 *Find the two year and ten year notionals N_2 and N_{10} for a 2s 5s 10s butterfly given that the five year notional N_5 is \$10 million, and the DV01s for the two year, five year and ten year swaps per \$10 million notional are \$1,770.37, \$4,801.25 and \$8,729.53. For a DV01-neutral and pitch-neutral butterfly find the two year notional N_2 and ten year notional N_{10} in terms of the five year notional N_5, the two year duration D_2 and the ten year duration D_{10}. Given that the two year, five year and ten year par swap rates are 0.7864%, 2.144%, and 3.418% construct the carry-neutral, pitch-neutral and DV01-neutral and carry-neutral butterflies.*
If the butterfly is DV01-neutral and pitch-neutral then

$$N_2 = - \frac{N_5}{2} \frac{D_5}{D_2}$$
$$= - \frac{10}{2} \frac{4801.25}{1770.37}$$
$$= - 13.56$$

And

$$N_{10} = -\frac{N_5}{2}\frac{D_5}{D_{10}}$$

$$= -\frac{10}{2}\frac{4801.25}{8729.53}$$

$$= -2.75$$

Just to check, our total DV01 is

$$-13.56 \times 1770.37 + 10 \times 4801.25 - 2.75 \times 8729.53$$

This is very close to zero, and so is the pitch sensitivity

$$2.75 \times 8729.53 - 13.56 \times 1770.37$$

Putting numbers into the other two butterflies gives:

	N_2	N_5	N_{10}
DV01 & Pitch	-13.56	10	-2.750
Carry & Pitch	-14.49	10	-2.939
DV01 & Carry	-431.6	10	-93.03

The extremely large notional for the DV01-neutral and carry-neutral butterfly is due to the extremely small par premium for the two year swap (0.7864%) compared to the ten year swap (3.418%).

45 *For a DV01-neutral and pitch-neutral butterfly find the two year notional N_2 and ten year notional N_{10} in terms of the five year notional N_5, the two year duration D_2 and the ten year duration D_{10}.*

If the butterfly is DV01-neutral then $D = 0$, and if it is pitch-neutral then $P = 0$, so we have to solve

$$N_2 D_2 + N_5 D_5 + N_{10} D_{10} = 0$$

$$N_{10} D_{10} - N_2 D_2 = 0$$

From the pitch-neutral constraint we know that $N_{10}D_{10} = N_2 D_2$ which we can substitute into the DV01-neutral constraint equation to get

$$N_2 D_2 + N_5 D_5 + N_2 D_2 = 0$$

$$2 N_2 D_2 = -N_5 D_5$$

$$N_2 = -\frac{N_5}{2}\frac{D_5}{D_2}$$

Substituting this into $N_{10}D_{10} = N_2 D_2$

$$N_{10} D_{10} = -\frac{N_5}{2}\frac{D_5}{D_2}D_2$$

$$N_{10} = -\frac{N_5}{2}\frac{D_5}{D_{10}}$$

46 *For a carry-neutral and pitch-neutral butterfly find the two year notional N_2 and ten year notional N_{10} in terms of the five year notional N_5, the two year duration D_2, ten year duration D_{10}, the two year swap rate r_2, five year swap rate r_5 and ten year swap rate r_{10}.*

If the butterfly is carry-neutral then $C = 0$, and if it is pitch-neutral then $P = 0$, so we have to solve

$$
\begin{aligned}
N_2 r_2 + N_5 r_5 + N_{10} D_{10} &= 0 \\
N_{10} D_{10} - N_2 D_2 &= 0
\end{aligned}
$$

From the pitch-neutral constraint we know that $N_{10} = \frac{D_2}{D_{10}} N_2$ which we can substitute into the carry-neutral constraint equation to get

$$
\begin{aligned}
N_2 r_2 + N_5 r_5 + N_{10} r_{10} &= 0 \\
N_2 r_2 + N_5 r_5 + \frac{D_2}{D_{10}} N_2 r_{10} &= 0 \\
N_2 &= -\frac{r_5}{r_2 + \frac{D_2}{D_{10}} r_{10}} N_5
\end{aligned}
$$

And

$$
N_{10} = -\frac{D_2}{D_{10}} \frac{r_5}{r_2 + \frac{D_2}{D_{10}} r_{10}} N_5
$$

47 *For a DV01-neutral, carry-neutral butterfly find the two year notional N_2 and ten year notional N_{10} in terms of the five year notional N_5, the two year duration D_2, ten year duration D_{10}, the two year swap rate r_2, five year swap rate r_5 and ten year swap rate r_{10}.*

If the butterfly is DV01-neutral then $D = 0$ and if it is carry-neutral then $C = 0$, so we have to solve

$$
\begin{aligned}
N_2 D_2 + N_5 D_5 + N_{10} D_{10} &= 0 \\
N_2 r_2 + N_5 r_5 + N_{10} r_{10} &= 0
\end{aligned}
$$

From the carry-neutral constraint we know that

$$
N_2 = -\frac{N_5 r_5 + N_{10} r_{10}}{r_2}
$$

which we can substitute into the DV01-neutral constraint equation

$$
\begin{aligned}
-\frac{N_5 r_5 + N_{10} r_{10}}{r_2} D_2 + N_5 D_5 + N_{10} D_{10} &= 0 \\
r_2 N_5 D_5 + r_2 N_{10} D_{10} &= N_5 r_5 D_2 + N_{10} r_{10} D_2 \\
N_{10} (r_2 D_{10} - r_{10} D_2) &= N_5 (r_5 D_2 - r_2 D_5) \\
N_{10} &= \frac{r_5 D_2 - r_2 D_5}{r_2 D_{10} - r_{10} D_2} N_5
\end{aligned}
$$

and

$$N_2 = -\frac{1}{r_2}\left(r_5 N_5 + r_{10} N_{10}\right)$$

$$= -\frac{1}{r_2}\left(r_5 N_5 + r_{10}\frac{r_5 D_2 - r_2 D_5}{r_2 D_{10} - r_{10} D_2}N_5\right)$$

$$= -\frac{1}{r_2}\left(r_5 + r_{10}\frac{r_5 D_2 - r_2 D_5}{r_2 D_{10} - r_{10} D_2}\right)N_5$$

48 *Find the par swap rate for the one year forward-starting two year swap (the 1×2 or "one into two" swap) if the one, two, three and four year zero rates are 1%, 2%, 3% and 4% respectively.*

As before we can find the discount factors and forward rates.

Year	1	2	3	4
Zero Rate	1%	2%	3%	4%
Discount Factor	0.9901	0.9612	0.9151	0.8548
Forward Rate	1%	3.01%	5.03%	7.06%

The cash flows of the two year forward starting swap look exactly like a spot-starting two year swap, which is a swap that starts life immediately. They are simply shifted one year into the future. This means that the first set of cash flows occur in year two and the last cash flows in year 3. As before we equate the present value of the fixed and floating leg.

$$\text{fixed leg value} = \text{floating leg value}$$

$$r_{par}\left(\delta_2 + \delta_3\right) = f_2\delta_2 + f_3\delta_3$$

$$r_{par}\left(0.9612 + 0.9151\right) = 0.0301 \times 0.9612 + 0.0503 \times 0.9151$$

$$r_{par} = \frac{0.0301 \times 0.9612 + 0.0503 \times 0.9151}{0.9612 + 0.9151}$$

The 1×2 rate is 4%.

Part IV

Credit

7 Credit Derivatives

7.1 Credit Default Swaps

Credit risk is created whenever someone promises to pay someone else in the future, and the risk persists until the promise is fulfilled and all the payments are complete. Credit risk arises because debtors may break their promise to pay their creditors. Once created, credit risk cannot be destroyed but it can be traded using various types of CREDIT DERIVATIVE. For example, bonds are a promise given by a bond issuer to pay principal and coupon payments to bond investors. Bonds generate credit risk because issuers of bonds sometimes fail to pay coupons or repay the principal. Bond investors may therefore want to sell this risk, along with the credit risk premium they receive to take the risk, to someone else. The credit derivative that allows investors to trade credit risk is called a CREDIT DEFAULT SWAP (CDS). There are three entities involved in every credit default swap trade: a buyer of credit protection, a seller of credit protection and the borrower whose credit is being bought and sold. The borrower whose credit is being traded is called the REFERENCE ENTITY and is not directly involved in the trade itself. The buyer of protection is trying to get rid of the reference entity's credit risk and the seller of protection is trying to buy that credit risk. Whoever owns the credit risk is paid a credit risk premium to take the risk. When the protection buyer and seller face one another directly the CDS is over-the-counter but CDS can also be traded through an exchange. Exchange traded CDS, unlike over-the-counter CDS, carry almost no counterparty risk.

The seller of credit protection promises to reimburse the buyer with the face value of a bond triggered by default of the reference entity. In return for this protection the buyer pays the seller a set of fixed premium payments that terminate on maturity of the contract or on default. The event that triggers payment of protection from the seller to the buyer is a CREDIT DEFAULT EVENT and is defined as failure of the reference entity to pay its debts. When a credit event occurs the buyer is paid in one of two ways depending on the type of CDS. If the CDS is PHYSICALLY SETTLED, the buyer delivers their heavily discounted bonds to the seller who returns their face value. If CASH SETTLED the buyer receives cash from the seller. The value of the contract is initially zero so no money changes hands when the deal is made, just like an interest rate swap. Credit default swaps are a pure credit instrument whose value depends only on the market's view of the probability of a company becoming unable to meet its debts. A CDS can be thought of as insurance against default for a bond, although unlike insurance there is no requirement to own any of the issuer's bonds. A common use of CDS is to reduce credit risk for bonds in a portfolio. Another common use is to buy or sell a CDS without owning any bonds to create a highly leveraged gamble on a single company's credit.

For example if the reference entity has the fateful name Risky Corporation then the payments and obligations of the buyer and seller would be as follows:

To the Buyer of Protection on Risky Corp. You pay nothing up front, but agree on $10 million notional protection. In return for protection you pay the seller an annual fee of 50 basis points paid in quarterly installments of $12,500, for five years. If Risky Corp. triggers a credit event the seller reimburses your full notional amount in return for the notional amount of Risky Corp. defaulted bonds, then the contract ends. You profit if Risky Corp.'s credit worsens and its credit spread increases because you are left holding cheap protection.

To the Seller of Protection on Risky Corp. You receive nothing up front. You receive regular payments from the buyer. If Risky Corp. triggers a default event you pay out a large amount in cash to the buyer and receive the defaulted bond which is now trading at a fraction of its notional amount. You profit if the Risky Corp. does not default in the five year lifetime of the contract, or if Risky Corp.'s credit improves and the credit spread decreases.

The CDS market has grown explosively in response to standardised trade documentation called the "Credit Derivatives Definitions" produced by the International Swaps and Derivatives Association (ISDA) in 1999 and updated in 2003. By standardising CDS contracts ISDA transformed a fragmented and illiquid market with large bid-offer spreads into the commoditised, highly liquid, trillion dollar market that we see today. When a CDS trade is done its details are defined in a trade confirmation based on the ISDA credit derivatives definitions. A CDS trade confirmation specifies a REFERENCE ENTITY whose credit worthiness is being sold, and the ISIN or CUSIP code of a REFERENCE OBLIGATION which is a bond issued by the reference entity. It must also define the precise CREDIT EVENTs that trigger a protection payment and terminate the contract. Credit events are usually bankruptcy, failure to pay, or restructuring of the reference entity's debt. It also specifies the notifying party who is able to create a "credit event notice" (usually either the buyer or the seller) that initiates the settlement process. The seller usually doubles as a CALCULATION AGENT who determines the recovery price of the defaulted bonds.

In order to determine the term of protection and payments that will be made a CDS trade confirmation will contain a trade date, an EFFECTIVE DATE when protection begins on T+1 (first calendar day after the trade date) and a TERMINATION DATE when protection ends. The term of a contract is the time between the effective date and termination date, and this is most commonly 5 or 10 years, although the most heavily traded entities have terms in the range 6 months to 30 years. In order to improve liquidity termination dates are standardised to fall on IMM dates[1]: the 20th of March, June, September and December e.g. a five year CDS struck on February 14th 2006 will not terminate on February 14th 2011 but is rounded up to terminate on March 20th 2011. If the 20th falls on a weekend it is moved to the next working day. The cost of protection is given by the annual fixed premium rate, also known as the ISSUE PREMIUM. The contract also gives the date of the first premium payment,

---

[1]IMM stands for International Money Market, and IMM dates are standard expiry dates for futures contracts that fall on the third Wednesday of March, June, September and December. Although strictly incorrect practioners still refer to CDS expiry dates as IMM dates.

payment frequency, and the notional of the contract e.g. a notional of $10 million and a fixed premium of 40 bps would result in quarterly payments of $10,000.

Figure 7.1 shows cash flows for someone buying five year protection with an effective date on St. Valentine's day in 2006, a notional of $10 million and an issue premium of 40 basis points. The downward outgoing payments are the quarterly premium payments paid to the seller of protection. Notice that they are all roughly equal except for the first payment. This is simply the hiccup payment that gets the CDS onto the standardised IMM payment schedule. This payment is for protection from the effective date to the first IMM payment a month and a half later. Protection for half the usual period results in a payment of half the

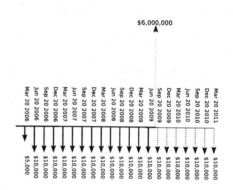

Figure 7.1:
Cash flows for a five year CDS effective on February 14, 2006.

size. The dashed payments are those that are affected by a default in August 2009. After the default date premium payments, shown as solid arrows, stop and a payment of $6 million is made to the buyer.

A critical concept in understanding CDS is the idea of CREDIT SPREAD. Bonds present a full spectrum of risk ranging from almost riskless dollar-denominated US Treasury bonds to extremely risky South American corporate bonds. The yield of risky bonds is greater than the yield of safer bonds because investors would not buy them unless they were compensated for the possibility of not retrieving their principal at maturity. The difference between the yield of a risky bond and a government bond of the same maturity is called a spread. An issuer's CDS spread will be roughly equal to the spread of the issuer's bonds. The rest of the spread is attributable to other risks such as liquidity.

Buyers of a CDS are buying credit protection or equivalently selling credit risk, and are said to be SHORT CREDIT, while sellers of CDS contracts are selling credit protection, or buying credit risk, and are LONG CREDIT. In order to make a profit with a CDS a buyer of protection wants credit spread to widen. If spreads widen then buying more credit protection on the same entity would require a higher issue premium, making the current contract seem a bargain.

| Buy protection | sold credit risk, short credit | profit if spreads widen |
| Sell protection | bought credit risk, long credit | profit if spreads tighten |

The interesting part of a CDS is the "D". If no default occurs during the life of a CDS it is a tedious set of constant, small, regular premium payments. When the reference entity triggers a CREDIT EVENT things become more interesting. Roughly speaking a credit event occurs if the reference entity does not meet one of its debt repayments. When a triggering event occurs the protection buyer stops paying premium and delivers the nominal face value amount of the reference entity's bond to the protection seller. After a credit event the bond would not be worthless, but it would be trading at a huge discount. The protection seller then pays the buyer an amount that allows her to recover her bond's par or face value. If a bond investor bought $10 million face value of a bond with $10 million notional protection and after default the bond is worth $4 million in the market, the protection payment would be $6 million. Since we recovered 40% of our par value this is known as a 40% RECOVERY RATE. If we have recovered 40% then we must have lost 60% which is our LOSS GIVEN DEFAULT. The protection buyer has some leeway in their choice of bond to deliver in the case of default and they will usually choose the cheapest eligible bond. The delivered bond must be from the correct issuer, must be denominated in the currect currency and must have the correct seniority, but the maturity allows some freedom of choice.

Credit Default Swap Quotes

CDS are quoted as a spread using this combination of factors:

Reference entity refers to the particular company, as a legal entity, for which credit protection is being sold.

Term is the duration for which protection is sought, typically five years.

Seniority is either senior or subordinated, with sub-classification of the subordinated category into senior subordinated and junior subordinated.

Restructuring determines whether debt restructuring is a credit event and constrains the attributes of the bond that is delivered by the protection buyer when a default occurs (if the CDS is physically settled).

Currency although this has a small effect on the spread.

In order to buy protection for Goldman Sachs you would phone a credit sales desk and say "I want to buy ten million dollars of subordinated five year protection on Goldman Sachs". The trader might say "One hundred and six basis points," meaning that the annual cost of your protection will be $0.0106 \times 10,000,000$ or $106,000. If he were to publish this quote internally at the bank, or send it to a price aggregator such as Markit, he would fill in the following fields.

The reference entity must have an unambiguous identifier, such as the ISIN or CUSIP of one of its reference obligations, or its Markit RED code (RED stands for Reference Entity Database). A RED code is a six character alphanumeric string that is unique to each reference entity in the credit market. Markit are extremely careful to "scrub" each reference entity to ensure that it is real and has the correct legal name. RED codes are very specific so that in a hierarchy of companies with a parent and multiple levels of subsidiaries each corporation has its own unique RED code. The RED code for The Goldman Sachs Group Incorporated is 3B955H. Each reference obligation has a unique CLIP code, or RED pair code, that consists of the six character RED code with an additional three digits. In the example the Goldman Sachs subordinated bond (ISIN US38141GEU40) has a CLIP code of 3B955HAE0 which is the RED code for Goldman with AE0 appended for this bond. RED codes can be found on the Bloomberg REDL page. Unfortunately RED codes are unique but not memorable, so Markit have created their own ticker code that is human-readable and similar to the Bloomberg corporate ticker except in cases where there are many reference entities with the same Bloomberg ticker.

Seniority is usually one of two values: senior or subordinated, with senior being sold more often than subordinated. When a bankruptcy occurs and a company is liquidated the proceeds are used to pay off the creditors in a strict order. Senior debt is first in line for repayment and once senior bond holders are fully paid off the remaining capital is paid to subordi-

Reference Entity	*Legal Name*	The Goldman Sachs Group, Inc.
	Reference Obligation	US38141GEU40
	RED Pair Code	3B955HAE0
Term		5Y
Seniority		Subordinated
Restructuring		No Restructuring
Currency		USD

Figure 7.2: Credit default swap quote attributes.

nated bond holders. Holding subordinated debt, which is lower down in the pecking order for repayment, means that the LOSS GIVEN DEFAULT is greater, so subordinated CDS have a greater spread than an equivalent senior CDS. Usually only entities with a comparatively low default risk have quotes for subordinated debt, such as investment banks.

Restructuring determines whether debt restructuring is a credit event and sets constraints on the particular bond that can be delivered for physically delivered CDS. When a default occurs the protection buyer has some leeway in the choice of bond they deliver. It must be issued by the reference entity specified in the CDS documentation for the trade, but some issuers have thousands of bonds outstanding. The protection buyer will deliver the cheapest bond they can find because this will be converted into more cash from the protection seller. To tighten constraints on the deliverable bond ISDA documentation has several types of restructuring. One choice is to have no restructuring, so that debt restructuring is not considered a credit event and any bond with a maturity of up to 30 years can be delivered. The other types of restructuring are "Modified" (delivered bond must mature 30 months or less after the CDS termination date or can be the reference obligation that was restructured regardless of maturity), "Modified Modified" (60 months after CDS termination date for restructured reference obligations and 30 months for other obligations) and "Complete" where any restructuring is a credit event and bonds with a maturity of up to 30 years can be delivered. After the CDS Big Bang no restructuring is used in the United States and after a default the determination committee will now specify exactly which bonds may be delivered. If the determination committee he choice of bond that is delivered is then in the hands of the buyer of protection and this DELIVERY OPTION has value.

There is a significant caveat to buyers of credit protection. To give an extreme example, it would make no sense for an investor to buy credit protection on an investment bank from the bank itself. If the bank becomes bankrupt then the protection will be worthless. Extending this idea it would also be wise to choose to buy insurance from an entity that has very little default correlation with the reference entity. For example it would be foolish to buy credit protection on a motor company from another company's motor finance subsidiary since these two entities would have a high default correlation. This pitfall is called WRONG-WAY RISK.

7.1.1 Credit Events

The essence of a credit default swap lies in the definition of a credit event in the CDS trade documentation created by ISDA. By laying out precise rules the documentation aims to protect lenders from losing their principal. There have to be two irrefutable, publicly available pieces of information to show that a credit event has occurred. A credit rating downgrade is not a credit event because it is a subjective opinion on the part of a credit analyst about an issuer's ability to meet its debt obligations. Similarly a widening of credit spread or a drop in the share price for an entity is not a credit event. So what are the events that show that an issuer will fail to pay its debts?

Bankruptcy Filing for bankruptcy is an obvious sign that bond holders are likely to suffer some loss. In the United States this is called "filing for Chapter 11 bankruptcy" and is a process whereby the company is put into administration while it tries to get its house in order. If this fails it may lead to sale of the company or liquidation. If it succeeds then the company can come back out of bankruptcy.

Failure to pay Failing to make a single coupon payment on any of its bonds can be enough to tip a company into bankruptcy.

Restructuring When a company is having trouble meeting its debt repayments it may try to strike an agreement with its creditors to pay them back later, or to reduce and extend the payments. This is called debt restructuring.

Acceleration If a single bond coupon is not paid on time bond holders may insist on receiving their principal back immediately before the finances of the issuer deteriorate further. If the issuer agrees to repay its debt sooner than scheduled this is known as acceleration. For example in December 2008 United Aircraft Corporation, a government-backed Russian aerospace company, missed coupon payments on $250 million of its bonds. Fearing loss of their principal bondholders sought accelerated repayment.

Repudiation/Moratorium Usually refers to governments that for reasons of internal unrest or financial distress or political expedience declare that they will either delay (declare a moratorium) or downright refuse to repay their debt. For example Ecuador defaulted on $3.2 billion worth of its bonds on December 12, 2008. President Rafael Correa stated that the debt was repudiated due to "evidence of criminal wrongdoing in the issuance of its foreign debt" by the previous administration.

7.1.2 CDS Settlement

CDS are either cash settled or physically settled. If cash settled the protection seller pays the protection buyer an amount that tops up the defaulted bond price to 100. If the face value of the bond is $100 and it is trading at $10, as determined by a poll of bond market makers or credit auction, then the payment would be $90. If physically settled the protection buyer delivers one of the defaulted issuer's bonds to the protection seller who pays them back the full face value of the bond. If the buyer of protection does not own the bond then they are forced to buy it in the secondary market after default has occurred for some fraction of its face value. Then they immediately sell it to the protection seller who pays them the full face value of $100.

Physical settlement poses a problem. The notional amount of CDS protection written on a issuer can be many times larger than the amount of physical bond available to buy in the secondary market. This means the bonds may be recycled many times before all positions are physically settled. In turn this rush to buy an issuer's defaulted bonds pushes up their price. In the period of time between purchasing and delivering a defaulted bond to a protection seller the value of the bond may have changed significantly due to its price volatility. This introduces some price risk into the settlement process for both the protection seller and the buyer. For these reasons the CDS market has moved away from physical settlement towards the majority of CDS trades being cash settled.

7.1.3 Credit Auctions

In order to avoid an unsightly scrabble for defaulted bonds and uncertainty as to the true value of the bonds the CDS market introduced the practice of credit auctions. Credit auctions are designed to provide a single market-wide agreed price for a defaulted issuer's bonds. The auction process has two stages. In the first stage bond dealers pool their tradable quotes for the defaulted bonds. This pool of quotes is called the inside market. The inside market quote size and bid-offer spread are agreed before any quotes are submitted. So for example the size might be to buy or sell $5 million with a bid-offer spread of 2%, for example $42 - $44. Notice that this is a steep discount to the $100 face value of the bond, as we are now dealing with distressed debt. Here are some imaginary quotes for the first stage auction in which five dealers participate. Quotes can have fractional amounts in multiples of $\frac{1}{8}$ and all are for a size of $5 million.

Dealer	Bid	Offer	Size
1	39.125	41.125	$5M
2	32	34	$5M
3	36.875	38.875	$5M
4	42.375	44.375	$5M
5	37.625	39.625	$5M

The dealer bids are sorted into descending order and the offers are sorted into ascending order,

Dealer	Bid		Dealer	Offer
4	42.375	Cross!	2	34
1	39.125	Cross!	3	38.875
5	**37.625**		5	**39.625**
3	**36.875**		1	**41.125**
2	32		4	44.375

Any crossing bid-offers are removed and the best half of the remaining quotes are averaged to give a number known as the Inside Market Midpoint (IMM). The four numbers that are averaged to give the IMM are shown in bold in the table above. The IMM in this example is $\frac{37\frac{5}{8}+36\frac{7}{8}+39\frac{5}{8}+41\frac{1}{8}}{4}$ or 38.8125, which is rounded to the nearest $\frac{1}{8}$ to give 38.875.

There is provision in the auction process to give dealers a rap over the knuckles for quoting too far off-market. For quotes where the bid crosses another dealer's offer or the offer crosses another dealer's bid the dealer pays a penalty called an adjustment. The punishment is proportionate to the crime: $(\text{bid}-\text{IMM})\times\text{notional}$. Our two crossed bids would incur adjustments of $5,000,000\times\frac{42.375-38.875}{100}$ or \$175,000 and $5,000,000\times\frac{39.125-38.875}{100}$ or \$12,500.

Dealers submit physical settlement requests alongside their quotes that are used to find the sign and size of open interest in the defaulted bond. Some dealers, either directly, or acting on behalf of clients, want to either buy or sell various amounts of the bond to settle their CDS contracts.

Dealer	Buy/Sell	Limit
1	Buy	\$4M
2	Sell	\$7M
3	Sell	\$2M
4	Buy	\$5M
5	Sell	\$3M

The net value of the buy and sell requests is $-4+7+2-5+3$, so the open interest is to sell \$3 million of the reference obligation. The inside market midpoint, size and direction of open interest are published to all market participants who can then decide whether to participate in the second half of the auction. In this case the open interest is to sell the bond so we are only interested in bid prices and the offer prices are discarded.

In the second part of the auction both dealers and investors submit limit orders. A limit order has both a price and an amount. In our example we are only interested in bids, so the bids from the first part of the auction are combined with any new bids from the second half of the auction. Then the bids are sorted in decreasing order and used to fulfill all the open interest. The last price reached that fulfills all open interest is the agreed price of the bond. In our example we may have the following new limit bids in the second part of the auction:

Bid Price	Size
33	$11M
43	$1M
36	$9M

All crossing quotes are replaced with the IMM price. Combining the new bids with the inside market bids (shown in bold) and sorting:

Bid Price	Size
43	**$1M**
38.875	$5M
38.875	$5M
37.625	$5M
36.875	$5M
36	**$9M**
33	**$11M**
32	$5M

In order to fulfill the open interest we would work down from the highest bid of 43 which would fulfill $1M of open interest and reach 38.875 to fulfill the rest of the open interest. The final market-wide price set by the auction would be 38.875.

7.1.4 Pricing CDS

The key to pricing CDS is to find the probability of a credit event occurring in the future. Once we have this probability for every future time the present value simply becomes the discounted value of the cash flows multiplied by some probability of default occurring in the case of the protection and accrued payments, or not occurring in the case of the premium payments. We derive this probability from the par credit spreads quoted by traders, and a simple model of default. Here we will see two models for backing out survival probability from par spreads. One is a discrete time model, the other continuous time.

It is possible to infer the default probability of a bond from its credit spread. If the yield of a bond is 5% higher than a comparable maturity risk-free bond (such as a Treasury) this tells us that the market expects to lose 5% of the principal on average due to default. In fact a large component of the spread will be due to other risks such as liquidity, nevertheless this is a useful approximation. The spread compensates us for the probability of default times the loss given default has occurred. We would not lose all our principal because some fraction R would be returned when the company's assets are liquidated, say 40%, meaning that our loss given default would be $1 - R$ which is 60%. So if the probability of default in one year is p and the spread over the risk-free rate is s and the recovery rate is R then

$$p(\text{default}) \times \text{loss given default} \quad \simeq \quad \text{credit spread}$$
$$p(1 - R) \quad = \quad r_{\text{risky}} - r_{\text{risk-free}} = s$$
$$p \quad = \quad \frac{s}{1 - R}$$

In our example where the spread is 5% and recovery is 40% the probability of default per year would be about $\frac{0.05}{1-0.4}$ which is 8.3%. The probability of default is proportional to the spread and increasing the recovery rate increases the default probability if spread remains constant.

Exercise 49 *A bank has two five year CDS spreads quoted in the market. One is for senior debt at 100 bp and the other is for subordinated debt at 400 bp. What does this tell you about the recovery rate for senior and subordinated debt issued by the bank?*

CDS Pricing on a Beermat

If you want to impress your colleagues with the ability to calculate the value of a CDS in your head, then read this section. The first trick is one for calculating annual payment amounts when rates are given in basis points. All you have to remember is that annual payments are $100 for each million of notional and each basis point. So for protection on a notional of $10 million and an issue premium of 40 basis points you would pay $100 \times 10 \times 40$ or $40,000 annually.

Calculating the present value (PV) of a CDS exactly is quite complicated, but there is a simple approximation. The three numbers you need are the issue premium, the current par premium and the notional. The PV is roughly the difference between the issue premium and the par premium multiplied by the remaining lifetime of the CDS contract in years. So if we bought protection at an issue premium of 100 basis points, and after a few days the entity is trading at 110 basis points with the same seniority, restructuring and term, then our PV is positive (our protection looks cheap now that spreads have widened) and over the five year lifetime of the contract we will make $(110 - 100) \times 5$ or 50 basis points. Using our approximation above 50 basis points on a notional of $10 million is $100 \times 10 \times 50$ or about $50,000. An exact calculation gives a PV of about $43,000. If notional is in millions, the issue premium in basis points is p_{issue} and current premium is $p_{current}$, time to maturity in years is T, then the PV is roughly

$$\text{PV} \simeq 100 \times \text{Notional (millions)} \times (p_{current} - p_{issue}) \times T$$

if buying protection. The sign is reversed if selling protection.

This approximation works because a par credit default swap, where $p_{current} = p_{issue}$ has, on average, future cash flows that cancel exactly. If $p_{current}$ increases slightly the result is a small imbalance in the cash flows with the result being a set of cash flows with an annual value of about $100N(p_{current} - p_{issue})$ for the life of the CDS, T. This is dealt with in more detail in Section 7.1.7.

Exercise 50 *You buy $10 million five year protection on Risky Corporation today for 100 bp. Tomorrow Risky Corporation's five year par spread widens to 110 bp. Did you*

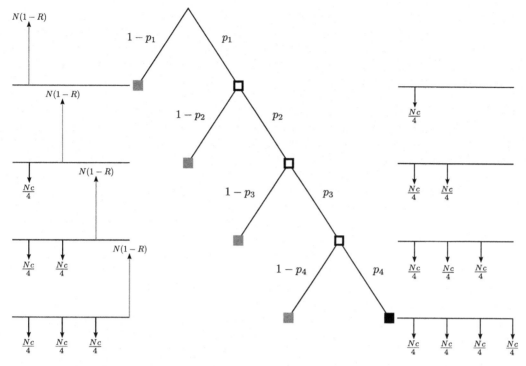

Figure 7.3: Credit default swap pricing tree.

make or lose money? Without using a calculator roughly how much did you make or lose?

7.1.5 Inferring Survival Probability From Par Credit Spread

Given a CDS pricing model it is possible to infer the survival probability of a CDS from the spread curve, the risk free curve (LIBOR) and the recovery rate. Survival to time t is defined as no default occurring before time t, and is a decreasing function of time in the future which we will call $p_s(t)$. At time zero there is no default so $p_s(0) = 1$, and at an infinite time in the future $p_s(\infty) = 0$ since no entity survives forever. Once we have $p_s(t)$ it becomes trivial to calculate the present value of the CDS. We have information about par spreads at discrete points in time from quotes given by traders for different terms. The most frequently quoted spreads are usually for terms of 6 months, 1, 2, 3, 4, 5, 7 and 10 years. These constrain survival probability for a few points in time and our model has to interpolate for all other times.

Discrete Time Model

Figure 7.3 shows the possible outcomes in the life of a credit default swap as a tree assuming that defaults always occur half-way between premium payments. A grey node indicates a default event and a black node indicates no default. A filled node indicates that the contract has terminated. This imaginary CDS has a life of one year and a coupon period of 3 months giving four quarterly payments if no default occurs. By each node are the cash flows up to that point in time. Black cash flows are premium payments paid regularly by the protection buyer to the protection seller. Grey cash flows are protection payments triggered by a default event. Notice that the premium cash flows are much smaller than the protection cash flows.

Our CDS starts life at the top of the tree on the effective date. The seller has agreed an issue premium c that remains fixed for the life of the contract, and the notional is N. After three months one of two events can happen: no default occurs in which case the protection buyer pays the protection seller a tiny premium payment of $\frac{Nc}{4}$, or a default occurs and the protection seller pays the protection buyer a huge sum of $(1 - R)N$. To give a sense of the size of these cash flows in a typical contract, the nominal might be $10 million and the issue premium 50 basis points, giving quarterly premium payments of $12,500 ($10,000,000 \times 0.0050 \times \frac{1}{4}$). Assuming a recovery rate of 40% the protection payment would be $6,000,000. The grey cash flows showing protection payments should be 480 times bigger than the black premium cash flows.

There are five ways this contract could end: after a default on the first, second, third or fourth coupon payments or by reaching the termination date without any defaults at all. We can find the probability of reaching any node on the tree by multiplying together the probabilities of all the branches to get there. The probability of having no defaults is $p_1 p_2 p_3 p_4$. The probability of the contract ending with a default occurring on the third premium payment is $p_1 p_2 (1 - p_3)$. To find the present value of the CDS we find all the terminal nodes and multiply the present value of their discounted cash flows by the probability of reaching that node.

Exercise 51 *Take a look at the top branch of the tree in Figure 7.3 on page 287. If this were a quarter year CDS contract with just one premium payment then find the value of p_1 that sets the expected present value of the contract to zero.*

Exercise 52 *To prepare the ground for the following explanation we will play a game. You are a CDS trader providing one year protection for Risky Corporation. The CEO of Risky Corp. throws a dice at the end of each financial quarter. If he throws a six he drives the company to bankruptcy and triggers a default payment of ten million dollars. If he does not throw six the company survives and you will receive a coupon payment c. You decide the fair value of c.*

Exercise 53 *Now find an expression relating survival probability p, coupon payment c and default payment d.*

We will infer the survival probability for the two-premium CDS in Figure 7.4 then generalise the method for any number of cash flows. There are three times of interest for this CDS: the effective date t_0 when protection begins, the first premium date t_1 and the second premium date t_2. Time spans between these times are denoted Δt, so $\Delta t_1 = t_1 - t_0$ and $\Delta t_2 = t_2 - t_1$. Notice in Figure 7.4 that the first period Δt_1 is significantly smaller than Δt_2 in order to line up the cash flows with the IMM premium schedule. Premium payments occur on a fixed schedule of IMM dates which is known and agreed on the day the contract is written. Protection payments are driven by default that occurs at an unknown time in the future. Models differ in the timing of protection payments, but the most commonly used model is that of JP Morgan (JPM) which places this cash flow halfway through each premium payment period. For the first period this would be $t_1^{mid} = \frac{t_0+t_1}{2}$ and for the second period $t_2^{mid} = \frac{t_1+t_2}{2}$.

The total present value consists of the present value of premium payments, protection payments and a tiny term for accrued premium. The premium payment for the first period is the product of notional N, issue premium c and the first coupon period Δt_1 running from the effective date t_0 to the first premium date t_1, giving $Nc\Delta t_1$. The second premium payment is significantly larger because the period Δt_2 is larger than Δt_1. To calculate present value we multiply by the discount factor at the time the payment is made, $\delta_1 = e^{-r_1(t_1-t_0)}$ and $\delta_2 = e^{-r_2(t_2-t_0)}$ so for these two premium payments the present values are $Nc\Delta t_1\delta_1$ and $Nc\Delta t_2\delta_2$. There is a subtlety in cal-

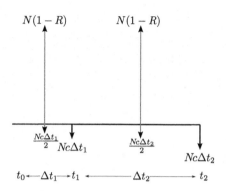

Figure 7.4:
Cash flow detail for a 6 month CDS under the JPM model.

culating the time difference for discounting and accruing premium because they may, and often do, have different day count conventions. Accrual is usually A/360 while discounting is usually A/365. Of course the premium payment will not occur if default occurs before it is paid, so we multiply the discounted payment by the probability of surviving to time t_1 which we call p_1. This gives a final value for the present value of premium payments of $Nc\Delta t_1\delta_1 p_1$ and $Nc\Delta t_2\delta_2 p_2$. For premium i the present value is

$$V_{\text{premium}} = Nc\Delta t_i\delta_i p_i. \tag{7.1}$$

Protection payments depend only on the notional N and the recovery rate R and are equal to $N(1-R)$. The $(1-R)$ term comes about because the reference obligation was originally worth N, is worth NR in its defaulted state, so requires a payment of $N(1-R)$ to top it back up to N. The probability of default occurring in the time period from t_0 to t_1 is $p_0 - p_1$, which is the drop in survival probability from t_0 to t_1. We multiply by the probability of defaulting in this time period $p_0 - p_1$ by the payment given default $N(1-R)$ to give the expected value of the protection payment $N(1-R)(p_0 - p_1)$. The present value is the discounted value of the cash flow which is $N(1-R)(p_0 - p_1)\delta_1^{mid}$, and for the second period is $N(1-R)(p_1 - p_2)\delta_2^{mid}$. Generally this gives protection present value of

$$V_{\text{protection}} = N(1-R)(p_{i-1} - p_i)\delta_i^{mid}. \tag{7.2}$$

The cash flow for accrued premium is $Nc\frac{\Delta t_1}{2}$ because we are assuming that default occurs half-way through the period. The probability of this payment occurring in time period t_0 to t_1 is exactly the same as the protection payment. This gives an expected cash flow of $Nc\frac{\Delta t_1}{2}(p_0 - p_1)$ and discounting gives an expected present value of $Nc\frac{\Delta t_1}{2}(p_0 - p_1)\delta_1^{mid}$. This value is very small with respect to the other two because it is scaled by the coupon c and the period default probability $p_0 - p_1$. Accrued value is

$$V_{\text{accrued}} = Nc\frac{\Delta t_i}{2}(p_{i-1} - p_i)\delta_i^{mid} \tag{7.3}$$

We now have expressions for the premium payment, the protection payment and the accrued payment. We can use these to infer the survival probability for each par spread by using the fact that by definition the present value of a CDS contract is zero on the effective date. The present value on the effective date is

$$V_{\text{total}} = V_{\text{premium}} + V_{\text{accrued}} - V_{\text{protection}} = 0.$$

Substituting from equations 7.1, 7.2 and 7.3 gives an expression for the decay of survival probability over one premium period.

$$
\begin{aligned}
V_{\text{protection}} &= V_{\text{premium}} + V_{\text{accrued}} \\
(1-R)\delta_1^{mid}(p_0 - p_1) &= c\Delta t_1\delta_1 p_1 + \frac{c\Delta t_1}{2}(p_0 - p_1)\delta_1^{mid} \\
p_0\left[(1-R)\delta_1^{mid} - \frac{c\Delta t_1}{2}\delta_1^{mid}\right] &= p_1\left[(1-R)\delta_1^{mid} + c\Delta t_1\delta_1 - \frac{c\Delta t_1}{2}\delta_1^{mid}\right] \\
\frac{p_1}{p_0} &= \frac{1 - R - \frac{c\Delta t_1}{2}}{1 - R + c\Delta t_1\left(\frac{\delta_1}{\delta_1^{mid}} - \frac{1}{2}\right)}
\end{aligned}
$$

We know the survival probability at time t_0 must be equal to 1. All the other terms in this expression are known except for p_1. Starting with the first par premium at time t_1 we can use equation 7.4 to find survival probabilities p_1 at time t_1, p_2 at time t_2, and all subsequent premium times. Generalising this equation to any pair of adjacent premium payments at times t_{i-1} and t_i we get

$$\frac{p_i}{p_{i-1}} = \frac{1 - R - \frac{c\Delta t_i}{2}}{1 - R + c\Delta t_i\left(\frac{\delta_i}{\delta_i^{mid}} - \frac{1}{2}\right)}. \tag{7.4}$$

To get a feel for the meaning of this equation, we can ignore discount factors by setting δ_i to 1 and ignore accrued altogether. This gives a rough guide to building the survival curve: survival probability decreases by a factor of about $(1-R)/(1-R+c\Delta t_i)$. Or thinking in terms of cash flows

$$\text{survival decay factor} \simeq \frac{\text{protection payment}}{\text{protection payment} + \text{premium payment}}$$

Exercise 54 *Set the discount factors to 1, $\delta_i = \delta_i^{mid} = 1$, and ignore the term for V_{accrued} and find the ratio $\frac{p_1}{p_0}$.*

So if our five year par spread is 50 basis points, $c = 0.005$, our recovery rate is 0.4 and we are looking at the drop in survival probability between five years and 10 years then the ratio will be about 0.96. We can also approximate the decay constant for survival in terms of the par quote and the recovery rate. Assuming that survival probability dies away exponentially with a decay constant λ then between time t_{i-1} and t_i we would expect a reduction in survival probability $e^{-\lambda \Delta t_i}$. Putting this into our simplified version of equation 7.4,

$$
e^{-\lambda_i \Delta t_i} \simeq \frac{1-R}{1-R+c_i \Delta t_i}
$$

$$
-\lambda_i \Delta t_i \simeq \ln \left(\frac{1-R}{1-R+c_i \Delta t_i} \right)
$$

$$
\lambda_i \Delta t_i \simeq \ln \left(1 + \frac{c_i \Delta t_i}{1-R} \right)
$$

Using the first order Taylor expansion of $\ln(1+x) \simeq x$,

$$
\lambda_i \simeq \frac{c_i}{1-R}.
$$

This means that survival probability decays at a rate which is roughly proportional to the par premium. If the recovery rate is zero then the decay constant is equal to the par spread. And the higher the recovery rate the faster the decay. The half-life of an entity is therefore $t_{\frac{1}{2}} = \frac{(1-R)\ln 2}{c_i}$. For a 50 basis point par spread and a recovery of 40% the half-life of a credit is about 83 years. When the spread increases to 500 basis points the half-life shortens to 8 years.

As a worked example we will calculate the survival probability for a one year CDS with a par premium of 50 basis points, notional $10 million and a recovery of 40%. The effective date is March 20, 2006 and maturity is on March 20, 2007. We will assume that the LIBOR rate is a flat 5%. The calculation is shown in table 7.1. First we calculate the time from the effective date to the premium payments using the A/360 convention. Then we calculate the mid-points between premium payments, as these are the default times in the JPM model. Discount factors for all the values of t_{365} and t_{365}^{mid} are calculated using $e^{-rt_{365}}$ and $e^{-rt_{365}^{mid}}$. Survival probability is calculated from 7.4. Premium, protection and accrued present values are calculated from equations 7.1, 7.2 and 7.3. If you add the premium, protection and accrued present values you will find they add to zero as we expect. The probability of default at the end of one year is 0.0084.

Continuous Time Model

Continuous time models offer another route to the survival curve. In a continuous time model we will interpolate by assuming that default on payments is a Poisson process with intensity λ. If λ were constant then our job would be simple because survival probability would simply decay exponentially with time constant $\frac{1}{\lambda}$, and so

Date	t_{360}	t_{365}	t^{mid}	$\delta_{365}(t)$	$\delta_{365}(t^{mid})$	$V_{premium}$	$V_{protection}$	$V_{accrued}$	$p_s(t)$
3/20/06	0	0		1	1				1
6/20/06	0.255556	0.252055	0.126027	0.987476	0.993718	-12591.07	12604.50	-13.42	0.997886
9/20/06	0.511111	0.504110	0.378082	0.975110	0.975110	-12407.11	12420.33	-13.23	0.995776
12/20/06	0.763889	0.753425	0.628767	0.963030	0.963030	-12094.87	12107.62	-12.75	0.993694
3/20/07	1.013889	1	0.876712	0.951229	0.951229	-11790.95	11803.24	-12.30	0.991639

Table 7.1: Survival probability from par spreads.

$p_s(t) = e^{-\lambda t}$ and our task would simply be one of fitting λ to the par premia. A single intensity λ would imply that the expected time to the first default is $\frac{1}{\lambda}$. For a spread of 50 basis points our expected time to first default would be $\frac{1}{0.0050}$ or 200 years. Even an unusually high spread of 1000 basis points would mean an expected time to first default of 10 years.

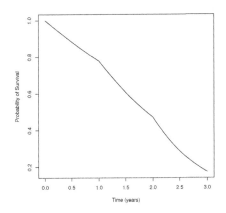

Figure 7.5:
Piecewise decay of survival probability.

A single intensity is too simple to model a real CDS because each par spread provides its own opinion about the risk of default for some period of time in the future. When a trader sells three year Ford protection the risk is that every day between the effective date and the termination date she may have to make a huge protection payment. The par spread that she sets for the contract depends only on her opinion of the likelihood of Ford defaulting from now until three years in the future. We will break up time into pieces and model each period of time with its own λ. Our one year par spread will set λ for the period $t = 0$ to $t = 1$, our two year par spread will set λ for the period $t = 1$ to $t = 2$, and so on. Each piece knows nothing about the other pieces and it is assumed that λ is constant in each piece. You can probably guess why mathematicians call this a PIECEWISE MODEL.

A piecewise model of default will result in piecewise exponential decay with the default intensity λ reset as we get new information from each par spread. This is illustrated in Figure 7.5 where there are three different default intensities. From time zero to one year the intensity is 2500 basis points ($\lambda = 0.25$), from one year to two years 5000 basis points ($\lambda = 0.5$) and from two years to three years 10,000 basis points ($\lambda = 1$). If the reference entity in Figure 7.5 were real it would clearly be on the verge of default. Each piece of the model picks up the decay where the last piece left off, so the first piece takes us from a survival probability of 1.0 to 0.78, the second picks up at 0.78 and decays to 0.47, and the third piece decreases the probability from 0.47 to 0.17. Intensities are exaggerated in this example to highlight the exponential shape of the survival curve, as more common values of λ make decay seem almost linear.

The present value of the premium payments can be derived from the following equation

$$V_{premium} = \int_{t=0}^{t=T} Nc\delta(t)d(-p_s(t))$$

where N is the notional, c is the issue premium and $\delta(t)$ is the discount factor. This is assuming we have continuous coupon payments rather than discrete payments every quarter. By making the simplifying assumption that default intensity is constant and that its value is λ, then $p_s(t) = e^{-\lambda t}$ and $d(-p_s(t)) = \lambda e^{-\lambda t}dt$. Our integral becomes

$$
\begin{aligned}
V_{premium} &= Nc\lambda \int_0^T e^{-rt}e^{-\lambda t}dt \\
&= Nc\lambda \int_0^T e^{-(\lambda+r)t}dt \\
&= -Nc\frac{\lambda}{\lambda+r}e^{-(\lambda+r)t}|_0^T \\
&= Nc\left[\frac{\lambda}{\lambda+r}e^{-(\lambda+r)T} - 1\right]
\end{aligned}
$$

Protection payments depend on default occurring so

$$
\begin{aligned}
V_{protection} &= \int_0^T N(1-R)\delta(t)d(-p_s(t)) \\
&= N(1-R)\int_0^T e^{-rt}\lambda e^{-\lambda t}dt \\
&= N(1-R)\frac{\lambda}{\lambda+r}\left(1 - e^{-(\lambda+r)T}\right)
\end{aligned}
$$

Accrued depends on default not occurring

$$
\begin{aligned}
V_{accrued} &= \int_0^T Nct\delta(t)d(-p_s(t)) \\
&= Nc\lambda \int_0^T te^{-(\lambda+r)t}dt \\
&= -Nc\frac{\lambda}{(\lambda+r)^2}e^{-(\lambda+r)t}\left[1 + (\lambda+r)t\right]|_{t=0}^T \\
&= Nc\frac{\lambda}{(\lambda+r)^2}\left(1 - e^{-(\lambda+r)T}\left[1 + (\lambda+r)T\right]\right)
\end{aligned}
$$

As with the discrete time model we use the fact that the present value on the effective date is zero to infer the value of $p_s(t)$ but this time inference is on the intensity parameter λ. We find the value of λ for which total value is zero on the effective date, for which $V_{premium} + V_{accrued} = V_{protection}$,

$$c\left[\frac{\lambda}{\lambda+r}e^{-(\lambda+r)t} - 1\right] + c\frac{\lambda}{(\lambda+r)^2}\left(1 - e^{-(\lambda+r)t}[1 + (\lambda+r)t]\right) = (1-R)\frac{\lambda}{\lambda+r}\left(1 - e^{-(\lambda+r)t}\right).$$

This can be solved numerically by using any root-finding algorithm.

7.1.6 Present Value From Survival Curve

We have calculated the survival curve for March 20, 2006 from par premia for a particular entity on a particular date. Now that we have the survival curve we can value any CDS for the same entity on that date. For example we might have a contract where we bought one year protection for this entity two weeks ago on March 6, 2006 for 40 basis points. We simply substitute the issue premium of 40 basis points instead of the par premium and calculate new values for $V_{premium}$ and $V_{accrued}$ ($V_{protection}$ does not depend on issue premium) for each premium payment. We know the answer is roughly 10bp $\times$ 10million $\times$ 1year $\times$ 100 or \$10,000. The exact present value is \$9787.14.

7.1.7 Credit Delta

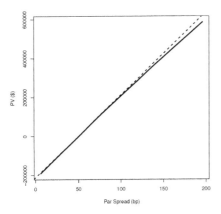

Figure 7.6:
Effect of credit spread on present value.

Owners of default swaps find it useful to know roughly how much the present value changes for each basis point shift in the credit curve. This number is called CREDIT DELTA or DV01, pronounced "dee vee oh one", which means the dollar value of a 1 basis point shift in the credit spread. The DV01 of a CDS is roughly equal to the DV01 of a par bond issued by the same reference entity, because a CDS is the credit risky part of a bond. As a rough rule of thumb the DV01 of a CDS is equal to the remaining life of the CDS multiplied by the notional multiplied by one basis point. So a five year CDS with notional \$10 million has DV01 of roughly \$5,000. If the credit spread were to increase by 1 basis point the present value would increase by \$5,000. Figure 7.6 shows that this approximation of present value is a good one for even large changes in par spread. The solid line is the exact present value, which is a curve, and the dashed line is the straight-line approximation $PV = DV01 \times (p_{current} - p_{issue})$ where today's par spread is $p_{current}$ and p_{issue} is the issue premium, which is 50 basis points in this example. The gradient of the red line is DV01 and it has zero PV for a par spread of 50 basis points.

The effect of issue premium and recovery rate on DV01 are illustrated in Figure 7.7 which is a five year CDS with a recovery rate of 0.4 and a notional of \$10 million. In (a) both the issue premium and the flat credit curve have been shifted to find the effect on DV01. This shows that less risky entities are more sensitive to curve shifts than those with higher credit spreads, everything else being equal. Recovery rate also affects DV01, as seen in (b), but only for very large values of more than 60%. Since the effect of increasing recovery rate is to decrease the size of the protection payment it acts to reduce the riskiness of the CDS. By reducing the risk of default we are reducing the value of the swap.

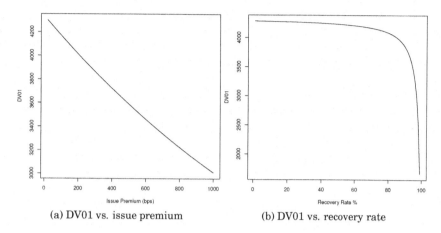

(a) DV01 vs. issue premium　　　　(b) DV01 vs. recovery rate

Figure 7.7: Effect of issue premium and recovery rate on DV01.

7.1.8 The CDS Big Bang

On April 8th 2009 the CDS market changed quite radically through a change in the ISDA documentation. The aim was to make CDS fungible. Fungible simply means interchangeable. If you buy five year protection on Sprocket Corporation and want to close out the position after one year you might expect that selling four year protection on Sprocket Corporation would be a perfect hedge. However this is not the case because of the following:

Restructuring There are several restructuring clauses: modified, modified modified, no restructuring.

Effective Date Protection may start on any day, and so two CDS are unlikely to have precisely the same effective date.

Par Coupon This can take any positive value.

Long/Short Stub The time between the effective date and the first premium payment will differ between contracts.

The Big Bang in North America and the Small Bang in Europe changed CDS documentation in order to make CDS more fungible. Firstly all North American CDS now have no restructuring clause, so restructuring of an entity's debt will not be classified as a credit event. Europe retained modified modified restructuring as the default because there is no equivalent of Chapter 11 bankruptcy laws in Europe with each jurisdiction treating bankruptcy differently.

The effective date of all CDS contracts is 90 days in the past for credit events and 60 days in the past for succession events. For North American CDS all deals have a spread either of 100 basis points or 500 basis points with an upfront payment that compensates for the difference between the true spread and the contract spread. European CDS have a wider range of running spreads: 25, 100, 300, 500, 750 and 1000 basis points. Finally all buyers of protection will pay the full first premium period payment but the seller of protection will repay the premium between the effective date and the previous IMM payment date. All these measures ensure that any two CDS with the same reference entity, currency and seniority will be fungible. In North America these terms form the STANDARD NORTH AMERICAN CORPORATE (SNAC) contract.

Another important change is the creation of a DETERMINATION COMMITTEE. When a credit event occurs the determination committee determines whether a credit event has actually occurred and if so what type of event. If a credit event has occurred the Determination Committee rules on when the event occurred. For physical settlement there are often arguments about which reference obligations (bonds) can be delivered, so again this is decided by the committee. All CDS are settled by credit auctions and the committee decides the number of auctions to be held for each entity. In Europe Determination Committees are able to decide whether or not to hold auctions for specific maturity buckets. Maturity buckets were established to limit the number of auctions while still maintaining optionality for buyers or sellers to trigger. Investors must trigger a CDS before the credit auction or they lose the restructuring clause, a concept called USE IT OR LOSE IT.

7.2 Measures of Credit Spread

Bonds carry information about their credit risk in their price. There are many ways of estimating this risk, three of which are listed in this section: ASSET SWAP MARGIN (ASM), Z-SPREAD and I-SPREAD. ASM and Z-Spread measure credit risk as a spread to the interest rate swap curve, which carries generic bank credit risk. I-Spread measures credit risk relative to government bonds or the swap curve by interpolating the curves at the bond's maturity. The most important measure of the three is ASM because it can be traded directly through an asset swap or liability swap.

Measure	Description	Spread Benchmark
ASM	Fixed coupon margin added to zero rates that equates present value of bond cash flows with dirty price of bond.	Interest rate swap curve
Z-Spread	Fixed coupon margin added to zero rates that equates present value of bond cash flows with dirty price of bond.	Interest rate swap curve
I-Spread	Spread of bond to maturity-matched, linearly interpolated government bond curve	Government bond curve or interest rate swap curve

7.2.1 Asset Swap Margin

If a bond investor wants exposure to the credit risk of an issuer but no exposure to interest rates they can buy a floating rate note. This would make sense if the investor thinks the credit spread of the issuer will tighten, increasing the price of the bond, and the investor thinks interest rates will increase. A floater will not suffer a loss in value as rates rise because its floating coupons will increase and as credit spread tightens with an improving credit story the bond price will rise. If the issuer has only issued fixed coupon bonds then it is possible to turn a fixed rate bond into a floater by paying away the fixed coupons on entering into a payer's swap. This trade is called an asset swap. The result is that the investor receives floating coupons plus a fixed spread that reflects the risk premium of the issuer. A floater would also pay a coupon of LIBOR plus some fixed spread that reflects its credit risk, so we would expect our synthetic floater to do the same. The fixed spread on top of the floating coupons in an asset swap is called the ASSET SWAP MARGIN (ASM).

If we discount a bond's cash flows using its own issuer curve, which will be made up of the risk-free curve plus some credit spread for that issuer, the price we get should very closely match the dirty price of the bond. If we discount with just the risk free part of the curve then we are discounting each cash flow less, and we will end up with a present value that is too large. This lump sum is compensation to the bond investor for taking the credit risk of the issuer over the remaining life of the bond. Instead of being paid a lump sum today we can spread out this excess as a spread over each floating coupon, and this spread is the asset swap margin. We also have to remember that the bond was probably not trading at par, which means the fixed coupon of the bond and the swap will not cancel exactly and so have to add another margin for the off-par-ness of the bond.

ASM is most easily explained using an example. In June 2005 the hotel company Marriott International issued \$350 million of an eight year bond with a fixed semi-annual coupon of $4\frac{5}{8}\%$ that matures on June 15th, 2012. If we own \$1 million face of this bond and we want to swap it, then we could enter into a par payer's swap with a notional of \$1 million. On May 12th, 2010 this bond had a clean price of 103.67, a yield to maturity of 2.79% and five remaining cash flows.

Notional	1,000,000.00 USD
Coupon	4.625%
Clean Price	103.67
Accrued	1.952778 USD
Full Price	105.62 USD
Yield to Maturity	2.79358%

If the bond were trading at par then the fixed leg of the swap would match, and exactly cancel, the fixed coupon of the bond. In that case the fixed leg of the swap would pay the bond coupon of 4.625%. However it is extremely unlikely that the bond happens to be trading at par. In practice the fixed leg of the swap and the fixed coupon of the bond will not cancel. The par swap rate for a two year swap on 17th of May 2010 was 1.20344% which is significantly less than the bond coupon of 4.625%. The Marriott bond is trading at a premium and is worth \$3.67 above par. Discounting the future cash flows of the bond using the swap curve gives a dirty price of

$$\frac{23,125}{1.00027065} + \frac{23,125}{1.00409002} + \frac{23,125}{1.01206100} + \frac{23,125}{1.01812011} + \frac{1,023,125}{1.02527463} = 108.96.$$

Date	Bond Pays	Swap Floating Leg 3M LIBOR + ASM	Net Flow	Present Value	Days	Discount Factor	Floating Coupon
17 May 10				-52,836.80	0	1.00000000	0.33618%
15 Jun 10	23,125.00	-4,951.90	18,173.10	18,168.19	29	1.00027065	0.52134%
15 Sep 10		-5,425.08	-5,425.08	-5,416.39	121	1.00160332	0.98217%
15 Dec 10	23,125.00	-6,531.01	16,593.99	16,526.40	212	1.00409002	1.48473%
15 Mar 11		-7,715.62	-7,715.62	-7,655.78	302	1.00781702	1.64780%
15 Jun 11	23,125.00	-8,303.83	14,821.17	14,644.54	394	1.01206100	1.16374%
15 Sep 11		-7,066.70	-7,066.77	-6,961.85	486	1.01507086	1.18839%
15 Dec 11	23,125.00	-7,052.26	16,072.74	15,786.68	577	1.01812011	1.21269%
15 Mar 12		-7,113.70	-7,113.70	-6,965.74	668	1.02124107	1.54552%
15 Jun 12	1,023,125.00	-1,008,042.43	15,082.57	14,710.76	760	1.02527463	

Table 7.2: Cash flows and discount factors in an asset swap.

Subtracting the accrued coupon of \$1.952778 gives an implied clean price of 107.01 which is too high as we expected. As we would pay par for the bond to enter into the asset swap we are getting a discount of \$3.67. In total per \$100 face we should receive \$7.01 for taking the credit risk of Marriott for the next two years and we pay \$3.67 because we buy the bond for \$100. For \$1 million face these values scale up to \$70,087.97 and \$36,700. That means we should receive a total of $70,087.97 - \$36,700$ or \$33,387.97 today. Instead of receiving this today we spread it out into nine fixed payments added onto the floating payments of the swap. The only question that now remains is how much spread on top of 3 month USD LIBOR will equate to a present value of \$33,387.97 today? There are 9 cash flows at times t_1 to t_9 and we know the discount factors $\delta(t_1)$ to $\delta(t_9)$, so that the value of a 1 basis point payment for a face value N today is

$$\text{PV01} = N \times 0.0001 \times (t_1 \delta(t_1) + (t_2 - t_1)\, \delta(t_2) + \ldots + (t_9 - t_8)\, \delta(t_9)).$$

If we have face value N of \$1 million then per basis point spread (0.0001) the value today would be

$$\frac{1,000,000 \times 0.0001}{360} \times \left(\frac{29}{1.00027065} + \frac{121 - 29}{1.00160332} + \frac{212 - 121}{1.00409002} + \frac{302 - 212}{1.00781702} \right.$$
$$\left. + \frac{394 - 302}{1.01206100} + \frac{486 - 394}{1.01507086} + \frac{577 - 486}{1.01812011} + \frac{668 - 577}{1.02124107} + \frac{760 - 668}{1.02527463} \right)$$

This is \$208.48 per million face per basis point. To convert a present value of \$33,387.97 into a spread we divide by the PV01 of \$208.48 to get a spread of 160.2 basis points, and this is our asset swap margin. On Bloomberg we can decompose this into an off-par-ness component of $-\$36,700$ which is -176.0 bp and a credit risk component of \$70,087.97 which is +336.2 bp. The cash flows and discount factors are summarized in Table 7.2.

Asset swap margin can be calculated in Bloomberg by pulling up a bond, then using the ASW function. Our Marriott International $4\frac{5}{8}\%$ of 2012 example is illustrated in

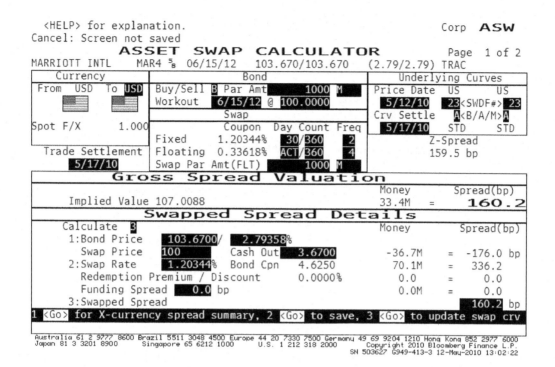

ASSET   SWAP   CALCULATOR   Page 1 of 2
MARRIOTT INTL   MAR4 ⅝ 06/15/12   103.670/103.670   (2.79/2.79) TRAC

Currency	Bond	Underlying Curves

From USD   To USD   Buy/Sell B Par Amt   1000 M   Price Date US   US
                     Workout   6/15/12 @ 100.0000   5/12/10 23<SWDF#> 23
                              Swap   Crv Settle A<B/A/M>A
Spot F/X   1.000   Coupon Day Count Freq   5/17/10   STD   STD
                     Fixed   1.20344% 30/360   2   Z-Spread
Trade Settlement   Floating 0.33618% ACT/360 4   159.5 bp
     5/17/10   Swap Par Amt(FLT)   1000 M

Gross   Spread   Valuation

                                                          Money   Spread(bp)
        Implied Value 107.0088   33.4M   =   **160.2**

Swapped   Spread   Details

Calculate B   Money   Spread(bp)
  1:Bond Price   103.6700/ 2.79358%
     Swap Price   100   Cash Out 3.6700   -36.7M   =   -176.0 bp
  2:Swap Rate   1.20344%   Bond Cpn   4.6250   70.1M   =   336.2
     Redemption Premium / Discount   0.0000%   0.0   =   0.0
     Funding Spread   0.0 bp   0.0M   =   0.0
  3:Swapped Spread   160.2 bp

1 <Go> for X-currency spread summary, 2 <Go> to save, 3 <Go> to update swap crv

Figure 7.8: Bloomberg asset swap margin calculation. Source: Bloomberg.

Figure 7.8. The ASW page is reached by first selecting the Marriott bond with MAR 4.625 12 <CORP> then typing ASW. The asset swap margin appears in the middle box labelled "Gross Spread Valuation" in large digits on the right hand side. We can see that this is displayed as a dollar amount today of $33,400 as well as a spread to LIBOR of 160.2 basis points "Money 33.4M = Spread (bp) 160.2" (note that M in Bloomberg is units of 1,000, so 33.4M is $33,400). Boxes in black show where the user can change inputs to the calculation, such as the bond price, whether we are buying the bond (asset swap) or selling the bond (liability swap) which curve to use for valuation, or the currency of the swap if the user wants a CROSS-CURRENCY ASSET SWAP. Calculation details are in the "Swapped Spread Details" box at the bottom of the screen.

7.2.2 Z-Spread

Figure 7.8 shows the Bloomberg asset swap pricing page. Just above the asset swap margin is another box that shows the Z-Spread, which in the case of the Marriott bond is 159.5 basis points, and this is a little bit less than the asset swap margin of 160.2 basis points. Z-Spread is the parallel shift to the swap curve that prices the future cash flows of the bond to the observed market dirty price of the bond. By parallel shift we mean that all the curve rates are shifted upward by the same amount. Z-Spread is similar to ASM in that it prices the fixed cash flows of the Marriott bond using the swap curve rather than the bond's own issuer curve. However ASM and Z-Spread

Date	Bond Pays	Zero Rate	Shifted Rate	Discount Factor	Present Value
17 May 10				1.000000	
15 Jun 10	$23,125.00	0.348234%	1.942884%	0.998497	$23,090.25
15 Dec 10	$23,125.00	0.707694%	2.302344%	0.986861	$22,821.15
15 Jun 11	$23,125.00	1.115466%	2.710116%	0.971404	$22,463.72
15 Dec 11	$23,125.00	1.141421%	2.736071%	0.958030	$22,154.44
15 Jun 12	$1,023,125.00	1.204923%	2.799573%	0.943871	$965,698.24

Table 7.3: Z-Spread calculation for Marriott $4\frac{5}{8}\%$ of 2012.

differ because Z-Spread shifts the swap curve leaving the bond cash flows unchanged whereas ASM adds a fixed amount to the bond cash flows while leaving the swap curve unchanged.

To demonstrate a Z-Spread calculation we will use the Marriott example above. Cash flows and discount factors are given in Table 7.3. The discount factor column gives the discount factor using each swap rate $r(t)$ shifted by the Z-Spread, z,

$$\delta(t) = \frac{1}{\left(1 + \frac{r(t)+z}{2}\right)^{2t}},$$

and discounting the bond cash flows by the swap curve shifted up by 1.5947% gives a dirty price of $105.6228 which is the observed dirty market price of the bond. The Z-Spread for this bond for this day is 159.47 basis points. Usually the Z-Spread and ASM match one another fairly closely, although they are calculated in quite different ways.

7.2.3 I-Spread

The third and final measure of credit spread that we will mention here is I-Spread. The "I" in "I-Spread" stands for interpolated because the I-Spread is simply the difference between the yield of the bond and the interpolated yield at the maturity time of the bond on another reference yield curve. If the maturity time of the bond is T with yield to maturity Y and our reference yield curve is $y(t)$ then the I-Spread is $Y - y(T)$. The reference curve is usually the government bond yield curve or the interest rate swap curve. Swap curves carry bank credit risk because they are wholesale uncollateralized rates at which a panel of banks lend to one another. Swap curves usually trade at higher rates than government bonds because banks carry more credit risk than the government. I-Spread measures the spread of a bond relative to the government curve.

To calculate I-Spread one must first find government bonds with maturities that are a little less and a little more than that of the bond. For a bond domiciled in the United States one would use US Treasuries, for UK corporate bonds one would use gilts. Then we find the yield to maturity of the government bonds and find a best fit line on a plot of maturity against yield. The curve is built so that it is smooth and yet passes through the government bonds as closely as possible. The I-Spread of the bond is the spread between the yield to maturity of the bond and the yield to maturity on the government bond curve at that maturity. On May 12th 2010 the yield to maturity of some US Treasury bonds was as follows:

Ticker	Coupon %	Maturity	Yield %	$t_{A/360}$
B	0	12-Aug-2010	0.160	0.2556
B	0	12-Nov-2010	0.226	0.5111
B	0	5-May-2011	0.385	0.9944
T	1	30-Apr-2012	0.871	1.9972
T	$1\frac{3}{8}$	15-May-2013	1.412	3.0528
T	$2\frac{1}{2}$	30-Apr-2015	2.282	5.0389
T	$3\frac{1}{8}$	30-Apr-2017	3.005	7.0694
T	$3\frac{5}{8}$	15-Feb-2020	3.575	9.9056
T	$4\frac{5}{8}$	15-Feb-2040	4.482	30.1972

The first three treasuries are T-bills because they are zero coupon bonds, hence the ticker "B" instead of the usual "T". Our Marriott bond matures on June 15th, 2012. The closest Treasury in terms of maturity is the one that matures on April 30th, 2012. The next Treasury maturity that sandwiches the Marriott bond is the $1\frac{3}{8}$ of May 15th, 2013. Since none of the treasuries match the maturity of the Marriott bond exactly we have to interpolate the Treasury curve to find the yield to maturity for a maturity of 2.0917 years. The answer will be somewhere between 0.871% and 1.412%, but closer to 0.871%.

Ticker	Coupon %	Maturity	Yield %	$t_{A/360}$
T	1	30-Apr-2012	0.871	1.9972
MAR	4.625	15-Jun-2012	2.794	2.1250
T	$1\frac{3}{8}$	15-May-2013	1.412	3.0528

The interpolated Treasury yield will be

$$y_T(2.1250) = 0.871 + \frac{2.1250 - 1.9972}{3.0528 - 1.9972} \times (1.412 - 0.871) = 0.9365$$

which gives an I-Spread of $2.794\% - 0.9359\%$ or 185.8 basis points, and this is wider than our asset swap margin of 160.2 bp by 25.6 basis points. This 25.6 basis point difference between ASM and I-Spread is due to the credit risk difference between the USD swap curve, which carries bank credit, and the US Treasury curve which carries almost no credit risk. We could also find the interpolated swap rate at a maturity of 2.125 years.

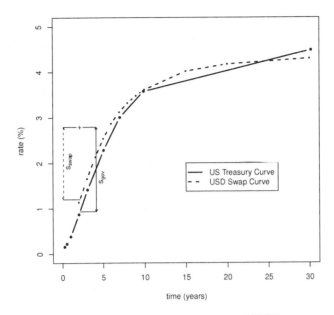

Figure 7.9: I-Spread vs. the US Treasury and USD swap curves.

Maturity	Yield %	Maturity	Yield %
2	1.136	8	3.321
3	1.657	9	3.480
4	2.133	10	3.612
5	2.537	15	4.016
6	2.866	20	4.172
7	3.122	30	4.295

The swap rate will be interpolated to lie between the two year and three year rates of 1.136% and 1.657%, as follows:

$$y_T(2.1250) = 1.136 + \frac{2.1250 - 2}{3 - 2} \times (1.657 - 1.136) = 1.2011$$

The interpolated swap rate is 1.2011 years and the I-Spread to the swap benchmark curve is $2.794 - 1.2011$ or 159.3 bp. Interpolation against both the US Treasury and swap curves is shown graphically in Figure 7.9.

7.3 Credit Linked Notes

Some real-money institutional investors such as pension funds, mutual funds and insurance companies are not allowed or are unwilling to buy credit derivatives such as credit default swaps. In order to provide such investors with access to tailored credit exposure a market has developed in CREDIT LINKED NOTES (CLN). A CLN investor would pay a notional amount up-front, just as they would if they were buying a bond. They then receive a floating interest payment of LIBOR plus a spread on this notional. The spread can be chosen to reference any single credit or basket of credits. The spread that the investor is paid will be a bit less than the credit default swap spread of the reference credit. If the reference credit defaults then the investor will lose their capital investment, and the amount they lose will depend on the recovery rate determined in the credit auction. An investor will choose their credit exposure just as they would with choosing the issuer of a bond, weighing the risk of losing their capital against the return that this risk will pay in the form of a CLN spread.

If a CLN pays a CDS spread that is roughly equal to the ASM of the linked credit cash bonds, then why not just buy the cash bonds? Sometimes the CDS spread of an issuer is greater than the asset swap margin of its bonds, a situation described as a positive credit basis. A positive credit basis means that it makes sense to buy CLNs rather than buying cash bonds issued by the reference credit. For taking the same credit risk the CLN investor is then able to receive a greater risk premium than the cash bond investor. Another reason to buy a CLN is that there may simply not be enough floaters in the market to satisfy investor demand.

CLNs can be issued by any player in the financial markets that is in a position to sell credit protection. Typically CLNs are issued by CDS market makers and this is mostly investment banks. It is crucial that CLN issuers have a good credit rating and small CDS spread themselves, as investors that buy credit linkers will be taking the additional credit risk of the CLN issuer. CLN issuers will choose linked credits that have an active and liquid CDS market as these notes will be attractive to investors. A CLN issuer will invest the notional provided by the investor and earn LIBOR on this deposit. The issuer will then sell protection on the reference credit through a credit default swap. Almost all of the premium that the issuer is paid for providing credit protection is passed on to the investor. If a default occurs the CLN issuer must pay the notional on the CLN minus the recovery rate and this is paid for from the notional that was paid by the investor. The investor will be paid their remaining notional. So if the recovery rate is 40% and notional is $100 million the CLN issuer has to pay $60 million to their CDS counterparty and will return the remaining $40 million to their CLN investors. A common CLN variant is to reference a basket of credits rather than a single reference entity. For example during the European sovereign debt crisis in 2010 a popular CLN with a high yield was a basket that gave the investor exposure to the credit risk of peripheral sovereigns such as Portugal, Ireland, Greece and Spain.

7.4 CDS Curve Play

If a credit curve is very steep such that the cost of three year protection is 50 basis points, but five year protection is 100 basis points then we might expect that the curve will flatten. In other words we may think that the difference between these two spreads will decrease in the future. We could put on a flattener trade. We would buy three year protection and sell five year protection. If our two trades have the same notional and the reference entity defaults we will receive a protection payment from our three year counterparty and pay the same protection payment to our five year counterparty. However if the curve steepens further we will lose money. If the curve flattens as we expect then we will make a profit.

Before we put on the trades we have to decide on the notionals. The decisions we make and the calculations are very similar to flatteners and steepeners for interest rate swaps (see Section 6.2 on page 254). If we want the premium payments to cancel, so that the premium we receive for selling protection exactly matches the premium we pay for buying protection, our position is called CARRY-NEUTRAL. Our five year CDS trades at twice the spread of our three year CDS so we buy twice as much three year protection as five year protection to balance the premium payments perfectly. The amount of notional we put on depends on how confident we feel about the curve flattening.

Alternatively we may decide that we want our position to be insensitive to parallel up and down shifts of the credit curve and only sensitive to change in the steepness of the curve. If this is the case we will choose our notionals so that they are proportional to the credit delta ratios of the two CDS. If the three and five year notionals are N_3 and N_5 and the credit delta, or DV01, of the two CDS are $DV01_3$ and $DV01_5$ then in order to be insensitive to parallel up and down shifts of the credit curve

$$N_3 DV01_3 = N_5 DV01_5$$
$$\frac{N_3}{N_5} = \frac{DV01_5}{DV01_3}$$

This position will not be carry-neutral, so we may end up paying premium or receiving premium while we wait for the curve to flatten. If we buy equal notional amounts then we will have positive carry of 50 basis points because we are receiving 100 basis points on the five year CDS and paying 50 basis points on the three year CDS.

7.5 Credit Default Swap Indices

Credit indices are of fundamental importance in the credit market. By analogy with equity indices like the S&P 500 and the Nikkei 225 they take the roles of barometer and yardstick: in their role as barometer they provide a succinct snapshot of the state of the credit market, and in their role as yardstick they provide a standard against which single name spreads can be compared. In addition credit indices have become important in the creation of structured products where they provide standardised pools of liquid entities. We can summarize their uses and their use to buyers and sellers of protection as follows:

Uses Transferring credit risk for a basket of names, hedging credit risk for a portfolio, taking a punt on credit spreads for a whole credit market, defining a standardised reference pool for structured credit products.

Deal to the Buyer of Protection You pay the present value of the index up front. You also pay fixed quarterly payments in return for default protection on a fixed basket of reference entities, each assigned some weighting. If any of the entities defaults you receive notional times the entity weighting, and your fixed payment reduces by the weighting. You profit as more defaults occur, reaching a maximum if all the names in the basket default.

Deal to the Seller of Protection You receive the present value of the index up front. Your profit is greatest if no defaults occur, and reduces with each default.

CDS indices are split geographically into two groups, CDX for North America and iTraxx for the rest of the world. CDX is maintained by Markit Partners and iTraxx by the International Index Company (IIC). Although IIC and Markit handle the logistics of indices the constituents are selected by consortia of investment banks who act as single-name and index market makers. Twice each year, every March and September, CDS indices change their constituents according to a vote by the consortium members, and this update is known as an INDEX ROLL. Indices have a series number that increments when a roll occurs, and the most current series is called the ON THE RUN index. CDS indices also have a version number that increments on default of an index entity. The version number resets to 1 when the index next rolls to a new series number because all defaulted entities are not included in the new index series.

CDS indices are fixed pools of reference entities. Each entity is given a weight according to its importance in the index. On the day an index is issued its coupon is fixed for its entire lifetime, and the spread is roughly the average spread of its constituents. The effective date of the index is its issue date, and various standardised maturities are issued such as five year and 10 year each with its own fixed coupon. On the day of issue the index will trade at a spread that is roughly equal to its fixed coupon, then market forces take over and drive the spread away from the fixed coupon.

CDX and iTraxx each have a main index, which are iTraxx Europe main and CDX North American Investment Grade (CDX.NA.IG). Other indices are defined according to market sector or risk. Some indices have been discontinued as they were not widely traded. These include the CDX North American High Yield High Beta (CDX.NA.HY.HB) and CDX North American crossover indices (CDX.NA.XO).

iTraxx Europe 125 investment grade European reference entities with highest trading volumes (i.e. highest liquidity) over the last six months. Ratings of BBB-/Baa3/BBB- (Fitch/Moody's/S&P) with negative outlook or below are excluded. Three important sub-indices are the iTraxx Non-Financials (100 entities), iTraxx Financials Senior and iTraxx Financials Subordinated indices. The financial indices both contain 25 reference entities and are used to trade senior and subordinated financial credit which represent two levels of financial debt capital structure (see Section 1.6 on page 67 for an explanation of capital structure and subordination).

iTraxx HiVol 30 entities with the widest 5-year credit default swap spreads from the iTraxx Europe Non-Financials index. The spreads used to determine eligibility are the average five year spreads over the last 10 days of the month prior to the roll date. BBB-/Baa3/BBB- (Fitch/Moody's/S&P) with stable outlook or higher are excluded.

iTraxx Crossover 50 European entities with high liquidity and the highest sub-investment grade rating below BBB-/Baa3/BBB- (Fitch/Moody's/S&P).

iTraxx Japan 50 investment grade Japanese entities with high liquidity.

iTraxx Asia ex-Japan Asia ex-Japan Investment Grade index contains 50 entities and Asia ex-Japan HY index comprises 20 non-investment grade entities.

iTraxx Australia 25 Australian investment grade entities with high liquidity.

> **iTraxx SovX Western Europe** 15 sovereign entities with the largest sum of weekly trading activity over the six months preceding an index roll. These are chosen from a list of 18 possible European countries: Austria, Belgium, Cyprus, Finland, France, Germany, Greece, Ireland, Italy, Luxembourg, Malta, Netherlands, Portugal and Spain, Denmark, Norway, Sweden and the United Kingdom.

> **iTraxx SovX CEEMEA** 15 countries with highest liquidity from a list of 26 in Central and Eastern Europe, Middle East, and Africa (CEEMEA) countries. These include: Abu Dhabi, Bahrain, Bulgaria, Croatia, Czech Republic, Dubai, Estonia, Hungary, Israel, Kazakhstan, Latvia, Lebanon, Lithuania, Morocco, Poland, Qatar, Romania, Russian Federation, Saudi Arabia, Serbia and Montenegro, Slovakia, Slovenia, South Africa, Tunisia, Turkey and Ukraine.

> **iTraxx SovX Asia Pacific** 10 most liquid sovereign entities from the Asia Pacific region including: Australia, China, Hong Kong, Indonesia, Japan, Korea, Malaysia, New Zealand, Philippines, Thailand, and Vietnam.

> **iTraxx SovX Global Liquid Investment Grade** a variable number of the most liquid and highly rated investment grade sovereign entities. There is a lower and upper limit on the number of names from each region: APAC (2 to 5 entities), Eastern Europe (2 to 5 entities), Latin America (2 to 5 entities), Middle East and Africa (2 to 5 entities), North America (1 to 2 entities), Western Europe (2 to 5 entities).

> **iTraxx SovX G7** an equally weighted index of seven industrialized countries. The G7 consists of Canada, France, Germany, Italy, Japan, the United Kingdom and the United States.

> **iTraxx SovX BRIC** an equally weighted index containing Brazil, Russia, India, and China (BRIC).

The CDX family consists of:

CDX North American Indices

> **Investment Grade** (CDX.NA.IG) 125 investment grade names that are domiciled in North America chosen from five sub-sectors.

> **Investment Grade High Volatility** (CDX.NA.IG.HVOL) 30 investment grade names selected from CDX.NA.IG with the largest average CDS spreads over the 90 days before the index rolled.

> **High Yield** (CDX.NA.HY) 100 non-investment grade entities domiciled in North America, chosen from ten sub-sectors. Has two sub-indices: CDX.NA.HY.BB for BB rated entities, and CDX.NA.HY.B for B rated entities.

Name	Series	Version	Term	RED	Coupon	Maturity
iTraxx Europe	6	1	3Y	2I666VAF2	20 bp	20-Dec-09
	6	1	5Y	2I666VAF2	30 bp	20-Dec-11
	6	1	7Y	2I666VAF2	40 bp	20-Dec-13
	6	1	10Y	2I666VAF2	50 bp	20-Dec-16
iTraxx Europe Non-Financial	6	1	5Y	2I667NAF9	35 bp	20-Dec-11
	6	1	10Y	2I667NAF9	55 bp	20-Dec-16
iTraxx Europe HiVol	6	1	3Y	2I667LAF3	35 bp	20-Dec-09
	6	1	5Y	2I667LAF3	55 bp	20-Dec-11
	6	1	7Y	2I667LAF3	70 bp	20-Dec-13
	6	1	10Y	2I667LAF3	85 bp	20-Dec-16
iTraxx Europe Senior Financials	6	1	5Y	2I667DAF1	10 bp	20-Dec-11
	6	1	10Y	2I667DAF1	20 bp	20-Dec-16
iTraxx Europe Sub Financials	6	1	5Y	2I667EAG7	20 bp	20-Dec-11
	6	1	10Y	2I667EAG7	30 bp	20-Dec-16
iTraxx Europe Crossover	6	1	5Y	2I667KAG3	280 bp	20-Dec-11
	6	1	10Y	2I667KAG3	345 bp	20-Dec-16

Table 7.4: iTraxx Europe Series 6 indices.

Name	Series	Version	Term	RED	Coupon
Dow Jones CDX.NA.HY	7	1	5Y	2I65BRAW0	325 bp
Dow Jones CDX.NA.IG	7	1	5Y	2I65BYAL9	40 bp
Dow Jones CDX.NA.IG.HVOL	7	1	5Y	2I65B3AL7	75 bp
Dow Jones CDX.NA.XO	7	1	5Y	1D764IAD9	165 bp
Dow Jones CDX.EM	6	1	5Y	2I65BZAF9	140 bp
Dow Jones CDX.EM.DIVERSIFIED	4	1	5Y	2I65EKAD1	95 bp
Dow Jones CDX.NA.HY.BB	7	1	5Y	2I65BVAM3	205 bp
Dow Jones CDX.NA.HY.B	7	1	5Y	2I65BSAL2	300 bp

Table 7.5: CDX indices.

CDX Emerging Markets 15 sovereign issuers from three regions: Latin America, Eastern Europe the Middle East and Africa, and Asia. This is the only index with non-equal weightings.

Figure 7.10 shows cash flows for the CDX.EM.5-V1, the CDX emerging market series 5 index from the point of view of the protection seller. In this apocalyptic hypothetical scenario the entire index defaults over its five year lifetime. This is very unlikely to happen in practice, but illustrates the mechanics of a CDS index. The contract has the following attributes:

Term Five years. Most indices have a five and ten year contract. Only the most liquid indices have intermediate tenors e.g. the main North American investment grade index CDX.NA.IG.6-V1 has 1Y, 2Y, 3Y, 5Y, 7Y and 10Y maturities.

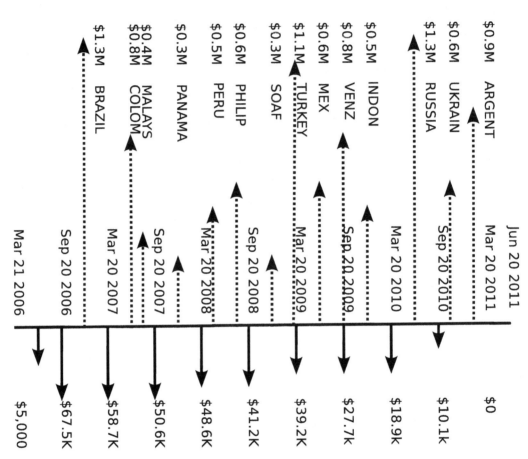

Figure 7.10: CDX EM S5 in an apocalyptic default scenario.

Fixed Rate An annual premium of 135 basis points, fixed on the issue date and paid by anyone who owns this version of the index. This is rather like a bond coupon.

Effective Date March 21st, 2006

Maturity Date June 20, 2011

Payment Frequency Every six months. This is unusual, as most indices pay quarterly.

Markit Trade ID DJCDX-EMS5V1-5Y

The 10 year contract DJCDX-EMS5V1-10Y would have a maturity date of June 20, 2016 and a premium of 190 basis points, but all other attributes of the contract would be exactly the same, such as the entities in the index and its effective date. The reference entities for EM Series 5 in order of decreasing weight are Russian Federation, Federative Republic of Brazil, Republic of Turkey, Argentine Republic, Bolivarian Republic of Venezuela, Republic of Colombia, United Mexican States, Ukraine, Republic of the Philippines, Republic of Indonesia, Republic of Peru, Malaysia, Republic of South Africa and the Republic of Panama. Russia and Brazil have the greatest weighting of 0.13 and South Africa and Panama the smallest weighting of 0.03.

A credit default swap is unfunded as the par premium is defined such that the value on the trade date is zero. In contrast a CDS index is bond-like in that it has a fixed premium, so a payment of the present value of the index plus accrued premium is paid up front. After the initial payment all protection buyers make the same regular premium payments of 135 basis points scaled by their own notional which decrease as the notional of the index is eroded by defaults. In fact, after the CDS Big Bang CDS started to be priced like CDS indices, with a set of standard, fixed premiums and an up-front payment on the settlement date. For this index the entity weights are obviously not equal as can be seen by the widely differing protection payments as each default occurs. Countries such as Brazil and Russia dominate the index with 13% weighting whereas Panama and South Africa have weights of just 3%. In this example the protection buyer would be very happy with his protection payments, but this happiness would probably be tempered with remorse were the emerging market to melt down.

The other extreme is to have no defaults at all over the life of this index. In this case the protection buyer pays the seller 135 basis points on their notional of $10 million, as this is the fixed premium. This gives an annual payment of $135,000 paid in two installments of $67,500 in March and September. An index does not have to be held until maturity, and money can be made by trading in and out as spread changes, just like a credit default swap. Indices have a bid offer spread which has to be taken into account when deciding whether to trade. A common practice is to roll the index to the new series every six months. Sellers of protection are usually willing to roll the index at a slight discount.

7.6 Pricing CDS Indices

Pricing CDS indices is done in the same way as pricing single name credit default swaps. Although a CDS index is a basket of reference entities and a single name CDS is just one entity, what matters when determining a price is the expected value of premium payments and protection payments. Assuming default of entities in the basket are not correlated it makes no difference to the expected cash flows whether nominal is eroded and protection paid out in 125 little pieces or in one piece. One little quirk is that CDS indices have always been priced assuming a flat credit spread curve, but since the introduction of the SNAC pricing convention single-name CDS are now also priced assuming a flat credit spread curve.

In theory the CDS index should have a spread that can be replicated by buying protection on all the names in the index with the correct weightings. Replicating an index in this way is common practice for equities, where exchange traded funds are constructed to track an index by buying the shares in the index with the appropriate weights. By the Law of One Price the basket of single-name CDS in the index and the index should have the same spread. However this is not always the case. The difference between the basket of single names and the index is called CREDIT SKEW. Hedge funds are usually responsible for keeping skew to a minimum by doing the arbitrage trade that aligns the index and its constituents. However during crises, such as the Credit Crisis, hedge funds and others were not able to do the arbitrage trade so the skew, which was a few basis points before the crisis, widened.

7.7 Further Reading

Markit has an excellent set of resources on their web site with primers for CDS and CDS indices, announcements of the constituents for CDS indices when they roll in March and September and also calculators for pricing CDS and CDS indices. These can be found at `http://www.markit.com/cds`. Markit also sponsors the CDS Standard Model open source project which defines how to price CDS with an Excel add-in that is free to download at `http://cdsmodel.com/cdsmodel`. The web site has definitions of the Standard North American (SNAC) pricing convention and the Standard European convention. To see all credit event auction announcements and the detailed results of each auction, including the final recovery rates, see `http://creditfixings.com`. Chaplin (2010) provides a good introduction to pricing credit derivatives.

Answers to Exercises

49 *A bank has two one year CDS spreads quoted in the market. One is for senior debt at 100 bp and the other is for subordinated debt at 400 bp. What does this tell you about the recovery rate for senior and subordinated debt issued by the bank?*

The probability of default for senior and subordinated CDS will be identical as they have the same reference entity and are triggered by the same credit events. We know that the senior and subordinated probability of default is the same,

$$p_{sub} = p_{sen},$$

and so

$$\frac{s_{sub}}{1 - R_{sub}} = \frac{s_{sen}}{1 - R_{sen}}$$

$$\frac{1 - R_{sub}}{1 - R_{sen}} = \frac{s_{sub}}{s_{sen}}$$

The ratio of loss given default is the same as the ratio of the credit spreads. So if the ratio of spreads is $\frac{400}{100}$ or 4 then the loss given default is about four times higher for subordinated debt than senior debt.

50 *You buy \$10 million five year protection on Risky Corporation today for 100 bp. Tomorrow Risky Corporation's five year par spread widens to 110 bp. Did you make or lose money? Without using a calculator roughly how much did you make or lose?*

If we buy protection then we have sold away Risky Corporation credit risk so we profit if Risky Corporation credit spread increases. Another way to think of it is that we are paying 100 bp but if we were to buy credit protection today we would have to pay 110 bp, so we have cheap protection which has grown in value since we bought protection yesterday.

We have made money. But how much? Since we are paying 100 bp while the current market par five year spread is 110 bp we are 10 bp better off each year over a period of five years. For a notional of \$10 million our 10 bp (10 bp as a decimal is $\frac{10}{10,000} = 0.0010$ because a basis point is 0.01%) benefit over five years is worth roughly

$$0.0010 \times 5 \times 10,000,000 = 50,000$$

So if we close out the CDS trade today we will have made about \$50,000.

51 *Take a look at the top branch of the tree in Figure 7.3 on page 287. If this were a quarter year CDS contract with just one premium payment then find the value of p_1 that sets the expected present value of the contract to zero.*

If the fair price is zero then

$$p_1 N \frac{c}{4} e^{-rt_1} = (1 - p_1) N (1 - R) e^{-rt_1}$$

$$p_1 = \frac{1 - R}{\frac{c}{4} + 1 - R}$$

52 *To prepare the ground for the following explanation we will play a game. You are a CDS trader providing one year protection for Risky Corporation. The CEO of Risky Corp. throws a dice at the end of each financial quarter. If he throws a six he drives the company to bankruptcy and triggers a default payment of ten million dollars. If he does not throw six the company survives and you will receive a coupon payment c.* You decide the fair value of c.

We price our premium c by calculating the expected payoff for all possible outcomes of the game. There are five possible outcomes: no default at all, or default on the first, second, third or fourth throw. We denote throwing a 6 as "D" for default and any other number from 1 to 5 as "N" for no default.

outcome	probability	payoff
NNNN	$\left(\frac{5}{6}\right)^4$	$4c$
NNND	$\left(\frac{5}{6}\right)^3 \frac{1}{6}$	$3c - d$
NND	$\left(\frac{5}{6}\right)^2 \frac{1}{6}$	$2c - d$
ND	$\frac{5}{6}\frac{1}{6}$	$c - d$
D	$\frac{1}{6}$	$-d$

In order to find the fair value of the coupon payment we set the expected value of the payoff to zero. If this is the case then you and the buyer of protection expect to make the same amount from the deal.s

$$\left(\frac{5}{6}\right)^4 4c + \left(\frac{5}{6}\right)^3 \frac{1}{6}(3c - d) + \left(\frac{5}{6}\right)^2 \frac{1}{6}(2c - d) + \frac{5}{6}\frac{1}{6}(c - d) - \frac{1}{6}d = 0$$

We can re-arrange this to find the relationship between c and d,

$$4.5^4 c + 3.5^3 c + 2.6.5^2 c + 5.6^2 c = 5^3 d + 5^2.6d + 5.6^2 d + 6^3 d$$
$$c = \frac{4.5^4 + 3.5^3 + 2.6.5^2 + 5.6^2}{5^3 + 5^2.6 + 5.6^2 + 6^3} d$$
$$c = \frac{d}{5}$$

If the protection payment d is \$10 million then the premium c should be \$2 million.

53 *Now find an expression relating survival probability p, coupon payment c and default payment d.*

As before we set the expected payoff to zero.

$$p^4 4c + p^3(1 - p)(3c - d) + p^2(1 - p)(2c - d) + p(1 - p)(c - d) - (1 - p)d = 0$$
$$\frac{p^3 - p^4 + p^2 - p^3 + p - p^2 + 1 - p}{4p^4 + 3p^3 - 3p^4 + 2p^2 - 2p^3 + p - p^2} = \frac{c}{d}$$
$$\frac{1 - p^4}{p + p^2 + p^3 + p^4} = \frac{c}{d}$$

But $p + p^2 + p^3 + p^4 = \frac{p(1-p^4)}{1-p}$ (see Section 3.7 on page 118) so

$$\frac{1-p}{p} = \frac{c}{d}$$

and

$$p = \frac{d}{c+d}$$

54 *Set the discount factors to 1, $\delta_i = \delta_i^{mid} = 1$, and ignore the term for $V_{accrued}$ and find the ratio $\frac{p_1}{p_0}$.*

If we set the discount factors to 1, $\delta_i = \delta_i^{mid} = 1$, and ignore the term for $V_{accrued}$ then

$$
\begin{aligned}
V_{\text{protection}} &= V_{\text{premium}} \\
(1-R)(p_0 - p_1) &= c\Delta t_1 p_1 \\
(1-R)p_0 &= p_1 \left[1 - R + c\Delta t_1\right] \\
\frac{p_1}{p_0} &= \frac{1-R}{1-R+c\Delta t_1}
\end{aligned}
$$

8 Structured Credit

8.1 The Deal

In 1144 the Knights Hospitaller were given a castle in modern-day Syria on a strategic site controlling the road from Antioch to the Mediterranean. They completely rebuilt the castle using a concentric design. This is shown in Figure 8.1 which is a drawing of Krak des Chavaliers. Clearly visible is an outer wall, and within that an inner wall and then a third wall. If attackers managed to breach the outer wall the defenders would retreat to the castle within a castle. The attackers would then find themselves in a well-designed killing zone. This concentric design made castles impregnable until the advent of gunpowder.

Now imagine that we were to store gold inside the castle in one of three zones: outer, middle or inner. The

Figure 8.1:
From Guillaume Rey, "Étude sur les monuments de l'architecture militaire des croisés en Syrie et dans l'île de Chypre (1871)".

Knights Hospitaller could provide an insurance policy against theft by attack. They would charge a different rate for each zone. Obviously the riskiest area would be the outer zone, where we would pay the highest rate of insurance, less for the middle zone and least for the innermost zone.

This seems simple enough, but a shrewd investor might see a problem. The problem is whether the inner walls are more likely to be breached if the outer wall is breached. How closely linked are the walls? A commonly used castle-busting technique, called sapping, was to dig tunnels under the castle walls supported by wooden props. Then fires would be lit in the tunnel that would burn the props undermining the wall and causing it to collapse. If the walls were very close to one another the collapse of one wall could trigger the collapse of the next like dominos. If this domino factor were very high then if one wall were breached then all would be breached. It would be as if we had just one wall after all. Our shrewd medieval investor might argue that the inner zone premium should be much closer to the outer zone premium.

A COLLATERALIZED DEBT OBLIGATION (CDO) is organized like a concentric castle. It is divided into tranches (*tranche* means "slice" in French). The slices are ordered according to their risk of taking losses through default. The ordering is called

SUBORDINATION. The riskiest tranche, akin to the outer zone of our castle, is the EQUITY TRANCHE. Next comes the MEZZANINE TRANCHE usually nicknamed the "mezz tranche". And safest of all is the SENIOR TRANCHE. Just as we would pay more insurance premium for the outer zones than we would for the inner zones, investors pay more premium to buy protection on the junior tranches than the senior tranches. And investors in a tranche are very interested in the domino effect, which is called CORRELATION. There are variations on this structure, such as multiple mezz tranches or varying tranche sizes, but this is the broad-brush organisation of a CDO.

When defaults occur they eat into the subordination structure from the bottom up. Each tranche has an attachment and detachment point denoted $[a, b]$ where a and b are expressed as percentages of the total CDO notional. For example a [3%,7%] tranche on a notional of $1 billion would start to take a hit when losses reach $30 million and be totally wiped out when losses reach $70 million. As the notional of a tranche is eroded by defaults the premium paid on the tranche decreases.

As mentioned in chapter 7.5, one of the uses of CDS indices is to form standard reference pools for structured credit. For iTraxx Europe main the standard tranches are [0,3], [3,6], [6,9], [9,12], [12,22] and for CDX main [0,3], [3,7], [7,10], [10,15] and [15,30].

8.2 CDO Pricing

Structured credit pricing depends on default correlation. A commonly used method for pricing CDOs is to Monte Carlo sample using a Gaussian copula. This is a simulation method, meaning that we generate thousands of possible futures. In each simulated future we know everything about the future, such as whether each entity will default and when it will default. What we are aiming for is a set of simple cash flows that can be discounted to give a present value.

To illustrate the method we can price a single-name default swap using simulation. If we assume a flat term structure for the par spread of 50 basis points then the survival curve $p_s(t) = e^{-0.005t}$. To price the CDS we need to know its survival time. We sample from a uniform $U(0, 1)$ distribution to give a survival probability then inverse-transform this probability into a survival time using the survival curve. We could generate a look-up table, but for this simple example we can simply re-arrange the equation to give the survival time $t = -\frac{\ln p_s}{0.005}$. Once we have the survival time t we know all the cash flows. If the contract is for five years protection then in the cases where $t > 5$ there was no default and the value of the contract is the present value of all the protection cash flows. If default occurs before the termination of the contract the cash flows will include the protection payment and the accrued interest between the preceding premium payment and the default time.

Pricing a CDO is more complex than simulating default of each CDS in the reference pool because we have to capture default correlation. This is the tendency of some entities to default together. The calculation can be broken down into the following steps for a reference pool containing p reference entities:

- The $p \times p$ covariance matrix has a leading diagonal equal to 1 and off-diagonal elements all equal to a single value ρ.

$$\Sigma = \begin{bmatrix} 1 & \rho & \rho & \rho & \rho \\ \rho & 1 & \rho & \rho & \rho \\ \rho & \rho & 1 & \rho & \rho \\ \rho & \rho & \rho & 1 & \rho \\ \rho & \rho & \rho & \rho & 1 \end{bmatrix}$$

- Given this $p \times p$ covariance matrix Σ generate one p-dimensional sample from a $N(0, \Sigma)$ multivariate normal distribution (see sections 3.3.2 and 3.3.3 if you don't understand what this means).

- Each of the p samples is normally distributed, and these are converted into probabilities using the inverse normal cumulative distribution function ϕ^{-1}.

- Convert each one of the p probabilities into a survival time using the survival curve $p_s(t)$ of each CDS in the reference pool, just as with the single-name CDS simulation pricing.

- Survival times for each entity give the cash flows and losses for each tranche.

8.3 Example

We will work through an example showing how it is possible to simulate default times for the credits in a pool and how to use the default times to calculate the breakeven spread of a tranche. Our example above had a covariance matrix of five names. We will also have five names with flat CDS spreads of 200, 500, 300, 100 and 400 basis points.

We will start by seeing how correlation ρ affects default times. Our covariance matrix has $\rho = 0$ initially, which means that the individual credit default probabilities are independent of one another.

$$\Sigma = \begin{pmatrix} 1 & 0 & 0 & 0 & 0 \\ 0 & 1 & 0 & 0 & 0 \\ 0 & 0 & 1 & 0 & 0 \\ 0 & 0 & 0 & 1 & 0 \\ 0 & 0 & 0 & 0 & 1 \end{pmatrix}$$

We can use a mathematical package such as R, or MATLAB, to find the Cholesky decomposition of Σ, which we will call C. Cholesky decomposition of a unit matrix gives another unit matrix, so in this example both Σ and C are unit matrices. Now we can use the Cholesky matrix to generate some default times. Say we want 3 samples. First we fill a 3×5 matrix with samples from a normal distribution with mean 0 and standard deviation 1.

$$S = \begin{pmatrix} -0.6265 & 1.5953 & 0.4874 & -0.3054 & -0.6212 \\ 0.1836 & 0.3295 & 0.7383 & 1.5118 & -2.2147 \\ -0.8356 & -0.8205 & 0.5758 & 0.3898 & 1.1249 \end{pmatrix}$$

To get samples from the multivariate normal distribution $N(0, \Sigma)$ we take the product $N = CS$. In this case C is a unit matrix so $N = S$. Each element of N is transformed into a probability using the inverse normal cumulative distribution function.

$$
P = \begin{pmatrix}
0.2655 & 0.9447 & 0.6870 & 0.3800 & 0.26722 \\
0.5729 & 0.6291 & 0.7698 & 0.9347 & 0.01339 \\
0.2017 & 0.2060 & 0.7176 & 0.6517 & 0.86969
\end{pmatrix}
$$

Finally probabilities in P are transformed into survival times using the five survival curves for the five credits in the pool. In this example the spreads are 200, 500, 300, 100, 400 basis points. So the survival probabilities for the five columns of P are transformed into the columns of T using the functions $-\frac{\ln(p_1)}{.02}, -\frac{\ln(p_2)}{.05}, -\frac{\ln(p_3)}{.03}, -\frac{\ln(p_4)}{.01}$ and $-\frac{\ln(p_5)}{.04}$.

$$
T = \begin{pmatrix}
66.31 & \mathbf{1.138} & 12.513 & 96.749 & 32.992 \\
27.86 & 9.269 & 8.719 & 6.752 & 107.831 \\
80.05 & 31.600 & 11.061 & 42.821 & \mathbf{3.490}
\end{pmatrix}
$$

Now we will increase the correlation ρ to 0.999, and see how this affects our samples. The covariance matrix is now

$$
\Sigma = \begin{pmatrix}
1 & 0.999 & 0.999 & 0.999 & 0.999 \\
0.999 & 1 & 0.999 & 0.999 & 0.999 \\
0.999 & 0.999 & 1 & 0.999 & 0.999 \\
0.999 & 0.999 & 0.999 & 1 & 0.999 \\
0.999 & 0.999 & 0.999 & 0.999 & 1
\end{pmatrix}.
$$

The Cholesky matrix is no longer a unit matrix,

$$
C = \begin{pmatrix}
1 & 0.999 & 0.999 & 0.999 & 0.999 \\
0 & 0.04471 & 0.02234 & 0.02234 & 0.02234 \\
0 & 0 & 0.03873 & 0.01290 & 0.012905 \\
0 & 0 & 0 & 0.03651 & 0.009126 \\
0 & 0 & 0 & 0 & 0.035354
\end{pmatrix}.
$$

And the product $C^T C = \Sigma$, by definition. Again, we fill a 3×5 matrix with samples from an $N(0, 1)$ distribution,

$$
S = \begin{pmatrix}
-0.04493 & 0.8212 & 0.78214 & 0.61983 & -1.4708 \\
-0.01619 & 0.5939 & 0.07456 & -0.05613 & -0.4782 \\
0.94384 & 0.9190 & -1.98935 & -0.15580 & 0.4179
\end{pmatrix}.
$$

We shape this distribution into a multivariate normal by multiplying S by the Cholesky matrix $N = SC$,

$$
N = \begin{pmatrix}
-0.04493 & -0.008172 & 0.00375010 & 0.006186 & -0.06279 \\
-0.01619 & 0.010379 & -0.00001635 & -0.003991 & -0.01936 \\
0.94384 & 0.983980 & 0.88638508 & 0.932066 & 0.95111
\end{pmatrix}.
$$

Notice that N has rows that are roughly equal as a consequence of the correlation being very high. These correlated samples are converted to probabilities using the inverse normal cumulative distribution function,

$$P = \begin{pmatrix} 0.4821 & 0.4967 & 0.5015 & 0.5025 & 0.4750 \\ 0.4935 & 0.5041 & 0.5000 & 0.4984 & 0.4923 \\ 0.8274 & 0.8374 & 0.8123 & 0.8243 & 0.8292 \end{pmatrix}.$$

And finally the survival probabilities are converted to survival times using the five survival curves, with default times that occur before the contract matures shown in bold,

$$T = \begin{pmatrix} 36.482 & 13.994 & 23.01 & 68.82 & 18.613 \\ 35.307 & 13.698 & 23.11 & 69.63 & 17.718 \\ 9.475 & \mathbf{3.548} & 6.93 & 19.32 & \mathbf{4.682} \end{pmatrix}.$$

So to summarize the sampling process, if we want to generate n samples and we have d names in our pool of credits:

Matrix	Dimensions	Description
S	$n \times d$	Independent normal $N(0,1)$ samples, $S_{ij} \sim N(0,1)$
Σ	$d \times d$	Covariance matrix $\Sigma = \begin{pmatrix} 1 & \cdots & \rho \\ \vdots & \ddots & \vdots \\ \rho & \cdots & 1 \end{pmatrix}$
C	$d \times d$	Cholesky matrix, $C^T C = \Sigma$
N	$n \times d$	Multivariate normal samples $N = S \times C$
P	$n \times d$	Survival probabilities
T	$n \times d$	Survival times

Our examples have only generated three samples, but it is easy to see how this method can be scaled up to thousands of samples. Instead of starting with an S matrix of dimension 3×5 we generate a matrix that is $n \times 5$. At the end of the process one would have a survival time matrix T that is also of dimension $n \times 5$. If we set $n = 100$ we can plot the survival times to see the effect of correlation ρ as shown in Figure 8.2. When there is no correlation default times are widely dispersed. Within one sample, which is one horizontal line in the graph, some credits default after a few years and some after 400 years. This is in stark contrast with the high correlation example where, within one sample (line) all the credits default together, with tightly clustered default times. In terms of number of defaults within the life of the contract, which is five years, the result is that for high correlation either all the credits default, or none of the credit defaults. There is no half-way house when correlation ρ is high.

Going back to our castle metaphor, if the castle walls are built close together it is as if there was one wall, not two. If one wall falls, so does the other. The effect of having walls built close together is that insurance premia converge because the extra wall offers no extra protection. Similarly, the effect of increasing the correlation ρ is that instead of multiple tranches there is effectively one tranche. In Figure 8.3 we see

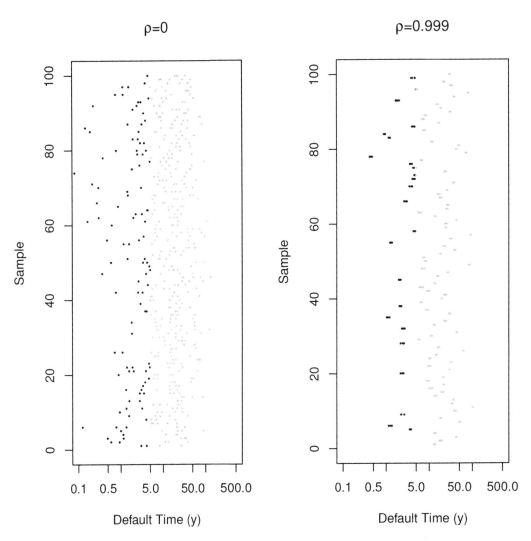

Figure 8.2:
Effect of correlation on default times. The pool of credits contains five names so each sample (row) has five dots. Defaults that occur within five years are black, those after five years grey.

the effect of increasing correlation on the number of defaults. For low correlation the distribution of defaults peaks at 4 out of the 20 entities in the pool, the senior tranche is never hit and the chance of their being one or more defaults over the life of the contract exceeds 99%. As correlation increases (moving further away in the Figure) the "hump" at 4 defaults flattens out and probability is shifted into the extreme 0 default and 20 default buckets, favouring the no default outcome.

We have seen the effect of correlation on default times, but what really matters in credit is the loss incurred when defaults occur. The job of the trader who sells protection is to work out what premium should be paid on each tranche given the survival curves of the credits in the pool and the assumed correlation ρ. The principle by which this BREAKEVEN SPREAD is calculated is the same as that of single-name credit default swaps. The expected payoff of the protection payments and premium payments is set to be equal, so that the value of a five year contract, say, is zero on the day that it is struck.

It is a simple matter to calculate the break-even spread of each tranch using our simulated default times T. For each sample one knows the time at which each credit defaults. We ignore defaults that occur after the contract has matured, because these do not generate any cash flows. We calculate the present value of the protection payments, then the present value of the premium payments. This is just the sum of their discounted cash flows. And then we work out the average of these two numbers over all our samples. The break-even spread is the ratio of the average present value of the protection payments over the average present value of the premium payments.

Assume we have bought $10 m protection on the [0,40%] equity tranche. Take the third sample (third row) from the simulated default times T, and sort the values into ascending order

$$3.548177 \quad 4.681583 \quad 6.929725 \quad 9.4749631 \quad 9.316168$$

Only two times are of interest because they occur before the contract ends and incur a loss for our tranche. The first default after 3.55 years wipes out half our tranche and the second at 4.68 years wipes out the tranche completely. After the first default the premium payments halve and after the second default they are zero because the tranche is wiped out. The cash flows that we would expect are shown in Table 8.1 where the notional is N and the premium of the tranche is c.

We know all the future cash flows so we now take the sum of their discounted values. This gives us the present value of the premium and protection legs. Now we could repeat this process for thousands of samples (rows) of the T matrix. To make things a little more interesting we will have a pool of 20 credits with attachment and detachment points of [0-25%] for the equity tranche, [25%-75%] for the mezz tranche and [75%-100%] for the senior tranche. All the names are assumed to have a flat spread of 500 basis points. The results of the simulations are shown in Figure 8.4. Correlation has a clear difference on tranches with differing seniority. For the senior tranche increasing correlation increases the expected loss and consequently also increases break-even spread. For the equity tranche we see the opposite effect, namely

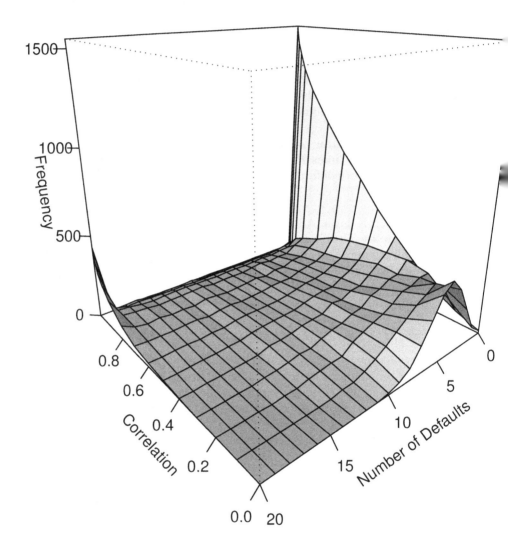

Figure 8.3: Effect of correlation on number of defaults.

Time	Premium	Protection
0.25	$-\frac{Nc}{4}$	0
0.50	$-\frac{Nc}{4}$	0
0.75	$-\frac{Nc}{4}$	0
$\vdots$	$\vdots$	$\vdots$
3.25	$-\frac{Nc}{4}$	0
3.50	$-\frac{Nc}{4}$	0
3.55	0	$\frac{N}{2}$
3.75	$-\frac{1}{2}\frac{Nc}{4}$	0
4.00	$-\frac{1}{2}\frac{Nc}{4}$	0
4.25	$-\frac{1}{2}\frac{Nc}{4}$	0
4.50	$-\frac{1}{2}\frac{Nc}{4}$	0
4.68	0	$\frac{N}{2}$
4.75	0	0
5.00	0	0

Table 8.1:
Simulated synthetic CDO tranche cash flows. Notional is N, tranche premium is c.

increasing correlation decreases expected loss and decreases the break-even spread. The mezzanine tranche is similar to the equity tranche in this example. Notably there is a unification of tranche behaviour as correlation approaches one. When $\rho = 1$ the three tranches become identical as all the credits survive or default simultaneously as if they were one credit.

It may seem surprising that increasing correlation decreases the chance of the equity tranche taking any losses. This is rather more intuitive if one considers that *something* has to happen. As correlation increases either every name defaults or no name defaults so more probability is swept into these two outcomes at the expense of the others. Because the probability of all the names defaulting is never 100% the result is that increasing correlation favours the "no defaults at all" outcome sparing the equity tranche. Another way of thinking about CDO tranches in a high correlation regime is in terms of a single-name CDS. For a correlation 0.9999 the probability of all 20 names defaulting is 22%, nothing defaulting 77% leaving just a 1% probability of having an intermediate number of defaults. As the correlation tends toward 1 the CDO transforms into a single-name CDS with a spread of 500 basis points. Because the recovery rate has been set to zero the survival probability over five years is $e^{-0.05 \times 5} = 0.78$ (see Section 7.1.5 on page 287 which explains how to infer survival curves from credit spreads). As the tranches converge to the same spread the equity tranche spread, which was very high when correlation was low, will decrease. Conversely the senior and super-senior tranches, which had low spreads when correlation was low, will see their spreads increase as correlation increases.

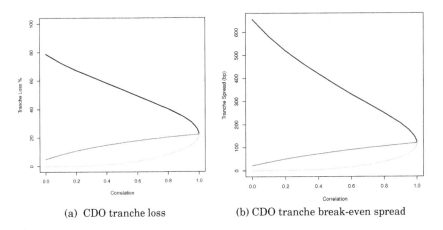

(a) CDO tranche loss

(b) CDO tranche break-even spread

Figure 8.4:
Effect of correlation ρ on tranche loss and break-even spread. Curves are equity tranche (black), mezzanine tranche (dark grey) and senior tranche (light grey).

Part V

Forwards, Futures & Options

9 Forwards and Futures

Forwards and futures are the simplest type of derivative. They are simply deferred purchases and sales. When we buy something we are used to handing over some cash and receiving our goods. In a forward purchase we agree today the price we will pay for the goods at a fixed date in the future. This means that we pay nothing today and yet the value of our contract will make or lose money as the price of the goods change day to day. The thing that we agree to buy or sell in the future is called the UNDERLYING. Historically the forward and futures markets evolved to help farmers lock in the price of their crop removing any uncertainty about the price they would be paid for their produce. The first fully-fledged futures market was established in Japan in the early eighteenth century with the creation of the Dōjima Rice Exchange in Osaka. Once the concepts for buying forward had become established the number of underlyings grew to encompass forwards and futures on non-agricultural commodities and financial instruments, and futures markets spread globally.

The reason why investors buy a forward or future is to get exposure to the price risk of the underlying without paying the full cash amount of the underlying up front. In other words forwards and futures provide leveraged exposure to the underlying. Instead of paying $100 today to get exposure to Sprocket shares you pay just $10 and get the same price risk. This means you have leveraged exposure to both the upside and the downside. The prices of forwards, futures and their underlying are intimately related. Forward and futures prices track the underlying price very closely. If the underlying spot price increases then so will its associated forwards and futures and, unfortunately, if the underlying spot price falls then so will its forwards and futures. Because they track the underlying price in a one-for-one manner forwards and futures are called DELTA ONE instruments.

Forwards are over-the-counter (OTC) assets. This means that they are traded directly between two counterparties and they carry the credit risk of the counterparty. Forwards can be tailored to suit the needs of the client so the size, underlying, delivery dates or any other aspect of the contract can be altered as required. Futures are traded through an exchange and therefore come with standardized notional sizes, dates and underlyings. Forwards are rather like tailor-made clothes, designed to fit the precise measurements of the individual and priced at a premium, whereas futures are like mass-produced clothes which are standardized and sold at a discount. The cash flows for a forward and a future are also quite different. A forward requires no payment at all until delivery, but a future requires maintenance of a margin account and a daily reckoning of profit and loss in the margin account. Despite these differences, a forward and a future with the same underlying and expiry date are related by arbitrage so understanding the pricing of one helps in the understanding and pricing of the other.

9.1 Forwards

A forward is an agreement to exchange a fixed amount of some underlying in return for a fixed amount of cash at a predetermined time in the future. A forward costs nothing when the trade is settled. It can be thought of as a deferred purchase or sale. The forward price is the amount of cash that will be paid for the underlying at expiry. The general pricing principle is that by buying a forward one has implicitly assumed costs and benefits of owning the underlying. This is known as COST OF CARRY. Sometimes cost of carry is converted into an annualized rate called the CARRY RATE. For example, if buying a Procter and Gamble Corporation equity forward one has given up the right to have the dividend and also the interest on the cash required to buy the share. To buy a forward for a commodity such as gold we have to fund the purchase of the gold, and our counterparty has to consider the storage costs of owning gold until delivery.

The difference between the spot and the forward price is called the SPOT-FORWARD BASIS. In the case of many commodities, forward basis is not a matter of opinion, it is fixed by the spot price, interest rates and storage costs. For other forwards the basis is more a matter of opinion because the cost of carry is uncertain. We can generalize the cost of carry argument to find a rule of thumb for pricing any forward where we can do a CASH-AND-CARRY ARBITRAGE trade. As an example here is cash-and-carry arbitrage for a one year forward on Sprocket Corporation stock.

- We agree to sell 1,000 Sprocket Corporation shares to Immense Investment Bank (our counterparty) for $102 each in one year. No money changes hands because the payment we receive is deferred. However the moment we agree the trade we are negatively exposed to the price fluctuations of Sprocket Corporation stock. We are effectively short 1,000 Sprocket shares.

- At the same time as we agree the forward contract we buy 1,000 Sprocket shares at today's market price of $100 to deliver in one year. We have to borrow $100,000 to buy the stock. Buying the stock counteracts the price risk of the short forward so we are no longer making and losing money as Sprocket's stock price fluctuates.

- During the period from the trade date and the settlement date in one year we will have to pay interest of 5% on our loan and this is a total cost of $5,000. Sprocket makes a dividend payment eleven months into the trade of $3 per share and this $3,000 dividend is a benefit. The interest on $3,000 is negligible but is a benefit.

- After one year has passed we will hand over the 1,000 shares we bought on the trade date to Immense Investment Bank and they will pay us $102 for each share, whatever the price of the stock in the spot market. We will repay our $100,000 loan plus $5,000 interest with the $102,000 cash we receive from Immense and the dividend of $3,000.

The fair price produced by a market maker will be their cost of hedging their forward position. More generally we can think in terms of symbols for costs C and benefits B of holding an underlying for forward delivery. If the underlying spot price is S, the forward price is F then we can summarize the trade as follows.

Today		At Expiry Time t	
Action	**Cash Flow**	**Action**	**Cash Flow**
Sell underlying forward for F	0		
Borrow S at the risk free rate r	$+S$	Pay back loan	$-S(1 + rt)$
Buy underlying at spot price S	$-S$	Deliver underlying, receive F cash	$+F$
		Receive benefit of holding underlying	$+B$
		Pay cost of holding underlying	$-C$
Total	0		0

If we set the cash flows at expiry to zero then

$$
\begin{aligned}
\text{Forward} &= \text{Spot} + \text{Costs} - \text{Benefits} \\
F &= S + Srt + C - B
\end{aligned}
$$

The difference between forward and spot is the cost of holding the underlying until expiry minus the benefits of holding the underlying until expiry. Cost includes the funding cost of purchasing and holding the underlying for time t, which is the product of spot price, interest rate and time to expiry Srt. As time to expiry approaches the forward and spot prices converge and at expiry $F = S$. Usually the costs and benefits of holding the underlying until expiry are small compared with the spot price, so that the forward and spot price are almost equal $F \simeq S$. If we look at daily changes in the forward price we would find that it tracks the daily changes in spot price, such that F and S usually have a correlation approaching +1. This is why the forward is used as a means of gaining exposure to the price of the underlying without having to pay the full spot price. In the following sections we describe the costs and benefits of holding various underlyings, but all conform to this general pricing framework based on the cost of carrying the hedged position until expiry.

9.1.1 Commodity Forwards

If gold is trading today at $800 per troy ounce, interest rates are 10%, and gold costs $2 per troy ounce per year to store, what price would we expect for the three month forward gold contract? There is a well-known arbitrage trade for commodity forwards called the cash-and-carry trade. It is constructed as follows, assuming that the price of gold today (the spot price) is S, the annual cost of gold storage is g, and the forward price is F.

Today		In 3 Months	
Action	**Cash Flow**	**Action**	**Cash Flow**
Sell gold forward for \$F	0		
Borrow \$S at the risk free rate r	$+S$	Pay back loan	$-S(1+rt)$
Buy gold	$-S$	Deliver gold, receive \$F cash	$+F$
		Pay gold storage fee	$-gt$
Total	0		0

The forward contract is worth zero today so

$$
\begin{array}{ccccccc}
\text{Forward} & = & \text{Spot} & + & \text{Funding Cost} & + & \text{Storage Cost} \\
F & = & S & + & rtS & + & gt.
\end{array}
$$

This means that the arbitrage-free forward price is the spot price, which is the price today, plus the interest paid on the spot price over the time to maturity t at rate r plus the storage cost g for time t. Interest and the storage cost are both positive, so in this case the forward price is always greater than the spot price. If $S = 800$ and $r = 0.1$ and $t = 0.25$ and $g = 2$, then $F = 800(1 + 0.1 \times 0.25) + 2 \times 0.25 = 820.50$. Over the three month life of the contract the cost of carry is \$20 for the cash required to buy the gold and \$0.50 to store the gold. The cash and carry trade ensures that the forward price will be kept tightly around \$820.50 by arbitrageurs.

The beauty of the trade is that it is completely insensitive to changes in the price of the underlying. Everything is fixed when the deal is set up: the forward price, the interest rate to borrow money to buy the gold and the gold storage cost. At expiry we are indifferent to the price of gold because we are receiving the pre-arranged forward price in return for our gold. Any significant deviation in the forward price from the arbitrage-free price guarantees a profit through the cash-and-carry trade.

9.1.2 Currency Forwards

The value of a currency forward involves two currencies: the domestic currency and the foreign currency. For example a company that trades in the United States may want to fix its USD to JPY exchange rate three months forward. In this case the company would buy a three month USD|JPY currency forward or FX FORWARD. How would the creator of the forward determine the forward rate? The answer is based on the principle of arbitrage. Consider the following two trades:

Trade A: Borrow Yen Borrow JPY 100 million for three months at the current Japanese Yen risk-free rate r_{JPY} .

Trade B: Invest Dollars Borrow 100 million JPY and convert into USD using the USD|JPY spot exchange rate. Invest this amount for three months at the current risk-free USD rate r_{USD}. Then convert the USD back into JPY at the three month forward rate.

The value of the two trades at the end of three months must be the same. Why? If they were not equal we would have an arbitrage opportunity. But in order to compare the value of the two trades we would need to convert JPY in the foreign currency USD back to our domestic currency JPY. We would do this using our locked-in forward rate. So we could equate the value of the two trades taking the spot exchange rate $USD|JPY_{spot}$ and three month forward exchange rate $USD|JPY_{3M}$ into account,

$$N\left(1 + r_{JPY}t\right) = \frac{N}{USD|JPY_{spot}} \times (1 + r_{USD}t) \times USD|JPY_{3M}$$

Re-arranging to get the three month forward rate

$$USD|JPY_{3M} = USD|JPY_{spot}\frac{1 + r_{JPY}t}{1 + r_{USD}t}.$$

To make our argument a little bit more general we can consider our domestic currency DOM has a cheap funding rate r_{DOM} and the foreign currency FOR has a higher interest rate $r_{FOR} > r_{DOM}$.

$$N\left(1 + r_{DOM}t\right) = \frac{N}{FOR|DOM_{spot}} \times (1 + r_{FOR}t) \times FOR|DOM_{3M} \qquad (9.1)$$

The left hand side of Equation 9.1 is just the domestic currency trade A. Trade A is the interest we would receive if we invest our notional in the domestic currency during the life of the forward. The right hand side is the foreign currency trade which involves converting the notional N of domestic currency into $\frac{N}{FOR|DOM_{spot}}$ of foreign currency at the spot rate $FOR|DOM_{spot}$, then investing this amount at the foreign t-year rate for time t. This gives a value in foreign currency at maturity of $\frac{N}{FOR|DOM_{spot}} \times (1 + r_{FOR}t)$. This is then converted back into the domestic currency using the t-year forward FX rate $FOR|DOM_t$.

$$FOR|DOM_t = FOR|DOM_{spot}\frac{1 + r_{DOM}t}{1 + r_{FOR}t} \qquad (9.2)$$

If we were using continuously compounded rates the relationship would be

$$FOR|DOM_t = FOR|DOM_{spot}e^{(r_{DOM} - r_{FOR})t}.$$

The relationship in Equation 9.2 is known as INTEREST RATE PARITY. This is how foreign exchange forwards are priced, and if we were to try and profit from the FX carry trade the break-even rate is the forward rate. Parenthetically we should note that the day count convention for the foreign and domestic currency may differ so the t in the numerator and denominator may not be the same. In terms of cash flows the arbitrage trade would be as follows:

Action	Today Cash Flow	
	DOM	FOR
Sell forward for $FOR|DOM_t$	0	0
Borrow DOM at rate r_{DOM}	+1	0
Buy FOR in spot market	−1	$+\frac{1}{FOR|DOM_{spot}}$
Total	0	$+\frac{1}{FOR|DOM_{spot}}$

Then at expiry,

Action	At Expiry Cash Flow	
	DOM	FOR
Deliver FOR	0	$-\dfrac{1+r_{FOR}t}{FOR|DOM_{spot}}$
Repay DOM loan	$-(1+r_{DOM}t)$	0
Total	$-(1+r_{DOM}t)$	$-\dfrac{1+r_{FOR}t}{FOR|DOM_{spot}}$

At expiry the cash flows must add to zero otherwise an arbitrage opportunity would exist. However we have to compare like with like and use a single currency. Arbitrarily choosing the domestic currency (the foreign currency would give the same answer) we convert the foreign currency back to the domestic currency at the forward rate $FOR|DOM_t$ and set the cash flows at expiry to be equal and opposite

$$1 + r_{FOR}t \quad = \quad \frac{1 + r_{DOM}t}{FOR|DOM_t} FOR|DOM_{spot}.$$

Rearranging

$$FOR|DOM_t \quad = \quad FOR|DOM_{spot} \frac{1 + r_{DOM}t}{1 + r_{FOR}t}. \tag{9.3}$$

Equation 9.3 assumes that the time to expiry t is less than a year because the rates are simple. If the forward is for a period of time greater than a year then we would use compound interest, and we then have to include the compounding frequency convention for each currency. We also have to allow for the fact that the day count convention could differ between the FOR and DOM currencies. So for longer periods our forward and spot relationship becomes

$$FOR|DOM_t = FOR|DOM_{spot} \frac{\left(1 + \frac{r_{DOM}}{f_{DOM}}\right)^{f_{DOM}t_{DOM}}}{\left(1 + \frac{r_{FOR}}{f_{FOR}}\right)^{f_{FOR}t_{FOR}}}.$$

FX forwards have their own quirks of quotation. They are usually quoted relative to FX spot rates. The smallest unit of change for an FX rate is 1 PIP, but the size of a pip depends on the currency pair. For EUR|USD 1 pip is 0.0001, so if the EUR|USD spot rate is 1.4895 and it increases by 1 pip the rate will be 1.4896. For a currency pair such as USD|JPY where the rates are much larger, say 93.01, 1 pip is 0.01 so if the USD|JPY rate were to increase by 1 pip it would be 93.02. If an FX rate increases by 100 pips this is called a BIG FIGURE. So if GBP|USD is trading at "1.50 the figure" that means the rate is 1.5000. FX forwards are quoted in pips relative to the spot rate. This makes a lot of sense because as we know the difference between spot and forward is just the cost of carry and this will not fluctuate hugely during a typical day unless the two interest rates fluctuate hugely.

Using a EUR⎮USD example say the spot rate is 1.4896, the USD three month rate is 0.3% and the EUR three month rate is 0.4%. We know that the three month forward will be lower than the spot rate because the domestic (USD) rate is smaller than the foreign rate (EUR). The EUR⎮USD three month forward rate is $1.4895 \times \frac{1+0.003\times\frac{90}{360}}{1+0.004\times\frac{90}{360}}$ or 1.489128 or the spot rate minus 3.72 pips. So the quote might be "-3.72". It is given in pips and as there is a bid ask spread the actual quote might be -5⎮-3 which is the mid-price of about 4 pips plus or minus one pip. If the spot rate 10 minutes later were to increase by 7 pips to 1.4903 and if the interest rates are about the same we can find the forward rate by just subtracting 4 pips, so we know the three month forward would be trading around 1.4899.

Some governments are wary of speculators in the FX market and have decided to put strong restrictions on movement of their currency offshore. These are usually emerging market currencies and these strong restrictions are probably in reponse to disruptive devaluations that occurred to some Asian countries during the Asian Crisis. For these currencies it is not possible to physically deliver the currency to settle an FX forward. Such contracts have to be cash settled in the currency that is deliverable, commonly US dollars, and are known as NON-DELIVERABLE FORWARDS (NDF). The list of non-deliverable currencies varies over time, but in 2010 it included the Argentinian peso (ARS), Brazilian real (BRL), Chilean peso (CLP), Chinese renminbi (CNR), Colombian peso (COP), Israeli shekel (ILS), Philippine peso (PNP), Russian ruble (RUR), Taiwan dollar (TWD), and the Venezuelan bolivar (VEB).

9.1.3 Equity Forwards

For single equity forwards the hedging trade when a market maker is short a forward is to borrow the money to buy the share today at the spot price S, invest any dividends received until expiry then deliver the share at expiry and repay the loan. The cost of the trade is interest paid on the money borrowed and the benefit is dividend payments received while the share is held. If a dividend D is received at time t_D and the term of the contract is T then the forward price is

$$F = S\left(1 + rT\right) - \left(1 + r\left[T - t_d\right]\right)D$$

The arbitrage trades used to derive this forward price are as follows:

Today		At Expiry T	
Action	Cash Flow	Action	Cash Flow
Sell forward for \$F	0	Deliver stock, receive cash	$+F$
Borrow at rate r	$+S$	Pay back loan	$-S(1+rT)$
Buy stock	$-S$	Receive dividend, interest	$+\left(1 + r\left[T - t_D\right]\right)D$
Total	0		0

Unfortunately dividends are often unknown so the value of D is often an estimate. For this reason the forward price on a single equity, or even an equity index forward, has some subjectivity.

9.1.4 Bond Forwards

Bond forwards have a cost of funding required to buy the bond and a benefit of accrued interest whilst holding the bond. The added complication with bond forwards is that there are two accrued interest amounts which have to be taken into consideration when the bond is bought and sold. The interest rate that is charged r will depend on the bond because the bond can itself be lent out as collateral in the repo market to reduce the cost of borrowing. The cost of carry is calculated using the following trades:

Today		At Expiry T	
Action	**Cash Flow**	**Action**	**Cash Flow**
Sell forward for $F	0	Deliver bond, receive cash	$+F + AI_{delivery}$
Borrow at rate r	$+P_{clean} + AI_{today}$	Pay back loan	$-(P_{clean} + AI_{today})(1 + rT)$
Buy bond	$-P_{clean} - AI_{today}$	Receive coupons	$+C$
Total	0		0

Setting the cash flows at expiry to zero,

$$
\begin{aligned}
F + AI_{delivery} + C &= (P_{clean} + AI_{today})(1 + rT) \\
F &= (P_{clean} + AI_{today})(1 + rT) - C - AI_{delivery}
\end{aligned}
$$

9.2 Futures

Forwards are over-the-counter (OTC) instruments and as such have inherent advantages and disadvantages. The advantage of being OTC is that any aspect of the contract can be modified to suit the client. The main disadvantage is that there is no secondary market for OTC assets. If you no longer want the instrument there is no market into which you can sell, so you have to agree directly with your conterparty to terminate the contract by paying them the current value or you can arrange for a third party to STEP-IN to your side of the trade. Another disadvantage of being OTC is credit risk because your counterparty may default if they owe you money or, if you have bought a commodity forward and want physical delivery they may fail to deliver. An alternative way to trade is through an exchange. This way you never face other traders directly because all transactions, both buying and selling, are with the exchange. The exchange carries almost no credit risk because it ensures that all traders settle their losses at the end of each trading day and that they maintain a cash account that can comfortably absorb a more-than-typical daily loss. The amount of cash in this account is called the MARGIN or alternatively the PERFORMANCE BOND.

Everything about a futures contract is standardized. This includes the expiry date, the quality and the amount of underlying. Expiry dates usually fall on the third Wednesday of March, June, September and December. The futures market has a set of codes for each delivery month so March is abbreviated H, June is M, September is

U and December is Z. The full set of delivery month codes is given in Table 9.6 on page 342. There is also a code for the underlying but unfortunately the underlying codes are not standardized so it is often the case that the code on the exchange web site will differ from those on, say, Bloomberg. A particular futures contract is identified with a ticker that starts with the underlying code, appends the delivery month code and ends with the last digit of the delivery year. Here are some examples using Bloomberg codes for the underlying:

Index	Exchange	Expiry	Ticker		
E-mini S&P 500 Futures	CME	December 2015	ES	Z	5
DJ Euro Stoxx 50	EUREX	June 2018	SX5E	M	8
S&P CNX Nifty	NSE	September 2017	NIFTY	U	7
Nikkei 225 mini Futures	OSE	March 2013	NO	H	3

The futures market is widely used to trade futures on financial instruments such as stock indices. The most widely traded equity index futures contract in the world is the E-mini S&P 500. In the table above the contract identifier is ESZ5 which is broken down into "ES" which is the symbol for the E-mini S&P 500 contract, "Z" which means expiry in December, and "5" which means the year of expiry is the next year ending in 5, which at the time of writing is 2015. If you buy one E-mini S&P contract then you have to place some margin into your margin account. Once you have the contract you are exposed to fluctuations in the price of the future but you have a 50-fold multiplier. This means that if the price of the future increases from 1000 to 1003 you will gain 50×3 or $150. There is a minimum amount that the price of the future can change and this is called one TICK. For the E-mini S&P the tick size is 0.25 points, so the smallest amount by which the price can move if it starts at 1000 is either an up-tick to 1000.25 or a down-tick to 999.75. If we are long the contract an up-tick will earn 50×0.25 or $12.50 and a down-tick will lose $12.50. If we are short the contract then an up-tick will lose $12.50 and a down-tick will earn $12.50. There are four monthly expiries for this contract so you can buy a future that expires in March (ESH5), June (ESM5), September (ESU5) or December (ESZ5) 2015, and expiry occurs on the third Friday of the delivery month. ESZ5 will expire on Friday December 18th, 2015. When we reach the third Friday of the delivery month the contract is cash-settled and terminates.

9.2.1 Price Discovery

Futures markets can be thought of as providing a platform for PRICE DISCOVERY. To understand what price discovery means consider the following question. What is the price of wheat? The question seems simple enough but in fact it is not simple at all. Firstly we would have to specify the precise type and quality of wheat as there are many different varieties and qualities of wheat. The Chicago Board of Trade accepts delivery of four types of wheat for its wheat future contract: soft red winter wheat, hanrd red winter wheat, dark northern spring wheat and northern spring wheat. There is an official body that defines and maintains standards for wheat, the Federal Grain Inspection Service (FGIS). Wheat quality is split by the FGIS into five grades ranging from "No. 1", the highest quality, to "No. 5" and the default quality for CBOT delivery is No. 2[1]. Wheat quality is defined by its density, whether there is any damage to the kernels, and the amount of foreign materials such as stones, glass, weeds or "animal filth". Delivering No. 1 quality is allowed and commands an extra 3 cents per bushel. The buyer would not want the wheat to be too moist because they are paying by weight[2] so wheat with a moisture content of greater than 13.5% is not deliverable. The seller will deliver wheat with a water content as close as possible to 13.5% because this maximizes their profit. Sometimes wheat contains a chemical known as vomitoxin produced by a wheat fungus, so the maximum tolerable level of vomitoxin is set at 4 parts per million and if wheat exceeds this level it is not deliverable.

Secondly we would have to specify when we want to buy the wheat because wheat is produced at particular harvest times and buying outside these harvest times would incur an additional storage cost. Wheat is grown all over the United States and harvest times vary for each geographic region. Wheat contract months on CBOT are March (H), May (K), July (N), September (U) and December (Z). As a futures contract approaches the expiry month the futures contract price and the spot price converge as the cost-of-carry approaches zero. If the two differ shortly before expiry then it should be possible to make a risk free profit. If the futures price is below the cash price we would buy the future, take delivery and sell into the cash market. If the future is higher than the cash market we would sell the future and buy in the cash market. However CBOT wheat contracts failed to converge for nine successive contract expiries after March 2008. The Chicago Mercantile Exchange modified the wheat contract to avoid this failure to converge. They did this by doubling the area over which wheat could be delivered, particularly in areas where soft red winter wheat was produced, making arbitrage more effective. In 2008 and 2009 there were record wheat harvests and the excess had to be stored. The cost of storage sky-rocketed but was not reflected in the carry rate priced into wheat futures contracts so this was another reason for failure of wheat future convergence. The CME introduced a variable storage rate into the contract to better reflect the true cost of carry.

Thirdly we would have to specify the quantity of wheat that we are buying because buying enough for a single loaf of bread would cost more per bushel than buying thousands of tonnes. Each CBOT wheat futures contract is for 5,000 bushels (about 136 metric tons). Finally we would have to specify where we want our wheat delivered by choosing from the following list: Chicago, St. Louis, Toledo, Ohio, or Burns Harbor, Indiana. If this delivery point is distant from the place where the wheat is grown we would expect to pay transportation costs. A futures exchange fixes all these variables, so that both buyer and seller know what they are delivering or receiving. The price of the contract is then driven by the price that buyers are willing to pay and sellers are willing to receive for a standard contract. To answer our question the price of wheat *is* the futures price as there is no better way to define the price of wheat.

---

[1]http://archive.gipsa.usda.gov/reference-library/standards/810wheat.pdf

[2]Wheat contracts on CBOT trade in size of 5,000 bushels per contract. A bushel was originally a unit of volume but is used as a weight for agricultural commodities. Because each commodity has a different density (mass = volume × density) a bushel represents a different weight for each commodity. For wheat a bushel is 60 lb (60 pounds is 27.2155 kg) but for oats a bushel is 32 lb in the USA and 34 lb in Canada.

Mon Jan 4	Tue Jan 5	Wed Jan 6	Thu Jan 7	Fri Jan 8
1128.75	1132.25	1133	1137.5	1141.5
Mon Jan 11	**Tue Jan 12**	**Wed Jan 13**	**Thu Jan 14**	**Fri Jan 15**
1142.5	1134	1141.5	1145.25	1132.25
Mon Jan 18	**Tue Jan 19**	**Wed Jan 20**	**Thu Jan 21**	**Fri Jan 22**
-	1145.75	1134	1111	1091
Mon Jan 25	**Tue Jan 26**	**Wed Jan 27**	**Thu Jan 28**	**Fri Jan 29**
1092.5	1087.25	1094.5	1079.25	1070.5

Table 9.1: Daily closing prices for E-mini S&P contract.

9.2.2 Margin and Mark to Market

Cash maintenance differentiates futures from other financial assets. The exchange insists that all people who trade futures have a margin account in order to reduce its risk to a minimum. When a future is bought or sold the trader puts up INITIAL MARGIN. This can be cash or cash-like liquid instruments such as US Treasuries. The price of the contract will change minute by minute and at the end of each day the official closing price is recorded. If the trader is long and the closing price is higher than the previous day's closing price then their margin account increases, and if they are long and the underlying price goes down their margin account decreases. This daily cleaning of the slate is called MARK TO MARKET. If the amount in the margin account falls below the MAINTENANCE MARGIN the trader will receive a MARGIN CALL whereby they are obliged to top up their margin account to the maintenance margin amount. If they fail to do so their position is closed out. By maintaining margin accounts the exchange limits the amount that can be lost or gained to single day mark to market changes. In addition, as the exchange is both long and short, these positions offset reducing its risk further. Traders may also benefit from diversification if they hold multiple positions in many different contracts because increases in one contract could offset losses in another. As they can combine their margin accounts this beneficial diversification effect is called CROSS-MARGINING.

To illustrate the effects of margining and to show the rollercoaster effect of leverage we will imagine that we have bought a single E-mini S&P futures contract. We buy the contract on January 4th, 2010 and we decide to buy rather than sell because we have a conviction that the S&P will increase in price strongly in January. Our broker tells us to put $5,625 initial margin into our margin account. We now have "skin in the game" and will be watching the S&P very closely over the next four weeks. The daily closing prices for the ESH0 contract over the following four weeks are shown in Table 9.1.

On Tuesday January 5th the futures price closes at 1132.25. This means a profit for us, and our P&L increases by the multiplier of 50 for the E-mini contract times the price difference. This is $50 \times (1132.25 - 1128.75)$ or 50×3.5 which is $175. On Wednesday we make another profit of $50 \times (1133 - 1132.25)$ or 50×0.75 which is $37.50. Our margin

	Mon Jan 4	Tue Jan 5	Wed Jan 6	Thu Jan 7	Fri Jan 8
Mark to Market	0	+$175	+$37.50	+$225	+$200
Margin Payment	$5,625	0	0	0	0
Margin Balance	$5,625	$5,800	$5,837.50	$6062.50	$6,262.5
	Mon Jan 11	Tue Jan 12	Wed Jan 13	Thu Jan 14	Fri Jan 15
Mark to Market	+$50	-$425	+$375	+$187.50	-$650
Margin Payment	0	0	0	0	0
Margin Balance	$6312.50	$5,887.50	$6,262.50	$6,450	$5,800
	Mon Jan 18	Tue Jan 19	Wed Jan 20	Thu Jan 21	Fri Jan 22
Mark to Market	-	+$675	-$587.50	-$1,150	-$1,000.0
Margin Payment	0	0	0	0	$762.50
Margin Balance	$5,800	$6,475	$5,887.50	$4,737.50	$4,500
	Mon Jan 25	Tue Jan 26	Wed Jan 27	Thu Jan 28	Fri Jan 29
Mark to Market	+75	-262.50	+362.50	-762.50	-437.50
Margin Payment	0	$187.50	0	$400	$437.50
Margin Balance	$4,575	$4,500	$4,862.50	$4,500	$4,500

Table 9.2: E-mini contract P&L.

account holds $5,800 once we mark to market on Wednesday. By the end of the week we have made a total of $637.50. The futures price, which tracks the underlying S&P almost one-for-one, has only increased by $12.75 but we are benefitting from our fifty-fold leverage. Week two is not so good as the price seems to hover around 1140. On Monday January 18th the exchange is closed for Martin Luther King day but picks up where it left off closing at 1145.75 on Tuesday January 19th. Then bad things start to happen and the market takes a nose-dive. The market moves down for the next three days where we lose $587.50, $1,150 and $1,000 on Wednesday, Thursday and Friday. Although this shakes our faith in the rally we decide to hold on for another week. Monday sees a modest gain of $75 but on Tuesday we lose $262.50. The gain of $362.50 on Wednesday January 27th is more than offset by losses of $762.50 and $437.50 on Thursday and Friday. At this point we decide to close our position and cut our losses. Our daily mark-to-market profits and losses, margin payments and margin account balances are shown in Table 9.2.

We had to put up $5,625 initial margin when we opened our position, and we closed the position on the minimum margin of $4,500 having paid a total of $1,787.50 in variation margin. In total we lost $-5,625 + 4,500 - 1,787.50$ or $2,912.50. Over this period the future price dropped from $1,128.75 to $1,070.50 which means a loss of $50 \times (1128.75 - 1070.50)$ which is also a loss of $2,912.50. Notice that the minimum margin of $4,500 comfortably covered all of our daily losses. Our largest daily loss was $1,150 but the maintenance margin was almost four times larger. We can see that the minimum margin requirement is not sized for a typical daily loss, but for an extreme loss, and it is extremely rare for the entire margin to be wiped out in one day. If markets become more volatile the exchange will increase the margin requirements

E-Mini Limit	ETH	5% $\updownarrow$		
		55		
	RTH	10% $\downarrow$	20% $\downarrow$	30% $\downarrow$
		110	220	330
DJIA Rule 80B Limit		1050	2100	3150

Table 9.3:
Limits for E-mini S&P futures. ETH is extended trading hours, RTH is regular trading hours, DJIA is the Dow Jones Industrial Average.

and extreme moves may trigger margin calls more than once per day.

If there is a precipitous fall in the futures market then trading is suspended for a period of time to allow people to calm down, then trading resumes. This is called a PRICE LIMIT or CIRCUIT BREAKER. In regular trading hours (RTH) circuit breakers are only for downward price movements of 10%, 20% and 30% and in extended trading hours (ETH) the breaker triggers for either up or down movements. The limits are reset every quarter based on the average futures price so that the absolute limit sizes remain sensible. The average price used to scale the limits is the average closing price of the lead month futures contract in December, March, June and September and the limits are rounded in multiples of 10 index points. For the E-mini S&P futures contract in the first financial quarter of 2010 the limits in extended and regular trading hours are shown in Table 9.3.

On Thursday January 21st the futures price of the E-mini fell 23 points from 1134 to 1111. This was a fall of just 2%. If instead the futures price had fallen 110 points to 1024 at some point in the trading day then the 10% trading limit would be imposed for 10 minutes. Trading is allowed during these ten minutes but only at prices at or above 1024. Would this have wiped out our margin? We would have lost $(1134 - 1024) \times 50$ or $5,500 which would have consumed our maintenance margin of $4,500. If trading was so volatile we would have received margin calls within the trading day to ensure our margin was topped up and that we could cover any further losses. After the ten minutes are over if the market is still limit offered then trading is suspended for two minutes then resumes with the 20% limit in place. If after trading resumed the price fell 220 points to 914 another ten minute period would apply where trading could only occur at or above the 20% limit of 914. The largest price limit is 30% so the futures price could not fall below 804 during the trading day on Thursday January 21st, 2010. Another event that can trigger the circuit breaker is if the New York Stock exchange suspends share trading. This event is called NYSE RULE 80B and Rule 80B also has 10%, 20% and 30% limits based on intra-day falls in the value of the Dow Jones Industrial Average Index. E-mini futures trading stops until the NYSE resumes share trading, then the next limit applies on the futures.

9.2.3 Futures Markets

Historically the futures market grew out of a need to lock in a fixed price for physically delivered agricultural products such as wheat, and even though the first futures markets originated in Japan in the early 18th century by the 20th century futures were a predominantly a US market. Chicago was the centre of the futures universe with its strategic position between population centres on the East coast of the United States and prime Midwestern farm land. The data in Table 9.4 shows that the futures market has now shifted East towards Europe and Asia and South toward Latin America. In terms of trading volume Eurex is now comparable with the Chicago Mercantile Exchange Group (CME), and Korea is close behind and still growing rapidly. Another radical change in the futures market is that the trading pit, with people in brightly coloured jackets shouting and hand-signalling at each other in a system called OPEN OUTCRY, has given way almost completely to ELECTRONIC TRADING. A trade for an electronic E-mini S&P futures contract is now executed in a matter of milliseconds. Some say this is a step backwards as it allows the market to react more quickly and this may increase volatility and even be a causal factor in market crashes. The majority of traders simply take rapid execution for granted and build it into their trading and execution strategy.

Some exchanges specialize in a few contracts and others have a broad range of contracts. For example the Korea Exchange (KRX) is dominated by exchange traded options on the Korea Composite Stock Price Index (KOSPI). In contrast the CME has a much broader range of contracts including options and futures on interest rates (Eurodollar futures, Treasury bond futures and options), equity indices (dominated by the E-mini S&P but also the Nasdaq 100 and Russell 2000 indices), and the traditional agricultural contracts (corn, soybean, wheat, hogs and cattle). The underlyings that are traded have also shifted from agricultural products to a global market dominated by equity indices, single equities and interest rate futures as shown in Table 9.5. In terms of volume agriculture, energy, currency, precious metals and non-precious metals lag far behind equity index futures, single equity futures and interest rate futures. Interest rate futures are described in detail in the part on fixed income (Section 4.5.4 on page 152) as are bond futures (Section 5.12 on page 204).

Commodity futures are usually sub-divided into things that are grown and things that are mined. Commodities that are grown are soft commodities, or SOFTS, which include agricultural commodities such as corn, soybean, barley, oats, wheat, rice, sugar, coffee, cocoa, wool, lumber, lean hogs, live cattle and orange juice. Softs are usually perishable and so cannot be stored for any length of time. HARD COMMODITIES are not perishable and include both industrial and precious metals, crude oil, heating oil, natural gas, and cotton (because it can be stored without spoiling). PRECIOUS METALS are gold, platinum, palladium and silver and almost any non-precious metals are considered INDUSTRIAL METALS such as copper, aluminium, lead, zinc, nickel and cobalt. Fossil fuels, such as West Texas intermediate (WTI) crude oil, Brent crude oil, heating oil and natural gas are called ENERGY COMMODITIES.

Physical commodities that have to be delivered to the contract buyer are priced based on the place where the commodity will be delivered. This is because any physical commodity must price in the cost of transportation. For example the DELIVERY

Exchange	2008	2007
CME Group (includes CBOT and Nymex) *	3,277,645,351	3,158,383,678
Eurex (includes ISE) *	3,172,704,773	2,704,209,603
Korea Exchange	2,865,482,319	2,777,416,098
NYSE Euronext (includes all EU and US markets) *	1,675,791,242	1,525,247,465
Chicago Board Options Exchange (includes CFE) *	1,194,516,467	945,608,754
BM&F Bovespa *	741,889,113	794,053,775
Nasdaq OMX Group (includes all EU and US markets) *	722,107,905	551,409,855
National Stock Exchange of India	590,151,288	379,874,850
JSE South Africa	513,584,004	329,642,403
Dalian Commodity Exchange	313,217,957	185,614,913
Russian Trading Systems Stock Exchange	238,220,708	143,978,211
IntercontinentalExchange (includes US, UK and Canada markets) *	234,414,538	194,667,719
Zhengzhou Commodity Exchange	222,557,134	93,052,714
Boston Options Exchange	178,650,541	129,797,339
Osaka Securities Exchange	163,689,348	108,916,811
Shanghai Futures Exchange	140,263,185	85,563,833
Taiwan Futures Exchange	136,719,777	115,150,624
Moscow Interbank Currency Exchange	131,905,458	85,386,473
London Metal Exchange	113,215,299	92,914,728
Hong Kong Exchanges & Clearing	105,006,736	87,985,686
Australian Securities Exchange (includes SFE) *	94,775,920	116,090,973
Multi Commodity Exchange of India	94,310,610	68,945,925
Tel-Aviv Stock Exchange	92,574,042	104,371,763
Mercado Español de Opciones y Futuros Financieros	83,416,762	51,859,591
Mexican Derivatives Exchange	70,143,690	228,972,029
Tokyo Financial Exchange	66,927,067	76,195,817
Singapore Exchange	61,841,268	44,206,826
Turkish Derivatives Exchange	54,472,835	24,867,033
Mercado a Termino de Rosario	42,216,661	25,423,950
Tokyo Commodity Exchange	41,026,955	47,070,169
Italian Derivatives Exchange	38,928,785	37,124,922
Bourse de Montreal	38,064,902	42,742,210
Tokyo Stock Exchange	32,500,438	33,093,785
National Commodity & Derivatives Exchange	24,639,710	34,947,872
Oslo Stock Exchange	16,048,430	13,967,847
Budapest Stock Exchange	13,369,425	18,827,328
Warsaw Stock Exchange	12,560,518	9,341,958
Tokyo Grain Exchange	8,433,346	19,674,883
Athens Derivatives Exchange	7,172,120	6,581,544
Malaysia Derivatives Exchange	6,120,032	6,202,686

Table 9.4:

Futures exchanges ranked by number of futures and options traded/cleared. Source: The Futures Industry Association.

Category	2008	2007
Equity Index	6,488,620,434	5,499,833,555
Individual Equity	5,511,194,380	4,400,437,854
Interest Rates	3,204,838,617	3,745,176,350
Agricultural	888,828,194	640,683,907
Energy	580,404,789	496,770,566
Currency	577,156,982	459,752,816
Precious Metals	180,370,074	150,976,113
Non-Precious Metals	175,788,341	106,859,969
Other	45,501,810	26,140,974
Total	17,652,703,621	15,526,632,104

Table 9.5:

Futures contracts traded/cleared Jan-Jun 2008 by category of underlying. Source: The Futures Industry Association.

January	F	July	N
February	G	August	Q
March	H	**September**	U
April	J	October	V
May	K	November	X
June	M	**December**	Z

Table 9.6: Delivery month codes for futures contracts.

Exchange / Contract	KRX	CME	Eurex	Liffe	Multiple	BM&F	NSE	CBOE	ZCE	Nymex	DCE	Taifex	TASE	
Kospi 200 Index Options	●													1137
Eurodollar Futures		●												356
E-mini S&P 500 Index Futures		●												276
DJ Euro Stoxx 50 Index Futures			●											195
DJ Euro Stoxx 50 Index Options			●											181
10 Year Treasury Note Futures		●												155
Euro-Bund Futures			●											150
Eurodollar Options on Futures		●												140
Euribor Futures				●										133
SPDR S&P 500 ETF Options					●									131
Powershares QQQ ETF Options					●									109
Euro-Schatz Futures			●											102
5 Year Treasury Note Futures		●												99
One Day Inter-Bank Deposit Futures						●								98
Euro-Bobl Futures			●											87
S&P CNX Nifty Index Futures							●							87
iShares Russell 2000 ETF Options					●									79
S&P 500 Index Options								●						78
White Sugar Futures									●					71
Light Sweet Crude Oil Futures										●				71
Short Sterling Futures				●										65
Euribor Options on Futures				●										58
Financial Select Sector SPDR ETF Options					●									57
E-mini Nasdaq 100 Futures		●												53
30 Year Treasury Bond Futures		●												52
No. 1 Soybeans Futures											●			51
Dax Index Options			●											50
Taiex Index Options												●		47
2 Year Treasury Note Futures		●												46
TA-25 Index Options													●	43
	1137	1177	765	256	375	98	87	78	71	71	51	47	434254.909437	

Figure 9.1:

Volume of contracts traded/cleared Jan-Jun 2008 broken down by exchange and underlying. Numbers in margins are in billions of contracts traded/cleared. Source: The Futures Industry Association.

POINT of US natural gas futures is the Henry Hub, a meeting point of many natural gas pipelines in Erath, Louisiana, a small town close to the Gulf of Mexico in the southern United States. The NYMEX light sweet crude oil contract has its delivery point at a junction of oil pipelines in Cushing, Oklahoma. Wheat futures traded on the CBOT have a choice of delivery areas, including long stretches of the Ohio River and Mississippi River. The reason why delivery dates for futures contracts span almost an entire month was originally to avoid congestion at the delivery point. Some physically settled contracts may not involve taking physical ownership, such as gold. Because of its high value gold is usually stored in a LICENSED DEPOSITORY with a record of ownership and regular audits to ensure that there is agreement between the physical amount stored and the recorded amounts. To ensure the quality of the gold is sufficient to satisfy the requirement of the contract there are APPROVED ASSAYERS, and to transport gold from the licensed depository the use of APPROVED CARRIERS is obligatory.

9.2.4 The Futures Curve

Part of the specification of a futures contract is its expiry date. For a single underlying, such as Brent crude oil, there will be a range of futures contracts quoted for expiries ranging from a few weeks up to several years in the future. By plotting the price of the contracts against their expiry times we can see the shape of the FUTURES CURVE. For underlyings where cash and carry arbitrage is possible we can calculate the futures price if we know the spot price and the cost of carry. This will include any underlying that can be bought in the spot market and "stored" until delivery such as equities (single-stock and indices), foreign currencies, precious and industrial metals, and bonds. The cost of carry for futures is just the same as the cost of carry for forwards that we have already described in detail. For underlyings where storage is not practical, such as live hog contracts, the futures price is a reflection of where the market expects the underlying will trade. It is important to stress that the futures curve is a poor predictor of where the actual spot price will trade in the future.

One reason why the shape of the futures curve matters is that in order to maintain exposure to, say, oil prices the investor must roll their futures contract. As one contract expires the investor will sell before the settlement date and buy a contract that expires later. The cost of rolling the contract will depend on whether the futures curve is upward or downward sloping. If upward sloping this will be a cost to the investor that is long and a benefit to the investor that is short. If downward sloping the roll cost will be a benefit to the investor that is long and a cost to the investor that is short. An upward sloping futures curve is called CONTANGO and a downward sloping curve is called BACKWARDATION. These two states are shown in Figure 9.2 for the West Texas Intermediate crude oil futures market. The usual explanation for backwardation, other than a negative carry rate, is that delivery today is worth a premium because of supply restrictions. It may be that the commodity will be unavailable when it is needed in the future, so it is best to buy now while it is available, and this spot-over-future premium is called CONVENIENCE YIELD. Convenience yield is a stronger determinant of futures prices in markets such as oil where storage is expensive and difficult, the value-to-volume ratio is low and where the working inventory

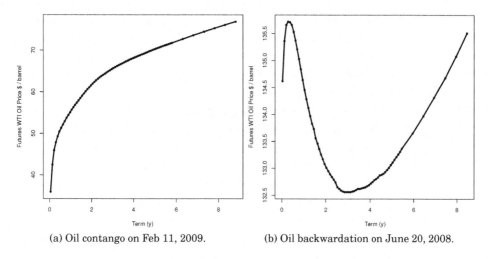

(a) Oil contango on Feb 11, 2009.   (b) Oil backwardation on June 20, 2008.

Figure 9.2: West Texas Intermediate crude oil futures. Source: Bloomberg.

of the commodity is a small fraction of annual consumption. In contrast gold is easy to store, has high value per unit volume, and the working inventory is a large fraction of consumption so the futures price is dominated by cost-of-carry.

The shape of the curve can be complex. If the futures curve is S-shaped then parts of the curve can be in backwardation while other parts are in contango, as seen in Figure 9.2 (b). This shows the price of WTI oil futures on the 20th of June, 2008. The futures curve fell steeply for expiries up to three years which meant that this part of the curve was in backwardation. For expiries from three to eight years the curve rose again, so that very long-dated futures were in contango.

10 Call and Put Options

10.1 Introduction

An option is a contract that gives its buyer a choice whether to buy or sell some asset in the future. In the movie industry producers frequently buy film rights for a book from the author. The deal gives a producer a choice, but no obligation, to produce a screenplay and a film based on the story. The contract usually comes with an expiry date, so that if the producer cannot raise the capital to produce the film the contract expires worthless. In this sense film options convey the *right* but not the *obligation* to turn a story into a movie in a time limit. What the producer is paying for is choice, and in the case of film rights exclusivity, because no other producer can use a story for which exclusive film rights have been sold. There is a secondary market in film rights, so that producer A could buy rights from producer B. The value of the option will depend on the popularity of the author and the story, but the value is indirect or derived from the value of the screenplay hence the name derivative.

In the financial domain options give the right, but not the obligation, to buy or sell some asset in the future. The contract specifies what will be bought or sold, the UNDERLYING, and whether the contract is to buy the underlying (a CALL OPTION) or sell the underlying (a PUT OPTION). To remember the meaning of call and put it may be useful to imagine that when you want to buy something you would *call* your broker. If you sell something you *put* it down. The agreed upon fixed price at which the underlying can be bought or sold is the STRIKE. The latest date that the option may be exercised is called the EXPIRY. Even in the textual description of an option it is possible to make out the description of a future. The difference between a future and option is that a future confers an *obligation* to buy or sell some asset at a fixed price in the future whereas an option confers an *option* to buy or sell. Another way of seeing an option is as a future with an embedded insurance policy to protect the buyer from adverse price changes. If it is not financially advantageous to EXERCISE an option by buying or selling the underlying then the owner of the option can allow it to expire worthless.

Some options allow the owner to exercise at any time before expiry, and these are known as AMERICAN OPTIONS. Alternatively the option could allow exercise only at the expiry date, and this is a EUROPEAN OPTION. If the option can be exercised on a fixed set of dates up to expiry this is a BERMUDAN OPTION because Bermuda is between Europe and America and closer to America. When an option is exercised shares in the underlying change hands in the case of PHYSICAL SETTLEMENT. Alternatively, if the option specifies CASH SETTLEMENT, there is an exchange of a cash amount representing the difference between the current market price and the strike. Putting the attributes together, here are four examples of option trades and two forwards:

	Long / Short	Underlying	Strike	Exercise Type	Expiry
European Call	A right	to buy	100 Sprocket shares	at $70 per share	on	March 11
European Put	A right	to sell	100 Sprocket shares	at $70 per share	on	March 11
American Call	A right	to buy	100 Sprocket shares	at $70 per share	on or before	March 11
American Put	A right	to sell	100 Sprocket shares	at $70 per share	on or before	March 11
Long Forward	An obligation	to buy	100 Sprocket shares	at $70 per share	on	March 11
Short Forward	An obligation	to sell	100 Sprocket shares	at $70 per share	on	March 11

If you want to buy an option in practice it can come in many forms. A common way for retail investors to get exposure to options is to buy a COVERED WARRANT. A covered warrant is issued by a financial services company such as an investment bank. Covered warrants can be calls or puts and the underlying can be individual blue chip stocks, stock indices, FX or commodities. For example Société Générale could issue call and put warrants with Exxon Mobil Corporation as the underlying and it would then maintain a two-way market in that option so investors can sell the option before expiry. In keeping with their target retail market, covered warrants only allow investors to buy and not sell options which limits their risk to the premium they pay up front. If a covered warrant is exercised no new shares are issued and the covered warrant issuer is responsible for settling the payoff with the investor as a cash payment. Covered warrants are quite different from regular CORPORATE WARRANTS where a company issues physically settled call warrants on its own stock[1]. If corporate warrants are exercised at expiry the company will issue new shares to the corporate warrant holders and this will raise capital for the issuing company and dilute the shares of existing shareholders. Compared to covered warrants corporate warrants are usually illiquid, longer dated and traded over-the-counter rather than on an exchange. Another wrapper is an EXCHANGE TRADED OPTION which is for the most liquid underlyings and necessarily has standardized maturities and strikes and like all exchange traded products requires the maintenance of margin. Finally investors can buy and sell options directly from and to an investment bank in the over-the-counter derivatives market. This carries counterparty risk so the OTC options market is usually limited to institutional investors.

10.2 Trading Game

To introduce the concept of options we will describe a game. This game is similar to hop-scotch (Ken-Ken-Pa in Japan), but far more interesting because it is played for money. The game is played with a clock that counts down to zero, and when the clock reaches zero the game ends. The game is played on a very long line of numbered squares drawn out on the ground starting at square zero. You start on the square labelled "Spot". One dollar is placed on all the squares starting with one some distance from your starting spot. The square where the money starts is labelled

---

[1]If a company were to issue put options on its own stock would send negative signals to the market.

"Strike" because if you reach this square you may strike it rich. Each time the clock ticks you toss a coin and if you throw heads you move one square forwards toward the money, or if the coin comes up tails you move one square backwards further from the money. If you reach the strike square where the dollar bills begin you are "in the money" which you signal by shouting "I'm in the money!". If you haven't reached that square you are "out of the money", and there's nothing to shout about. When the game ends you can keep all the money on your square and behind you. The money you win is called your payoff.

It is not free to play this game. All those dollar bills have to come from somewhere. How much money would you expect to make if you played the game? If we knew this we could set a fair price to pay per game. One way to find out would be to play the game many times and see how much money you make. We can go through one game just to get the idea, then simulate the game on a computer. For this game our spot is 5, which means we will start the game standing on square 5. We set the strike to 10, which means that one dollar is laid out on square 10, one dollar on square 11, and so on into the distance. The clock counts down from 10 seconds. The game begins. On the first tick you throw tails and move backwards to square 4, then throw heads and move forwards back to square 5, forwards again to square 6, and forwards again to square 5. The game goes as follows:

Clock	Start	10	9	8	7	6	5	4	3	2	1
Hop		B(ack)	F(orward)	F	F	B	F	B	B	F	F
Square	5	4	5	6	7	6	7	6	5	6	7

So the game ends and you are left on square 7, three squares out of the money. Your payoff is zero. How can you modify the game so that you are more likely to win? The game could run for a longer time. If we set the clock to say 20 seconds you would be more likely to win. We could move the strike closer to your starting spot. If the money had started at square 7 you would have made a dollar. We could even start the game so deep in the money that you would be guaranteed to win. Or we could change the game so that you hopped two squares forward or backward on each turn. Making the steps bigger would increase your chance of winning.

Figure 10.1 shows the average amount you would win by playing the game 10,000 times with the spot set to 5, varying the strike value and running the game for different numbers of ticks. As we suspected we win more money by running the game for longer. Even starting 30 steps out of the money we expect to win about $3 if we run the game for 1000 ticks. We win least when we start furthest out of the money and run the game for the shortest time and most when we start in the money and run the game for the longest time. It is interesting that the surface is non-linear, so doubling the time for which the game runs or halving the strike does not double the payoff.

Another way that we might increase our expected payoff is to take bigger jumps. The best we can possibly do is to hop forward towards the money for every turn, although this is very unlikely. This intuition is confirmed in Figure 10.2 where we run the game for 200 ticks varying the hop size from 1 to 10 squares and the strike from 0 to +100. Just as we found for the payoff when varying ticks and strike the

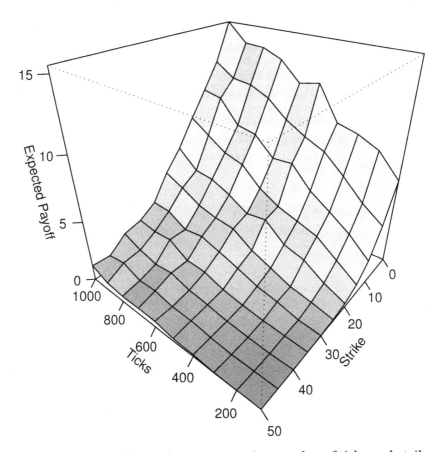

Figure 10.1: Payoff for option game varying number of ticks and strike.

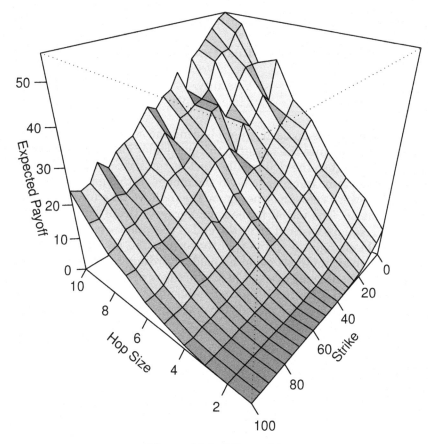

Figure 10.2: Effect of hop size on payoff.

relationship is non-linear. Doubling the hop size does not double the payoff. The biggest payoff occurs when we start deeply in the money and have the largest hop size.

This game is similar to an option. An option has an expiry date which is like the number of ticks until the game ends. It has a strike which is the share price at which the option comes into the money, and the size of the steps is like the volatility of a share price. The value of the option increases with maturity and volatility. The strike of a real option is the dollar value of a stock. For example, if the price of Sprocket Corporation today is $100 the strike may be $120. Of course there are also many differences between the game and a real option. If we were to plot the distribution of distances travelled in each game it would be a normal distribution. For share prices the distribution is slightly skewed to favour positive jumps because the price of a share can never be less than zero. Share price movements are more accurately modelled with a log-normal distribution which has such a skewed shape. Another difference is that the game lasted just a few minutes. Because the payoff of a real option occurs months in the future we would have to discount the payoff using the risk-free rate.

This table shows how attributes in the game map onto a real option:

Game		Real Option
Position	→	Stock Price
Size of jump	→	Volatility
Clock	→	Time to expiry

We chose to lay down dollar bills on each square beyond the strike. The amount of money we lay on each square defines the payoff in this particular game. Alternatively we could change the game so that the dollar bills start at the strike and are laid on each square down to square zero. In order to be in the money in this game we would have to move backwards toward zero. In either game the path we take until the clock reaches zero does not matter. The payoff is the same however deeply we move into and out of the money; the square we land on at the end of the game solely determines our payoff. Now we could change the game slightly so that the payoff depends on the path that we take. For example we could be paid according to the value of the highest square that we reach, or some average of the numbers of the squares that we landed on, or some fixed payoff if we reach the strike during the course of the game. All these possibilities have been used as payoffs for real options but they are usually given esoteric names, as we will discover.

10.3 European Call Option

A European call option is an option to buy the underlying at a fixed price, the strike, at some time in the future. To describe a call option we can draw the payoff at expiry. To make the example concrete, we describe a one month 100 call on Sprocket Corporation. By "100 call" we mean that the strike is $100. Today we do not know what price Sprocket Corporation will be trading at in one months time. But we do know, for each possible price of Sprocket stock, the value of our call option. If the price of Sprocket shares in a month's time is less than $100 then our 100 call will be out of the money. We would be insane to exercise the option to buy Sprocket shares for $100 if we could buy them in the market at $80. If the price of Sprocket shares were more than $100 then the option is in the money and it becomes worthwhile to exercise the option. Say the price of Sprocket at expiry was $120, then our call option would give us the right to buy Sprocket shares at a price of just $100 which would be a bargain. The relationship of our 100 call payoff to the underlying share price at expiry is shown in this table and in Figure 10.3, with the strike price shown in bold.

Sprocket Share Price ($)	70	80	90	**100**	110	120	130
100 Call Payoff at Expiry ($)	0	0	0	0	10	20	30

Payoff is different from the profit and loss (P&L) graph at expiry. P&L incorporates the price of the option. So if our Sprocket 100 call cost $10 then the P&L at expiry for each expiry share price would be

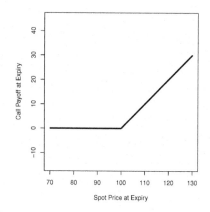 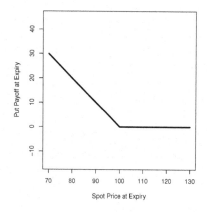

Figure 10.3: Call and put option payoffs at expiry.

Sprocket Share Price ($)	70	80	90	**100**	110	120	130
100 Call P&L at Expiry ($)	-10	-10	-10	-10	0	10	20

Notice that in order to break even the underlying share price has to increase to 110. Above this price we start to make money on the call. The price of the underlying at which we make back the value of the premium is known as the BREAK-EVEN price. For share prices between 100 and 110 we are in the money but still not breaking even because of the cost of the option premium. Both of the tables above assume that we have bought a Sprocket 100 call. Of course someone must have sold us the 100 call, so we are long the 100 call and they are short the 100 call. For someone short the 100 call payoff and P&L will have the opposite sign. Notice that while the person long the call has unlimited potential gains the person short the call has unlimited possible losses, so being short a call can be disastrous if prices move quickly before the position can be closed. A large jump in stock price, known as GAPPING, often happens overnight when trading is impossible so it is safer to also hold the underlying stock rather than write a naked call.

10.4 European Put Option

A call is similar to a forward in that increases of the underlying price increase its value. The difference is that the call has downside insurance. But what if we wanted an option that would actually increase in value if the share price decreased? This is a put option. If we were to buy a Sprocket Corporation 100 put our payoff at expiry would look as follows.

Sprocket Share Price ($)	70	80	90	**100**	110	120	130
100 Put Payoff at Expiry ($)	30	20	10	0	0	0	0

Below the strike the payoff increases. However, unlike a 100 call which has unlimited upside (the share price can increase infinitely in value) the upside of this put is capped because the lowest value of the share price is 0. If Sprocket stock is worthless at expiry the put reaches its maximum value of $100. As with a call the P&L at expiry is lower than the value of the payoff by the premium value. If the premium is $10, as with the call then the P&L is as follows.

Sprocket Share Price ($)	70	80	90	**100**	110	120	130
100 Put P&L at Expiry ($)	20	10	0	-10	-10	-10	-10

10.5 Moneyness

The strike of an option can be compared with the current spot or forward price. For European options it makes sense to compare the strike with the forward price. If a put or call option has a strike that equals the forward price it is AT-THE-MONEY-FORWARD (ATMF). As an example we return to Sprocket Corporation showing the effect of forward price on the moneyness of a 100 call and a 100 put.

Sprocket Forward Price ($)	70	80	90	100	**110**	120	130
100 Call Moneyness	←		OTM	→	ATMF	← ITM	→
100 Put Moneyness	←		ITM	→	ATMF	←OTM	→

The forward price of Sprocket, determined completely by carry cost, is 110. If a call or put option has strike equal to 110 then it is said to be at-the-money-forward. A call option is IN THE MONEY (ITM) if the forward price is greater than the strike price and out of the money if the forward price is less than the strike price. A put option is in the money if the forward price is less than the strike price and OUT OF THE MONEY (OTM) if the forward price is greater than the strike price.

It may be helpful to think of moneyness in the following way. A call option is a right to buy at the strike price. If we have a right to buy at 110 and the stock is trading at 130 then our call is valuable because we can buy stock more cheaply than the market price. If we have a right to buy at 110 and the market price is 90 then our call is no longer valuable, it is out of the money. A put on the other hand is a right to sell at 110. If we can sell at 110 and the market price is 90 then our put is valuable, it is in the money. If we can sell at 110 and the market price is 130 then our put is not valuable, it is out of the money.

10.6 Put Call Parity: Relating Call, Put and Forward

Imagine that we were to buy the 100 call and sell the 100 put for Sprocket Corporation and that both contracts had the same expiry. Our payoffs would add up as follows.

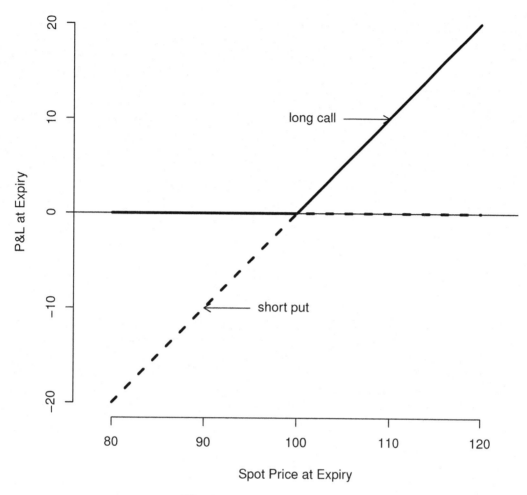

Figure 10.4: Put call parity.

Sprocket Share Price ($)	70	80	90	**100**	110	120	130
100 Long Call P&L at Expiry ($)	-10	-10	-10	-10	0	10	20
100 Short Put P&L at Expiry ($)	-20	-10	0	10	10	10	10
Total P&L at Expiry ($)	-20	-10	-10	0	10	20	30
100 Forward P&L at Expiry ($)	-20	-10	-10	0	10	20	30

In other words by going long the 100 call and short a 100 put we have reproduced the payoff of a 100 forward. The upshot is that if we can price the call and forward the value of a put is the difference between the two. If this were not the case then this would be a situation that would attract the attention of arbitrageurs. The fact that there is equivalence, or parity, between a long-call short-put position and a forward is known as PUT-CALL PARITY and the identity in payoff is illustrated in Figure 10.4.

We can find the numerical relationship between the put, call and forward price for an equity by trading the synthetic forward against stock. We buy a stock which means we are long the underlying. At the same time we create a synthetic short forward position by buying a put and selling a call. In total we have a flat position that should make no money at all because it carries no price risk. The stock purchase will dominate our cash flows and we will have to borrow enough money to buy the stock and the put. Selling the call will generate a small profit. The trades are as follows:

Today		At Expiry T	
Action	**Cash Flow**	**Action**	**Cash Flow**
Buy stock	$-S$	Receive dividend, interest	$+\left(1 + r\left[T - t_D\right]\right) D$
Sell X strike call	$+C$	Settle option	$+X$
Buy X strike put	$-P$		
Borrow/Invest	$S - C + P$	Repay/Receive	$-\left(S - C + P\right)\left(1 + rT\right)$
Total	0	Total	0

Note that when the options are settled at expiry we will receive the strike price whatever the price of the underlying. If the underlying is worth less than X then will exercise our put and sell the underlying for $+X$. If the underlying is worth more than X then the person to whom we have sold the call will exercise their call, we will be assigned on the call and again will sell the underlying for $+X$. If there is no arbitrage opportunity then this trade should make no money. This means that the total cash flows at expiry should add up to zero.

$$
\begin{aligned}
X + \left(-S + C - P\right)\left(1 + rT\right) + \left(1 + r\left[T - t_D\right]\right) D &= 0 \\
X - S\left(1 + rT\right) + \left(1 + r\left[T - t_D\right]\right) D &= \left(P - C\right)\left(1 + rT\right) \\
P - C &= \frac{X - S\left(1 + rT\right) + \left(1 + r\left[T - t_D\right]\right) D}{1 + rT}
\end{aligned}
$$

This can be simplified by noticing that the numerator contains

$$
-S(1 + rT) + \left(1 + r\left[T - t_D\right]\right) D
$$

which is minus the forward price F for a single equity (see Section 9.1.3 on page 333). So the put call parity equation simplifies to

$$
P - C = \frac{X - F}{1 + rT}
$$

In words, the difference between the put and the call price must equal the present value of the difference between the strike and the forward price. The difference $X - F$ is sometimes called PARITY TO FORWARD. So more succinctly the put-call price difference is the present value of parity to the forward. For *any* option market the put and call are related to one another by this arbitrage trade so there are always arbitrageurs scouring the market looking for these opportunities to make risk-free profits. Of course there will always be a little leeway in the put-call price difference due to the cost of putting on the arb trade. When it becomes legally impossible to short the underlying because of a short selling ban, as we saw with financial stocks during and after the Credit Crisis, the put and call can trade out of line.

Another way of doing the arb trade is via the forward rather than buying the underlying. This would look slightly different. Because we are buying forward there is no large cash flow when the trade begins. Instead there is a small cash flow initially due to the difference between the call and put premia. Then the large cash flow $-F$ required to buy the underlying forward moves to expiry time. Recall that F is S plus or minus a typically small carry cost so as S is large relative to the option premium then F will also be large relative to the option premium.

Today		At Expiry T	
Action	**Cash Flow**	**Action**	**Cash Flow**
Buy Forward	0	Pay forward price	$-F$
Sell X strike call	$+C$	Settle option	$+X$
Buy X strike put	$-P$		
Borrow/Invest	$-C+P$	Repay/Receive	$(C-P)(1+rT)$
Total	0	Total	0

Setting the cash flows at expiry to zero gives the same result as before,

$$
\begin{aligned}
X + (C - P)(1 + rT) - F &= 0 \\
(P - C)(1 + rT) &= X - F \\
P - C &= \frac{X - F}{1 + rT}.
\end{aligned}
$$

Again, the difference in value between the put and the call is equal to the present value of parity to the forward. And notice that this relationship depends only on the call and put premia, strike and forward price. Put call parity does not make any assumptions about the behaviour of the underlying. It is completely model-independent. Put call parity exists because of the symmetric shape of the put and call payoff around the strike price.

Another way of understanding put-call parity is in terms of off-market forwards. If we buy a call and sell a put we have created a synthetic forward position. If the strike of the call and put are equal to the forward price then we have an on-market forward. An on-market forward is worth nothing today because this is how forwards are priced (see Section 9.1.3 on page 333). If buying a call and selling a put is worth nothing today then we know the call and put prices must be exactly equal to one another. If you see a table of European call and put prices for different strikes you will notice that the calls and puts have the same price when the strike is equal to the forward price. If the strike is above the forward price then we are agreeing to buy the underlying at maturity at a high price so we would expect to receive a positive cash flow of $X - F$ for this off-market forward at expiry. Discounting back to today the off-market forward is worth $PV(X - F)$ which is positive. This means the put is worth more than the call because it is in the money. If the strike is below the forward price then we get a negative cash flow at expiry and a negative present value. This means the call is worth more than the put because the call is in the money.

Put call parity applies to European options on any underlying. Here we have shown the form of put-call parity for equities but the same applies for bond options, options on commodities, options on interest rates such as caps and floors, or options on foreign exchange. All that varies is the cost of carry that in turn affects the value of the forward.

10.7 Share Price Return Distribution

It is worth giving an example of a share price because some option pricing models assume certain distributions. We have chosen Google as an example, but other stocks show similar characteristics. Figure 10.5 shows just over three years of daily share price data. Over that period of time the price goes up from 100, peaks at 700 then falls back to around 500. For the purpose of investment we are concerned about monetary return so we look at the ratio of the price today over the price yesterday $\frac{p_t}{p_{t-1}}$. Because the distribution is supposedly log normal we take the logarithm of this value $\ln \frac{p_t}{p_{t-1}}$.

The log return series is displayed in the top right graph. The bottom left graph shows a histogram of the return values with a line showing the normal distribution that best fits the data. Notice that there are three large negative outliers that are very unlikely if the log returns are normally distributed. The bottom right graph shows the quantile plot of the return distribution versus the quantiles of a normal distribution. If the returns were normally distributed the points would fall on the straight line. Compared to a normal distribution the tails are larger and the distribution is more "pointy" or leptokurtic in statistical jargon. This manifests itself in the quantile plot as an upper tail that lies above the point expected by the normal distribution and a lower tail that lies below. The tails are shifted away from the mean. Close to the mean the opposite is true, Google's returns are shifted toward the mode making the peak higher than expected for a normal curve. The tails are moved out and the central density is moved in, which increases the kurtosis above that of a normal distribution.

Nassim Taleb has coined the phrase BLACK SWAN to describe very extreme events that fall deeply into the downside tail. The quantile plot shows several of these black swan outliers. In periods of crisis, when volatility is high we tend to see clusters of these outliers which suggests that black swans tend to flock together. Furthermore we also see very high positive returns, or snow-white swans, in periods of high volatility. Unfortunately a gain of $x\%$ followed by a loss of $x\%$ will lose x^2 basis points in value overall. So a gain and loss of 10% will lose 100 bp in value overall.

The log normal assumption is not particularly accurate in this case, nor for many other equities. The fit is good enough to put *some* faith in models that make a log normal assumption. It is not good enough to put one's *entire* faith in such models. Be wary of calculating option prices to many decimal places using a model that makes the log normal assumption, such as Black-Scholes.

Another typical behaviour is clearly apparent in Figure 10.5. As the Credit Crunch hit Google's share price into 2008 and 2009 notice that the volatility of the share price, as seen in the fluctuation of returns in the top right figure, increase markedly. During periods of steady price increases volatility is usually relatively low. Many option pricing models, including the Black-Scholes model, do not take this into account and assume a constant volatility that is independent of price trends.

10.8 Synthetics

It is possible to recreate payoffs using combinations of options and puts and calls. For example we have already seen in Section 10.6 how to replicate a forward by buying a call and selling a put with the same strike and maturity. This was used to derive put-call parity. To recreate the payoff of a put we could sell a forward and buy a call with the required strike. And to recreate a call we could buy a forward and buy a put with the same strike. The value of the synthetic put must equal the value of the real put and similarly for the synthetic call. This is just a way of re-stating put-call parity.

It is possible to recreate almost any payoff at expiry by buying and selling a combination of calls and puts. One can reproduce the payoff of either a call, put or forward by buying and selling a combination of the other two instruments. So the expiry payoff of a forward can be reproduced by buying a call and selling a put. At expiry either the call will be in the money or the put will be in the money. If the call is in the money we will exercise it and buy the underlying at the strike price X. If the put is in the money our counterparty will exercise and we will be assigned on the put and again, we will buy the underlying at the strike price X. Whatever the value of the underlying at expiry we will end up buying the underlying at the strike price and our payoff will be as if we had bought the underlying forward at X. Buying a call and selling a put is like buying a synthetic forward. Similarly one can construct a synthetic call as shown in Table 10.1.

Of course it is also possible to create a synthetic short version of all the synthetics in the table by reversing the trades. Selling a call and buying a put would result in a synthetic short forward, selling forward and selling a put would result in a synthetic short call and buying forward and selling a call would give a synthetic short put.

10.9 Breakevens

If we were to buy a call on some stock believing it would increase in value we would have to pay a premium. The premium is usually a fraction of the price of the stock. In order to make a profit either by closing out the position by selling the call before expiry or exercising the call at expiry the value of the underlying has to increase. If the strike price is 100 and the premium is 5 then the stock price would have to be greater than 105 before we could close out our position at a profit, as shown in Figure 10.6. The value of the underlying at which we just start to make money is known as the BREAKEVEN. For more complex portfolios of options and underlying there may be more than one breakeven value as the payoff weaves above and below zero.

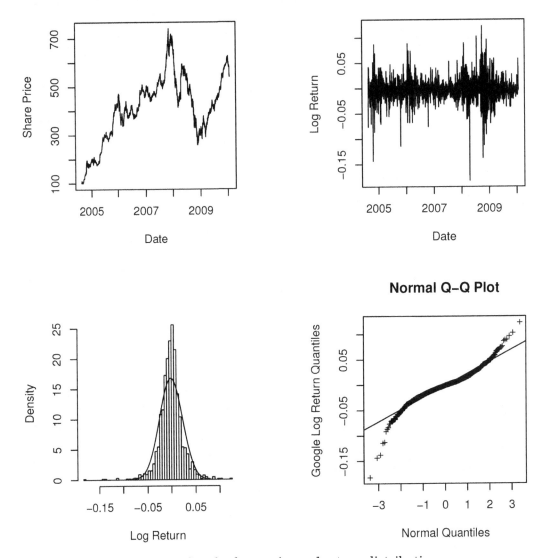

Figure 10.5: Google share price and return distribution.

Synthetic	Replicating Portfolio	Payoff at Expiry
Forward	Buy call, sell put	
Call	Buy forward, buy put	
Put	Sell forward, buy call	

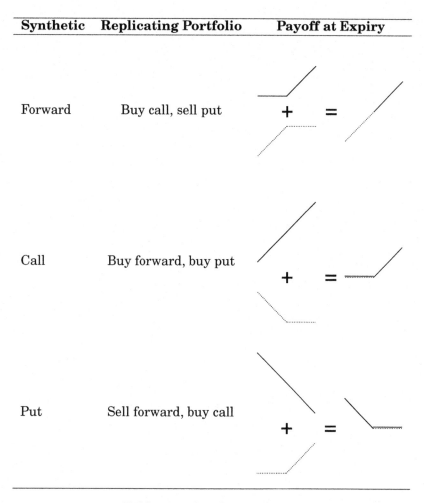

Table 10.1: Synthetic options.

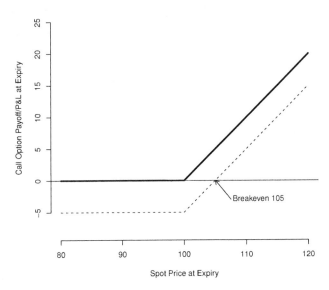

Figure 10.6: Profit and loss diagram for a 100 call, premium $5.

11 Option Pricing & Risk

To price a future we did not need a model. All we needed was to consider the cost of carrying a hedged position into the future. To price an option we need to model the value of the underlying. For European options we are only interested in modelling the value of the underlying at maturity, and here we will look exclusively at European options. The lure of high salaries and a ready army of disaffected mathematicians and physicists have created thousands of option pricing models. Some are analytical, relying on stochastic calculus to model the state of markets and come up with pricing equations, others are more computational. We will restrict our discussion here to pricing vanilla call and put options. The adjective "vanilla" in finance means standard or simple, and its antonym is "exotic". EXOTIC OPTIONS are more difficult to price because their payoff depends on the price path taken by the underlying until maturity. If we were to imagine that our pricing method is a black box then the inputs to the black box would be:

- Spot price of the underlying, the price of the stock today.

- Strike price at which we agree to buy or sell the underlying at expiry.

- Expiry, which is usually less than a year in the future.

- Risk-free interest rate.

- Costs and benefits of owning underlying (funding cost, dividend for equities, storage costs for commodities).

- Volatility of the underlying.

All option pricing models take these inputs in some form and produce a price. Notice that the first five inputs are exactly those required to price a forward. The sixth input, which is the volatility of the underlying, is the extra ingredient required to price the insurance provided by an option. Volatility is a statistical measure of how much a variable changes, on average, over a given period of time (see Section 3.1 on page 97 for a formal definition of volatility).

It is always useful to have a sanity check when pricing. The prices of options are bounded by arbitrage trades. For example, for call options:

- The price of a call option must be greater than the forward basis (forward price minus spot price).

- The price of a call option is less than the forward price.

11.1 Binomial Trees

The future price of the underlying is unknown. Tree-based models simulate the future value of the underlying by discretizing changes in time and price into the form of a branching tree. The option price is calculated by considering all possible future paths through the tree[1]. Say we have a three month 100 call on Sprocket shares struck at the money. The change in price over one day could be either up to 101 or down to 99. In other words there are two paths the share price could take in this model, so this would be a BINOMIAL TREE. If we allowed the share price to stay the same at 100 or go up to 101 or go down to 100 we would have a TRINOMIAL TREE. Notice that we have also broken down time into discrete steps, although in reality share prices can change whenever market makers quote a new price.

For a binomial tree the price in the first time step can move to 99 or 101. In the next time step the price for the up path can again go up to 102 or back down to 100. For the down path the price can go up to 100 or down to 98. Notice that we can follow two paths to 100 in the second time step, the two branches have recombined, so this is a RECOMBINING TREE. After three time steps we have the following tree.

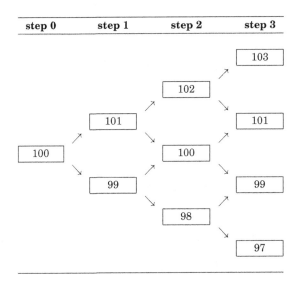

To make the tree more "realistic" we could make it more granular by decreasing both the size of the time step and the size of the steps in the share price. This comes at the price of more computation because it requires simulating more time steps and increasing the depth of the tree. The drawback with tree pricing models is that they are computationally costly, more so for non-recombining trees than recombining trees because they have more nodes. The number of nodes increases rapidly as the depth of the tree increases. In this recombining tree the number of nodes scales as $n(n + 1)/2$ whereas a non-recombining tree scales as $2^{n+1} - 1$. For a depth of 10 the recombining tree has only 55 nodes compared with 2047 nodes for the non-recombining tree.

---

[1]Physicists will see an analogy with the sum over states in quantum mechanics.

Adding just ten levels to a depth of 20 the recombining tree has 210 nodes compared with 2,097,151 for the non-recombining tree.

11.1.1 Building a Replicating Portfolio

Recall that if we can reproduce the payoff of an option then the price of our replicating portfolio must equal the price of the option. This is simply the law of one price. So we can try to replicate the payoff of a call option by buying some of the underlying stock and some zero coupon bonds. If you are not comfortable with bonds just imagine that we have an unlimited investing and lending facility from a bank. We need some investment strategy that will reproduce the option payoff at expiry. We will start with a tree that has just one branch. Our share price starts at 100 and will either go up to 101 with probability p_u or down to 99 with probability $1 - p_u$. We buy s shares and b bonds at time 0 so that at time 1 our portfolio will be worth either

$$101s + be^{rt}$$

with probability p_u or

$$99s + be^{rt}$$

with probability p_d. We also know that the payoff of the portfolio must equal that of a 100 call, so

$$
\begin{aligned}
101s + be^{rt} &= 1 \\
99s + be^{rt} &= 0
\end{aligned}
$$

Subtracting the top equation from the bottom gives $s = \frac{1}{2}$ and substituting this into the second equation gives $b = -\frac{99}{2}e^{-rt}$. If interest rates are 5% then $b = -\frac{99}{2}e^{-\frac{0.05}{4}} = -48.8851$. So to recap, if we were to buy a portfolio with half a share of Sprocket and short about \$49 of zero coupon bonds, then in three months our portfolio will reproduce the payoff of our 100 Sprocket call option.

The price paid to construct the portfolio today must be the price of the option. This price would be

$$100s + b = 100 \times \frac{1}{2} - \frac{99}{2}e^{-\frac{0.05}{4}} = 1.114899.$$

Exercise 55 *Calculate the value of the replicating portfolio if the price of the share goes up to 101, and the price if it goes down to 99. Does it replicate the call option payoff?*

In the limited universe of this model, where the Sprocket share price can only take one of two values in three months time, this is the fair, arbitrage-free price of the 100 Sprocket call. To make the model more realistic we must increase the depth of the tree. If we increase the depth to two time steps by halving the time step size to 1.5 months then the share price can have one of four values: 97, 99, 101 and 103 with payoffs of 0, 0, 1 and 3 respectively. Taking the top right branch first we treat it exactly like the single branch case. Our spot share price is 101 and it can either increase to 102 (payoff 2) or decrease to 100 (payoff 0).

$$102s_1 + b_1 e^{rt} = 2$$
$$100s_1 + b_1 e^{rt} = 0$$

Solving these equations gives $s_1 = 1$ and $b_1 = -100e^{-0.05 \times 0.125} = -99.37695$ and the value of the portfolio at node 1 is $P_1 = s_1 S_1 + bB_1 = 101 - 99.37695$ which is 1.62305. We repeat the exercise for node 2, equating the payoff of each branch with the value of the replicating portfolio for each branch and solving for b_2 and s_2.

$$100s_2 + b_2 e^{rt} = 0$$
$$98s_2 + b_2 e^{rt} = 0$$

Solving gives $s_2 = 0$ and $b_2 = 0$, so a payoff of zero is easy to replicate. Finally we calculate the option price today

$$101s_0 + b_0 e^{rt} = 1.62305$$
$$99s_0 + b_0 e^{rt} = 0$$

Solving gives $s_0 = \frac{1.62305}{101-99} = 0.811525$ and $b_0 = -99 \times 0.811525 \times e^{-0.05 \times 0.125} = -79.84041$. The value of the option $P = s_0 S + b_0 B = 0.811525 \times 100 - 79.84041$. The value of the option today is 1.312090.

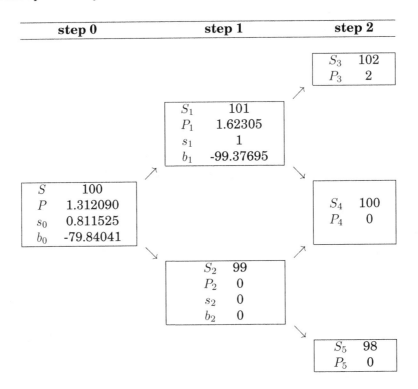

11.1.2 Probability Revisited

Somehow we lost the probability of an up-step and down-step in price, p_d and $p_u = 1 - p_d$. We can resuscitate probability by noting that the expected payoff should be of the form

$$P = e^{-rt}\left[p_u P_u + p_d P_d\right].$$

This is the discounted value of the expected payoff. To get the expected payoff we multiply the payoff for each branch P_u and P_d by the probability of reaching that payoff, p_u and p_d respectively. Rearranging and abbreviating p_d as p

$$
\begin{aligned}
P_u - pP_u + pP_d &= Pe^{rt} \\
p(P_d - P_u) &= Pe^{rt} - P_u \\
p &= \frac{Pe^{rt} - P_u}{P_d - P_u}
\end{aligned}
$$

We know that the value of the option today $P = sS + bB$, that is the number of shares multiplied by the share price plus the number of bonds multiplied by the bond price. Substituting our values for s and b above

$$
\begin{aligned}
p &= \frac{\frac{P_d - P_u}{S_d - S_u} Se^{rt} + P_u - \frac{P_d - P_u}{S_d - S_u} S_u - P_u}{P_d - P_u} \\
p &= \frac{Se^{rt} - S_u}{S_d - S_u}.
\end{aligned}
$$

In other words by using this branch probability the discounted expectation of the payoff is the fair option price. We could use a different definition of probability but this one ensures that the expected value of the payoff is the arbitrage-free price of the option. The precise choice of p is called the probability MEASURE and our entire tree of possible share prices is called a PROCESS. Arbitrage constraints ensure that p lies between 0 and 1. Notice that the measure depends on the size of the up-step and down-step, the risk-free interest rate and the size of the time-step. So our measure (branch probability) is dependent on our process (tree).

Another way to understand this branch probability is in terms of risk. The reason why people risk their capital in stocks is to receive a higher return than risk-free investments such as government bonds. If we take no risk at all then we would expect our investments to increase at the risk-free rate. So the expectation of the stock price S under our risk-neutral probability measure p should be the forward price of the stock F.

$$pS_d + (1 - p)S_d = Se^{rt} = F$$

If the stock pays no dividend then r above is just the risk-free rate. If there is a dividend then r is the carry rate so we would reduce the interest rate by some annualized dividend yield $r_{carry} = r_{risk-free} - r_{dividend}$. But this is actually how the risk-neutral probability is calculated - in terms of the forward price.

Generalized Branch

We can generalize the treatment of a single branch. If the number of shares we buy is s and the number of bonds is b, the share price and bond price now are S and B and the share price for an up-step is S_u and a down step S_d, and the option payoff for an up-step is P_u and P_d for a down-step then

$$
\begin{aligned}
sS_u + bBe^{rt} &= P_u \\
sS_d + bBe^{rt} &= P_d.
\end{aligned}
$$

Solving for s by subtracting the top from the bottom gives

$$
s = \frac{P_d - P_u}{S_d - S_u}.
$$

Solving for b gives

$$
\begin{aligned}
bBe^{rt} &= P_u - sS_u \\
bBe^{rt} &= P_u - \frac{P_d - P_u}{S_d - S_u}S_u \\
b &= \frac{e^{-rt}}{B}\left[P_u - \frac{P_d - P_u}{S_d - S_u}S_u\right].
\end{aligned}
$$

Generalized Tree

It would be nice to have a closed form equation for the price of a call option based on our binomial tree model. The problem with the trees above is that the share price at each branch point increases or decreases by a fixed amount. This means that if we have sufficient tree depth the price will become negative. Of course this is unrealistic. So instead the price will have a multiplicative factor by which it increases or decreases at each branch. If the increase factor is u and the decrease factor is d then the probability of a down branch, for *all* nodes, is according to our definition of a measure for this tree

$$
p = \frac{Se^{r\Delta t} - uS}{dS - uS} = \frac{e^{r\Delta t} - u}{d - u}.
$$

Our tree will look like this:

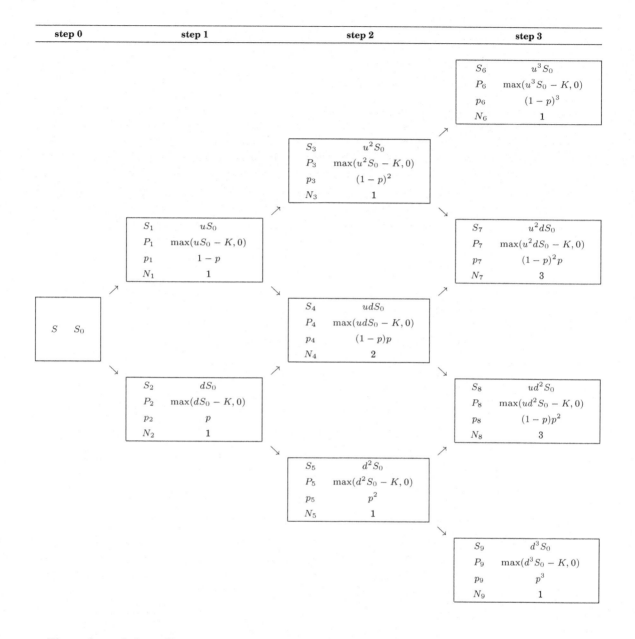

The value of the call option is the discounted expected value of the payoff. The discount factor is simply $e^{-rn\Delta t}$ for a tree of depth n. We have already seen that the probability of a down branch is $\frac{e^{r\Delta t}-u}{d-u}$. There is one other thing to put in the mix, which is the number of possible paths to the leaf nodes. For the top and bottom nodes there is only one path in which the share price rose three times to $u^3 S_0$ or fell three times to $d^3 S_0$. For nodes 7 and 8 however there are three different paths through the tree that lead to the same terminal price. For example node 7 has price $u^2 d S_0$. But this price could be arrived at by the following paths:

- up, up, down

- up, down, up

- down, up, up

As the tree depth increases the number of paths to the central nodes multiply and form a pattern that you may recognize as Pascal's Triangle. For a tree of depth n we are seeking the number of paths to leaf node k. Note that we are re-indexing the leaf nodes, so node $6 \to 0$, $7 \to 1$, $8 \to 2$, and $7 \to 3$. The number of paths N is the binomial coefficient $C(n,k) = \frac{n!}{j!(n-j)!}$ (see Section 3.2.4 on page 107). So for our case $n = 3$ and node 7 has $k = 1$ and $C(3,1) = \frac{3!}{1!2!} = 3$. We have to weight the probability for this leaf node by the number of paths that lead to the node. As everything is being discounted at the leaf nodes which are at time $n\Delta t$ we can set $T = n\Delta T$.

So putting it all together our discounted, expected payoff is

$$C = e^{-rT} \left[N_6 p_6 P_6 + N_7 p_7 P_7 + N_8 p_8 P_8 + N_9 p_9 P_9 \right]$$

Substituting values for the number of paths N, probability of reaching each node p, payoff P and strike X we get

$$
\begin{aligned}
C \;=\; & e^{-rT} \frac{3!}{0!3!}(1-p)^3 \max\left[0, u^3 S_0 - X\right] \\
& +e^{-rT} \frac{3!}{1!2!}p(1-p)^2 \max\left[0, u^2 d S_0 - X\right] \\
& +e^{-rT} \frac{3!}{2!1!}p^2(1-p) \max\left[0, u d^2 S_0 - X\right] \\
& +e^{-rT} \frac{3!}{3!0!}p^3 \max\left[0, d^3 S_0 - K\right]
\end{aligned}
$$

Expressing this more generally as a summation over the leaf nodes

$$c = e^{-rT} \sum_{j=0}^{n} C(n,j)(1-p)^{n-j} p^j \max\left[0, u^j d^{n-j} S_0 - X\right]$$

Finally we can get rid of the $\max[0, S_j - X]$ term by noticing that if any of the terminal nodes have a payoff of zero we can remove them from the summation altogether. If the number of up-steps required to make the payoff non-zero is m then we can now rewrite the summation as follows

$$C = e^{-rT} \sum_{j=m}^{n} C(n,j)(1-p)^{n-j} p^j \left(u^j d^{n-j} S_0 - X\right) \qquad (11.1)$$

If we simplify the expression by defining two variables

$$d_1 \;=\; e^{-rT} \sum_{j=m}^{n} C(n,j)(1-p)^{n-j} p^j u^j d^{n-j}$$

$$d_2 \;=\; \sum_{j=m}^{n} C(n,j)(1-p)^{n-j} p^j$$

Then Equation 11.1 simplifies to

$$C = d_1 S_0 - d_2 X e^{-rT}. \tag{11.2}$$

This may remind you of the present value of a forward $S_0 - Xe^{-rT}$. The first term shows that we can replicate the value of a call option by buying d_1 amount of stock. The second term shows how much cash we need to replicate the payoff of a call option. Equation 11.2 is also very similar to the Black-Scholes equation, as we will see later (Section 11.2 on page 373). This is hardly surprising as Black-Scholes is the limiting case of this binomial tree as the time-steps become very small.

Calibrating the Tree

If equity prices follow an exponential pattern of growth, then we can model the share price as steady, smooth exponential growth $S(t) = S_0 e^{\mu t}$ with some noise that has volatility σ. In a binomial model we simulate volatility as the breadth of the up and down movements of the tree, where greater volatility will result in a larger up and down step in a given time interval.

$$\begin{aligned} u &= e^{+\sigma \sqrt{\Delta t}} \\ d &= e^{-\sigma \sqrt{\Delta t}} \end{aligned}$$

Here we have made the choice that $u = \frac{1}{d}$ with the rather pleasing consequence that if the stock price moves up then down it returns to its starting position. Our measure, which is the probability of a downward move, is

$$p = \frac{e^{r\Delta t} - u}{d - u}$$

Substituting for u and d we find that

$$p = \frac{e^{r\Delta t} - e^{\sigma \sqrt{\Delta t}}}{e^{-\sigma \sqrt{\Delta t}} - e^{\sigma \sqrt{\Delta t}}}.$$

11.1.3 Building the Tree Using Risk-Neutral Probability

We can mechanically price any option without calculating the replicating portfolio. This alternative method for binomial tree pricing is therefore easier and relies on the assumptions that the probability of an up and down jump at each branch is the same throughout the tree. This in turn assumes that volatility and interest rates remain constant throughout the tree. The value of the option for the terminal nodes can be written down easily. Then the value for previous times can be calculated based on the discounted, expected value of the option (see Section 11.1.2).

$$P = (p_d P_d + p_u P_u) e^{-r\Delta t}$$

The tree is built using these steps:

1. Build the share price tree from the value of the stock today, the up-jump factor u and the down-jump factor d.

2. Write down the payoff of our option for all the leaf nodes at the top of the tree.

3. Calculate the payoff for all previous nodes using the terminal payoffs and the probability of down-jumps p and discount at each step by $e^{-r\Delta t}$.

The following example and exercise illustrate how this works in detail. We will price a 100 strike call option on a stock that is currently trading at 100 with 3 months until maturity. The volatility of the stock is 30%, interest rates are a flat 5% (actual continuous). The depth of the tree will be two, so our time step Δt is half of three months $\Delta t = \frac{1}{2}\frac{3}{12} = \frac{1}{8}$, an eighth of a year. First we build our stock process. The factor by which the stock price increases in one time step is $e^{\sigma\sqrt{\Delta t}} = e^{0.3\times\sqrt{\frac{1}{8}}}$ which is 1.111895, and the factor by which the stock price decreases is the reciprocal of the increase factor, 0.8993653. This is all we need to build our stock process:

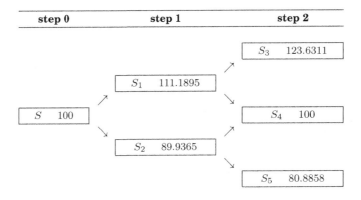

To build the option process we need the probability of a down jump, which is

$$
\begin{aligned}
p &= \frac{e^{r\Delta t} - e^{\sigma\sqrt{\Delta t}}}{e^{-\sigma\sqrt{\Delta t}} - e^{\sigma\sqrt{\Delta t}}} \\
&= \frac{e^{0.05\times\frac{1}{8}} - e^{0.3\times\sqrt{\frac{1}{8}}}}{e^{-0.3\times\sqrt{\frac{1}{8}}} - e^{0.3\times\sqrt{\frac{1}{8}}}} \\
&= 0.496992
\end{aligned}
$$

These are the detailed calculations for the option process:

$$
\begin{aligned}
P_1 &= [pP_4 + (1-p)P_3]\,e^{-r\Delta t} = [0.4970 \times 0 + (1 - 0.4970) \times 23.6311] \times e^{-0.05\times\frac{1}{8}} = 11.8126 \\
P_2 &= [pP_5 + (1-p)P_4]\,e^{-r\Delta t} = [0.4970 \times 0 + (1 - 0.4970) \times 0] \times e^{-0.05\times\frac{1}{8}} = 0 \\
P &= [pP_2 + (1-p)P_1]\,e^{-r\Delta t} = [0.4970 \times 0 + (1 - 0.4970) \times 11.8126] \times e^{-0.05\times\frac{1}{8}} = 5.9048
\end{aligned}
$$

And we can place these into the combined stock and option tree diagram:

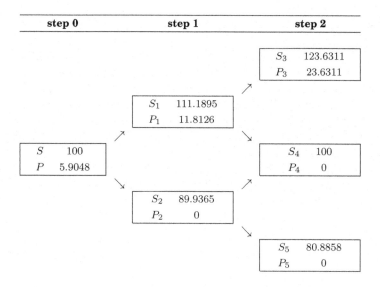

	step 0		step 1		step 2	

The final value for the 100 call is 5.90.

Exercise 56 *Build a binomial tree for pricing a three month 100 strike call stock option with a depth of three, so each time step will be one month with 31 days per month and 365 days per year. Volatility for the underlying stock is 30% and interest rates are a flat 5% (actual continuous). The price of the stock today is 100.*

11.2 Black-Scholes

If we let the time-step drop to an infinitesimally small amount the binomial model converges to the Black-Scholes model (Baxter and Rennie, 1996). The value of a European call option C derived using Black-Scholes is

$$C = SN(d_1)e^{-(r_l - r_c)t} - Xe^{-r_l t}N(d_2), \qquad (11.3)$$

Where $N(.)$ is the cumulative normal distribution function (see Section 3.2.1 on page 104), S is the spot price of the underlying, X is the strike price, r_c is the carry rate, r_l is the cash (long) rate and $N(d_1)$ and $N(d_2)$ measure the moneyness of the option. If an option is deeply in the money $N(d_1)$ and $N(d_2)$ approach 1 and the call value approaches that of an off-market forward with value $e^{-r_l t}(F - X)$. If deeply out of the money both $N(d_1)$ and $N(d_2)$ approach 0, as does the value of the call option.

There are two terms in the call value: an underlying term in S and a cash term in X. We will assume that the underlying is a stock. These two terms tell us how to replicate the payoff of the call. The first term is $SN(d_1)e^{-(r_l-r_c)t}$ which is the underlying share price today S multiplied by the number of shares to buy $N(d_1)e^{-(r_l-r_c)t}$. This tells us how to hedge the call because the $N(d_1)e^{-(r_l-r_c)t}$ "number of shares to buy" term is the sensitivity of the call to changes in the share price. So by selling $N(d_1)e^{-(r_l-r_c)t}$

shares of the underlying we can hedge the call against sensitivity to the underlying, and this term is called delta.

The second term $Xe^{-r_l t}N(d_2)$ is a cash term telling us that if the call is in the money at expiry we will have to buy the underlying at the strike price X. This has a term $e^{-r_l t}$ to discount X from time t to the present at the cash rate r_l, so if we invest this amount today it will return enough at expiry to fund the purchase of a stock. It is multiplied by the probability of the call ending in the money $N(d_2)$ because we need not buy the stock unless the call is in the money. By analogy to the stock delta this term is sometimes called the cash delta.

The value of the call option is reproduced by buying a bit of stock and investing some money. The Black-Scholes equation tells us precisely how much stock to buy and how much money to invest.

$$
\begin{array}{ccccccc}
C & = & S & \times & N(d_1)e^{-(r_l-r_c)t} & - & Xe^{-r_l t} & \times & N(d_2) \\
\text{Call Value} & = & \text{Stock Price} & \times & \text{Stock Delta} & - & \text{PV(Strike)} & \times & p(\text{ITM at Expiry})
\end{array}
$$

There are two rates in the pricing formula. The first is the cash rate, or long rate, r_l and the second is the carry rate r_c. The cash rate is the cost of borrowing money and this is usually taken to be the LIBOR rate but this term is subjective. Your funding rate r_l may be higher than LIBOR with the spread to LIBOR dependent on your credit worthiness. The carry rate r_c is the cost of carrying the spot price into the future. For example for an equity option r_c is the dividend expressed as an annualised rate. For a commodity the carry rate would include storage costs. Again this rate r_c is often subjective because it is your cost to carry a position to expiry. This would incorporate uncertainty through estimating the as yet unknown dividend of a stock. If the carry rate and the cash rate are equal, as they would be for a stock with no dividend, then delta for a call option is equal to $N(d_1)$.

The price of a put option according to the Black-Scholes model is

$$P = -Se^{-(r_l-r_c)t}N(-d_1) + Xe^{-r_l t}N(-d_2). \tag{11.4}$$

The terms are similar to those for a call, but notice the difference in some of the signs. Delta has the opposite sign to a call, as we would expect because the slope of the payoff of a put is negative. If the put expires in the money we would be forced to sell a share which would pay $+X$ at time t and the probability of the put ending in the money is $N(-d_2)$. Note that the distribution function $N(x)$ has the property $N(-x) = 1 - N(x)$ so that the probability of a call being in the money $N(d_2)$ is one minus the probability $N(-d_2)$ of a put being in the money $N(-d_2) = 1 - N(d_2)$. In words the put pricing formula is

$$
\begin{array}{ccccccc}
P & = & S & \times & -N(-d_1)e^{-(r_l-r_c)t} & + & Xe^{-r_l t} & \times & N(-d_2) \\
\text{Put Value} & = & \text{Stock Price} & \times & \text{Stock Delta} & + & \text{PV(Strike)} & \times & p(\text{ITM at Expiry})
\end{array}
$$

Whereas a put option was replicated by buying some stock and borrowing some cash, a put is replicated by selling some stock and lending some cash. Importantly "some" differs for a call and a put because the stock delta and cash delta differ. Call deltas depend on $N(d_1)$ and $N(d_2)$ whereas put deltas depend on $N(-d_1)$ and $N(-d_2)$. The definitions of "moneyness", d_1 and d_2, are

$$d_1 = \frac{\ln \frac{S}{X} + \left(r_c + \frac{\sigma^2}{2}\right) t}{\sigma \sqrt{t}}$$

$$d_2 = \frac{\ln \frac{S}{X} + \left(r_c - \frac{\sigma^2}{2}\right) t}{\sigma \sqrt{t}} = d_1 - \sigma \sqrt{t}.$$

We can make the Black-Scholes value for calls and puts into a much neater form by looking at their value at expiry and using the forward price instead of the spot price. Instead of looking at the value of the call today, C, we look at the future value at expiry $FV(C)$ and instead of using the spot price S we use the forward price $F = Se^{r_c t}$. The values of the call and put at expiry are

$$\begin{array}{ccccccc} FV(C) &=& +F & N(d_1) & - & X & N(d_2) \\ FV(P) &=& -F & N(-d_1) & + & X & N(-d_2) \end{array}.$$

In this new form it is easy to see that Black-Scholes satisfies put-call parity. The difference between the future values of the put and the call at expiry should be parity to the forward, $FV(C - P) = F - X$.

$$FV(C - P) = F[N(d_1) + N(-d_1)] - X[N(d_2) + N(-d_2)]$$

One of the properties of the normal distribution is that it is symmetric about its mean, so that $N(x) = 1 - N(-x)$. This means that the terms in square brackets are equal to one and we have put-call parity.

Exercise 57 *Find the value of a call option on Sprocket Corp. with strike $X = 100$, spot price $S = 95$, carry rate and long rate 5% $r_c = r_l = 0.05$, volatility 30% $\sigma = 0.3$ and three months to maturity $t = 0.25$. Assume Sprocket pays no dividends over the life of the contract.*

Exercise 58 *Find the value of the put option on Sprocket Corp. with the same strike and maturity as the previous example. Do the put and call values obey put-call parity?*

Exercise 59 *Find the three month forward price of Sprocket with a three month continuously compounded interest rate of 5% (A/360) and a spot price of 98.758. Assume that Sprocket Corp. pays no dividends.*

Exercise 60 *Calculate the value of the 100 call on Sprocket corporation given that Sprocket is now trading at $S = 98.75778$. So $X = 100$, $r_l = r_c = 0.05$, volatility is unchanged at 30% $\sigma = 0.3$, maturity is still three months $t = 0.25$. Then calculate the value of the 100 put.*

Exercise 61 *What happens to the value of the call and the put when volatility approaches zero?*

Exercise 62 *What happens to the value of the call and the put when volatility approaches infinity?*

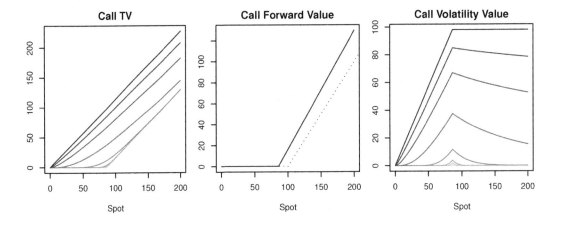

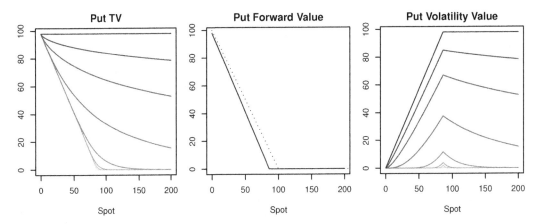

Figure 11.1:
Theoretical value for a call and a put decomposed into forward and volatility value.

11.2.1 A Graphical Description of Call and Put Value

We can decompose the value of European call and put options into two pieces. One is the forward value, the other the volatility value. If we turn down volatility to zero we are left with the forward value which is the value of an option due to its being in the money. This value looks like the hockey-stick payoff at expiry with some modifications due to discounting and carry cost. The payoff of a one year 100 call and put are illustrated in Figure 11.1, along with their zero volatility and volatility value graphs. In this example the long rate is 2% and the carry rate is 15%. Firstly we can see that the spot value at which the theoretical value drops to zero is not 100 even though this is a 100 strike option. This is because the forward value at expiry for a European option is $\max(F - X, 0)$. For an equity the forward price $F = Se^{r_l t} - D$. Here r_l is the long rate charged for funding the stock purchase and D is the dividend. We can roll up the long rate r_l and dividend D into one continuous carry rate r_c so the forward price paid at expiry is $F = Se^{r_c t}$. Today the present value of this payoff, discounted using the long rate r_l, is $\mathrm{PV}(F) = Se^{(r_c - r_l)t}$. We can find the value of spot for which the forward value is zero, which we can call $S_{FV=0}$, by setting $\mathrm{PV}(F - X) = 0$ then

$$
\begin{aligned}
S_{FV=0}e^{(r_c - r_l)t} - Xe^{-r_l t} &= 0 \\
S_{FV=0} &= Xe^{-r_c t}
\end{aligned}
$$

In our example the carry rate is 15%, so $S_{FV=0} = 100e^{-0.15} = 86.07$. The other difference between this payoff and the payoff at expiry is that the gradient in the money is not 1, it is

$$
\begin{aligned}
\frac{\partial}{\partial S}\mathrm{PV}(F - X) &= \frac{\partial}{\partial S}e^{-r_l t}\left[Se^{r_c t} - X\right] \\
&= e^{(r_c - r_l)t}
\end{aligned}
$$

In the special situation where the carry rate is equal to the long rate the gradient is one, but in our example the carry rate is 15% and the long rate is 2% so the gradient is $e^{0.15-0.02} = 1.1388$ which is significantly greater than one. As time passes and time to expiry decreases the intercept moves from $Xe^{-r_c t}$ to X and the gradient for values of spot in the money changes from $e^{(r_c - r_l)t}$ to 1. In our example the intercept increases from 86.07 to 100 and the gradient decreases from 1.1388 to 1. As a consequence the value of a European option can change over time even if the volatility of the underlying is zero. For our example the call loses forward value as it approaches expiry, and loses most forward value for values of spot deepest in the money. The put also loses forward value as it approaches expiry and loses most value for values of spot that are close to $Xe^{-r_c t}$.

If volatility is not zero we have an additional value component that arises purely from volatility. This is greatest at-the-money-forward and decreases for spot values far from the money. The volatility value of a call and a put with the same strike and maturity is exactly equal as shown in Figure 11.1. So decomposing a put and a call with the same strike into forward value and volatility value

$$
\begin{aligned}
C &= V_{vol} + C_{fwd} \\
P &= V_{vol} + P_{fwd}
\end{aligned}
$$

For a particular value of spot either the call will be in the money or the put will be in the money. In the example we have used the one year forward is $F = Se^{r_c t} = 100e^{0.15} = 116.18$ and our call and put option are struck at-the-money-forward. If spot is 100 and the forward is trading at 116.18 and the call strike is 100 then the call is in the money because the forward is greater than the strike. The value of the call is 37.12 broken down into a forward value of 34.29 and a volatility value of 2.83. The value of the put is 2.83, and as the put has no forward value this is pure volatility value. So for a spot value of 100

		volatility value		forward value		
C	$=$	2.83	$+$	34.29	$=$	37.12
P	$=$	2.83	$+$	0	$=$	2.83

This is another way of re-stating put-call parity by noticing that

- The volatility value of a call and put option with the same strike, underlying and maturity is equal

- The difference in value between the same-strike call and put must equal the forward value of the in-the-money option

11.3 Risk Measures: The Greeks

Using the Black-Scholes model it is possible to work out the sensitivity of the option price to each of its variables. Option market makers use these sensitivities to hedge their risk exposure, so although many people assume price is the most important output of a pricing model, sensitivities are just as important. These sensitivities are known as the "Greeks" even though one of them, vega, is a fictional but plausible-sounding member of the Greek alphabet. Vega is in fact the name of a bright star in the constellation Lyra, Alpha Lyrae. Although vega is a fictional greek letter it is easy to remember because the first letter of vega is "v", and vega is sensitivity to "**v**olatility". Vega is denoted in this book by the greek letter nu, ν, but is also denoted by others with the letter kappa, κ. Rho, ρ, describes price sensitivity with respect to change in interest "**r**ate". Theta is sensitivity to "**t**ime" to expiry (even though tau might have been a better choice).

Delta	Δ	Sensitivity to underlying price
Gamma	Γ	Sensitivity of Δ to underlying price
Theta	Θ	Time decay
Vega	ν	Sensitivity to volatility of underlying
Rho	ρ	Interest rate sensitivity

A large investment bank will have thousands of derivatives in its trading book at any time. These will have different underlyings and they will be in many different currencies. The way that the derivatives trading desk at a bank manages their risk is by calculating the total risk exposure of their trading book to each factor, and then buying and selling instruments to reduce their risk. The market maker aggregates their greeks daily and the total value of each greek tells them how much of the underlying they need to reduce their risk close to zero. Delta is the sensitivity of the value of an option to the changes in the price of the underlying. Delta is also known as the HEDGE RATIO because it tells us exactly how much of the underlying has to be bought or sold in order to hedge against price moves in the underlying. Delta is probably the most important greek and the daily process of buying and selling the underlying to reset the overall position delta to zero is DELTA HEDGING. It is possible to derive each of the greeks for the Black Scholes model by differentiating the Black Scholes formula with respect to each of its inputs. These are given as fully worked exercises in the following sections on each of the greeks, but are summarized for reference in Tables 11.311.4 in simplified form when the carry rate r_c is equal to the cash rate r_l, and in slightly more complex form when r_c is not equal to r_l in Tables 11.1 and 11.2.

Δ	$N(d_1)e^{-(r_l-r_c)t}$
Γ	$\frac{1}{S\sigma\sqrt{2\pi t}}e^{-\frac{d_1^2}{2}}e^{-(r_l-r_c)t}$
Θ	$Se^{-(r_l-r_c)}\left[-(r_l-r_c)N(d_1)+\frac{\left(r_c+\frac{\sigma^2}{2}\right)3t+\ln\frac{S}{X}}{2\sigma t^{\frac{3}{2}}}N'(d_1)\right]$
	$+Xe^{-r_lt}\left[r_lN(d_2)-\frac{\left(r_c-\frac{\sigma^2}{2}\right)3t+\ln\frac{S}{X}}{2\sigma t^{\frac{3}{2}}}N'(d_2)\right]$
ν	$\frac{1}{\sqrt{2\pi}}\sqrt{t}Se^{-(r_l-r_c)t}e^{-\frac{d_1^2}{2}}$
ρ	$tXe^{-r_lt}N(d_2)$

Table 11.1: Black-Scholes greeks for a call option.

Δ	$-N(-d_1)e^{-(r_l-r_c)t}$
Γ	$\frac{1}{S\sigma\sqrt{2\pi t}}e^{-\frac{d_1^2}{2}}e^{-(r_l-r_c)t}$
Θ	$Se^{-(r_l-r_c)t}\left[(r_l-r_c)N(-d_1)-\frac{\left(r_c+\frac{\sigma^2}{2}\right)3t+\ln\frac{S}{X}}{2\sigma t^{\frac{3}{2}}}N'(-d_1)\right]$
	$-Xe^{-r_lt}\left[r_lN(-d_2)-\frac{\left(r_c-\frac{\sigma^2}{2}\right)3t+\ln\frac{S}{X}}{2\sigma t^{\frac{3}{2}}}N'(-d_2)\right]$
ν	$\frac{1}{\sqrt{2\pi}}\sqrt{t}Se^{-(r_l-r_c)t}e^{-\frac{d_1^2}{2}}$
ρ	$-tXe^{-r_lt}N(-d_2)$

Table 11.2: Black-Scholes greeks for a put option.

For those who are not comfortable with differentiation we could think of Black-Scholes as a black box taking six inputs and producing one output which is the price of the option. We can "wiggle" each input and see how it affects the price. If we wiggle the spot price, S, and the mathematical notation for the S wiggle is $\frac{\partial}{\partial S}$, then the size of the price wiggle $\frac{\partial}{\partial S}$PV is delta. Gamma is the wiggle of the spot price wiggle $\frac{\partial}{\partial S}\frac{\partial}{\partial S}$PV (a wiggle of a wiggle is called a SECOND ORDER derivative), theta is the time-to-expiry-wiggle $\frac{\partial}{\partial t}$PV, vega is the volatility wiggle $\frac{\partial}{\partial \nu}$PV and rho is the interest rate wiggle $\frac{\partial}{\partial \rho}$PV. More esoteric measures of sensitivity are used sometimes, particularly for FX derivatives, such as VANNA, which is the sensitivity of delta to volatility $\frac{\partial}{\partial \sigma}\frac{\partial}{\partial S}$PV, and VOMMA which is $\frac{\partial}{\partial \sigma}\frac{\partial}{\partial \sigma}$PV or the second order sensitivity of the option price with respect to volatility.

Δ	$N(d_1)$
Γ	$\dfrac{1}{S\sigma\sqrt{2\pi t}}e^{-\frac{d_1^2}{2}}$
Θ	$S\dfrac{\left(r+\frac{\sigma^2}{2}\right)3t+\ln\frac{S}{X}}{2\sigma t^{\frac{3}{2}}}N'(d_1)$
	$+Xe^{-rt}\left[rN(d_2)-\dfrac{\left(r-\frac{\sigma^2}{2}\right)3t+\ln\frac{S}{X}}{2\sigma t^{\frac{3}{2}}}N'(d_2)\right]$
ν	$\dfrac{1}{\sqrt{2\pi}}\sqrt{t}Se^{-\frac{d_1^2}{2}}$
ρ	$tXe^{-rt}N(d_2)$

Table 11.3: Simplified Black-Scholes greeks for a call option.

Δ	$-N(-d_1)$
Γ	$\dfrac{1}{S\sigma\sqrt{2\pi t}}e^{-\frac{d_1^2}{2}}$
Θ	$-S\dfrac{\left(r+\frac{\sigma^2}{2}\right)3t+\ln\frac{S}{X}}{2\sigma t^{\frac{3}{2}}}N'(-d_1)$
	$-Xe^{-rt}\left[rN(-d_2)-\dfrac{\left(r-\frac{\sigma^2}{2}\right)3t+\ln\frac{S}{X}}{2\sigma t^{\frac{3}{2}}}N'(-d_2)\right]$
ν	$\dfrac{1}{\sqrt{2\pi}}\sqrt{t}Se^{-\frac{d_1^2}{2}}$
ρ	$-tXe^{-rt}N(-d_2)$

Table 11.4: Simplified Black-Scholes greeks for a put option.

11.3.1 Delta Δ

Delta is the sensitivity of the option value to changes in the price of the underlying. It is critical to know delta for an option because this allows traders and investors to hedge their option position. If a call option has a delta of 20% then we know that we have to sell one fifth of a stock to be hedged against movement in the price of the underlying. The Black-Scholes formula tells us that the value of a call option is replicated by buying delta of the underlying and borrowing some cash. As a call option is long the underlying, which means that it makes money as the underlying increases in value, we can hedge by going short the underlying, more precisely by selling delta amount of underlying. Similarly, if a put option has a delta of 40% then we have to buy 0.4 of the underlying to hedge our position. Delta for a call is always positive and delta for a put is always negative because a call is like being long the underlying and a put is like being short the underlying. In other words increasing the price of the underlying always increases the value of a call and decreases the value of a put as shown in Figure 11.1.

It is informative to think of extreme cases. A deeply out of the money option becomes insensitive to the underlying so delta approaches zero. An at-the-money option has a delta of about 50%. A deeply in the money call behaves just like the forward so delta approaches that of the forward. Delta for the forward is $e^{-(r_l-r_c)t}$ which in our example, where long rate is 2% and carry rate is 15%, is $e^{-(0.02-0.15)}=1.1388$. When this call is deeply in the money delta approaches 114%, not 100%. The top-left graph in Figure 11.4 shows the value of delta vs. spot price of the underlying. Different volatilities are shown in shades of grey ranging from low volatility in light grey to high volatility in black. When volatility is zero delta is either zero or 1.1388. The spot value where the value of delta abruptly changes is the strike price discounted at the carry rate $Xe^{-r_c t}$ which is $100e^{-0.15} = 86.07$. Delta is zero for spot values below 86.07 and 1.1388 for spot values above 86.07. As volatility increases delta starts to become a smoother, S-shaped curve. This means that as we increase volatility, values of delta increase for spot values less than $Xe^{-r_c t}$ and decrease for spot values greater than $Xe^{-r_c t}$.

For very large volatility values we know that the value of a call option approaches that of the forward. So for very large volatilities delta becomes that of the forward for all values of spot. This means that delta behaves differently for spot values above and below $Xe^{-r_c t}$. For values of spot below $Xe^{-r_c t}$ delta always increases as volatility increases up to a limit of $e^{-(r_l-r_c)t}$ for infinite volatility. For values of spot above $Xe^{-r_c t}$ delta initially decreases away from the limit $e^{-(r_l-r_c)t}$ but as volatility increases it starts increasing again until for infinite volatility delta converges to $e^{-(r_l-r_c)t}$.

Exercise 63 *Derive the value of delta for a call option by differentiating the expression for the value of a call (Equation 11.3) with respect to S using the Black-Scholes model.*

11.3.2 Gamma Γ

Gamma is the sensitivity of delta to changes in the price of the underlying. When an option is delta-hedged it is only hedged against small moves in the underlying. If the underlying moves then the delta of the delta-hedged position is no longer zero because delta is itself sensitive to the value of the underlying. This is why market makers must re-hedge their positions on a daily basis. If they do not re-hedge daily their positions will not be delta-hedged and they will be taking on directional risk. Gamma to mathematicians is the curvature of the theoretical value of an option with respect to the underlying price. Gamma is exactly the same for a call and a put with the same strike, expiry and underlying. If we are long an option, be it a call or a put, then gamma is always positive. If we are short a call or a put then gamma is negative. A simple way to read the sign of gamma from a plot of option value against the underlying price, is to compare the shape of the line with a smile. If the line is curved upward in a smile then gamma is positive. If the line is curved downwards then gamma is negative.

When volatility is very small gamma is zero for almost all values of spot and spikes around a spot value of $Xe^{-r_c t}$. This is because for small volatilities the value of delta abruptly jumps from zero to $e^{-(r_c-r_l)t}$ at this point so the gradient of delta against spot price is almost infinite. Increasing volatility spreads out the value of gamma. The spot value with maximum gamma decreases as volatility increases until for infinite volatility gamma is all concentrated at a spot value of zero.

Exercise 64 *Derive the value of gamma for a call option by differentiating delta with respect to S again.*

Exercise 65 *Now show that Γ for the call and put option are equal.*

11.3.3 Theta ⊖

Theta is the rate at which an option loses value as time to expiry decreases. By market convention theta is positive if an option position loses value over time, it is a value decay rate. If we are long a call or a put then our option will lose value as we approach expiry so theta is almost always positive. And if we are short a call or put then theta is almost always negative. If cost of carry is strongly negative and volatility is low, as sometimes happens with FX options, then it is possible for the sign of theta to be reversed i.e. theta can be negative if we are long a call or put. Generally theta is greatest as we approach expiry because volatility value drops more quickly just before expiry.

Starting with the case where volatility is very low then our option value is composed almost completely of forward value, as the volatility value is almost zero. Consequently our option value changes in exactly the same way as the forward. Because the forward has no value below the spot value $Xe^{-r_c t}$, theta is zero for these spot values. For spot values above $Xe^{-r_c t}$ theta jumps abruptly to $r_c Xe^{-r_l t}$ (see exercise below) then increases with a gradient of $e^{-(r_l - r_c)t}$. If carry rate is 15%, long rate is 2%, strike is 100 and we have one year to maturity in the case where volatility is zero theta is zero below $100e^{-0.15} = 86.07$. For a spot value exactly equal to 86.07 theta jumps up to $0.15 \times 100e^{-0.025} = 14.70$.

Exercise 66 *Derive the value of theta for a call option by differentiating the expression for the value of a call (Equation 11.3) with respect to t using the Black-Scholes model.*

Exercise 67 *What happens to the value of theta for a call and a put when volatility approaches zero?*

11.3.4 Vega ν

Vega is the sensitivity of option value to change in volatility. Just like gamma, vega is the same for a call and a put. As we have seen in Section 11.2.1 on page 376, option value can be decomposed into forward value and volatility value. Only volatility value is affected by volatility and volatility value is the same for a call and put, so we would expect that vega is identical for a call and a put. From Figure 11.4 it seems that vega is rather similar to gamma. For low volatility vega is greatest around the strike X, or more accurately around the strike discounted at the carry rate $Xe^{-r_c t}$. For deeply in the money options volatility is unimportant as the option value is dominated completely by forward value. Consequently deeply in the money options have small vega. Similarly, deeply out of the money options have small vega because the underlying is unlikely to move above strike before expiry. As volatility increases the value of vega flattens out into a bell-shaped curve, just like gamma. However as volatility increases further vega and gamma behave quite differently. For extremely high volatilities around 100%, which seldom occur, vega is largest for large spot values whereas gamma is greatest for small spot values.

Exercise 68 *Derive the value of volatility sensitivity, vega, for a call option by differentiating the expression for the value of a call (Equation 11.3) with respect to σ using the Black-Scholes model.*

Exercise 69 *Show that the volatility sensitivity, vega, for a put option is the same as that of a call option by differentiating the expression for the value of a put (Equation 11.4) with respect to σ.*

Exercise 70 *Express vega in terms of gamma.*

11.3.5 Rho ρ

Rho is the sensitivity of option price with respect to changes in interest rate. Options can have considerable interest rate sensitivity because they can lead to a large cash flow $\pm X$ at maturity if a stock is bought or sold at the strike price, but this payment only occurs if the option is exercised. If we were certain that exercise was going to take place then the cash flow for the option is just a zero coupon bond with face value X and duration equal to the expiry time t. Consequently rho should increase in a linear fashion with expiry time t. Of course exercise may not occur, and we know that the risk-neutral probability of exercise is $N(d_2)$. So we would expect that the greater the probability of exercise the greater the value of rho.

For a call option rho is $tXe^{-r_l t}N(d_2)$, which is the interest rate sensitivity of the strike X which might be paid to buy the underlying at time t with probability $N(d_2)$. As the strike paid at expiry is an outward payment, $-X$, increasing interest rates decreases its negative value and this is a benefit today, so rho is positive. Rho for a put is similar except that it is opposite in sign, $-tXe^{-r_l t}N(-d_2)$, and the probability term is $N(-d_2)$. As we receive a payment of $+X$ for selling the underlying if we exercise the put at expiry increasing interest rates decreases the present value of this payment, hence rho for a put is negative. The "duration" of a call option is $tN(d_2)$ which increases in a linear fashion with expiry time t and probability of exercise $N(d_2)$.

Exercise 71 *Derive the value of rho for a call option by differentiating the expression for the value of a call (Equation 11.3) with respect to the long rate r_l using the Black-Scholes model.*

11.4 Approximate Value of ATMF Options

It is useful to have an idea of the rough value of an option without using the full Black-Scholes formula. The at-the-money-forward call (or put) value ignoring discounting is roughly

$$C_{ATMF} = P_{ATMF} \approx \frac{2}{5}X\sigma\sqrt{t}.$$

All we need to calculate the approximate value of a call or put at-the-money-forward is the strike, the volatility of the underlying and the time to expiry. This approximation is a succinct summary of option value. The approximate value of ATMF call and put options is proportional to volatility so doubling volatility doubles the value of ATMF call and put options. Time appears with a square root, which means that in order to double the value of the option we would have to quadruple time to expiry. The value of the option scales up or down in direct proportion with the strike.

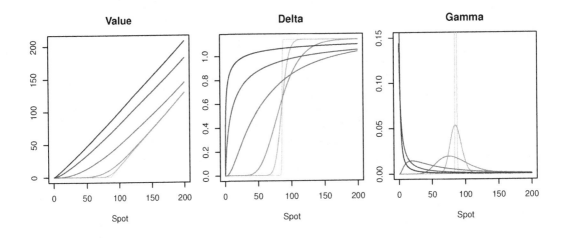

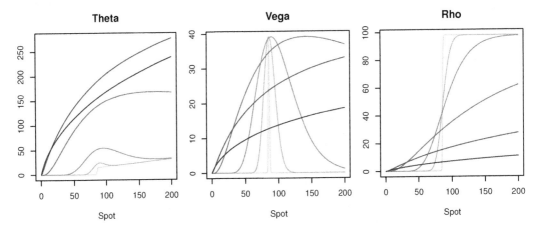

Figure 11.2:
    Value, delta, gamma, theta, vega and rho vs. spot for a 100 call option, volatility 1% (light grey), then darker shades of grey for volatility 10%, 30%, 100%, 200%, and 300% (black). Carry rate is 15%, long rate is 2%.

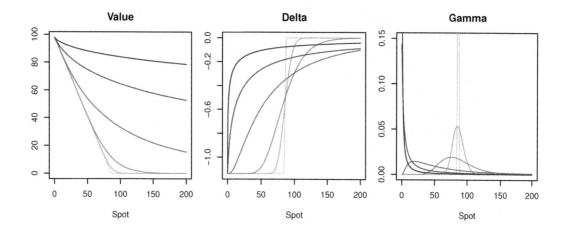

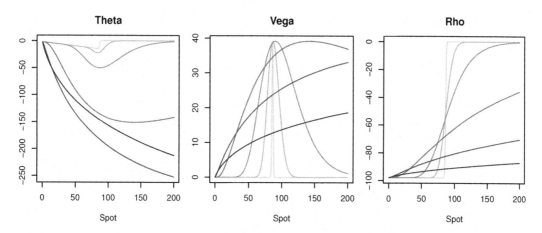

Figure 11.3:
Value, delta, gamma, theta, vega and rho vs. spot for a 100 put option, volatility 1% (light grey), then darker shades of grey for volatility 10%, 30%, 100%, 200%, and 300% (black). Carry rate is 15%, long rate is 2%.

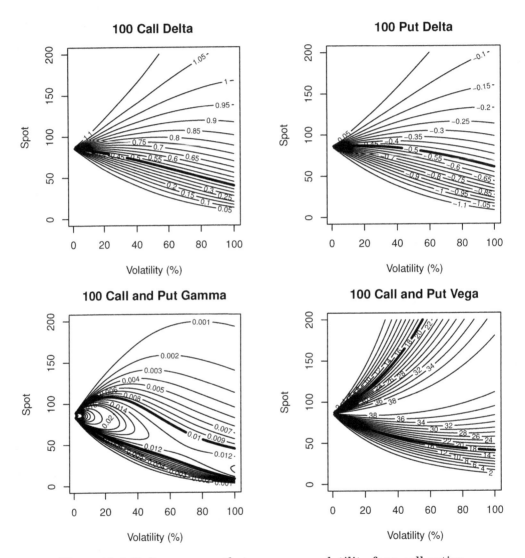

Figure 11.4: Delta, gamma, theta, vega vs. volatility for a call option.

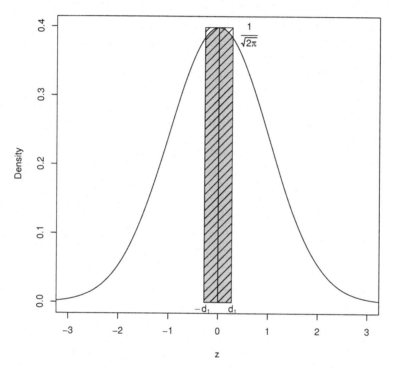

Figure 11.5: At-the-money-forward option price approximation.

We can also use this approximation to calculate the value of delta for ATMF calls and puts. The value of delta for a call at-the-money-forward is

$$\Delta_{\text{ATMF}}^{\text{call}} \approx 0.5 + \frac{\sigma\sqrt{t}}{5},$$

and for the ATMF put delta is roughly

$$\Delta_{\text{ATMF}}^{\text{put}} \approx 0.5 - \frac{\sigma\sqrt{t}}{5}.$$

It is therefore not the case that ATMF calls and puts have delta equal to 50%. Delta for a call is a little higher than a half and for the put a little lower than a half. If volatility is very high or the option has a long time to expiry the delta of the at-the-money call and put differ significantly from 0.5.

As we have such a simple expression which is linear in volatility we can see that for the at-the-money call and put the value of the option is proportional to volatility. If we double volatility we double option value. So the sensitivity of the option price to volatility, vega, does not itself depend on volatility.

$$\frac{\partial C_{\text{ATMF}}}{\partial \sigma} = \frac{\partial P_{\text{ATMF}}}{\partial \sigma} = \frac{2}{5} X \sqrt{t}.$$

Finally we can use our approximation to think about theta, which is time decay, or the rate at which our option loses money as time passes. This is

$$\Theta_{\text{ATMF}} \simeq \frac{2}{5} \frac{X \sigma}{\sqrt{t}}$$

This shows that the longer the time to expiry the slower the decay of option value. Just before expiry decay of value due to the passage of time is fastest.

Exercise 72 *For at-the-money-forward calls and puts where $X = F$ find the value of d_1 and d_2 in the Black-Scholes option pricing formula on page 373.*

Exercise 73 *Given your values for d_1 and d_2 find an expression for the value of the ATMF call and put.*

Exercise 74 *Draw a normal density curve and mark the values of d_1 and d_2. Shade in the areas $N(d_1)$ and $N(d_2)$. What area corresponds to the value of the ATMF call and put options? Can you approximate this area?*

Exercise 75 *Delta for a call option is $N(d_1)$. Sketch this area on your normal density graph. Can you approximate this area?*

Exercise 76 *Can you find an approximation of delta for the ATMF put option?*

11.5 Volatility Smile

Black-Scholes makes many unrealistic assumptions. One of the assumptions is that there can only be one volatility for a given underlying. If we think of historic volatility then obviously there can only be one volatility for a given underlying because historic volatility is the annualized standard deviation of returns over some period of time. IMPLIED VOLATILITY has to be backed out of option prices using a pricing model and there are option prices for each strike and maturity. According to Black-Scholes all call and put options with the same underlying and maturity should have the same implied volatility. If we plot the implied volatility of options against strike it turns out that it is not constant at all. At-the-money options are usually cheaper than out-of-the-money options, as measured by Black-Scholes implied volatility. The shape of the curve is U-shaped, and this is called the VOLATILITY SMILE. If one side is steeper than the other people talk about a VOLATILITY SMIRK. The smile or smirk is usually more pronounced for shorter-dated options.

If most people are long the underlying then they are concerned about downside risk. In order to protect themselves these investors will buy out-of-the-money puts as a hedge. A protective put is like an insurance policy that will limit their loss if the underlying drops in value. Similarly if investors believe a stock will increase in value they can increase their profit if they are correct by buying an out-of-the-money call because the cheap option will give them leverage. These two groups of investors will bid up the price of out-of-the-money puts and calls leaving the at-the-money options behind. Higher option prices for out-of-the-money options relative to at-the-money options must mean higher implied volatility if all other inputs to Black Scholes are constant, so this results in a U-shaped smile. Furthermore when a crisis occurs people will be more likely to buy puts than calls so this will shift up the left hand side of the smile into a smirk where puts trade over calls. If on the other hand people are bullish this will push up the value of calls over puts and raise the right hand side of the smile into a smirk.

There are two dimensions that are commonly used to characterize the shape of the volatility smile. If the shape of the smile is an asymmetric smirk, then equally out of the money calls and puts, where moneyness would be compared using option delta, would have different implied volatilities. For example 25 delta calls might be more valuable than 25 delta puts, so this market would be described as CALLS OVER PUTS. If the smirk is reversed this is called PUTS OVER CALLS. Buying the 25 delta call and selling the 25 delta put is an option strategy called a RISK REVERSAL (see Section 12.1.7 on page 434). Another way of characterizing the volatility smile is to compare the implied volatility of out-of-the-money calls and puts compared to at-the-money calls and puts. If there is no smile at all then two at-the-money options will have the same implied vol as a 25 delta call and a 75 delta call. Buying two at-the-money call options and selling the 25 delta and 75 delta calls is called a BUTTERFLY because the payoff vaguely resembles the insect (see Section 12.1.8 on page 12.1.8). If the smile is steeply curved then the wings of the butterfly will be much more expensive than the head. FX option smiles are often described in terms of combinations of riskies (risk reversals) and flies (butterflies).

An interesting application of the volatility smile is that it can be used to infer the risk-neutral probability density of the underlying at expiry. Breeden and Litzenberger showed (1978) that if the value of a call option is the discounted expected payoff with a risk-neutral distribution $f(S_T)$ of the underlying stock price at expiry,

$$C = e^{-rT}\mathbf{E}\left[\max\left(S_T - X, 0\right)\right] = e^{-rT} \int_0^\infty \max\left(S_T - X, 0\right) f(S_T) dS_T$$

then if we differentiate the value of the call option twice with respect to strike we get an expression that is the discounted risk-neutral probability density

$$\frac{\partial^2 C}{\partial X^2} = e^{-rT} f(S_T).$$

In other words the curvature of the volatility smile is a direct way of measuring the risk-neutral probability density of the underlying at expiry $f(S_T)$. In practice a reasonable density can only be obtained for underlyings with a liquid options market otherwise the density reflects lumpy liquidity rather than market expectations. This includes stock index options and options on interest rate futures. The distribution is shown for three month S&P 500 call options in Figure 11.6. The distribution is skewed toward the upside with almost no probability density below 1080 or above 1400. This should not be interpreted as a real probability density because risk-neutral density is subjective, depending on things such as funding costs and dividend expectations. But this is a useful way of roughly visualizing the strikes where the "action" is in the options market.

A common confusion arises about the sign of skew. When an equity market trades puts over calls traders call this positive skew. However if you were to back out the risk-neutral density it would show a distribution with a long tail on the downside. Referring to Figure 3.1 on page 99 we can see that statisticians would call this negative skew. The best way to avoid confusion is to use the language of puts over calls or calls over puts because this is unambiguous.

11.6 Volatility Term Structure

In fixed income the term structure of interest rates shows the relative cost of borrowing or lending money for different periods of time. A plot of the interest rate against the term of the loan is called a yield curve, and as lenders expect a greater rate of interest if they lend money for a greater period of time the yield curve is usually upward sloping. All the rates on the yield curve are annualized so the three month rate is actually an annualized three month rate. Options are usually quoted in terms of Black-Scholes implied volatility, and if we plot the implied volatility for a fixed strike against the option expiry we have the VOLATILITY TERM STRUCTURE. In Figure 11.7 we plot the implied volatility of at-the-money options on the S&P 500 index against expiry. Each implied volatility is annualized, just as all rates on interest rate yield curves are annualized. The two term structure curves shown are for January 24th 2007, which had a low level of volatility, and November 20th 2008 which was just after the collapse of Lehman Brothers when volatility across the entire term structure

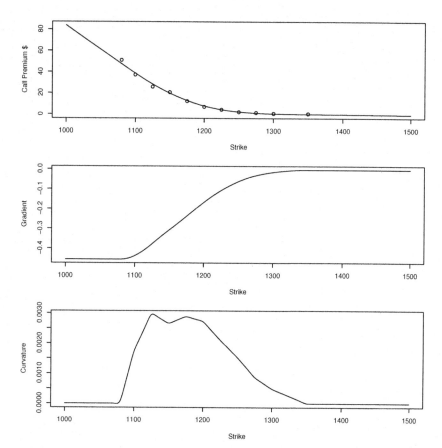

Figure 11.6:
Premia for September 2010 call options on the S&P 500 index with three months until expiry (top), gradient of price vs. strike and curvature of price vs. strike.

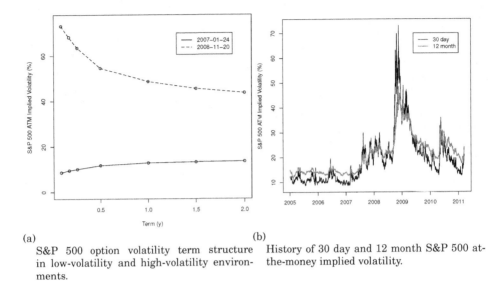

(a)

(b)

S&P 500 option volatility term structure in low-volatility and high-volatility environments.

History of 30 day and 12 month S&P 500 at-the-money implied volatility.

Figure 11.7:
At-the-money volatility term structure for the S&P 500. Source: Bloomberg.

was very high. Options on the S&P and other equity indices are usually slightly upward sloping at-the-money, as shown for 2007. During crises volatility increases for all expiries and the term structure inverts as attention focuses on short-term protection. Shorter term implied volatility tends to fluctuate more rapidly than longer term implied volatility.

If we plot the implied volatility against both term and strike price we would have a VOLATILITY SURFACE, although these contain a great deal of information and are difficult to read. Generally what the volatility surface shows is a skew for short maturities that fades for longer maturities. For single-equity or equity index volatility surfaces the shorter maturities usually exhibit a put-over-call skew that fades as we move to longer dated expiries. For FX volatility surfaces the skew is also usually more pronounced for shorter maturities, but the sign of the skew depends on the currency pair and macroeconomic conditions. The reason why the term structure matters is that it tells the investor at which term volatility is cheap or expensive. As with any investment buyers of vol (buyers of call or put options) will prefer to buy vol when it is cheap and sellers of vol (seller of call or put options) will prefer to sell vol when it is expensive. By exploiting the term structure investors can increase the profitability of any derivative strategy.

11.7 Option Market Making

Individuals who delve into the world of options are expressing their beliefs about the future behaviour of the underlying. These retail investors are hoping that their beliefs will be correct and that they will make a profit if the market agrees with them. Such beliefs are often directional. For example you may believe that a particular company will perform well and want to profit from future increase in its stock price, so you may buy a call option. Or if you believe the share price will decrease you could buy a put option. These are directional plays because they are designed to profit from an increase or decrease in the value of the underlying.

Institutions that make a market in options do not make their money from taking directional plays. The market maker's job is to provide liquidity to the market, so that if an investor wants to buy or sell options on a company they are always able to do so. The market maker earns profit from their EDGE. Edge is the bid-offer spread. If you were to buy an option and sell it immediately you would lose money because you buy high at the offer price and sell low at the bid price. The offer price is always higher than the bid price and the difference between the two is the bid-offer spread. A small bid-offer spread is the sign of a highly liquid market where many deals are done each day, and a wide bid-offer spread is a sign of illiquidity.

A market maker has to hedge their position at all times by buying and selling the underlying. A newcomer to an options trading desk is often surprised to find that the traders are buying and selling forwards and underlying stocks all day as they continually hedge and re-hedge their positions. A hedge can be either a static hedge or a dynamic hedge. If there is a lot of volume in a market then inventory will not sit on the trader's book for long so a dynamic hedging approach is better in this situation. For less liquid markets, inventory may sit on the books for a while so it may not be cost-effective to re-hedge frequently so this situation is better suited to a static hedge.

11.7.1 Static Hedging

Imagine you are a market maker and you are told to make a market on three month 100 strike call options for company XYZ. You have to set a bid price and an offer price. How do you decide on the bid-offer spread? The market in the underlying stock is 99 | 101 and the 100 strike put is 4.7 | 4.8 and interest rates are a flat 10%. You do not want to take any directional risk at all, so you must hedge your position. So you take a guess and set your market at 5.5 | 6.5. This means that people can sell XYZ call options to you at 5.5 and buy XYZ call options from you at 6.5.

Immediately someone sells you a call option at your bid price. You have been "hit" on your bid. So you pay 5.5 and are left with an XYZ call option. By holding the option you now have a directional position on XYZ which you do not want. To start you can sell one underlying share of XYZ. As you do not make a market in the underlying stock you are a market taker for the share and have to pay the bid price to sell your stock, so you sell at 99. Above your strike price your position is now flat, but you are left with a short position below your strike. To flatten your position completely you have to sell a 100 strike put, and again you are a market taker so you sell for 4.7. Finally you are no longer exposed to any changes in the XYZ share price, and if you have put on the right trades you can wait until expiry to reap your profit.

Cash flows today

Hit on bid, buy 100 call	-5.5
Sell 100 put	$+4.7$
Sell XYZ share	$+99$
Invest	$+5.5 - 4.7 - 99 = -98.2$

Cash flows at expiry

Settle options	-100
Receive	$98.2(1 + 0.1 \times 0.25) = 100.66$

At expiry in 3 months time we receive \$100.66 and have to pay \$100 to settle our options so we make \$0.66. Our market was a guess that worked out. What if we were to set the trade up so that our edge is zero? If we turn our trade into symbols we can come up with a general expression for our bid price.

Cash flows today

Hit on bid, buy 100 call	$-C_{\text{bid}}$
Sell 100 put	$+p_{\text{bid}}$
Sell XYZ share	$+s_{\text{bid}}$
Borrow	$-s_{\text{bid}} + C_{\text{bid}} - p_{\text{bid}}$

Cash flows at expiry

Settle options	$-X$
Receive	$(s_{\text{bid}} - C_{\text{bid}} + p_{\text{bid}})(1 + rt)$

Note that our own market is in capitals to make it clear that this is ours and that we are a market taker in all other markets. In order to just break even the amount we invested to buy the call and hedge our position on the day we were hit on our bid must equal the strike price

$$(s_{\text{bid}} - C_{\text{bid}} + p_{\text{bid}})(1 + rt) = X.$$

Re-arranging

$$C_{\text{bid}} = s_{\text{bid}} + p_{\text{bid}} - \frac{X}{1 + rt}.$$

So our zero-edge price for the bid is $99 + 4.7 - \frac{100}{1+0.1\times0.25}$ or \$6.14. Just to check we can calculate the future value of $s_{\text{bid}} - C_{\text{bid}} + p_{\text{bid}}$ and this is $(99 - 6.14 + 4.7) \times 1.025$ which is \$100. We can follow through the same logic to come up with the offer price for our call. We are lifted on our offer which means we are forced to sell a call option. We immediately hedge by buying one stock and buying a put option.

Cash flows today

Lifted on offer, sell 100 call	$+C_{\text{offer}}$
Buy 100 put	$-p_{\text{offer}}$
Buy XYZ share	$-s_{\text{offer}}$
Borrow	$s_{\text{offer}} - C_{\text{offer}} + p_{\text{offer}}$

Cash flows at expiry

Settle options	$+X$
Repay	$(-s_{\text{offer}} + C_{\text{offer}} - p_{\text{offer}})(1 + rt)$

The offer price for the call is

$$C_{\text{offer}} = s_{\text{offer}} + p_{\text{offer}} - \frac{X}{1 + rt}$$

This is $101 + 4.8 - \frac{100}{1+0.1\times0.25}$ or $8.24. So our market for the call option assuming we are perfectly hedged and have no edge whatsoever is 6.14 | 8.24. If we were to make a market for put options the argument is largely the same but the hedging procedure is different. If we are hit on our bid for a put option we would have to buy a 100 put from our customer at p_{bid}. Then we would buy the stock at the offer price flattening our position below the strike price. To flatten the position above the strike price we would sell a call option at the bid price.

Cash flows today

Hit on bid, buy 100 put	$-P_{\text{bid}}$
Sell 100 call	$+c_{\text{bid}}$
Buy XYZ share	$-s_{\text{offer}}$
Borrow	$s_{\text{offer}} - c_{\text{bid}} + P_{\text{bid}}$

Cash flows at expiry

Settle options	$+X$
Repay	$(-s_{\text{offer}} + c_{\text{bid}} - P_{\text{bid}})(1 + rt)$

Which gives

$$s_{\text{offer}} - c_{\text{bid}} + P_{\text{bid}} = \frac{X}{1 + rt}$$

$$P_{\text{bid}} = \frac{X}{1 + rt} - s_{\text{offer}} + c_{\text{bid}}$$

Exercise 77 *Find the zero-edge put offer price using the method above. You are lifted on your put offer price P_{offer} and have to hedge your position. Do you buy or sell stock and calls and at bid or offer price? Find your offer price by setting the payoff at expiry to zero.*

Collecting the formulae together for our call option market we have

$$C_{\text{bid}} = s_{\text{bid}} + p_{\text{bid}} - \frac{X}{1+rt} \qquad C_{\text{offer}} = s_{\text{offer}} + p_{\text{offer}} - \frac{X}{1+rt}$$

and for our put option market we have

$$P_{\text{bid}} = \frac{X}{1+rt} - s_{\text{offer}} + c_{\text{bid}} \qquad P_{\text{offer}} = \frac{X}{1+rt} - s_{\text{bid}} + c_{\text{offer}}$$

Notice that all of our prices are in terms of other market makers' bids and offers, so that in every market but our own we are a market taker, not a market maker. The market we have made here is very conservative. We are taking almost no risk because we are fully hedged. In practice our market would have to be tighter in order to be competitive and would therefore take some price risk.

11.7.2 Dynamic Hedging

Option market makers exist to provide a market for buying and selling options on some underlying such as stock. They make their profit by having a spread between their bid and ask price. These traders usually rely on dynamic hedging to remove any directional risk from their positions. By hedging they are indifferent to the direction in which the underlying moves, though their positions are not totally flat because of one of the Greeks that we met earlier called gamma. We will demonstrate using the previous example where we were making a market in the three month 100 call on XYZ corporation. Say we are hit on our bid and forced to buy one 100 call. This means that we have a directional position on XYZ corporation which we have to hedge. Because we are long the underlying we expect that we have to sell XYZ stock. To find out exactly how much stock we have to sell we calculate delta for our call option using a model like Black-Scholes. If the call is 50 delta then we need to sell half a stock of XYZ in order to flatten our position. We can now consider what may happen to our hedged position as time passes.

Black-Scholes gives a value for the 100 call (given 0.25 years to expiry, volatility 30%, carry rate 2%, long rate 5%, strike 100 and stock price 100) of $6.17 and delta 0.5391. So in order to delta hedge the call we sell 0.5391 of XYZ stock. This will earn $53.91 and we pay $6.17 for the call premium so our overall cash position is $47.74. One day passes and the stock price drops to $99.27. Our call option value decreases because of the drop in stock price, but also due to time value decay (theta decay), and our short stock position gains in value. The short stock position has now increased in value from -$53.91 to -0.5391×99.27 or -$53.51. Re-calculating the value of the call option using the new stock price of $99.42 and the reduced time to expiry of 0.2472 years gives a reduction in value from $6.17 to $5.75. Now that the value of the stock has changed our stock hedge no longer "works" because delta has now decreased from 0.5391 to 0.5194. Our call option's new sensitivity to changes in the stock price has decreased so we need to reduce our short position in stock which requires buying 0.0197 stock. At the new stock price of $99.27 this will cost 0.0197×99.27 which is $1.95.

Time	Stock Price	Short Stock		100 Call Option		Delta		Hedge Cost
		Value	Change	Value	Change	Value	Change	
Day 0	100	-53.91		6.17		0.5391		+53.91
Day 1	99.27	-53.51	+0.40	5.75	-0.42	0.5194	-0.0197	-1.95

Notice that the gain in the short stock position of 40 cents is roughly cancelling out the lost value of the call option of -42 cents as we would expect for a hedged position. The next day the stock price increases from $99.27 to $99.42. Now the roles are reversed because the call option increases in value and the short stock position loses value. The short stock position has decreased 8 cents in value from -$51.56 to -$51.64 and the call option has increased 4 cents in value from $5.75 to $5.79.

Time	Stock Price	Short Stock			100 Call Option		Delta		Hedge Cost
		Value	Change	Re-Hedged	Value	Change	Value	Change	
Day 0	100	-53.91		-53.91	6.17		0.5391		+53.91
Day 1	99.27	-53.51	+0.40	-51.56	5.75	-0.42	0.5194	-0.0197	-1.95
Day 2	99.42	-51.64	-0.08	-52.02	5.79	+0.04	0.5232	+0.0038	+0.38

The picture that emerges as we hedge, wait to see what the market throws at us, then re-hedge is a nickel and dime change in profit on a daily basis. So how does a market maker make their money? Their profit depends on the size of the daily moves in the underlying. If the underlying price does not move at all the market maker will not recoup the premium that they paid for this call option. If the underlying moves more than expected they will claw back their premium and make a profit. Our measure of movement is of course volatility which tells us the average movement in a year. Priced into the option premium is an IMPLIED VOLATILITY. If REALIZED VOLATILITY exceeds implied then the market maker that is long a delta-hedged option will make a profit. If we take the previous example we can see what would happen to the value of our short stock position and our call option for various one-day stock price movements. To convert from an annualised volatility of 30% to a daily volatility we divide by the square root of the number of days in a year, $\sigma_{daily} = \frac{\sigma_{annual}}{\sqrt{260}} = \frac{30}{\sqrt{260}}$ or about 2% [2]. So if we see the underlying move by 2% in one day we would not be surprised at all, but a 6% move would be very surprising.

---

[2]A useful rule of thumb: to convert from annualized to daily volatility divide by sixteen ($\sqrt{260} \simeq 16$).

| Stock | | Short Stock | | 100 Call Option | | Hedged Position | |
Return	Price	Value	Change	Value	Change	Value	Delta
$-3\sigma_{daily}$	94.57	-50.98	2.93	3.61	-2.56	0.36	-0.1461
$-2\sigma_{daily}$	96.35	-51.94	1.97	4.35	-1.82	0.14	-0.0980
$-\sigma_{daily}$	98.16	-52.91	0.99	5.19	-0.98	0.01	-0.0490
0	100	-53.91	0.00	6.13	-0.04	-0.04	0.0000
σ_{daily}	101.88	-54.92	-1.01	7.19	1.02	0.01	0.0484
$+2\sigma_{daily}$	103.79	-55.95	-2.04	8.36	2.19	0.15	0.0954
$+3\sigma_{daily}$	105.74	-57.00	-3.09	9.64	3.47	0.38	0.1404

Whether the stock moves up or down we make a profit. The further it moves the more money we make. When the stock price increases delta is positive and we are long the underlying just as we would wish. When the stock price decreases we are short the underlying just as we would wish. Only if the stock price remains unchanged or moves a little bit do we lose money due to time decay of the option. If we graph the payoff of our position against stock price as in Figure 11.8 we can see the profit and loss looks like a parabola. This shape is largely due to option gamma because we have hedged away all the first order delta exposure to the underlying and what remains is second and higher order exposure which is dominated by gamma. Gamma is the same for a call and put option with the same strike, so if the market maker is delta-hedged then whether she is long a call or long a put her position looks the same. As we can see the only way that the position in Figure 11.8 can lose money is if the underlying does not move or moves by a small amount.

Day to day the market maker tries to lock in profits due to gamma, a process called SCALPING GAMMA. The more volatile the underlying the more money this position will make, so a long-gamma position is also a long-volatility position. The market maker starts off paying the option premium and has to make this money back by scalping gamma. Those with a military frame of mind might see this as a war, not between good and evil, but between theta and gamma. As time passes the call's value trickles away due to theta and must be recouped by movement in the underlying combined with the dish-shaped payoff due to gamma. This is why traders sometimes say that theta is the rent for gamma because those that are long a call or put have to pay theta in order to make profit with gamma. Others describe scalping gamma as being akin to picking up nickels on a train track. Usually this makes small profits but you have to watch out in case you get wiped out completely.

If the market maker has sold an option and is therefore short the option then she starts out with the premium in her hand. Being short the option means that she will lose a little money every time she re-hedges her position. Gamma is now no longer a benefit but a cost because the market maker must buy stock when the price rises and sell stock when the price drops, buying high and selling low. Her job in this case is to keep as much of the premium as possible. She cannot stop delta hedging because this would expose her to the much greater risk of having a directional position in the underlying. Directional means that she is either long or short the underlying. Having a directional position is the job of the prop trader who has a view and capital to invest, it is not the job of the market maker. So being short a call or short a put is a short-

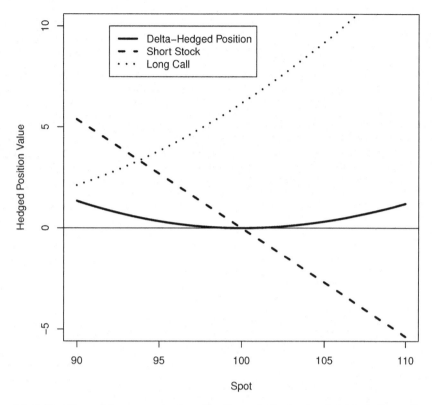

Figure 11.8: Profit and loss vs. stock price for a delta-hedged 100 strike call option.

gamma and short-volatility position. Fortunately theta is now a benefit and the short position gains value through time decay. So the market maker is hoping that the volatility will be lower than the implied volatility and that theta will outdo gamma until expiry so that she holds onto her premium.

11.8 FX Options

When buying a call option on a stock such as Google we *could* think of the transaction as the option to exchange one Google stock for $500. This is easy to understand because we are used to buying stuff for cash. People would be confused if we started to talk about an option to buy $500 with one Google stock because we use cash to buy things not things to buy cash. A trader from the Bronze Age would not have any difficulty seeing it either way. In fact there is no reason why there could not be an active options market if we were to scrap currencies altogether and reinstate a system of barter. Say there was an active market swapping sheep for cows then the only tricky question might be how we would pay for the option. Would the option to buy one thousand cows be expressed in cows or sheep? People today have difficulty understanding FX options because we are buying one currency with another and both are, in some sense, cash.

Say we want an option to buy Euros and we will buy our Euros with US dollars. If the spot rate for EUR | USD is 1.5 then it will cost us $1.50 to buy one euro today. If we want to buy a three month option on EUR | USD then we must specify what we want to buy and sell, so we would describe our option as a EUR call USD put because we are buying EUR and selling USD to pay for them. Our strike would be expressed in the same terms as spot so we would call it a 1.50 strike three month EUR call USD put. What is interesting is that we could quote the premium in USD or in EUR. Alternatively the option premium can be expressed as a percentage of the face value in USD or EUR. We can use Black-Scholes to price the option, but we have to re-interpret some of the variables. We have to be clear about what we mean by the long rate r_l and carry rate r_c in this equation:

$$
\begin{array}{ccccccc}
C & = & S & \times & N(d_1)e^{-(r_l - r_c)t} & - & Xe^{-r_l t} & \times & N(d_2) \\
\text{Call Value} & = & \text{Spot Price} & \times & \text{Delta} & - & \text{PV(Strike)} & \times & p(\text{ITM at Expiry})
\end{array}
$$

If we are buying EUR using USD as cash then the long rate, or cash rate, r_l is the interest rate in USD. The carry rate is the cost of carrying a long EUR short USD position through time. We have to borrow cash in USD so that will be a cost, and we hold EUR which is a benefit. So the cost minus the benefit will be $r_c = r_{USD} - r_{EUR}$, and the difference $r_l - r_c = r_{USD} - (r_{USD} - r_{EUR}) = r_{EUR}$. We have already seen how to find the forward price using interest rate parity (see Section 9.1.2 on page 330). For our FX call option the Black-Scholes formula can be written as

$$
C = Se^{-r_{EUR}t} \times N(d_1) - Xe^{-r_{USD}t} \times N(d_2),
$$

where

$$
d_1 = \frac{\ln \frac{S}{X} + \left(r_{USD} - r_{EUR} + \frac{\sigma^2}{2}\right)t}{\sigma\sqrt{t}}
$$

$$
d_2 = \frac{\ln \frac{S}{X} + \left(r_{USD} - r_{EUR} - \frac{\sigma^2}{2}\right)t}{\sigma\sqrt{t}} = d_1 - \sigma\sqrt{t}.
$$

For a EUR put USD call where we are selling EUR and buying USD the long or cash rate $r_l = r_{EUR}$ because EUR is now our "cash" currency, and the carry rate is $r_c = r_{EUR} - r_{USD}$. The difference $r_l - r_c = r_{EUR} - (r_{EUR} - r_{USD}) = r_{USD}$. The value of this put is

$$
P = -Se^{-r_{USD}t} \times N(-d_1) + Xe^{-r_{EUR}t} \times N(-d_2).
$$

Putting everything in more general terms if the currency pair is FOR | DOM then our "cash" is DOM, our underlying is FOR, our carry rate is $r_c = r_{DOM} - r_{FOR}$, and

Black-Scholes is as follows:

$$
\begin{aligned}
C &= Se^{-r_{FOR}t} \times N(d_1) - Xe^{-r_{DOM}t} \times N(d_2) \\
P &= -Se^{-r_{DOM}t} \times N(-d_1) + Xe^{-r_{FOR}t} \times N(-d_2) \\
d_1 &= \frac{\ln\frac{S}{X} + \left(r_{DOM} - r_{FOR} + \frac{\sigma^2}{2}\right)t}{\sigma\sqrt{t}} \\
d_2 &= \frac{\ln\frac{S}{X} + \left(r_{DOM} - r_{FOR} - \frac{\sigma^2}{2}\right)t}{\sigma\sqrt{t}} = d_1 - \sigma\sqrt{t}. \quad (11.5)
\end{aligned}
$$

The FX form of the Black-Scholes pricing equations are known as the Garman and Kohlhagen option pricing formulae (Garman and Kohlhagen, 1983).

Exercise 78 *Find the value of an at-the-money forward three month EUR call USD put on €10,000,000 face given that EUR|USD spot is trading at 1.4752, the three month USD interest rate is 0.288%, the three month EUR interest rate is 0.416% and the EUR|USD rate volatility is 10%. Start by calculating the three month forward EUR|USD exchange rate then either use Black-Scholes or the ATMF approximation of Black-Scholes (see Section 11.4 on page 383) to find the value of the call option.*

Exercise 79 *In what units was the previous call premium? Complete the sentence: _ is the cost in _ for the right but not the obligation to buy _ EUR for _ USD in three months time.*

Exercise 80 *Express the premium in EUR, then as a percentage of the EUR face amount.*

11.9 American Options

The difference between a European option and an American option is that the American allows EARLY EXERCISE at any time before expiry. Black-Scholes can only price European options so pricing Americans requires Monte Carlo simulation or tree-based pricing methods. Because optionality has value and because Americans provide more optionality than Europeans, American options are always worth at least as much as equivalent Europeans. American options usually trade at the same price as European options except in special circumstances where it is beneficial to exercise before expiry. The value of an American option has a lower bound which is the value of the underlying. If you own a 300 strike American call on Sprocket Corporation and Sprocket is trading today at \$305 then you could exercise your 300 call today to buy Sprocket stock for \$300 and immediately sell that stock for \$305. You would pocket \$5, so your 300 American call must be worth at least \$5. If the spot price of the underlying is S then an American call will always be worth more than parity to the spot price, $S - X$ and an American put will always be worth more than $X - S$. The value $|X - S|$ is called INTRINSIC VALUE. Notice that for a European option the lower bound is not parity to spot $|X - S|$ but is instead parity to forward $|X - F|$ because a European can only be exercised at expiry and the only way to lock in a price for the underlying is to trade forward. In addition American options will have value due to the volatility of the underlying and this is called TIME VALUE and this is always positive for American options. Some text books try to use intrinsic value $|X - S|$ for European options and run into confusion when time values turn negative.

Although accurate pricing does require fairly sophisticated pricing algorithms we can gain some intuitive understanding of American pricing by considering the costs and benefits of early exercise. Firstly it is important to appreciate that exercise does not remove your risk exposure to the underlying. This is because when you exercise an option it is usually in the money so delta will be more than 50% and possibly well on its way to 100%. After exercise you will be long the underlying if you had a call or short the underlying if you had a put, so your exposure to the underlying has changed very little. The only way to reduce your price risk to zero is to sell the option. Secondly the only reason why you would consider early exercise is to own the rights that you gain from owning the underlying. If the underlying is a stock then the right which investors desire is the right to dividend payments. In order to be eligible for a dividend you must exercise the day before the stock EX-DIV DATE and this ensures that by the settlement date your name will be on the share register making you eligible for the dividend. If a stock pays no dividend then the price of its American and European options will be the same as there is no reason to exercise early.

In the case of an American call option the cost is twofold: you will give up downside protection when you switch from a call option to the underlying, and you have to fund the purchase and holding of the stock until the ex-div date. The cost of giving up protection, or equivalently the time value of the option which is lost on exercise, can be estimated by the value of a put P with strike price equal to the call. When you exercise an option you have to raise cash for the purchase and this will incur a funding cost. The cost of funding the stock purchase at strike price X will be $Xr\frac{t_{Xdiv}-t}{360}$ where the r is the funding rate and $\frac{t_{Xdiv}-t}{360}$ is the time to the ex-div date as a year fraction with the appropriate day count. The benefit is the discounted value of the dividend. We will only consider early exercise if the benefits exceed the costs

$$
\begin{aligned}
\text{benefit} &> \text{cost} \\
\text{dividend} &> \text{funding cost} + \text{time value} \\
\frac{D}{1+rt} &> Xr\frac{t_{Xdiv}-t}{360} + P
\end{aligned}
$$

Note that the cost of funding can be minimized by exercising at the last possible moment before the ex-div date. This means that the optimal time for exercising an American is usually the day before the ex-div date. The day before the ex-div date we can effectively ignore the one day funding cost and discounting the dividend which means that exercise is worthwhile if the dividend exceeds the time value that is being lost $D > P$.

American puts can be analyzed in a similar manner to calls. Early exercise of a put would result in a short position in the underlying stock. The benefit would be that shorting the stock would generate cash in the form of short proceeds. The cost would be that the investor would lose their upside protection, so that if the underlying rallies they face unlimited losses. The protection that is being given up is the value of a call.

The dividend is a cost when your are short a stock as you have to pay a synthetic dividend to the person from whom you have borrowed the stock. It makes sense to exercise if the put is in the money and

$$
\begin{aligned}
\text{benefit} \quad &> \quad \text{cost} \\
Xrt \quad &> \quad \frac{D}{1+rt} + C
\end{aligned}
$$

11.10 Exotic Options

One broad classification of options is into VANILLA OPTIONS and EXOTIC OPTIONS. The price of a vanilla option depends on where the underlying price is today. Vanilla options have no memory of where the underlying has traded in the past. In contrast exotic options do have such a memory and for this reason their price is PATH DE-PENDENT. The most commonly traded exotic options are ones that either activate or inactivate depending on whether the underlying crosses some threshold price and these are called BARRIER OPTIONS. Barrier options are always cheaper than equiv-alent vanilla options because introducing a barrier reduces the chance of the option paying out at expiry, and this is why they are popular. There are four variations of barrier option depending on whether they start out active or inactive and whether they have to rise above or drop below the barrier. If they have to rise above the bar-rier these are UP AND IN or UP AND OUT options. If they have to drop below the barrier they are DOWN AND OUT or DOWN AND IN options.

Up and in	Become active if spot rises above in-strike
Up and out	Become inactive if spot rises above out-strike
Down and in	Become active if spot drops below in-strike
Down and out	Become inactive if spot drops below in-strike

Once an in-option becomes active after the underlying crosses the in-strike it be-haves exactly like a vanilla option. An out-option ceases to exist if the underlying crosses the out-strike and does not come back into existence even if the underlying moves back across the barrier. The value of out-options drops dramatically as they approach their out-strike as it becomes more likely that they will be knocked out. An-other variation of barrier options are DOUBLE LOCKOUTS where the investor receives a fixed payout if the underlying trades within a range and never touches the two out-strikes. Obviously someone who is long such an option is short volatility because a high volatility increases the chance that one of the barriers will be touched and the option becomes worthless.

Another popular path-dependent exotic option is an ASIAN OPTION. The payoff of an Asian option is based on the average price of the underlying over the life of the option. It is as if the underlying were replaced by the averaged price of the underlying over the life of the option. Asian options are attractive to risk-averse investors because as they approach expiry the effect of price averaging is to reduce volatility making them cheaper than vanillas.

A Lookback Option maximizes the payout at expiry by resetting the strike to the best possible price over the life of the option. In other words the option has a Floating Strike. In the case of a lookback call the strike is the lowest value of the underlying over the life of the option. For a lookback put the strike is the highest value of the underlying over the life of the option. For example, if we have a three month lookback call option on the S&P 500 index and the index trades at a minimum of 1010 in that period and expires at 1300 our payoff will be $1300 - 1010$ or $290 because the strike will be set at 1010. It is as if we had a money manager with perfect timing that always buys at the lowest possible price. Due to this optimal timing lookbacks are very likely to give a large payoff at expiry but this is priced into their premium which will be very large compared to an at-the-money vanilla option with a fixed strike.

A Basket Option has a payoff that depends on the value of several underlyings. For example it could contain a basket of currencies, a basket of stocks, or a basket of commodity prices. Although they sound rather esoteric, if you have a company that is exposed to the price risk of many market variables, such as the price of oil and say, the USDJPY exchange rate, then it may make sense to hedge this risk with a basket of oil and USDJPY. The major difference in pricing a basket of underlyings compared with individual underlying options is that we have to consider how the movements in price are dependent on one another. In other words we have to know the covariance of the underlying asset prices. Once we know the covariance matrix pricing a basket option is very similar to pricing a CDO using Monte Carlo simulation (see Section 8.2 on page 316). This involves generating thousands of possible price paths for the underlyings. Each path is priced using the payoff function resulting in a distribution of prices. Because we have to quote a single price we use the expected payoff from the payoff distribution.

11.11 Further Reading

The standard introductory textbook for derivatives is Hull (2008). It is worth getting the latest edition of Hull, if you can afford it, as he has made sure to keep his book up to date with developments in the derivatives market. If you want to get your hands dirty and try pricing derivatives for yourself Haug (2007) provides pricing methods with an Excel implementation.Weithers (2006) provides a lively and clearly explained introduction to FX options. For people with a mathematical background I would recommend Baxter and Rennie (1996). This is another slim book that skilfully leads the reader from binomial trees to discrete time then continuous time stochastic calculus.

Answers to Exercises

55 *Calculate the value of the replicating portfolio if the price of the share goes up to 101, and the price if it goes down to 99. Does it replicate the call option payoff?*

If the share price goes up to $101 then the shares are worth $101 \times \frac{1}{2}$ or $50.50 for the share and the bond is worth $-48.8851 \times e^{\frac{0.05}{4}}$ which is -$49.50 giving a total of $1. If the share price goes down to $99 then the shares are worth $99 \times \frac{1}{2}$ or $49.50 and the bonds are again worth $-48.8851 \times e^{\frac{0.05}{4}}$ which is -$49.50. The total portfolio value is $0 because the share value is balanced by the cost of repaying our loan of $48.89 for three months. So whichever path the share follows the portfolio is worth exactly the same amount as the call option, and we have indeed replicated the call option payoff. The cash required to set up this replicating portfolio must equal the value of the call option by the law of one price.

56 *Build a binomial tree for pricing a three month 100 strike call stock option with a depth of three, so each time step will be one month with 31 days per month and 365 days per year. Volatility for the underlying stock is 30% and interest rates are a flat 5% (actual continuous). The price of the stock today is 100.*

Volatility is 30% ($\sigma = 0.3$), interest rates are 5% ($r = 0.05$) and our time step is one month $\Delta t = \frac{31}{365} = 0.08493$. The factor by which the stock price increases in one time step is $e^{\sigma\sqrt{\Delta t}} = e^{0.3 \times \sqrt{\frac{31}{365}}}$ which is 1.091365, and the factor by which the stock price decreases is the reciprocal of the increase factor, 0.9162839. The probability of a down jump is

$$
\begin{aligned}
p &= \frac{e^{r\Delta t} - e^{\sigma\sqrt{\Delta t}}}{e^{-\sigma\sqrt{\Delta t}} - e^{\sigma\sqrt{\Delta t}}} \\
&= \frac{e^{0.05 \times \frac{31}{365}} - e^{0.3 \times \sqrt{\frac{31}{365}}}}{e^{-0.3 \times \sqrt{\frac{31}{365}}} - e^{0.3 \times \sqrt{\frac{31}{365}}}} \\
&= 0.4975
\end{aligned}
$$

The stock process tree will look like this:

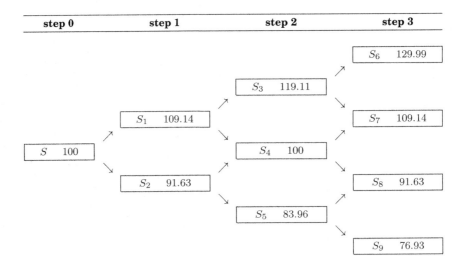

step 0	step 1	step 2	step 3

Filling in the option values at maturity, the stock price is either 129.99 in which case the 100 strike call payoff is 29.99, or the stock price is 109.14 giving a payoff of 9.14. The other two possible stock prices are 91.63 or 76.93 which are both below the strike price and therefore have zero payoff. The value of the call option at node 3 is

$$
\begin{aligned}
P_3 &= \left[pP_7 + (1-p)\,P_6 \right] e^{-r\Delta t} \\
&= \left[0.4975 \times 9.1365 + (1 - 0.4975) \times 29.99 \right] \times e^{-0.05 \times \frac{31}{365}} \\
&= 19.5315
\end{aligned}
$$

These are the detailed calculations:

$$
\begin{aligned}
P_3 &= \left[pP_7 + (1-p)P_6 \right] e^{-r\Delta t} = \left[0.4975 \times 9.1365 + (1 - 0.4975) \times 29.99 \right] \times e^{-0.05 \times \frac{31}{365}} = 19.53\!\mathrm{1} \\
P_4 &= \left[pP_8 + (1-p)P_7 \right] e^{-r\Delta t} = \left[0.4975 \times 0 + (1 - 0.4975) \times 9.1365 \right] \times e^{-0.05 \times \frac{31}{365}} = 4.5713 \\
P_5 &= \left[pP_9 + (1-p)P_8 \right] e^{-r\Delta t} = \left[0.4975 \times 0 + (1 - 0.4975) \times 0 \right] \times e^{-0.05 \times \frac{31}{365}} = 0 \\
P_1 &= \left[pP_4 + (1-p)P_3 \right] e^{-r\Delta t} = \left[0.4975 \times 4.5713 + (1 - 0.4975) \times 19.5315 \right] \times e^{-0.05 \times \frac{31}{365}} = 12.\!0 \\
P_2 &= \left[pP_5 + (1-p)P_4 \right] e^{-r\Delta t} = \left[0.4975 \times 0 + (1 - 0.4975) \times 4.5713 \right] \times e^{-0.05 \times \frac{31}{365}} = 2.2872 \\
P &= \left[pP_2 + (1-p)P_1 \right] e^{-r\Delta t} = \left[0.4975 \times 2.2872 + (1 - 0.4975) \times 12.037 \right] \times e^{-0.05 \times \frac{31}{365}} = 7.15
\end{aligned}
$$

Our combined stock process and option process trees will look like this:

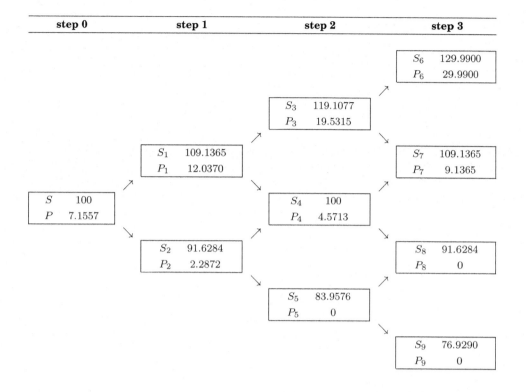

	step 0		step 1		step 2		step 3

S 100, P 7.1557

S_1 109.1365, P_1 12.0370

S_2 91.6284, P_2 2.2872

S_3 119.1077, P_3 19.5315

S_4 100, P_4 4.5713

S_5 83.9576, P_5 0

S_6 129.9900, P_6 29.9900

S_7 109.1365, P_7 9.1365

S_8 91.6284, P_8 0

S_9 76.9290, P_9 0

The final value for the 100 call is 7.16. If we were to use the Black-Scholes model the value of the option would be 6.58.

57 *Find the value of a call option on Sprocket Corp. with strike $X = 100$, spot price $S = 95$, carry rate and long rate 5% $r_c = r_l = 0.05$, volatility 30% $\sigma = 0.3$ and three months to maturity $t = 0.25$. Assume Sprocket pays no dividends over the life of the contract.*

First we calculate the values of d_1 and d_2.

$$
\begin{aligned}
d_1 &= \frac{\ln \frac{S}{X} + \left(r_c + \frac{\sigma^2}{2}\right)t}{\sigma\sqrt{t}} \\
&= \frac{\ln \frac{95}{100} + \left(0.05 + \frac{0.3^2}{2}\right)0.25}{0.3\sqrt{0.25}} \\
&= \frac{-0.05129 - 0.02375}{0.15} \\
&= -0.18362
\end{aligned}
$$

And

$$
\begin{aligned}
d_2 &= d_1 - \sigma\sqrt{t} \\
&= -0.18362 - 0.3\sqrt{0.25} \\
&= -0.33362
\end{aligned}
$$

The value of a call option is, for spot price $S = 95$,

$$
\begin{aligned}
C &= SN(d_1)e^{-(r_l - r_c)t} - Xe^{-r_l t}N(d_2) \\
&= 95N(-0.18362) - 100e^{-0.05 \times 0.25}N(-0.33362) \\
&= 95 \times 0.42716 - 100 \times 0.98758 \times 0.36933 \\
&= 4.1053
\end{aligned}
$$

58 *Find the value of the put option on Sprocket Corp. with the same strike and maturity as the previous example. Do the put and call values obey put-call parity?*

The values of d_1 and d_2 are the same for the 100 call as for the 100 put. The value of the call option is, for spot price $S = 95$,

$$
\begin{aligned}
P &= -SN(-d_1)e^{-(r_l - r_c)t} + Xe^{-r_l t}N(-d_2) \\
&= -95N(0.18362) + 100e^{-0.05 \times 0.25}N(0.33362) \\
&= -95 \times 0.57284 + 100 \times 0.98758 \times 0.63066 \\
&= 7.86305
\end{aligned}
$$

Using put-call parity the difference between the put and the call should be the present value of the parity to the forward, $P - C = (X - F)e^{-r_l t}$. The forward value is $F = Se^{r_l t}$ so $P = C + Xe^{-r_l t} - S = 4.1053 + 100e^{-0.05 \times 0.25} - 95 = 7.8631$ as we expected, so put-call parity applies.

59 The forward price incorporates the cost of carry for three months which is the interest on borrowing the future value of the stock which we will have to pay in three months time. This is

$$
\begin{aligned}
F &= Se^{rt} \\
&= 98.758e^{0.05 \times 0.25} \\
&= 100.00
\end{aligned}
$$

60 *Calculate the value of the 100 call on Sprocket corporation given that Sprocket is now trading at $S = 98.75778$. So $X = 100$, $r_l = r_c = 0.05$, volatility is unchanged at 30% $\sigma = 0.3$, maturity is still three months $t = 0.25$. Then calculate the value of the 100 put.*

First we calculate the values of d_1 and d_2.

$$
\begin{aligned}
d_1 &= \frac{\ln \frac{S}{X} + \left(r_c + \frac{\sigma^2}{2}\right)t}{\sigma\sqrt{t}} \\
&= \frac{\ln \frac{98.75778}{100} + \left(0.05 + \frac{0.3^2}{2}\right)0.25}{0.3\sqrt{0.25}} \\
&= \frac{-0.012498 + 0.02375}{0.15} \\
&= 0.075000
\end{aligned}
$$

And

$$d_2 = d_1 - \sigma\sqrt{t}$$
$$= 0.075000 - 0.3\sqrt{0.25}$$
$$= -0.075000$$

The value of a call option is, given spot price $S = 98.75778$,

$$C = SN(d_1)e^{-(r_l-r_c)t} - Xe^{-r_lt}N(d_2)$$
$$= 98.75778 \times N(0.075000) - 100e^{-0.05\times0.25}N(-0.075000)$$
$$= 98.75778 \times 0.52989264 - 100 \times 0.9875778 \times 0.47010736$$
$$= 5.9043$$

And the value of the 100 put is

$$P = -Se^{-(r_l-r_c)t}N(-d_1) + Xe^{-r_lt}N(-d_2)$$
$$= -98.75778 \times N(-0.075000) + 100e^{-0.05\times0.25}N(0.075000)$$
$$= -98.75778 \times 0.47010736 + 100 \times 0.9875778 \times 0.52989264$$
$$= 5.9043$$

Or we could use put-call parity with forward price $F = Se^{rt} = 98.75778e^{0.05\times0.25} = 100$.

$$P = C + (X - F)e^{r_lt}$$
$$= 5.9043 + (100 - 100)e^{0.05\times0.25}$$
$$= 5.9043$$

This exercise illustrates the point that if the strike is equal to the forward price i.e. our options are "at-the-money-forward" (ATMF), the put and call values at the same strike are equal.

61 *What happens to the value of the call and the put when volatility approaches zero?*

First we consider what happens to d_1 when volatility σ is very small. The definition of d_1 is

$$d_1 = \frac{\ln\frac{S}{X} + \left(r_c + \frac{\sigma^2}{2}\right)t}{\sigma\sqrt{t}}$$
$$= \frac{\ln\frac{S}{X}}{\sigma\sqrt{t}} + \frac{r_ct}{\sigma\sqrt{t}} + \frac{\sigma t}{2\sqrt{t}}$$

So when σ is close to zero the last term becomes much smaller than the other two

$$d_1 \approx \frac{\ln\frac{S}{X}}{\sigma\sqrt{t}} + \frac{r_ct}{\sigma\sqrt{t}}$$
$$d_1 \approx \frac{\ln\frac{S}{X} + r_ct}{\sigma\sqrt{t}}$$

Similarly

$$d_2 \approx \frac{\ln\frac{S}{X} + r_c t}{\sigma\sqrt{t}} = d_1,$$

and this number is large and positive if $\ln\frac{S}{X} + r_c t$ is greater than zero and large and negative if $\ln\frac{S}{X} + r_c t$ is less than zero. The limiting case occurs when

$$\ln\frac{S}{X} + r_c t = 0$$
$$\ln\frac{S}{X} = -r_c t$$
$$S = X e^{-r_c t}$$

So the value of $N(d_1)$ and $N(d_2)$ will be

$$N(d_1) = N(d_2) = \begin{cases} 0 & S < X e^{-r_c t} \\ 1 & S > X e^{-r_c t} \end{cases}$$

and the value of the call option will be

$$C \approx N(d_1)\left[S e^{-(r_l - r_c)t} - X e^{-r_l t}\right]$$

Since we know that $N(d_1)$ in the two regions will be 0 and 1, the value of the call will be

$$C = \begin{cases} 0 & \text{if } S < X e^{-r_c t} \\ S e^{-(r_l - r_c)t} - X e^{-r_l t} & \text{if } S > X e^{-r_c t} \end{cases}$$

which is a hockey-stick payoff which has zero value at values of spot below $X e^{-r_c t}$ and rises in value above this spot value with a gradient of $e^{(r_c - r_l)t}$. Alternatively, since $F = S e^{r_c t}$, $C = \max(0, \mathrm{PV}(F - X))$. For a put option

$$P \approx N(-d_1)\left[-S e^{-(r_l - r_c)t} + X e^{-r_l t}\right]$$

and the regions will be reversed relative to the call as the value depends on $N(-d_1)$. Where the value of the call is zero the value of the put will be non-zero and vice versa. So

$$P = \begin{cases} -S e^{-(r_l - r_c)t} + X e^{-r_l t} & \text{if } S < X e^{-r_c t} \\ 0 & \text{if } S > X e^{-r_c t} \end{cases}$$

This has zero value at and above a spot value of $X e^{-r_c t}$ and has a negative gradient of $-e^{-(r_l - r_c)t}$ for values of spot below $X e^{-r_c t}$. Again this can be rewritten as $P = \max(0, \mathrm{PV}(X - F))$.

62 *What happens to the value of the call and the put when volatility approaches infinity?*

First we consider what happens to d_1 when volatility σ is very large. The definition of d_1 is

$$d_1 = \frac{\ln \frac{S}{X} + \left(r_c + \frac{\sigma^2}{2}\right)t}{\sigma\sqrt{t}}$$

$$= \frac{\ln \frac{S}{X}}{\sigma\sqrt{t}} + \frac{r_c t}{\sigma\sqrt{t}} + \frac{\sigma t}{2\sqrt{t}}$$

When σ is very large the first two terms become very small leaving the third term

$$d_1 \approx \frac{\sigma\sqrt{t}}{2}$$

Similarly

$$d_2 \approx -\frac{\sigma\sqrt{t}}{2} = -d_1,$$

Our values for d_1 and d_2 are now insensitive to the spot price S. Now $N(d_1)$ will approach 1 for large values of σ and $N(d_2)$ will approach 0 and the value of the call option will be

$$C \approx Se^{-(r_l - r_c)t} = Fe^{-r_l t}$$

which is the present value of the forward price, so the call behaves just like the forward. If the carry rate is equal to the long rate $r_c = r_l$ then the value of the call option converges on the spot price. For a put option $N(-d_1) \approx 0$ and $N(-d_2) \approx 1$ and

$$P \approx Xe^{-r_l t},$$

which shows that the put value is constant for all values of spot and equal to the strike discounted at the long rate.

63 *Derive the value of delta for a call option by differentiating the expression for the value of a call (Equation 11.3) with respect to S using the Black-Scholes model.*
Starting with our expression for the call value

$$C = SN(d_1)e^{-(r_l - r_c)t} - Xe^{-r_l t}N(d_2)$$

We differentiate with respect to S,

$$\frac{\partial C}{\partial S} = N(d_1)e^{-(r_l - r_c)t} + Se^{-(r_l - r_c)t}\frac{\partial}{\partial S}N(d_1) - Xe^{-r_l t}\frac{\partial}{\partial S}N(d_2)$$

But we know that $\frac{\partial}{\partial x}N(x) = \frac{1}{\sqrt{2\pi}}e^{-\frac{x^2}{2}}$ because $N(x)$ is defined as the cumulative normal density $N(x) = \frac{1}{\sqrt{2\pi}}\int_{-\infty}^{x} e^{-\frac{z^2}{2}}dz$. So

$$\frac{\partial C}{\partial S} = N(d_1)e^{-(r_l - r_c)t} + \frac{Se^{-(r_l - r_c)t}}{\sqrt{2\pi}}e^{-\frac{d_1^2}{2}} - \frac{Xe^{-r_l t}}{\sqrt{2\pi}}e^{-\frac{d_2^2}{2}}$$

$$= N(d_1)e^{-(r_l - r_c)t} + \frac{e^{-r_l t}}{\sqrt{2\pi}}\left(Se^{r_c t}e^{-\frac{d_1^2}{2}} - Xe^{-\frac{d_2^2}{2}}\right)$$

We will show that the expression in parentheses is zero. Firstly, as $d_2 = d_1 - \sigma\sqrt{t}$, and $d_2^2 = d_1^2 - 2d_1\sigma\sqrt{t} + \sigma^2 t$ we can substitute for the d_2^2 term

$$Se^{r_c t}e^{-\frac{d_1^2}{2}} - Xe^{-\frac{d_2^2}{2}} = Se^{r_c t}e^{-\frac{d_1^2}{2}} - Xe^{-\frac{d_1^2}{2}}e^{d_1\sigma\sqrt{t}}e^{-\frac{\sigma^2 t}{2}}$$

The final step is to substitute the value of d_1 in the $e^{d_1\sigma\sqrt{t}}$ term

$$
\begin{aligned}
e^{d_1\sigma\sqrt{t}} &= e^{\ln\frac{S}{X}+\left(r_c+\frac{\sigma^2}{2}\right)t} \\
&= \frac{S}{X}e^{r_c t}e^{\frac{\sigma^2 t}{2}}
\end{aligned}
$$

So

$$
\begin{aligned}
Se^{r_c t}e^{-\frac{d_1^2}{2}} - Xe^{\frac{d_2^2}{2}} &= Se^{r_c t}e^{-\frac{d_1^2}{2}} - Xe^{-\frac{d_1^2}{2}}e^{d_1\sigma\sqrt{t}}e^{-\frac{\sigma^2 t}{2}} \\
&= Se^{r_c t}e^{-\frac{d_1^2}{2}} - Xe^{-\frac{d_1^2}{2}}\frac{S}{X}e^{r_c t}e^{\frac{\sigma^2 t}{2}}e^{-\frac{\sigma^2 t}{2}} \\
&= Se^{r_c t}e^{-\frac{d_1^2}{2}} - Se^{r_c t}e^{-\frac{d_1^2}{2}} \\
&= 0
\end{aligned}
$$

And we arrive at a value for delta of

$$\Delta = \frac{\partial C}{\partial S} = N(d_1)e^{-(r_l - r_c)t}$$

64 *Derive the value of gamma for a call option by differentiating delta with respect to S again.*

Starting with our expression for delta

$$\Delta = N(d_1)e^{-(r_l - r_c)t}$$

we differentiate with respect to S again

$$
\begin{aligned}
\Gamma &= \frac{\partial \Delta}{\partial S} \\
&= \frac{\partial N(d_1)}{\partial S}e^{-(r_l - r_c)t} \\
&= N'(d_1)\frac{\partial d_1}{\partial S}e^{-(r_l - r_c)t}
\end{aligned}
$$

The expression for d_1 in terms of S is

$$d_1 = \frac{\ln\frac{S}{X} + \left(r_c + \frac{\sigma^2}{2}\right)t}{\sigma\sqrt{t}},$$

and

$$\frac{\partial d_1}{\partial S} = \frac{1}{S\sigma\sqrt{t}},$$

so

$$\Gamma = \frac{1}{S\sigma\sqrt{t}}N'(d_1)e^{-(r_l-r_c)t}$$

$$= \frac{1}{S\sigma\sqrt{2\pi t}}e^{-\frac{d_1^2}{2}}e^{-(r_l-r_c)t}$$

65 *Now show that Γ for the call and put option are equal.*

To find Γ for a put option, recall that

$$\Delta_{\text{put}} = -N(-d_1)e^{-(r_l-r_c)t}.$$

If we differentiate this with respect to S once again we get

$$\frac{\partial\Delta_{\text{put}}}{\partial S} = -\frac{\partial N(-d_1)}{\partial S}e^{-(r_l-r_c)t}$$

$$= N'(-d_1)\frac{\partial d_1}{\partial S}e^{-(r_l-r_c)t}.$$

All that remains is to note that due to the symmetry of the normal density $N'(-d_1) = N'(d_1)$ so

$$\frac{\partial\Delta_{\text{put}}}{\partial S} = N'(d_1)\frac{\partial d_1}{\partial S}e^{-(r_l-r_c)t} = \frac{\partial\Delta_{\text{call}}}{\partial S}.$$

66 *Derive the value of theta for a call option by differentiating the expression for the value of a call (Equation 11.3) with respect to t using the Black-Scholes model.*

Starting with our expression for the call value

$$C = SN(d_1)e^{-(r_l-r_c)t} - Xe^{-r_lt}N(d_2)$$

We differentiate with respect to t,

$$\frac{\partial C}{\partial t} = -(r_l-r_c)SN(d_1)e^{-(r_l-r_c)t} + Se^{-(r_l-r_c)t}\frac{\partial}{\partial t}N(d_1) + Xr_le^{-r_lt}N(d_2) - Xe^{-r_lt}\frac{\partial}{\partial t}N(d_2)$$

$$= Se^{-(r_l-r_c)t}\left[-(r_l-r_c)N(d_1) + \frac{\partial}{\partial t}N(d_1)\right] + Xe^{-r_lt}\left[r_lN(d_2) - \frac{\partial}{\partial t}N(d_2)\right]$$

The expression for d_1 in terms of t is

$$d_1 = \frac{\ln\frac{S}{X} + \left(r_c + \frac{\sigma^2}{2}\right)t}{\sigma\sqrt{t}},$$

and

$$\frac{\partial d_1}{\partial t} = \frac{\left(r_c + \frac{\sigma^2}{2}\right)\sigma\sqrt{t} + \frac{\sigma}{2\sqrt{t}}\left(\ln\frac{S}{X} + \left(r_c + \frac{\sigma^2}{2}\right)t\right)}{\sigma^2 t}$$

$$= \frac{\left(r_c + \frac{\sigma^2}{2}\right)t + \frac{1}{2}\left(\ln\frac{S}{X} + \left(r_c + \frac{\sigma^2}{2}\right)t\right)}{\sigma t^{\frac{3}{2}}}$$

$$= \frac{\left(r_c + \frac{\sigma^2}{2}\right)3t + \ln\frac{S}{X}}{2\sigma t^{\frac{3}{2}}}$$

The expression for d_2 in terms of t is

$$d_2 = \frac{\ln \frac{S}{X} + \left(r_c - \frac{\sigma^2}{2}\right)t}{\sigma\sqrt{t}},$$

and

$$\frac{\partial d_2}{\partial t} = \frac{\left(r_c - \frac{\sigma^2}{2}\right)\sigma\sqrt{t} + \frac{\sigma}{2\sqrt{t}}\left(\ln \frac{S}{X} + \left(r_c - \frac{\sigma^2}{2}\right)t\right)}{\sigma^2 t}$$

$$= \frac{\left(r_c - \frac{\sigma^2}{2}\right)t + \frac{1}{2}\left(\ln \frac{S}{X} + \left(r_c - \frac{\sigma^2}{2}\right)t\right)}{\sigma t^{\frac{3}{2}}}$$

$$= \frac{\left(r_c - \frac{\sigma^2}{2}\right)3t + \ln \frac{S}{X}}{2\sigma t^{\frac{3}{2}}}$$

Theta for a call is therefore

$$\frac{\partial C}{\partial t} = Se^{-(r_l - r_c)t}\left[-(r_l - r_c)N(d_1) + \frac{\partial}{\partial t}N(d_1)\right] + Xe^{-r_l t}\left[r_l N(d_2) - \frac{\partial}{\partial t}N(d_2)\right]$$

$$= Se^{-(r_l - r_c)}\left[-(r_l - r_c)N(d_1) + \frac{\left(r_c + \frac{\sigma^2}{2}\right)3t + \ln \frac{S}{X}}{2\sigma t^{\frac{3}{2}}}N'(d_1)\right]$$

$$+ Xe^{-r_l t}\left[r_l N(d_2) - \frac{\left(r_c - \frac{\sigma^2}{2}\right)3t + \ln \frac{S}{X}}{2\sigma t^{\frac{3}{2}}}N'(d_2)\right]$$

67 *What happens to the value of theta for a call and a put when volatility approaches zero?*

As we have already seen when volatility σ is very small the value of the call option will be

$$C = \begin{cases} 0 & \text{if } S < Xe^{-r_c t} \\ Se^{-(r_l - r_c)t} - Xe^{-r_l t} & \text{if } S > Xe^{-r_c t} \end{cases}$$

Differentiating with respect to t

$$\frac{\partial C}{\partial t} = \begin{cases} 0 & \text{if } S < Xe^{-r_c t} \\ -S(r_l - r_c)e^{-(r_l - r_c)t} + r_l Xe^{-r_l t} & \text{if } S > Xe^{-r_c t} \end{cases}$$

For a put option

$$P = \begin{cases} -Se^{-(r_l - r_c)t} + Xe^{-r_l t} & \text{if } S < Xe^{-r_c t} \\ 0 & \text{if } S > Xe^{-r_c t} \end{cases}$$

Differentiating with respect to t

$$\frac{\partial P}{\partial t} = \begin{cases} S(r_l - r_c)e^{-(r_l - r_c)t} - r_l Xe^{-r_l t} & \text{if } S < Xe^{-r_c t} \\ 0 & \text{if } S > Xe^{-r_c t} \end{cases}$$

414

When $S = Xe^{-r_c t}$

$$\left.\frac{\partial C}{\partial t}\right|_{S=Xe^{-r_c t}} = -Xe^{-r_c t}(r_l - r_c)e^{-(r_l-r_c)t} - r_l Xe^{-r_l t}$$

$$= -Xe^{-r_l t}(r_l - r_c) + r_l Xe^{-r_l t}$$

$$= r_c Xe^{-r_l t}$$

68 *Derive the value of volatility sensitivity, vega, for a call option by differentiating the expression for the value of a call (Equation 11.3) with respect to σ using the Black-Scholes model.*

To find vega we start with our expression for the call

$$C = SN(d_1)e^{-(r_l-r_c)t} - Xe^{-r_l t}N(d_2)$$

We differentiate with respect to σ,

$$\frac{\partial C}{\partial \sigma} = Se^{-(r_l-r_c)t}\frac{\partial d_1}{\partial \sigma}N'(d_1) - Xe^{-r_l t}\frac{\partial d_2}{\partial \sigma}N'(d_2).$$

The expression for d_1 is

$$d_1 = \frac{\ln\frac{S}{X} + \left(r_c + \frac{\sigma^2}{2}\right)t}{\sigma\sqrt{t}},$$

and

$$\frac{\partial d_1}{\partial \sigma} = \frac{\sqrt{t}}{2}.$$

The expression for d_2 is

$$d_2 = \frac{\ln\frac{S}{X} + \left(r_c - \frac{\sigma^2}{2}\right)t}{\sigma\sqrt{t}},$$

and

$$\frac{\partial d_2}{\partial \sigma} = \frac{-\sqrt{t}}{2}.$$

$$\frac{\partial C}{\partial \sigma} = Se^{-(r_l-r_c)t}\frac{\sqrt{t}}{2}N'(d_1) + Xe^{-r_l t}\frac{\sqrt{t}}{2}N'(d_2)$$

$$= Se^{-(r_l-r_c)t}\frac{\sqrt{t}}{2}\frac{e^{-\frac{d_1^2}{2}}}{\sqrt{2\pi}} + Xe^{-r_l t}\frac{\sqrt{t}}{2}\frac{e^{-\frac{d_2^2}{2}}}{\sqrt{2\pi}}$$

$$= \frac{e^{-r_l t}}{2}\sqrt{\frac{t}{2\pi}}\left(Se^{r_c t}e^{-\frac{d_1^2}{2}} + Xe^{-\frac{d_2^2}{2}}\right)$$

We have already seen when deriving a value for delta that $Se^{r_c t}e^{-\frac{d_1^2}{2}} = Xe^{-\frac{d_2^2}{2}}$, so

$$\frac{\partial C}{\partial \sigma} = \frac{e^{-r_l t}\sqrt{t}}{\sqrt{2\pi}}Se^{r_c t}e^{-\frac{d_1^2}{2}}$$

$$= \sqrt{\frac{t}{2\pi}}Se^{-(r_l-r_c)t}e^{-\frac{d_1^2}{2}}$$

69 *Show that the volatility sensitivity, vega, for a put option is the same as that of a call option by differentiating the expression for the value of a put (Equation 11.4) with respect to σ.*

To find vega we start with our expression for the put

$$P = -SN(-d_1)e^{-(r_l-r_c)t} + Xe^{-r_lt}N(-d_2)$$

and we differentiate with respect to σ,

$$\frac{\partial P}{\partial \sigma} = Se^{-(r_l-r_c)t}\frac{\partial d_1}{\partial \sigma}N'(-d_1) - Xe^{-r_lt}\frac{\partial d_2}{\partial \sigma}N'(-d_2).$$

We already know from calculating vega for a call in the previous question that $\frac{\partial d_1}{\partial \sigma} = \frac{\sqrt{t}}{2}$ and $\frac{\partial d_2}{\partial \sigma} = \frac{-\sqrt{t}}{2}$. So

$$
\begin{aligned}
\frac{\partial P}{\partial \sigma} &= Se^{-(r_l-r_c)t}\frac{\sqrt{t}}{2}N'(d_1) + Xe^{-r_lt}\frac{\sqrt{t}}{2}N'(d_2) \\
&= Se^{-(r_l-r_c)t}\frac{\sqrt{t}}{2}\frac{e^{-\frac{d_1^2}{2}}}{\sqrt{2\pi}} + Xe^{-r_lt}\frac{\sqrt{t}}{2}\frac{e^{-\frac{d_2^2}{2}}}{\sqrt{2\pi}} \\
&= \frac{e^{-r_lt}}{2}\sqrt{\frac{t}{2\pi}}\left(Se^{r_ct}e^{-\frac{d_1^2}{2}} + Xe^{-\frac{d_2^2}{2}}\right)
\end{aligned}
$$

This is identical to the expression for vega for a call so $\frac{\partial P}{\partial \sigma} = \frac{\partial C}{\partial \sigma}$ as we would expect as a call and a put have identical volatility value.

70 *Express vega in terms of gamma.*

Vega is

$$\nu = \frac{\sqrt{t}S}{\sqrt{2\pi}}e^{-(r_l-r_c)t}e^{-\frac{d_1^2}{2}},$$

and gamma is

$$\Gamma = \frac{1}{S\sigma\sqrt{2\pi t}}e^{-(r_l-r_c)t}e^{-\frac{d_1^2}{2}},$$

so

$$
\begin{aligned}
\frac{\nu}{\Gamma} &= S\sigma\sqrt{2\pi t}\frac{\sqrt{t}S}{\sqrt{2\pi}} \\
&= \sigma S^2 t,
\end{aligned}
$$

and

$$\nu = \sigma S^2 t\Gamma$$

71 *Derive the value of rho for a call option by differentiating the expression for the value of a call (Equation 11.3) with respect to the long rate r_l using the Black-Scholes model.*

Starting with our expression for the call value

$$C = SN(d_1)e^{-(r_l-r_c)t} - Xe^{-r_l t}N(d_2)$$

We differentiate with respect to r_l,

$$
\begin{aligned}
\frac{\partial C}{\partial r_l} &= -tSN(d_1)e^{-(r_l-r_c)t} + Se^{-(r_l-r_c)t}\frac{\partial}{\partial r_l}N(d_1) + tXe^{-r_l t}N(d_2) - Xe^{-r_l t}\frac{\partial}{\partial r_l}N(d_2) \\
&= Se^{-(r_l-r_c)t}\left[-tN(d_1) + \frac{\partial}{\partial r_l}N(d_1)\right] + Xe^{-r_l t}\left[tN(d_2) - \frac{\partial}{\partial r_l}N(d_2)\right]
\end{aligned}
$$

The expression for d_1 is

$$d_1 = \frac{\ln\frac{S}{X} + \left(r_c + \frac{\sigma^2}{2}\right)t}{\sigma\sqrt{t}},$$

and if this has no terms in r_l the derivative $\frac{\partial d_1}{\partial r_l} = 0$. But if the carry rate r_c has a dependency on the long rate r_l the derivative $\frac{\partial d_1}{\partial r_l}$ will not be zero. For an equity that pays a dividend the carry rate is the difference between the long rate and the dividend $r_c = r_l - r_d$ and d_1 in this case would be $\frac{\partial d_1}{\partial r_l} = \frac{\sqrt{t}}{\sigma}$, and $\frac{\partial}{\partial r_l}N(d_1) = N'(d_1)\frac{\partial d_1}{\partial r_l} = \frac{\sqrt{t}}{\sigma\sqrt{2\pi}}e^{-\frac{d_1^2}{2}}$. Similarly, $\frac{\partial d_2}{\partial r_l} = \frac{\sqrt{t}}{\sigma}$ and $\frac{\partial}{\partial r_l}N(d_2) = \frac{\sqrt{t}}{\sigma\sqrt{2\pi}}e^{-\frac{d_2^2}{2}}$. For an equity the difference between the long rate and the carry rate is the continuous dividend rate $r_l - r_c = r_d$ which means one of the terms drops out of our derivative because it lacks dependence on r_l. Rho for a call on a dividend paying equity is therefore

$$
\begin{aligned}
\frac{\partial C}{\partial r_l} &= Se^{-r_d t}\frac{\partial}{\partial r_l}N(d_1) + tXe^{-r_l t}N(d_2) - Xe^{-r_l t}\frac{\partial}{\partial r_l}N(d_2) \\
&= Se^{-r_d t}\frac{\sqrt{t}}{\sigma\sqrt{2\pi}}e^{-\frac{d_1^2}{2}} + tXe^{-r_l t}N(d_2) - Xe^{-r_l t}\frac{\sqrt{t}}{\sigma\sqrt{2\pi}}e^{-\frac{d_2^2}{2}} \\
&= \frac{\sqrt{t}}{\sigma\sqrt{2\pi}}\left[Se^{-r_d t}e^{-\frac{d_1^2}{2}} - Xe^{-r_l t}e^{-\frac{d_2^2}{2}}\right] + tXe^{-r_l t}N(d_2) \\
&= \frac{\sqrt{t}}{\sigma\sqrt{2\pi}}e^{-r_l t}\left[Se^{r_c t}e^{-\frac{d_1^2}{2}} - Xe^{-\frac{d_2^2}{2}}\right] + tXe^{-r_l t}N(d_2)
\end{aligned}
$$

It turns out that the value in parentheses $Se^{r_c t}e^{-\frac{d_1^2}{2}} - Xe^{-\frac{d_2^2}{2}} = 0$ (see exercise for the derivation of delta). So

$$\frac{\partial C}{\partial r_l} = tXe^{-r_l t}N(d_2)$$

For a put

$$P = -SN(-d_1)e^{-(r_l-r_c)t} + Xe^{-r_l t}N(-d_2),$$

and for an equity in particular

$$P = -SN(-d_1)e^{-r_d t} + Xe^{-r_l t}N(-d_2)$$

So

$$\begin{aligned}
\frac{\partial P}{\partial r_l} &= -Se^{-r_dt}\frac{\partial}{\partial r_l}N(-d_1) - tXe^{-r_lt}N(-d_2) + Xe^{-r_lt}\frac{\partial}{\partial r_l}N(-d_2) \\
&= -Se^{-r_dt}\frac{\sqrt{t}}{\sigma\sqrt{2\pi}}e^{-\frac{d_1^2}{2}} + \frac{\sqrt{t}}{\sigma\sqrt{2\pi}}Xe^{-r_lt}e^{-\frac{d_2^2}{2}} - tXe^{-r_lt}N(-d_2) \\
&= -\frac{\sqrt{t}}{\sigma\sqrt{2\pi}}e^{-r_lt}\left[Se^{r_ct}e^{-\frac{d_1^2}{2}} - Xe^{-\frac{d_2^2}{2}}\right] - tXe^{-r_lt}N(-d_2) \\
&= -tXe^{-r_lt}N(-d_2).
\end{aligned}$$

72 *For at-the-money-forward calls and puts where $X = F$ find the value of d_1 and d_2 in the Black-Scholes option pricing formula on page 373.*

For at-the-money-forward options with strikes equal to the forward price the Black-Scholes formula simplifies. The forward price $F = Se^{r_ct}$ so d_1 can be rewritten

$$d_1 = \frac{\ln\frac{S}{X} + \left(r_c + \frac{\sigma^2}{2}\right)t}{\sigma\sqrt{t}} = \frac{\ln\frac{F}{X} + \frac{\sigma^2 t}{2}}{\sigma\sqrt{t}}.$$

When the forward price is equal to strike $F = X$, then $\ln\frac{F}{X} = 0$ and this term drops out of the equation for d_1. The expression for d_1 simplifies to $d_1 = \frac{\sigma\sqrt{t}}{2}$ and $d_2 = d_1 - \sigma\sqrt{t} = -\frac{\sigma\sqrt{t}}{2}$.

73 *Given your values for d_1 and d_2 find an expression for the value of the ATMF call and put.*

The value of a call option $C = e^{-r_lt}[FN(d_1) - XN(d_2)]$ and as $F = X$ we can derive the following expression for at-the-money-forward call and put options

$$C_{ATMF} = P_{ATMF} = Xe^{-r_lt}\left[N\left(\frac{\sigma\sqrt{t}}{2}\right) - N\left(-\frac{\sigma\sqrt{t}}{2}\right)\right].$$

Of course these are equal because ATMF calls and puts must have equal value due to put call parity.

74 *Draw a normal density curve and mark the values of d_1 and d_2. Shade in the areas $N(d_1)$ and $N(d_2)$. What area corresponds to the value of the ATMF call and put options? Can you approximate this area?*

The term $N\left(\frac{\sigma\sqrt{t}}{2}\right) - N\left(-\frac{\sigma\sqrt{t}}{2}\right)$ is the area under the normal density curve lying a small distance $\frac{\sigma\sqrt{t}}{2}$ above and below a forward value of zero. This can be roughly approximated with a rectangle with height equal to the peak value of the normal density $\frac{1}{\sqrt{2\pi}}$ and width equal to $2 \times d_1$ as illustrated in Figure 11.5. We know that $d_1 = \frac{\sigma\sqrt{t}}{2}$ so the width of the rectangle is twice this, $\sigma\sqrt{t}$. The area of the rectangle is then $\frac{\sigma\sqrt{t}}{\sqrt{2\pi}}$. One over the square root of 2π is roughly $\frac{2}{5} = 0.4$ (actually 0.3989). So the at-the-money-forward call (or put) value ignoring discounting is roughly

$$C_{ATMF} = P_{ATMF} \approx \frac{2}{5}X\sigma\sqrt{t}$$

75 *Delta for a call option is $N(d_1)$. Sketch this area on your normal density graph. Can you approximate this area?*

We know that delta for a call when carry rate is zero is $N(d_1)$. We also know that d_1 is positive because volatility is always positive, as is the square root of time to expiry. So the value $N(d_1)$ can be split into the area to the left of the mid-point of the normal distribution, which must have an area of 0.5, and the rectangle to the right of the mid-point. This rectangle has half the area of the one we used to value the ATMF call and put. So its area is $d_1 \times \frac{1}{\sqrt{2\pi}}$ and as $d_1 = \frac{1}{2}\sigma\sqrt{t}$ the area is $\frac{\sigma\sqrt{t}}{2\sqrt{2\pi}}$. The approximate value of $\frac{1}{2\sqrt{2\pi}} = 0.1995$ is $\frac{1}{5}$. The ATMF call option delta approximation is therefore

$$\Delta_{\text{ATMF}}^{\text{call}} \approx 0.5 + \frac{\sigma\sqrt{t}}{5}.$$

76 *Can you find an approximation of delta for the ATMF put option?*

For a put the expression for delta is $-N(-d_1)$ if we assume the carry rate and the long rate are zero. In this case the area of interest is can again be broken into two components. The first component is the area to the left of the mid-point, which is a half. But now as $-d_1$ lies to the left of the mid-point we subtract the area in our d_1 by $\frac{1}{\sqrt{2\pi}}$ rectangle to give

$$\Delta_{\text{ATMF}}^{\text{put}} \approx 0.5 - \frac{\sigma\sqrt{t}}{5}.$$

77 *Find the zero-edge put offer price using the method above. You are lifted on your put offer price P_{offer} and have to hedge your position. Do you buy or sell stock and calls and at bid or offer price? Find your offer price by setting the payoff at expiry to zero.*

Consider our hedging strategy when we are lifted on our put offer. We would sell the put at price P_{offer} and simultaneously sell stock at the bid price s_{bid} and buy a call at the offer price c_{offer}.

Cash flows today

Lifted on offer, sell 100 put	$+P_{\text{offer}}$
Buy 100 call	$-c_{\text{offer}}$
Sell XYZ share	$+s_{\text{bid}}$
Borrow	$-s_{\text{bid}} + c_{\text{offer}} - P_{\text{offer}}$

Cash flows at expiry

Settle options	$+X$
Repay	$(s_{\text{bid}} - c_{\text{offer}} + P_{\text{offer}})(1 + rt)$

Which gives

$$s_{\text{bid}} - c_{\text{offer}} + P_{\text{offer}} = \frac{X}{1 + rt}$$

$$P_{\text{offer}} = \frac{X}{1 + rt} - s_{\text{bid}} + c_{\text{offer}}$$

78 *Find the value of an at-the-money forward three month EUR call USD put on €10,000,000 face given that EUR | USD spot is trading at 1.4752, the three month USD interest rate is 0.288%, the three month EUR interest rate is 0.416% and the EUR | USD rate volatility is 10%. Start by calculating the three month forward EUR | USD exchange rate then either use Black-Scholes or the ATMF approximation of Black-Scholes (see Section 11.4 on page 383) to find the value of the call option.*

Firstly the three month forward EUR | USD rate calculated using interest rate parity (see Section 9.1.2 on page 330),

$$EUR|USD_{3m} = 1.4752 \times \frac{1 + 0.00288 \times \frac{90}{360}}{1 + 0.00416 \times \frac{90}{360}} = 1.47473$$

If we approximate the value of the ATMF call using the two fifths rule

$$
\begin{aligned}
C_{ATMF} &\simeq \frac{2}{5} X \sigma \sqrt{t} \\
&= \frac{2}{5} \times 1.47473 \times 0.1. \times \sqrt{\frac{1}{4}} \\
&= 0.02949
\end{aligned}
$$

So the right to buy 1 EUR for 1.47473 USD in three months time costs 0.02949 USD today. Using the FX form of the Black-Scholes formula

$$
\begin{aligned}
d_1 &= \frac{\ln \frac{1.4752}{1.474728} + \left(0.00288 - 0.00416 + \frac{0.1^2}{2}\right) \frac{1}{4}}{0.1 \times \sqrt{\frac{1}{4}}} = 0.02499437 \\
d_2 &= 0.02497303 - 0.1 \times \sqrt{\frac{1}{4}} = -0.02500563 \\
C &= 1.4752 \times e^{-0.00416 \times 0.25} \times N(0.02497303) - 1.47473 \times e^{-0.00288 \times 0.25} \times N(-0.02502697) \\
&= 0.02939213
\end{aligned}
$$

The ATMF approximation was 0.02949 which was close to the Black-Scholes value.

79 *In what units was the previous call premium? Complete the sentence: _ is the cost in _ for the right but not the obligation to buy _ EUR for _ USD in three months time.*

The premium was expressed in USD. "0.02939 is the cost in USD for the right but not the obligation to buy 1 EUR for 1.47473 USD in three months time."

80 *Express the premium in EUR per 1 USD, then as a percentage of the EUR face amount.*

The premium for the "right to buy 1 EUR for 1.47473 USD in three months time" is 0.02939213 USD. To find the premium for the right to buy 1 USD, expressed in USD, we divide by the strike

$$\frac{0.02939213}{1.4747} = 0.01993092$$

To find the premium to buy 1 USD in EUR we divide by the spot rate

$$\frac{0.01993092}{1.4752} = 0.01351066$$

The premium is 0.01351066 EUR per 1 USD.

12 Option Strategies & Structured Notes

12.1 Option Strategies

Options come into their own when combined to produce complex payoffs. These are called strategies and reflect varying investment goals. Some option strategies enhance yield, others limit risk yet others do both. Yield enhancement involves selling options and receiving premium and limiting risk involves buying options to remove the possibility of large losses. We will list some of the more common, named strategies here but in practice over time a trader or investor will build up extremely complex payoff profiles as they buy and sell in response to changes in the market.

12.1.1 Straddle

A straddle is one of the oldest strategies and involves buying both a put and a call with the same strike and maturity. Of course buying two options implies a hefty premium paid out up front, particularly as the two options are usually bought at-the-money-forward. This results in a V-shaped payoff as shown in Figure 12.1. The strategy pays off if the underlying either rises or falls beyond two breakeven limits and will lose money if the underlying does not expire outside the breakeven range. This position is not directional. The owner is indifferent whether the underlying increases or decreases, but simply wants change in either direction. Straddles are "long vol" because they are more likely to profit if volatility is high and the underlying is likely to expire far from the strike.

Being long a straddle is fairly low risk because the most that the investor can lose is their premium. Being short a straddle is extremely risky because the investor has unlimited losses if the underlying shoots off in either direction. For this reason brokers will seldom allow retail investors to be short a straddle. Some investors find the straddle to be too expensive because the investor has to buy both the call and the put and these investors may choose a cheaper variant of the straddle called a STRANGLE (see Section 12.1.2 on page 424). Straddles are usually chosen to be at-the-money-forward so that we can use the approximate value in Section 11.4 (page 383). By put-call parity the value of the ATMF call and put are equal. The approximate price of a straddle with strike X, implied volatility σ and expiry time t is roughly

$$\text{Straddle} \approx \frac{4}{5}X\sigma\sqrt{t}$$

In order to break even the underlying must move by $\frac{4}{5}X\sigma\sqrt{t}$ in either direction. For a volatility of 30% and a maturity of three months this is a move of $\frac{4}{5} \times 0.30 \times \sqrt{\frac{1}{4}}$ or

12% of the strike so that the underlying must increase beyond 112% of strike or below 88% of strike before we start to profit from the straddle.

Figure 12.2 shows the value and greeks of a long 100 strike straddle position as a contour plot varying spot price and volatility. Carry rate r_c is 15% and the long rate r_l is 2%. The top-left panel shows the value of the straddle. When volatility is zero the V-shaped payoff of the straddle is visible with the bottom of the V centred at the call and put strike of 100. Adding volatility and moving toward the right hand side of the graph makes the value profile against spot become curved into a U-shape around the strike rather than a sharp V-shape. The lowest value also shifts downward to values of spot below the strike as volatility increases. The middle-top panel shows delta, which is zero at the bottom of the V- or U-shaped value profile. When volatility is zero delta is constant and negative when spot is below strike and switches sharply to positive and constant above strike as we would expect for a V-shaped value profile. Consequently the instantaneous switch from a negative to a positive delta results in an infinite gamma which is shown in the top right graph. This gamma spike is softened as volatility increases and the peak of the gamma vs. spot profile shifts to lower values of spot as volatility increases.

Vega is shown in the bottom left hand contour plot and as we would expect the straddle has a very large volatility sensitivity because it is long two options which are themselves long volatility. Vega is greatest at the bottom of the V-shape when volatility is low. However as volatility increases the value of spot with greatest vega increases. Vega reaches a maximum at a spot value of $Xe^{-\left(r_c - \frac{\sigma^2}{2}\right)t}$ which increases as volatility increases, so the spot value where the straddle has greatest volatility sensitivity detaches from the bottom of the U-shaped value profile. Theta is shown in the bottom middle panel and shows that the bottom of the U-shaped straddle payoff has theta equal to zero which means there is no time decay. The sign and magnitude of theta above and below this point depend on the cost of carry, but in this case theta is positive for spot values above the zero point, which means the straddle loses value as time passes, and negative below the zero point which means the straddle gains value as time passes. Finally rho is shown in the bottom right hand panel and shows that the interest rate sensitivity is positive for spot values above the strike and negative below the strike. Above the strike the straddle value is dominated by the call option which has positive rho because an increasing interest rate reduces an outward payment and is a benefit. Below the strike the straddle value is dominated by the put option which has negative value because increasing interest rate will reduce the size of the expiry payment which results in loss.

12.1.2 Strangle

A strangle is like a straddle but the strike of the put and the call are separated. A strangle, like a straddle, involves buying a call and a put with the same underlying and maturity but different strikes. This makes an expiry payoff that is flat at the bottom with two upward ramps as shown in Figure 12.3. More importantly it reduces the price of the strategy compared with the straddle. Increasing the call strike and decreasing the put strike reduces the moneyness of both options, and consequently reduces their premia. The drawback is that in order to make a profit the underlying

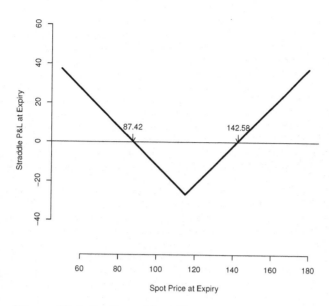

Figure 12.1: Profit and loss diagram for a straddle.

has to move further for a strangle than it would with a straddle. At the risk of sounding more like a reference on fetishes than finance, a strangle is a poor man's straddle because it is a cheaper way to get a non-directional volatility position.

12.1.3 Buy-Write or Over-Write

If an investor is bullish about a stock they may buy a call option. This gives them unlimited participation in the upside of the stock above the strike and limits their loss to the premium they pay up front. But what if the investor believes in limited upside? For example they may believe that in the next three months Apple would increase by 10%. But do they really believe that it would increase by 20%, or 30% or 1000%? This potential upside is factored into the premium, but the investor does not have to pay for eventualities which they consider outlandish. They can buy the stock and simultaneously sell an out of the money call option on the stock. This flattens out their upside beyond the strike because they have sold away all the extremely high returns. This leaves them with a limited upside and all the downside, and an enhanced yield by receiving the call option premium. The payoff is shown in Figure 12.4. This is called a buy-write because you buy the stock and write a call option.

If the stock increases up to and slightly beyond the strike price the premium received for selling the call option enhances the yield of the stock. If the stock is trading above the strike price at expiry the investor will be assigned on the call option and have to sell the stock they already own at the strike price so this is not as dangerous as writing a naked call option. One drawback with this strategy is that the investor is keeping all of the downside risk of the stock. When considering the strike there is a tradeoff between the premium received and the maximum return. If the call strike

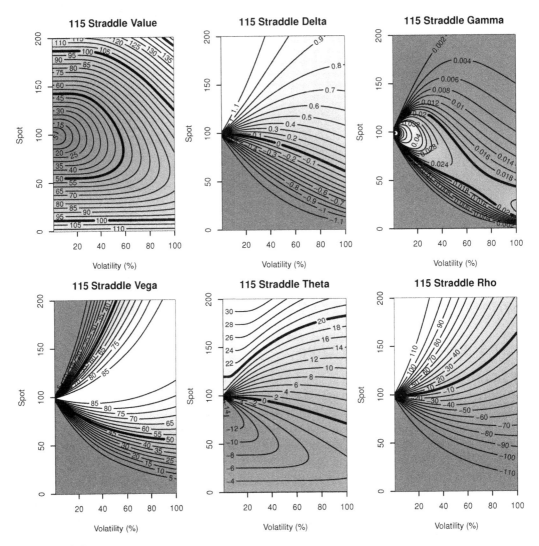

Figure 12.2:
Straddle risk measure plots varying volatility and spot price. Strike is 100, carry rate is 15%, long rate is 2%.

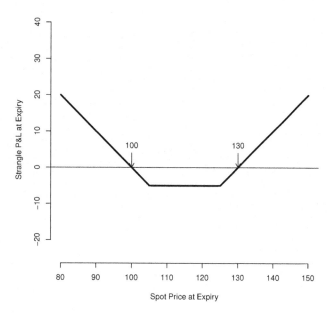

Figure 12.3: Profit and loss diagram for a strangle.

chosen is to be high and out of the money it would have a tiny premium but the maximum return cap would be very high. If the call strike is low and deep in the money it will generate a large premium but impose a very restrictive upside cap on returns.

12.1.4 Protective Put

A protective put is the opposite stance to a buy-write. Whereas a buy-write sells off unbelievably high upside and keeps all the downside, a protective put buys insurance against extreme downside and keeps all the upside. In the florid language of finance this is called "KILLING THE TAIL RISK". This strategy involves buying the underlying and buying an out of the money put at a strike below the current spot. The overall position participates in all the unlimited upside of the stock, albeit slightly reduced by the premium of the put. The benefit of the put is that it caps losses at the strike price of the put. This is clearly a hedging strategy. Although the payoff of the overall strategy resembles a call (see Figure 12.5) the funding of the position is quite different because it requires a large initial outlay of capital both to buy the stock and to buy the put. In the figure the dotted line is the payoff for the stock on its own. This highlights the fact that all upside returns are decreased compared with the "naked" stock position, as a consequence of paying the put premium.

Given that the payoff of the protective put strategy is the same as a call you may wonder why investors do not simply buy a call. One reason is dividend payments. By putting up capital to buy the stock the investor is entitled to receive dividend payments whereas the owner of a call option would not receive dividends. For a stock that does not pay dividends, call options may be a better way to express bullish beliefs. Many investors choose not to kill their tail risk with a protective put because they do

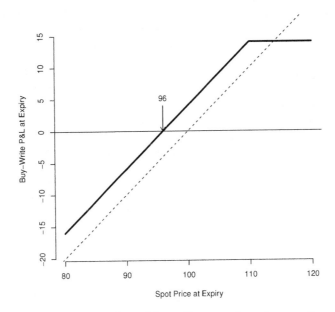

Figure 12.4: Profit and loss diagram for a buy-write.

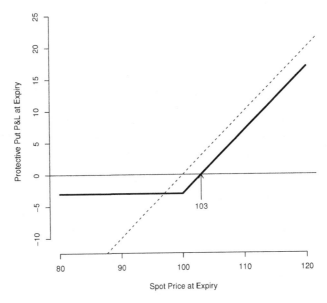

Figure 12.5: Profit and loss diagram for a protective put.

not want to pay the put premium on top of the cost of buying the stock. There is some leeway in this strategy. When choosing the put strike we have a tradeoff between the size of potential losses against the cost of buying the put. The put premium can be reduced by choosing a put option that has a lower strike and is further out of the money but this is at the cost of increased potential losses.

12.1.5 Collar

A collar is a bullish strategy with limited downside and limited upside. A collar involves buying the underlying, buying a low strike protective put and selling a high strike call. Buying the underlying gives the strategy a long exposure profiting when the underlying increases in value and losing money when the underlying decreases in value. Buying a protective put limits the loss on this strategy to the low strike with the disadvantage of having to pay a premium for the put at the outset of the trade. Selling the high strike call partially pays for the premium of buying the put but this comes at the price of limiting the return on the strategy. This strategy is most advantageous in cases where owning the underlying generates a benefit, such as holding a stock that pays a high dividend. If owning the underlying comes with little or no benefit, or even a cost, then a call spread would be a better strategy because the payoff of a collar and call spread are identical. One disadvantage of a collar is that the investor has to buy the underlying at the outset which can be expensive compared to buying a call spread.

12.1.6 Call Spread & Put Spread

To make a BULL CALL SPREAD we buy a low-strike call and sell a high strike call. The overall position is flat below the low strike and above the high strike, as shown in Figure 12.6. The zone of interest lies between the two strikes. This position is directional and bullish because it profits from an increase in the value of the underlying. It limits the maximum loss to the premia paid and received for the two options but also caps the maximum gain to the difference between the strikes. The low-strike call is deeper in the money and therefore more expensive than the high strike call. This means that the cost of buying the low-strike call is partially offset by receiving the premium for selling the high-strike call.

This strategy is like a collar which is a combination of the buy-write, which is long the underlying but sells off improbably large returns, and the protective put which kills the tail risk. Although the payoff of a collar is the same as a call spread the cash flows are quite different. A collar involves the costly purchase of a stock as the trade is put on, whereas a call spread is leveraged and requires a smaller up-front payment of option premium. The maximum profit of a call spread at expiry is determined by the high strike minus the low strike minus the total premia required to put on the strategy. Strictly speaking the sum of premia would be future valued to expiry. Constructing a call spread involves careful choice of the two strikes. If the high strike is too close to the spot price today then we will take in a large premium for selling the call but we are severely capping our upside. If the high strike is too high then we will

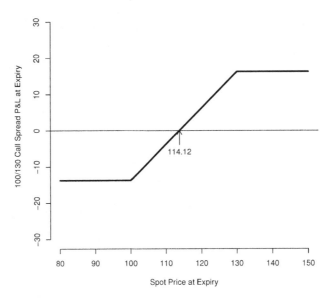

Figure 12.6: Call spread expiry profit and loss diagram.

not take in much premium for its sale although we will keep a lot of upside. Similarly the strike of the low-strike call cannot be too low, because it becomes expensive.

We construct a BEAR CALL SPREAD by reversing the two call positions; that means we sell a low-strike call and buy a high-strike call. This is an attractive trade because we are selling an expensive in-the-money low-strike call option and buying a cheaper out-of-the-money high-strike call option. So we take in a net premium as the trade starts and keep the premium if the stock price does not move upward beyond our breakeven price. Because we take in money on day one of the trade this is also called a CREDIT SPREAD (not to be confused with the credit spread of a bond in the world of fixed income and credit).

The BEAR PUT SPREAD payoff is the mirror image of the bull call spread, as shown in Figure 12.8. This strategy is constructed by buying a high-strike put and selling a low-strike put; the sale of the low-strike put partially pays for the more expensive and deeper in the money high-strike put. The overall position is bearish because it profits when the underlying decreases in value. The maximum loss is limited to the premia of the options and the maximum gain is capped at the difference between the strikes of the puts. Just as we saw for the bear call spread we can reverse the trades and sell a high-strike put and buy a low-strike put and this is a BULL PUT SPREAD. Just like the bear call spread the bull put spread strategy takes in a premium up-front because we are selling an expensive option and buying a cheaper option.

Put call parity means that any payoff that is constructed with calls can be constructed with puts. We have seen that the bull spread can be made with call options or put options. Similarly a bear spread can be constructed with call options or put options. A bull call spread expiry profit and loss graph looks identical to a bull put spread expiry profit and loss graph. However the timing of cash flows is quite different

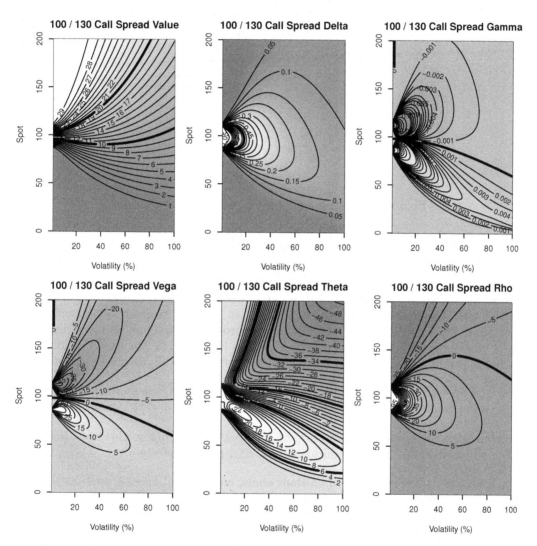

Figure 12.7: Call spread risk measure plots varying volatility and spot price.

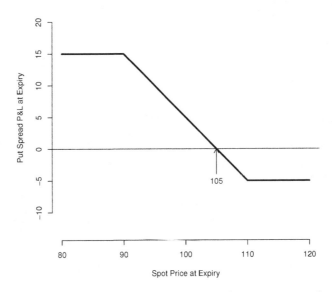

Figure 12.8: Profit and loss diagram for a put spread.

for the two strategies. A bull call spread involves buying an expensive in-the-money low-strike call option and selling a cheaper out-of-the-money high-strike call option. The initial premium outlay for a bull call spread is negative. A bull put spread involves selling an expensive high-strike put and buying a cheaper low-strike put. The initial outlay for a bull put spread is positive, so we take in money when we put on the trade. The expiry theoretical value, expiry profit and loss and cash flow diagrams for a both forms of bull spread are illustrated in Figure 12.9. The cash flow diagram in the top right and bottom right graphs show that the cash flows are reversed:

Bull Call Spread Pay net premium of $13.77 to put on the trade and receive at expiry a payment between $0 and $30 depending on the value of the underlying.

Bull Put Spread Receive net premium of $16.23 when putting on the trade then lose between $0 and $30 depending on the value of the underlying.

For a broker it is more risky when their client has a credit spread, such as the bull put spread. This is because the client is being *paid* to put on the trade so it will be tempting to put on a very large trade. The larger the trade the greater the potential loss at expiry, and the investor may not have the discipline to put money aside to cover their potential loss. The bull call spread is much safer to the broker because the client gives their premium when the trade begins and can lose no more than this premium at expiry. For this reason brokers may demand some margin when their investors have a credit spread.

Exercise 81 *The market for Sprocket Corp 100 and 130 strike call and put options is as follows:*

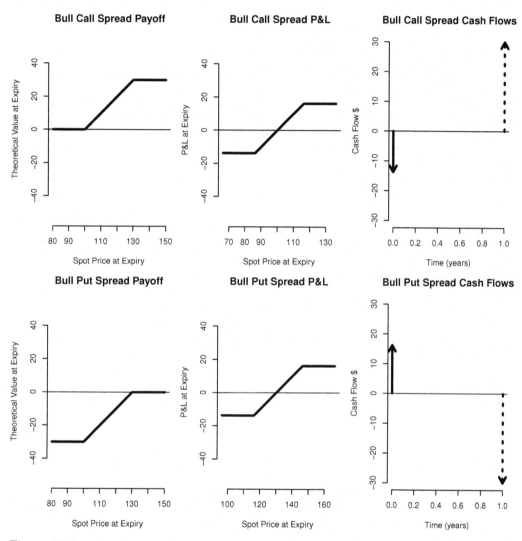

Figure 12.9:
Bull call spread and bull put spread expiry payoff, expiry profit and loss and cash flows.

| 100 Call | 22.10 | 130 Call | 8.60 |
| 100 Put | 6.23 | 130 Put | 22.15 |

What options would you buy to construct a 100/130 bull call spread? How much would this cost? Could you construct the same payoff with put options, and if so how much would the position cost?

12.1.7 Risk Reversal

A RISK REVERSAL, known informally as a RISKY, is an option position that is designed to profit from the skew of an underlying. If you buy an out-of-the-money put option and sell an out-of-the-money call option and both are equally out-of-the-money, say 30 delta, then they should have equal value in the Black Scholes world. However this is frequently not true due to the VOLATILITY SMILE. The smile can simply be driven by supply and demand. In the world of equity options people are mostly long stock so they will be most concerned by down crashes, so there is a high demand for out of the money puts. At the same time people want to buy out of the money call options to profit from the upward drift of stock prices. These tendencies push up the price of the low and high strike options relative to at-the-money options so a plot of implied volatility against strike resembles a smile.

The shape of the smile may not be symmetric, making it look more like a smirk. Traders summarize the pricing of risk reversals by describing the market as PUTS OVER CALLS or CALLS OVER PUTS. If the market is trading puts over calls then buying a 30 delta put will cost more than is made by selling a 30 delta call even though both options have the same moneyness. The risk reversal expiry profit and loss diagram for a puts over calls market is shown in Figure 12.10. Here we bought a 30 delta put and sold a 30 delta call and as volatility at the put strike was worth more than volatility at the call strike the overall premium was negative. We will profit if the market starts to trade more toward puts over calls, which means that the implied volatility of the downside put increases relative to the upside call.

12.1.8 Butterfly

A BUTTERFLY, known informally as a FLY, is a strategy for harvesting the kurtosis of an underlying. One way to construct a butterfly is to be long a straddle which forms the V-shaped head of the butterfly and short a strangle that creates the flattened wings. Alternatively a butterfly can be constructed entirely of calls or entirely of puts. A CALL BUTTERFLY involves selling a low-strike call, buying two mid-strike calls and selling a high-strike call. A PUT BUTTERFLY involves buying a high-strike put, selling two mid-strike puts and buying a low-strike put. An IRON BUTTERFLY consists of a long straddle (buy a call and a put at the mid-strike) and short strangle position (sell the high-strike call and sell the low-strike put). The profit and loss diagram at expiry for a 90/100/110 call butterfly is shown in Figure 12.11. When deciding which way to put on the trade people usually think in terms of BUY THE BELLY and SELL THE WINGS if they expect the mid-strike to go up in price relative to the wings, or they sell

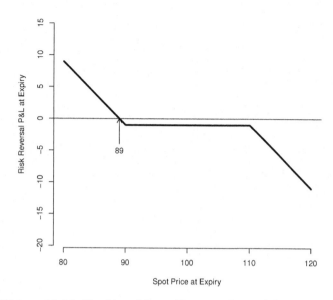

Figure 12.10: Profit and loss diagram for a risk reversal.

the belly and buy the wings if they expect the mid-strike option to go down in price relative to the wings.

A butterfly is not a directional strategy because the payoff has symmetric flat wings and a mini-straddle as its head and neither the flat wings nor the straddle are directional. The strategy is long volatility because of the V-shaped payoff of the head. If the spot price is sitting at the bottom of the V then the strategy will lose money unless spot moves, so volatility is a desirable thing and vega is positive. Just as the spot price climbs out of the head onto the plateau volatility can only lose money by moving back into the head so vega is negative. Further out into the wings volatility sensitivity drops to zero because spot price moves hardly affect the position's value at all.

Figure 12.11 shows the value graph and greeks for a 110/115/130 call butterfly with volatilities of 1%, 10%, 30% and 100%. When volatility is low the value graph is the familiar butterfly shape with the strikes shifted downward because they are discounted at the carry rate. As volatility increases the bottom of the value well becomes more shallow and value starts to spread out into the wings. Increasing volatility changes the value graph from a V-shape to a U-shape. This shape change is reflected in the value of delta. When volatility is low the gradient of the value graph is -1 between 110 and 115, +1 between 115 and 130 and zero elsewhere just as we would expect for a V-shaped value profile. As volatility increases this digital behaviour smooths out into lower peak values of delta. In terms of gamma the graph is dominated by sharp kinks in value at the strikes for low volatility. The gamma spikes are negative for the 110 and 130 strikes where we are short call options and positive and twice as large for the central 115 strike where we are long two call options. Again this gamma profile becomes smoother and less extreme as we increase volatility.

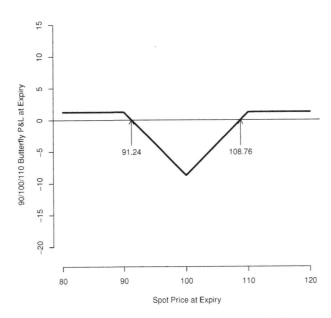

Figure 12.11: Butterfly expiry profit and loss diagram. Strikes are 90/100/110.

Exercise 82 *The market for one year Sprocket Corp 90, 100 and 110 strike call and options is as follows:*

90 Call	28.94	100 Call	22.10	110 Call	16.47

How much would it cost or earn in premium to construct a 90/100/110 butterfly today? If the continuous long rate is 2% calculate the future value of the total premium. Draw the payoff at expiry and find the breakevens.

12.1.9 Condor

A condor is a strategy that profits if the underlying expires within a range and makes a loss if the underlying expires outside that range. It is named after the rather dubious resemblance of its payoff diagram to a New World vulture. This strategy takes in a premium on the day it is constructed because it consists of a bull put spread and a bear call spread. To make the bull put spread we sell a high-strike expensive put, and buy a cheaper low-strike put. To make the bear call spread we sell the expensive low-strike call and buy the cheaper high-strike call. The strikes of the bull put spread are lower than the strikes of the bear call spread.

The expiry profit and loss diagram is shown in Figure 12.14. Here the strikes chosen are 80/90 for the bull put spread and 110/120 for the bear call spread. Today we take in $1.84 for the put spread and $4.45 for the call spread, a total of $6.29. If we calculate the future value of the total premium proceeds at expiry in one year at a continuous long rate of 2% it is $6.42. By taking in all this premium we have a high starting point

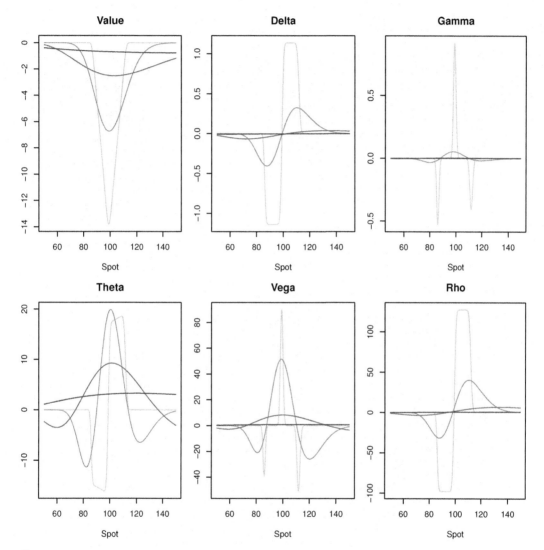

Figure 12.12:
Greeks for a butterfly. Strikes are 100/115/130, volatility 1% (light grey), 10% (dark grey), 30% (darker grey), 100% (black).

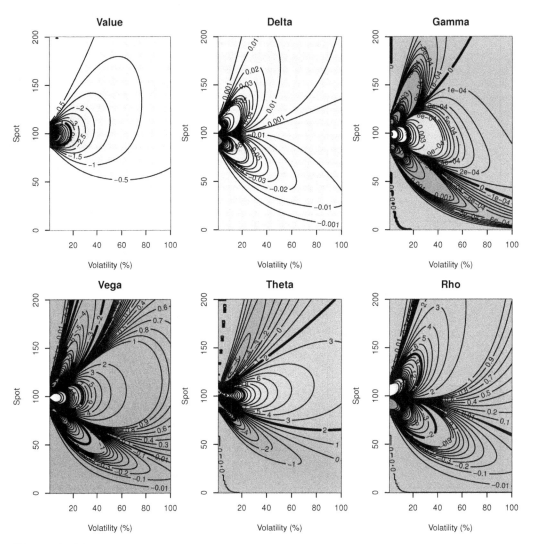

Figure 12.13:
Butterfly greeks contour diagram vs. volatility and spot. Strikes are 110/115/130.

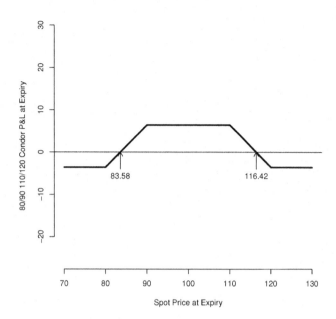

Figure 12.14: Condor expiry profit and loss diagram. Strikes are 80/90 and 110/120.

so that the underlying has to move a long way before we lose money. The breakevens are 83.58 and 116.42, so if the underlying expires in this large range we will make a profit.

12.1.10 Box

A box provides a means of profiting from mis-pricing of calls and puts when put-call parity is violated. A box is a position that is long a synthetic forward with one strike and short a synthetic forward with another strike. This means buying a call and selling a put with one strike creating a long synthetic forward, and simultaneously buying a put and selling a call with another strike creating a short synthetic forward. The payoff of this strategy at expiry is the least interesting of all strategies because it is completely flat. However the cash flows show that this is essentially a zero coupon bond.

It is very difficult to find a pair of strikes that will give a profit for this trade. This is because bid-offer spreads and commission costs are likely to be greater than very small violations of put-call parity. Institutional investors such as prop trading desks at banks, or hedge funds, are likely to spot these mis-pricings first and also be able to trade in size with low commission costs. Automated systems are usually watching for just such opportunities so they are unlikely to last for more than a few minutes.

12.1.11 Call Time Spread & Put Time Spread

A call time spread involves buying a far month expiry call option and selling a shorter expiry or near month expiry option with the same underlying and same strike. All

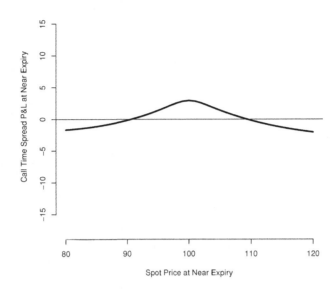

Figure 12.15: Call time spread profit and loss one day before near option expiry.

that differs between the two options is their expiry dates. This means that just before expiry of the near option the payoff is mostly the volatility value of the far option. The "hockey-stick" payoffs of the two options almost cancel one another but their volatility values do not cancel one another. Just before expiry the near option has almost no volatility value but the far option has a lot of volatility value, so the position is dominated by the volatility value of the far option. So call time spreads are a way of trading the volatility value of options, or vega.

Figure12.15 shows the profit and loss diagram of the following call time spread position:

Long far call		Short near call	
Underlying	XYZ stock	**Underlying**	XYZ stock
Strike	100	**Strike**	100
Expiry	0.5 years	**Expiry**	0.25 years
Value	$7.58	**Value**	$5.56

The continuous cash rate is 2%, the carry rate is -3%, the volatility of XYZ stock is 30% and the value of the call time spread is calculated on the day before the near option expires. Black-Scholes gives the value of the near option as $5.56 and the far option as $7.58. The future value of the total premium on the day before near expiry is -$2.03.

Volatility value is greatest near the strike of the option so this strategy has a payoff at the near option expiry date that is greatest near the strike. This strategy is profitable if the spot price is near the strike at the near option expiry date. The greater the volatility the greater the volatility value at the strike. From our approximation of the at-the-money-forward option value (Section 11.4 on page 383) we know that

$C_{\text{ATMF}} \simeq \frac{2}{5} X \sigma \sqrt{t}$ so the payoff when spot is equal to the strike price $S = X$ is directly proportional to volatility with a scaling constant of $\frac{2}{5} X \sqrt{t_{\text{near}}}$. This linearity of value with respect to volatility can be seen in the value graph of Figure 12.16 which has volatilities of 1%, 10%, 30%, 100%, 200% and 300%. In the Figure $X = 100$ and $t_{\text{near}} = 0.25$ so the call time spread values when spot is equal to strike should be roughly 0.2, 2, 6, 20, 40, and 60 as indeed they are, although the actual values are slightly lower than the estimates.

One peculiarity of call time spreads is that vega and gamma have opposite signs. For plain vanilla calls and puts vega and gamma have the same sign so if you are long gamma then you are also long vega and *vice versa*. At the near option expiry the near option has a very large gamma because of the discontinuity in the gradient of the hockey-stick payoff. As we are short this near option we have a large negative gamma near the strike price. At the same time vega of the near to expiry option is almost zero and negative and vega is large and positive for the far option, so we are net long vega near the strike. Hence our overall option position near the strike is long vega and short gamma. Short gamma is also visible in the value graph due to the negative curvature of the option value near the strike.

Note that the forward values of the two options do not cancel exactly. This is because the point at which the forward value kinks is not the strike but the strike discounted at the carry rate. For the near option this is almost exactly equal to the strike because it is only discounted for a single day at the carry rate. For the far option, however, there can be a considerable difference between the strike and the discounted value of the strike. Also the gradient of the far option forward value is not 1 but $\frac{1+r_l t}{1+r_c t}$ (see Section 11.2.1 on page 376 for an explanation) so there is some hockey-stick forward value leaking into the call time spread value. If the carry rate is equal to the long rate, as is the case for a stock that pays no dividend, then the forward value of the options cancel and all that remains is volatility value. The vega panel in Figure 12.16 shows the kink in vega near the strike because the carry rate was not equal to the long rate in this example.

Call and put time spreads, where the strikes are the same but expiries differ are called HORIZONTAL SPREADS or CALENDAR SPREADS. A spread where the expiry is the same but the strikes are different, such as a bull call spread or bear put spread, is called a VERTICAL SPREAD. If a spread varies both strike and expiry it is called a DIAGONAL SPREAD. The rationale behind these names is to imagine a table of option prices with expiry in columns and strikes in rows. So the June/September 90 strike call spread would be a horizontal spread (HH), the March expiry 100/110 call spread would be a vertical spread (VV) and the June/September 100/110 call time spread would be a diagonal spread (DD).

	March	June	Sep
90		H	H
100	V	D	
110	V		D

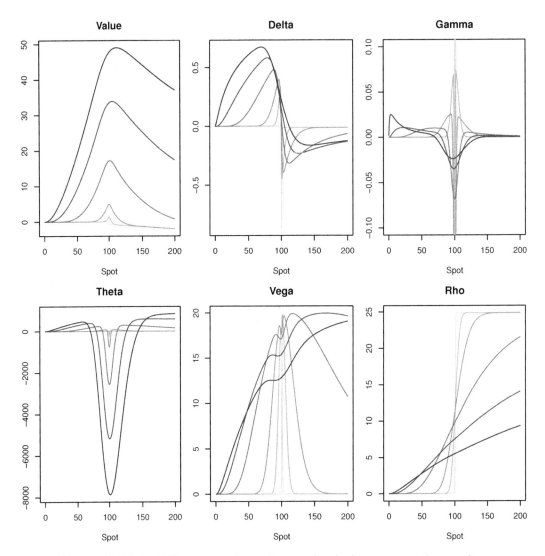

Figure 12.16: Call time spread greeks one day before near option expiry.

12.2 Structured Products

Options provide a way of turning beliefs about the behaviour of an underlying into trades. However option positions need to be monitored closely otherwise a winning position can quickly become a losing position. Banks have produced pre-packaged option packages that achieve common goals and which are well-defined in terms of risk and reward. These are known as structured products. There are three aspects to structured products: the underlying, the wrapper and the payoff. The underlying can be any market variable that interests a client such as the value of an index, an FX rate, or even the performance of an investment strategy. The wrapper can be a certificate issued by a bank or a warrant. Then according to the risk appetite of the client the payoff can either be protected on the downside offering a guaranteed minimum return and capital protection for the risk-averse, or it can offer any degree of leverage for those with a high appetite for risk. By varying these three ingredients sales staff have huge flexibility for crafting products to suit almost any investor and in return for creating the structure the issuer takes a fee.

12.2.1 Principal Protected Note

Some investors want a guaranteed return. They have $100 to invest and they want their $100 back whatever happens. At the same time they want the upside of some underlying, such as a stock index. In order to satisfy such investors investment banks came up with principal protected notes. Say we are on the structured desk at a bank and we are constructing a one year principal protected note with an initial value of $100. According to the sales person the client thinks the market is about to undergo a huge rally and so they are bullish about the S&P 500 index, which is trading at 700 today. At the same time the client is terrified about losing their money. We suggest to the sales person that a principal protected note might meet the client's requirements. The sales person agrees, pitches the product to the client who agrees to buy it. The client gives the bank their $1000 and in return receives a principal protected note. The bank buys a zero coupon bond issued by the government at a discount to its face value of $1000. Say the bank pays just $950 for the zero coupon bond today. The bank can now guarantee that the client can have their $1000 back at maturity because that is how much the zero coupon bond will pay in one year. The remaining $50 will not buy much of the S&P 500 if we were to buy a basket of the stocks outright. However we can buy one or more out-of-the-money options on the S&P 500. This makes use of the inherent leverage in an option which provides a cheap way of buying exposure to the index. If we can afford to buy a call option for $50 then that would achieve our goal of giving the client a guaranteed payoff of $1000 at expiry and the full upside of the S&P above the strike price of the option. The term sheet of our structured note would look as follows:

Maturity	1 year
Issue price	$1000
Index price on issue date	700
Minimum value at expiry	$1000
Maximum return	unlimited
Payoff	$1000 + \max[\text{S\&P at expiry} - 800, 0]$

The payoff is guaranteed to be $1000 or more. If the S&P trades below 800 at expiry the call option expires worthless and the client receives their $1000. If the S&P trades above 800 on the expiry date then the client gains $1 for each point, so if the S&P is at 850 at expiry the client will receive $1000 + \max[850 - 800, 0]$ which is $1050. Note that we can buy any option or combination of options with our $50. For example if the client is bearish on the S&P 500 then we would buy an out of the money put option with a strike of 600, so the payoff would then be $1000 + \max[600 - \text{S\&P at expiry}, 0]$. The client would gain one dollar for each point drop of the S&P below 600 at expiry or just receive their $1000 back if the S&P trades above 600. So if the S&P were trading at 570 at expiry then the bearish client would receive $1000 + \max[600 - 570, 0]$ which is $1030.

It may be that the call option is too expensive in which case we could start to become more creative with our $50 play money. One way to make our option strategy cheaper is to sell options and take in the premium. Recalling our option strategies for the bullish customer we might come up with a call spread (see Section 12.1.6 on page 429). Instead of just buying an out of the money and cheap call option we could buy a more expensive, lower strike, call option that is more likely to end in the money and simultaneously sell a higher strike call option. The higher strike call option will not pay completely for the low strike call option but it could reduce the overall cost of the options and make the product more attractive to the client. Our maximum payoff on the call spread is the difference between the strikes. By selling the high strike call option we have sold some of the upside and capped our maximum payoff at the high strike. So instead of unlimited upside we now have a maximum upside. Say we can now afford an at-the-money-spot call option with strike 700 and we sell the 1000 strike call. Our maximum payoff is 300, and the term sheet would now look as follows:

Maturity	1 year
Issue price	$1000
Index price on issue date	700
Minimum value at expiry	$1000
Maximum value at expiry	$1300
Payoff	$1000 + \min[\max[\text{S\&P at expiry} - 700, 0], 300]$

When would this product be difficult to structure? Remember that our play money was determined by interest rates. If rates are very low then T-bills will trade close to their face value and our play money, which is the difference between the price of the T-bill today and its face value, will shrink to almost zero. The reason why rates are low is that the central bank is trying to stimulate the economy when times are tough, and when times are tough the stock market is volatile and options are expensive. An environment with low rates and high volatility is the worst case for structurers of principal protected notes. There are three ways in which we can remedy the situation. Firstly we can reduce the guaranteed minimum return because this boosts our play money. If we receive $100 from the client and guarantee only 80% of their capital then we have only to buy $80 face of a zero coupon bond and this gives us more money for the option part. Secondly we can increase the maturity of the note. The value of options scale as the square root of their time to maturity, but interest rates are roughly linear because, sadly, interest rates are usually small and $\left(1 + \frac{r}{f}\right)^{ft}$ is roughly linear when $\frac{r}{f}$ is small. Our play money increases linearly with time but the option price scales at just $\sqrt{t}$. Quadrupling time to expiry quadruples our play money but only doubles the price of options, so this works in our favour. Thirdly we can buy cheaper options, such as exotic options that cease to exist or come into existence if the underlying touches a certain level en route to expiry.

The choice of underlying is vast. The examples we have shown contain an embedded call option on the US equity market, but it is possible to buy a note that gives USD investors a payoff in dollars that is linked directly to the value of the Nikkei index in JPY. This note would contain a QUANTO for handling the FX conversion. The option part could be a multi-asset option where the payoff is the best return of a set of, say, 5 telecom stocks. High net worth individuals may be exposed to the FX market so could be interested in taking a position of one currency versus another. So according to prevailing fashion or the needs of each investor, principal protected notes are a versatile way to give investors access to markets while preserving some portion of their capital.

There are two caveats that investors should bear in mind when considering investments in principal protected notes. The first is hidden costs. For example consider a principal protected note that gives an investor exposure to the upside of a dividend paying stock. The stock pays dividends but the note seller would probably hang on to the dividend payments. This would be in the documentation for the note but may be overlooked. Secondly investors are taking a credit risk when handing over their capital to buy such notes. This is because the note issuer may become bankrupt and the assets inside the structure belong to the issuer and sit on their balance sheet as assets. Consequently the investor could lose their investment. Before the Credit Crisis this would never have been a concern, but it is a real risk and should be taken into consideration.

12.2.2 Reverse Convertible

A good way to understand a reverse convertible is to understand a convertible bond (see Section 5.14 on page 211). A convertible bond offers the investor a right to convert their bonds into equities. In effect the investor buys a call option on the stock along with their bond. For this reason the coupon on convertible bonds is slightly lower than the coupon of comparable bonds from the same issuer. The reduction in coupon is a payment to the issuer from the investor of the value of the call option, because optionality comes at a price. What if we as an investor were to do the opposite, that is to say we boost the value of the coupon by selling a call option. Now what we have is a bond where the coupon is higher than comparable issues. At expiry we may be assigned on the call if spot ends above strike and forced to sell the stock at the strike price. This means that we end up with cash in our hands and no stock. If spot ends below strike the call option expires worthless and we end up with the stock in our hands. So if the stock performs poorly we end up with the stock and if the stock performs well we end up with a fixed amount of cash, which is the strike price, but the most important thing is that we receive a high coupon regardless of the stock price.

Spot	Call Option	Receive at expiry
Below strike at expiry	Worthless	Stock
Above strike at expiry	In the money	Cash

In order to buy a reverse convertible an investor has to like the underlying and to believe that its stock price will increase. If this were not the case then they would be rather upset if spot expires below strike and they are delivered the sickly stock. Most investors buy a reverse convertible because it gives a very large yield and they are not at all interested in having the stock at expiry. The greater the value of the option that is sold the greater the yield enhancement so times of high volatility provide greater yield enhancement. What we have done is to monetize the volatility of the stock by selling the call option. Tax efficiency may also be a consideration. For Swiss taxpayers the coupon payments of a reverse convertible are divided into interest and premium boost because the Swiss pay no tax on capital gains but they do pay tax on interest.

Say we are a structurer and the a sales person comes to us to ask us to structure a product for one of their high net worth clients. The client wants to invest $10 million for three years. Yields are low and volatility is high because we are in the aftermath of a financial crisis. The yield curve has one, two and three year rates of 0.1%, 0.5% and 1%. The client sort of likes Sprocket Corporation stock because he has heard that they have good long-term prospects but he really just wants a good return on his 10 million for three years. He does not particularly want to end up with Sprocket Corp stock. So we suggest a reverse convertible note on Sprocket corporation. How do we work out the boosted coupon on the note? The reason why the note pays a high coupon is that the client has sold an option and this premium is amortized, or smeared out, over three years. Our note will pay coupon annually.

The annual volatility of Sprocket Corp stock is 80% and the stock is trading at a spot price of $100 today so we know that the at-the-money-forward price of the three year call and put options is about $\frac{2}{5}X\sigma\sqrt{t}$ which is $0.4 \times 100 \times e^{0.01 \times 3} \times 0.8 \times \sqrt{3}$, or about $57. The Black-Scholes price of the call option is $51.89. So we can amortize this 51.89 into a boost in the coupon of say, c_{boost} over three years.

$$54.80 = c_{\text{boost}}e^{-0.001} + c_{\text{boost}}e^{-0.005 \times 2} + c_{\text{boost}}e^{-0.01 \times 3}$$

$$c_{\text{boost}} = \frac{51.89}{e^{-0.001} + e^{-0.005 \times 2} + e^{-0.01 \times 3}} = 17.53$$

If the client were to receive a three year par government note their risk-free coupon c_{govvie} would be

$$100 = c_{govvie}e^{-0.001} + c_{govvie}e^{-0.005\times 2} + (100 + c_{govvie})e^{-0.01\times 3}$$

$$c_{govvie} = \frac{100\left(1 - e^{-0.01\times 3}\right)}{e^{-0.001} + -e^{0.005\times 2} + e^{-0.01\times 3}} = 0.9986$$

So we take the rather feeble annual government coupon of $1 and boost it by selling a call option which we spread out into three payments of $17.53. This boosts the client's total coupon payment to $18.53. If the client lives in a country such as Switzerland they only pay tax on the interest component of $1, not on the coupon boost of $17.53. If the worst happens and Sprocket Corp stock trades below 100 in three years time then the client still receives their boosted coupon and receives a Sprocket share instead of their principal of $100. As they were keen on the stock this may not be a such a problem. The client may have some regrets if Sprocket shares soar well above $100 because they have given away this upside when they sold the call option. The ideal situation is if the stock ends just above the strike because the client gets back their principal and has not missed out on much upside. This strategy works best with a volatile stock that has no strong upward or downward price trend.

12.2.3 Range Accrual Note

A Daily Range Accrual Note (DRAN) offers a way for fixed income investors to boost their return above standard market rates. A DRAN is like a bond where the coupon depends on the value of some fixed income index, usually LIBOR. The coupon paid is proportional to the number of days per period that the index has traded within some range. If the index is within the range for the entire period the coupon will exceed market returns. If the maximum possible coupon is c_{max} and there are N trading days per period and for n of those days the index is trading within range then the coupon will be $c_{max}\frac{n}{N}$ for each period. For example say the maximum semi-annual coupon is 10% and the note depends on three month LIBOR trading in the range 0% to 5%. We pay $10,000 for the note and in the first six months the value of three month LIBOR was in range for 73 of the 180 days our coupon will be $10000 \times \frac{73}{180} \times 0.1$ or $405.56. If LIBOR had traded in the range 0% to 5% for the entire 180 days we would receive the maximum coupon of $1,000.

The index used is commonly the value of 3 month or 6 month LIBOR, but it could be a combination of rates, such as the difference between two swap rates. If the index is a difference between two rates such as the 5 and 10 year constant maturity swap rates then it becomes a play on the steepness of the yield curve and this is a SPREAD DRAN. DRANs usually have long maturities often five or ten years. A shorter-term version of a DRAN is the Money Market DRAN. Whereas DRANs have long maturities of five years or more Money Market DRANs will have maturities of one or two years.

The day-to-day value of a DRAN depends on the behaviour of the yield curve. When it is issued the DRAN is priced expecting that the yield curve will evolve as predicted by the foward curve on its issue date. If this is the case the price of the DRAN will remain fairly constant. If rates start to "beat" the values predicted by that initial forward curve then the DRAN will gain in value, and conversely if rates fall behind their forward-predicted values the DRAN will lose in value. However these daily fluctuations in value only matter if the investor intends to sell the structure before maturity. If the investor holds the structure until maturity or until is called. The investor in a DRAN has actually sold one option per day for the life of the structure. Each option is digital because it pays either nothing or a fixed amount of the notional if the index expires within the specified range.

If the DRAN is made callable by the issuer the value of c_{max} can be even higher. This structure is called a Callable Daily Range Accrual Note (CDRAN). However the risk that the investor faces is that the note will be called after just a few coupons and they will not receive their high coupon for long. The probability of being called increases when the value of the coupons is high. If the note is called the investor may have to invest in a new note with lower returns. The reason why the CDRAN pays a higher coupon than a DRAN is that it puts the coupons at risk of being called early.

12.2.4 Auto-callable

Auto-callables are structured notes that allow a degree of capital protection with a potentially highly leveraged upside. As their name suggests auto-callables are called by the issuer automatically if the underlying trades above some strike price on a set of fixed observation dates. Say we have a three year auto-callable note on the S&P index and that the index is trading at 1200 today. The strike of the auto-callable is 1200 and the investor buys $100 face of the note. The following table describes the possible outcomes:

Spot	Call Time	Payoff
S>1200 in 1 year	called after 1 year	Earn 15% coupon, $115
S>1200 in 2 years	called after 2 years	Earn 30% coupon, $130
S>1200 in 3 years	matures	Earn 45% coupon, $145
S<1200 in 3 years	matures	Earn no coupon, $100

If the underlying is above strike in one year then the structure is called and the investor receives their principal and a 15% coupon. If the underlying is below strike in one year then they receive no coupon but the coupon is accumulated for the next period. If in two years the underlying is trading above strike the structure is called and the investor receives coupon for both years, a total of 30%, and their principal. If the underlying is below strike in two years the coupon is not paid and rolled over again. Each year the structure is either called and the cumulative coupon is paid or not called and the coupon is rolled. If at maturity the underlying is below strike the investor simply receives their principal and no coupon, so there is a degree of capital protection. If during the life of the structure the underlying trades below some threshold, say 60% of spot at issue, the capital protection disappears. Once protection disappears the investor will lose one for one below the strike. If the S&P were trading at 600 at maturity then the investor would receive $50 because this is half of the strike. If the structure loses its capital protection and the underlying drops significantly then the investor has lost both the coupon and a potentially significant amount of their capital.

Although this auto-callable seems to offer an eye-watering 45% coupon it is extremely unlikely that this will be paid. This is because the underlying would have to trade below strike for two observation days at the end of year one and year two, then stage a recovery that would take it past strike in the third year. The most likely outcome, although this would obviously depend on the structure parameters and behaviour of the underlying, is usually that the autocallable is called after one year paying $115. Figure 12.17 shows the distribution of payoffs obtained by Monte Carlo simulation of the share price varying drift and volatility. At and above $100 payoffs are discrete and can only take the values $100, $115, $130 and $145 described above. Below $100 the continuous distribution of payoffs is the result of losing capital protection when a path touches the out-strike. If the underlying is rising strongly then the autocallable is not an attractive product because its maximum profit is $145, as shown in the bottom right hand histogram when drift is +20% per year. If the underlying is falling in value strongly then the autocallable is again not an attractive product because capital protection disappears as soon as the underlying reaches the out-strike. In this case volatility is beneficial because it increases the chance of the underlying rallying up above strike for one of the high-payoff observation dates. Without volatility the underlying simply drifts downwards and the note matures at a low price with no capital protection as if one had bought the underlying directly.

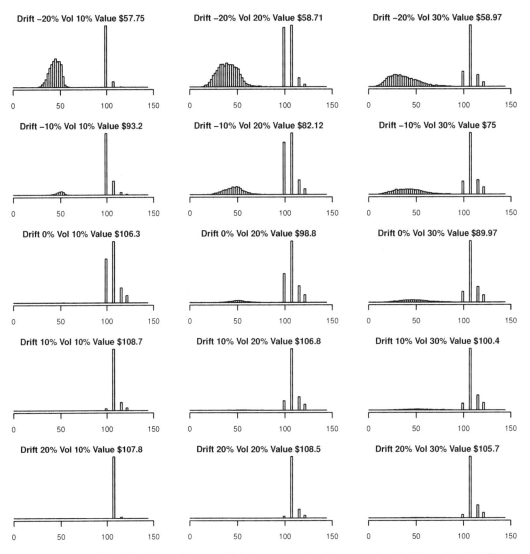

Figure 12.17: Distribution of autocallable present value varying drift and volatility.

Answers to Exercises

81 *The market for Sprocket Corp 100 and 130 strike call and put options is as follows:*

100 Call	22.10	130 Call	8.60
100 Put	6.23	130 Put	22.15

What options would you buy to construct a 100/130 bull call spread? How much would this cost? Could you construct the same payoff with put options, and if so how much would the position cost?

To construct the 100/130 bull call spread we would buy the 100 strike call for $22.10 and sell the 130 call for 8.60 which in total costs $13.49. We could construct exactly the same payoff by selling the 130 put for $22.15 and buying the 100 put for 6.23, earning a total of $15.92.

82 *The market for one year Sprocket Corp 90, 100 and 110 strike call and options is as follows:*

90 Call	28.94	100 Call	22.10	110 Call	16.47

How much would it cost or earn in premium to construct a 90/100/110 butterfly today? If the continuous long rate is 2% calculate the future value of the total premium. Draw the payoff at expiry and find the breakevens.

To construct the 90/100/110 call butterfly we would sell one 90 strike call for $28.94, buy two 100 strike calls for $22.10 each and sell one 110 strike call for $16.47. In total we receive $1.21 when we put on the trade. At expiry in one year the future value of $1.21 is $1.21 \times e^{0.02}$ which is $1.24. The payoff is shown in Figure 12.11 on page 436. Because the gradient in the wings is -1 and +1 the profit and loss diagram breaks even when the spot value at expiry is at 90+1.24 which is 91.24, and 110-1.24 which is 108.76.

A Interest Calculations

These formulae relate future value FV, present value PV, interest rate r, time t and compounding frequency f. Note that simple compounding is usually used for lending periods up to one year, and complex compounding for periods greater than one year. Continuous rates are usually used only in theoretical finance. For all of these rates the ratio of the present value and future value is called the discount factor which we represent by the greek symbol $\delta = \frac{PV}{FV}$, so $PV = \delta FV$ and $FV = \frac{PV}{\delta}$.

	Simple	**Compound**	**Continuous**
Discount Factor	$\delta = \frac{1}{1+rt}$	$\delta = \frac{1}{\left(1+\frac{r}{f}\right)^{ft}}$	$\delta = e^{-rt}$
Future Value	$FV = PV(1+rt)$	$FV = PV\left(1+\frac{r}{f}\right)^{ft}$	$FV = PVe^{rt}$
Present Value	$PV = \frac{FV}{1+rt}$	$PV = \frac{FV}{\left(1+\frac{r}{f}\right)^{ft}}$	$PV = FVe^{-rt}$
Rate	$r = \frac{1}{t}\left(\frac{FV}{PV} - 1\right)$	$r = f\left(\sqrt[ft]{\frac{FV}{PV}} - 1\right)$	$r = \frac{1}{t}\ln\frac{PV}{FV}$
Time	$t = \frac{1}{r}\left(\frac{FV}{PV} - 1\right)$	$t = \frac{\ln\frac{FV}{PV}}{f\ln(1+\frac{r}{f})}$	$t = \frac{1}{r}\ln\frac{PV}{FV}$
Discount Factor Derivative $\frac{\partial\delta}{\partial r}$	$-\frac{t}{(1+rt)^2} = -t\delta^2$	$-\frac{t}{1+\frac{r}{f}}\frac{1}{\left(1+\frac{r}{f}\right)^{ft}} = -\frac{t}{1+\frac{r}{f}}\delta$	$-te^{-rt} = -t\delta$

A.1 Day Count Convention

Day count comes in two parts. The first part is the method for calculating the number of interest-bearing days between two calendar dates. The second part is the divisor which converts the number of days into a fraction of a year. Rates are always quoted as annual rates, but interest is calculated on a daily basis.

Year fractions are not meant to reflect real time that you would measure on a calendar, so do not be alarmed if you see days missing or strange values for the time in years between two dates. The complicated part of a day count is the first part, as the second is simply a divisor to express days as a fraction of a year. The following list contains the most commonly used day count conventions.

Actual

This means that the day count is the number of calendar days between two dates. This is easily calculated in a spreadsheet application.

30 (ISDA)

Each month is assumed to have 30 days. The number of days between January 1, 2000 and February 1, 2000 is 30. The number of days between February 1, 2001 and March 1, 2001 is again 30, even though the number of actual calendar days is 28.

Complications arise when the start and end dates fall on the 31st of a 31 day month.

- If the first date falls on the 31st day of the month, and the second does not, move the first date to the 30th.

- If the first and second dates fall on the 31st day of the month move the second date to the 30th.

30E (30 ISMA)

- If the first or second date falls on the 31st the date is moved to the 30th.

- If the second date falls on the last day of February the actual number of days in February is used.

30E+

- If the first date falls on the 31st it is moved to the 30th.

- If the second date falls on the 31st it is moved to the 1st of the next month.

30 (SIA)

- If the first and second dates are the last day of February then the second date is changed to the 30th

- If the first date falls on the 31st or the last day of February it is changed to the 30th.

- If the first date is bumped to the 30th by the previous rule and the second date falls on the 31st the second date is moved to the 30th.

A.2 Date Adjustments

If a date falls on a weekend or a holiday it is not a business day and interest periods have to be adjusted for this possibility. Of course holidays differ between countries so instruments will detail which holiday calendar to use for interest calculations. The exact modification rule is also specified for a security, and is one of the following four variants:

Following If the date is not a business day then move it forward to the next available business day.

Preceding If the date is not a business day then move it backwards to the preceding business day.

Modified Following If the date is not a business day then move it forward to the next business day unless this day falls in the next month in which case move it backwards to the previous business day.

Modified Preceding If the date is not a business day then move it backwards to the preceding business day unless this day falls in the previous month in which case move it forwards to the next available business day.

B Useful Bloomberg Pages

News			
READ	Most widely read news stories of the day	TOP	Top headlines of the day
NRR	News spikes	TNI	News search
ECFC	Economic forecasts	WECO	World economic calendar

Fixed Income			
WBM	List all major government bonds	WBMF	List all bond futures
F <CORP>	List all corporate bonds issued by Ford Motor Company (ticker F)	F 9.98 47 <CORP>	Find the single corporate bond issued by Ford Motor Company with coupon 9.98% maturing in 2047
WIR	World interest rate futures	WIRP	World interest rate implied probabilities
IYC	Yield curve menu	BTMM	Treasury and money market summary
HG	Hedge corporate bond with CDS and IRS	LR	Today's LIBOR rates
SWPM	Swap and interest rate derivative calculator	CDSW	CDS calculator
CT5 <GOVT>, CT10 <GOVT>	US Treasury 5 year bond, 10 year bond	CB1 <GOVT>, CB3 <GOVT>	US Treasury 1 month T-bill, 3 month T-bill
USGG5YR <INDEX>, USGG10YR <INDEX>	Generic United States 5 year / 10 year on-the-run government bond yield	US0003M <INDEX>	USD three month LIBOR rate
FDTR <INDEX>	US Fed target funds rate	RPGT01D <INDEX>	US Treasury general collateral repo rate
LOIS USD, LOIS EUR	LIBOR-OIS swap spread for USD, EUR	ASW	Asset swap margin

Equity			
WEI	World equity indices	WEIF	World equity index futures
FA	Financial analysis	EE	Earnings estimates
CH1, CH2, CH3	Financial history, income statements, balance sheets	ANR	Analyst recommendations

RELS	List related securities	OMON	List of call and put option prices
TRA	Total return analysis	BETA	Correlation to stock index
CN	Company news	CACS	Corporate actions
DDIS	Debt distribution	BQ	Individual trades, intra-day price data, news flow and competitor performance
BDVD	Dividend forecasts	ECCG	Equity/credit comparison graphs

Graphs

GP, GIP	Daily price history, intra-day price history	GY	Daily yield history
GPO, GPC	Daily high/low /close price bar-chart or candlestick history with traded volume	IGPO, IGPC	Intra-day high/low /close bar-chart or candle-stick price history with traded volume
IVAT 5	Five days of intra-day volume at time, average volume at time, with price history	HS	Historical spread between any pair of variables

Useful Spread Time Series

US0001M <INDEX> FDTR <INDEX> HS2	Plot USD 1 month LIBOR rate vs. the Fed target funds rate	UKT CDS USD SR 5Y <CORP> GP	UK Treasury 5 year CDS spread in USD
FDTR <INDEX> RPGT01D <INDEX> HS2	Plot one week Fed target funds rate vs. the USD repo rate	CBRYLN CDS EUR SR 5Y <CORP> GP	Cadbury's 5 year CDS spread
.TEDSP <INDEX> GP D	TED spread	LOIS USD, LOIS EUR	LIBOR-OIS spread for major currencies
YCMM0074 <INDEX>	Repo rate for US Govt. Securities GC		

Foreign Exchange

FXC	Show real-time updating cross-currency rates for major currencies	WCR	World currency rates
EURUSD	Select EUR|USD as a currency pair	EUR TKC	FX rates for EUR
EUR FRD	Spot and forward FX rates for EUR	FRD	Forward FX rates

Index

Nomenclature

Accredited investor Accredited investors in the US are people with a net worth of at least a million dollars or a joint income of $300,000 for the past two years ($200,000 if unmarried) and the expectation of the same salary in the coming year.

ALM Asset liability management. This is the art of balancing future costs against future income. ALM is central to the operation of life insurers and pension funds.

American Option An option that may be exercised at any time up to expiry.

Basis point One percent of one percent, which is 0.01%. Abbreviated as "bp" and pronounced as "bip" or "beep".

Bear market A market in which value is dropping.

Bearish Of the belief that value will fall in a given market.

Bermudan Option An option that may be exercised on a fixed set of dates up to expiry.

Bid-offer spread Difference between the price at which a market maker will buy (offer) and sell (bid) a security. Bid price is always higher than offer price.

Binomial Tree Option pricing tree in which each node branches into two child nodes.

Break-Even Price Price of the underlying at which an option payoff equals the premium required to buy the option.

Bull market A market in which value is rising.

Bullish Of the belief that value will rise in a given market.

Call Option An option to buy some asset at a fixed price (strike) at or before some expiry date in the future.

Call Option An option to sell some asset at a fixed price (strike) at or before some expiry date in the future.

Cash Settlement Derivative contract which stipulates that there will be an exchange of the cash value of the derivative upon exercise.

Downside Percentage decrease in the future value of a security. This is always a matter of opinion.

Edge   Means by which market makers earn their living. This is either in the form of commissions or bid-offer spread.

European Option An option that can only be exercised at expiry, in contrast to an American option that can be exercised at any time up to expiry.

Exchange-traded Standardised assets sold in bulk on an exchange. The opposite of OTC assets.

Exercise The owner of an option may choose to exercise their right to buy (call option) or sell (put option) the underlying if it is in the money.

Gilt   Bond issued by the UK Treasury, named after the distinctive silver edging that used to be embossed on the bond certificates.

Hedge A position that cancels out some of the risk from another position, reducing the overall risk to an investor.

Hedge funds Unregulated investment companies that manage the wealth of ultra-rich individuals and companies.

Interest rate parity An arbitrage relationship between two currencies involving the risk-free interest rate, the spot FX rate and the duration of the investment. Interest rate parity is used to price currency forwards and ensures that it is not possible to make risk-free profit from forward FX trades.

Interest Rate Swap An agreement between two counterparties to swap fixed for floating rate cash flows on some notional amount.

IPO   An initial public offering is the first time a privately held company sells shares in order to raise capital.

Leverage Borrowing money to make (or lose) money. Has the effect of amplifying possible returns or losses.

OTC (Over The Counter) A trade that is individually tailored for a direct transaction between a buyer and seller. For example, credit default swaps and interest rate futures are OTC securities.

Par Bond A bond that trades with a price equal to its face value, and a coupon equal to its yield to maturity.

Point   One point is 1%. In the context of stock indices a point is on index unit. So if the S&P index was at 1010 yesterday and is at 1011 today it has gone up one point.

Pull to Par The tendency of bond prices to approach their face value as they get closer to maturity.

Put-Call Parity By being long a call and short a put on the same underlying with the same strike and expiry we can reproduce the payoff of a forward with that strike. This relates the value of a call, put and forward.

Recombining Tree An option pricing tree in which more than one path can lead to the same node.

Spot-Forward Basis The difference between the spot price (price paid today) and forward price (price for delivery at a fixed time in the future). Basis is also known as cost of carry because it depends on funding costs to buy and in the case of commodities to store the underlying asset.

Strike Price at which an option is agreed to be bought (call option) or sold (put option).

Trinomial Tree Option pricing tree in which each node branches into three child nodes.

Underlying Asset that underlies an option and upon whose value the value of an option indirectly depends. If the option is physically settled the underlying trades hands if the option is exercised.

Upside Percentage increase in the future value of a security. This is always a matter of opinion.

Venture Capital Private equity company that specialises in helping fledgling companies expand in return for a share of the company. Usually the VC sells its share of the company when there is an IPO.

Volatility A measure of the risk of an investment. Calculated using the standard deviation of the return series over a time interval.

Yield to Maturity A single flat rate that discounts future cash flows to the current market price of an instrument.

List of Figures

List of Tables

References

Ahamed, L.
  2010. *Lords of Finance: 1929, The Great Depression, and the Bankers who Broke the World*. Windmill Books.

Baxter, M. and A. Rennie
  1996. *Financial Calculus: An Introduction to Derivative Pricing*. Cambridge University Press.

Breeden, D. and R. Litzenberger
  1978. Prices of State Contingent Claims Implicit in Options Prices. *Journal of Business*, 51:621–651.

Burrough, B. and J. Helyar
  2004. *Barbarians At The Gate: The Fall of RJR Nabisco*, new edition. Arrow.

Calamos, N. P.
  2003. *Convertible Arbitrage: Insights and Techniques for Successful Hedging*. John Wiley & Sons.

Chaplin, G.
  2010. *Credit Derivatives: Trading, Investing, and Risk Management*, 2nd edition. John Wiley & Sons.

Deacon, M., A. Derry, and D. Mirfendereski
  2004. *Inflation-indexed Securities: Bonds, Swaps and Other Derivatives*, 2nd edition. John Wiley & Sons.

Drobny, S. and N. Ferguson
  2009. *Inside the House of Money: Top Hedge Fund Traders on Profiting in the Global Markets*, 2nd revised edition edition. John Wiley & Sons.

Fabozzi, F. J.
  2005. *The Handbook of Fixed Income Securities*, 7th edition. McGraw-Hill Professional.

Fabozzi, F. J.
  2009. *Bond Markets, Analysis, and Strategies*, 7th edition. Pearson Education.

Garman, M. B. and S. W. Kohlhagen
  1983. Foreign Currency Option Values. *J. International Money and Finance*, 2:231–237.

Hagan, P. and G. West
  2006. Interpolation methods for curve construction. *Applied Mathematical Finance*, 13(2):89–129.

Haug, E. G.
  2007. *The Complete Guide to Option Pricing Formulas*, 2nd edition. McGraw-Hill Professional.

Hull, J. C.
  2008. *Options, Futures, and Other Derivatives*, 7th edition. Prentice Hall.

Jaeckel, P.
  2002. *Monte Carlo Methods in Finance*. Wiley.

John B. Taylor
  1993. Discretion Versus Policy Rules in Practice. *Carnegie-Rochester Conference Series on Public Policy*, 39:195–214.

Press, W. H., S. A. Teukolsky, W. T. Vetterling, and B. P. Flannery
  2007. *Numerical Recipes 3rd Edition: The Art of Scientific Computing*, 3rd edition. Cambridge University Press.

Reinhart, C. M. and K. Rogoff
  2009. *This Time Is Different: Eight Centuries of Financial Folly*. Princeton University Press.

Student
  1927. Errors of Routine Analysis. *Biometrika*, 19:151–164.

Tuckman, B.
  2002. *Fixed Income Securities: Tools for Today's Markets*, 2nd edition. John Wiley & Sons.

Weithers, T.
  2006. *Foreign Exchange: A Practical Guide to the FX Markets*. John Wiley & Sons.

Wiseman, J. A.
  2001. *Pricing Money: A Beginner's Guide to Money, Bonds, Futures, and Swaps*. John Wiley & Sons.

Lightning Source UK Ltd.
Milton Keynes UK
UKOW04f0557150317

296677UK00009B/242/P